*Ecclesiastical Polity in the
Church of God Mountain Assembly*

Michael Padgett

Middlesboro, Kentucky

Copyright © 2021 by Michael Padgett / Middlesboro, Kentucky.
All Rights Reserved. No part of this book may be reproduced in any form without written permission from the publisher.
First Edition.

Front Cover: Image from the rear cover of the 1914 Minute Book
Rear Cover: Photograph courtesy of Photography By Maria

Library of Congress Control Number: 2021909794
ISBN: 978-0-9646344-9-7

Table of Contents

Figures and Tables ii

Acknowledgments viii

Dedication x

Preface xi

1 Introduction 1

2 Baptist Roots 22

3 The Influence of the Church of God (Cleveland) 60

4 Centralized Polity and Tension with the Church of God 95

5 Parallel Histories: Successful and Failed Leadership Transition 117

6 An Informal Triumvirate 134

7 Toward a Denominational Government 165

8 Surviving a Schism 198

9 Toward a Worldwide Movement 242

10 Rise Up and Build 273

11 Fruit That Remains 314

12 Grounded and Settled 362

13 Strong Local Churches 384

14 Summary, Analysis, and Conclusion 418

Appendix 1: General Officials 427

Appendix 2: General Assembly Speakers 464

Bibliography 495

Figures and Tables

Figure 0.1: The author (ca. 1977) viii
Figure 0.2: James Cox with the author x
Figure 0.3: Elk Valley CGMA xiii
Figure 1.1: John H. Parks 17
Figure 1.2: John Thomas 17
Figure 2.1: John H. Parks and Andrew J. Silcox 23
Figure 2.2: Stephen N. Bryant 24
Figure 2.3: Mary Storey 27
Figure 2.4: Sherrod, Francis, Michael, and Daniel Thomas 28
Figure 2.5: The Church at Wolf Creek 32
Figure 2.6: Newton K. Parks 35
Figure 2.7: Aaron Thomas 35
Figure 2.8: Thomas D. Moses 35
Figure 2.9: James Allen Moses 35
Figure 2.10: Cornelius house at Ryan's Creek 37
Figure 2.11: William B. Douglas 38
Figure 2.12: James J. Sammons 39
Figure 2.13: Joseph T. Richardson 40
Figure 2.14: Jacob C. Taylor 40
Figure 2.15: Jellico Creek Church 49
Figure 2.16: Map of the first ten churches (1907) 50
Table 2.1: Delegates at the First Assembly 58-59
Figure 3.1: R.G. Spurling 61
Figure 3.2: A.J. Tomlinson 61
Figure 3.3: W.R. Hamlin 70
Figure 3.4: Hayes Creek Church 70
Figure 3.5: Charlie T. Pratt 74
Figure 3.6: Tom Moses' ordination 76
Figure 3.7: Barthena & Newton Parks, John & Rachel Parks 79
Figure 3.8: Jonah Shelton and family 82
Figure 3.9: Jonah Shelton 83
Figure 3.10: James Dusina 86
Figure 4.1: John H. Parks 96
Figure 4.2: The first tabernacle in Jellico 100

Figure 4.3: Andrew Silcox 103
Figure 4.4: Henry Mobley 112
Figure 4.5: J.H. Parks 112
Figure 5.1: George A. Fore 119
Figure 5.2: James L. Goins 119
Figure 5.3: Starling Smith 120
Figure 5.4: Francis M. Thomas 120
Figure 5.5: John Sharp 124
Figure 5.6: Charles H. Standifer...124
Figure 5.7: B.H. Enix...125
Figure 6.1: Curd Walker 135
Figure 6.2: C.L. Price 139
Figure 6.3: Lewis Broyles..139
Figure 6.4: Everett H. Ross 140
Figure 6.5: Everett Creekmore 142
Figure 6.6: Drue Stanifer 144
Figure 6.7: M.E. Woolum 145
Figure 6.8: Monroe Church, 1932..145
Figure 6.9: Levi M. White..146
Figure 6.10: Richard & Mary Litton 147
Figure 6.11: E.B. Bryant..148
Figure 6.12: Earnie E. Yeary...148
Figure 6.13: Cale Yeary Family, ca. 1916..149
Figure 6.14: Virgil and Mattie Akins...152
Figure 6.15: McKinley Baird 152
Figure 6.16: Thomas Woods 153
Figure 6.17: Joshua Baird...154
Figure 6.18: Stephen Bryant 156
Figure 6.19: John Parks & Ernie Yeary 157
Figure 6.20: J.C. Taylor automobile, ca. 1917................................158
Figure 7.1: J.H. Bryant 166
Figure 7.2: Kim Moses 166
Figure 7.3: A.J. Long...168
Figure 7.4: Ira H. Moses...168
Figure 7.5: J.E. Hatfield..170
Figure 7.6: Luther Gibson 170
Figure 7.7: Clayton Lawson..171

Figure 7.8: The Gospel Herald, Issue 1 173
Figure 7.9: Olive & Abraham Tribble 177
Figure 7.10: Edward Woolum 181
Figure 7.11: Robert Thomas 181
Figure 7.12: Floyd Jordan and YPE 181
Figure 7.13: R.N. Ballinger 188
Figure 7.14: Roy and Mary Cornelius 188
Table 7.1: 1940 US Census Data for Ordained Ministers 196-197
Figure 8.1: Clayton and Lassie Lawson 200
Figure 8.2: PFC Cordell Partin 204
Figure 8.3: Dave Hammitte & Ottis Ellis 206
Figure 8.4: John H. Bryant 207
Figure 8.5: Andrew J. Long 211
Figure 8.6: Kim Moses 211
Figure 8.7: Paul Grubbs 212
Figure 8.8: James Walden 214
Figure 8.9: Willis Yeary 214
Figure 8.10: Luther Gibson 216
Figure 8.11: Oscar Bunch 217
Figure 8.12: Harvey Rose 216
Figure 8.13: E.B. Rose 223
Figure 8.14: Jellico Main Street Church 223
Figure 8.15: Ottis Ellis 224
Figure 8.16: Fate Creasman 226
Figure 8.17: Floy Marie Bell 227
Figure 8.18: Jessie Fearrl 227
Figure 8.19: Jackie Ethridge 228
Figure 8.20: 15th & Race Street Church 229
Figure 8.21: 15th & Race Street Music Department 230
Figure 9.1: E.L. Cyrus 247
Figure 9.2: Chester I. Miller 247
Figure 9.3: Middlesboro CGMA with Pastor Ulyess Graham 248
Figure 9.4: Charles L. Weaver 250
Figure 9.5: Jennings Baird 252
Figure 9.6: Claude Baird 252
Figure 9.7: Jerome Walden 252
Figure 9.8: Roger Powell 254
Figure 9.9: C.A. Freeman 255

Figure 9.10: Wade M. Hughes 257
Figure 9.11: Arvil Rountree 257
Figure 9.12: Haskel Swain 259
Figure 9.13: Helper, Utah CGMA..260
Figure 9.14: James Walden, Jr. 261
Figure 9.15: Lake City Homecoming, 1958 262
Figure 9.16: Clayton Lawson 263
Figure 9.17: Auza Vinson 263
Figure 9.18: Executive Board, 1958 264
Figures 9.19-9.20: General Council, 1958 266
Figure 10.1: Ira Moses 273
Figure 10.2: Fred Cornelius 273
Figure 10.3: John Longsworth 274
Figure 10.4: Efford Enix 277
Figure 10.5: Camp Matrina Flier 277
Figure 10.6: Leon Petree 279
Figure 10.7: Arlie Petree...279
Figure 10.8: Some of the ministers at the Lake Placid retreat.........281
Figure 10.9: Jasper Walden 282
Figure 10.10: Donnie Hill 282
Figure 10.11: YWC Groundbreaking 283
Figure 10.12: Breaking Ground for the New Tabernacle, 1966.....286
Figure 10.13: C.B. Ellis, Jr. 289
Figure 10.14: Ira Moses & J.E. Prewitt...290
Figure 10.15: the Amos Family...292
Figure 10.16: James L. Cox, Sr. 296
Figure 10.17: J.E. Hatfield 299
Figure 10.18: C.B. Ellis, Jr. 300
Figure 10.19: Fred Cornelius with the Prewitt Brothers................301
Figure 10.20: Glenn Rowe 302
Figure 10.21: Jerome Walden 302
Figure 10.22: Kenneth Massingill...303
Figure 10.23: Jasper Walden 304
Figure 10.24: James L. Cox, Jr. 304
Figure 11.1: Jack Cates 315
Figure 11.2: Elder M. Blair 315
Figure 11.3: James Walden, Jr. 316

Figure 11.4: James Walden, Jr. 316
Figure 11.5: Jerome, James, & Jasper Walden 317
Figure 11.6: Myrlene & James Walden 317
Figure 11.7: Glenn Rowe at Salt Springs 319
Figure 11.8: The Massingill Family.. 321
Figure 11.9: Cleveland Walcott 324
Figure 11.10: Conroy Adams 324
Figure 11.11: Mona Cornet 326
Figure 11.12: Nozor Augustin 326
Figure 11.13: Mrs. J.P. Strong 327
Figure 11.14: Sam Daniel 328
Figure 11.15: Laura Taylor 329
Figure 11.16: Janey Hackler 329
Figure 11.17: Clayton Lawson 330
Figure 11.18: J.E. Prewitt 334
Figure 11.19: Donnie Hill 334
Figure 11.20: Danny Jones 335
Figure 11.21: David Cornelius 335
Figure 11.22: Paulette & Reggie 337
Figure 11.23: Ray Landes, Jr. 338
Figure 11.24: Michael Bartee 338
Figure 11.25: Dennis McClanahan 341
Figure 11.26: Richard Massingill 341
Figure 11.27: Henry C. Taylor 344
Figure 11.28: James Bartee 344
Figure 11.29: Ray A. Freeman 346
Figure 11.30: A.G. Padgett 347
Figure 11.31: Charlene Walden 349
Figure 11.32: Linda Massingill 349
Figure 11.33: CGMA Logo 350
Figure 11.34: Jackie Cox 351
Figure 11.35: Beulah Fry 351
Figure 12.1: Kenneth Massingill 364
Figure 12.2: Jasper Walden 364
Figure 12.3: Bob J. Vance 365
Figure 12.4: Cecil Johnson 367
Figure 12.5: Lonnie Lyke 367
Figure 12.6: Kenneth Ellis 371

Figure 12.7: Jay Walden 371
Figure 12.8: Paulette McClanahan 372
Figure 12.9: Nancy Vance 372
Figure 12.10: Henry Taylor 376
Figure 12.11: James W. Kilgore 377
Figure 12.12: Kevin Human 378
Figure 13.1: Executive Board, 2000 384
Figure 13.2: Merle & Marlin Laws 386
Figure 13.3: Jerry Wilson 386
Figure 13.4: James Walden, Jr. 387
Figure 13.5: Ray Landes, Jr. 387
Figure 13.6: Leon Petree 388
Figure 13.7: James Earl McKinney 388
Figure 13.8: Fred Cornelius 388
Figure 13.9: David Cornelius 388
Figure 13.10: Lloyd Camp 389
Figure 13.11: Tim McGlone 389
Figure 13.12: Michael Cornelius 390
Figure 13.13: J.H. Douglas 390
Figure 13.14: Wayne Ison 391
Figure 13.15: Donnie Hill 391
Figure 13.16: Jasper Walden 391
Figure 13.17: Jerome Walden 391
Figure 13.18: CGMA Tabernacle, 1999 392
Figure 13.19: Jellico CGMA Tabernacle, 2007 392
Figure 13.20: Ministers' Memorial 393
Figure 13.21: Elders & Officials 393
Figure 13.22: Dedication of New Office 394
Figure 13.23: Diamond Hosiery Mills 398
Figure 13.24: 2001 Thomas Trask with Lonnie Lyke 399
Figure 13.25: 2001 Men of Integrity Retreat 401
Figure 13.26: Tim Bartee 409

Acknowledgments

Figure 0.1: *The author (ca. 1977) approaching the old tabernacle*

This book represents the culmination of more than 35 years of passionate interest in the history of the Church of God Mountain Assembly. Neither the academic pursuit that began 15 years ago and concluded with a doctoral dissertation nor this final project could have been possible without the cooperation and encouragement of my wife, Dedra, who has supported me unquestionably every step along the way. Our three children have followed her lead in showing me deference and patience. Thank you, Carissa, Lauren, and Andrew. The congregation I have pastored for the past 29 years has been especially understanding and, for that, I am thankful.

Several professors prepared me for the historical research required for a project of this scope. For their impact on my academic career, I offer my gratitude to Drs. John Lowry, Ronald Huch, Bradford Wood, Carolyn Dupont, David Coleman, and Thomas Appleton at Eastern Kentucky University and Drs. Ronald Eller and Ron Formisano at the University of Kentucky. I especially appreciate Dr. Todd Hartch at Eastern Kentucky who first proposed that I could achieve the goal of an earned Ph.D. I continue to treasure his friendship. I am deeply indebted to Dr. David Hollingsworth and Dr. Nathan Coleman for the time invested in reading, editing, and suggesting ways to improve my dissertation. I am also convinced that this goal would have remained unrealized without my recruitment to the University of the Cumberlands by Dr. Jennifer Simpson. For her interest and her willingness to serve on my dissertation committee, I am forever grateful.

Many sources cited in this book were provided from personal collections of ministers and members of the Church of God Mountain Assembly over the past three decades. Most of the minute books and issues of *The Gospel Herald* in my possession were obtained through gifts from the following individuals and/or their families: Alice Chitwood, Fred & Mary Cornelius,

Ray Freeman, James Earl McKinney, Roger Powell, James Earl Prewitt, James Walden, and Jerome Walden. I appreciate the confidence these individuals and families have shown by entrusting me with the preservation of these records. Numerous other sources have been available to me with assistance from the staff of various institutions and members of individual families. Special thanks is offered to James Walden, Jr. II and James Kilgore of the Church of God Mountain Assembly; David Roebuck of the Dixon Pentecostal Research Center; Darrin Rodgers of the Flower Pentecostal Heritage Center; Jim Stephens, Raymond Hodge, Debbie Parker, and B.J. Roberson of the Church of God (Cleveland) Headquarters; Stephanie Owens of God's Bible School; Adam Winters at the James P. Boyce Centennial Library; Stephen Jett and Janus Jones at the South Union / Mount Zion Baptist Association; Mark Amos and Stephen Amos (Ron and Mavis Amos); Romona Barger (Floy Marie Bell); Robin Bryant, Philip Patrick Bryant, and Barry Bryant (E.B. Bryant); Jeff Bryant (S.N. Bryant and J.H. Bryant); David Cady (C.T. Pratt); David Duncan (Mark and W.R. Byrge); Linnea Rains and Carolyn Georgiton (Lee Caddell); Kim Walden (Cornelius and Grubbs families); Earl Dusina (James Dusina); Brenda Demps (Jackie Ethridge); Monika Arvin, Charles Crowe, and Jon Fore (G.A. Fore); Jimmy and Angel Justice (C.A. Freeman and Ray Freeman); Harold Gibson, Merle Gibson, and Mike Gibson (Luther Gibson); Jerry Grubbs (Paul Grubbs); Gerald Holmes (Drue Stanifer); Harold Long (A.J. Long); Debra Longsworth (John T. Longsworth); Glenda Hotchkiss (Ira Moses); Roger Lands (John Parks); Mark Moses, Wesley Moses, and Kenny Carr (Thomas D. Moses Family); Phillip Moses (Moses and Rountree families); Nicki Smith (Harvey & E.B. Rose); Roger Glenn Rountree (Arvil Rountree); Frankie Wilson (J.J. Sammons); Deb Switzer (Jonah Shelton); Kay Bohara (Robert Thomas); Evon Hatfield Tipton (J.E. Hatfield); Larry Branstutter, John Thomas and Claudia E. Thomas (Thomas family); Merele Vinson (Auza Vinson); Tim Walden and Kevin Walden (Jerome Walden); Jon Walden (James Walden, Jr.); Polly Byers, Carla Walker, Stephen Curd Walker, and James Salter (Curd Walker); and Philip Yeary, Tony Yeary, Francis Yeary, and Fred Cornelius (Yeary Family); Debbie Cochran (Cincinnati); Jon Walden (Cleveland); Jerry Grubbs (Fonde); Crystal Eld (Harlan); William Kilby (General Assembly Church of God); Joy Ball (Hayes Creek); Donnell and Lisa Sellers (Holiness Baptist Church); Scott Landes (Jellico); Alice Chitwood (Jellico, Jellico Creek); Rick & Tammy Massingill (Monroe); Bonnie Bishop (Pleasant View); Janet Cassada (Sidney); Sharon Vance (Rittman); and Kenneth Ellis (Melbourne).

Over the past thirty years, I have had numerous personal conversations with individuals that have helped me interpret primary sources from the perspectives of eyewitnesses. I am thankful for the friendships and the insights provided by Michael Cornelius, James Cox, J.H. Douglas, Donnie Hill, Cecil Johnson, Lonnie Lyke, Kenneth Massingill, Dennis McClanahan, Alfred Newton, Leon Petree, Arlie Petree, James Earl Prewitt, Glenn & Leatha Rowe, James Walden, Jasper Walden, Jay Walden, and Bob Wilson.

Finally, I remember Jesus's words in John 15:5 and acknowledge that He is right. His help has been a constant source of strength. To God be the glory!

Dedication

When I attended the annual convention of the Church of God Mountain Assembly in 1985 after having just accepted the call to ministry at the age of 14, I was so intrigued by the business sessions that I asked the General Secretary & Treasurer for a copy of the delegate booklet. James L. Cox, Jr. happily obliged me, and that booklet became the springboard from which my pursuit of this organizational history began. After, I received my minister's license from the denomination in 1988 and was nearing the completion of high school, I had a conversation with Jim in his home that changed my life forever. The passion for ministry was all that consumed me. I had given no thought to higher education because I saw college attendance as a delay to my quest for active ministry. Jim called attention to the historical purpose of higher education in America to train clergy, to the rising number of college graduates in our society, and the need for competent preachers to reach them. His persuasion led to my enrollment in college that fall. Through the past thirty years, I have relied often upon his personal experiences and relationships with Mountain Assembly leaders to assist me with the interpretation of sources.

In His infinite wisdom, God chose to call home His servant and my dear friend on April 8, 2020, just as my dissertation was being concluded. For his impact on my life and education, his friendship, and constant encouragement, this book is affectionately dedicated to the memory of James L. Cox, Jr.

Figure 0.2: James Cox with the author before his 1992 ordination examination

Preface

John Thomas rose to preach the introductory sermon at the Eighth Annual Mountain Assembly on the morning of October 2, 1914, after the service at Elk Valley, Tennessee began with "several songs and prayer and speaking in tongues." Thomas admonished his fellow pastors to feed the Church of God.[1] To Thomas, and those who listened to him preach, *Church of God* was understood as a renewal movement that sought to restore Biblical doctrines of personal sanctification, the baptism of the Holy Ghost, and spiritual gifts. Many used the term interchangeably with *Holiness* or *Pentecostal*.

Thomas had embraced Wesleyan holiness a decade earlier when "a man by the name of White" preached the message of sanctification in Whitley County, Kentucky. Thomas later conducted a Holiness revival of his own at a newly organized church at Ryan's Creek in 1907.[2] Delegates from that congregation convened at Little Wolf Creek, Kentucky that October with those from nine other churches and adopted the name, "Church of God," for the association they created. They were unaware that a group of Holiness believers in Cleveland, Tennessee had also adopted that name earlier in the year. When A.J. Tomlinson, General Overseer of the group in Cleveland, attended the Fifth Annual Assembly at Siler's Chapel in 1911, Thomas's Church of God added the words "Mountain Assembly" to distinguish its association meeting from the one held in Cleveland. By that time, both groups were fully Pentecostal. As ministers from the two associations exchanged visitation over the next decade, the Church of God (Cleveland, Tennessee) came to exert a significant influence on the Mountain Assembly.

The minutes of the Eighth Annual Mountain Assembly contain no mention of any Church of God (Cleveland) ministers in attendance at that meeting. However, delegates voted to send "a letter of correspondence to the Cleveland assembly and send it by the hands of some of our brethren asking them to receive our letter and messengers." In addition, the rear cover was printed with an illustration and curious inscription: "Ther [sic] was a bowe [sic] tie'd [sic] in the Assembly of the Churche's [sic] of God at Elk Valley that will never be understood until the Son of God is revealed from Heaven."[3]

When writing the first history of the Church of God Mountain Assembly (CGMA) forty years later, Luther Gibson pondered "just what they had in mind when they wrote that" but offered no speculation.[4] Johnie Douglas explained many years later that growing up in the Mountain Assembly congregation at Elk Valley, members there interpreted the phrase to mean that there would always be a Church of God in Elk Valley.[5] This book contends that by 1914 the history of the CGMA, especially with respect to the development of ecclesiastical polity, was inexplicably *tied* to the Church of God (Cleveland). It is the author's conjecture, then, that the phrase should be interpreted in that manner.

At the same time, the Mountain Assembly's roots in the Baptist church cannot be ignored. After its founders prepared an order of business for its first assembly patterned after the same to which they were accustomed in the South Union Association of United Baptist, they chose to preserve the record by publishing a minute book of the event. The South Union met for its 93rd Annual Session two weeks before the Mountain Assembly met for its first, and Clerk Joseph Meadors chose Courier Print in Williamsburg to publish its minute book. At the conclusion of the text, Courier filled the empty space with a garland crest, not usual for an offset printer.[6] That the Mountain Assembly chose Courier Print to publish its first minute book in 1907, or that the printer used the same crest at the end of both books should not be thought of as more than a coincidence.[7] However, like the curious bow tie on the back of the 1914 minute book, the crest below remains a symbol of the Mountain Assembly's connection with its Baptist roots. This book aims to demonstrate both of those historic influences.

Figure 0.3: Elk Valley CGMA with Stephen N. Bryant & William Douglas
c/o Douglas Family

---

[1] Church of God Mountain Assembly (CGMA), *Minutes of the Eighth Annual Session of Churches of God* (n.p.: by the association, 1914), 2.

[2] Luther Gibson, *History of the Church of God Mountain Assembly* (Jellico, Tenn.: Church of God Mountain Assembly, Inc., 1954), 5, 51.

[3] CGMA, *Minutes* (1914), 5, rear cover.

[4] Gibson, 11.

[5] Johnie Douglas, conversation with the author, circa 1995. Eleven decades after it was founded, the Elk Valley CGMA continues to meet near the same location where much larger crowds attended in the 1910s and 1920s.

[6] South Union Association of United Baptists (SUAUB), *Minutes of the Ninety-third Annual Session of the South Union Association of United Baptists* (n.p.: by the association, 1907), 1, 9, 11.

[7] Church of God [Mountain Assembly], *A Minute of the Council Meeting of the Church of God [Mountain Assembly]* (n.p.: by the association, 1907), 4.

1

Introduction

When John Parks, Andrew Silcox, Stephen Bryant, and others met in Ryan's Creek, Kentucky, on August 24, 1907, to organize what would become the Church of God Mountain Assembly (CGMA), they intended to create an association like the one with which they had been affiliated for years. These men had pastored various United Baptist congregations in Southeastern Kentucky and had participated in the annual meetings of the South Union Association of United Baptists until that association, on September 23, 1905, blacklisted them and four others—Allen Moses, Thomas Moses, Newton Parks, and Aaron Thomas—for preaching "doctrine contrary to the word of God." The association's Committee on Resolutions further advised that churches remove them from pastoral office and not allow them to preach in their pulpits or be "considered out of harmony with this Association."[1]

Parks and the others had embraced the doctrine of entire sanctification through the preaching of Wesleyan Holiness by Methodist Episcopal evangelists in Whitley County, Kentucky a few years earlier. The Baptist church taught that sanctification begins at salvation, "increases throughout life," and "is completed at death."[2] John Wesley "described sanctification as a lifelong process of daily cooperation with God's grace in which the believer grows in love of God and neighbor ... and joy in the presence of the Holy Spirit." "As holiness in heart and life gradually increases," Wesley taught, "there can come a moment when 'in an instant, the heart is cleansed from all sin, and filled with the pure love to God and man." This immediate experience he referred to as "entire sanctification," and suggested it was a second work of grace by faith, after salvation.[3]

In the fervor of the holiness revival, Parks and others claimed to have experienced entire sanctification and began to preach the danger of apostasy, which they understood as *falling away* and losing one's salvation. Such doctrine contradicted the teachings of the United Baptist churches to which they belonged. The South Union Association's Articles of Faith held to the Calvinist view of the "final perseverance of the Saints in grace and holiness, and that none of them shall be lost."[4] Excluded by their churches, Parks and the others formed a new association in 1907 named, the Church of God.

When this group met in Little Wolf Creek, Kentucky, that October, they had no knowledge of another recently constituted association using the same name. Two decades earlier Richard G. Spurling rejected the Landmarkism espoused by the Holly Springs Baptist Church where he pastored in Monroe County, Tennessee.[5] Excluded by the Missionary Baptist Church, Spurling organized the Christian Union in 1886 and determined to reject all creeds but love. Ten years later, a revival at the Schearer Schoolhouse in Cherokee, North Carolina, introduced Wesleyan Holiness to that region. For many, the experience of sanctification also prompted ecstatic tongues speech. This group began meeting in the home of William F. Bryant, who had been a Baptist deacon. Spurling worshipped with them often, and his influence ultimately led to the organization of the Holiness Church at Camp Creek in 1902. The following June, Ambrose Jessup Tomlinson joined the congregation. Tomlinson had been raised a Quaker in Indiana but embraced the holiness movement and became an itinerant evangelist and Bible salesman. Over the next few years, he established similar churches in southeastern Tennessee and northern Georgia.[6] The first Assembly of the "Churches of East Tennessee, North Georgia and Western North Carolina" took place at Camp Creek in January 1906.[7] The following year, this group adopted the name, Church of God.

As Spurling's leadership role gave way to that of Tomlinson's, the Church of God's polity and ecclesiology further developed. Shortly before arriving in western North Carolina, Tomlinson had studied at Frank Sandford's Bible school in Maine. There, Tomlinson's ecclesiology began to shift from the congregationalism of his Quaker past to a "theocratic authoritarian" view of church leadership where God led the church through "divinely appointed leaders."[8] Tomlinson had moderated each General Assembly since the Church of God's inception; but beginning in 1909, the Church expanded the Moderator's duties to include service throughout the year. In 1910, the name "general moderator" was replaced by "General Overseer." Tomlinson preferred this nomenclature because it described more aptly the role he envisioned for the office, and because "overseer" was a biblical term, unlike "moderator." In 1911, Tomlinson appointed State Overseers to assist him in the general oversight of all the churches. Five years later, the General Assembly created the first Elders Council to transact any business that might occur between the annual assemblies.[9] Although Tomlinson recognized that the visible church depended on hierarchy with officers and ranks, he differentiated "theocracy from episcopacy."[10]

Introduction

By autumn 1911, Tomlinson had heard of the Church of God led by Parks and Bryant in southeastern Kentucky and attended the Fifth Annual Assembly of that group in October in Whitley County. In the opening devotional service, Tomlinson led in prayer and then conducted the election of moderator in the business session.[11] He also "preached two sermons besides other talks and interpretations of messages in tongues."[12] At this meeting, the delegates voted to add the words "Mountain Assembly" to the name of its associational meeting.[13] This distinguished the association and the assembly in Kentucky from the one in Cleveland, Tennessee. In January 1912, Parks, Bryant, Jonah L. Shelton, William Hicks, and Josiah M. Thomas attended the Seventh Annual Assembly of the Church of God in Cleveland.[14] In October, Tomlinson again visited the Mountain Assembly when it met at Lower Elk Valley outside of Jellico, Tennessee, where he preached twice. At the Sunday service, Tomlinson followed Parks' 65-minute sermon with more than 90 minutes of preaching of his own. Nearly 1,500 people gathered at the outdoor meeting and most stood in the "hot sun" to hear Tomlinson's message and to have him pray for them.[15]

Though Tomlinson did not attend another Mountain Assembly, he maintained a cordial friendship with Parks and continued to influence ministers in that fellowship for quite some time. The polity of Tomlinson's Assembly enticed many pastors in the Mountain Assembly. In 1922, the Assembly elected George A. Fore, Moderator; James Lee Goins, Assistant Moderator; Starling Smith, Clerk; and Francis M. Thomas, Assistant Clerk and General Treasurer. Before the annual minute book could be printed, Fore, Smith, and Thomas had left the Mountain Assembly and joined the group in Cleveland.[16] Three years later, Goins followed them.

For many who stayed, the impulse to model their association after the Church of God continued. The Baptist Association from which Parks and Bryant came valued independent congregationalism so much that they embodied this principle into their constitution in two separate articles. Article Five stated that "This body shall exercise no ecclesiastical authority" and Article Ten stated that Article Five could not be altered or amended.[17] At its core, the Mountain Assembly consisted of independently governed congregations who voluntarily joined the association annually. As its ministers became aware of the Church of God and its hierarchical episcopal-like polity, they began to modify aspects of their organizational leadership structure. The history of the Church of God Mountain Assembly is best understood as a narrative in tension between two competing ecclesiastical polities: the congregationalism of its Baptist roots and the episcopalism from the influence of the Church of God (Cleveland). The account that follows examines that tension over the organization's first one hundred years.

Brief Review of Literature

This study examines the development of polity in the CGMA and emphasizes the congregationalism of its Baptist roots and the growth of episcopalism from its relationship with the Church of God (Cleveland). The relevant literature discusses Baptist and Pentecostal origins and models of ecclesiastical polity. Discussion of Baptist origins generally falls into four distinct explanations, while some historians incorporate aspects of one while emphasizing another. The first view holds that Baptists developed out of the Separatist movement in the Anglican Church. Ordained a priest in 1594, John Smyth espoused Puritanism within the Church of England. His criticism of infant baptism and the episcopacy soon transformed him into a Separatist. Under persecution from King James I, Smyth and layman Thomas Helwys led a group of Separatists to Amsterdam in 1607. Two years later Smyth flatly rejected pedobaptism and insisted that the true church consisted only of believers baptized upon profession of their faith. Smyth constituted a new church after baptizing himself, Helwys, and the other members. Months later, dissatisfied with his self-baptism, Smyth sought baptism among the Mennonites. Separated from Smyth, Helwys led the newly constituted church back to England in 1611.[18] H. Leon McBeth contends that the congregation constituted by Smyth and Helwys based on believer's baptism represents the first Baptist church. He argues that "following Separatist teachings to their logical conclusions" perfectly accounts "for Baptist theology and practice."[19]

A second view recognizes the significance of Smyth and Helwys but places more emphasis on the influence of Anabaptists on the development of Baptist churches. William R. Estep attempts to "examine the relationship of continental Anabaptism and early English Baptists and to measure the influence of Anabaptism upon English and American Separatism."[20] He suggests that Anabaptists initially influenced Smyth toward believer's baptism. He recognizes that Smyth "could have arrived at this position from his own private study of the Scriptures, apart from any outside stimulus," but finds this highly unlikely given that he was near three Mennonite churches in Holland for at least a year before he reached this conclusion. Estep concludes that at the very least the exposure to Anabaptist teachings forced Smyth to reexamine his own views about baptism.[21] While Estep emphasizes the Mennonites

Introduction

particularly, A.C. Underwood generalizes all Anabaptist sects as "forerunners of the Baptists." Like Anabaptists, Baptists also championed the idea of soul liberty, or an individual's "immediate and direct accountability to God" and "insisted strongly on the freedom of the human will."[22]

On this point, McBeth admits that "*some* English Baptists (the General Baptists) may have been influenced by *some* of the Anabaptists (the Dutch Mennonites) at a *specific time* (the early seventeenth century);" but because Regular Baptists embraced the five points of Calvinism, Anabaptism influence cannot account totally for the rise of Baptist churches. He limits any influence of Anabaptism to "preparing the way for Separatism and by leading some to go beyond Separatism to believer's baptism."[23] Winthrop S. Hudson flatly rejects the Anabaptist influence thesis. He demonstrates that early Baptists constantly denied affiliation with Anabaptists. Baptists rejected many hallmarks of Anabaptist life, such as refusing to take oaths and going to court, and of certain doctrines of early Anabaptists, such as soul sleep and the basic goodness of humanity. Furthermore, nearly all early Baptist leaders began as Separatists, not Anabaptists. Hudson also points out that, upon returning to England the Helwys' congregation disclaimed Smyth for gravitating toward the Anabaptists. Finally, Hudson maintains that embracing believer's baptism does not demand Anabaptist influence.[24] William H. Whitsitt concurs on the denial of Anabaptist influence and recognizes a later starting point for the first recognizable Baptist church. For Whitsitt, legitimate Baptist baptism necessitates a profession of faith, but it also requires the correct mode, immersion. Smyth and the Dutch Mennonites surrounding him practiced baptism by affusion.[25] Henry Jessey performed the first recorded baptism by immersion at the Ancient Independent Church of London in 1641. For Whitsitt, this marks the beginning of the Baptist Church.[26]

A third view, Baptist perpetuity, suggests a historical succession of Baptist teachings and practice back to the early church. This continuity of Baptist thought may be found in dissenting groups throughout the middle ages, but the reformation provided the religious and cultural context for the genuine Baptist church to manifest through congregations like Smyth's. One of the first Baptist historians, Thomas Crosby, demonstrates examples of believer's baptism and rejection of infant baptism throughout church history. He contends that even pedobaptists themselves recognize the basis of their practice rests in tradition and not in any explicit scriptural instructions.[27]

In the fourth view, Baptist secessionism argues that these dissenters throughout church history did not merely preserve Baptist thought and practice. Instead, although called various names through the centuries, these nonconformists represent an unbroken line of Baptists back to John the Baptist. James Robinson Graves, James M. Pendleton, and Amos C. Dayton championed this viewpoint in the mid-nineteenth century in the American South and their understanding of ecclesiology came to be known as Old Landmarkism.[28] James Milton Carroll crafted *The Trail of Blood* in 1931 and documented the persecution of "Baptists" throughout the centuries.[29]

One more historian merits attention. J.H. Spencer's two-volume history of Baptists in Kentucky contextualizes the religious culture in which the CGMA was born. Spencer traces the history of Baptists in the Commonwealth from the first sermons preached by Thomas Tinsley at Harrodsburg in 1776 until the publication of his book just over a century later.[30] He offers details on conventions and associations, local churches and itinerant preachers, and the doctrine and practices of Kentucky Baptists.

Out of the Baptist Church, Parks and others became adherents of the Holiness movement before they became fully Pentecostal. John Wesley's Methodism migrated from England across the Atlantic in the eighteenth century and laid the foundation for the Second Great Awakening and the American Holiness movement. As a result, religious revival ensued, and scores of holiness societies and new denominations developed. The modern Pentecostal movement, which began in Los Angeles shortly after the turn of the twentieth century spread around the world and claimed more adherents than every other Protestant group by the turn of the twenty-first. Randall Stephens examines the movements as they developed in the regional context of the southern United States and offers "clear theological and cultural reasons for believers' adversarial roles in the region." Stephens argues that the Holiness and Pentecostal movements, once imported from the North and West, respectively, adapted to the South and subsequently impacted Southern culture. He suggests that "conflict, dissent, and antagonism marked both early movements."[31] Southerners found in the Holiness and Pentecostal movements more than just religious experiences absent from their Methodist or Baptist practices. Stephens presents the ways in which Southern culture and the Pentecostal and Holiness movements influenced each other. Both country music and rock and roll were influenced by Holiness and Pentecostalism. Tammy Wynette, Johnny Cash, Jerry Lee Lewis, Little Richard, and Elvis Presley all grew up in within these religious traditions.[32]

While scholars generally identify the beginning of the modern Pentecostal movement with the events leading to the Azusa Street Revival in

Introduction

Los Angeles in 1906, Grant Wacker argues that the sources of the movement can be pictured as "four distinct though frequently confluent streams that had been flowing across the American religious landscape for many decades." He identifies these "streams" as an "emphasized heartfelt salvation," "Holy Ghost Baptism," "Divine healing," and "anticipation of the Lord's soon return." The "Holy Ghost Baptism" stream had three "tributaries: Wesley's doctrine of entire sanctification, Charles Finney's notion of Christian perfectionism, and the influence of Keswick, England's "higher life conferences." Though these "experiences" were significantly different, they were each referred to as the "Holy Ghost baptism," and the pursuit of a concrete understanding of that term led to the Pentecostal movement.[33]

While some studies on early Pentecostalism appear more focused on foundational elements and organizational developments, Wacker views the first twenty-five years of the movement from a different perspective. He looks at the early adherents themselves and the lives they lived rather than the ideas they formulated into doctrinal statements, the religious institutions they founded, or the major events that launched the worldwide movement known today. "In brief," this social history on early Pentecostals searches for the answer to, "what did the world look and feel like in that first intense burst of enthusiasm just before and after World War I?"[34] Wacker argues that "the genius of the Pentecostal movement lay in its ability to hold two seemingly incompatible impulses in productive tension." One impulse, the author identifies as primitivist and refers to Pentecostals' otherworldly inclinations and "yearning to be guided solely by God's Spirit in every aspect of their lives, however great or small." The other impulse, Wacker acknowledges as pragmatism. He uses this term to describe the real or practical side of the Pentecostals' life. By living the Pentecostal life within this healthy tension, "the life beyond in all its fullness, and the life at hand with all its richness," early believers experienced a taste of "heaven below."[35]

Walter Hollenweger examines the theological, cultural, and practical peculiarities of Pentecostal believers around the world. Scholars most commonly attribute the origins of twentieth century Pentecostalism to the Wesleyan Holiness movement of the previous century. Hollenweger, however, argues that Pentecostalism is "a denomination *sui generis*: its roots in the black, oral tradition of the American slaves, in the Catholic tradition of Wesley, in the evangelical tradition of the American holiness movement (with its far-reaching political, social, and ecumenical programs), in the critical tradition of both the holiness movement and critical Western theology, and in the ecumenical tradition."³⁶ To Hollenweger, Azusa Street pioneer William Joseph Seymour was the Father of Pentecostalism, typifying the movement in its infancy as well as the current worldwide phenomenon. Thus, Seymour typifies the author's "black root." Hollenweger attributes this tradition with bestowing upon Pentecostals such things as "orality of liturgy," the call to "prayer and decision-making," the "inclusion of dreams and visions," and the "ministry of healing by prayer and liturgical dance."³⁷

To the "Catholic Root," Hollenweger contends Pentecostalism owes its "strict Arminianism," belief in both the natural and supernatural world, "hierarchical church structure," and the "doctrine of two (or sometimes) three stages" in the order of salvation. These include regeneration, sanctification, and the baptism in the Holy Spirit.³⁸ The "Evangelical Root" gave to the Pentecostal movement its revivalism, dispensationalism, fundamentalism, and scholarship.³⁹ On the "Critical Root," Hollenweger discusses Pentecostals and their relationship to matters such as social justice, pneumatology, divine healing, soteriology, ecclesiology, public worship, missiology and hermeneutics.⁴⁰ In his treatment of the final root, the author establishes "the fact that Pentecostalism started in most places as an ecumenical renewal movement in the mainline churches" and describes the "four phases in the ecumenical development of Pentecostalism."⁴¹

Church of God (Cleveland) historiography begins with the writings of Spurling and Tomlinson. Spurling's *The Lost Link* calls for Christian unity in response to the apostasy of denominationalism.⁴² Tomlinson's seminal work, *The Last Great Conflict*, chronicles his spiritual biography and the development of his personal theology.⁴³ Ernest L. Simmons produced the first narrative history of the Church of God in 1938 and viewed the denomination's origins as rooted "in the conviction of a number of people of different denominations." He argued that it was "not a reformation of any special church or denomination but rather the response to a call of many for the doctrine and tenets set forth by the organization."⁴⁴ Charles W. Conn authored *Like a Mighty Army: A History of the Church of God* in 1955, revised it in 1977, and produced a third edition in 1996. Conn situates the Church of God within the context of the holiness movement in the American South and at the forefront of modern Pentecostalism, while paying attention to its relationship with fundamentalism.⁴⁵ In 1923, the Church of God split over the leadership of Tomlinson, and he and his followers re-organized as the Church of God of Prophecy. In 1973, Charles T. Davidson produced a three-volume history of the Church of God that follows the Tomlinson-led

Introduction

branch of the Church of God. Davidson sees the Church of God growing out of the religious unrest in the American South after the Civil War.[46]

In 1990, Mickey Crews wrote a "social history" of the Church of God and argues that the denomination represents the transformation of "poor Pentecostals" in the Appalachian hills into the "middle-class suburbs of the New South."[47] He suggests that the social and cultural outcasts of the early Church of God had abandoned their former churches "because they identified the historic denominations with the middle-class aspirations of the New South. These class-conscious 'come-outers' felt alienated, isolated from sources of power, and surrounded by an unfriendly culture."[48] Crews observes that since mid-century the Church of God moved from "Back Alleys to Uptown" and the perception of "an obscure religious sect composed of sincere but fanatical believers" evolved into a denomination that deserved its place in "mainstream conservative evangelicalism."[49]

The most recent contribution to the literature by Wade H. Phillips, *Quest to Restore God's House*, comprises a three-volume set. The first covers the formational years up to "the disruption of the church in 1922-23" that led to division within the denomination. His second volume begins "with the reform movement of A.J. Tomlinson" called the Church of God of Prophecy under the leadership of Tomlinson and his sons and concludes with the resignation of Milton Tomlinson in 1990. Volume three examines the tumultuous years that followed until a "restoration and reorganization of the church in April 2004" as the "Zion Assembly Church of God." Phillips views the Church of God as the church of the Bible with its roots at Mount Sinai and its modern visible manifestation as a fulfillment of prophecy.[50]

In 1954, Luther Gibson first attempted to chronicle the history of the Church of God Mountain Assembly.[51] For "compiling and writing" the book, the Assembly paid him $250.[52] Gibson presents a chronological summary of each general assembly taken from the annual minutes supplemented with personal and collected anecdotes and photographs. He attests that he "had the information furnished me from 1895 to 1911 and I have the records from our minute books from 1911 to 1953."[53] Gibson offers no bibliography or footnotes to identify his sources. Savannah Taylor's testimony and John H. Bryant's sermon in the appendix suggest that they provided him with some of the anecdotal material.[54] Parks' grandson, Ira H. Moses, also offered personal recollections as he supplied Gibson with copies of two of the oldest minute books.[55] Gibson suggests that the "Church of God, Mountain Assembly, like many other Pentecostal Organizations, is a continuation of the Great Revival that began at the early outpouring of the Holy Ghost on the Day of Pentecost, when the hundred and twenty were filled with the Holy Ghost, and began to speak with other tongues as the spirit gave them utterance." He points to periods of revival through the centuries and contends that the renewal movement that became the CGMA began when "Rev. J. H. Parks, Rev. Steve Bryant, Tom Moses, William Douglas, and others that were affiliated with the United Baptist Church, of the South Union Association, began to preach Sanctificition [sic]."[56] Delegates to the 64th General Assembly authorized Gibson to "bring the Church History up to date" and designated $400 from the general fund to assist him.[57] In his second edition, Gibson began where he left off, reprinted the first edition, and doubled the size of the book.[58] Personal and church histories supplement the summarization of the general assemblies.

At the 81st General Assembly, the General Council authorized the publication of a "pictorial history of the Church of God Mountain Assembly" to include "all former directors of the various departments" and update the 1970 edition of Gibson's work. As editor of the denominational periodical, James E. Prewitt undertook the assignment to be funded by receipts from the magazine.[59] The following year, Prewitt solicited the General Council for permission to "take on this project as a private enterprise, allowing him to sell the books on his own for one year" before the organization could begin to sell them. The Assembly agreed to the request and contracted the purchase of 1,000 copies at $1.00 above the printing cost for each. It also stipulated that the manuscript must be approved by the Board of Twelve Elders prior to its publication.[60] Prewitt envisioned a work patterned after Gibson's but supplemented with a complete history of each local church inserted chronologically at its founding. Also, like Gibson, Prewitt understood the organization as a continuation of Day of Pentecost in the book of Acts. He wrote:

> Revivals must be a continuing process as the influence of secularism, formalism, and moral impurity takes its toll on the spiritual fiber of the church. The church, like the mythological Pheonix [sic] Bird, seems to have a certain length of spiritual life before it dies of multiple illnesses and then through another revival springs from its own ashes to new life. Just as the eagle stirs her nest in preparation for the flight of her young, so the Holy Spirit began stirring the hearts of men for another revival just prior to the turn of the twentieth century.[61]

Unfortunately, Prewitt, frustrated by the lack of responses to his call for local church histories, never finished the project.[62]

Introduction

Discussion of Ecclesiology and Church Leadership Models

All religious history requires theological context. Ecclesiology includes the nature of the church, its discipline and doctrine, and its authority and leadership. Several recurring themes warrant an introduction. First, many evangelicals understand the church as "the community of all true believers for all time."[63] The invisible church refers to its spiritual nature because God, alone, knows who include the true believers. The "visible church includes all who profess faith in Christ and give evidence of that faith in their lives."[64] Theologians also describe the church as both "local and universal."[65]

God has entrusted the "fellowship of the church" with "certain activities, ceremonies, or functions" that serve as "means of grace," that is, the way in which God demonstrates His favor to mankind. For Roman Catholics, God uses the Church as a vehicle to bestow His favor upon His people through the seven "sacraments" or "means of salvation." These include baptism, confirmation, the Eucharist, penance, extreme unction, holy orders, and marriage. Evangelicals, on the other hand, recognize God's love through such things as Bible teaching, water baptism, the Lord's Supper, prayer, worship, church discipline, giving, spiritual gifts, fellowship, evangelism, and service to one another. From their perspective, Christ commanded his followers to observe these ordinances to edify his church.[66]

Ecclesiastical polity refers to church government and leadership. From the New Testament era until the Protestant Reformation, episcopal polity governed the medieval church. In this hierarchical system, rectors lead local congregations under the jurisdiction of a bishop. All the local congregations under the bishop form a diocese. An archbishop maintains authority over bishops and dioceses in his jurisdiction. In the Roman Catholic Church, the pope stands at the head of the church with authority over all the archbishops.[67] Catholics understand Peter as the shepherd appointed by Christ over "the whole flock" and Peter's successor, the pope, "as pastor of the entire Church" with "full, supreme, and universal power over the whole Church, a power which he can always exercise unhindered."[68] Episcopal polity continues to govern the Roman Catholic Church, Orthodox churches, and Anglican and Episcopalian Churches.

The Reformation brought new church denominations and new styles of polity, including Presbyterianism. In this system, leadership in the local church consists of "elders" elected to a "session" by the members of the congregation. The session governs the local church. Some or all the elders of the session may also serve on a presbytery, which oversees all the congregations under its authority. Some members of the presbytery then represent it at the "general assembly" which governs "all the presbyterian churches in a nation or region."[69] Many Reformed churches and various Presbyterian churches employ this leadership method today.

Connexionalism (or Connectionalism) refers to the polity employed by most Methodist churches. United Methodists define "connexion" as "a network of classes, societies, and annual conferences." Local congregations form an "interconnected network of organizations that join together in mission and ministry."[70] Local congregations within a geographic area form districts. "Each district is led by a district superintendent ("DS"), an elder appointed by the bishop, usually for a six-year term." The DS "works with the bishop and others in the appointment of ordained ministers to serve the district's churches."[71] The bishop presides over the "annual conference" comprised of all the districts within its regional boundary. At the annual conference sessions, the conference elects lay and clergy delegates to represent it at the jurisdictional and general conferences every four years.[72] As the "primary legislative body", the general conference "speaks officially for the church." The "council of bishops" forms the spiritual leadership of the United Methodist Church, and the "judicial council" forms its highest court.[73] Connectionalism differs significantly from Episcopalism in the absence of a single leader at the head. It arose in the 1820s out of the desire to give a democratic voice to local pastors and laymen. The offices of Anglican episcopalism were retained, but the method by which they were chosen was redirected from the top to the bottom.[74]

The Reformation also gave rise to Congregationalism. Sometimes congregational churches utilize a single pastor at the head of the church with a board of elders or deacons serving alongside him. The members of the church select their leadership. Some congregational models see the deacon board as the leadership mechanism with the pastor subservient to the board or to the church. The most democratic congregational churches choose not to appoint a governing board and relegate the pastor's role to that of the primary Bible teacher. In this system, the members vote on every decision. Regardless of the leadership dynamic within the local body, congregational churches govern themselves autonomously and recognize no authority outside the membership of that congregation.[75]

As Anglican Separatism grew, the separatists who became Baptists adopted congregationalism as their preferred church polity. The lengthy reign of Queen Elizabeth I provided stability for the Church of England, but also contributed to the rise of Puritanism. As many Puritans became discouraged at the possibility of full reformation, Separatists organized their own self-governing congregations. One such Puritan, Robert Browne, established a separate church with a congregational form of government in the late sixteenth century. While lecturing at Cambridge, Browne insisted that civil authorities had no jurisdiction in matters of ecclesiastical government. He proposed that the church consisted of a gathering of believers who had entered a covenant with one another to live under Christ's rule. He recognized that God called church leaders and gave them their authority, but also insisted that their appointment to office came from the consent of the church by majority vote. These principles guided Particular Baptists and General Baptists in the following century as they established congregationally governed churches.[76]

Five theological convictions direct Baptist congregational polity. First, Jesus Christ is the true head of the Church and the only mediator between God and man. All humanity then has direct access to God through His Son. Second, each local body must govern itself. No ecclesiastical authority exists outside the local church. Third, the church membership serves as the final arbiter in church government. The congregation judges false and correct doctrine, true ministers, and matters of personal conduct. Fourth, the authority of leadership rests in the power of persuasion. The New Testament recognizes three offices in the church, apostle, elder, and deacon. Baptists believe the office of Apostle ceased to exist with the death of the men Christ chose to fulfill that office. Because the office of elder or pastor depends on the assent of the congregation, church leaders have no authority on their own to compel obedience. Instead, the pastor must influence followers by the Word of God. Finally, church authority naturally divides into three spheres. Christ exercises ultimate authority and will one day judge all humanity. The congregation rules in the earthly affairs of the church, while the pastor provides influential leadership in the daily lives of believers.[77]

Once transplanted from Europe, Congregationalism was transformed by several uniquely American factors. The first of which was the Great Awakening. The effects of the colonial revival differed by geographical regions. In New England, many Congregationalists detached themselves from state establishment and became Baptists, and converts in the South came to see the Baptist churches as an evangelical alternative to the Church of England. Religious diversity was present in the middle colonies from the beginning, and congregationalism flourished there during the Great

Awakening. If religious enthusiasm provided congregationalism with a spark, the American Revolution and the creation of the federal republic gave it the fuel to set it aflame. Colonial Americans knew too well the abuses that accompany unchecked power, whether political or ecclesiastical. If they were not aware, Colonial clergymen often brought attention to them in sermons leading up to the war for independence. With the principle of liberty at the heart of the Revolution, evangelicals especially championed the disestablishment of the church. Thomas Jefferson's letter to the Danbury Baptist Association in 1802 interpreting the First Amendment as "a wall of separation between Church and State" was celebrated by its recipients. In the spirit of democratic populism that thrived in the early nineteenth century, Bible-reading and unconstrained self-interpretation led to the formation of numerous denominations and the abandonment of written creeds. "No creed but the Bible" became commonplace in America. The Second Great Awakening provided a platform for the spread of Methodism in America and contributed to explosive growth of Baptists in the first half of the century. The egalitarian nature of the revival gave rise to the American "farmer-pastor" as an alternative to seminary-trained clergy.[78]

By the twentieth century, Baptists had developed a sophisticated theology of the church and had been long establishing churches based on it. Pentecostalism, however, grew out of an experience before a theology had time to form. Early Pentecostals, then, often formed churches first and allowed ecclesiology to grow from the experience. Veli-Matti Kärkkäinen suggests that early adherents of the modern Pentecostal movement focused primarily on evangelism in preparation for the soon return of Christ and that their busyness left little time for theological reflection and therefore little has been written about Pentecostal ecclesiology.[79]

Dale Coulter takes exception to that generalization of all Pentecostals and argues that during "the first thirty-seven years of its existence as a movement, ecclesiology permeated the theological milieu of the Church of God (1886-1923)." Coulter views the development of ecclesiology in the Church of God in two stages: the formative phase under R.G. Spurling and the maturation phase under A.J. Tomlinson. Spurling's ecclesiology developed as he rejected the Landmarkism of his Baptist upbringing and an emphasis on doctrinal statements and creeds. He began to rethink his view of church membership as something accomplished by water baptism and saw it as the product of having received "the right hand of fellowship" when one enters the church covenant.[80] Coulter argues that Tomlinson further developed Church of God ecclesiology by emphasizing the need for centralized government. For Tomlinson, "hierarchy, structure, organization, and government" formed important themes for his understanding of the church. "Hierarchy also implied officers and ranks" and "one could not have government without officers." Tomlinson eventually described the church's polity as a "theocracy" with Christ at the head, and with every decision confirmed by witness of the Holy Spirit. Through this latter Pentecostal distinction, Tomlinson differentiated between the episcopacy of the Roman Catholic Church and his own hierarchical structure that featured him as the General Overseer who appointed regional State Overseers who had direct authority over the pastors and congregations within their jurisdiction.[81]

Harold Hunter responds to Coulter and argues that Tomlinson's ecclesiology should not be understood as a further development or refinement of Spurling's but instead should emphasize the theological contributions Frank Sandford, Alexander Dowie, Frank Porter, B.H. Irwin, and others. Hunter identifies two "distinctive pillars of Tomlinson's ecclesiology." First, the visible church constitutes an exclusive body, the one true church. Second, the General Overseer should serve this body for life. This idea formed much of what Tomlinson meant by "theocracy," for like Sandford, he believed that God ruled "His Church through divinely appointed leaders who were to be obeyed as absolutely as if they were God Himself."[82]

Tomlinson maintained that his understanding of theocracy deviated from the hierarchy of episcopalism. At the urging of many in attendance at the Seventh General Assembly of the Church of God, Tomlinson relented to share his opinion on a matter before that body. The Moderator typically refrained from taking part in such discussions, and Tomlinson hesitated from breaking that tradition to avoid criticisms that he desired to "make" himself "a king or pope." He continued, "Some may say 'I know now what you are aiming at, you want to organize a body like the Catholic Church,'" consisting of a hierarchy of ministers with Tomlinson at the top.[83] Though Tomlinson denounced such claims, his repudiation did little to deter his critics. By the early 1920s, one former Church of God minister insisted that "the Church of God is like the Catholic Church and Tomlinson is the pope."[84]

Baptist churches today maintain congregational government by the members of the local church. While many voluntarily choose to participate in regional associations and state and national conventions, Baptist churches are autonomous. In the Church of God (Cleveland), membership is more universal. While members in a local church govern the affairs of that congregation, they also participate in the institutional government of the whole Church through the General Assembly. The General Overseer and leadership elected at the national level appoint and direct leaders on the state level. State and district overseers appoint leaders in the local churches. The polity of the Church of God Mountain Assembly lies between these two models. The degree to which an overseer directs the affairs of the local church depends on several factors, including the personality of the overseer and the makeup of the local church. Notwithstanding, the tension between local governance and the authority of ecclesiastical hierarchy remains.

Summary and Outline

The religious association of ten churches that Parks, Bryant, and others founded in Whitley County, Kentucky in 1907 ultimately developed into a worldwide organization. The tension between two very different expressions of ecclesiology, the congregationalism of its Baptist founders and the theocratic episcopalism from the influence of the Church of God (Cleveland), provides a context for understanding the CGMA's historical leadership. Part one (chapters two through eight) of this book analyzes how ecclesiastical polity developed within the organization and explores that tension through the first 40 years of its history leading up to a major schism over church government in 1946 and how its leaders responded to it. Part two (chapters nine through thirteen) examines the slow shift back toward congregationalism over the next 60 years culminating with a fissure in 2004 that swung the pendulum back again.

Chapter two will demonstrate the distinctive Baptist characteristics of the Mountain Assembly during its first few decades. Chapter three will show the influence of the Church of God (Cleveland) on the development of denominational leadership in the Mountain Assembly. Chapter four will discuss further progression toward centralized government in the CGMA until it encountered its first conflict with the Church of God (Cleveland) in the 1920s. Chapter five will consider the setback the Mountain Assembly experienced when its leaders left to join the Church of God (Cleveland). Chapter six will focus on the informal leadership structure in the 1930s that rose from the departure of key ministers the previous decade and the spread of the organization outside the Appalachian coal fields. Chapter seven will examine how the establishment of youth and women's auxiliaries and a new church periodical further developed the association into a centralized denomination and will conclude with the adoption of a new form of

Introduction

government in 1944. Chapter eight will analyze the conditions that led to an organizational split in 1946.

Chapter nine explains how the Mountain Assembly rebounded from the schism of 1946 by recruiting new ministers and starting new churches. Chapter ten describes the building of an international denomination through the development of a national youth program and the establishment of the first foreign missions work. Chapter eleven analyzes the long-lasting benefits of these two auxiliaries and two new ones, Christian education and national ladies' ministries. Chapter twelve discusses the financial growth and stability achieved by maintaining these ministries. Chapter thirteen examines the restored emphasis on local congregations and its disruptive reaction. The final chapter summarizes the findings and analyzes the thesis.

Figure 1.1: John H. Parks
c/o Jellico CGMA

Figure 1.2: John Thomas
c/o CGMA

---

[1] South Union Association of United Baptists (SUAUB), *Minutes of the Ninety-First Annual Session of the South Union Association of United Baptists* (n.p.: by the association, 1905), 11.

[2] Wayne Grudem, *Bible Doctrine: Essential Teachings of the Christian Faith*, ed. Jeff Purswell (Grand Rapids, MI: Zondervan, 1999), 326-329.

[3] J. Lawrence Brasher, *The Sanctified South: John Lakin Brasher and the Holiness Movement* (Chicago: University of Illinois Press, 1994), 27.

[4] SUAUB, *Minutes* (1905), 4.

⁵ Landmarkism describes an ecclesiology espoused by some Baptists that suggests that the Baptist church is the true church of the New Testament and that there exists an unbroken chain of Baptist churches from the Apostolic age until the present. Further description of the theology and history of Landmarkism follows later in this chapter.

⁶ David G. Roebuck, "Restorationism and a Vision for World Harvest: A Brief History of the Church of God (Cleveland)," *Cyberjournal for Pentecostal-Charismatic Research* 5 (February 1999): 1-5.

⁷ Church of God, *Minutes of the Annual Assembly of the Churches of East Tennessee, North Georgia and Western North Carolina, Held January 26 & 27 1906, at Camp Creek, N.C.* (n.p.: 1906), 1.

⁸ Dale M. Coulter, "The Development of Ecclesiology in the Church of God (Cleveland, TN): A Forgotten Contribution?" *Pneuma* 29 (2007): 72-73.

⁹ Roebuck, 9; Wade H. Phillips, *Quest to Restore God's House: A Theological History of the Church of God (Cleveland)*, Vol. 1, 1886-1923, *R.G. Spurling to A.J. Tomlinson: Formation-Transformation-Reformation* (Cleveland, TN: CPT Press, 2014), 244-248.

¹⁰ Coulter, 79.

¹¹ CGMA, *Minutes of the Fifth Annual Mountain Assembly of the Churches of God* (n.p.: by the association, 1911).

¹² A.J. Tomlinson, *Diary of A.J. Tomlinson: 1901-1924*, ed. Hector Ortiz and Adrian Varlack (Cleveland, TN: White Wing Publishing House, 2012), 183.

¹³ CGMA, *Minutes* (1911), 2.

¹⁴ Church of God, *Echoes from the General Assembly* (Cleveland, TN: Church of God Publishing House, 1912), 20.

¹⁵ Tomlinson, 197.

¹⁶ CGMA, *Minutes of the Sixteenth Annual Session of the Mountain Assembly of the Churches of God* (Jellico, TN: CGMA, 1922), 1.

¹⁷ South Union Association, *Minutes* (1905), 2.

¹⁸ H. Leon McBeth, *The Baptist Heritage* (Nashville: Broadman Press, 1987), 32-38.

¹⁹ Ibid., 49.

²⁰ William R. Estep, *The Anabaptist Story* (Nashville: Broadman Press, 1963; revised ed., Grand Rapids, MI: William B. Eerdmans Publishing Company, 1975), 3-4 (page citations are to the revised edition).

²¹ Ibid., 217-221.

²² A.C. Underwood, *A History of the English Baptists* (London: Kingsgate Press, 1947), 20-22.

²³ McBeth, 53.

²⁴ Winthrop S. Hudson, "Baptists Were Not Anabaptists," *The Chronicle* 16 (October 1953): 171-179.

²⁵ With baptism by affusion, the clergy pours water on the head of the baptized. With immersion, the minister submerges the believer in water.

²⁶ William H. Whitsitt, *A Question in Baptist History* (New York: Arno Press, 1980), 9-11, 80, 90.

Introduction

²⁷ Thomas Crosby, *The History of the English Baptists*, vol. 1 (London, 1738-1740), *i-lxi*.

²⁸ James E. Tull, *A History of Southern Baptist Landmarkism in the Light of Historical Baptist Ecclesiology* (New York: Arno Press, 1980), 128-137.

²⁹ James Milton Carroll, *The Trail of Blood… Following the Christians Down Through the Centuries* or *The Present History of Baptist Churches: From the Time of Christ, Their Founder, to the Present Day* (Lexington, KY: Ashland Baptist Church, 1931), 6-53.

³⁰ J.H. Spencer, *A History of Kentucky Baptists*, vol. 1 (Cincinnati, 1885; reprint, Gallatin, TN: Church History Research & Archives, 1984), 13 (page citations are to the reprint edition).

³¹ Randall J. Stephens, *The Fire Spreads: Holiness and Pentecostalism in the American South* (Cambridge: Harvard University Press, 2008), 7.

³² Ibid., 4.

³³ Grant Wacker, *Heaven Below: Early Pentecostals and American Culture* (Cambridge: Harvard University Press, 2001), 1-3, 9.

³⁴ Ibid.

³⁵ Ibid., 10-14, 269.

³⁶ Walter J. Hollenweger, *Pentecostalism: Origins and Developments Worldwide* (Peabody, MA: Hendrickson Publishers, Inc., 1997), 2.

³⁷ Ibid., 18.

³⁸ Ibid., 143. Not all Pentecostals view sanctification as work of grace, but rather see it as a progressive work that commences at the new birth.

³⁹ Ibid., 183-200.

⁴⁰ Ibid., 203-325.

⁴¹ Ibid., 334, 355.

⁴² Richard G. Spurling, *The Lost Link* (Turtletown, TN: by the author, 1920).

⁴³ Ambrose J. Tomlinson, *The Last Great Conflict* (Cleveland, TN: White Wing Publishing House, 1913).

⁴⁴ Ernest L. Simmons, *History of Church of God: With Headquarters at Cleveland, Tennessee* (Cleveland, TN: Church of God Publishing House, 1938), 153.

⁴⁵ Charles W. Conn, *Like a Mighty Army: A History of the Church of God,* Definitive Edition (Cleveland, TN: Pathway Press, 1996), *xxvii-xxviii*.

⁴⁶ Charles T. Davidson, *Upon This Rock*, vol. 1 (Cleveland, TN: White Wing Publishing House, 1973), 286-289.

⁴⁷ Mickey Crews, The Church of God: A Social History (Knoxville: University of Tennessee Press, 1990), *xii-xiii*.

⁴⁸ Ibid., 173.

⁴⁹ Ibid., 172.

⁵⁰ Phillips, *xvi-xxii*.

⁵¹ Gibson.

[52] CGMA, *[Minutes of the] Church of God Mountain Assembly: Sixty-Fourth Annual Assembly* (Jellico, TN: CGMA, 1970), 55.

[53] Gibson, 47.

[54] Ibid., 50-53.

[55] [Ira] Moses, [Monroe, MI], to [Luther Gibson], [Sidney, OH], [1953], in the personal collection of Mike Gibson, Knoxville, TN.

[56] Gibson, 5.

[57] CGMA, *Minutes* (1970), 21, 23.

[58] Luther Gibson, *A History of the Church of God Mountain Assembly, 1906-1970* (Jellico, TN: Church of God Mountain Assembly, Inc., 1970). All future citations of Gibson will be from this edition.

[59] CGMA, *[Minutes of the] 81st Annual Assembly of the Church of God Mountain Assembly, Inc.* (Jellico, TN: CGMA, 1987), 24.

[60] CGMA, *[Minutes of the] 82nd Annual Assembly of the Church of God Mountain Assembly* (Jellico, TN: CGMA, 1988), 28.

[61] James E. Prewitt, "Upon This Rock I Will Build My Church," unfinished manuscript, 1, in the personal collection of the author.

[62] In 1995, this author self-published a modern narrative history of the Church of God Mountain Assembly. This work takes a fresh look at primary sources, incorporates personal recollections from second-generation interviews, and attempts to situate the narrative into its cultural context. It examines the movement as a response, rather than a renewal. See Michael Padgett, *A Goodly Heritage: A History of the Church of God Mountain Assembly, Inc.* (Middlesboro, KY: self-published, 1995).

[63] Wayne Grudem, *Systematic Theology: An Introduction to Biblical Doctrine* (Leicester, England: Inter-Varsity Press, 1994), 853.

[64] Ibid., 856.

[65] Ibid., 857.

[66] Ibid., 950-951.

[67] Ibid., 923-925.

[68] Catholic Church, "The Hierarchal Constitution of the Church," in *The Catechism of the Catholic Church*, 2nd ed. (Vatican: Libreria Editrice Vaticana, 2012), 880-882.

[69] Grudem, *Theology*, 925-927; see also Presbyterian Church (USA), *The Book of Order 2017-2019* (Louisville: The Office of the General Assembly Presbyterian Church [USA], 2017), F-3.0201-0203, G-1.0103, G-3.01-05.

[70] United Methodist Church, "Organization: The Church as Connection," accessed 7 April 2019, http://www.umc.org/who-we-are/organization-church-as-connection.

[71] UMC, "Districts," accessed 7 April 2019, http://www.umc.org/who-we-are/districts.

[72] UMC, "Annual Conferences," accessed 7 April 2019, http://www.umc.org/who-we-are/annual-conferences.

[73] UMC, "Constitutional Structure," accessed 7 April 2019, http://www.umc.org/who-we-are/constitutional-structure.

Introduction

74 Russell E. Richey, Kenneth E. Rowe, Jean Miller Schmidt, *American Methodism: A Compact History* (Nashville, TN: Abingdon Press, 2010), 76-79.

75 Grudem, *Theology*, 928-936.

76 Michael A.G. Haykin, "Historical Roots of Congregationalism" in Mark Dever and Jonathan Leeman, eds. *Baptist Foundations: Church Government for an Anti-Institutional Age* (Nashville: B&H Publishing Group, 2015), 31-41.

77 Stephen J. Wellum and Kirk Wellum, "The Biblical and Theological Case for Congregationalism," in ibid., 62-77.

78 Mark A. Noll, *A History of Christianity in the United States and Canada* (Grand Rapids: William B. Eerdmans Publishing Company, 1992), 98-99; 119-122; 144-148, 151, 169-180.

79 Veli-Matti Kärkkäinen, "Church as Charismatic Fellowship: Ecclesiological Reflections from the Pentecostal-Roman Catholic Dialogue," *Journal of Pentecostal Theology* 9, no. 1 (2001): 102.

80 Coulter, 60, 62-67, 69.

81 Ibid., 77-81.

82 Harold D. Hunter, "A.J. Tomlinson's Emerging Ecclesiology" *Pneuma* 32, no. 3 (2010): 373-378.

83 Church of God, *Echoes* (1912), 16

84 J.P. Hughes, "The Church of God a Great Mystery," *CGE* 12, no. 18 (30 April 1921): 1.

2

The Baptist Roots of the Church of God Mountain Assembly

John Parks, Andrew Silcox, and Stephen Bryant were Baptists. They came to know Christ as their Savior in Baptist altars, were baptized by Baptist preachers, and began preaching in Baptist pulpits. As their leadership potential developed, it did so within a United Baptist Church polity. United Baptist Churches in the American South were the product of a reunification of "Separates" and "Regulars" in the nineteenth century. Just prior to the American Revolution, the Great Awakening simultaneously increased the number of Baptists in the colonies and divided them into two parties. Regular Baptists, or "Old Lights," "adhered to the old ways and disparaged revivals," while Separate Baptists, or "New Lights," adopted the methods of George Whitefield and Jonathan Edwards. As the spiritual climate in America waned, the schism between Baptist groups subsided. In the nineteenth century, many gradually dropped "United" and simply became "Baptists." The preservation of "United Baptist" in the South, was especially characteristic of Kentucky.[1]

After Parks, Silcox, and Bryant joined the Holiness Movement, they departed from United Baptist faith, but never departed fully from Baptist practice. The Baptist roots of the founding ministers of the Church of God Mountain Assembly form the basis for understanding the ecclesiological development of the movement. Parks and Bryant maintained some key Baptist doctrines and practices which significantly influenced the identity of the organization. Many of the historical features of the South Union Association of United Baptists were retained in the new denomination. The association Parks, Silcox, and Bryant. formed in Whitley County, Kentucky in 1907 must be understood in the context of a Baptist association framework comprised of Holiness churches.

The Baptist Roots of John Parks, Andrew Silcox, and Stephen Bryant

John Hansford Parks was born near Marsh Creek in Whitley County (present day McCreary County), Kentucky on July 5, 1861, the fourth of five children born to Helen (Thomas) and James Uriah Parks, Jr. Shortly before his second birthday, his father died, leaving his family faced with many hardships. When he was 16, his mother married their neighbor, Griffin Morgan, an older man recently widowed, and gave birth to four more children. By 1880, Parks had moved to Little Wolf Creek, Kentucky, to live and work with his mother's brother, Daniel Thomas. On July 16 that year, Parks eloped to Scott County, Tennessee, with Daniel's daughter, Rachel, at the home of Hiram Trammell who solemnized the marriage rites. Rachel gave birth to their first child, Birtha, in 1884, and their second, Jalie, in 1886. Perhaps the burden of fatherhood impressed upon Parks an urgency of spiritual matters as he dedicated his life to Christ and joined the United Baptist Church at Little Wolf Creek, Kentucky on November 21, 1886. He was baptized there on January 12, 1887 and began preaching the gospel of Christ not long after. On May 11, 1889, Elders Caswell Lovitt, Alvin Jones Ross, and Wesley Perry ordained him to gospel ministry at Little Wolf Creek.[2]

Andrew Jackson Silcox was born in Scott County, Tennessee on November 5, 1863 to Elizabeth (Shoopman) and Riley Silcox. At age 6, his father died and left his mother to care for five children alone. On June 3, 1883, Silcox married Jane Thomas, Rachel Parks's sister, in Campbell County, Tennessee. Soon after the Parks family dedicated themselves to Christ, the Silcoxes followed. Andrew was baptized and joined the United Baptist Church at Little Wolf Creek on October 9, 1887. Like his brother-in-law, Silcox began preaching the gospel shortly after his conversion and was ordained August 8, 1891 by Parks and Lovitt.[3]

Figure 2.1: John H. Parks and Andrew J. Silcox

c/o CGMA

While Parks and Silcox joined the United Baptist Church in their 20s, Stephen Nathan Bryant was raised in the church. Bryant was born in Whitley

County, Kentucky on July 30, 1868 to Amey (Cox) and John Bryant. His parents were members of Pleasant Hill United Baptist Church in Whitley County in the 1860s before transferring their membership to the newly constituted Bethel United Baptist Church in 1878. Bryant married Mary Davenport in Whitley County on December 20, 1887, and the following October their first child, John Harrison Bryant, was born at their new home on Sheep Creek. The Bryants had joined Wolf Creek United Baptist Church not far from Sheep Creek and became acquainted with the ministries of Parks and Silcox. In 1900, Bryant also accepted a call to gospel ministry.[4]

Figure 2.2: Stephen N. Bryant
c/o CGMA

Parks, Silcox, and Bryant began preaching within twelve years of each other in Whitley County, Kentucky. Many of the United Baptist Churches in which they preached, and ultimately pastored, were affiliated with the South Union Association of United Baptists. Just months after joining the church, Parks represented his home church as a delegate when Little Wolf Creek hosted the annual association meeting in September. Caswell Lovitt moderated the meeting and preached the introductory sermon. Two years later, Silcox joined Parks as a delegate at Ryan's Creek on September 26. The Moderator appointed Parks, along with W.H. Cornelius and F.M. Cornelius, to a correspondence committee to represent the association and carry its letter of greeting to the West Union Association when that group met later in the fall. Additionally, before the business session concluded, Parks "was chosen by private ballot to preach the next introductory sermon." To be asked to preach the keynote message preceding the business session of the association indicated the great respect Parks had already found among his peers even before he was ordained. Over the next fifteen years, Parks and Silcox attended every annual association meeting and grew increasingly involved.[5]

At Wolf Creek on September 25, 1891, Parks preached the introductory sermon of the 77th Annual Session of the South Union Association of United Baptists. He read from 1 Peter 5:1-3, "The elders which are among you I exhort, who am also an elder" and preached about feeding God's flock and leading by example. The following day, the association "ordered that A.J.

Silcox preach the next introductory sermon," which he did on September 23, 1892 at Jellico Creek from Revelation 22:14. Over the next decade Parks and Silcox represented the South Union Association by carrying corresponding letters to the West Union Association (1892, 1900, 1902), New River Association (1892, 1900), Mt. Zion Association (1893, 1894), North Concord Association (1893), Lynn Camp Association (1894), and East Union Association (1894, 1902). Over the same period, Parks preached the introductory sermon two more times (1897, 1901), and Silcox preached it three more (1896, 1900, 1902). In addition to the keynote address, both ministers frequently preached at the appointment of the "committee on divine services" during the sessions.[6]

In recognition of his leadership potential, the South Union Association elected Parks to serve as assistant to the moderator, Caswell Lovitt, in 1893 at Good Hope Church, just outside Jellico, Tennessee. In the next three annual sessions, the association re-elected Parks to the position. The 83rd Annual Session of the South Union Baptist Association at Paint Creek in Whitley County on September 24, 1897 began with Silcox conducting the devotional service with hymn singing and scripture reading before Parks preached the introductory sermon. When the business session opened, delegates elected Parks as Moderator and Silcox as his Assistant. The two were reelected again the following year. In 1899 and again in 1900, the delegates chose Silcox to be the Moderator before reelecting Parks again in 1901 and 1902. The 1902 association meeting at Little Wolf Creek was also significant in that it was the first one attended as a delegate by Stephen Bryant. Bryant represented the Wolf Creek Church and preached one of the divine services on the second night.[7]

Bryant had been acquainted with the ministry of Parks for at least a decade before that association meeting. His son, John, recollected as one of his earliest memories Parks preaching at Wolf Creek when he was a toddler.

> Jane Holt, a colored sister, and Barbara Siler began to shout and ran upon the stage where stood Brother Parks. When they slapped their hands right in his face and praised the Lord in a loud voice, it so scared me that I began crying and squalling. When mother was unable to calm me down, some boys from the outside of church reached in at the window to take me outside. Really I was glad to get out, and when they asked me what they were doing in there, I gave them this story, "They are having the biggest fight I ever saw, and that man with the long beard was the one who raised it."

At home that night, Stephen and Mary explained the excitement to their young son and religious fanaticism never frightened John again.[8]

Baptist Preachers, Holiness Doctrine, and Holiness Churches

The longtime mutual respect between Parks, Bryant, and Silcox proved critical when they and four other ministers were excluded from the Baptist association and sought to organize an association of churches of like faith. At the peak of his popularity in the Baptist association, Parks embraced the doctrine of entire sanctification and began encouraging his congregants to seek the second blessing and to warn them of the danger of apostasy if they allowed sin to dominate them. In the last decade of the nineteenth century, several Methodist ministers conducted evangelistic crusades in the Whitley County area and won many converts to Holiness teachings. Among these revivalists was Martin Wells Knapp, one of the most influential leaders of the Holiness movement.[9]

After a long struggle with his own inner inclination toward sin, the Methodist pastor, Knapp, experienced entire sanctification at a revival in Michigan conducted by William Taylor in November 1882.[10] Four years later, Knapp moved to Cincinnati where he published a Holiness newspaper, *God's Revivalist*, and conducted Holiness crusades. One such campaign was launched in the summer of 1894 near Flat Rock in Pulaski (now, McCreary) County, Kentucky. Knapp established an annual camp meeting at "Beulah Heights" three miles east of Flat Rock. He was so burdened "for the people in the South, and the first time he went down there and found old men who could neither read nor write, he was greatly moved." An elderly convert donated 200 acres for Knapp to build a campground, Christian school and orphanage.[11]

When the Beulah Heights Holiness Camp Meeting opened the second week of August 1894, its principal participants were Asbury College President John Wesley Hughes and Evangelists Kate Keith and Mary Storey of Cincinnati.[12] Storey was born in Ireland in 1852, was saved at the age of eight, and immigrated to the United States thirteen years later where she worked alongside her brother managing a large department store in Cincinnati.[13] In her pursuit of sanctification, she left her "large salary" and answered God's call to "give up all" and to "tell it." She perceived Knapp's arrival in Cincinnati as an answer to her prayers for God to send help to "rebuild the walls of wasted holiness."[14] Knapp also highly regarded Storey's ministry.[15]

Baptist Roots

From its earliest days, the Wesleyan Holiness Movement "championed the equality of women both in society and in God's redemptive plan for mankind." For this reason, suffragists Elizabeth Cady Stanton and Lucretia Mott found a welcome host at the Wesleyan Methodist Church to conduct the Seneca Falls Convention in 1848. The ordination of Antoinette Brown in 1853 by Methodist Minister Luther Lee was one of the first female ordinations in America.[16] Although among some early Baptists women taught and preached, most Baptists limited to men the task of expositing scripture.[17]

Storey returned to Beulah Heights in 1895 as the "preaching evangelist," and Keith returned as the "children's evangelist."[18] The success of the holiness meetings at Beulah Heights earned Storey additional opportunities to preach Holiness in Southeastern Kentucky. In late December 1898, Storey and another evangelist, Elizabeth Hartley, led a successful revival in Williamsburg.[19] After this meeting, Hartley went to Holy Hill and conducted a "holiness convention" for a young pastor, William Jesse Wilder, where "a number were converted and sanctified" through the efforts of this "zealous, thorough and able advocate of entire sanctification."[20] Meanwhile, Storey went to nearby Pleasant View where "the trustees opened their house, and from the very first the Lord gave victory."[21]

The revival at Pleasant View was held at "the Gospel Congregational Church." This church was constructed in 1884 on land donated by Robert Boone Bird who had hosted Methodist circuit riders in his home for forty years. It was the first church building erected in Pleasant View and served as a meeting house for multiple congregations when families of many denominations moved into the community after the rise of the coal mining industry in the 1890s. Although most United Baptists in southeastern Kentucky in the late 19th century did not endorse women in ministry, Storey's revival at the Congregational Church that summer drew "large numbers" from both the Methodist and Baptist congregations and "many Christians from both churches professed this second blessing." Many "found they had never been converted and others had long since lost their salvation." Two men "that had not

Figure 2.3: Mary Storey
c/o God's Bible School

spoken to each other for years, and the last time had been to draw knives on each other" experienced sanctification and "took each other in their arms." When the United Baptist Church at Pleasant View "dismissed their members" who professed sanctification, many stayed with the Congregational Church. Among those who claimed the experience of entire sanctification in Mary Storey's revival at Pleasant View in 1898-1899 were John Parks and his first cousins, the Thomas brothers.[22]

Parks' maternal uncle, Aaron Thomas, had served as a deacon at the United Baptist Church at Little Wolf Creek for 25 years prior to his death in 1892.[23] His four sons, Sherrod, Francis, Daniel, and Michael, were actively involved in church life at Little Wolf Creek and Pleasant View. Their experience that summer generated such piety in the lives of the Thomas brothers that many assumed they were all preachers.[24] The zeal of these new converts to the Holiness movement soon led to friction with the "more conservative members of the congregation." After an attempt to conduct separate services failed, Bird donated additional land for the construction of a new Methodist Church, and the "extreme group" continued meeting in the Congregational Church.[25]

Figure 2.4: Sherrod, Francis, Michael, and Daniel Thomas
c/o Claudia E. Thomas

As Storey's popularity spread throughout southeastern Kentucky, attitudes about women in ministry sometimes changed. In January 1900, the Presiding Elder of Middlesborough District of the Methodist Episcopal Church remarked, "When she holds a meeting once at a place, it is no more trouble for the people to make arrangements for a woman to preach."[26] Storey's three-week revival in Middlesboro the previous January had featured "large crowds" and the "altar full of seekers for Holiness."[27] From Middlesboro, Storey went to Pineville where "there were fifty or sixty conversions."[28] Next, she preached in Barbourville where "all the young men at the [Union] college who are preparing for the ministry, with the president, got the blessing."[29] Storey continued to preach additional revivals in Whitley, Bell, and Knox Counties throughout the summer.[30]

One of ministry students at Union College in Barbourville was William Jesse Wilder.[31] After school, Wilder returned to Whitley County and began conducting holiness revivals of his own. A revival at Whitley City in June 1901 saw people "coming to church who have not been before in years" with many "being saved and sanctified."[32] This successful meeting was followed by another at Clear Creek Campground near Pine Knot on August 16-28.[33] The following month, Wilder conducted a revival at Pleasant Hill United Baptist Church, which had been organized and pastored by his maternal great-grandfather, Andrew Jackson Patrick, 33 years earlier.[34]

One of the attendees of this revival was his mother's first cousin, 24-year-old Curd Walker. When he was a boy, Walker was baptized at the church their grandfather started but was excluded as an adult for drunkenness. After attending several nights of the revival, Walker was converted under the preaching of that "good old fire-baptized Methodist preacher" on September 13, 1901.[35] Early the following morning, the zealous new convert visited his brother's sick wife, to sing and pray for her. "Seemingly shocked" at the change she observed in one who "had been so rough in the past," the sister-in-law presumed Walker had been "sanctified." Until then, he had not contemplated the subject, but on the eight-mile trip back to Pleasant Hill for the evening service, Walker "pondered it over and over." At church that night, he experienced "consecration to advance my new life in righteousness" and "started in a sanctified life the best" he "knew."[36]

The holiness revival in Whitley County brought persecution, and the Pleasant Hill Church faced "division over the doctrine of holliness [sic]." The church eventually excluded the Walkers and others for embracing the doctrines of "sinless perfection" and the danger of apostacy that would jeopardize the "final perseverance of the saints." The "great divide came to such an extent that people of holiness faith got another burrying [sic] ground and some talked of taking up their dead and moving them."[37] After their expulsion from the Baptist church, the Walkers returned to Cane Creek. His brother and his wife's uncles were members of the Baptist church at nearby Saxton and were active in the East Union Association.[38] As the holiness movement spread in that community, members excluded from the Saxton church began worshipping together and organized a Holiness church with James Jackson Sammons as pastor and Curd Walker as clerk.[39] On September 21, 1907, Curd, his wife, and James Patton Smith, were baptized at Cane Creek by John Parks.[40]

Walker was not the only member of Wilder's family to embrace Wesleyan Holiness. In 1904, Wilder's sister, Nora, married James Bruton Kendall and relocated for a time to Wilmore, Kentucky. Kendall later evangelized out of Lexington until his death in 1956.[41] Also in 1904, Wilder's sister, Mary Belle, married Emmett Kyle Arnold, who pastored churches in central Kentucky until his retirement to Florida in 1956.[42] His sister, Martha Lena, married Frank Christy Soper in 1908, and the two embarked on a ministry career that took them to Florida, Michigan, and West Virginia, before settling in retirement near Wilmore.[43] The eldest sister, Martha Elizabeth, married Nicholas Noah White in Whitley County on October 17, 1885.[44] Around 1909, White moved to Conway Springs, Kansas, and later to Little Johnny, Colorado, where he died around 1920.[45]

The White family had long been associated with the Baptist churches at Pleasant Hill, and nearby Alsile and Red Bird, where the Holiness doctrine was already creating conflict for the congregations of the Mount Zion Association of United Baptists. On September 9, 1899 at Bethlehem Church, the 15th Annual Mount Zion Association adopted a resolution that stated:

> Whereas there is among the people of some of our churches and in our community a spirit of unrest, and some good people seem to be troubled about the matter of entire sanctification, sinless perfection, second blessing, etc., for which there is neither reason, scripture, or occasion. Therefore, Resolved, That we hereby warn our people and churches against preachers, so-called whether men or women, whose business it is to propagate said doctrines.[46]

Nicholas White may have been the "man by the name of White" that Stephen Bryant's son recollected had introduced the preaching of sanctification to "our part of the country," and under whose preaching Anderson Alder and John Thomas "got the blessing."[47]

On December 15, 1900, the large United Baptist congregation at Jellico Creek called on Parks to pastor almost two years after he experienced entire sanctification. On January 18, 1903, Parks was reelected to a third term after snow forced the cancellation of the regular monthly meeting in December. During these two years, Parks also served as pastor to the United Baptist Church at nearby Ryan's Creek, and "preached a clost [sic] Christian life and freedom from sin" and "a clost [sic] life in Christ Jesus" to both congregations.⁴⁸ His preaching won many converts to Wesleyan Holiness, but also attracted much opposition.

When the church at Jellico Creek met to choose a pastor for the following year, Parks was elected to a third term. The church also nominated Mike Lay who lost the secret ballot vote to Parks, 19 to 49. Before the next monthly meeting, a small minority of the more than 250 members sought to dispute and overturn the election. The protest was led by a man whom a church committee had investigated the previous month "for drinking too much." Despite the popularity indicated by the vote and the dubious character of what Parks called the "nearly set drunkards" who opposed him, the church overturned the results of the election. Similarly, at Ryan's Creek, one preacher whose near drunkenness "was witnessed by 15 witnesses" persuaded enough of the congregation to turn away from what Parks declared was "Gospel truth" in "protest for articles of Baptist faith."⁴⁹ After being expelled as pastor of Jellico Creek and Ryan's Creek, Parks began pastoring the United Baptist Churches at Zion Hill and Little Wolf Creek where his holiness preaching found a more receptive audience.

When the South Union Association met at the Bethel Church in September 1903, Parks called the meeting to order as he had been elected Moderator the previous year. The committee on divine services appointed him to preach the first night at the "Ball school house," but Parks did not figure as prominently in the proceedings as he had for more than a decade. While the minister received little direct notice, much of the business conducted nevertheless centered on him. The committee on resolutions offered two measures directed at Parks without naming him specifically. On September 26, the association resolved

> that we advise the Pastors of the churches of this Association to beware of men who are members of the Baptist church and who are advancing doctrine contrary to the constitution and articles of faith of the United Baptists and not invite such one to preach and advise all our churches to exclude and call in credentials of any member or members who teach doctrines contrary to the articles of faith of the United Baptist churches.

The second resolution appointed a committee of eight "to go to the churches where they understand that brethren have been preaching doctrine that is contrary to the Baptist Articles of Faith and investigate same and report to our next annual meeting."⁵⁰

One such church was Wolf Creek, where Silcox and Bryant were members. Parks had joined his brother-in-law as co-pastor there and preached the holiness message. As a result, Jane Silcox testified to having experienced entire sanctification for herself. Andrew Silcox began preaching against the danger of apostasy. That a Christian could fall from grace and be lost after regeneration gravely contradicted Article of Faith 11 of the South Union Association, "We believe in the final perseverance of the Saints in grace and holiness, and that none of them shall be lost." After receiving the advice from the recent association meeting, the church met on December 26, 1903 to conduct the regular election of pastor for the following year. Before the election, Parks proposed to the church, "They claim we are preaching heresies, a doctrine contrary to the Articles of Faith, and rule of decorum of the Baptist Churches." The Pastor defended the doctrine he and Silcox preached as "nothing but the Bible." Like Elijah calling Israel to choose Jehovah over Baal, Parks called on the church members to decide between the traditions of man and the "truth of the Gospel." His charge also indicated that a vote for the Bible was a vote for Parks and Silcox to remain pastors. A vote for the Articles of Faith was a vote to change pastors, "for we are going to stay with the Bible." The vote revealed a majority at Wolf Creek rejected the Holiness doctrine and preferred to remain Baptists in good standing. After the vote, Alexander "Alec" Dickerson requested his and his wife's letter of dismission. When the church granted their request, another 30 members followed suit. This group organized the "Holiness Baptist Church" at nearby Sheep Creek school the following year.[51]

Figure 2.5: The Church at Wolf Creek

c/o Ianetta Tincher Wilson

The next South Union Association meeting began on September 23, 1904 at Pleasant Hill. Silcox had been selected the previous year to preach the introductory sermon. Before the address could be given, the "regular order of business" was suspended in order to "hear the report of the committee appointed last year to investigate certain doctrine." After the report, the association voted to defer the sermon and to appoint a committee of nine to "consult with Elders J.H. Parks, A.J. Silcox and others in regard to the disputed doctrine." The investigative committee reported the following day that its attempt to correct the doctrinal errors of Parks and Silcox had failed. Having examined the faith of the churches still under Parks's pastoral care, the association voted to withdraw its "fellowship from Little Wolf Creek and Zion Hill churches," and they became unaffiliated Holiness churches.[52]

Despite the setbacks, Parks seemed relentless in his attempt to bring holiness to the Baptist association. When the association met in September 1905 at Wolf Creek, Parks presented a letter from a church he pastored at Maple Creek, east of Williamsburg. The association rejected the letter and refused to seat Parks as a delegate, while they accepted another letter from the true Baptist Church at Maple Creek with J.F. Sullivan and Isaac Woods as delegates. As the appointed tellers continued reading the remaining letters, the validity of Patterson Creek's letter with Pastor Stephen Bryant was questioned. Having concluded that Bryant was "not under censure," the letter and delegates were received. As the meeting continued into the second day, however, associational leaders questioned the soundness of the doctrine of Patterson Creek, Maple Creek, and Crooked Creek (in Campbell County, Tennessee). The association appointed a committee of three "to investigate their faith and report" the following year.[53]

While Bryant had participated in the business meeting at Wolf Creek that led to a church split over holiness, had voted in favor of Parks and Silcox, and had called for his membership, he remained conflicted over the doctrine of sanctification until an experience at Patterson Creek settled his conscience in 1905. Anderson Alder attended service one Sunday to hear Bryant preach. During the sermon, Alder burst out with spontaneous shouts of "glory hallelujah." After several such fervent outbursts, Bryant called him to order and requested he cease with the disturbances, and Alder acquiesced to his appeal. Bryant walked down the aisle after the service closed feeling rather "grand" at his display of authority until he met Alder at the door. When Alder grabbed the pastor's hand and exclaimed, "God bless you Brother Bryant, I love you," something pierced Bryant's heart. Outside the church, he watched until Alder disappeared over the hilltop. When one more "glory hallelujah" echoed down the hollow to where Bryant stood, his conscience said, "He has something you haven't got, or he couldn't be feeling so good after the way you have treated him." The long trip back to Sheep Creek gave the pastor plenty of time to ponder what happened. His family could tell something bothered him that evening when he gathered them together for a rare bedtime prayer that seemed to last indefinitely. Long after they had retired for the night, the whole home was awoken with shouts of "glory hallelujah." His mother-in-law bid him to be silent, lest the whole neighborhood think he was "sanctified." He responded that he wished "the whole world knew" that he had prayed through and experienced the second blessing.[54]

In 1905, the association recognized that these new holiness preachers had direct influence on at least six of its member churches and adopted a resolution formally condemning them. It resolved

> that we advise all our churches to beware of all men who preach doctrine contrary to the word of God—such doctrine as modern sanctification and apostasy. Be it further resolved, that; we advise them not to allow them to be pastors of their churches, or preach in their church houses; and advise all of our churches in our bounds not to call John Parks, A.J. Silcox, Allen Moses, T.D. Moses, Stephen Bryant, N.K. Parks, A. Thomas, or anyone else guilty of heresy as pastor, or to preach in our churches. Any church holding one of the above brethren as pastor is advised to remove them at once. Any church not obeying this advice will be considered out of harmony with this association.[55]

Of the seven, all but Silcox and Bryant were members at Little Wolf Creek. James Allen Moses had long been a participant in the South Union Association Meetings. His brother, Thomas Deberry Moses, had been ordained by Parks, Silcox, and Caswell Lovitt on January 8, 1898.[56] Shortly thereafter, Tom Moses accepted the holiness doctrine and followed Parks as pastor at Little Wolf Creek. Though the ministries of Newton K. Parks and Aaron Thomas were largely overshadowed by the former's younger brother and the latter's brothers-in-law, the two zealously sought to advance the holiness message especially in western Whitley County where they were born. In a building recently purchased from the Methodist Episcopal Church, "Newt" Parks, Aaron Thomas, and Stephen Bryant organized the Holiness Church of God at Hayes Creek on August 19, 1907 with 17 members. Thomas served as pastor and Parks as Moderator.[57]

Figure 2.6: Newton K. Parks
c/o Sandy Beavers

Figure 2.7: Aaron Thomas
c/o Sandy Beavers

Figure 2.8: Thomas D. Moses
c/o CGMA

Figure 2.9: James Allen Moses
c/o the Moses Family

When the committee appointed to investigative the faiths of Maple Creek, Patterson Creek, and Crooked Creek reported to the South Union Association in 1906, the association voted to "endorse the work of Maple Creek church as stated by Bro. J.F. Sullivan of those that hold to the articles of faith of United Baptists." The association received the letter and delegates of Patterson Creek, but offered no such endorsement, indicating that while they were considered in good standing, some questions lingered.[58] Although he could no longer pastor in the Baptist association, Bryant's influence upon Patterson Creek was significant. From 1906 to 1907, the church's membership dropped from 208 to 165, with six dismissed by letter and 37 excluded. Members dismissed for departing from the Baptist faith organized a Holiness church at Patterson Creek and selected Bryant to be their pastor. On March 18, 1908, Lorenzo Dow Siler donated land on which to build a church, and the "the Holiness Church of God (near Patterson Creek)" became known as Siler's Chapel.[59]

Crooked Creek, near Wooldridge, last sent its letter and delegates to the association in 1904. The following year, the association opened an investigation into its faith. John Smiddy had carried correspondence from the New River Association to the Annual Meetings of the South Union Association in 1894, 1897, and 1900 and heard Parks and Silcox preach in those meetings.[60] Smiddy had also pastored the church at Pleasant View just before Mary Storey's revival came to the community.[61] He embraced the doctrine of entire sanctification and preached it at Crooked Creek. In 1908, the South Union Association formally excluded the congregation for "departing from the faith."[62]

Smiddy's influence in the area also affected the church at Good Hope, just a few miles away. Alvin Jones Ross had begun preaching entire sanctification at Good Hope, for which the church revoked his ordination and excluded him and his followers. Ten were excluded and eleven were dismissed by letter.[63] On September 12, 1907, Parks and Silcox organized a Holiness church at the "Hackler School House" at nearby Oswego. Charter members included Ross and Smiddy's father, Calvin, and his daughter and son-in-law, Rosa and Starling Donaldson. The church purchased the school building, began meeting there with Smiddy as their pastor, and became known as the Lower Elk Valley Church of God.[64]

After its expulsion from the Baptist association, the Zion Hill church maintained consistency in membership for many years to come, despite losing some members via transfer. Jacob "Jake" and Savannah Taylor were members at Zion Hill when Parks began preaching holiness. Around 1907, the Taylors opened a general store when they moved to Ryan's Creek where "holiness was being evil spoken of by certain people." Those members of Jellico Creek and Ryan's Creek who had supported Parks and endorsed his preaching "stayed together and began to have prayer meetings out in the groves." Bryant often came over the mountain from Sheep Creek to worship with them and to preach, as did Edom "Neadom" John Rountree. They began to have regular meetings in an empty house belonging to James Alexander "Elick" Cornelius and made plans to organize a church with members who had left the Baptist churches at Ryan's Creek and Jellico Creek.[65]

Figure 2.10: Cornelius house at Ryan's Creek

c/o CGMA

At a business meeting at Jellico Creek United Baptist Church on February 16, 1907, Thomas Higginbotham requested a letter of dismission for himself and his wife, Polly, which the church granted. The church also granted letters of dismission for his daughter-in-law, Hannah, and his daughters, Surelda and Eliza, along with Henry Newton Creekmore and wife, Hannah, and Clark Campbell. On March 16, 1907, Polly Higginbotham's brother, John C. Criscillis requested his and his wife's letters. The Baptist church required members to secure a letter of dismission when they desired to relocate to another church of like faith where they could carry out the spirit of the covenant.[66] By asking for such letters, Higginbotham and the others implied that they intended to take fellowship with another Baptist congregation. Instead, they joined themselves with those who had left Ryan's Creek Baptist Church and organized a Holiness church. By May, the Baptist church realized what they had done and brought "charges against all the members that got letters from this church & joind [sic] at lower rians [sic] creek." In July, the church requested that its members notify the rest of the body if they were aware of "any parties taking letters from this church to lower ryans creek." In July and August, the church formally excluded the offending members.[67]

As the Holiness revival expanded throughout the region, it effected the West Union Baptist Association as well. At its 32nd Annual Session in October 1901, William Baird Douglas was among the delegates chosen to visit the South Union Association's next annual session as a corresponding messenger.[68] The following September, Douglas carried his association's letter to Little Wolf Creek and heard Silcox preach the introductory sermon and

Parks preach the final service. During the business session, he was asked to serve as one of the tellers that saw Parks reelected as moderator.[69] One year later, Douglas's home church, Elk Fork, reported that it had excluded 41 members for departing from the Baptist faith. The West Union Association adopted a resolution in 1903 that "we advise our churches that have any members that preach, teach or advocate any doctrine contrary to the Articles of Faith of United Baptists, to demand of such members their credentials and admonish them; if not heeded to after the first and second admonition reject them."[70]

Figure 2.11: William B. Douglas
c/o the Douglas Family

For the rest of the decade, the resolutions and queries committees at the West Union Association responded to questions contrary to Baptist faith. It resolved "that we advise our churches not to allow the doctrine of apostasy, modern sanctification advocated in their churches, school houses or homes."[71] It further advised its churches to reject churches that teach divine healing, "to have nothing to do with ministers who have been excluded for departing from the Faith," to "exclude members who claim a second work of grace, or believe in apostasy," and to "mark" as a "heretic" those who "speak the unknown tongue."[72] Some of those excluded from Elk Fork Baptist Church in 1903 were among the number that Parks, Douglas, and James Frank Baird later organized as the Mountain Assembly Church at Elk Valley on February 21, 1909.[73]

The Baptist association mourned the loss of its ministers and members. The personal and familial relationships within the small communities where its churches were located meant many were affected. As a result, the South Union Association adopted a resolution that "we are sorry that our Brethren have gone from us and recommend that we do not persecute them but treat them with respect."[74] Not everyone shared the same sentiment. In one early meeting where Parks was preaching, a group of men brought weapons to disrupt the service and intimidate the preacher. Eyewitnesses recounted many years later that Parks was elevated from the floor above them, and the sight of that was enough to deter those men who would do him harm.[75]

At the urging of the new Holiness churches at Little Wolf Creek and Zion Hill, a meeting was held at Ryan's Creek on August 24, 1907 to organize a new association of Holiness churches. Silcox was appointed chairman, and Joseph Thomas Richardson from Patterson Creek was appointed clerk. The participants at this meeting selected three committees. A committee on articles of faith consisted of Silcox, Parks, Bryant, Rountree, and Sammons. Five men served on a "committee on constitutional name," including Smiddy and Parks.

Figure 2.12: James J. Sammons
c/o Frankie Wilson

James Jones, Isaac Newton Jones, and Allen Moses rounded out the committee. Parks, Bryant, and Moses were also "appointed to prepare an order for the proceedings of the Association" which was set to convene October 11-12, 1907 at Little Wolf Creek. Parks was appointed to preach the introductory sermon.[76]

When the first assembly met in October, ten churches sent letters and delegates to the meeting (see map / figure 16 at the end of chapter). In addition to Pleasant View, Little Wolf Creek, Zion Hill, Ryan's Creek, Hayes Creek, Patterson Creek, Sheep Creek, Lower Elk Valley, and Crooked Creek ("Wooldridge"), the Saxton church also sent a letter and delegates. Delegates to the first assembly chose Silcox to moderate the meeting with Sammons as his assistant. Richardson was elected clerk, assisted by Taylor. A committee on resolutions was appointed. It included Allen Moses, Curd Walker, and Milton Franklin Ross. The "Holiness Union Association" adopted eight resolutions including four related to personal holiness, one on temperance, two emphasizing Christian benevolence, and one expressing gratitude for the hospitality of the host community. The association also approved six articles of faith offered by the committee. The foundational doctrines of the new churches consisted of the supremacy of the Scripture, regeneration by faith, water baptism, the doctrine of entire sanctification, the danger of apostasy, and open communion. A second council meeting was scheduled to commence on September 12, 1908 at Zion Hill.[77]

Figure 2.13: Joseph T. Richardson
c/o the Richardson Family

Figure 2.14: Jacob C. Taylor
c/o Alice Chitwood

Baptist Faith and Practice

The Holiness Union Association metamorphosed into the Church of God Mountain Assembly, but it was rooted in Baptist doctrine and practice. Elements of Baptist ideology persisted in the faith and practice of the holiness believers. Among these core values were spiritual equality, congregational authority, covenantal church membership, the two ordinances of the church, and the two offices of the church. Participation in an association also remained central to the experience of those holiness leaders.

Baptist polity focused on congregational authority and spiritual equality. Baptists understood congregationalism as the Biblical model of church government. All authority rested in the members cooperatively. Democracy prevailed in Baptist churches at a time when civil government suppressed it. In many antebellum churches, slaves voted along with their masters. The ratification of the Thirteenth Amendment in 1870 granted blacks the right to vote, but many southern states disenfranchised blacks through poll taxes, literacy tests, and other measures. It took 80 years for the women's suffrage movement to realize its aim with the ratification of the Nineteenth Amendment in 1920. Though some congregations continued to suppress women, in most Baptist churches, women members voted along with men. Although segregated churches multiplied in the Jim Crow South, Baptist thought championed the ideal of equality in race and gender even if many congregations never realized it as a matter of practice. No matter the socioeconomic status, every member was a "brother" or a "sister."[78]

The Baptist-turned-Holiness members brought the concept of spiritual equality with them into the new churches they organized, and the association represented that diversity. Among the 51 delegates to the First Assembly, nearly 60 percent owned their homes. Most earned their livings farming, and many also worked in coal mines. Two were merchants. As many as ten could not read or write.[79] Two women took seats with the men as delegates at the First Assembly: Maggie Swaney of Wooldridge, and Rachel Hackler of Lower Elk Valley.[80] It might have taken 18 years for the first African American to attend an Assembly as a delegate, but when a "colored church" at Kenvir, Kentucky sent its "letter" with Horace Maynard Bates, pastor of the "white" church, the Assembly received both churches into the fellowship in the same motion.[81] The following year, Ed Johnson, African American pastor of the Kenvir church, brought the letter himself and preached one night's service at the appointment of the committee on divine services.[82]

When the 32nd Mountain Assembly adopted its first rules of decorum for "behavior in the house of God" to set guidelines for the transaction of the business in the assembly and in the local churches, it incorporated ideas from the Constitution of the South Union Association of United Baptists. Article 12 of the Constitution stated that members should address the Moderator with "brotherly respect" and when referring to another member should "use no other appellation than that of brother." In 1938, the Assembly adopted rules that declared members wishing to speak should arise and "address the Moderator with brotherly respect. The word brother shall be the only title of address in a motion permissible, in the church or assembly."[83] It further stated that speakers should "in no wise reflect or make remarks about the imperfection in the person who spoke before him."[84] Though it took three decades for them to formally include it in their governing document, the policy had long been their practice. The printed minutes of the preceding Assembly, for example, used the word, "brother," as a title 170 times, while "Rev." was used once.[85]

Baptists believed the sole authority in church affairs rested in the members. The church possessed the privilege of self-government and bore the responsibility for it. Baptists believed that the church possessed "the right to choose its own officers," "the right of discipline, formative and corrective," and the duty to "interpret for itself the laws of Christ, and to enforce obedience, on the part of its members, to the system of faith and practice which it derives from the word of God."[86] Baptist ecclesiology emphasized that "no outside ecclesiastical authority possesses jurisdiction over the local church" and that "the final court of appeal is the congregation."[87]

These principles also followed the holiness preachers into their new churches. These Baptists-turned-Holiness people cherished the right to choose their own officers in the church. Delegates to the 8th Annual Mountain Assembly at Elk Valley, Tennessee, made sure to emphasize that pastoral selection remained the privilege of the local church with a resolution "that each church in our bounds choose for their pastors, ministers that are able to care for the churches."[88] When the founding pastor of the Mountain Assembly Church in Fonde, Kentucky, resigned after five years of service, the distraught church voted to "see Brother J.H. Parks for the purpose of getting him to serve us as pastor." When he agreed to accept the care of the church, the members unanimously elected him on December 9, 1922.[89] The appointment of deacons was equally as important as the selection of pastors. Lower Elk Valley had grown to more than 250 members in 1920 as Parks entered the 60th year of his life. In recognition that the pastor needed help, the church ordained Aaron Gaylor, W.C. Brock, and Arthur Parks to the office of deacon.[90]

Those who came out of the Baptist Church also highly regarded the right of church discipline. The Lower Elk Valley Church, for example, regularly disciplined its unruly members. With Parks as its pastor, on July 28, 1917, the church "resolved that all members of the church" who were "breaking the covenant of the Church" by "using tobacco" or "going to shows" or "drinking strong drinks" should "come before the church" and "answer to such charges as may be brought against them." The following month, seven were excluded for such things as "the use of tobacco," "going to shows and not refraining from it," making false reports concerning tobacco use, "swearing," and "fighting." The church also appointed committees to visit three other members to answer to similar charges brought against them.[91] At the 15th Annual Mountain Assembly four years later, delegates passed a motion to reinforce this policy of the right of the local church to discipline members. The Assembly resolved that "each local Church shall have the final decision as to excluding their members."[92]

Baptist churches generally conducted church business one Saturday night each month at the "conference meeting." Typically, this provided the opportunity for new converts to present themselves for membership. The applicant would recount the testimony of his or her conversion and respond to any questions the congregation posed. Should a convert produce satisfactory evidence of the conviction of sin, repentance, and faith in Christ, the church would vote to receive them into the fellowship upon water baptism. Upon joining the church, members subscribed to the church covenant. The covenant recognized the commitment members made to God, to each other, and to their community.[93] When Baptists relocated, the covenant required that they seek another congregation of like faith with which to carry out the spirit of this covenant. Having already satisfied one congregation of the genuineness of their conversion and having been baptized on profession of faith, the transient member secured a letter of commendation from his church to present to the members of the new congregation.[94]

Mountain Assembly churches universally adopted this method of membership. When the new church at Fonde, Kentucky, was set in order by Henry Mobley and James Daniels on December 8, 1917, at least fifteen of its charter members had letters of dismission from Lower Elk Valley.[95] At its regular monthly meeting the following June, six new members were received by baptism.[96] Within five years of its organization, each Mountain Assembly church routinely reported to the Assembly its membership statistics, including numbers received by baptism, received by letter, restored, dismissed by letter, excluded, deaths, and current membership.[97]

Mountain Assembly members, like good Baptists, took seriously membership transfer protocol as evidenced by a conflict between the Mountain Assembly churches at Siler's Chapel and Emlyn. The Emlyn church was organized in 1914 by George Fore and property was purchased from Terrell Foley Hamlin to build a building there in December.[98] When several members left the church at Emlyn, Kentucky, and joined the Siler's Chapel Church in Pollyeton, Kentucky, in 1916 without letters of dismission, the Assembly adjudicated and determined that their membership should remain at Emlyn.[99] Churches continued to expect disciplined members to respond to the judgment of the church and be restored. In 1921 the Assembly ordered that "each member that has been exculded [sic] shall first be reconsiled [sic] to the Church that excluded them before becoming a member of another Church of the same Faith and order."[100]

The idea of membership by subscription to a church covenant developed out of sixteenth century congregationalism. As Separatists left the Church of England and established independent congregations, they developed such charters to guide the consciences of their members. For more than a century, each church crafted the wording of its own covenant and declaration of faith. Gradually, associations began adopting standard confessions of faith and writing sample covenants. In 1833, the prominent Baptist minister John Newton Brown helped draft the New Hampshire Confession of Faith at the New Hampshire Baptist Convention. Two decades later, he published it in his *Baptist Church Manual* along with a church covenant.[101] Many nineteenth century Baptists congregations utilized this manual and this covenant, including many in the South Union Association. The Mountain Assembly churches at Hayes Creek and Jellico Creek incorporated it into their minutes when they organized in the summer of 1907.[102] At a meeting of Mountain Assembly ministers at Pleasant View on November 30, 1917, the ministers voted "that each church have the same covenant" and the Brown Covenant was "agreed upon by the ministers of this meeting."[103] With few variations, it has been printed in the annual minute book ever since.

Baptists held that there were two ordinances of the church, water baptism and observance of the Lord's Supper. By ordinances, Baptists meant the "exercises of divine worship, enjoined upon the disciples in their stated meetings."[104] This understanding differentiated between the Catholic understanding of sacraments, as the impartation of divine grace necessary for salvation. Perhaps nothing distinguished Baptists from other Protestants more than the doctrine of water baptism, hence the emphasis in their name. Baptists believed that "immersion of professing believers" constituted the only legitimate baptism. Not only was it vital to be immersed in water upon profession of faith in Christ, it also helped to be baptized by a Baptist minister. Presbyterians and Methodists made no claim that baptized infants were saved, so Baptists considered them out of order because they often practiced infant baptism, thereby receiving unregenerate persons into the church as members. To Baptists, this distorted the meaning of water baptism, which they regarded as exclusively reserved for those who have trusted Christ for salvation. Since Presbyterians and Methodists viewed baptism differently, Baptists did not recognize the baptism of Methodists and Presbyterians and required a believer to be baptized again if they had a previous "alien baptism."[105]

The founding ministers of the Mountain Assembly remained as ardent about water baptism as they had been in the Baptist church. "What ought to be done with brethren who teach that pouring or sprinkling will do as well as immersion?" they asked at the Sixth Annual Mountain Assembly. "We do not indorse [sic] any other baptism but a burial in water and we recommend that brethren who teach otherwise be disciplined." As fervently as Baptists resisted Methodist or Presbyterian baptisms, early Church of God ministers held contempt for those who refused to accept their newfound way. "Ought the Churches of God recieve [sic] members from other churches that have been baptised [sic] by preachers who fight holiness?" they asked at the same Assembly. "Be it resolved No."[106] This zeal for right baptism prompted the Mountain Assembly preachers to adopt a measure in 1921 "that those who wish to become a member of the Church of God must be Baptized by a legal ordained Minister of the Church of God before becoming a member of the Church of God." At the same time, they also began to restrict baptism to only those who would join the church.[107]

Baptists believed that one must be baptized to participate in the observance of the Lord's Supper. Since Baptists rejected the baptism of most non-Baptists, they practiced "close communion" where only those with legitimate baptism could participate. Baptists commonly took communion once per quarter. Some Baptists churches, especially Landmark Baptists, did not permit visitors to take communion with them even if they were members of another Baptist church.[108] Significantly, at the First Assembly the articles of faith proposed by Parks, Silcox, Byrant, Rountree, and Sammons proposed that "all regenerated persons should be admitted to the Lord's table" and thereby removed the proscription of water baptism as prerequisite for admission to communion. The article also added "that the ordinance of foot washing should be observed in connection with the Lords' Supper."[109]

Baptists held that the New Testament Church had two offices, deacon and elder. The scripture sometimes refers to elders as bishops and pastors, and Baptists used these terms interchangeably.[110] The Baptist elder functioned as a servant-leader, a caring shepherd, and able teacher.[111] Pastors officiated the ordinances and provided most of the teaching and preaching. Deacons oversaw the temporal affairs of the church, met the pastor's needs, prepared for the observance of the ordinances, maintained the church property, and relieved the poor.[112] Baptists often emphasized the latter, especially, since it so closely resonates "with the original responsibility of the Seven in Acts 6."[113]

The Mountain Assembly retained these offices in the church and viewed them with equal importance. Of the 25 churches who reported to the General Assembly in 1924, there were 29 ordained ministers and 29 deacons. The Assembly recommended that year that the deacons serve as treasurers for the churches and "have charge of the tithes" by keeping a record of members' tithes contributions and distributing first to the needs of the pastor.[114] The following year, a question was asked concerning the legality of deacons administering the Lord's Supper. The Assembly admonished "pastor and deacons work together in harmony under the pastor."[115] Some pastors had the care of more than one church and would attend services on alternating Sundays. In the pastor's absence, deacons often took care of the church.

Baptists believed every church was autonomous in that they were "independent of each other with regard to power," but they also recognized that Christians had "an indisputable right to share in each other's gifts and graces, so have churches in this joint capacity." Baptists, then, recognized their need to unite with other Baptist churches "so far as their local situation and other circumstances will admit." They accomplished this by constituting associations to convene once a year with delegates representing each congregation. Baptist churches benefited from joining an association by utilizing the collective wisdom of other saints to clear any confusion or doubts that might have arisen with the congregation. Churches without a minister might have acquired one through the help of the association. Christian unity increased through participation in the association. The association often commissioned ministers to preach in destitute areas or to establish churches in communities without one. The association sometimes settled contention between congregations. The association also provided local churches with presbyters to assist in the ordination of their ministers and deacons.[116] For these reasons, Parks, Silcox, and Bryant, organized an association of holy Baptist churches like the one they had been a part of since their conversions.

Even the idea of separation from the association to create a new one was rooted in their experience with the South Union Association. In its first 100 years of existence, the South Union Association had dismissed churches to establish additional associations. Five churches from the South Union Association left to help constitute the Laurel River Association in September 1831. North Concord Association was formed in 1844 with at least three South Union churches. The South Union Association split geographically in 1870 by a "dividing line ... beginning at the mouth of Jellico Creek on the Cumberland River, and running south with the Jellico Mountain all the way to Elk Fork in Campbell County, Tennessee." Churches in the western half instituted the West Union Association. Mount Zion Association was organized in 1885 with one existing church from the South Union Association and several new congregations. In 1891, East Union Association was formed from seven South Union Association churches. Finally, at Parks's last South Union Association meeting in 1904, a committee was appointed to determine if launching a new "Elk Fork Association" was necessary. Two years later, the new association was established and later became the Campbell County, Tennessee Association.[117] Generally, churches needed a letter of dismission from the South Union Association to join or constitute a new association, which Zion Hill and Little Wolf Creek obviously lacked when they called for the constitution of a new Holiness association in 1907. From one perspective, Parks and Bryant thus organized the Mountain Assembly under this broad principle, though with the absence of formal authorization of their mother association to do so.

A Baptist Association of Holiness Churches

The South Union Association of United Baptists was formed at the Clear Fork Meeting House in Whitley County, Kentucky, on September 15, 1815, by delegates from the Cumberland River Church (now known as First Baptist of Barbourville) and others located in Knox and Whitley Counties. Among the oldest churches in the association were Jellico Creek (1808), Wolf Creek (1809), and Patterson Creek (1828). and the association met annually for two days on the Friday before the fourth Saturday in September.[118]

The South Union Association meetings began at 10:00 a.m. with an introductory sermon delivered by the minister so chosen the previous year. After the devotional lesson, appointed tellers read the letters from each church, and their messengers were enrolled. After member churches had been enrolled, the moderator called for any new churches to present letters. If found to be sound in faith, the association admitted new churches into its fellowship and enrolled the additional messengers. Next, the association elected its officers by ballot. The moderator and assistant moderator conducted the business, and the clerk and assistant clerk recorded the minutes of the meetings. The new moderator then called for any corresponding letters from other Baptist associations who might have sent representatives. Visitors were often given seats as fraternal delegates and might participate in any discussion but would not be entitled to vote.[119]

Next, the moderator appointed committees on divine services, on resolutions, and on correspondence. The Committee on divine services selected men to preach during times of worship. Often, the church buildings lacked adequate space to accommodate all that might wish to attend, so various sites in the community would be selected and multiple services would take place simultaneously. The committee on resolutions drafted measures of doctrinal or practical importance for the association to consider. The committee on correspondence was charged with drafting letters to sister associations that they might report to them the welfare and happenings within their own bounds.[120]

Once the committees began their work, the association would choose a place for its next meeting and select a minister to preach the next introductory sermon, along with an alternate. The association then proceeded to hear the reports of standing committees. These often included its executive board and committees on Sunday schools, orphan's home, and minister's aid. Another standing committee collected obituaries of members who had died since the last meeting to be printed in the annual minute book of the association. After announcements, the first day's business was adjourned.[121]

After the second morning's devotional services, the minutes were read and corrected, and appointments were made to the standings committee for the following year. Then the correspondence committee would present the letters it had written to the various associations and the moderator appointed representatives to carry them to the respective association meetings. The divine service committee announced its appointments before the association considered resolutions presented by that committee. When the routine business was completed, the association appointed someone to print and distribute the minutes to the various churches. Any miscellaneous business preceded the reading and correcting of the minutes before adjournment.[122]

The association of Holiness churches that Parks, Silcox, and Bryant founded in 1907 was structured along this same pattern. Delegates chose the "name of Council Meeting instead of Association." Courier Print in Williamsburg printed a minute book of the "Council Meeting of the Church of God" in 1907.[123] At the second annual conference on September 12, 1908, delegates at Zion Hill reversed this decision and renewed their preference for "Association." The third annual meeting was held at Hayes Creek on October 1-2, 1909 and began using "General Assembly" to describe its annual convention.[124] After the Fourth General Assembly convened on September 30, 1910 at Jellico Creek, the group met at Siler's Chapel on October 6-8, 1911 for the Fifth General Assembly of the Churches of God.[125] At Siler's Chapel, delegates voted that the "name of this Assembly shall be called the Mountain Assembly of the Churches of God."[126]

The order of business that guided the Mountain Assembly during these early conventions and subsequent years bore a striking resemblance to that of the South Union Association. First, the CGMA continued the practice of choosing a speaker for the introductory sermon a year in advance until 1964. That year, the Assembly voted to have the General Overseer preach the

Figure 2.15: Jellico Creek Church

c/o Tim Walden

introductory sermon each year.[127] The process of reading the letters and enrolling messengers persisted until 1944. The Assembly then instated a "roll call of churches" with statistical letters presented by the churches and read, but the formal enrollment of delegates was suspended.[128] The Assembly discontinued the formal reading of the letters in 1975.[129] From 1975 to 2019, churches mailed their statistical report to the General Secretary & Treasurer who assembled the data in one table to be distributed among the delegates. Though the process changed, the historical basis was rooted in the Baptist association tradition.

The annual election of moderators and clerks continued until a new system of government was instituted in 1944.[130] The Assembly adopted biennial elections for its officers six years later.[131] The committee on divine services continued to select preachers during the week of the convention until 1953, when the organization voted to create a "Program Committee" appointed at the last Elders Meeting before the Assembly.[132] The Program Committee selected preachers and published the schedule before the convention began. In 1971, the Assembly began electing the committee for the following year at the end of its business meeting.[133] The organization continued the tradition of a standing committee on Sunday schools until 1931 when it appointed Sunday School evangelists for each state.[134] By 1940, nearly all its churches reported strong Sunday schools, and it discontinued this practice.[135] The tradition of gathering and printing obituaries in the annual minute book persisted until 1939.

The annual election of a committee on resolutions which presented proposals during the same session persisted until 1964. That year, the Assembly voted to elect the committee to serve a two-year term to better prepare amendments to the constitution of the organization.[136] The tradition of selecting a location for the next meeting ended in 1922 when the Assembly erected a tabernacle in Jellico, Tennessee for that purpose. The Lower Elk Valley Church relocated to this tabernacle in 1926.[137] When the Assembly outgrew a second tabernacle in the late 1940s, the need for alternative locations was discussed. Though delegates resumed the practice of annual voting for the next year's location, the 44th Annual Assembly held in Cincinnati, Ohio, in 1950 was the only one not held in Jellico. In the 1960s, additional property was purchased adjoining the tabernacle lot, and the Assembly planned the construction of a new gathering place. After authorizing the construction of a much larger open-air tabernacle, the annual vote on the selection of a meeting place was once more discontinued.

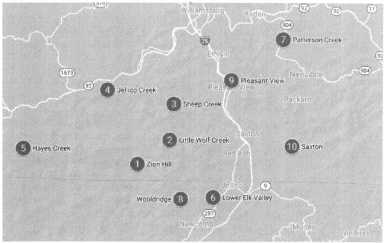

Figure 2.16: 2021 map showing the locations of the first ten churches (1907)
Map © 2019 Google.

Conclusion

Parks, Silcox, Bryant, and others began preaching doctrines contrary to the articles of faith of the United Baptist Church shortly after the turn of the twentieth century. This "heresy," as the Baptist leaders called it, forced the South Union Association to adopt measures to disfellowship them. The churches who received their message preserved some very Baptist practices. When they banded together to form their own association, they created one that maintained many conspicuous resemblances to the association that had expelled their leaders. As the Church of God Mountain Assembly encountered the Church of God (Cleveland) and further transformed, a proclivity to its Baptist heritage produced tension.

---

[1] Henry C. Vedder, *A Short History of the Baptists* (Valley Forge, PA: Judson Press, 1907), 308-309, 387.

[2] Michael Padgett, "Honoring Our Fathers," *Mountain Preacher Magazine* (Jan – Mar 2019): 3; J.E. Hatfield, "Rev. J.H. Parks, Beloved Minister Called By Death," *The Gospel Herald* 2, no. 3 (September 1943): 1; [2] *Tennessee Marriage Records, 1780-2002*, s.v. "John Parker," Ancestry.com; John H. Parks, Unpublished Journal: 1917-1937, in the personal collection of Jason Lands, Cookeville, TN., 218-219; 1880 United States Census, Whitley County, Kentucky, s.v. "John Parks," Ancestry.com.

[3] *Tennessee Marriage Records, 1780-2002*, s.v. "A J Silcox," Ancestry.com; James E. Prewitt, "In Appreciation of Their Many Years of Service," *GH* 34, no. 4 (April 1973): 2.

[4] James E. Prewitt, "In Appreciation of Their Many Years of Service," *GH* 34, no. 3 (March 1973): 3; Bethel Baptist Church, *History of Bethel Baptist Church, McCreary Co., KY 1870-1996* (Pine Knot, KY: Bethel Baptist Church 1996); *Kentucky County Marriage Records, 1783-1965*, s.v. "Stephen Bryant," Ancestry.com; John H. Bryant, "My Life Story in Brief," *GH* 25, no. 11 (November 1965): 3; "S.N. Bryant Dies Saturday Night," obituary clipping from an unidentified newspaper in the possession of Chester Spradlin, Coalfield, TN.

[5] SUAUB, "Minutes of the Annual Sessions of the South Union Association of United Baptists," handwritten association records at South Union / Mt. Zion Association Mission Office, Williamsburg, KY, 118,149-156.

[6] Ibid., 163, 165, 170-229.

[7] Ibid., 177, 212; SUAUB, *Minutes of the Eighty-Eighth Annual Session of the South Union Baptist Association of United Baptists* (n.p.: by the association: 1902), 4.

[8] Bryant, "Life Story," 3.

[9] For more on the significance of Knapp's ministry to the radical Holiness movement, see Wallace Thornton, "The Revivalist Movement and the Development of a Holiness/Pentecostal Philosophy of Missions," *Wesleyan Theological Journal* 38, no. 1 (Spring 2003), 160-186.

[10] Aaron Merritt Hills, *A Hero of Faith and Prayer; or, Life of Rev. Martin Wells Knapp* (Cincinnati: Mrs. M.W. Knapp, 1902), 53-55.

[11] Ibid. 129-142.

[12] Martin Wells Knapp, "Beulah Heights Holiness Camp Meeting," *The Revivalist* 8, no. 9 (August 1894): 1.

[13] "Mary Storey, Servant of God," *God's Revivalist* 114, no. 1 (Winter 2000): 15.

[14] Ibid.; Hills, 130, 249.

[15] Knapp so regarded Storey's ministry that upon his death in 1901, he designated Storey as one of the three trustees of God's Bible School, which he had founded the previous year. She became its superintendent until her death in 1906.

16 The Wesleyan Church, "Women in Ministry," accessed April 9, 2020, https://www.wesleyan.org/ecd/women-ministry-leadership

17 For more on the history of social acceptance of Baptist women in ministry, see Susan M. Shaw, *God Speaks to Us, Too: Southern Baptist Women on Church, Home, and Society* (Lexington: University of Kentucky Press, 2008) and Curtis W. Freeman, ed., *A Company of Women Preachers: Baptist Prophetesses in Seventeenth-Century England* (Waco: Baylor University Press, 2011).

18 "Bulah Heights Holiness Camp Meeting," *The Revivalist* 9, no. 7 (July 1895): 4.

19 "Revival Prayer Answered," *The Revivalist* 11, no. 1 (January 5, 1899): 12.

20 W.J. Wilder, "Revival Prayer Answered," *The Revivalist* 12, no. 4 (January 26, 1899): 12.

21 Mary Storey, "Revival Prayer Answered," *The Revivalist* 11, no. 2 (January 12, 1899): 12.

22 Ibid.; Carolyn Chatfield Hensel, "History of Pleasant View Methodist Church," Pleasant View United Methodist Church Homecoming Bulletin, July 6, 1980, 1-2.

23 Jones, *150th Anniversary*, 107.

24 An unidentified newspaper clipping in the possession of Claudia E. Thomas highlights the peculiarity of the four brothers marrying four sisters and repeats this misconception that they were preachers.

25 Hensel, 2.

26 J.S. Miller, "Revival Prayer Answered," *The Revivalist* 12, no. 2 (January 11, 1900): 11.

27 "Church News," *Middlesborough News*, February 11, 1899; Mary Storey, "Revival Prayer Answered," *The Revivalist* 11, no. 5 (February 2, 1899): 12.

28 G.E. Hancock, "Revival Prayer Answered," *The Revivalist* 11, no. 14 (April 6, 1899): 12.

29 Mary Storey, "Revival Prayer Answered," *The Revivalist* 11, no. 16 (April 20, 1899): 12.

30 Lafayette Davis, "Revival Prayer Answered," *The Revivalist* 11, no. 36 (September 7, 1899): 12; Mary Storey, "Revival Prayer Answered," *The Revivalist* 11, no. 44 (November 2, 1899): 12.

31 1900 United States Census, Knox County, Kentucky, s.v. "William J. Wilder," Ancestry.com.

32 W.J. Wilder, "Revival Prayer Answered," *The Revivalist* 13, no. 26 (June 27, 1901): 11.

33 W.J. Wilder, "Revival Prayer Answered," *The Revivalist* 13, no. 33 (August 15, 1901): 12.

34 Janus Jones, ed., *Happenings Around Pleasant Hill: Pleasant Hill Baptist Church (1868-2018) Celebrating 150 Years* (Williamsburg, KY: Pleasant Hill Baptist Church, 2018), 52.

35 Curd Walker, "Just a Bit of History," November 14, 1956, in the personal collection of Stephen Curd Walker, Durango, CO, 4.

36 Curd Walker, "The Beginning of My Experience as the Pastor of Johnson Chapel Holiness Church," January 26, 1956, in the personal collection of Stephen Curd Walker, Durango, CO, 1-2.

37 Curd Walker, "The Beginning of My Experience as the Pastor of Johnson Chapel Holiness Church," January 26, 1956, in the personal collection of Stephen Curd Walker, Durango, CO, 3-4.

38 East Union Association of United Baptists (EUAUB), *Minutes of the Tenth Annual Session of the East Union Association of United Baptists* (n.p.: by the association, 1900), 5; EUAUB, *Minutes of the Twelfth Annual Session of the East Union Association of United Baptists* (n.p.: by the association, 1902), 5, statistical table; EUAUB, *Minutes of the Thirteenth Annual Session of the East Union Association of United Baptists* (n.p.: by the association, 1903), 5, statistical table.

39 CGMA, *Minutes* (1907), 2.

40 Parks, 190.

41 1910 United States Census, Jessamine County, Kentucky, s.v. "James Kendall," Kentucky, Death Records, 1852-1965, s.v. "James Bruton Kendall," and U.S. City Directories, 1822-1995, s.v. "Rev. James B. Kendall," Ancestry.com.

42 1910 United States Census, Nicholas County, Kentucky, s.v. "Emmet K. Arnold," Ancestry.com; "Obituaries," *The [Stanford, Kentucky] Interior Journal*, July 23, 1964.

43 1910 United States Census, Hillsborough County, Florida, s.v. "Frank C. Soper," 1920 United States Census, Cass County, Michigan, s.v. "Frank C. Soper," 1930 United States Census, Tucker County, West Virginia, s.v. "H. C. Soper," and 1940 United States Census, Jessamine County, Kentucky, s.v. "Frank Soper," Ancestry.com. "Obituaries," *Danville Advocate-Messenger*, May 13, 1969.

44 Kentucky, County Marriage Records, 1783-1965, s.v. "N.N. White," Ancestry.com.

45 1910 United States Census, Sumner County, Kansas, s.v. "Miklas M. White," and 1920 United States Census, Las Animas County, Colorado, s.v. "Nicholas N. White," Ancestry.com.

46 Mt. Zion Association of United Baptist, *Minutes of the Fifteenth Annual Session of the Mt. Zion Association of United Baptists* (n.p.: by the association, 1899), 15-16.

47 John Harrison Bryant, "The Building of God" in Gibson, 51.

48 "Minutes of the Jellico Creek Baptist Church, Book 3 from Jan. 1891 thru April 1908, 16-20, transcribed in *Church Records: Jellico Creek Baptist Church, Whitley County, Kentucky, 1846 to 1928*, History and Genealogy Room, Whitley County Public Library, Williamsburg, KY; Parks, 215.

49 Ibid.

50 SUAUB, *Minutes of the Eighty-Ninth Annual Session of the South Union Association of United Baptists* (n.p.: by the association, 1903), 6, 9.

51 Ibid., 4; Parks, 216; J.H. Bryant, "Building," in Gibson, 52.

52 SUAUB, *Minutes of the Ninetieth Annual Session of the South Union Association of United Baptists* (n.p.: by the association, 1904), 6, 8.

53 SUAUB, *Minutes of the Ninety-First Annual Session of the South Union Association of United Baptists* (n.p.: by the association, 1905), 6-8, 11.

54 Bryant, in Gibson, 51.

55 SUAUB, *Minutes* (1905), 11.

56 Thomas D. Moses certificate of ordination, January 8, 1898 in the possession of Wolf Creek Baptist Church, Williamsburg, KY.

57 Minutes of the Holiness Church of God at Hayes Creek: Book One, Hayes Creek, KY, 9 in the possession of Joy Ball, clerk; General Assembly Churches of God, Inc., *Centennial History Book: 1906-2006* (Pine Knot, KY: General Assembly Churches of God, Inc., 2007), 12.

58 SUAUB, *Minutes* (1907), 8.

59 Deed of Conveyance, *Whitley County Deed Book* 74, March 18, 1908, 304, Whitley County Court House, Williamsburg, KY.

60 SUAUB Minutes (1894), 186, 212; SUAUB, *Minutes of the Eighty-Sixth Annual Session of the South Union Association of United Baptists* (n.p.: by the association, 1900), 4.

61 EUAUB, *Minutes of the Eighth Annual Session of the East Union Association of United Baptists* (n.p.: by the association, 1898), statistical table.

62 SUAUB, *Minutes of the Ninety-second Annual Session of the South Union Association of United Baptists* (n.p.: by the association, 1906), 6; SUAUB, *Minutes* (1907), 6; Janus Jones, ed., *1990 Annual of South Union Baptist Association: 175th Anniversary* (Williamsburg, KY: South Union Baptist Association, 1990), 115.

63 SUAUB, *Minutes* (1907), 9.

64 Minutes of the Jellico Church of God Mountain Assembly (Book Two: 1916 to 1943), 9 available at the church.

65 Savannah Taylor, "Testimony of Mrs. J.C. Taylor" in Gibson, 50; Parks, 223; Gibson, 5.

66 Charleston Association, *A Summary of Church Disciple* (Charleston, 1774), in Mark E. Dever, ed., *Polity: Biblical Arguments on How to Conduct Church Life* (Washington: Nine Marks Ministries, 2001), 124-125.

67 Jellico Creek Minutes, 26-27; CGMA, *Minutes of the Ninth Annual Session of the Church of God [Mountain Assembly]* (n.p.: by the association, 1915), 3.

68 West Union Baptist Association (WUBA), *Minutes of the Thirty-Second Annual Session of the West Union Baptist Association* (n.p.: by the association, 1901), 4.

69 SUAUB, *Minutes* (1902), 5.

70 WUBA, *Minutes of the Thirty-Fourth Annual Session of the West Union Baptist Association* (n.p.: by the association, 1903), 8, statistical table.

71 WUBA, *Minutes of the Thirty-Fifth Annual Session of the West Union Baptist Association* (n.p.: by the association, 1904), 8.

72 WUBA, *Minutes of the Thirty-Sixth Annual Session of the West Union Baptist Association* (n.p.: by the association, 1905), 5; WUBA, *Minutes of the Thirty-Seventh Annual Session of the West Union Baptist Association* (n.p.: by the association, 1906), 9-10; WUBA, *Minutes of the Fortieth Annual Session of the West Union Baptist Association* (n.p.: by the association, 1910), 9.

73 Elizabeth Brown Lynch, *A History of Elk Valley, Tennessee* (Knoxville, TN: by the author, 1991), 61.

74 SUAUB, *Minutes* (1904), 11.

75 Gibson, 6; Padgett, *A Goodly Heritage*, 12; Arlie Petree, "John Parks," *GH* 39, no. 7 (July 1978): 4. No primary source accounts exist for this story. Parks rarely spoke of it. Years later, he confessed to a member that "for three days after that, I couldn't talk about it, else I'd feel that upward pull again." The story was repeated by those who heard it second-hand for many years. Daniel Moses was in his early 20s at the time and testified of the event often in the Jellico Church until his death in 1961. He claimed to have been seated near the front of the building "and when [Parks] came down, he put his hand on my shoulder." Nellie (Croley) Moses was a small child in attendance the night it happened and shared the story with her children and grandchildren until her death in 1995. Lora (Davenport) Ross was a teenager and was also present at the time. She recounted the event before her death for Pastor Jerome Walden on an audio recording in the early 1980s. The exact time and place of the event is unknown. It most likely occurred between 1905 and 1908. Little Wolf Creek is the most likely location as Daniel Moses was a member of that church. It is also possible that the event took place at Zion Hill, where Parks was also pastoring at the time.

76 CGMA, *Minutes* (1907), 1.

77 Ibid., 2-4.

78 Greg Wills, "The Church: Baptists and Their Churches in the Eighteenth and Nineteenth Centuries," in Dever, *Polity*, 21-22.

79 1910 United States Census, Campbell County, Tennessee and 1910 United States Census, Whitley County, Kentucky, Ancestry.com; See Table 2.1 at the end of the chapter.

80 CGMA, *Minutes* (1907), 2.

81 CGMA, *Minutes of the Church of God, Inc.: Minutes of the Eighteenth Annual Session of the Mountain Assembly of the Church of God* (Jellico, TN: CGMA, 1924), 7.

82 CGMA, *Minutes of the Church of God, Inc.: The Nineteenth Annual Session of the Mountain Assembly of the Churches of God* (Jellico, TN: CGMA, 1925), 6, 10.

83 CGMA, *Minutes of the Mountain Assembly of the Churches of God (Incorporated): The Thirty-Second Annual Assembly of the Churches of God* (Jellico, TN: CGMA, 1938), 30.

84 SUAUB, *Minutes* (1905), 2.

85 CGMA, *Minutes* (1938).

86 J.L. Reynolds, *Church Polity or The Kingdom of Christ, in its Internal and External Development* (Richmond, 1849), in Dever, *Polity*, 328-342.

87 Wellum and Wellum in Dever and Leeman, *Foundations*, 64, 67.

88 CGMA, *Minutes: Eighth Annual Session of Church of God [Mountain Assembly]* (n.p.: by the association, 1914), 3-4.

89 Minutes of the Fonde Church of God Mountain Assembly, Book One: 1917 to 1940, 87 in the possession of Jerry Grubbs, Lincoln Park, MI.

90 Jellico Minutes, 57.

91 Ibid., 17-18.

92 CGMA, *Minutes of the Fifteenth Annual Session of the Mountain Assembly Churches of God* (n.p.: by the association, 1921), 4.

93 Wills in Dever, *Polity*, 22-23.

94 Charleston Association, in Ibid., 124-125.

95 Fonde Minutes, 293; Jellico Minutes, membership roster.

96 Fonde Minutes, 13.

97 CGMA, *Minutes* (1911), 8.

98 CGMA, *Minutes* (1914), 2, statistical table; Deed of Conveyance, *Whitley County Deed Book* 102, March 2, 1923, 542, Whitley County Court House, Williamsburg, KY.

99 CGMA, *Minutes of the Tenth Annual Session of the Mountain Assembly of the Churches of God* (n.p.: by the association, 1916), 5.

100 CGMA, *Minutes* (1921), 4.

101 Marshall Davis, *The Baptist Church Covenant: Its History and Meaning* (Sandwich, NH: by the author, 2013), 18, 20; John Newton Brown, *The Baptist Church Manual: Containing the Declaration of Faith, Covenant, Rules of Order and Brief Forms of Church Letters* (Philadelphia: American Baptist Publication Society, 1853).

102 Hayes Creek minutes, 1; Gibson, 5. In his description of the "first assembly," Gibson says that "Rev. S.N. Bryant read the covenant at that time" and "the delegates unanimously accepted it as read." As the church covenant is not mentioned in the minutes of the first assembly, nor does it appear in the minute book until 1917, the author speculates that Gibson had access to the organizational minutes of the Jellico Creek Church (possibly from Savannah Taylor) in 1953-4 and it is to that meeting that Gibson refers. Further evidence to support this conjecture is Gibson's listing of "delegates" at this meeting who do not appear in the minutes of the first assembly, but likely would have been members at Jellico Creek.

103 CGMA, *Minutes of the Eleventh Annual Session of the Mountain Assembly of the Churches of God* (n.p.: by the association, 1917), 5.

104 W.B. Johnson, *The Gospel Developed Through the Government and Order of the Churches of Jesus Christ* (Richmond, 1846), in Dever, *Polity*, 204.

105 Wills, in Dever, *Polity*, 24.

106 CGMA, *Minutes of the Sixth Annual Session of the Churches of God [Mountain Assembly]* (n.p.: by the association, 1912), 3-4.

107 CGMA, *Minutes* (1921), 4.

108 Wills, in Dever, *Polity*, 25-26.

109 CGMA, *Minutes* (1907), 4.

110 Benjamin L. Merkle, "The Scriptural Basis for Elders," in Dever and Leeman, *Foundations*, 246-247.

111 Merkle, "The Biblical Role of Elders," in Dever and Leeman, *Foundations*, 271-276.

112 Wills, in Dever, *Polity*, 33-35.

113 Andrew Davis, "Practical Issues in Deacon Ministry," in Dever and Leeman, *Foundations*, 327-328.

114 CGMA, *Minutes* (1924), 3-7, 15, 19.

115 CGMA, *Minutes* (1925), 16.

116 Charleston Association, in Dever, *Polity*, 131-133.

117 Janus Jones, *200 Years of Associational Missions: A History of the South Union Association 1815-1997 And the South Union Mount Zion Association 1997-2015* (Williamsburg, KY: South Union Mount Zion Association, 2015), 13-14.

118 Jones, *1990 Annual*, 13-14.

119 SUAUB, *Minutes of the Eighty-seventh Annual Session of the South Union Association of United Baptists* (n.p.: by the association, 1901), 3.

120 Ibid.

121 Ibid.

122 Ibid.

123 CGMA, *Minutes* (1907), 1.

124 Church of God [Mountain Assembly], *A Minute of the Second Association of the Church of God [Mountain Assembly]* (n.p.: by the association, 1908), 2. As of the time of this writing, no minute book of the Third General Assembly (1909) is known to exist. The 1910 minute book uses "General Assembly," but does not contain a reference to the name of the association being changed. This leads to the assumption that the change took place the preceding year.

125 Church of God [Mountain Assembly], *Minutes of the General Assembly of the Church of God [Mountain Assembly]* (n.p.: by the association, 1910), 1; CGMA, *Minutes* (1911), 1.

126 CGMA, *Minutes* (1911), 1.

127 CGMA, *Minutes of the Church of God Mountain Assembly, Inc.: Fifty-Eighth Annual Assembly* (Jellico, TN: CGMA, 1964), 23.

128 CGMA, *Minutes of the Church of God Mountain Assembly Incorporated: Thirty-Eighth Annual Assembly* (Jellico, TN: CGMA, 1944), 11.

129 CGMA, *Annual Minutes of the Church of God Mountain Assembly* (Jellico, TN: CGMA, 1974), 23.

130 Ibid., 8.

131 CGMA, *Minutes of the Church of God Mountain Assembly Incorporated: Forty-Fourth Annual Assembly* (Jellico, TN: CGMA, 1950), 11.

132 CGMA, *Minutes of the Church of God Mountain Assembly Incorporated: Forty-Seventh Annual Assembly* (Jellico, TN: CGMA, 1953), 13.

133 CGMA, *Minutes of the Church of God Mountain Assembly Incorporated: Sixty-Fifth Annual Assembly* (Jellico, TN: CGMA, 1971), 21.

134 CGMA, *Minutes of the Mountain Assembly of the Churches of God (Incorporated): The Twenty-Fifth Annual Assembly of the Mountain Assembly of the Churches of God* (Jellico, TN: CGMA, 1931), 2.

135 CGMA, *Minutes of the Mountain Assembly of the Churches of God Incorporated: The Thirty-Fourth Annual Assembly of the Mountain Assembly of the Churches of God* (Jellico, TN: CGMA, 1940), 14.

136 CGMA, *Minutes* (1964), 22.

137 Jellico Minutes, 112.

A Bow Tied

Full Name	Church	Age	Profession
John W. Beams	Pleasant View	59	farmer
John Bryant	Sheep Creek	62	farmer
John H. Bryant	Sheep Creek	21	laborer
Stephen N. Bryant	Sheep Creek	42	farmer
George D. Caddell	Sheep Creek	37	miner
Ambrose Campbell	Ryan's Creek	48	farmer
Emby K. Creekmore	Hayes Creek	45	farmer
Henry N. Creekmore	Ryan's Creek	70	farmer
Marion F. Dickerson	Sheep Creek	32	farmer
Cleve Douglas	Lower Elk Valley	42	farmer
John Griffitts	Sheep Creek	67	farmer
Aaron Hackler	Lower Elk Valley	44	farmer
Rachel Hackler	Lower Elk Valley	43	laborer
John Hickman	Saxton	49	miner
William Hicks	Wooldridge	63	farmer
Thomas Higginbotham	Ryan's Creek	71	*illegible*
Joe L. Jones	Saxton	32	farmer
John D. Kidd	Zion Hill	27	miner
John M. Laws	Little Wolf Creek	33	farmer
James Lay	Zion Hill	52	farmer
John Long	Zion Hill	50	farmer
Ransom D. Lovitt	Hayes Creek	34	farmer
James Martin	Saxton	36	miner
Daniel E. Moses	Little Wolf Creek	28	farmer
James Allen Moses	Little Wolf Creek	53	farmer
Tom D. Moses	Little Wolf Creek	53	farmer
John H. Parks	Pleasant View	48	farmer
Newton K. Parks	Zion Hill	51	farmer
Joseph T. Richardson	Patterson Creek	54	farmer
Alvin G. Ross	Ryan's Creek	27	farmer
Alvin J. Ross	Lower Elk Valley	52	laborer
Melton F. Ross	Zion Hill	51	farmer
James M. Rountree	Sheep Creek	53	merchant
Melton F. Rountree	Sheep Creek	57	farmer
Edom J. Rountree	Sheep Creek	35	farmer
William H. Rountree	Little Wolf Creek	33	miner
James J. Sammons	Patterson Creek	35	miner
John P. Smiddy	Wooldridge	66	cargoman
J. Patton Smith	Saxton	51	farmer
William E. Strunk	Hayes Creek	38	farmer
Frank W. Sullivan	Pleasant View	39	clerk
Maggie Swaney	Wooldridge	52	none
Daniel Taylor	Zion Hill	40	farmer
Aaron Thomas	Ryan's Creek	52	farmer
Francis M. Thomas	Pleasant View	51	miner
Josiah M. Thomas	Little Wolf Creek	26	farmer
Mike Thomas	Zion Hill	49	farmer
Sherrod Thomas	Little Wolf Creek	53	farmer
Curd Walker	Saxton	32	farmer

R	W	O	M	County, ED, Pg, Ln
✓	✓	O	F	Whitley, 258, 1, 15
✓	✓	R		Whitley, 259, 16, 3
✓	✓			Whitley, 258, 10, 42
✓	✓	O	F	Whitley, 258, 10, 40
✓	✓	R		Whitley, 255, 12, 39
✓	no	O	M	Whitley, 241, 18, 15
✓	✓	O	F	Whitley, 238, 13, 32
no	no	O	F	Whitley, 241, 5, 8
✓	✓	O	F	Whitley, 258, 9, 23
✓	✓	O	F	Campbell, 50, 8, 75
✓	✓	O	M	Whitley, 269, 11, 8
✓	✓	O	F	Campbell, 50, 10, 17
✓	✓			Campbell, 50, 10, 18
no	no	R	F	Campbell, 49, 23, 37
✓	✓	O	F	Campbell, 42, 8, 57
✓	✓	O	F	Whitley, 259, 19, 100
✓	✓	O	F	Whitley, 254, 3, 84
✓	✓	R		Whitley, 256, 6, 77
no	no	O	F	Whitley, 258, 13, 66
no	no	R		Whitley, 241, 20, 47
no	no	O	F	Whitley, 241, 20, 55
✓	✓	O	F	Whitley, 240, 3, 57
✓	✓	R		Whitley, 252, 14, 57
✓	✓	R		Whitley, 260, 31, 26
✓	✓	O	F	Whitley, 258, 13, 36
no	no	O	F	Whitley, 258, 13, 74
✓	✓	O	F	Whitley, 258, 14, 55
✓	✓	O	F	Whitley, 240, 1, 58
✓	✓	O	F	Whitley, 259, 4, 29
✓	✓	O	F	Whitley, 241, 7, 70
✓	✓	O	F	Campbell, 50, 13, 69
✓	✓	R		Whitley, 241, 6, 16
✓	✓	O	M	Whitley, 258, 13, 1
✓	✓	R		Whitley, 251, 5, 51
✓	✓	R	F	Whitley, 258, 14, 38
✓	✓	O	F	Whitley, 256, 9, 24
✓	✓	R		Campbell, 49, 30, 8
✓	✓	R		Campbell, 45, 11, 54
✓	✓	O	F	Whitley, 254, 3, 56
✓	✓	O	F	Whitley, 240, 2, 96
✓	✓	O	F	Whitley, 258, 1, 23
✓	✓	O	F	Campbell, 50, 13, 55
✓	✓	O	F	Whitley, 241, 6, 72
✓	✓	R		Whitley, 241, 20, 98
✓	✓	O		Whitley, 258, 3, 50
✓	✓	R		Whitley, 256, 9, 19
✓	✓	O	F	Whitley, 243, 5, 65
✓	no	R		Whitley, 256, 9, 13
✓	✓	O	M	Whitley, 254, 3, 90

Table 2.1: Delegates at the First Assembly

1910 U.S. Census Data for delegates at the 1st Assembly.

Key:
Read?
Write?
Own or Rent?
Free or Mortgage?
Enumeration District, Page number, Line number

Note: Calvin L. Caddell of Sheep Creek and John Selvia of Wooldridge cannot be located in the 1910 Census and are not listed in this table as a result.

3

The Influence of the Church of God on the Mountain Assembly

When the Fifth Annual Mountain Assembly opened on October 6, 1911, two guests from the Church of God (Cleveland) were conspicuously present. Ambrose Jessup Tomlinson of Cleveland, Tennessee and Joseph Steel Llewellyn of Knoxville attended the meeting at Siler's Chapel.[1] In the South Union Association, guest ministers were often invited to participate in the divine services and to assist in the conduct of business. Following this custom, Tomlinson led the congregation in prayer prior to the introductory sermon. At the opening of the business session, he was appointed to read the church letters and enroll the messengers before he took the vote for moderator and Llewellyn took the vote for clerk. The committee on divine services also selected Tomlinson to preach that night.[2] In a single day, Tomlinson had played a significant role in both the worship services and the business session of the Mountain Assembly. A.J Tomlinson's impact on the group was both immediate and enduring. The Church of God (Cleveland) would continue to influence the CGMA for decades to come.

Parallel Histories: The Church of God Mountain Assembly and the Church of God (Cleveland)

When Richard Green Spurling established Christian Union in 1886, he clung tightly to the values of his Baptist heritage that emphasized soul liberty and congregational autonomy. Every believer was accountable to God directly, and the church was governed by the members collectively. As the Christian Union began to add churches, these congregations and their members championed that rugged individualism as well. Spurling's ecclesiology lacked "a firm and objective basis for fellowship, both in regard to the members' relationship to one another and the churches' relationship to one another."[3] In contrast, the Mountain Assembly's original churches were organized within a few years of each other from members who shared both their Baptist history and the holiness experience. In addition, numerous family relationships connected members and churches together.[4] Spurling's vision also failed to communicate a clear purpose of the church in the world and

The Influence of the Church of God

Figure 3.1: R.G. Spurling
c/o Dixon Pentecostal Research Center

Figure 3.2: A.J. Tomlinson
c/o Dixon Pentecostal Research Center

lacked any central government necessary to direct the congregations to that end. Spurling's association was also missing "an inspirational leader with the organizational skills to bring about these results."[5] Tomlinson provided the latter and transformed Spurling's church into the Church of God (Cleveland).

While Tomlinson's Church of God moved toward institutionalization through centralized government and Parks's Church of God clung to its congregationalism, both groups moved the same direction doctrinally. By the time Tomlinson visited the Mountain Assembly in 1911, both his and Parks's church had completed the transformation from Holiness to Pentecostalism. According to Acts 2:4, about fifty days after Christ's crucifixion, his disciples "were all filled with the Holy Ghost and began to speak with other tongues" on the Day of Pentecost. Baptists believed that the gifts bestowed by the Holy Spirit to the New Testament Church met "a temporary emergency in the incipiency of Christianity" and were "intended to cease when the necessity for them should cease," never "to be revived in the church."[6] Pentecostals, and others, have argued that though sporadic and marginalized, tongues speech continued from the Apostolic Age through the Reformation and up to the modern Pentecostal movement.[7]

Although Spurling's Christian Union Church reportedly had manifestations of tongues speech in its revivals in the 1880s, the significance of the phenomenon was not recognized at the time.[8] When the revival broke out at Schearer Schoolhouse in Cherokee County, North Carolina in 1896, several claimed to speak in "other tongues when they *prayed through*."[9] The revival was conducted by three ministers affiliated with Benjamin Hardin

Irwin's fire-baptized holiness movement.[10] Irwin's holiness association began in Iowa in 1895 and spread like fire into the American South within three years. The doctrine he preached included various experiences where the believer might be effused with several "baptisms of fire" that included entire sanctification, physical healing, and tongues speech.[11] It was the doctrine of speaking with other tongues in association with the baptism of the Holy Ghost that had a doctrinal impact on the Church of God movement in North Carolina and Tennessee. After Tomlinson read about the 1906 Azusa Street Revival, he took a keen interest in the Pentecostal baptism. In June 1907, Tomlinson attended a Pentecostal revival in Birmingham, Alabama, and began earnestly seeking the blessing for himself upon his return. On January 12, 1908, he claimed the personal experience of Spiritual baptism. "After this glorious immersion into the Spirit, Tomlinson began zealously to promote the Pentecostal movement's interpretation of Spirit-baptism and endeavored to transform the Church of God completely into a Pentecostal body."[12]

In southeastern Kentucky, Parks and Bryant had also "heard of the people receiving the Holy Ghost baptism in Los Angeles, California in the year 1906." To them, "speaking in the other tongues" seemed "to be a lot of foolishness." They still believed in the cessation of the spiritual gifts they had been taught in the Baptist church.[13] In February 1909, however, Bryant's 20-year-old son, John Harrison Bryant, received the baptism of the Holy Ghost. Johnny Bryant had been converted in 1905 about the same time his father embraced the doctrine of sanctification. He was the youngest delegate at the First Assembly at Little Wolf Creek in 1907. A young and zealous Christian, Bryant ascended a mountain cliff to pray, despite the "big snow on," and "received the Baptism of the Holy Ghost." The following Sunday, February 7, 1909, Bryant was called upon to lead prayer at Sunday school and began to speak in tongues while he prayed. His father had stayed home to assist his wife with the care of her 90-year-old mother, who would die a week later. By the time John had returned home, the senior Bryant had already heard about the experience from one of his members and inquired of his son what it was like. John explained, "Dad, I just can't tell how I felt and the only way you will ever know is to get it yourself." Later that year, the elder Bryant did experience it for himself.[14] Within a few years, the Mountain Assembly meetings regularly featured "some praying for the Holy Ghost" and many people "speaking in tongues."[15] In 1913, the Mountain Assembly formally endorsed "speaking with tongues as the spirit gives utterance" in its first set of teachings.[16]

The Influence of the Church of God

Tomlinson's spiritual empowerment coincided with the increase in actual authority in the church. When he joined the Holiness Church at Camp Creek in North Carolina in June 1903, Tomlinson brought a leadership style that blended several influences, including his Quaker roots, the ideals of American government, and Frank Sandford's authoritarianism.[17] The congregation chose Tomlinson to be its pastor upon recognition of his charismatic leadership. The following year, Tomlinson helped establish three more churches in Georgia and Tennessee, and by 1905 served as pastor to two of them as well as Camp Creek.[18] By the end of that year, "the work" of the churches "had so prospered that there began to be a demand for a general gathering together of members from all the churches to consider questions of importance and to search for additional light and knowledge."[19]

On January 26-27, 1906, the first General Assembly convened at the home of J.C. Murphy at Camp Creek with 21 delegates present.[20] These delegates understood the nature of their assembly as a judicial body which met to interpret scripture and make important decisions. The "findings" of the Assembly were understood as recommendations to the churches, its members, and its ministers. Tomlinson led the delegates in discussion of ecclesial matters, such as the pressing need for evangelism, the importance of regular weekly church prayer meetings and daily family devotions, the worth of Sunday schools, and the observance of feet washing with the ordinance of the Lord's Supper. Each local church was also advised to keep accurate account of its own records and to grant letters of recommendation to members moving from one area to another. The delegates also stressed the value of gathering annually in further assemblies of the church.[21]

Over the next seven Januarys, Tomlinson convened a General Assembly in Bradley County, Tennessee. During that time, the institutionalization of the church became a reality. "The General Assembly became authoritative and from it developed a hierarchy of Episcopal authority over the churches" with Tomlinson at the top of the hierarchy.[22] Tomlinson embraced the name "Church of God" during a mountaintop revelation in June 1903 when he joined the church at Camp Creek.[23] By the time the Second General Assembly met in 1907 at Union Grove and formally adopted the name, it was already in common usage.[24] A common name subtly moved the group toward centralization, as did the recognition of credentials. The Second General Assembly also addressed the proper mode for the selection of pastors. R.G. Spurling expressed his belief that generally every "church should choose their pastor," but conceded that the Apostle Paul also often sent ministers to some congregations. The Assembly agreed that the Holy Spirit was the ultimate authority in the selection of pastoral leadership, but that sometimes this was manifest through the choice of the local congregation and sometimes another responsible party guided the church.[25] The subject came up again the following year in Cleveland. The Third General Assembly upheld the right of the church to choose its pastor but determined that additional inquiry on the subject was necessary.[26] By January 1909, sufficient study produced a solution, and the Church of God adopted this plan:

> The church desiring a pastor should earnestly pray for God to give them the person that He, with His infinite wisdom, knows would be the propper [sic] one for them under the existing circumstances. After prayer to agree upon one, if possible, as they feel divinely guided. To consult in person or by mail with the person desired and finally as they make out the yearly report for the general assembly to fill in the space, "Call for Pastor," the names of two ministers, either one of which they would gladly receive. This should be done so the report could reach the Moderator 2 or 3 days before the date on which the assembly convenes. The assembly, after prayers and consultation with the delegates from the churches and the ministers desired, to place the pastors as nearly as possible according to the requests or desires of the churches to be supplied. In case it is not possible for the assembly, in its short time for deliberation, to make arrangements for the pastors for all churches, those vacant will be submitted to the care of the Moderator of Assembly to confer with such vacant churches and arrange to supply such vacancies to the best of his ability.[27]

By implementing this procedure, the local churches yielded one of their most fundamental privileges to the episcopal leadership of the Church of God.

The leader vested with this authority became Tomlinson. While the Fourth General Assembly discussed the possible office of General Overseer, it took no action to create it. For the time being, instead, it extended the "term" of the "General moderator" to last a full year. His responsibilities included acting as moderator and clerk for the General Assembly, issuing ministerial credentials, keeping a record of all the ministers of the assembly, and filling vacancies in local church leadership. Upon creating the office, the Assembly selected Tomlinson to serve in that capacity.[28] After the completion of his first term, the title of the office was changed to "General Overseer," and Tomlinson was given authority to "appoint pastors for the different churches, as they consent to go, feel led of the Lord, etc."[29] Over the next few years, the power and influence of the General Overseer's office increased as Tomlinson used the General Assembly pulpit to articulate his vision. He envisioned the church council at Jerusalem in Acts 15 in which James served as "moderator" and "General Overseer" as a prototype of the General Assembly of the Church of God.[30] He compared the Church of God to the military and made frequent use of the terms, "rank" and "position."[31]

As committed as Tomlinson seemed to the expansion of his authority, he was equally zealous for the growth of his church. In 1911, Tomlinson reported that the Church of God was represented in six states and the Bahamas. With churches in North Carolina, Tennessee, Kentucky, Georgia, Alabama, and Florida, the General Overseer sought to extend the work further. He reported contacts and the possibility of bringing the organization to California, Mississippi, Arkansas, Iowa, Indiana, Virginia, and Cuba.[32] As he traveled in ministry, he looked for opportunities to enlist additional churches, ministers, and members. When he heard about the Church of God meeting in southeast Kentucky, he purposed to know more about them.

The Influence of A.J. Tomlinson on the Mountain Assembly

Jonah Love Shelton was born in White Rock, North Carolina, on December 10, 1876, had been converted as a child, and was ordained as a minister of the gospel by the Freewill Baptist Church at Dry Branch, North Carolina, on August 29, 1904.[33] Shelton's itinerant ministry brought him to Harlan County, Kentucky, shortly thereafter, and he claimed the experience of entire sanctification. By the time his fourth son, William Apollos, was born in 1908, his ministry had brought him to Whitley County where he got acquainted with John Parks. The Wooldridge church disbanded around 1909 with many of its members transferring to Lower Elk Valley. Its clerk, William Hicks, owned 150 acres near Caryville, Tennessee, and he and Parks founded the Rains Grove Church of God on a half-acre plot.[34] Shelton was a member of this church until November 1909 when he moved to Dickson County, Tennessee.[35] Delegates at the Fourth General Assembly in 1910 so regarded his ministry that they moved to "retain Bro. Shelton as a member of the holiness ranks" despite him living so far away.[36]

While living in Dickson County, Shelton acquired a bundle of "sample papers" from A.J. Tomlinson and began corresponding with him.[37] He attended the Sixth Annual General Assembly of the Church of God (Cleveland) in January 1911 and participated in the discussion on the need for a ministers training school. The following week, Tomlinson issued Shelton an evangelist's license.[38] When Shelton returned to Whitley County later that year, he joined the church at Emlyn, attended the Mountain

Assembly at Siler's Chapel, and was elected clerk.[39] It was probably through Shelton's correspondence that A.J. Tomlinson first learned of the Mountain Assembly and determined to visit the Fifth Annual Assembly.[40] The impact of Tomlinson's first visit was demonstrated by the new name adopted by the Kentucky group, by the exposure of its men to the General Assembly of the Church of God (Cleveland), and by its position on the use of tobacco.

When Parks, Silcox, and Bryant, organized what they called the "Church of God" in 1907, they did not know that earlier that year in Bradley County, Tennessee, another group had adopted that same name. Upon Tomlinson's arrival, they discovered another group of likeminded believers. To distinguish their meeting from the one that met in Cleveland, they adopted the name "Mountain Assembly" on Friday, October 6, 1911.[41] This name was intended to be an informal differentiation between the gatherings of the two groups. When the Mountain Assembly applied for its charter in the state of Tennessee on July 17, 1917, it incorporated under the name "The Church of God."[42] The convention continued to be known as the "Mountain Assembly of the Churches of God" until the 1940s when the name of the organization was changed on the charter to the "Church of God Mountain Assembly, Inc."[43]

When Tomlinson and Llewellyn attended the Mountain Assembly in 1911, they were received in the same manner visiting brethren had been received by the Baptist associations in the area. Parks had been accustomed to representing the South Union Association and preaching at other associational meetings, and he had often invited visiting ministers to sit with the delegates when he moderated the business sessions. Tomlinson was afforded the same ministerial courtesy by Bryant serving as Moderator.[44] He undoubtedly invited representatives from the Mountain Assembly to come to Cleveland for the Seventh General Assembly of the Church of God.

On the afternoon of January 9, 1912, Tomlinson told the General Assembly of his October visit to Kentucky and introduced Parks and Bryant, who each spoke and shared their testimonies of embracing holiness and their exclusion from the Baptist church. Tomlinson indicated that Parks and Bryant had come with Shelton, Hicks, and Josiah Martin Thomas (of Jellico) "for the purpose of forming a union" and appointed a committee to confer with them. On the last day of the General Assembly, the committee reported with a letter on terms of acceptance of a union. The terms included a wholesale incorporation of the Mountain Assembly into the Church of God. All ministers and deacons were recognized "in their respective positions" provided they did not use tobacco and had not been divorced and remarried.

The Influence of the Church of God

The Mountain Assembly was given permission to continue to hold its annual meeting, so long as it recognized the General Assembly in Cleveland as the supreme council. After the representatives "accepted the conditions of union they were asked to come forward and take their places on the rostrum." Tomlinson formally received the Mountain Assembly into the Church of God and then had the ministers and deacons offer "the right hand of fellowship" to its messengers.[45] From the appearance of the printed Church of God record, the Mountain Assembly united with the Church of God in 1912.

This formal union, however, was never consummated. Tomlinson claimed the Mountain Assembly had sent messengers to consider a union, yet no record exists of such authorization from the meeting at Siler's Chapel. Firmly rooted in the ecclesiology of their Baptist upbringing, the idea of congregational autonomy made clear that the association itself had no power to act on behalf of the individual churches. The tradition of receiving and sending visiting associational messengers was never intended to demonstrate a formal merger of two groups of churches. Rumors that Parks and Bryant delivered the Mountain Assembly to Tomlinson persisted into the 1930s. Parks wrote to Tomlinson to clear up the matter. His reply indicated that the Church of God's minutes showed the names of the five men attending the General Assembly in 1912, but he remembered "very well that yourself and Brother Bryant did leave and we only acted by what the other three Brethren said." He added that "the very fact that we never did work together according to the plans outlined is enough to show that the matter of union was not finally decided upon, and we never did recognize its final consummation."[46]

Though the consolidation of the two groups into one body never took place, the relationship between the two groups continued to develop as Tomlinson returned for the Sixth Annual Mountain Assembly in October 1912 at Lower Elk Valley. Attending with him were Thomas L. McLain, Martin S. Haynes, George F. Lucas, and Samuel C. Perry, and Bryant invited all five to be seated with the delegates. The committee on divine services invited McLain, Haynes, Lucas, and Tomlinson to preach. Tomlinson had made such an impression that the committee asked him to preach Friday night at nearby Tannery Hollow, Saturday morning at the church, Saturday night back at Tannery Hollow, and Sunday evening at the church.[47] So many gathered on Sunday night that the small church could not hold them all. Tomlinson reflected on the experience in his personal diary:

> I went up and preached for an hour and a half, or more, after [Parks] had preached an hour and five minutes. A great crowd, estimated at 1,500. The seats were taken out of the house and placed out of doors in front of the house, and a thousand people stood up while we preached. We had to stand on a platform in the hot sun, and most of the congregation was in the hot sun the most of the time. They stayed right there, and God wonderfully helped to deliver the truth. After the discourse I was called on to pray for and anoint quite a number for healing right out in the hot sun. I was almost exhausted.[48]

Although this was Tomlinson's last visit to the Mountain Assembly, the sending and receiving of messengers in the Baptist association tradition continued for the rest of the decade. In 1914, the Eighth Annual Mountain Assembly resolved to "write a letter of correspondence to the Cleveland assembly and send it by the hands of some of our brethren asking them to receive our letter and messengers." Appointed to carry the letter were John Parks, Newt Parks, William R. Hamlin, George A. Fore, Matt H. Morgan, Josiah Thomas, and William Hicks.[49] In 1919, seven brothers and sisters from the Church of God were enrolled as visiting messengers at the 13th Annual Mountain Assembly.[50]

One final impact of Tomlinson's 1911 visit can be seen in its stance on the issue of tobacco. The Church of God dealt with it at its first assembly:

> This assembly agrees to stand, with one accord, in opposition to the use of tobacco in any form. It is offensive to those who do not use it; weakens and impairs the nervous system; is a near relative to drunkenness; bad influence and example to the young; useless expense, the money for which ought to be used to clothe the poor, spread the gospel or make the homes of our country more comfortable; and last we believe its use to be contrary to the teaching of Scripture, and as Christ is our example we cannot believe that He would use it in any form or under any circumstances.[51]

In recognition that nicotine addicts continued to struggle two years later, the Church of God "decided that those in the Church who use tobacco should be dealt with kindly, fairly, and squarely and given a little time for consideration" before they were excluded from the church for their refusal to give up "the filthy stuff."[52] In 1909, the General Assembly became even more tolerant as they struck out the limitations on church membership.[53] Finally, in January 1911, the Church of God returned to its strict prohibition against members using tobacco in any form.[54]

Having firmly settled the issue within the Church of God after five years of deliberation, Tomlinson was present for the business session when the subject arose at the Mountain Assembly on October 5, 1911. In the South Union Association, although members visiting from other associations were not entitled to vote on matters, they were given the same privileges of speech as the messengers from the member churches. Tomlinson certainly weighed in when the resolution committee consisting of Pleasant Isaiah Cox, James Madison Rountree, Neadom Rountree, and William Hicks presented an advice that the Churches of God "will not recognize preachers that do not preach a full Gospel." Its amendment included that "the Churches of God ordain no Minister that will not abstain from the use of tobacco." When the question was asked about those who presently used tobacco, the Assembly advised that they should quit. "After a long discussion by both sides which lasted till [sic] in the evening with many sobs, groans, amens, and shouts and prayers to God for victory," the Moderator called for the vote and it was adopted 18 to 15. Several members abruptly left the house without permission.[55] Like the Church of God (Cleveland), the Mountain Assembly would have to return to the subject multiple times before the matter was final, but the first encounter with the Church of God indirectly led to the first split in the Mountain Assembly over the issue of tobacco.

The General Assembly Church of God

So close was the vote over tobacco that it was certain to come back up again. At the Seventh Annual Mountain Assembly in Saxton, Kentucky in 1913, the resolution committee of John Parks, Curd Walker, G.A. Fore, Melt Ross, and J.T. Richardson presented two resolutions related to tobacco. First, the Assembly "resolved that it be a debore [sic] of fellowship for the ministers of the churches of God to advocate the use of tobacco in any way." They also issued a rebuke to ministers who claimed "that the Lord took the taste away" or that He told them to quit using tobacco and then picked back up the habit.[56] When such measures still did not prevent ministers from using tobacco, the Assembly took further action. At the Ninth Annual Mountain Assembly at Jellico Creek in 1915, the Assembly passed a motion to "withdraw its fellowship from every preaching brother that will not abstain totaly [sic] from the use of tobacco from this time on." The Assembly also appointed ministers to visit the churches pastored by tobacco users to seek compliance with this resolution.[57]

Figure 3.3: W.R. Hamlin
c/o the Hamlin Family

Figure 3.4: Hayes Creek Church
where W.R. Hamlin reorganized as the
General Assembly Church of God in 1917
c/o Joy Ball

William Riley Hamlin had moved from Scott County, Tennessee to Whitley County, Kentucky and organized a new Holiness church at Gold Bug, Kentucky in 1910.[58] He was among its messengers at the Mountain Assembly the following year at Siler's Chapel and presumably voted "no" on the adoption of the anti-tobacco resolution. In October 1912, he was elected to replace Newt Parks as the Pastor of Hayes Creek when Parks started a new church a few miles away at Upper Rock Creek.[59] The following April, Hayes Creek ordained Edom Lonzo Lovitt, and he replaced Hamlin as pastor.[60] Hamlin replaced Parks at Upper Rock Creek and also assumed the pastorate at Zion Hill.[61] To no avail, the Assembly dispatched ministers to meet with Hamlin and Lovitt about their use of tobacco.

While the Tenth Annual Mountain Assembly convened at Lower Elk Valley on October 6-8, 1916, Hamlin gathered Rock Creek and Zion Hill to Hayes Creek. With Melton Ross moderating and Alvin J. Ross serving as clerk, these churches reorganized what became known as the General Assembly Church of God.[62] John Parks referred to Hamlin as a "tobacco slave" and blamed him for the "strong fight against the brethren" and the drawing away of three churches.[63] So infamous did Hamlin become in the Mountain Assembly that his name became synonymous with "excluded preacher." Ten years after Hamlin's last assembly, the Mountain Assembly adopted a motion not to receive "members into our body that are baptized by excluded preachers, such as W.R. Hamlin, etc., until they are baptized again by legal ordained ministers."[64]

The split with the General Assembly Church of God took place before the Mountain Assembly had firmly established its Pentecostal theology. While the practice of speaking with other tongues was readily associated with the experience of the baptism of the Holy Ghost, the Mountain Assembly had not yet formulated its doctrinal statement that recognized it as the initial "evidence" of the baptism.[65] As a result, the General Assembly Church of God never adopted this view.[66]

The Church of God of the Union Assembly

While the Church of God (Cleveland) directly influenced The Mountain Assembly's position on the use of tobacco, it also inspired the formulation of doctrinal statements in the Mountain Assembly. Spurling's Christian Union was founded on a rejection of creeds as he felt the invention of such led to the divisions and schisms of the medieval church. As time passed, however, the Church of God codified its doctrinal statements. This process was decades long and was impacted by several important factors. The First General Assembly in 1906 offered the opportunity for reflection and consensus on many important beliefs. Next, a lawsuit against the Church of God by the city of Cleveland presented a platform for Tomlinson to demonstrate that his sect was not as unorthodox as had been charged. Finally, the General Assemblies of 1910, 1915, 1917, and 1922 engaged the delegates in critical thinking that led to the adoption of additional standard teachings.[67]

The Mountain Assembly had adopted six articles of faith at its first assembly in October 1907.[68] At each successive assembly, various resolutions were adopted that further defined what the group believed, but with no formal cumulative list. In 1913 at Saxton, the Mountain Assembly made several doctrinal statements through the answering of submitted Bible questions and also printed a list of about ten standard teachings.[69] Tomlinson's church first published a set of standard "Teachings" in its 1917 minute book.[70] Later that year, John Parks presented a new list of eleven "articles of faith" at a ministers meeting at Pleasant View on November 30, which were readily adopted by the Mountain Assembly. A few years later, the 1920 minute book published an updated list of about 30 "articles and doctrines of the Church of God." Of this list, the first 27 were nearly identical in wording and appeared in the same order as those adopted by the Church of God (Cleveland).[71]

The 1917 "articles of faith" of the Church of God Mountain Assembly contained, in some form, eight declarations adopted in previous years and a statement reaffirming the "principles and doctrins [sic] of the said church of

God herein from the date of its organization the 24th day of August, 1907, down to the present date." In addition, the Mountain Assembly included two new doctrinal statements as a result of the United States' entry into the World War in April, one on pacifism and another on the second coming of Christ.[72] The Mountain Assembly's views on pacifism may be attribute to Tomlinson. His Quaker roots formed his conviction, and he led his church accordingly. Sensing the imminence of American involvement, Tomlinson wrote:

> Our attitude toward war can be no other way than that taught by our lord. If we are of the world so we can take part in the wars then we are not of His kingdom. We cannot be of the world and of the Lord at the same time ... As for me, I cannot fight Germany, nor lend my influence in that direction and support such a movement. I can be imposed upon, but I cannot fight. No doubt many of our people are wondering what to do in case our country gets into war. Shall we enlist in the governmental service and fight for our rights? Can we shoulder a gun and march to the battle front and point our gun toward our enemy and fire into his ranks and send his soul to hell, when Jesus, our King, tells us to love our enemies?[73]

The General Overseer reminded his followers that Jesus warned "that we will hear of wars and rumors of wars" as His second coming approached.

Seven months after the United States entered the Great War, the Mountain Assembly adopted Park's presentation of a new teaching that "we believe it to be wrong for Christians to take up war arms and go to war, for Jesus said thou shall not kill, therefore, we forbid that any of our members engage in war."[74] The church officially maintained this position for fifty years.[75] By the Second World War, enforcement of the military prohibition had laxed to the point that the new denominational periodical included a prayer list of those on active duty.[76] When the teaching was first enacted in 1917, however, Mountain Assembly churches strictly followed it. When Ora Jones, for example, joined the United States Army in September 1920, the church at Fonde "dropped" his membership "from the roll."[77]

With the world around them engaged in the *War to End All Wars*, Mountain Assembly preachers carefully contemplated its eschatological implications. Parks adhered to the millenarian view that the imminent physical return of Jesus would end all wickedness and Christ would reign for one thousand years on an earthly throne. In his personal journal, Parks reflected on "the Kingdom of God at hand" as something "within reach or not far distant." The aged minister studied what the New Testament said about the great tribulation and what some preached "that the saints will be caught away before the tribulation come." His own interpretation of "what the scriptures teach" led him to conclude that "the saints will be here in the earth in the tribulation days."[78] Parks became obsessed with the "signs of the times." From his home in Jellico, Tennessee on March 7, 1918, Parks presumably witnessed an occurrence of the aurora borealis. Now approaching sixty years of age, the minister felt that the "great lights in the heavens" which appeared as if the sun was "rising in the north" was what Jesus meant when he said that "great signs shall there be from heaven" (Luke 21:11). A second sighting the following February seemed to confirm his first assumption.[79] Amid the influenza pandemic of 1918, Parks wrote on November 17, that the "worldwide deaths of many thousands" about which he read fulfilled the prophecy of Amos 8:3, "there shall be many dead bodies in every place," and described the "pestilences" predicted by Jesus in Matthew 24:7.[80]

The adoption of a formal article of faith, "We believe in the millennial reign in accordance as the scriptures refered [sic] to," was, in part, due to the Church of God (Cleveland) having published its teaching on the "pre-millennial second coming of Jesus" earlier that year.[81] The exact wording employed by the Church of God would appear in the Mountain Assembly's teachings in 1930. Its wording in 1917, however, seems to have stemmed primarily from a controversy involving one of its ministers, Charlie Pratt, and his erroneous preaching that the millennial reign had already begun.

Charles Thomas Pratt was born near Monticello, Kentucky, on August 11, 1879, to George Washington Pratt and Margaret Elizabeth Lair. On April 8, 1904, Pratt married Mary Minnie Broyles, the 14-year old daughter of Lewis Marion Broyles and Martha "Tiny" Prewitt. The marriage of their eldest daughter to a man ten years her senior with a reputation for "drinking hard liquor, carousing, and fighting" devastated the devout Methodists. The following year, Pratt was converted at Piney Grove Methodist Church where his wife attended in Goldbug, Kentucky, and felt a call to the ministry. Over the next four years, Pratt backslid into alcoholism and renewed his commitment to Christ multiple times. Each time he returned to the church, the call to preach pressed upon him. In 1909, he "began training to become a minister in the Methodist Church." His inability to read, however, seriously impeded ordination in the Methodist conference. Pratt then turned to the Mountain Assembly, which he presumably heard about from Minnie's first cousin, Squire Broyles, who was John Parks's son-in-law. Pratt joined Hamlin's newly organized congregation at Gold Bug and was ordained on October 18, 1910.[82]

Sam Jones Guyton relocated to Kentucky from Bartow County, Georgia, in the early 1900s to work on the railroad. He and his wife befriended the Pratts and followed Charlie's ministry. In 1911, Guyton persuaded Pratt to hold a revival in his hometown of Cass Station near Cartersville. With the 44 souls converted in this revival, Pratt organized a church. His return to Kentucky was intended to be temporary until he could earn enough money to move to Cass Station permanently. Financial setback brought about another relapse with alcoholism until Pratt finally rededicated his life to service in ministry in 1912.[83] Pratt and his father-in-law represented Gold Bug at the Sixth Annual Session of the Mountain Assembly at Lower Elk Valley in October 1912.[84] The Pratts soon returned to Cass Station to pastor the church Charlie organized in a building that had been erected on land donated by a relative of Guyton.[85] The Cass Station Church presented itself for membership in the Mountain Assembly at its Seventh Annual Session at Saxton on October 3, 1913.[86]

Figure 3.5: Charlie T. Pratt
c/o David Cady

In early 1915, Pratt moved his family to Knoxville, Tennessee, to establish a church there.[87] At some point that year, Pratt entertained the possibility of joining the Church of God (Cleveland). Tomlinson wrote to his members and readers of *The Church of God Evangel,* "We have before us some fine recommendations of one C.T. Pratt, of Cass Station, Ga., who has offered himself and his churches for membership." The General Overseer reported that he was investigating the "successful preacher and evangelist" and that "if he proves perfectly in harmony with us he will be received."[88] Three months later, however, Tomlinson informed his readers that "facts about [Pratt] and his teaching showed he could not become a members with us." Pratt "bought a small printing press" but "knew nothing about printing, and nothing about setting up the type." However, the same night he "dreamed how to set up that type" and "got up the next morning" with the knowledge.[89] When Tomlinson learned that Pratt had published a paper named "The Church of God Evangel," he called the act an "encroachment" and an "intrusion" and advised Pratt to "change the name of his paper at once or stop publishing it." Tomlinson charged Pratt with starting an "imitation" church and declared that "his counterfit [sic] affair will not prosper" and warned "honest souls" not "to be deceived and duped by it."[90] About the same time, Pratt was forced to return to Georgia. In his absence, the church dismissed the owner of the property, even though he had never actually been a member. In response, the landowner donated the property to the Church of God (Cleveland). Despite having no deed, the court ruled in favor of Pratt, and he was able to secure the property once again.[91]

Pratt resumed fellowship with the Mountain Assembly until 1917. At a minister's meeting in Middlesboro on April 15, 1917, nine days after the United States entered World War I, Pratt proclaimed a doctrine that led to his expulsion from the Mountain Assembly and to the adoption of its teaching on the millennial reign. That night Pratt proclaimed that "In a vision, God showed me Satan bound in chains; therefore the millennial reign of Christ has already begun." The preachers present at the meeting tried to silence Pratt and called on him to recant "his sins of blasphemy," but he continued until he had said enough to warrant his dismission from the church.[92] In November 1919, Pratt and seven others applied for a charter in Bartow County, Georgia, for the "Union Assembly of the Church of God, Inc.," which was granted on May 18, 1920.[93] At its peak, the Union Assembly had over 50 churches and Pratt served as its moderator until his son, Jesse Franklin Pratt, took over the church in October 1961.[94]

Within ten years of the Mountain Assembly's first encounter with A.J. Tomlinson, it experienced two separate splits over doctrine. The General Assembly of the Churches of God formed over the strict anti-tobacco policy the Mountain Assembly copied from the Church of God (Cleveland). Charlie T. Pratt formed what became the Church of God of the Union Assembly after he was defrocked by the Mountain Assembly over his unorthodox eschatological views. In reaction to the setback with Pratt, the Mountain Assembly ultimately adopted the Church of God's precise wording regarding its teaching on the second coming of Christ and His millennial reign.

The Continued Influence of the Church of God on the Mountain Assembly

Although Tomlinson himself attended only two Mountain Assembly meetings, his organization continued to influence the development of the CGMA in several significant ways. First, the Mountain Assembly began to deviate in the credentialing process of its ministers from the tradition of its Baptist roots to that of the Church of God. When a potential ministry candidate accepted a call and appeared promising, the Baptist church formally recognized his giftedness, placed him on "trial," and "gave him a letter of license, for the exercise of his gifts abroad, his encouragement and further improvement, and to obtain the opinion of others concerning his gifts." After sufficient time, a formal vote of the church membership commended the minister to the ordaining presbytery for a public ceremony. Often these presbyters consisted of ordained ministers and deacons from the church or from the association gathered in the local church where the minister's membership was held. The service consisted of a sermon "suited to the occasion," interrogation of the minister to ascertain his qualifications, a formal charge to be faithful to gospel ministry, and the laying on hands of the presbytery for an ordination prayer. Typically, the church presented the newly ordained elder with a certificate and authorized him to preach, to baptize, to administer the Lord's Supper, and to pastor.[95] The United Baptist Church at Little Wolf Creek used this process to ordain Thomas Deberry Moses on January 8, 1898. "After examination," Moses "was found sound concerning the gospel faith of Christ, and was ordained according to the Bible, by prayer and by laying on of hands by the Presbytery" of Andrew Silcox, John Parks, and Caswell Lovitt.[96]

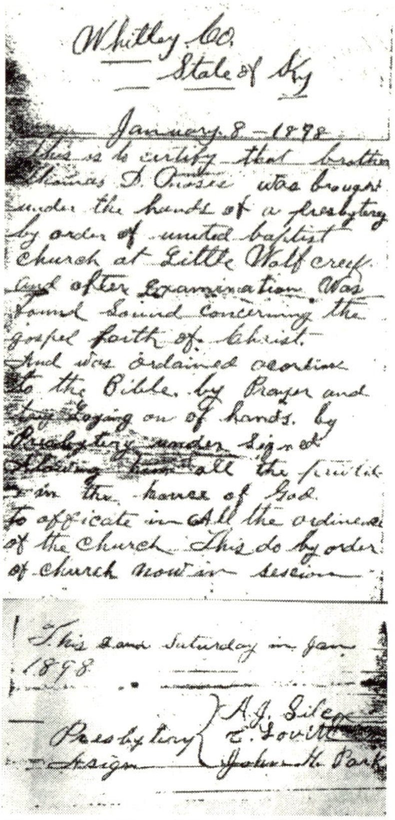
Whitley Co.
State of Ky
January 8 - 1898
This is to certify that brother
Thomas D. Moses was brought
under the hands of a presbytery
by order of united baptist
Church at Little Wolf creek
and after examination Was
found Sound Concerning the
gospel faith of Christ
And was ordained acording
to the Bible by Prayer and
by laying on of hands. by
Presbytery under sign
Allowing him all the privilege
in the house of God.
To officiate in All the ordinance
of the Church This do by order
of church now in session

This same Saturday in Jan
1898
Presbytery assign — A.J. Silcox, C. Lovitt, John H. Park

Figure 3.6: Tom Moses' ordination
c/o Mark Moses

When Richard G. Spurling established Christian Union in 1886, his father formally ordained him to the ministry. To Spurling, the ordination legitimized his leadership in the church. "According to Baptist polity and tradition," this act was necessary to "effect a church organization and to moderate business sessions."[97] Once organized, Christian Union "decided to receive persons into membership who were possessed with a good Christian character, and that ordained and licensed ministers from other churches could retain their same position or office without being reordained."[98] Two decades later, however, the Second General Assembly formally endorsed Spurling's 1886 credentials, indicating that the Assembly saw itself as "a new and higher tribunal of authority."[99] On the same day, Saturday, January 12, 1907, the Assembly raised "the question of ordaining Alex[ander] Hamby."[100] Hamby had joined the Christian Union at Camp Creek in 1902 and had been a delegate at the First General Assembly in 1906.[101] Therefore, when all the ministers present indicated their confidence in Hamby's ministry, he was examined to their satisfaction and ordained to the office of elder on the following day. At the same service, another minister "was also formally given a minister's License."[102] This procedure represented a significant departure from the tradition of the local church authorizing its ministers and demonstrated that the polity of the Church of God recognized the Assembly as one church that perhaps met in different geographic locations. Two years later, the General Assembly began issuing credentials for bishops, deacons, and evangelists (men and women).[103]

Tomlinson's attendance at the Mountain Assembly in 1911 coincided with the first credentials issued by that body when the delegates voted to "give all the ordained [ministers] of this assembly a certificate from the Mountain Assembly of the churches of God."[104] Two years later at Saxton, the Seventh Annual Mountain Assembly voted "to ordain brother Chris Irvin to Ministery [sic] Gospel," and after an admonition on the role of elder, he "was ordained by the hands of the Presbytery," John Parks, Stephen Bryant, Anderson Alder, Curd Walker, John Thomas, Michael Thomas, Newt Parks, and Lewis Broyles.[105] The next three Mountain Assemblies featured the ordinations of Walter Hughes, James Lee "J.L." Goins, and James Mowery, respectively. The "ordination of ministers" was removed from the assembly's "order of business" a few years later, and the ordination process returned exclusively to the local churches for some time.[106] While the procedure returned to the local church, the endorsement remained a matter of the association. In 1925, the delegates to the 19th Mountain Assembly voted to print 500 blank ordination certificates.[107] Sixteen years later, the process of examining and approving ordination candidates returned to the organization. The new method called for a recommendation by the candidate's local church and examination and acceptance by the Assembly's Board of Elders. Once approved by the Elders, the minister would "return to his home church to be ordained in presence of his pastor and church."[108] By adopting this practice, the Mountain Assembly maintained a balance between the congregational polity of its Baptist roots and the episcopal polity of the Church of God.

As Tomlinson's authority increased in the Church of God, so too did concerns about his power. The General Overseer capitulated to the desire of the 12th General Assembly to create a Council of Elders "to help guide and administrate the affairs of the growing organization." The plan called for Tomlinson to appoint two members of the council and for the three of them to select the remaining ten. Ultimately, Major Sterling Lemons, Tillman Seitz Payne, Thomas Lloyd McLain, Flavius Josephus Lee, Samuel Clement Perry, George Tyre Brouayer, Edward John Boehmer, James Benton Ellis, Samuel William Latimer, Samuel Oram Gillaspie, Joseph Steel Llewellyn, and Martin Scott Haynes served on this Elders' Council when it met for its first session in October 1917.[109] Of those twelve, Llewellyn, Haynes, McClain, Perry, and Brouyaer had attended an annual Mountain Assembly by 1920.

Brouyaer's presence at the 13th Annual Mountain Assembly at Lower Elk Valley was significant. On Saturday, October 4, 1919, the Mountain Assembly appointed twelve men "to plan together with each church as far as our work will extend." Their duties consisted of "keeping the churches in progress" and the "right to call meetings with any church for any cause, to investigate the conduct of pastors or churches in case of a question that may arise." Parks "was appointed a minister or servant of the 12 brethren." The others included Stephen Bryant, Newton Parks, Curd Walker, Kim Moses, Levi Milton White, Joshua Baird, George A. Fore, J.L. Goins, Henry Mobley, Starling Smith, and John Thomas.[110] Two years later, the Mountain Assembly recognized they had created a polity that stood in opposition to the congregationalism of its roots and adopted a new plan of church government proposed by Parks, Bryant, and Mobley. This plan recognized "that each legal ordained elder that fills the office of a bishop in each local church shall have equal gospel rights in the house of God." In the event a pastor fell "out of divine order," leadership in the local church bore the responsibility of admonition and correction. The Assembly would only get involved when a pastor and his congregation could not be corrected. In such a case, the Assembly withdrew its "fellowship from the said church."[111]

In 1922, the Mountain Assembly moved back toward centralized government when discussion at minister's meetings in Williamsburg in April called on Parks, Bryant, Mobley, Fore, and Smith to present reports on the merits of an Elder Board. When the reports were read to the Mountain Assembly on October 7, 1922, a committee of Francis Marion Thomas, Lewis M. Broyles, Kim Moses, J.L. Goins, and Joshua Baird was appointed to determine whether the office was needed. When their favorable report was accepted by the delegates, thirteen men felt they were qualified and volunteered to serve. Mobley and Bryant were appointed as a committee to select six elders, and they appointed Fore, Bryant, Mobley, Broyles, Goins, and Baird.[112] At the following Mountain Assembly, a new Elder Board of twelve men was appointed as "servants for the Assembly or Churches in case of questions." They were to "look after the interest of the said Mountain Assembly" and to "be subject to the orders of said Assembly." The Assembly chose John Parks, Newt Parks, Charles Hampton Standifer, C.L. Price, Levi White, John Sharp, William Douglas, Lewis Broyles, J.L. Goins, Joshua Baird, and Stephen Bryant.[113] The duties of the Elders and composition of the Board would evolve over the next couple of decades, but the office would be retained from 1923 forward.

Figure 3.7: Barthena & Newton Parks, John & Rachel Parks

c /o Sandy Beavers

A fourth area where the Church of God (Cleveland) impacted the CGMA in the 1910s was in the development of a financial system. The Baptist Church had long been averse to the coercion of giving. Soul liberty freed the church member to contribute to the church cheerfully and without compulsion. Baptists recognized that church members were scripturally bound "to provide a comfortable Maintenance for" their pastors "and their Families, suitable to their State and Condition." This pastoral care was not dependent upon tithes, as they viewed that as an Old Testament institution.[114] God intended for the Levitical tithe system to provide for the priests and their families. Baptists rejected the mediaeval doctrine that "ministers of the Christian church were the successors of the Jewish priesthood."[115]

At the Third General Assembly in 1908, the Church of God (Cleveland) discussed the pressing need for pastors to devote "themselves entirely to the ministry of the word and prayer." While, recognizing that it was not always possible for ministers to earn a living from full-time pastoral work, preference was still given for "preachers to not be entangled too much with the affairs of this life."[116] To accomplish this, church members needed training in financial stewardship. Three years later, the Assembly advised that liberty be granted to teach tithing and giving with the understanding that the church should not enforce tithing on the members but teach them the blessedness of tithing and that they may practice it from choice.[117]

That same year, the first State Overseers were appointed to assist Tomlinson with the centralized church government. The increase in bureaucracy created a great financial need at the state and national levels. Carl M. Padgett proposed a plan at the General Assembly in November 1913 whereby "every member should pay a tenth of his income" to his local church, each local church should send one tenth of its tithes received to the State Overseer, and each State Overseer should send ten percent of his receipts to the General Overseer.[118] This proposal was not formally adopted by the General Assembly, but several of the churches implemented the suggestion and began supporting the State Overseer accordingly.[119] At the General Assembly in Harriman, Tennessee, in November 1917, Tomlinson admitted that "the money system" utilized by the Church of God was "crude and incomplete." He proposed that the "tithe of tithes shall be sent to headquarters. The remaining nine-tenths shall be used to supply the needs at home including the overseers."[120] The General Assembly adopted the system recommended by its General Overseer and empowered him to work out with his Council a plan to implement it. By May, the execution of the plan called for ten percent of the tithes from the local church to be sent to the general fund and another ten percent to be sent to the State Overseer.[121]

This financial plan was discussed by the Mountain Assembly at a minister's meeting in Pleasant View the following month, most likely the result of conversations with Jonah Shelton. Shelton had attended the 1912 General Assembly of the Church of God (Cleveland) when the potential merger with the Mountain Assembly was first discussed and conducted worship one morning.[122] He attended again the following year and was listed as a Church of God Evangelist living in Harlan, Kentucky.[123] Shelton returned to the Mountain Assembly as a visiting minister in 1913.[124] In 1915, Shelton moved his family to Black Mountain, North Carolina, and evangelized the area while also teaching broom-making at Montreat College nearby. During this time, his wife, Betty, "grew weaker and weaker from the pellegra [sic] that ravaged her body."[125] For three years, she suffered with it

> until her fingernails were already gone and her fingers were numb and raw to the first joints. The tips of her ears were red, raw and angry. The tip of her nose was raw, red and sore. Her eye-brows and eye-lashes were gone. She could not keep any food down.[126]

The doctor advised Jonah to feed her anything she could tolerate and expect the disease to attack her internal organs and brain. Paul, the eldest son, had already assumed the duties of household chores and "became a second mother" to his younger siblings. One day in the early fall of 1915, Betty instructed Paul to prop her up with "three or four goose-down pillows" with her Bible laid out before leaving her alone to pray. As she questioned whether God would take her from this "wicked world" with her "little girl to be left alone," she felt pressed of the Spirit to turn to the Scripture. Too weak to search, she asked God to guide her to the "right one," opened to Acts 19:11-12, and read of the "special miracles by the hands of Paul" that God wrought from "handkerchiefs or aprons, and the diseases departed from them."[127]

Her immediate response was "there's [sic] nobody that does that yet today," and then she remembered those "Holy Roller people over in Jellico, Tennessee." She called for Paul to return and retrieve some "un-bleached muslin" from "the second drawer of the buffet" and "make some mittens to fit my hands." Once crafted, Paul sent them by "afternoon train" with the package simply addressed to "the Pentecostal People at the Jellico Pentecostal Church." The mittens arrived in time for the Ninth Annual Mountain Assembly at Jellico Creek, where Parks and others anointed them with olive oil. The mittens were returned the Shelton family a few days later and Betty asked for her husband to place them on her hands that had become a "solid mass of scab, oozing" with infection. Jonah initially assumed this was the onset of senility that her doctor warned him about, but relented with "Betty, according to your faith and at your request, I put these mittens on you, in the name of Jesus." The family retired from the room leaving their wife and mother to sleep and expecting her imminent death.

Betty was the only one who slept that night. At daybreak, she called for Paul to bring her a wash basin and peeled the oil-soaked mittens from her hands and began to wash them in the basin. As she washed, "the oozing, scabby skin rolled off like biscuit dough until her hands were as new-born baby skin." Jonah fell to the floor overcome with emotion until Betty asked

Figure 3.8: Jonah Shelton and family
c /o Deb Switzer

for something to eat. Ten days later, a visitor called upon the Sheltons. Knowing that Jonah was a minister and acquainted with the residents in the community, he explained that they were in the process of building a textile mill nearby to manufacture counterpanes and was looking for someone he could hire to cook for the "ten young men they were bringing in to work at the mill." Betty overheard the conversation in the kitchen and volunteered. With this income, the Sheltons were able to pay off the debts they had acquired during Betty's long illness.[128]

In 1916, Shelton moved back to Emlyn, returned to the Mountain Assembly as a delegate, and was elected Assistant Clerk in October 1917.[129] The following month, he attended the Church of God General Assembly in Harriman where Tomlinson presented the new financial plan.[130] Three weeks later the plan was discussed at a minister's meeting at Pleasant View, Kentucky.[131] The host pastor, George A. Fore, served as moderator for the meeting. Pleasant View's clerk, Francis Marion Thomas, had been appointed as the "General Treasury-man" for the Mountain Assembly in October.[132] The ministers carefully considered this proposal for two years before implementing their own version of it in 1919. The Mountain Assembly's "tithes of tithes" system called on members to pay ten percent of their income to the local church. The church then forwarded one tenth of its tithe receipts to "the general treasury." This income would be used to support evangelists, while the tithes in the local church would be paid to the pastor.[133]

The fluidity of Shelton's membership and ministry demonstrated the ambiguity of the relationship between the Church of God (Cleveland) and the Mountain Assembly. Many in the mountains understood *Church of God* as a movement, rather than as an institution. The term was used synonymously with *Holiness* or *Pentecostal*. The exchange of fraternal

The Influence of the Church of God

delegates and informal talks of a union persisted for a decade between the two groups. In 1914, the Mountain Assembly drafted "a letter of correspondence to the Cleveland assembly ... asking them to receive our letter and messengers."[134] Four years later, the Mountain Assembly had sixteen volunteers to attend the General Assembly at Harriman in November 1918.[135] The 14th General Assembly of the Church of God was canceled, however, when the mayor of Harriman expressed concerns over the influenza epidemic.[136] Seven "visiting brothers and sisters from the Cleveland Assembly were invited to seats" with the delegates of the 1919 Mountain Assembly.[137] Ultimately, the Mountain Assembly abandoned the consideration of "a union with the Cleveland Assembly" in the absence of their sending "Messengers from their Assembly to one of" the Mountain Assembly meetings.[138]

Perhaps nothing better demonstrated the ambiguous boundaries of the two groups or the direct influence of the Church of God (Cleveland) on the members of the CGMA than the circulation of *The Church of God Evangel*. At the Third General Assembly in 1908, the Church of God discussed the need for "a church organ (paper)."[139] Tomlinson "had already experienced the benefits of" a paper. He had published *Samson's Foxes* in 1901-1902, *The Way* in 1904-1905, and been a "corresponding editor" of *The Bridegroom's Messenger* in 1908.[140] No action was taken by the General Assembly to create a church periodical until a publishing committee was appointed on January 15, 1910.[141] On March 1, the first issue of *The Evening Light and Church of God Evangel* was published with inspirational messages and testimonials from church members.[142] Tomlinson saw the bulletin as a vehicle for church growth. At the next General Assembly, he described the paper as "a great factor in spreading the news of the church into new fields" and encouraged its circulation.[143]

When Jonah Shelton first acquired a bundle of "sample papers" from Tomlinson in 1910 while he was living in Dickson County, Tennessee, *The Evangel* "appealed to [him] so much, because [he had] had a work like that on [his] heart for some time" and believed "that God would be well pleased with a small Paper established in mountains of Kentucky on the Pentecostal lines."[144]

Figure 3.9: Jonah Shelton
c /o Deb Switzer

When he relocated to Whitley County, Kentucky, the following year, the opportunity presented itself when Shelton was appointed postmaster at Emlyn.[145] Shelton joined the Mountain Assembly Church at Emlyn and was elected clerk at the 1911 Assembly attended by Tomlinson. Before the close of business, the delegates voted to "recommend *The Mountain Evangel*, published by John Thomas & Johan L. Shelton at Emlyn, Ky. to all the churches in the assembly."[146]

When Shelton attended the General Assembly in Cleveland and joined the Church of God the following January as one of the messengers sent from the Mountain Assembly, he "offered his subscription list to the *Church of God Evangel*" and to "lend his influence to the latter, and have one paper instead of two."[147] When Shelton returned to the Mountain Assembly in 1916, he also resumed publication of a periodical at Jellico. Shelton advertised *The Old Paths* as "the only real Pentecostial [sic] Holiness paper published in the mountains."[148] Tomlinson praised the "sheet" for its "good news about the brethren and their work in South Eastern, Ky."[149] Its publication was discontinued the following year when Shelton returned to the Church of God (Cleveland) and once again proposed "to discontinue [his] paper published at Jellico, Tenn., and throw his influence all toward the *Evangel* and its circulation."[150] Twice in five years, subscribers to a Mountain Assembly periodical became subscribers to the *Church of God Evangel*. As a result, many Mountain Assembly members became directly affected by the Church of God, sometimes without realizing the institutional difference.[151]

One example of how the delineation between the two Churches of God was obscured by the combination of church papers may be found in a letter to the *Evangel* by William M. Hicks in 1915. Hicks represented the church at Wooldridge as a delegate at the first Mountain Assembly in 1907.[152] By 1909, he was serving as the clerk at the recently constituted Rain's Grove church near Caryville.[153] Hicks had attended the 1912 General Assembly in Cleveland as a messenger from the Mountain Assembly. He wrote to the *Evangel* to report the persecution the church had experienced. In a revival in November 1913, "about seventeen were saved, sanctified, and baptized with the Holy Ghost and the devil got awfully mad." A mob "of about ten men ... whipped the preacher with hickory withes," and the church had been without preaching ever since.[154]

Another example of fluidity between the CGMA and the Church of God (Cleveland), may be seen in the death of Pleasant Isaiah Cox of the Mountain Assembly church at Pleasant View. After Cox died on January 24, 1917, his daughter, Nettie Brown, shared the news with the readers of *The Old Paths* and *The Church of God Evangel*.[155] Cox had helped draft the tobacco resolution at the 1911 Assembly attended by Tomlinson, and the Church of God General Overseer assured the grieving daughter that he remembered her father well and offered comfort in the knowledge that his family does "not sorrow as those who have no hope."[156] Nettie's expectation "to see him by and by" was realized much more quickly than anticipated, and her own death notice was printed in *The Evangel* the following month.[157]

At the Tenth Annual Mountain Assembly at Lower Elk Valley in 1916, the Buffalo Church at Walden, Kentucky presented itself for membership. The church was pastored by George Fore, and James L. Cupp served as its clerk.[158] The following year, Starling Smith was elected to serve as pastor.[159] Fore, Cupp, and Smith were all avid readers of the *Church of God Evangel*. Cupp wrote to the paper in June 1917 to express his gratitude upon receiving each issue and said he could "hardly read one without shouting and praising God."[160] Smith testified to its readers how God had healed him of pellagra three years earlier and sent him "to preach His word and [that he was] trying to not shun to declare the whole council of God."[161]

The *Evangel* was also used as a medium to publish Mountain Assembly news by the church in Harlan, Kentucky. On October 5, 1917, the new congregation petitioned the Mountain Assembly for membership. The delegates from Harlan included Benjamin Harrsion Enix, James Harvey Maples, and William Sherman Sizemore who had been members of the church at Jellico.[162] The same week, Bertha Martin reported to the *Church of God Evangel* on the church that was being built in Harlan. She reported many false teachers in the area, but that the church was strong because God had sent "Brother Broyles" there to instruct the people.[163] Lewis Marion Broyles had been "sent as Evangelist" by the Mountain Assembly.[164] To further strengthen the church, the Mountain Assembly sent George A. Fore there to pastor, and the Jellico church ordained Sizemore to the ministry on October 20, 1917.[165] When Enix's eight-year-old son, William Sherman Enix, died the following March, his death notice was sent to the *Evangel*.[166]

When Mountain Assembly subscribers to Shelton's *Old Paths* in Emlyn, Kentucky, became readers of the *Church of God Evangel* through the combined subscriptions, the paper grew into a means to share their testimonies. In January 1918, one appeared in the paper from James Dusina of Emlyn.[167] Dusina was born in Northern Italy on May 4, 1880, and immigrated to the United States on the ship, *La Savoie*. He arrived at Ellis

Island on January 11, 1904, with $20 in his pocket, destined for Jellico where a relative had preceded him to work in the coal mines.[168] In 1910, he married Mary Jane Blythe, the daughter of coal miner Thomas A. Blythe.[169] Her older sister, Bertha, had married another Italian coal miner, John Calchera, seven years earlier.[170] Calchera had arrived on *La Gascogne* at Ellis Island on December 3, 1900, bound for the coal mines in Jellico.[171]

Dusina testified to the readers of the *Evangel* of "a meeting" of "a few Holiness people here at Emlyn." One of the converts was Calchera, who came with others to his home to sing and pray. Uninterested in their activities, Dusina "read the newspaper" until the "power of God fell upon [his] brother-in-law and he began to dance." After leaving the room, Dusina began to contemplate his soul. A few days later, Mary attended the revival in progress at Emlyn and "got saved and danced too." When she came through the door at home that evening "the power of God fell upon her and the others who were there and all began to dance." This convinced Dusina that "this was of God." After a sleepless night, he went to the revival. Having been raised Catholic, he "could hardly understand anything the preacher said," but earnestly desired "the people to pray for [him]." He was the first to respond to the altar call that night and "stayed until the burden rolled away." A few days later, "the Lord baptized [him] with the Holy Ghost."[172]

Ten months later, Calchera's testimony appeared in *The Evangel*. He testified how he had seen a vision one night of his mother who had died when he was an infant in Italy. In the vision, she prayed at the foot of the bed where he lay sleeping and then began to read a book. When she had finished her reading, she went to the bed where Calchera's two young daughters lay sleeping, kissed them both, turned to smile at her son, and then disappeared. The vision caused Calchera to contemplate the life he was living. Not long after he relocated to Emlyn, Kentucky, God "saved" him, and he was "baptized with the Holy Ghost and spoke with other tongues."[173] Calchera represented the Emlyn Church as a delegate to the Mountain Assembly from 1916 to 1918.[174] The following year, Thomas Blythe was a delegate from

Figure 3.10: James Dusina
c /o Rita Bailey

Emlyn, and James Dusina represented the church in 1920.[175] Through the combination of church papers, the Church of God continued to wield influence over Mountain Assembly members. The *Evangel* demonstrated that the Church of God (Cleveland) was a worldwide movement reaching far beyond southeastern Kentucky. Perhaps, this appeal ultimately led Dusina, Calchera, and Enix to leave the Mountain Assembly for the Church of God within a few years after their testimonies were published in the *Evangel*.

The Church of God Evangel accomplished Tomlinson's aim of promoting his church in areas where no members and ministers were present. It also served as a medium for Mountain Assembly members to share what God was doing in their communities and churches. While it sometimes obscured the identities of the churches represented, it also subtly assisted in the proselytization of many members from the Mountain Assembly to the Church of God (Cleveland). One reader wrote in 1921 that she had discovered that "the Church of God at Cleveland, Tenn." was "the only and oldest church." She had, therefore, abandoned her membership with the "Mountain Assembly at Jellico" acknowledging that God "will lead us in the right way if we live true to Him." She certainly exaggerated when she declared that "the saints that went into the Mountain Assembly have all scattered abroad," but the Mountain Assembly was about to see its first significant migration to the Church of God the following year.[176]

Conclusion

Within a decade of his first encounter with the CGMA, A.J. Tomlinson had impacted the group led by Parks and Bryant in several significant ways. As a direct result of Tomlinson's presence, "Mountain Assembly" was added to the name of the association meeting and ultimately to the name of the organization. His attendance began a decade of fellowship that featured talks of consolidation and the exchange of ideas and ministers. Tomlinson's hardline stance against tobacco use led to the first split in the Mountain Assembly and the creation of another association within the Church of God movement. A second split the following year and the creation of another "Church of God" resulted from the discipline of a minister with unorthodox eschatological views. As a result of exposure to the Church of God (Cleveland), the Mountain Assembly began a shift toward centralized polity. This shift included a change in the ordination and credentialing process, the creation of a financial system, the publication of a standard set of teachings, and the development of a Board of Twelve Elders. Finally, the absorption of the Mountain Assembly's first two periodicals into the magazine of the Church of God sometimes muddled the distinctiveness of the two organizations.

---

[1] Phillips, 256. Llewellyn was also present at the Fourth General Assembly in 1910 at Jellico Creek. Though he had not yet joined the Church of God (Cleveland), Llewellyn would become a central figure in the organization as Tomlinson's "right hand man" over the next decade.

[2] CGMA, *Minutes* (1911), 1-2.

[3] Phillips, 171-172.

[4] Of the 51 delegates at the First Assembly in 1907, more than half were related by blood or marriage to the Thomas, Moses, Rountree, or Cox families.

[5] Phillips, 172.

[6] William Williams, *Apostolical Church Polity* (Philadelphia, 1874) in Dever, *Polity*, 530.

[7] Wade Horton, ed., *Glossolalia Phenomenon* (Cleveland, TN: Pathway Press, 1966), 69-139.

[8] Phillips, 107-108.

[9] Many early Holiness / Pentecostal believers utilized the term, "praying through," to denote a session of prayer that lasted until the person felt a sense of relief or breakthrough that came with assurance of the answer to their request.

[10] Vinson Synan, *The Pentecostal-Holiness Tradition: Charismatic Movements of the Twentieth Century,* 2nd ed. (Grand Rapids, MI: Eerdman's Publishing Company, 1997), 72.

[11] Ibid., 55-58.

[12] Philips, 234-237.

[13] Bryant, "Building of God," in Gibson, 51.

[14] Bryant, "Life Story," 3.

[15] CGMA, *Minutes* (1912), 4.

[16] CGMA, *Minutes of the Seventh Annual Mountain Assembly of the Churches of God* (n.p.: by the association, 1913), 5.

[17] Phillips, 174-210.

[18] Ibid., 217-220.

[19] Tomlinson, *Conflict*, 192.

[20] Ibid.

[21] Church of God, *Minutes*, 13-18.

[22] Phillips, 223-225.

[23] Ibid., 215.

[24] Church of God, *Minutes*, 22.

25 Ibid., 23.

26 Ibid., 33.

27 Ibid., 39-40.

28 Ibid., 43-44.

29 Ibid., 48-49.

30 Church of God, *Echoes from the Eighth General Assembly* (Cleveland, TN: Church of God Publishing House, 1913), 29.

31 Church of God, *Echoes from the Ninth General Assembly* (Cleveland, TN: Church of God Publishing House, 1914), 6-14.

32 Church of God, *Minutes of Sixth Annual Assembly of the Churches of God* (Cleveland, TN: Church of God Publishing House, 1911), 4.

33 Application for Ordination Certificate, Deceased Ministers file - Jonah L. Shelton, Flower Pentecostal Heritage Center, Springfield, Missouri; Certificate of Ordination, Jonah L. Shelton file, Central Files and Records of the Church of God, Cleveland, Tennessee.

34 Deed of Conveyance, *Campbell County Deed Book* X, Volume 1, October 14, 1887, 612, and Deed of Conveyance, *Campbell County Deed Book*, October 20, 1915, 471-472, Campbell County Court House, Jacksboro, TN.

35 "U.S. WWII Draft Cards, young men, 1940-1947," s.v. "William Apollos Shelton," Ancestry.com; William Hicks (church clerk), J.L. Shelton letter of dismission, November 21, 1909, Jonah L. Shelton file, Central Files and Records of the Church of God, Cleveland, Tennessee.

36 CGMA, *Minutes* (1910), 1.

37 *The Evening Light and Church of God Evangel (CGE)* 1, no. 15 (October 1, 1910): 5.

38 Church of God, *Minutes* (1911), 8; Evangelist's License, Jonah L. Shelton file, Central Files and Records of the Church of God, Cleveland, Tennessee.

39 CGMA, *Minutes* (1911), 2.

40 Phillips suggests that the link between Tomlinson and the Mountain Assembly was probably J.B. Mitchell who was living in Jellico in 1911. Mitchell and Tomlinson had worked as traveling Bible salesmen (See Philips, 256). Another possibility is J.S. Llewellyn who had attended the 1910 Assembly before attending the Assembly in 1911 with Tomlinson.

41 CGMA, *Minutes* (1911), 2.

42 The Church of God Charter of Incorporation, *Tennessee Corporation Record Book P-13* (State of Tennessee, August 2, 1917), 254.

43 Church of God Mountain Assembly, Inc. Charter of Incorporation, *Tennessee Corporation Record Book P-29* (State of Tennessee, April 15, 1947), 123. Note: on October 20, 1943, the organization was first renamed "The Mountain Assembly of the Churches of God." It was changed back to "The Church of God" on December 27, 1944 before its final name change in 1947.

44 CGMA, *Minutes* (1911), 3.

45 Church of God, *Echoes* (1912), 10, 20.

46 A.J. Tomlison, Cleveland, Ohio, to John H. Parks, Jellico, Tennessee, November 20, 1933 in CGMA, *Minutes of the Mountain Assembly of the Churches of God (Incorporated): The Twenty-Eighth Annual Assembly of the Churches of God* (Jellico, TN: CGMA, 1934), 3.

47 CGMA, *Minutes* (1912), 2-4.

48 Tomlinson, *Diary*, 202.

49 CGMA, *Minutes* (1914), 4.

50 CGMA, *Minutes of the Thirteenth Annual Session of the Mountain Assembly of the Churches of God* (n.p.: by the association, 1919), 3.

51 Church of God, *Minutes*, 15

52 Ibid., 35.

53 Ibid., 39.

54 Church of God, *Minutes* (1911), 7.

55 CGMA, *Minutes* (1911), 6.

56 CGMA, *Minutes* (1913), 4.

57 CGMA, *Minutes* (1915), 5.

58 Parks, Journal, 223.

59 Hayes Creek Minutes, 32; CGMA, CGMA, *Minutes* (1913), 6.

60 Hayes Creek Minutes, 34.

61 CGMA, *Minutes* (1914), 6.

62 Parks, 223.

63 Ibid.

64 CGMA, *Minutes* (1925), 12.

65 CGMA, *Minutes of the Fourteenth Annual Session of the Mountain Assembly of the Churches of God* (n.p.: by the Association, 1920), 8.

66 General Assembly Church of God, *Minutes of the 111th Annual Assembly of the General Assembly Churches of God, Inc.* (Pine Knot, KY: General Assembly Church of God, 2017), 6.

67 Phillips, 363-370.

68 CGMA, *Minutes* (1907), 4.

69 CGMA, *Minutes* (1913), 5.

70 Church of God, *Minutes of the Thirteenth Annual Assembly of the Church of God* (Cleveland, TN: Church of God Publishing House, 1917), 65.

71 CGMA, *Minutes* (1920), 8-9; Phillips, 368-370.

72 CGMA, *Minutes of the Twelfth Annual Session of the Mountain Assembly of the Churches of God* (n.p.: by the association, 1918), 6.

73 A.J. Tomlinson, "The Awful World War," *CGE* 8, no. 8 (February 24, 1917), 1.

74 CGMA, *Minutes* (1918), 6.

75 As American involvement in the War in Vietnam escalated in the 1960s and many more members of the church were pressed into service through the draft, attitudes toward pacifism drastically changed. On August 15, 1968, the Church of God Mountain Assembly amended its teaching against members going to war to read: "The Church of God believes that nations can and should settle their differences without going to war; however in the event of war, if a member engages in combatant service, it will not affect his status with the church. In case a member is called into military service who has conscientious objections to combatant service the Church will support him in his constitutional rights." CGMA, *Minutes of the Sixty-Second Annual Assembly* (Jellico, TN: CGMA, 1968), 22.

76 J.E. Hatfield, "Our Boys in Uniform," *GH* 1. no. 6 (December 1942): 8.

77 Fonde Minutes, 49.

78 Parks, Journal, 155-157.

79 Ibid., 224.

80 Ibid., 232.

81 CGMA, *Minutes* (1918), 8; Church of God, *Minutes* (1917), 65.

82 David Cady, *Religion of Fear: The True Story of the Church of God of the Union Assembly* (Knoxville: University of Tennessee Press, 2019), 8-13.

83 Ibid., 14-15.

84 CGMA, *Minutes* (1912), 3.

85 Cady, 15.

86 CGMA, *Minutes* (1913), 3.

87 Cady, 16.

88 A.J. Tomlinson, "Editorial Notes," *CGE* 6, no. 34 (August 21, 1915): 2.

89 [Minnie] Pratt, *We Walked Alone: Part of the Story of My Life* (Dalton, GA: Southerner Press, 1955), 7.

90 Tomlinson, "Editorial Notes," *CGE* 6, no. 47 (November 20, 1915): 2.

91 Cady, 16; Pratt, 7.

92 Cady, 1-3.

93 Ibid., 23.

94 Ibid., 112-114.

95 Samuel Jones, *A Treatise of Church Discipline, and a Directory* (Lexington, 1805) in Dever, *Polity*, 143-144.

96 Tom Moses ordination certificate.

97 Phillips, 69.

98 Tomlinson, *Conflict*, 186.

99 Phillips, 224.

100 Church of God, *Minutes*, 25.

101 Phillips, 169.

102 Church of God, *Minutes*, 25, 28.

103 Ibid., 40.

104 CGMA, *Minutes* (1911), 5.

105 CGMA, *Minutes* (1913), 3.

106 CGMA, *Minutes* (1914), 4.; CGMA, *Minutes* (1915), 5; CGMA, *Minutes* (1916), 1, 5.

107 CGMA, *Minutes* (1925), 12.

108 CGMA, *Minutes of the Mountain Assembly of the Churches of God, Incorporated: The Thirty-Fifth Annual Assembly of the Churches of God* (Jellico, TN: CGMA, 1941), 27.

109 Phillips, 412-417.

110 CGMA, *Minutes* (1919), 5.

111 CGMA, *Minutes* (1921), 4-5.

112 CGMA, *Minutes of the Sixteenth Annual Session of the Mountain Assembly of the Churches of God* (Jellico, TN: CGMA, 1922), 5-6.

113 CGMA, *Minutes of the Church of God, Inc.: The Seventeenth Annual Session of the Mountain Assembly of the Church of God* (Jellico, TN: CGMA, 1923), 16.

114 Benjamin Keach, *The Glory of a True Church, and Its Discipline Displayed* (London, 1697) in Dever, *Polity*, 68.

115 Reynolds, in Dever, *Polity*, 401.

116 Church of God, *Minutes*, 33.

117 Church of God, *Minutes* (1911), 6.

118 Church of God, *Echoes* (1913), 146.

119 Conn, 180.

120 Church of God, *Minutes* (1917), 17, 33.

121 *CGE* 9, no. 18 (May 4, 1918): 1-2.

122 Church of God, *Echoes* (1912), 17.

123 Church of God, *Echoes* (1913), 26; Church of God, *Echoes* (1914), 41.

124 CGMA, *Minutes* (1913), 3.

125 Lois [Shelton] Gribling, "An Inheritance Money Can't Buy," reminiscences shared with Peggy England, in the possession of Deb Switzer, Phoenix, AZ, 1.

126 Ibid., 5.

127 Ibid., 3-4.

128 Ibid., 5-7.

129 CGMA, *Minutes* (1916), 4; CGMA, *Minutes* (1917), 3; According to the Minutes of the Jellico Church (p. 11), Shelton's membership was transferred by letter from the Mountain Assembly church at Pleasant View to Jellico on January 27, 1917.

130 Church of God, *Minutes* (1917), 26.

131 CGMA, *Minutes* (1919), 5; According to the Jellico Minutes, (p. 20), Shelton was granted "a letter of dismission for to go to the Cleveland Assembly" on November 24, 1917. He may not have been at the minister's meeting at Pleasant View the following week, but he

almost certainly made his pastor, John Parks, aware of the Church of God's new financial plan prior to his final departure from the Mountain Assembly. According to *CGE* 9, no. 8 (January 19, 1918), the Church of God sent Shelton to Whitter, California, to pastor in January 1918.

[132] CGMA, *Minutes* (1917), 4-5.

[133] CGMA, *Minutes* (1919), 5.

[134] CGMA, *Minutes* (1914), 4

[135] CGMA, *Minutes* (1918), 5.

[136] *CGE* 9, no. 43 (October 26, 1918), 3.

[137] CGMA, *Minutes* (1919), 3.

[138] CGMA, *Minutes* (1925), 9.

[139] Church of God, *Minutes*, 32.

[140] Phillips, 257.

[141] Church of God, *Minutes*, 49-50.

[142] *CGE* 1, no. 1 (March 1, 1910).

[143] Church of God, *Minutes* (1911), 4-5.

[144] *CGE* 1, no. 15 (October 1, 1910): 5; 1900 United States Census, Harlan County, Kentucky, s.v. "Jonah Shelton," Ancestry.com.

[145] U.S., Appointments of U. S. Postmasters, 1832-1971, s.v. "Jonah Shelton," Ancestry.com.

[146] CGMA, *Minutes* (1911), 5.

[147] Church of God, *Echoes* (1912), 20.

[148] CGMA, *Minutes* (1916), back cover.

[149] *CGE* 8, no. 39 (October 6, 1917): 2.

[150] Church of God, *Minutes* (1917), 26.

[151] *CGE* 8, no. 46 (November 24, 1917): 3. The notice announcing the absorption of *The Old Paths* subscriptions amounted to a few lines amid letters from *Evangel* readers.

[152] CGMA, *Minutes* (1907), 2.

[153] CGMA, *Minutes* (1911), 8.

[154] *CGE* 6, no. 9 (February 27, 1915): 2.

[155] *The Old Paths* 1, no. 4 (February 1917): 2, reprinted in *GH* 44, no. 7 (July 1984): 8; *CGE* 8, no. 10 (March 10, 1917): 3.

[156] *CGE* 8, no. 10 (March 10, 1917): 3.

[157] Ibid.; *CGE* 8, no. 16 (April 28, 1917): 3.

[158] CGMA, *Minutes* (1916), 4, 7.

[159] CGMA, *Minutes* (1917), 9.

[160] *CGE* 8, no. 23 (June 16, 1917): 4.

[161] *CGE* 8, no. 20 (May 26, 1917): 4.

[162] CGMA, *Minutes* (1917), 3.; Jellico Minutes, membership roster.

[163] *CGE* 8, no. 39 (October 6, 1917): 3.

[164] CGMA, *Minutes* (1917), 4.

[165] CGMA, *Minutes* (1917), 4; Jellico Minutes, 20.

[166] *CGE* 9, no. 14 (April 6, 1918): 2.

[167] *CGE* 9, no. 1 (January 5, 1918): 3.

[168] https://www.findagrave.com/memorial/37747921; New York, Passenger and Crew Lists (including Castle Garden and Ellis Island), 1820-1957, s.v. "Giacomo Dusina," Ancestry.com.

[169] 1900 United States Census, Knox County, Tennessee, s.v. "Thomas A. Blith," Ancestry.com.

[170] Tennessee, Marriage Records, 1780-2002 s.v. "Bertha Blythe," Ancestry.com.

[171] New York, Passenger and Crew Lists (including Castle Garden and Ellis Island), 1820-1957, s.v. "Giovanni Calchera," Ancestry.com.

[172] *CGE* 9, no. 1 (January 5, 1918): 3.

[173] *CGE* 9, no. 44 (November 12, 1918): 4.

[174] CGMA, *Minutes* (1916), 3; CGMA, *Minutes* (1917), 2; CGMA, *Minutes* (1918), 2.

[175] CGMA, *Minutes* (1919), 3; CGMA, *Minutes* (1920), 3.

[176] *CGE* 12, no. 32 (August 8, 1921): 4.

4

Centralized Polity and Tension with the Church of God

When the 16th Annual Session of the Mountain Assembly of the Churches of God opened at Jellico, Tennessee, on October 6, 1922, the CGMA more closely resembled the Church of God (Cleveland) than it did the South Union Association of United Baptists in three significant ways. First, it had found a permanent meeting place when it selected Jellico as its headquarters. Second, the nature of its leadership structure had deviated from its Baptist roots to something like that of the group in Cleveland. Third, its first constitutional declaration revealed a government that encompassed more than a loose federation of churches which met annually. While the Mountain Assembly modeled its corporate government after the pattern of the Church of God (Cleveland), some of its congregations experienced conflict with Church of God congregations in their communities. Hostility at the local level served to impede further progress toward centralization. Thus, while the influence of the Church of God (Cleveland) moved the Mountain Assembly toward episcopalism in the 1910s, local strife curbed this impulse and gravitated the Mountain Assembly back toward congregationalism.

The Move to Jellico and the Move toward Centralization

One important matter of business on the annual agenda at the South Union Association was the selection of a meeting place for the following year. No single church edifice was large enough to accommodate the crowds expected for the annual association meeting, but a good location often included enough meeting places nearby where alternate worship services could be held simultaneously. The Baptist association historically recognized the privilege of each church and community to host the meeting and, in 1884, "advised churches wanting the annual meeting in their church next year to state their intention in their letter." In the twelve years leading up to Parks's and Bryant's exclusion from the Baptist association, no church hosted the annual session more than once.[1] The Mountain Assembly attempted to follow this pattern in its first decade. The first eight general assemblies were held at Little Wolf Creek, Zion Hill, Hayes Creek, Jellico Creek, Siler's Chapel, Lower

Elk Valley, Saxton, and Elk Valley before returning to Jellico Creek in 1915. At the 10th Annual Session of the Mountain Assembly of the Churches of God at Lower Elk Valley in 1916, the precedent was broken when the delegates agreed "that the assembly be held again with the church at Lower Elk Valley" and the length of the meeting was extended to "hold seven days."[2] After relocating to Emlyn for the 1918 assembly, the convention was moved back to Lower Elk Valley for the next three years.[3]

Figure 4.1: John H. Parks
c/o Joe Asbury

The preference for Lower Elk Valley for six of ten general assemblies may have been, in part, out of deference to John Parks, its pastor. The size of its congregation also played a role. Within ten years, Lower Elk Valley had grown from ten charter members to the largest church in the Mountain Assembly with 284 members, after baptizing more than 200 from 1913 to 1917.[4] Residents of the Lower Elk Valley community outside of Jellico also proved to be a very hospitable people. Among the resolutions offered by the 1912 committee, one undertook to "tender our thanks to the church and vicinity at Lower Elk Valley for their kindness to us during our stay with them."[5] When the assembly meeting expanded to seven days, the need for hospitality increased and the community responded in kind. At the conclusion of the first day's service at the 14th Mountain Assembly, "a free invitation was given by 62 well furnished homes" to the many attendees.[6] The number of visitors continued to rise as the convention progressed until the final day when "the house would receive no more, so preaching was both in the house and out of doors, which lasted the greater part of the day."[7] Within another decade, the local pastor had assumed the unofficial duty of arranging accommodations for visiting ministers and members. Business sessions often concluded with Parks advising visitors "where they could get dinner and find lodging."[8]

The preference for a single annual meeting place was a result of an evolving ecclesiology. With its congregational polity, alternating convention sites, and annual leadership elections, the Baptist association withstood any tendency toward centralization in government. When the Mountain Assembly came under the influence of the Church of God (Cleveland), this began to change. On November 26, 1904, A.J. Tomlinson purchased a home at 2525 Gaut Street in Cleveland, Tennessee and soon relocated his family from Culberson, North Carolina.[9] The city was small, "but it was a scheduled stop on the Norfolk and Western Railroad," which proved conducive to the itinerancy of Tomlinson's ministry and crucial to the expansion of the Church of God.[10] The First General Assembly of the Church of God met at Camp Creek, North Carolina, the second was at Union Grove in Bradley County, Tennessee, but the next eight were in Cleveland.

In 1913, the Church of God changed its meeting time from January to November. Natural church growth and the more moderate weather in the fall, led to increased attendance at the General Assembly. In 1916, the Church of God purchased the former Women's Christian Temperance Union (WCTU) Temple in Harriman, Tennessee and held the next two Assemblies there.[11] The temple had been erected in the 1890s with a seating capacity of "about one thousand" and served as a meeting place for the WCTU Tennessee State Convention.[12] Dissatisfaction with the building prompted the General Assembly to return to Cleveland in 1919.[13]

Tomlinson's ecclesiology had been shaped by his experience with Frank W. Sandford at the Holy Ghost and Us Bible School in Durham, Maine. There, Sandford infused two critical principles vital to a religious movement: a divinely appointed leader with undisputed authority and a geographic center of operations. Tomlinson's move to Cleveland and the recurring General Assemblies in that city were more than matters of personal preference or practical convenience. To Tomlinson, God had chosen Cleveland, and the General Overseer communicated such to his members. In his message to the 6th General Assembly, Tomlinson explained how Jerusalem had been the seat of government for the united kingdom of Israel and how it had been the seat of church government for the apostles. He contended that God had chosen Cleveland "to be the center for God's church in the last days."[14] The opening of Bible Training School (now, Lee University) in 1918 and the construction of a new auditorium to seat 4,000 in time for the 1920 General Assembly solidified the status of Cleveland in the Church of God.[15]

The same year a new auditorium was built in Cleveland, the Mountain Assembly appointed a committee "to select a place to hold our assembly each year." The committee consisted of Francis M. Thomas, Henry Mobley, George A. Fore, J.L. Goins, John Thomas, Squire Broyles, Stephen N. Bryant, and John Parks. Despite the predilection for the Jellico area the past several years, the committee reported after deliberation that it had determined that "Williamsburg is the place for our assembly building." This decision "seemed to satisfy all present," so the Assembly proceeded with plans for the house to "go up at Williamsburg in the name of the Lord." The following morning Benjamin Harrison Enix, Jake Taylor, and George A. Fore were appointed as a committee to receive finance and pay for the construction of the new assembly building. A building committee of Bryant, Thomas, Broyles, Fore, Goins, John Bunch, William C. Brock, and Matt Witt was appointed to oversee its construction.[16] Though Jellico and Williamsburg were roughly the same size in 1920, the latter possessed at least three advantages.[17] Williamsburg was a county seat, it was more centrally located, and it had direct access to the railroad.

Williamsburg was the seat of Whitley County, Kentucky. When the Mountain Assembly began seeing itself as something more than an association of independently governed congregations, it realized for the first time the potential of jointly holding property. In response, the first trustees were appointed at a minister's meeting in Emlyn four weeks later. Thomas, Fore, and Taylor, residents of Whitley County, were appointed trustees "to look after the property for the assembly known as the Mountain Assembly of the Churches of God."[18] The proximity to a county courthouse would facilitate the registration of deeds. At the center of Whitley County, Williamsburg also found itself at the geographic center of the Mountain Assembly. Of the 29 Mountain Assembly churches in 1920, eight were in Whitley County. McCreary County to the west had two, Bell County to the east had five, and Campbell County, Tennessee, to the south had five.[19]

No less important than geography was Williamsburg's convenient access to the railroad. Jellico had gained railroad access in the late nineteenth century when the Southern Railroad and the Louisville & Nashville Railroad raced to see who could gain entry to its rich coal fields first. By 1905, L&N had bought out enough of its competition to own a continuous line between Cincinnati and Atlanta. The Jellico depot was connected by a short track to the main line at Lot, Kentucky. Situated near the state line, it also left the Lower Elk Valley church nearly the same distance to the station at Newcomb.[20] The convenience of a nearby depot would have simplified travel to and from the headquarters for the annual assembly. By the time the Elders met at Emlyn, a prime location in Williamsburg had been found. Adjoining property owned by Fore's brother, a vacant lot less than half a mile from the train depot, promised to be everything the Mountain Assembly would need for future growth.[21] The ministers voted to purchase the lot under the care of the newly appointed trustees and appointed Brock and Bunch to oversee the planning and construction of the building.[22]

Over the next year, however, the Mountain Assembly changed directions. In February, Fore and Thomas purchased the Williamsburg lot.[23] By October, the Assembly announced that a lot had been "bought, in the city of Jellico, and staked off, and ready to build." Members were encouraged to send their building fund donations to John Parks or Squire Broyles.[24] In addition to what was received by their solicitation, the Lower Elk Valley Church borrowed the money to complete the construction of a new tabernacle on Florence Avenue in Jellico. At a local church business meeting at Lower Elk Valley three weeks after the 1921 General Assembly was held there, the church appointed Parks, Broyles, Brock, and J.M. Ross as a "building committee for the assembly building." Everett H. Ross, John Creekmore, Gilbert Weaver, and Will Sharp were also appointed a committee to solicit funding for the building.[25] In September before the General Assembly would convene in the newly constructed tabernacle, Parks appointed a committee to audit his financial records of the building fund.[26] When the 16th Annual Session of the Mountain Assembly of the Churches of God met in the new tabernacle in October 1922, the delegates voted to assume the debt of $3,272.18 (out of the total cost of $4,121.92) and to allow the Lower Elk Valley Church to "take charge of the Assembly building."[27] The following year, the Assembly appointed three new trustees, Gilbert Weaver, John Shephard, and J.T. Richardson, to assume the "duty in looking after the property of the Mountain Assembly of the Churches of God" and to work in cooperation with the trustees of the local churches. The Assembly recommended each church have three trustees as well to protect the property of the local congregations.[28]

After maintaining two buildings for two years, the Lower Elk Valley church voted in June 1924 to "change the meetings from the Hackler Church to the tabernacle and have all their meetings there for the present time."[29] As the ministers and members gathered for a third consecutive assembly in the new tabernacle, they were pleased to learn that the indebtedness on the building had been reduced to $1,221.30. With the debt manageable, delegates were willing to consider another building project and a motion was made to "arrange some plan to take care of the people of this Assembly, and it was moved that we build a mess hall." Parks, Goins, Broyles, and Curd Walker were appointed a committee to formulate a plan. They reported it would cost an estimated $1,000 to erect such a hall, and Parks, Brock, and Will Sharp

Figure 4.2: The first tabernacle in Jellico

c/o CGMA

were appointed a building committee.[30] A small fire, however, later necessitated that funds be diverted to repair the tabernacle, and the committee was released.[31] The damage forced the Lower Elk Valley Church to return to the old Hackler church for a time, but in July 1926, the church permanently moved into the tabernacle and began referring to itself as the "Jellico Church" from that point forward.[32]

Jellico was first referred to as "headquarters" for the Mountain Assembly in 1918 when "all communications" were directed to John Parks' address.[33] Over the next decade, the Tabernacle itself would become headquarters.[34] As the center of operations and primary meeting place, it had become to the Mountain Assembly what Cleveland was to the Church of God. The Jellico Church had for its pastor John Parks who was by far the most influential minister in the Mountain Assembly despite holding no office but Elder. The establishment of headquarters at Jellico proved a vital step toward the Mountain Assembly's transformation into a denomination.

Centralized Leadership and the Move Toward Centralization
The Mountain Assembly patterned the office of moderator after that of the Baptist association. After its encounter with the Church of God (Cleveland), it incorporated aspects of the office of General Overseer into the Mountain Assembly's leadership. Ideally, the Baptist association chose a moderator sufficiently skilled in the rules of order to conduct business without prejudice. Impartiality was especially necessary when the association served as an arbiter between congregations, ministers, or sometimes even other associations. On

one such occasion, September 24, 1892, the South Union Association dispatched John Parks, Andrew Silcox, and J.M. Meadors to the West Union Association with a letter of correspondence admonishing the association to "settle the difficulty between her and the New River Association."[35] The clerk omitted from the minutes the nature of the conflict between the two associations, but it apparently lingered for two more decades. Moderating his last South Union Association session, Parks appointed Allen Moses to draft a letter to the West Union Association and then appointed Silcox, Mike Lay, and others to bear it to the association meeting two weeks later.[36] When the correspondence was read at the Buffalo church in Huntsville, Tennessee, "a motion was put before the body to ask South Union to have no further correspondence with New River Association." After the motion was defeated, Lay was given the opportunity to speak about "some of the causes of non-correspondence between" West Union and New River. Lay's personal appeal made a difference. Later that day, a motion to "correspond with New River Association" survived an attempt to lay it on the table, the moderator appointed someone to draft the letter, and "the ministers of New River Association present were invited to seats."[37]

The role of the association to resolve conflict and the duty of the moderator to pilot the delegates through tense moments demonstrated the arduous task of serving in that capacity. It was no place for a novice. The delegates, therefore, elected seasoned pastors and confident pulpiteers. Their ability in the pulpit frequently earned them an appointment by the committee on divine services to preach in the association worship services as well as the coveted introductory sermon. These conditions positioned a charismatic leader to become something more than a moderator had it not been that Baptist polity recognized no such office. Its constitution made clear that the South Union Association "shall exercise no ecclesiastical authority" and that "the business of this body" was to serve as "an advisory council to advise with each church in its bounds for the advancement of the cause of Christ."[38] For this reason, when the committee of nine appointed by Lay at the South Union Association meeting in 1904 to "consult with Elders J.H. Parks and A.J. Silcox and others in regard to disputed doctrine" reported that it had been unsuccessful, the association was forced to withdraw its fellowship from Little Wolf Creek and Zion Hill churches.[39] No moderator, committee, nor associational body could compel submission to authority that did not exist outside the voting members of the local churches.

Though the men who served as moderators in the Baptist association retained their prestige by virtue of their aptitude for preaching and leadership, their official responsibilities terminated with the conclusion of the association meeting. The previous moderator customarily opened the association meeting and enrolled the delegates to elect officers for the current session, but during the year-long adjournment he held no more power than another minister. Shared responsibility and equality among brethren helped safeguard Baptists against potential encroachments by any who might dare to claim some apostolic authority over others. The members of the South Union Association recognized that not everyone had the necessary leadership skills to serve as moderator, but they also recognized several capable men among them. From 1895 to 1904, the association elected five different men to serve as moderator, and none was elected more than two years in a row.[40]

From the First General Assembly, A.J. Tomlinson had a different vision for the ecclesiastical polity of the Church of God (Cleveland). Tomlinson moderated the council meeting which he declared was a judicial body only and continued to moderate subsequent assemblies as well. At the Fourth Annual Assembly in 1909, the Church of God decided a "general moderator" should serve "full-time instead of only at the annual Assembly." His term commenced at the close of each assembly and expired at the same time the following year. The duties of the general moderator included the issuance of ministerial credentials and maintenance of ministerial records, oversight of the general welfare of all the churches and fulfillment of ministerial vacancies, and service as moderator and clerk of the annual assembly. The following year, the assembly changed its title to "General Overseer."[41] In 1914, a lifetime appointment of Tomlinson as General Overseer supplanted the one-year term and annual election of the office.[42]

Tomlinson's vision of theocratic government recognized Jesus reigned over his church, but in Christ's physical absence the General Overseer resembled "a kind of head of state awaiting the return of an exiled king." Though *General* Overseer indicated broad or universal administration, to Tomlinson it also suggested rank in a military sense. His annual addresses to the General Assembly often incorporated such ideas as well. The church was a "mighty army," and submission to authority was imperative. Tomlinson viewed himself as God's head of command divinely appointed to execute His laws within His kingdom. Tomlinson's theology significantly differed from Roman Catholicism in that he emphasized the primacy of James, instead of Peter. Tomlinson viewed the General Assembly in Cleveland, much like he interpreted the Jerusalem Council of Acts 15. After all assembled had interjected their views and reached a consensus, Tomlinson (like James) could state conclusively that such "seemed good to the Holy Ghost, and to us."[43]

When the General Overseer of the Church of God (Cleveland) attended his first Mountain Assembly at Siler's Chapel in 1911, Stephen Bryant was elected to his first term as moderator after Andrew Silcox had moderated the first four assemblies.[44] The Mountain Assembly continued to name Bryant moderator each year for the next decade. Perhaps this departure from the Baptist association's tradition of frequent turnover was the result of limited availability of capable seasoned men at the time. Parks had served four times as moderator of the South Union Association but had limited his leadership role in the Mountain Assembly. His lone election as moderator of the Mountain Assembly came in 1934, the first year that elections were held by open nomination.[45] Silcox had twice served as moderator of the Baptist association and had also moderated the first four Mountain Assemblies. In 1911, Silcox read the Bible lesson at the beginning of the assembly, preached a Saturday service, and was appointed to preach the introductory sermon the following year.[46] However, it would be his last Mountain Assembly. The following year, Silcox apparently renounced his preaching of apostasy and rejoined Baptist Church at Wolf Creek where he had been excluded in 1904.[47] The South Union Association also readily received Silcox, elected him Assistant Moderator in 1912, and chose him to preach the introductory sermon the following year.[48] In 1919, the South Union Associated elected Silcox as moderator again.[49]

Figure 4.3: Andrew Silcox
c/o CGMA

Bryant proved himself a capable and impartial moderator and, whether by necessity or by patterning itself after the Church of God (Cleveland), the Mountain Assembly retained his services in this capacity for most of the rest of his life.[50] As the tenure of the moderator's office lengthened, the breadth of his duties widened. These expanded responsibilities included administering ministerial credentials, chairing additional meetings, serving as an official evangelist for the Mountain Assembly, and overseeing all the churches.

When the Mountain Assembly began issuing standard credentials to its ordained ministers in 1911, it represented the first step away from associational congregationalism toward a denominational polity for two reasons. First, in the Baptist church, licensing and ordination represented the endorsement of the congregation. Baptists believed that "the essence of ordination consists in the call of the church, in their voting in his favour [sic], and designating him by said vote to the ministerial work" and that no man might enter gospel ministry "without the approbation of others, and this power was lodged in the church."[51] The newly ordained minister reasonably expected documentation of that commendation. The certificate included the date, location, name of the recommending church, and the signatures of the ordaining presbyters. By issuing credentials from the association, the Mountain Assembly began to recognize an ecclesiastical authority outside the local church. Second, issuing and maintaining records of authorized ministers required some administrative leadership. For the first time, the elected officials at the Mountain Assembly would have some minor duties to attend after the conclusion of the convention.

The moderator's role further expanded in 1914, when the Mountain Assembly resolved to hold "three ministers' meetings between the assemblies."[52] The assembly moderator was generally expected to chair these conferences. The quarterly meetings served to transform the ministers' view of the Mountain Assembly as something more than an annual association and to provide inclusiveness by offering local churches an opportunity to host them at a time when Lower Elk Valley was becoming the primary meeting place for the annual Assembly.

The following year, the Mountain Assembly appointed its first evangelist who was expected to preach in destitute places and assist struggling churches. A freewill offering was received to help support Henry Mobley in this work.[53] In 1919, the Mountain Assembly adopted a financial system intended to aid the work of evangelists. Each church would send one tenth of its members' tithes receipts to the general treasury at headquarters to fund the work of its evangelists.[54] While this system demonstrated another step toward centralized government, it proved ineffective in the support of evangelists, and the Mountain Assembly dropped the appointment of evangelists from its order of business. On October 3, 1924, however, delegates to the 18th Annual Mountain Assembly voted to "select an evangelist for the purpose of visiting all the churches and helping them out in whatever way needed" and committed his selection to the Board of Twelve Elders. The following day, the Elders announced their unanimous selection, Moderator Stephen Bryant. "It must have pleased everybody to have such a sound man for our evangelist to oversee all the churches and preach among them." For "all men and women who favored this selection were asked to stand, and all stood, as far as we could see, to signify that it was their selection." The congregation then sang a song and offered Bryant their prayerful support for prosperity for the task.[55] The following year, Bryant was retained as the evangelist for the Mountain Assembly, and pastors were advised to "cooperate with" him when he came "to their church and help him financially." The delegates also selected Bryant to preach the next introductory sermon.[56] This expanded responsibility of the moderator to serve the Mountain Assembly and all its churches throughout the year, along with the clerk's use of the word "oversee" in the 1924 minutes, showed a significant step toward hierarchical polity similar to the Church of God (Cleveland).

While not with the same scope or at the same pace, the Mountain Assembly began enlarging the responsibilities of its moderator within a few years of the Church of God (Cleveland) expanding A.J. Tomlinson's power. Additionally, its creation of a Board of Elders in 1919 was the direct result of the Church of God's installment of a Council of Twelve in 1917. The Elder Board of the Mountain Assembly underwent multiple transformations that distinguished it from the body which inspired its creation. However, even as its duties and composition changed, the Board of Twelve Elders represented a move toward centralized government. Tomlinson envisioned his Council of Twelve as a mere "advisory council" that he might convene when he deemed appropriate. The Elders themselves saw their role as a "check" on the "General Overseer's tendency to act unilaterally."[57]

In the Mountain Assembly, the Twelve Elders originally functioned in 1919 as a board of directors and a judiciary when questions of ministerial or ecclesiastical conduct arose.[58] When the board was dissolved in 1921 and reconstituted in 1922, it became a board of six. The new Board of Elders replaced the committee on grievances, called to settle any matters of dispute among churches or ministers.[59] In 1923, the board expanded to twelve members again. Now, its purpose was to serve "the Assembly or Churches in case of questions."[60] Two years later, the Mountain Assembly added to the twelve elders' duties to "go out in the work of the Gospel, and work in cooperation with each pastor and church." The new motion made it clear that the Twelve Elders were to serve the interests of the local churches.[61] In 1926, the Mountain Assembly voted to replace the quarterly ministers' meetings with quarterly Elders meetings.⁶² This measure placed the board in the local churches more frequently and provided ample opportunities for it to hear matters of concern that required its judgment or counsel. At the second such elders' meeting at Emlyn in December, the board advised "churches to place forth their strongest efforts to have and maintain a Sunday School." At the third meeting, the board upheld that pastor's elections should be determined by a majority vote of the members present, and that "if the minority rebel they will consider them out of order."⁶³ In 1929, the Mountain Assembly created a subcommittee on the Board of Twelve Elders to "supervise the work of the evangelists of the Mountain Assembly, sending them where they see fit, allowing them the use of the funds of the General Treasure [sic] to pay their expenses."⁶⁴

In 1930, the Mountain Assembly reconstituted its Board of Twelve Elders and charged them with cooperating "with all and every line of business of the churches of this assembly." The delegates appointed Parks, Bryant, and Curd Walker as Elders and empowered them to select another nine to serve with them. The three chose C.L. Price, John B. Spears, Morris E. Woolum, Andrew J. Long, Thomas Woods, William M. Sharp, Drue Stanifer, John H. Bryant, and Lewis Baird.⁶⁵ After 1930, the Mountain Assembly continued to modify the duties of the Elders, added qualifications for election, and reduced the Elder's appointment to an eight-year term. Despite the changes, the lines of succession from these twelve seats established in 1930 remained unbroken.

By creating ecclesiastical leadership outside the local congregation, the Mountain Assembly continued its path from an association of independent congregations to a denominational organization. Stephen Bryant's power in the Mountain Assembly fell drastically short of A.J. Tomlinson's in the Church of God, but it far surpassed Mike Lay's in the South Union Association. Though not hierarchical like the episcopal polity of the Church of God (Cleveland), the establishment of a Board of Elders added another dimension of leadership to the Mountain Assembly. Its calendar of events had expanded beyond one annual gathering to include quarterly meetings of its ministers and Elders. As the Mountain Assembly developed denominational leadership, it also developed governing statutes for its leaders to execute.

Standardized Rules and the Move Toward Centralization

The constitution of the South Union Association of United Baptists set forward its simple purpose with no more rules than necessary to accomplish its objectives. A mere fifteen articles, each one a single sentence, governed the association. Article 5 formed the foundation of the constitution: "This body shall exercise no ecclesiastical authority." As a result, the scope of its rules was limited to the few days when the association was in session. To ensure that the association never encroached upon the congregationalism of the Baptist churches that comprised it, Article 5 unamendable.

At the First General Assembly of the Church of God (Cleveland), Tomlinson and his followers recognized that the body assembled in North Carolina was judicial only. Nevertheless, each judgment adopted by the Assembly became a guiding principle for the local congregations. Officially, the Church of God declared that these judgments were not "laws made by the assembly, but only the laws given us by Christ and His disciples searched out by that body and brought to light that the Churches might take action upon the same as they see fit."[66] The Fourth General Assembly in 1909 reiterated that "this Assembly is not legislative, nor executive, but judicial only," but also demonstrated that it viewed the actions of the previous sessions as an informal constitution by striking out two clauses in the minutes of the previous assembly.[67] When a question arose before the General Assembly concerning a matter already decided, the record from the previous minutes was referenced and quoted in the current minutes.[68] Maintenance of Assembly records was necessary to stay abreast with its regulations.

In 1921, the Church of God (Cleveland) enacted three measures intended to limit the growing power of the General Overseer. First, it created a Council of Seventy that along with the Council of Twelve composed the "official Assembly." Other ministers and members retained the right to attend the General Assembly and participate in discussion, but voting power rested in this group of bishops. Second, the General Assembly created a "Court of Justice" with seven "supreme judges" to hear appeals from lower courts on matters brought to it. Third, the Church of God adopted a formal constitution.[69] Tomlinson assured the Assembly that the eight articles and numerous sections included in the constitution set forth no "laws or creeds that are binding us," but that it merely represented "that which we have been practising [sic] for years."[70]

At the first Mountain Assembly in 1907, six resolutions were adopted offering advice to the local churches in the same fashion that resolutions had been adopted in the Baptist association.[71] Tomlinson's presence at the 1911 Mountain Assembly coincided with its first resolution that had implications of ecclesiastical authority over the local churches. The infamous "tobacco" resolution restricted "Churches of God" from ordaining ministers "that will not abstain from the use of tobacco."[72] This move started the Mountain Assembly on a course toward denominational bylaws. The following year, the resolution committee presented a measure that required re-ordination for ministers who sought to "join the Church of God and having credentials from other churches" and another that required "members of the Churches of God" to "abstain from all strong drinks and soft drink stands."[73] In addition to a resolution in 1913 which required the local churches to investigate the cause of divorce for members who had "two husbands or two wives," the Mountain Assembly also adopted a resolution to retain four resolutions from the previous year and encouraged members to "take good care of your minute for reference."[74]

By 1915, the Mountain Assembly recognized the impracticability of preserving an endless number of reference books and moved to read the resolutions from previous minutes and retain such "as would be best for the churches," and sixteen were identified.[75] This formed the basis for the Mountain Assembly's decision ten years later to take "out of the old Minutes" the resolutions "which have been neglected being brought forward each year" and "to be carried out in each Minutes unless part or all of them should be changed." Of the 20 which became the first set of "Standard Resolutions" of the Mountain Assembly, the vast majority demonstrated the move toward centralized government. The Mountain Assembly, for example, recommended each local church to organize a Sunday school, required each church to maintain a treasury, required excluded members to be reconciled to the excluding body before joining another Mountain Assembly church, and created the organizational leadership positions of general trustees and a board of twelve elders.[76] Through its establishment of a permanent headquarters, its creation of rudimentary ecclesiastical leadership, and its organization-centric statutes, the Mountain Assembly had taken three steps toward the episcopal government of the Church of God (Cleveland) during its first two decades. It also took one major step back.

Friction with the Church of God (Cleveland)
The Mountain Assembly warmly received Tomlinson and Llewellyn when they attended its meeting at Siler's Chapel in 1911, and formal relations with the Church of God (Cleveland) remained cordial for the rest of the decade. Part of this conviviality was demonstrated through the reception of visiting messengers at the conventions and by the transference of membership and credentials between the groups. The Mountain Assembly sent John Parks,

Tension with the Church of God

Stephen Bryant, Josiah Thomas, William Hicks, and Jonah Shelton to Cleveland in January 1912.[77] That October, Tomlinson, T.L. McLain, M.S. Haynes, George F. Lucas, and Sam C. Perry came to the Sixth Annual Session of the Mountain Assembly at Lower Elk Valley.[78] In 1914, the Mountain Assembly resolved to "write a letter of correspondence to the Cleveland assembly and send it by the hands of some of our brethren asking them to receive our letter and messengers" and dispatched John Parks, Newt Parks, Matt H. Morgan, William R. Hamlin, Josiah Thomas, William Hicks, and George A. Fore for that purpose.[79] The 1918 Mountain Assembly "approved that this assembly send some of the brethren to the Harriman assembly," and Parks, Fore, John Thomas, Curd Walker, Hubert Harris, Starling Smith, Lewis Broyles, Evan Anderson, Mark Meadors, J.L. Goins, Richard Dewey Litton, James Cale Yeary, John H. Maples, J.D. Martin, Harrison Enix, and C.L. Price volunteered to go.[80] This General Assembly of the Church of God (Cleveland) was canceled because of concerns over the influenza epidemic.[81] That Harriman was half the distance from Jellico than was Cleveland partially explained the large number of volunteers ready to attend this Assembly, but it also represented a growing interest in the sister church of some Mountain Assembly ministers. Within a decade, nearly half of the volunteers from 1918 had joined the Church of God (Cleveland).

Jonah Shelton's membership and credentialing vacillated between the Mountain Assembly and the Church of God (Cleveland) from 1909 until November 24, 1917 when the Lower Elk Valley Church granted Shelton "a letter of dismission for to go to the Cleveland Assembly."[82] On that same date, *The Evangel* published a notice announcing the absorption of Shelton's magazine, *The Old Paths*, and its subscriptions.[83] The increased exposure of Church of God (Cleveland) news and testimonies contributed to enticing away some members of the Mountain Assembly, and this led eventually to the cessation of amicable membership transfers between the churches.

Perhaps no community experienced more hostility between the Mountain Assembly and the Church of God (Cleveland) than did Fonde, Kentucky. Two weeks after Lower Elk Valley granted Shelton a letter of dismission, it granted at least another sixteen letters of dismission to join the newly constituted Mountain Assembly church at Fonde.[84] Clear Fork Coal & Coke Company built the coal camp at Fonde when it opened a mine there in 1912.[85] Once these coal fields were accessible by rail, many relocated from Jellico to the new camp houses in Fonde, including several members of the Lower Elk Valley Church. As they began to evangelize their coworkers and communities, their home church saw an increase in membership from members living in Fonde. Fifteen of the charter members at Fonde who transferred their membership from Lower Elk Valley had joined the latter between June 1914 and January 1915.[86] Among the Fonde coal miners who traveled by train to attend the church at Lower Elk Valley was Joseph Daniels, who represented the church as a delegate at the 1916 Mountain Assembly.[87] His brother, Rev. James Madison Daniels, lived nearby in the coal camp, and the following year represented the new church at Balkan, another coal camp in Bell County, at the Mountain Assembly.[88] On December 8, 1917, Henry Mobley, a member at Lower Elk Valley, and James Daniels organized the Mountain Assembly church at Fonde and served as its first pastors. Both, Joe Daniels, the first deacon, and John Meeks the first clerk and treasurer, had received letters of dismission from Lower Elk Valley.[89]

On June 14, 1919, the church met for its regular business session and excluded its pastor, James Daniels, for hugging another man's wife. The church also called for his credentials and received them.[90] In response, Daniels and 16 supporters, including his brother, started another church and affiliated with the Church of God (Cleveland).[91] On October 11, Pastor Henry Mobley and the church excluded Joe Daniels for "talking against the church" and adopted a series of resolutions designed to curtail further exoduses. First, the church resolved to exclude any "members without further notice who may enter into worship in any form with any excluded member." Second, members who allowed "any excluded member to hold service of any kind in their homes" would be immediately excluded from the church. Third, the church resolved to "exclude any member who speaks against this church or its works."[92] The church kept those rules in effect for four years and enforced them. As a result, at least 20 members were excluded from the church for violating these rules, and another four were excluded at their own request.[93]

While Mobley co-pastored Fonde with Daniels, he also co-pastored Lower Elk Valley with John Parks, where the tension with the Church of God (Cleveland) had been felt since Shelton left and abandoned the church paper for the *Evangel*. Luther Elijah Jones was a member of Lower Elk Valley living in the coal camp at Fonde in January 1918 when he reported to the *Evangel*: "There is a band of baptized saints here and how I long to see them come together. I believe in the Church of God and the assembly. I long to become a member."[94] The next week, Jellico church "directed the clerk to write Bro L.E. Jones conserning [sic] his testimony published in the Cleveland paper and ask him to be present next meeting and explain why he so ignored

Tension with the Church of God

his own church." On February 23, 1918, "the case concerning Bro Jones was put before the church" and after "the spirit of God came upon the saints with great power," Jones "made his ecnoledgement [sic] to the church." The church forgave him and retained his membership. The following month, however, he was granted a letter of dismission to the Fonde church.[95] His wife, Sarah, however, remained a member at Lower Elk Valley. She had testified that "God had led her into that church and she would never leave it."[96] Luther Jones left the Mountain Assembly at Fonde and was excluded on January 10, 1920 for "taking up membership with [the] Cleveland folks."[97] When the members of Lower Elk Valley Church realized Sarah had later joined there as well, they excluded her on May 28, 1921 for "joining the Cleveland church and claiming and telling the pastors that God led her into that church and she would never leave it for that reason."[98]

With Mobley still in pastoral leadership at both churches, the measure adopted in 1919 by Fonde was also enforced at Lower Elk Valley. Two months after Fonde adopted the resolution, Lower Elk Valley excluded Matt Mason and Ida Irvin "for worshipping with members who was [sic] out of order and joining the Cleveland Assembly."[99] This joint-responsibility for the care of each other's members was first proposed by the Lower Elk Valley Church the preceding year when it voted to "give the church of God at Fonde Ky all rights to look after and to take care of the members of this church and if any of them walk disorderly that church has a right to call them to order and transact business as this church should."[100] As the conflict in Fonde increasingly created issues for both churches, it invited the Mountain Assembly to address the matter at its annual convention. At the 17th Annual Session of the Mountain Assembly of the Churches of God in 1923, the committee on miscellaneous business posed the question of what should be done "with members or preachers who take sides with excluded members" who speak "evil of the church or pastor where they belong." The Mountain Assembly considered such members out of order.[101]

In the fall of 1922, a lingering matter of gossip in Lower Elk Valley led Mobley to request that his name "be droped [sic] from the roll" on December 23.[102] In the midst of this conflict, Mobley also offered his resignation as pastor of the Fonde Church.[103] When Parks assumed the pastorate at Fonde, he attempted to bring about a peaceful resolution to the conflict caused by the Daniels' church start-up. At a business meeting two months later, the church voted to rescind the resolutions adopted in October 1919 and replace them with a new rule that members should still not worship with those who started a church in opposition to the Mountain Assembly, but now they would not be excluded until after the first and second admonition.[104] Parks's decision to show more indulgence on this matter was predicated on the practicality of living and working in a small community with so many close personal and familial relationships affected. He also made the decision at a time when multiple communities faced similar conflict because of the migration of ministers and churches to the Church of God (Cleveland) after the defection of George Fore and others following the 1922 Mountain Assembly.

Figure 4.4: Henry Mobley
c/o CGMA

Figure 4.5: J.H. Parks
c/o CGMA

Conclusion

The influence of the Church of God (Cleveland) on the organizational development of the Mountain Assembly began with A.J. Tomlinson's first visit in 1911 and continued throughout the decade. By the early 1920s, the CGMA had expanded the role of the moderator and created a Board of Twelve Elders patterned after the polity of the Church of God (Cleveland). The Mountain Assembly had found in Jellico a permanent headquarters like the Church of God had in Cleveland. The CGMA Standard Resolutions de-emphasized local congregational autonomy in favor of a developing centralized government. As the polity of the Mountain Assembly unified the congregations after the episcopal model of Tomlinson's church, several of its congregations were disrupted by conflict with Church of God (Cleveland) bodies in their communities. These simultaneous experiences hampered the development of hierarchical denominational leadership in the Mountain Assembly.

Tension with the Church of God

[1] Jones, *1990 Annual*, 14, 170-171.

[2] CGMA, *Minutes* (1916), 4.

[3] Padgett, *Heritage,* 30.

[4] See statistical tables at the end of each annual CGMA Minute Book, 1913-1917.

[5] CMGA, *Minutes* (1912), 4.

[6] CGMA, *Minutes* (1920), 4.

[7] Ibid., 6.

[8] CGMA, *Minutes of the Mountain Assembly of the Churches of God (Incorporated): The Twenty-Second Annual Assembly of the Mountain Assembly of the Churches of God* (Jellico, TN: CGMA, 1928), 3; CGMA, *Minutes of the Churches of God (Incorporated): The Twenty-Third Annual Assembly of the Mountain Assembly of the Churches of God* (Jellico, TN: CGMA, 1929), 3-4; CGMA *Minutes of the Mountain Assembly of the Churches of God (Incorporated): The Twenty-Fourth Annual Assembly of the Mountain Assembly of the Churches of God* (Jellico, TN: CGMA, 1930), 6.

[9] Davidson, 322.

[10] Conn, 84.

[11] Ibid., 177-178.

[12] East Tennessee Land Company, *Two Years of Harriman, Tennessee* (New York: The South Publishing Company, 1892), 54.

[13] Conn, 188.

[14] Phillips, 418-421.

[15] Conn, 150, 198.

[16] CGMA, *Minutes* (1920), 4.

[17] US Census Bureau, Fourteenth Census of the United States: 1920 Bulletin (Population: Tennessee), 15; US Census Bureau, Fourteenth Census of the United States: 1920 Bulletin (Population: Kentucky), both at https://www.census.gov/library/publications/1920/dec/bulletins/demographics.html

[18] CGMA, *Minutes* (1920), 9.

[19] Ibid., 6-8.

[20] James Hayden Siler, "A History of Jellico, Tennessee: Containing Historical Information on Campbell Co., Tenn., and Whitley Co., Ky," unpublished manuscript, 1938, 16-17.

[21] Deed of Conveyance, *Whitley County Deed Book* 101, February 5, 1923, 594, Whitley County Court House, Williamsburg, KY.

[22] CGMA. *Minutes* (1920), 9.

[23] Deed of Conveyance, *Whitley County Deed Book* 98, February 23, 1921, 630, Whitley County Court House, Williamsburg, KY. It is unclear what motivated the purchase of this property by Fore and Thomas. It is possible that they intended to buy the land on behalf of the Mountain Assembly. It is also possible that Parks encouraged the backout on

the Williamsburg purchase in order to build closer to his home in Jellico. By 1922, Fore and Thomas had built a building on the Williamsburg lot and moved the Pleasant View church to this location.

[24] CGMA, *Minutes* (1921), 6.

[25] Jellico Minutes, 69.

[26] Ibid., 76.

[27] CGMA, *Minutes* (1922), 6.

[28] CGMA, *Minutes* (1923), 10-11.

[29] Jellico Minutes, 92.

[30] CGMA, *Minutes* (1924), 8-9.

[31] CGMA, *Minutes* (1925), 8.

[32] Jellico Minutes, 112.

[33] CGMA, *Minutes* (1918), cover.

[34] CGMA, *Minutes* (1928), 1.

[35] SUAUB Handwritten Minutes, 173.

[36] SUAUB, *Minutes* (1902), 5-6.

[37] Ibid., 3-4.

[38] SUAUB, *Minutes* (1905), 2.

[39] SUAUB, *Minutes* (1904), 6, 8.

[40] Jones, *1990 Annual*, 170-171.

[41] Conn, 109-110.

[42] Ibid., 216.

[43] Phillips, 391-395.

[44] Gibson states that Bryant was elected moderator for these assemblies, information he admits was "furnished to him." However, the October 2020 discovery of the 1908 and 1910 minute books shows that Silcox continued to serve in this capacity until 1911.

[45] CGMA, *Minutes* (1934), 2. Prior to 1934, the nomination of officers was by ballot.

[46] CGMA, *Minutes* (1911), 1-2.

[47] Parks, 216.

[48] SUAUB, *Minutes of the Ninety-Eighth Annual Session of the South Union Baptist Association of United Baptists* (n.p.: by the association: 1912), 2-3.

[49] Jones, *1990 Annual*, 71.

[50] When Bryant died in 1939, he had moderated Mountain Assembly business sessions in all but two years from 1911 to 1938.

[51] Jones, in Devers, *Polity,* 143.

[52] CGMA, *Minutes* (1914), 4.

[53] CGMA, *Minutes* (1915), 6.

[54] CGMA, *Minutes* (1919), 5.

55 CGMA, *Minutes* (1924), 12, 15.

56 CGMA, *Minutes* (1925), 13.

57 Phillips, 412.

58 CGMA, *Minutes* (1919), 5.

59 CGMA, *Minutes* (1922), 6.

60 CGMA, *Minutes* (1923), 16.

61 CGMA, *Minutes* (1925), 10-11.

62 CGMA, *Minutes of the Church of God, Inc.: The Twentieth Annual Assembly of the Churches of God* (Jellico, TN: CGMA, 1926), 9.

63 CGMA, *Minutes of the Church of God, Inc.: The Twenty-First Annual Assembly of the Churches of God* (Jellico, TN: CGMA, 1927), 9-10.

64 CGMA, *Minutes* (1929), 9.

65 CGMA, *Minutes* (1930), 2, 7, 8.

66 Church of God, *Minutes* 35-36.

67 Ibid., 38-39.

68 For example, the General Assembly raised the subject of divorce and remarriage in 1911 and the discussion of the subject from the 1908 minute book was read. "The sentence of this Assembly, therefore, is to let the minute of 1908 remain unchanged" with the insertion of another clause. See Church of God, Minutes (1911), 11.

69 Conn, 208-209.

70 Church of God, *Minutes of the Sixteenth Annual Assembly of the Church of God* (Cleveland, TN: Church of God Publishing House, 1921), 60.

71 CGMA, *Minutes* (1907), 3.

72 CGMA, *Minutes* (1911), 4.

73 CGMA, *Minutes* (1912), 3-4.

74 CGMA, *Minutes* (1913), 4.

75 CGMA, *Minutes* (1915), 3-4.

76 CGMA, *Minutes* (1925), 15-16.

77 Church of God, *Echoes* (1912), 10, 20.

78 CGMA, *Minutes* (1912), 2-4.

79 CGMA, *Minutes* (1914), 5.

80 CGMA, *Minutes* (1918), 5.

81 Davidson, 501.

82 Jellico Minutes, 20.

83 *CGE* 8, no. 46 (November 24, 1917): 3.

84 Fonde Minutes, 293; Jellico Minutes, membership roster.

[85] Kentucky Coal Education, "Bell County, Kentucky Coal Camps," accessed September 16, 2019. http://www.coaleducation.org/coalhistory/coaltowns/coalcamps/bell_county_coal_camps.htm

[86] Fonde Minutes, 1; Jellico Minutes, membership roster.

[87] CGMA, *Minutes* (1916), 2.

[88] 1910 United States Census, Whitley County, Kentucky, s.v. "James Daniel," Ancestry.com; CGMA, *Minutes* (1917), 3.

[89] Fonde Minutes, 1; Jellico Minutes, membership roster.

[90] Fonde Minutes, 32-33.

[91] Church of God, *Minutes of the 14th Annual Assembly of the Church of God* (Cleveland, TN: Church of God Publishing House, 1919), 69.

[92] Fonde Minutes, 39.

[93] Ibid., 39-91.

[94] *CGE* 9, no. 8 (January 19, 1918): 2.

[95] Jellico Minutes, 23-25.

[96] Ibid., 64.

[97] Fonde Minutes, 43.

[98] Jellico Minutes, 64.

[99] Ibid., 47.

[100] Ibid., 30.

[101] CGMA, *Minutes* (1923), 16.

[102] Jellico Minutes, 76-79. The nature of the gossip was not recorded in the minutes but was apparently grievous enough to harm Mobley's influence irreparably.

[103] Fonde Minutes, 87.

[104] Ibid., 91.

5

Parallel Histories: Successful and Failed Leadership Transition

In just over a decade, the Church of God (Cleveland) had effected significantly the development of the Mountain Assembly. Positive and negative influences had helped define what the movement of Parks and Bryant was becoming. First, it had experienced its split with the General Assembly of the Churches of God by adopting Tomlinson's hardline stance against tobacco use. Second, the consistent exposure to the Church of God formally through ministerial visits to the General Assembly and informally through reading the *Evangel* sometimes obscured the distinction between the two groups and facilitated the transfer of Mountain Assembly ministers to Tomlinson's church. With every few strides the Mountain Assembly made toward a centralized polity, it felt the tug back toward congregational independence. For the most part, its experiences with the Church of God (Cleveland) had been positive until some local churches encountered division when the community had congregations from both groups. Relations between the Church of God Mountain Assembly and the Church of God (Cleveland) cooled significantly in the 1920s as the result of a setback from failed leadership transition in the Mountain Assembly and a disruption from a leadership change in the Church of God (Cleveland). When all four officials elected at the 1922 Mountain Assembly ultimately left for the Cleveland group, it opened a floodgate of minister and church transfer. The accompanying loss of real property further soured relations. Meanwhile, the Church of God (Cleveland) faced a similar crisis on a grander scale when it replaced A.J. Tomlinson as General Overseer, and he and his followers seceded to form what later would be called the Church of God of Prophecy.

New Leadership and a New Exodus

By the 16th Annual Mountain Assembly, Parks and Bryant had a combined 60 years of ministry. Parks was over 60 years old, and Bryant was in his mid-50s. Parks once mistakenly attributed to Scripture an ancient proverb, "Old men for counsel, young men for war." When corrected by his grandson that this phrase was not in the Bible, Parks responded that it "orta [sic] be."[1]

Having been recognized by the Mountain Assembly as "Elders" in 1919, Parks and Bryant felt like they should transition to an advisory role and allow the Assembly's younger ministers to take more active positions of leadership. On October 6, 1922, the Mountain Assembly selected George A. Fore as moderator, and J.L. Goins, as his assistant. It also chose Starling Smith as clerk, and Francis M. Thomas, as his assistant and general treasurer of the newly adopted tithe of tithes fund.[2]

George Arlow Fore was born near Woodbine in Knox County, Kentucky on July 30, 1888, the son of Amanda Jane (Childress) and Stephen Francis Fore.[3] Fore dedicated his life to Christ in 1907, began preaching the following year, and experienced the baptism of the Holy Ghost in 1912.[4] Fore had joined the new church at Gold Bug, Kentucky, in 1911, and two years later, the church called upon him to pastor.[5] Fore's leadership potential was quickly recognized. Bryant appointed him to the committee on resolutions in 1913 and 1914.[6] By 1914, Fore was pastoring three different churches in Whitley County: Gold Bug, Emlyn, and Pleasant View. After pastoring three churches for two years, Fore retained the leadership of Pleasant View and also took charge of a newly constituted Buffalo Creek church near Walden in Whitley County.[7] In 1917, the Mountain Assembly sent him to pastor the newly constituted church in Harlan, Kentucky, while also maintaining the church at Pleasant View. That year, Fore was elected to serve with Bryant as assistant moderator. When the quarterly ministers' meeting was held at Pleasant View in November, Fore moderated the session when the assembly's eventual financial plan was presented and the church covenant and articles of faith were adopted.[8] In 1919 and 1921, Fore preached the important introductory sermon.[9] He continued to pastor multiple churches and added Middlesboro in Bell County, and Twila in Harlan County to his pastoral record.[10] After five years as assistant moderator, the Mountain Assembly elected Fore as its third moderator.

James Lee Goins was born in Pollyeton, Kentucky, on January 6, 1888, to Louisa Jane (Thomas) and Isham Goins.[11] His mother's brother, John Thomas, had been among the first Mountain Assembly preachers to claim an experience of entire sanctification and had served on the first Board of Twelve Elders.[12] John Thomas and Jane Thomas Goins were maternal first cousins of John Parks. J.L. Goins professed faith in Christ in 1912 and experienced Spirit baptism and began preaching the following year.[13] He attended his first Mountain Assembly in 1915 as a delegate from Emlyn with Fore as his pastor. At the conclusion of the service on October 2, Goins was ordained by Fore,

Parks, Bryant, Mobley, and others.[14] In 1917, he accepted his first pastorate at Hicks Station near Jacksboro, Tennessee.[15] An itinerant coal miner, Goins also helped establish churches in southeastern Kentucky coal mining communities from 1919 to 1922 at McRoberts in Letcher County, Blue Diamond in Perry County, Heidelberg in Lee County, and Mize in Morgan County.[16] Goins had been selected to the first Board of Twelve Elders in 1919 and in 1922 was elected as assistant moderator.[17] At Blue Diamond, Goins worked in the mines with John Sharp. Sharp joined the church at Blue Diamond and began preaching in 1921.[18] Two years later, Sharp transferred to the coal fields of Franklin County in eastern Illinois and started Mountain Assembly churches in Sesser and Christopher.[19] By 1925, Goins had joined Sharp in Illinois and was pastoring the church at Christopher.[20]

Figure 5.1: George A. Fore
c/o CGMA

Figure 5.2: James L. Goins
c/o Church of God

Starling Smith was born in Whitley County on June 19, 1885, to Synthia (Broyles) and Isaac S. Smith.[21] His mother was a maternal first cousin of John Parks. Smith was converted and baptized in the holiness church in 1903. He experienced the baptism with the Holy Ghost and spoke in other tongues seven years later and began preaching in 1911.[22] Smith was ordained in 1917 at Pleasant View and began his pastoral ministry at Gold Bug and Walden.[23] In 1919, Smith was appointed to the first Elder Board, and later pastored at Jellico Creek and Whitley City.[24] In 1922, he was elected clerk.

Francis Marion Thomas was born at Wolf Creek on December 18, 1858 to Mary (Broyles) and Aaron Thomas.[25] He was a maternal first cousin of John Parks, and both a maternal and paternal cousin of his wife, Rachel Parks. At the first Mountain Assembly in 1907, Francis represented the church at

Pleasant View where he served as clerk.[26] At the 11th Mountain Assembly in 1917, Bryant appointed Thomas to be the first "General Treasury-man" for the assembly.[27] In 1922, Thomas was elected assistant clerk and also assigned the responsibility of the newly adopted tithe of tithes treasury.

Figure 5.3: Starling Smith
c/o CGMA

Figure 5.4: Francis M. Thomas
c/o Claudia E. Thomas

By 1922, Fore had attended the General Assembly of the Church of God (Cleveland) four times and had been a "regular reader of the Church of God *Evangel*."[28] His immersion in Tomlinsonian thought was demonstrated by his sermon topic the morning after his appointment as moderator. At the request of Bryant, Fore preached the morning message on October 7, 1922, and advocated "that the Assembly have a 'Theocratic Government' that is laws given by God Himself."[29] Tomlinson had introduced the term to the Church of God (Cleveland) in 1912 by insisting that

> the form of church government was not democratic, that is government by the people by a majority vote, neither was it republican in form, that is governed by the people by representatives selected by them, but it was theocratic in form, a government by the immediate direction of God.[30]

Fore had probably read Tomlinson's lengthy discourse on the government of God in the *Evangel* a few years earlier, and the account of the General Overseer's annual address at the 1921 General Assembly.[31] In the latter, Tomlinson clearly articulated "the difference between theocratic and monarchic" governments. "The single person that rules in theocratic government is God." Tomlinson contended that Christ stood at the "head of the Church" as the "supreme ruler," but also insisted that James occupied "the executive chair under God, and the twelve apostles of the Lord in submission to him." He contended that the disciples "recognized him as their superior in governmental affairs" and that the New Testament repeated an Old Testament model. In the office of the General Overseer, therefore, lay the fulfillment of the biblical government God instituted for His church. The state and district overseers, along with local pastors corresponded to "Moses' organization of the Church in the wilderness."[32] Fore desired to complete the transformation of the Mountain Assembly's polity into that which he saw in Tomlinson's church.

Six weeks after the conclusion of the 16th Annual Mountain Assembly, Fore, Smith, and Thomas, and the Williamsburg church, left the Mountain Assembly and joined the Church of God (Cleveland).[33] Fore had pastored the church at Pleasant View seven of the previous nine years, Smith joined him there as a co-pastor in 1922, and Thomas had been its clerk since its inception. In 1921, Fore and Thomas relocated the Pleasant View church into the city limits of Williamsburg and erected a new building on the lot where the tabernacle had been proposed the previous year.[34] After 1922, the church became the Green Street Church of God (Cleveland). Fore retained his affinity with several Mountain Assembly ministers and their congregations over the next year. As a result of his influence, the congregations he had pastored at Twila and Harlan also joined the Church of God, as did ministers Blaine Adams, Benjamin Harrison Enix, James Longsworth, John Bunch, Archie Daniels, and others.

Enix reported to the *Evangel* in April 1923 of Fore's successful revival in Harlan. He also reported that "the Church of God of the Mountain Assembly which Brother Fore has been pastor of over five years came in under the government of the Church of God with headquarters at Cleveland, Tenn."[35] One week after the Harlan church left the Mountain Assembly, Adams reported that the church in Twila had "just recently transferred from the Mountain Assembly to the Church of God with headquarters at Cleveland" after having wanted "this done for a year or more."[36] At the General Assembly in Cleveland in 1923, Fore was appointed State Overseer of Kentucky and later served on the Board of Twelve.[37] The Kentucky churches received the new overseer well and "spoke in glowing terms of Brother Fore." Tomlinson confessed "the Church of God should congratulate itself for getting such a man as he for State Overseer" and advised "faint-hearted discouraged" pastors to call on Fore, assuring them that he would "do his best to heal the wounded broken heart."[38] Smith was also appointed a district overseer for the Jellico, Tennessee District and to the Council of Seventy.[39]

The decision to leave the Mountain Assembly for the group in Cleveland had been in the making for some time. For a decade, the two groups had sent and received visiting ministers to the other's assemblies, and at least informal talks of a possible merger had persisted. The decision to build a tabernacle and establish headquarters in Jellico instead of Williamsburg certainly affected Fore personally. He chaired a significant ministers' meeting at his home church in 1917. He pastored the church at Emlyn when it hosted the Mountain Assembly in 1918. Two years later, when the decision to build an assembly tabernacle was made, he was appointed to the three relevant committees: the building committee to plan its construction, a finance committee to raise funds for its completion, and trustee board to obtain and hold property on behalf of the Mountain Assembly.[40] When the 1921 Mountain Assembly returned to Lower Elk Valley instead of the newly constructed church at Williamsburg, not even Fore's election as moderator in 1922 at the new tabernacle in Jellico could quell his disappointment. Fore was certainly poised to become an overseer like Tomlinson, should the Mountain Assembly ever fully embrace *theocratic government* and adopt an episcopal polity like the Church of God's. When the delegates voted on the final day's business that "the Lower Elk Valley church take charge of Assembly building and further agree that said church have a right to dispose of her church house as she pleases," it became apparent that the Jellico church and its pastor, John Parks, would remain at the forefront of the association. To add insult to injury, the delegates also voted to assume "the debt off the Tabernacle and lot on the assembly instead of the [Jellico] church."[41]

The rapid departure of most of the Mountain Assembly's elected officials filled Bryant and Parks with remorse. The burden of preparing the annual minute book for publication fell to them, and they began it with a preface explaining that "our brethren have left the Mountain Assembly and have gone to the Cleveland Assembly, leaving the work of the Mountain Assembly in bad condition." They expressed sorrow "to give our brethren up but it seemed to be their choice." Members and churches were encouraged to send their tithes to Parks at Jellico and to "let the work go on as well as possible and all of us do our best."[42] The following year, Bryant was elected moderator again, and the Mountain Assembly selected three new trustees: Gilbert Weaver, John Shephard, and J.T. Richardson.[43]

Goins was the lone official elected in 1922 who did not immediately join the Church of God (Cleveland). Instead, Goins spent the next few years working "for a union of the two Assemblies." He desired that the Mountain Assembly "unconditionally unite with the Church of God." On September 3, 1925, Goins introduced a motion at the 19th Annual Session of the Mountain Assembly of the Churches of God to that effect. By a small margin, the motion was defeated.[44] Instead the delegates voted "that we will not consider a union with the Cleveland Assembly unless they send Messengers from their Assembly to one of our lawful assemblies." When Goins's motion failed, the minister asked the Mountain Assembly to "grant him a letter of recommendation as he was leaving."[45] Goins met with Fore that same day and was examined by him for credentials with the Church of God.[46]

As a result, the Mountain Assembly church in Christopher, Illinois, followed its pastor to the Church of God. Goins wasted no time proselytizing additional Mountain Assembly ministers and churches. In November, he held a revival at Blue Diamond, Kentucky, where he had once pastored. At the conclusion of the revival on November 14, 1925, "the church made a transfer from the Mountain Assembly of the Church of God into the Church of God, Headquarters, Cleveland, Tennessee." Five days later, he began a four-night meeting at Fleming, Kentucky, with Pastor James Anderson Cole. Goins preached "on the Church and the whole church agreed that this was formerly a Mountain Assembly church." On November 23-24, he preached at Mize, Kentucky, another former pastorate, and "presented the church and they all with one accord agreed."[47]

In 1926, Goins was appointed to the Council of Seventy and as State Overseer of Indiana.[48] Still living in Illinois, Goins conducted a three-week revival attended by "thousands" at Benton, Illinois, in August 1927. At its conclusion, Pastor John Sharp and the "Mt. Assembly decided to unite with the Church of God."[49] At the Assembly in Jellico the following month, a letter was read "from Bro. John Sharp, Benton, Ill., saying that him and his church had changed assemblies."[50] The Mountain Assembly's lone congregation in Indiana had been founded by Elder Charles H. Standifer when he relocated from Middlesboro, Kentucky to Shelburn, Indiana, in 1920.[51] As State Overseer, Goins convinced Standifer and his congregation to join the Church of God (Cleveland) in 1928. Then together, Goins and Standifer organized two more churches in Indiana, at Coalmont and Paxton.[52] Fore, Goins, Smith, Standifer, and Sharp all left the Mountain Assembly while serving on its Board of Twelve Elders. In addition to the ministers who left the Mountain Assembly with Fore, Goins also took Sharp, Standifer, Cole, Charlie Morgan, James Dixon, Becham Bailey, H.M. Bates, G.P. Gower, and others. In all, Goins was credited with bringing "9 churches from the Mountain Assembly" and "about 1000 members" into the Church of God.[53]

Figure 5.5: John Sharp
c/o the Sharp Family

Figure 5.6: Charles H. Standifer
c/o CGMA

A Property Dispute and Its Role on Centralization

In 1920, as the Mountain Assembly was moving toward centralization by contemplating the purchase of corporate real estate for its headquarters tabernacle, it created its first General Trustee Board to hold property jointly owned by the churches in the association. The congregationally governed autonomous churches which voluntarily joined and voluntarily remained in the Mountain Assembly retained possession of their own real property. By the end of the decade, this changed as property disputes arose when churches left the Mountain Assembly to join the Church of God (Cleveland). The General Trustee Board began to hold properties of local churches in a drastic departure from the congregationalism of its Baptist roots. Ironically, this time a negative experience with the Church of God (Cleveland) influenced the Mountain Assembly toward centralized government.

The loss of ministers, churches, and members was costly emotionally and spiritually to the Mountain Assembly, especially to the ministers who had invested their own time and resources in those congregations. It also brought financial loss. The church at Harlan was established in 1917 with 21 members and grew to 158 in five years.[54] The church purchased property on Clover Street from Marshall Ball for $350 on July 9, 1917. John Henderson Maples,

John Bunch, and Benjamin H. Enix acted as trustees on behalf of the church to make the purchase, and all three joined Sherman Sizemore as delegates from the church at the Mountain Assembly in October.[55] Fore's revival in November 1922 brought most the members into the Church of God (Cleveland) with Enix as pastor, but contention over the property ensued. All three trustees named on the deed had joined the Church of God.

The Mountain Assembly remnant indicated Lewis Broyles was the pastor of the 18 members who stayed.[56] Broyles raised the issue of the property at the 19th Annual Mountain Assembly in 1925. The delegates voted "that the Church of God at Harlan take the matter in hand with the Cleveland folks and decide the business without any resentment from the Assembly."[57] Ultimately, the court would play a role in the adjudication. While Enix and his members met at the Harlan County Education Building, the reduction of members at the Mountain Assembly church devastated it financially and made it impossible to meet the payments on the building they had erected.[58] When Bailey Construction initiated a lawsuit against Harlan CGMA in February 1926, the Harlan County Circuit Court directed that the property be exposed "for sale at public auction, to the highest and best bidder" in order to settle the debt. As a result, Biven M. Lee purchased the property on March 15, 1926, for $900.[59] Seven months later, Lee sold the property to the Harlan Church of God (Cleveland) for $750, and Enix and his congregation obtained full possession of the building.[60]

Figure 5.7: B.H. Enix

c/o Bill Enix

Benjamin Harrison Moses assumed the pastorate of the remnant of the Mountain Assembly congregation in Harlan and built the congregation back up to 124 members by the 1929 Assembly.[61] James Arthur Enix, the brother of B.H. Enix and John Parks's son-in-law, relocated about that same time from the coal mines in Jellico to work in Harlan. He served the Mountain Assembly church as clerk and assisted Moses with the restoration of a congregation there.[62] A few months later, they were able to purchase another church building just a few hundred yards from the L & N depot in Harlan.[63] After the Harlan congregation survived the challenges of a property dispute, the Mountain Assembly determined to approach the future more proactively.

At Siler's Chapel on February 10, 1928, the Board of Twelve Elders "moved in order that all our churches who hold church property and deeds not bearing the name Mountain Assembly of the Church of God be changed to read thus." The Elders also advised that properties should be deeded to the local trustees, "but not bearing any personal name" to avoid further conflicts like the one at Harlan. At the following quarterly Elders Meeting at Emlyn, the Board authorized "the Assembly Trustees to fee lawyers to protect our church property rights when necessary and carry such cases to the highest court if necessary to hold that which is ours." The Elders maintained that they did "not advocate litigation but believe it to be right to use the law in defense of our property rights." The Board further moved "that the local trustees of each church send their deeds" to be placed "in a safety vault at the First National Bank at Jellico, Tenn., for safe keeping."[64]

Leadership Transition and Conflict in the Church of God

While the Mountain Assembly experienced its own growing pains because of a failed leadership transition, the Church of God (Cleveland) faced an even greater crisis. As the church grew, Tomlinson's responsibilities grew with it. By 1921, in addition to preaching regularly, the minister served as General Overseer, editor and publisher, business manager of the publishing house, and superintendent of the Bible Training School, and oversaw the Church of God's orphanage and children's home.[65] As the church enacted measures intended to limit his authority, the General Overseer grasped for more. Amidst this struggle for power, financial reverses sparked a change of leadership in the Church. In 1920, the General Assembly revised its financial system. Under the new plan, each local church sent its members' tithes directly to headquarters, and a seven-man committee would oversee the funds and distribute them as needed. Despite its approval with no opposition, this plan for "Christianized communism" quickly revealed its flaws.[66]

After the plan's adoption, the Council of "elders did not feel like taking the responsibility of selecting seven men to do the business."[67] Instead, they left it to Tomlinson to oversee and distribute the tithes at his discretion. As a result, some pastors received little-to-no financial support. To make matters worse, Tomlinson redirected some of tithe treasury to make payments on the newly erected assembly tabernacle and even more to offset the deficit of the publishing house and the *Evangel*. Tomlinson explained his actions to the Assembly, "I only used the tithes little at a time, each time with a hope that I would get enough back in a few days to replace them and save the ministers, as well as the Publishing house and Church."[68] The General Overseer insisted that saving the church from bankruptcy left him with no alternative.[69]

In March 1921, Elders J.S. Llewellyn, M.S. Lemons, T.L. McCLain, and J.B. Ellis requested Tomlinson to convene a meeting of the board of Elders "for consideration of important matters that may be brought before them." They expressed their concern "for the welfare of the church and in view of the fact that there is a growing and widespread dissatisfaction on account of some recent developments of vital interests to the Church."[70] By the time the Overseer called the meeting in September, the men "made their complaints public and demanded answers to what appeared to be discrepancies in regard to the receipts and disbursements of monies." Tomlinson possessed poor book-keeping skills and tended to "think and act unilaterally." While this faction on the board of elders hoped for a quick remedy, the contention spread to ministers outside the board over the next several months.[71] The General Assembly instituted the Council of Seventy and adopted the Constitution as a measure intended to check Tomlinson's power.

At the Elders' Council Meeting in September 1922, Tomlinson responded to the formal charges brought against him by Llewellyn. When Lemons exploded into what Tomlinson called a "tirade of abusive words" and accusations of "mismanagement, misappropriation of funds, and a number of other things," the General Overseer "broke over and cried like a baby."[72] The incident drove the final wedge between Tomlinson and the faction that seemed intent on divesting him of his power. When Tomlinson addressed the General Assembly in November, he divulged to the members his financial blunders, but he also bolstered his position with a sermon that reinforced theocracy as the legitimate biblical model of church leadership. The General Overseer blamed the constitution for the opposition he faced and emphasized in his address that God had given him a lifetime appointment to his office no matter what men or a constitution might say to the contrary. He called on the Assembly to abandon the constitution it adopted the previous year and to change the process by which the Council of Elders was appointed by giving him sole authority to select the twelve.[73]

Instead, Llewellyn convinced the Committee on Better Government and the Council of Seventy to endorse a plan to create two new offices—Editor and Publisher of the *Evangel* and Superintendent of Education—to "serve with the General Overseer as an Executive Council." Tomlinson's appeal to rescind the constitution was denied as was his request to appoint the Council of Twelve himself. When the vote on the amendment was forced, it passed despite the knowledge of many leaders that the General Overseer was against it. When the Council of Twelve met to appoint the new leaders, "it was a foregone conclusion that Llewellyn would be the new Editor and Publisher, and it was just as likely that F.J. Lee would be selected as the new Superintendent of Education."[74] Indeed, on the morning of November 7, the recommendations of Tomlinson as General Overseer, and Llewellyn and Lee in their respective offices were accepted by the Assembly and the three became the first Executive Council of the Church of God (Cleveland). As the afternoon session ended, however, "The General Overseer tendered his resignation as General Overseer to take effect as soon as his successor was installed." When the Assembly refused to accept his resignation, Tomlinson that "he would reconsider the matter and at the night service he would inform the Assembly of his decision." That evening, he announced to the church that he would continue to serve for another year.[75]

In June 1923, the Council of Twelve was called to session to hear the final report of a committee—Lee, Ellis, and Llewellyn—appointed at the last Assembly to investigate all the Church of God's departments to ensure that all their affairs were in order. Along with the Twelve, the Council of Seventy was invited, as were any other ministers who were interested. The General Overseer endeavored to preempt the proceedings by first entertaining charges against Lemons, Ellis, and Llewellyn for "sacriligious [sic] indignities heaped upon our kind and patient General Overseer, as well as putting Lord Jesus to an open shame" and asked that they "be divested of all station and honor and trust in the Church of God, and a charge of disloyalty be presented to their respective places of local membership, for action in the Church." The charges were initiated by C.T. Anderson, but Tomlinson had spent the past few months preaching and traveling to add some seventy signatories to it. After the trial continued into the afternoon of the second day, Tomlinson dismissed the three in question that the other nine might deliberate in closed session on the validity of the charges. After another four hours, the Council determined that presentation of charges was "out of order," in that the purpose of this meeting was to hear the report of the Investigation Committee, including the auditor's report on Tomlinson's bookkeeping.[76]

When the proceedings turned to the matters for which the meeting was called, the auditor's report was read, and numerous previously disclosed inconsistencies were repeated. Tomlinson and his supporters attempted to defend his actions or offered explanations for them for two days. After all the issues were raised and discussed, the Council of Twelve retired to deliberate in closed session. On the tenth day of the "June Council," ten of the Elders brought 15 charges against Tomlinson, including misappropriating orphanage funds, misapplying several thousand dollars for other than what the funds were raised, refusing to cooperate with the Executive Council, copywriting in his own name publications that belonged to the Church, holding secret councils to oppose actions of the General Assembly, and more.[77]

Tomlinson refused to step down and insisted that God had elevated him to the office and man could not take him from it. The impeachment was turned over to the Court of Justice to determine whether he should be removed from office. The Court agreed to meet on July 26. Tomlinson meanwhile wrote to the ten Elders who voted to impeach him through Llewellyn and informed them that their actions were illegal and that they had dispersed from the meeting before they had finished business. He called them back into session on July 24 to complete the matters at hand. When that date arrived, Tomlinson met with the two elders who had supported him, George Brouayer and S.O. Gallaspie, and called the council meeting to order. Acting as General Overseer, he declared the two a quorum and determined that the others by their failure to attend were "disloyal and disobedient and had vacated their positions." Tomlinson then published a notice that the ten had been removed from all their respective offices, including those who served as officials of the Bible Training School, mission work, and orphanage.[78]

Two days later, the Court of Justice met and upheld the Council of Twelve's charges and officially removed Tomlinson from his position. Later that day, The Council of Seventy elected Flavius J. Lee to succeed Tomlinson as General Overseer of the Church of God (Cleveland) and J.B. Ellis to replace Lee as Superintendent of Education.[79] Tomlinson, of course, did not attend nor respond to the actions that he deemed out of order.

Instead, Tomlinson called a Council for his followers in Chattanooga on August 8-10, 1923. Together with Brouayer and Gallaspie, they appointed C.H. Randall, H.A. Pressgrove, Guy Marlow, T.A. Richard, J.O. Hamilton, J.A. Wilkerson, J.H. Brooks, J.N. Hurley, G.T. Stargel, and T.J. Richardson to the Council of Elders. The Call Council also repealed the Constitution and dissolved the Council of Seventy and Court of Justice. Most significantly, those in attendance reaffirmed the divine lifetime appointment of A.J. Tomlinson as General Overseer of the Church of God. When Tomlinson's faction met in Cleveland for its General Assembly in November, the Council of Twelve was formally dissolved as the office of General Overseer was restored its original autocratic authority.[80]

Lee continued to lead the Church of God (Cleveland) until his death from liver cancer in 1928.[81] During the 1920s the two factions were embroiled in bitter conflicts. Funds arriving in Cleveland designated for the "Church of God" remained a constant source of contention until a chancery court ruled that "the group that had impeached Tomlinson gained rights to the name "Church of God." The "Tomlinson Church of God" would become the "Church of God of Prophecy" after more lengthy litigation was finally settled in 1952. A.J. Tomlinson would not live to see the church use that name. The "General Overseer for life" finally fulfilled his term when he died on October 2, 1943. Contention over who should succeed Tomlinson as General Overseer led to his oldest son, Homer, creating another schism known as the Church of God, World Headquarters. The younger son, Milton Ambrose Tomlinson, followed his father as General Overseer of the Church of God of Prophecy.[82]

The Mountain Assembly ministers who joined the Church of God (Cleveland) in the early 1920s were more attracted to its government than they were to the person of A.J. Tomlinson. As a result, they remained loyal to the organization's polity and leadership. The schism in Cleveland and the setback in Jellico worked together to limit the influence of the Church of God on the Mountain Assembly for nearly two more decades. The formal visitation of messengers at the annual conventions ceased as the Church of God prioritized recovery and the Mountain Assembly remained circumspect. As the two groups centered in Cleveland recovered, they refined their ecclesiastical structure. In Jellico, the Mountain Assembly maintained the status quo until most of the founding generation passed and new leadership emerged in the 1940s.

Conclusion

The disruption in the Church of God (Cleveland) in 1922-23 was the result of several significant changes to its polity over the few years leading up to it. Tomlinson's insistence on his divinely exalted position atop the church's hierarchical centralized government contributed to a growing distrust among some of his ministers for what they viewed as dictatorial leadership. The Church of God (Cleveland) had recognized centralized government at its first assembly in 1906 and had entrusted most of the church's power in the single office of General Overseer in 1910. Over the next dozen years, the authority of the church was disseminated to varying degrees to the Council of Twelve Elders, then to the Council of Seventy, and then to the three-member

Executive Council. By 1923, two irreconcilable ecclesiastical polities had emerged within the Church of God (Cleveland). The result was division.

While this schism was forming over ideological differences, the Mountain Assembly was also developing a new form of ecclesiastical leadership. The episcopal government of Tomlinson's group charmed so many Mountain Assembly preachers that they began to incorporate aspects of it within their own association. So appealing was this polity that several ministers entirely abandoned the Mountain Assembly for the Church of God (Cleveland). The loss of ministers and churches because of the failed leadership transition in 1922 and its negative repercussions delayed further tendencies toward centralization for another decade.

---

[1] This anecdote was shared with the author by Parks's great-grandson in June 1990.

[2] CGMA, *Minutes* (1922), 2, 6.

[3] U.S., World War I Draft Registration Cards, 1917-1918, s.v. "George A Fore," and 1880 United States Census, Knox County, Kentucky, s.v. "George Fare," Ancestry.com.

[4] Ministers Examination Certificate, George A. Fore file, Central Files and Records of the Church of God, Cleveland, TN.

[5] CGMA, *Minutes* (1913), statistical table.

[6] Ibid., 4; CGMA, *Minutes*, (1914), 3.

[7] CGMA, *Minutes* (1916), statistical table.

[8] CGMA, *Minutes* (1917), 3-7.

[9] CGMA, *Minutes* (1919), 2; CGMA, *Minutes* (1921), 2.

[10] CGMA, *Minutes* (1921), 6; CGMA, *Minutes* (1922), 6.

[11] U.S., World War I Draft Registration Cards, 1917-1918, s.v. "Lee Goins," and 1900 United States Census, Whitley County, Kentucky, s.v. "Lee Goins," Ancestry.com.

[12] Gibson, 51; CGMA, *Minutes* (1919), 5.

[13] Ministers Examination Certificate, James L. Goins file, Central Files and Records of the Church of God, Cleveland, TN.

[14] CGMA, *Minutes* (1915), 1, 5.

[15] CGMA, *Minutes* (1917), statistical table.

[16] CGMA, *Minutes* (1920), 3, 7; CGMA, *Minutes* (1922), 3.

[17] CGMA, *Minutes* (1919), 5.

[18] Ministers Examination Certificate, John Sharp file, Central Files and Records of the Church of God, Cleveland, TN.

[19] CGMA, *Minutes* (1923), 7, 11.

[20] CGMA, *Minutes* (1925), 5.

[21] Find A Grave Memorial, "Isaac S. Smith," https://www.findagrave.com/memorial/54818545

[22] Ministers Examination Certificate, Starling Smith file, Central Files and Records of the Church of God, Cleveland, TN.

[23] CGMA, *Minutes* (1917), statistical table.

[24] CGMA, *Minutes* (1919), 5, statistical table; CGMA, *Minutes* (1922), 2.

[25] Kentucky, Death Records, 1852-1965, s.v. "Francis Larion Thomas," Ancestry.com.

[26] CGMA, *Minutes* (1907), 2.

[27] CGMA, *Minutes* (1917), 4.

[28] Examination, Fore file.

[29] CGMA, *Minutes* (1922), 5.

[30] Church of God, *Echoes* (1912), 15.

[31] A.J. Tomlinson, "The Government of God," *CGE* 10, no. 24 (June 14, 1919): 1.

[32] A.J. Tomlinson, "Address Before the Assembly," *CGE* 12, no. 4 (January 22, 1921): 1.

[33] Examination, Fore file.

[34] CGMA, *Minutes* (1921), 3.

[35] *CGE* 14, no. 15 (April 14, 1923): 4.

[36] *CGE* 14, no. 16 (April 21, 1923): 3.

[37] Church of God, *Minutes of the Eighteenth Annual Assembly of the Church of God* (Cleveland, TN: Church of God Publishing House, 1923), 85; Church of God, *Minutes of the Twenty-Third Annual Assembly of the Church of God* (Cleveland, TN: Church of God Publishing House, 1926), 76.

[38] *CGE* 15, no. 21 (May 24, 1924): 1.

[39] *CGE* 14, no. 47 (November 17, 1923): 2; CG, *Minutes* (1926), 76.

[40] CGMA, *Minutes* (1920), 4, 9.

[41] CGMA, *Minutes* (1922), 6.

[42] Ibid., 1.

[43] CGMA, *Minutes* (1923), 9-11.

[44] [James Lee Goins] to [The Officials of the Church of God], [ca. May 24, 1950], Goins file.

[45] CGMA, *Minutes* (1925), 9.

[46] Examination, Goins file.

[47] *CGE* 17, no. 1 (January 9, 1926): 3.

[48] Church of God, *Minutes of the Twenty-First Annual Assembly* (Cleveland, TN: Church of God Publishing House, 1926), 40, 77.

[49] *CGE* 18, no. 37 (September 10, 1927): 3.

[50] CGMA, *Minutes* (1927), 12.

51 CGMA, *Minutes* (1920), 4.

52 *CGE* 19, no, 16 (April 21, 1928): 4.

53 J.L. Goins to H.L. Chesser, February 5, 1952, Goins file.

54 CGMA, *Minutes* (1917), statistical table; CGMA, *Minutes* (1922), 3-4.

55 Deed of Conveyance, *Harlan County Deed Book* 33, July 9, 1917, 190, Harlan County Court House, Harlan, KY.

56 CGMA, *Minutes* (1923), 5.

57 CGMA, *Minutes* (1925), 9.

58 *The Church of God of Kentucky: A History, 1911-1987* (Charlotte: The Delmar Company, 1987), 178.

59 Deed of Conveyance, *Harlan County Deed Book* 55, April 8, 1926, 146, Harlan County Court House, Harlan, KY.

60 Deed of Conveyance, *Harlan County Deed Book* 57, October 1, 1926, 61, Harlan County Court House, Harlan, KY.

61 CGMA, *Minutes* (1929), statistical table.

62 CGMA, *Minutes* (1924), 4; CGMA, *Minutes* (1928), 12.

63 Deed of Conveyance, *Harlan County Deed Book* 67, November 6, 1929, 529, Harlan County Court House, Harlan, KY.

64 CGMA, *Minutes* (1928), 5.

65 Conn, 211.

66 Phillips, 438.

67 CG, *Minutes* (1921), 29.

68 CG, Minutes (1922), 29.

69 Phillips, 448.

70 Davidson, 543.

71 Phillips, 481-482.

72 Ibid., 495-496.

73 Ibid., 503-507.

74 Ibid., 511-512, 518.

75 Church of God, *Minutes of the Seventeenth Annual Assembly* (Cleveland, TN: Church of God Publishing House, 1922), 51-52, 58.

76 Phillips, 574-583.

77 Ibid., 592-594.

78 Ibid., 608-611.

79 Conn, 214-216.

80 Phillips, 616-618.

81 Conn, 242-243.

82 Synan, 198-199.

6

An Informal Triumvirate Gives Way to the Next Generation

While the Church of God (Cleveland) recovered from its rift governed by a new three-member Executive Council, the Mountain Assembly rebounded from its own setback under the informal leadership of a trio of its own. Sometimes by serving in official capacities and sometimes merely by influence, the triad of John Parks, Stephen Bryant, and Curd Walker guided the Mountain Assembly from the mid-1920s through the 1930s. In its third decade, the association added more centralized leadership by the appointment of full-time evangels/evangelists working under the auspices of the organization rather than as ministers appointed by the congregations of local churches. As the Mountain Assembly expanded geographically beyond the coalfields, centralized government further progressed through the financial support system adapted from the Church of God (Cleveland). By 1940, new leadership emerged, replacing the triumvirate of Parks, Bryant, and Walker.

Curd Walker

Alec Curd Walker was born in a "little log cabin" two miles "from the mouth of Jellico Creek" on August 7, 1877, the youngest of fourteen children born to Polly (Patrick) and Pleasant Phillip Walker.[1] His maternal grandfather, Andrew Patrick, had helped organize the United Baptist Church at Pleasant Hill in 1868 and served as its first pastor.[2] While Curd was a small child, his father lost the large farm and store he had built on it by "selling on credit." After Polly died in 1886, Pleasant remarried Margaret "Peggy" Petrey the following year and relocated his family to Cane Creek near Saxton, Kentucky. Curd attended elementary school there at the Clearkfork Baptist Church House for about five years. He quit school in the fall of 1891 and soon began courting a distant cousin of his step-mother, Theodocia "Dosha" Petrey, whom he married in Whitley County on March 22, 1893. Peggy Petrey Walker was a determined and industrious woman who "set her mind to redeeming" Pleasant's "old home" for his children. By peddling produce on "horseback" she managed to pay off the mortgage on the farm near Jellico Creek, where Curd and Dosha moved to a tract of land in 1896.[3]

After his conversion in 1901 and the ensuing controversy at Pleasant Hill, Walker returned to Cane Creek and helped organize the Holiness church at Saxton where he served as its first clerk. On September 21, 1907, Curd and Dosha, along with James Patton Smith, were baptized at Cane Creek by John Parks.[4] Three weeks later, Smith, Walker and his brother-in-law, Joe L. Jones, were among the delegates from Saxton at the first Mountain Assembly at Little Wolf Creek, and Walker served on the Resolutions Committee.[5] When the Saxton church relocated and reorganized in 1912 with John Parks as pastor, Walker again represented the church as a delegate and served on the Resolutions Committee.[6] He was on the committee the following year when the assembly was held at Saxton.[7] In 1915, Walker was appointed by the moderator to visit Hayes Creek over the issue of tobacco use and by the Divine Services Committee to preach one morning at the assembly.[8] In 1916, the Mountain Assembly appointed Parks, Walker, and John Thomas to "buy a tent to be used by the traveling preachers of this assembly."[9] Not long after, Walker began evangelizing in addition to pastoring at Saxton.

Figure 6.1: Curd Walker
c/o Stephen Walker

In the mid-1920s, Walker moved to Vidalia, Georgia, evangelized the southern part of the state, but returned each year for the annual assembly. For the rest of the decade, he was "gladly received in many localities and different churches among many different professions of both White and Colored" and asked "to preach to a number of convicts at a convict camp."[10] Walker was a frequent guest minister at Johnson's Chapel, a Baptist-turned-Holiness church near Adrian, Georgia. James William Daniel Johnson had organized this church in 1925 and served as its clerk and deacon but had trouble keeping a regular pastor.[11] The church was a member of the Holiness Baptist Association of Georgia and Florida. This association was formed from two churches and several preachers who "were expelled from the Little River Association upon the charge of 'heresy' or the doctrine of 'sinless perfection'" in October 1893. After two new churches were established, an 1894 convention at Pine City Church in Wilcox County, Georgia, organized the association "still retaining Missionary Baptist articles of faith and Decorum."[12]

On September 9, 1927, the Mountain Assembly voted to send Walker to "the annual assembly of the Holy Baptist Church" with "a letter of recommendation to them from us to consider a unity."[13] A month later, the association met at Bethany Church in Coffee County, Georgia, and its moderator, J.H. McCullough, "extended the right hand of fellowship" to "Elder Curd Walker and wife as visitors from the Mountain Assembly of the Churches of God, of Kentucky and Tennessee." Walker was invited to preach in the Friday morning service, and he "brought the message fresh from the presence of the Omnipotent. Shouts of praise and tears of joy were the order, as the message was delivered."[14] When Walker returned to Jellico the following September for the Annual Mountain Assembly, he brought back his report and also "asked permission to use a few minutes of the Assembly's time to present *The Gospel Standard* paper." This publication served as an official voice of the Holiness Baptist Association, edited by members, Joseph and Nola Sellers, and was printed by Ham Printing Company in Cordele, Georgia. Walker "distributed a few copies of said paper among the brethren for them to read and advised each church to subscribe for the paper." The Mountain Assembly acquiesced and approved the "order that at least one copy be subscribed for by each church in our ranks and that our pastor brethren advise their members to subscribe for same." The delegates also asked Walker to "confer" with Ham Printing Company "for the purpose of getting their price on printing our minutes."[15] As a result, the next ten minute books were printed in Cordele, Georgia.[16]

Walker "was called for pastor of Johnson's Chapel church" on August 29, 1928, and "it changed from Holliness [sic] Baptise [sic] to the Church of God" Mountain Assembly on February 8, 1930.[17] At the Mountain Assembly that September, a "letter of solicitation for fellowship" from Johnson's Chapel "was read and the new church was received" into the Assembly. Walker preached the introductory sermon the same morning "instructing the people how to love true holiness."[18] By the time the 24th Annual Mountain Assembly concluded that Sunday, it would become clear that Walker, with Parks and Bryant, formed a new leadership approach in the organization.

The Big Three

From the organizational meeting at Ryan's Creek in 1907, it was evident that Parks and Bryant would lead the new association. As moderator, Bryant led formally while Parks served primarily through influence. After Fore and Goins left the Mountain Assembly, Bryant and Parks reclaimed their status as evidenced by the "notice" they included as a preface to the 1922 minute book. Fore and the others had "gone to the Cleveland Assembly, leaving the work of the Mountain Assembly in bad condition." Bryant and Parks exhorted churches to send finance to Jellico and "let the work go on as well as possible."[19] By 1930, Bryant, Parks, and Walker settled into regular leadership roles.

As pastor of the Jellico church, Parks assumed the duties of hosting the annual assembly. He frequently made announcements after the worship services, especially aimed at directing guests where "refreshments could be gotten" or "placing those that have come to the assembly in the homes of the Jellico church folks."[20] Parks was also a popular preacher and was called upon by the committee on divine services to fill the pulpit at least once during the convention. Bryant's ministry, likewise, appealed to the attendees. It seemed the Assembly could not conclude without hearing the moderator deliver a sermon. From 1926 to 1930, Bryant preached the Sunday morning service to close the Assembly. Walker, on the other hand, was desired at the opening of the convention. During the same period, he preached on the first night three times, the second night in 1929, and the introductory sermon in 1930. Walker's "usual old time sermons" became so popular that by 1936, the divine services committee received "several outside requests for Brother Walker to preach."[21] In addition to Walker's preaching, the Mountain Assembly was often edified by manifestations of "speaking in tongues" with interpretations and prophetic utterances from his wife, Dosha.[22]

Bryant moderated the Mountain Assembly from 1923 to 1938, except for the 1934 Assembly when Parks was elected. During that same period, Parks was also Assistant Moderator for two years and frequently served on committees on resolutions, grievances, and bible questions. In addition to serving often on these committees with Parks, Walker was called upon almost annually to read the letters from the various churches reporting to the Mountain Assembly. As a result, he was elected Clerk or Assistant Clerk eight times and served as Assistant Moderator in 1927.

At the first business session of the 24th Annual Assembly in 1930, the Mountain Assembly appointed Bryant, Parks, and Walker to the committee on resolutions. Their first proposal called for a reconstitution of the Board of Twelve Elders to "cooperate with all and every line of business of the churches of this assembly." Next, they recommended that the Assembly appoint a committee of three to work with "the pastors and churches on Sunday School work and see that each church has a Sunday School." Both committees would be appointed on the third day.²³ On the second day, the Assembly accepted the resignation of two trustees, John Shepherd and Gilbert Weaver, and appointed Bryant, Parks, and Walker to select two men to replace them. The following day, they chose Stephen Bryant and William Sharp to "fill the vacancies" and vested them "with the same authority as was held by trustees resigning" to sit "equally with the other trustee [Lewis Miller Sharp] now holding this office."²⁴

On Friday, September 5, 1930, the Mountain Assembly appointed Bryant, Parks, and Walker to the reorganized Board of Twelve Elders and gave "them the power to select nine other qualified Elders of our body to make out the full number." The three were also authorized to appoint the committee on Sunday schools. They selected C.L. Price, John B. Spears, Morris Woolum, Andrew Long, Thomas Woods, William M. Sharp, Drue Stanifer, John H. Bryant, and Lewis Baird as Elders and John Melton Laws, George Kidd, and Gilbert Weaver as the Sunday School Committee.²⁵ With the new Elder Board came new standard resolutions governing them. The three proposed that "any decision made by the Board of Elders be final when as many as three in number have met in conference, provided that the full twelve have been legally notified."²⁶

In a move toward greater centralization, Bryant, Parks, and Walker proposed that each member of the local churches send a free will offering of one dollar "for the purpose of bearing the expenses of the Assembly for the coming year." This offering was understood to "not interfere with tithe paying."²⁷ The resolution committee also proposed a new directive asking each pastor and preacher to "pay tithes and teach tithe paying" and were asked by the Assembly to "put forth an example from the bible, how that tithes paid in should be distributed in the house of the Lord."²⁸ For a decade, the Mountain Assembly had attempted to implement the tithing system it observed in the Church of God (Cleveland), but with little effect. The emphasis on financial support to headquarters by the triumvirate at the 24ᵗʰ Mountain Assembly represented a turning point in the transition from a congregationalist association to a denominational organization.

Interchurch Officers and a Centralized Financial System

Baptist churches recognized no officer outside the local congregation. When the Mountain Assembly appointed Henry Mobley as its first evangelist in 1915, it expected the churches to support his mission of assisting struggling churches by providing him with a freewill offering of $7.60 that week.²⁹

Mobley reported the following year that "he did the best he could under the present conditions," and the Assembly retained his services for another year.[30] Pastoring at Emlyn gave Mobley little time to devote to evangelism, and the Mountain Assembly appointed C.L. Price and Lewis Broyles as evangelists in 1917.[31] From the donations that were sent to headquarters that year, the association paid Price twelve dollars for his ministerial services.[32]

Figure 6.2: C.L. Price
c/o CGMA

Figure 6.3: Lewis Broyles
c/o CGMA

Determined to spread the reach of its influence, the 12th Annual Mountain Assembly added John Parks, John Thomas, George Fore, James Goins, and Hubert Harris to the two it commissioned in 1917.[33] Francis Thomas was appointed "the General Treasury-man" and bore the responsibility of receiving the assembly's donations for distribution to the evangelists.[34] Thomas was able to pay three evangelists a combined $52.75 that year. After having brought in only $47.43 from the donations, the Mountain Assembly realized it could not continue the ministry of associational evangelism on a deficit.[35] As a result, the association depended on the new Board of Twelve Elders to fill the role that evangelists had played the past few years.

As Baptists, Parks and Bryant had not practiced the discipline of tithing. After the Church of God (Cleveland) adopted its tithe of tithe system in 1917, the Mountain Assembly approved such a method of financial support to its headquarters two years later to be used for the support of evangelists.[36] The tithe of tithes system brought in $605.89 the first year, but the outlay of $176.45 for the Elders and evangelists appointed by them combined with a $476.20 for printing costs left the treasury with a deficit again. Thomas resigned in frustration, and the practice of sending evangelists and receiving tithe of tithes ceased for the next two years.³⁷ In 1922, the Mountain Assembly renewed the tithe of tithe system and convinced Thomas to accept the reappointment to "treasurer with the assistance of the Elders." This appointment, however, was short-lived as Thomas left the Mountain Assembly with Fore the following month.³⁸ At its monthly business meeting on November 25, the Jellico church made a motion to notify Assistant Moderator J.L. Goins "to call the Elders together at the most convenient place and appoint a general treasureman [sic] for the Mountain Assembly."³⁹ At this time, Parks reluctantly assumed the responsibility of collecting and distributing the tithes until the next general assembly.⁴⁰

On October 3, 1923, Parks turned over a balance of $8.46 in the general treasury to the newly appointed treasurer, Everett Harmon Ross. Ross was the clerk from the Jellico church. His father, Alvin Jones Ross, had served as the church's first clerk and was a delegate at the first Mountain Assembly in 1907. E.H. Ross maintained the general treasury for the Mountain Assembly for the next eight years, but little was received. His report the following year "showed only a few churches living up to this obligation" of remitting a tithe of tithes to headquarters. Instead, most funds the churches sent

Figure 6.4: Everett H. Ross
c/o CGMA

during the 1920s were transmitted to the "assembly treasurer," Will Brock (and later, Lewis Sharp).⁴¹ This treasury bore the burden of the expense of the general assembly, including retiring the debt on the tabernacle. By maintaining two treasuries, one for ministry support and the other for maintenance and operational expenses, financial growth was frustrated.

In 1924, the Mountain Assembly returned to the practice of maintaining an evangelist and the Board of Twelve Elders appointed the Moderator, Stephen Bryant, to this office. That year the treasury operated in the black as Bryant was paid $189.68 from the $255.10 sent to tithe of tithes, and the Moderator was retained as Evangelist for another year.⁴² From 1926 to 1930, the Mountain Assembly returned to the practice of appointing evangelists. Ross received relatively little from the churches over that period, but also paid little out to the evangelists. During Ross's last five years as general treasurer, the Mountain Assembly averaged a mere $66 per year in tithe of tithes and less than $49 per year in expenses. The number of churches fluctuated between 25 and 29 during that span, but more than half sent no tithe of tithes at all, and two of churches who did—Shelburn and Cincinnati—accounted for more than 60 percent of the total receipts.[43]

After the efforts of Bryant, Parks, and Walker to increase financial participation in 1930, the Mountain Assembly introduced a new officer, "a Church Evangel to co-operate with the Field Evangelists and the Board of Elders," and selected Kim Moses "for the coming year." Moses, the son of Thomas D. Moses, was instructed to "see after the destitute churches and assist in obtaining pastors for such."[44] This move improved the effectiveness of the ministry of the field evangelists. In 1931, Morris Woolum, C.L. Price, Curd Walker, and Drue Stanifer reported on their work as field evangelists before Stephen Bryant "followed their reports" with "many rich comments explaining how the world at large needed the cup of salvation tilted into their lives and hearts and how important it is for our neglected churches to be looked closer after and furnished a pastor from our body of ministers."[45] Moses's report so pleased the delegates that they retained him and appointed Woolum and Andrew Long as Church Evangels also.[46] Long was the son-in-law of Andrew Silcox and his father, John Long, had been a delegate at the first assembly.

In 1932, the Mountain Assembly voted to retain the three Church Evangels and ask them not to pastor a church so they could "visit all the local churches, hold meetings and cooperate with the pastors." In addition, the delegates expected them to "bring about reconciliation" any place where they found pastors "to be out of order." In such cases where resolution was not possible, the assembly authorized the Church Evangels to "demand such preacher's credentials and take charge of the church." So, for the first time, the Mountain Assembly officially asserted it had authority over the congregational government of a local church. At the same time, the delegates empowered Parks, Bryant, and Thomas Woods to appoint "two Field Evangels from our number, who are not to be pastors of any church" to "set up churches and call pastors to take care of" them. The three selected William M. Sharp of Elk Valley and C.L. Price of Oneida, Tennessee. Afterward, the assembly prayed over "the Field and Church Evangels, asking God to prosper them in their work the coming year."[47]

A Bow Tied

In addition to Field and Church Evangels, the Mountain Assembly also created Sunday School Evangels for each state in 1933 to "communicate with each other and work in co-operation, one with the other" and "make their report at our next annual Assembly."[48] The three types of evangels functioned as officers of the association throughout the 1930s. Headquarters continued to compensate its centralized polity financially as the tithe of tithes and Sunday school funds increased. By 1939, "practically all churches in the Assembly reported good Sunday Schools in lettering up to the assembly, showing a good work," so the following year the Mountain Assembly voted to discontinue the office.[49] Two years later, the standard resolutions authorizing the offices of Church Evangel and Field Evangel were "annulled," and the Mountain Assembly adopted a measure whereby church planters could apply to headquarters and the "moderator and other proper assembly officials" could grant "assistance" from the "tithe of tithes treasury."[50]

Figure 6.5: Everett Creekmore
c/o CGMA

As the various evangel offices expanded throughout the 1930s, so too did the fields in which they labored and the finances that supported them. In 1930, Ross left the coal mines in Jellico to work in a recently opened mine at Bardo, in Harlan County, Kentucky.[51] After attempting to maintain the tithe of tithes treasury inconveniently away from headquarters, Ross offered "his resignation on account of him being located at a point which is not very handy and for no other reason." Charles "Everett" Creekmore was appointed to replace Ross in 1931 and served as General Treasurer until the office was discontinued in 1944.[52] Creekmore operated a grocery store in Jellico and was a member of the church there.[53] Three of his uncles, Emby King Creekmore, Ransom Dallentine Lovitt, and James Madison Rountree, were delegates at the first Mountain Assembly.[54]

Creekmore's first five years as General Treasurer saw a significant increase in receipts to the tithe of tithes treasury. The number of churches in the Mountain Assembly fluctuated between 32 and 38, and 27 different churches supported the fund at least once during that time with receipts averaging $187 per year.[55] During the 1937-38 assembly year, tithe of tithes receipts reached almost $600, and 80 percent of this was sent from nine churches north of the Ohio River, all started between 1928 and 1937.[56] The directive Bryant, Parks, and Walker emphasized on tithing coincided with the organization's geographic expansion. As members of the Mountain Assembly moved north at the onset of the Great Depression, the jobs they acquired provided the financial means for the churches. These new congregations became the largest fiscal supporters of the Assembly program, and this economic growth contributed to the further development of centralized ecclesiastical polity.

Leaving the Mountains

Just as the expansion of the Louisville and Nashville railroad contributed to the growth of the Mountain Assembly during its first two decades, the Dixie Highway and United States Numbered Highway System took the organization to areas outside the coalfields. By the late 1920s, many Mountain Assembly members who had depended on subsistence farming and coal mining to provide for their families began to look to factories in the north to provide a better life, especially after the stock market crash of 1929 launched the Great Depression. Over the next decade the Mountain Assembly planted churches in Cincinnati, Akron, Cleveland, and Sidney, Ohio, and Detroit and Monroe, Michigan. The good wages their members enjoyed prospered the churches and benefited headquarters through their tithe of tithes support.

Charles Hampton Standifer was working in the coal mines of Bell County, Kentucky when he began pastoring the Mountain Assembly church at Middlesboro in 1918. His father's sister, Mary, and her husband, William Lucas, had recently moved from nearby Claiborne County, Tennessee to Sullivan County, Indiana, to work in the coal mines near Shelburn. Mary had experienced the baptism of the Holy Ghost and longed for a Pentecostal church to be established in Shelburn. As she and a friend prayed and fasted for many days, she felt impressed to write to her nephew to come and hold a revival. Standifer arrived in Shelburn in late spring 1920 "with a couple changes of clothes and a guitar and a bible." The partitions of a two-room shotgun style house on South Buckley Street were removed and the revival commenced. After a slow start, the evangelist "kept on preaching, picking his guitar and singing" until "Retha Mills was baptized with the Holy Ghost and that set the town on fire."[57] One early convert was Morris Edgar Woolum, a neighbor of Retha and Rus Mills and fellow coal miner.[58] Woolum was baptized by Standifer in 1921 and served as the church clerk at Shelburn in 1925.[59]

A Bow Tied

When the revival outgrew the house on South Buckley Street, Standifer rented the Redman's Hall and gained more converts. Morris Street Methodist church had launched its own revival without success before its pastor, George Garbett Peel, another coal miner, approached Standifer about consolidating their efforts. Soon the hall was too small to accommodate the crowds, and property was acquired at 222 W. Maple Street to construct a church building.[60] On October 1, Standifer presented a letter to the 14th Annual Session of the Mountain Assembly from the newly organized church at Shelburn with 42 members. Peel served as church clerk and accompanied Standifer to Jellico to serve as delegates.[61] The revival continued throughout construction of the new building. By the time it was completed in 1925, with 250 members, Shelburn had surpassed Jellico as the largest congregation in the Mountain Assembly.[62] Two years later, tithe of tithes receipts from Shelburn accounted for more than half of the total received at headquarters.[63]

Standifer's success at Shelburn gained notice at the annual convention. In 1923, he was elected Assistant Moderator and to the Board of Twelve Elders. From 1922 to 1927, he preached at least once at each assembly, including the introductory sermon in 1924.[64] After the assembly met in September 1927, however, Standifer decided to leave the Mountain Assembly and join the Church of God (Cleveland). J.L. Goins had been appointed State Overseer for the Church of God in Indiana despite not having any congregations in the state. Goins persuaded Standifer and the Shelburn congregation to join the Church of God.[65] Standifer's nephew, Joseph Drue Stanifer, however, chose to remain in the Mountain Assembly.[66] With about sixty loyal members, another church in Shelburn with Drue Stanifer as pastor sent its letter by mail to the 22nd Mountain Assembly.[67] In 1930, the church relocated five miles east to Hymera.

Drue Stanifer had followed his uncle to Shelburn to work in the coal mines in 1923 and was a delegate from Shelburn at the Mountain Assembly that year.[68] Stanifer and Woolum were listed as ordained ministers from the church at Shelburn in 1928, but Woolum had hitch-hiked to Monroe, Michigan looking for work outside the coal mines

Figure 6.6: Drue Stanifer
c/o CGMA

that July. Finding no Church of God there, he organized one at 1302 East Third Street in September and immediately mailed a letter for inclusion in the Mountain Assembly.[69] Woolum's letter reported nine members, with Hobe Mayes as clerk, and listed two deacons, Jess Allen and Jim Mayes.[70] From the time he started pastoring, Woolum began preaching at the general assembly almost annually for 25 years and was appointed by Bryant, Parks, and Walker to the Board of Twelve Elders in 1930. In 1935, he

Figure 6.7: M.E. Woolum
c/o The Youth Gateway

relocated the church to a stone building at 1024 East First Street and began construction on a new sanctuary at 1009 Franklin Street.[71] The stability he provided the young church enabled them to begin supporting headquarters with tithe of tithes in 1936. Its contribution amounted to just over 10 percent of the total received.[72] Three years later it was the top supporting church in the Mountain Assembly.[73]

Figure 6.8: Monroe Church, 1932
c/o North Monroe Street Church of God

When the Monroe church presented its letter for admittance to the 22nd Annual Assembly, it was joined by a church in Sidney, Ohio, recently organized primarily from Mountain Assembly members who had relocated from McCreary County, Kentucky.[74] When this county was formed in 1912

Figure 6.9: Levi M. White
c/o CGMA

from parts of western Whitley County, the Mountain Assembly had two churches in the new county, Hayes Creek in Creekmore and Laurel Creek in Pine Knot, the latter of which was organized around 1909.[75] Over the next four years, three more churches were started in the vicinity. In 1912, Levi Milton White took charge of the Laurel Creek church and planted a new church at nearby Yamacraw. His wife's cousin, Jesse Shepherd, a brother-in-law to Stephen Bryant, served as its first clerk. Two of Shepherd's sons represented the new church as delegates at the annual assembly.[76] In 1915-1916, C.L. Price planted two churches in McCreary County, Shepherd's Grove at Flat Rock and Solomon's Chapel at Greenwood.[77] Lewis Calvin "Cal" King had been a member at Jellico Creek under Bryant and took charge of the Laurel Creek Church in 1918. The following year, he was called upon to pastor the Yamacraw church when the two merged and relocated to Whitley City.[78] Over the next few years, Shepherd's Grove and Solomon's Chapel dissolved and members gravitated toward Whitley City as that church's leadership alternated annually between White and King.

From 1921 to 1923, King's daughters, Myrtle, Nannie, and Eva, married Ezekiel Snowden, Benjamin Franklin Baker, and George Watters, respectively. Shortly after their marriages, their husbands moved them to Sidney, Ohio, and found work in machine shops and in aluminum manufacturing.[79] In the summer of 1928, this group persuaded Stephen Bryant's eldest son, John Harrison Bryant, that he could find employment in Sidney and that he should organize a church there. The younger Bryant had been pastoring at Whitley City since an automobile struck and killed White on Sunday afternoon, June 7, 1925.[80] Bryant relocated to Sidney long enough to organize a church on the 600 block of Main Street on August 29, 1928. The charter members included Bryant, the three King girls, Elbert and Janie Hughes, Charles and Leona Kendal, and Lou Jones. In November, the church elected Louis Zebedee Woods as its new pastor when he relocated from the Mountain Assembly church in Oneida, Tennessee.[81]

The Sidney church was unable to send delegates to the annual assembly in 1929, so it mailed its letter instead and reported that it was without a pastor after Woods had resigned. In its business session, the Mountain Assembly showed its inclination toward centralized polity by appointing Richard D. Litton to "take pastorial [sic] care of the Sidney, Ohio church."[82] Richard and Mary Litton left the coal mines of Jellico on December 7, 1929, with "a sewing machine, a barrel of canned goods, and a few other small belongings" to assume leadership of the fledgling congregation.[83] The Sidney church grew slowly until a 14-week revival in 1935 saw many converts, and the church's membership doubled that year.[84] As a result, the Sidney church began regular giving to the tithe of tithes fund. Although the congregation experienced numerical setbacks over the next decade, its financial support remained consistent.

Figure 6.10: Richard & Mary Litton
c/o Northtowne CGMA

The church destined to become the greatest source of financial support for the Mountain Assembly's centralized government was formed 90 miles south of Sidney in 1929. The Mountain Assembly church in Cincinnati began with the conversion of Charlie Yeary in 1928.[85] Charlie's father, James Caleb "Cale" Yeary, moved to Whitley County from Hancock County, Tennessee about 1895.[86] In 1901, Cale married Nancy Skeen, the daughter of Julia (Caddell) and John Skeen.[87] Cale and Nancy Yeary embraced the holiness revival that swept through Whitley County, and Nancy was among the first to experience the baptism of the Holy Ghost when the Mountain Assembly became Pentecostal. When George Fore organized the Buffalo Church at Walden, Kentucky in 1916 while pastoring at nearby Gold Bug, the Yearys were among the first members. Cale then donated land upon which to build a church and represented Buffalo as a delegate to the Mountain Assembly the following year.[88] Nancy's untimely death to typhoid fever in 1917 left Cale to care for nine children under the age of 15.[89] In 1927, he remarried Amanda Golden, represented the Buffalo church at the Mountain Assembly one more time, and then moved his family to Goshen township in Clermont County, Ohio.[90]

A Bow Tied

On June 3, 1928, 21-year-old Charlie Yeary dedicated his life to Christ and determined to see a Mountain Assembly church established in Cincinnati. Esom Bert Bryant II had pastored the Yeary family at Buffalo for three years, so Charlie Yeary came to Jellico for the 22nd Annual Assembly on a mission to persuade Bryant to come to the Queen City and start a church. He succeeded. Bryant held a revival at the Church of God (Cleveland) on Third Avenue and Plum Street where he met members of the Williams and Lawson families. Herman David Williams had been converted in Jellico earlier that year and moved to Cincinnati to work in a cold storage plant. He would begin preaching a few years later.[91] Minnie Baird Lawson had numerous relatives in the Mountain Assembly church at Elk Valley when it was organized in 1909.[92] Her husband, Andrew Jackson Lawson, had relocated his family from Elk Valley to Knoxville to work on the railroad just prior to the establishment of the church. By 1920, the family moved to Cincinnati.[93] Their son, Francis Everett Lawson, was the first church clerk when it was organized in early 1929 with twelve members.[94]

Figure 6.11: E.B. Bryant
c/o Philip Bryant

Figure 6.12: Earnie E. Yeary
c/o CGMA

The church began meeting at 303 West Court Street but moved to 711 Freeman Avenue after it began facing persecution. Harassment followed the congregation to 1522 Linn Street when "people threatened to storm the church there," so the church found another building on the corner of Wade Street and Central Avenue.[95] In September 1929, Bryant presented the church's letter to the Mountain Assembly where it was received with "Christian love and fellowship." Charlie Yeary's first cousin, Rachel Creekmore Morgan, had moved to Hamilton County, Ohio earlier that year with her husband, Rev. Matthew Hayden Morgan, to secure better jobs for their sons.[96] Morgan, the half-brother of John Parks, was listed among the ordained ministers on the letter sent from the new Cincinnati church.[97]

As the church in Cincinnati grew, the Yeary family became increasingly involved. Cale Yeary's brother-in-law, Floyd Bays, was elected clerk in 1930.[98] Cale's son, Willis Yeary, worked with E.B. Bryant at that time and finally responded to the pastor's pleadings to attend church and was converted in a revival service that year, as was Cale's brother, Ernest "Earnie" Esco Yeary.[99] The following year, the church elected Willis as the clerk.[100] In its first five years, the Cincinnati church sent Earnie and Cale Yeary, and three of Cale's sons, Ira, Willis, and Charlie, to represent it as delegates at the Mountain Assembly. In 1933, Cale's daughter, Mary Ellen Yeary, married Roy Cornelius, who had been converted in a revival the previous year.[101] Roy's parents, Walter and Hannah Baird Cornelius, had moved their family from Whitley County, Kentucky to Cincinnati in 1929. Hannah had been a member of the church at Jellico Creek and, like Nancy Yeary, was among the first in the Mountain Assembly to experience the baptism of the Holy Ghost. In 1934, Roy's brother, Ernest Cornelius, joined Earnie Yeary as a delegate along with Francis Lawson's younger brother, Clayton, who had just been elected church clerk.[102]

Figure 6.13: Cale Yeary Family, ca. 1916
Charlie, Minnie, Bessie, Nancy, Mary, Clyde, Willis, Cale, Ira, Paris, Elmer
c/o Francis Yeary

That same year, the church reported a membership of 74, making it the seventh largest church in the Mountain Assembly. From its inception also, the church in Cincinnati supported the financial program. In its first year, tithe of tithes receipts from Cincinnati accounted for more than half of the total received at headquarters. In its first five years, the church sent $337.58 of the $654.98 received in tithe of tithes. Its prominence was soon recognized, and the assembly agreed to hold an Elders' meeting there on April 1, 1933.[103] By then, the church had called upon H.D. Williams to pastor. During his tenure, Squire Broyles came from Jellico to hold a revival and helped the church locate an unused Presbyterian church on the corner of Poplar Ave and Dudley Street near Crosley Field. There, the church began to draw even larger crowds.[104]

Revival and its growth did not come without setbacks. Williams left in 1934 to start another church in Goshen township in Clermont County, Ohio and E.B. Bryant was re-elected as pastor. In the enthusiasm of revival, saints in Cincinnati danced, "shouted," and fell in the floor. A faction in the church, led by Morgan, was "opposed to the Spirit knocking people in the floor." Frustrated, Bryant called on the church to "withdraw from the Assembly," and most of the members voted to do so. Within days, however, news reached Jellico and Elder William M. Sharp came to Cincinnati to visit his family who were affected by the decision. In the end, the church remained with the Mountain Assembly and the Morgan faction left. Bryant also left and joined the Church of God (Cleveland). Andrew Long took care of the church until it elected Sharp as its pastor that fall. About the same time, the Presbyterian church wanted its building again, and the church relocated to another storefront mission on Central Avenue.[105]

After five years, commuting to downtown Cincinnati from rural Goshen became an inconvenience for much of the Yeary family. Once again, Charlie Yeary persuaded a pastor to establish a Mountain Assembly church. H.D. Williams and E.B. Bryant organized a church at Goshen with twelve members from the Cincinnati congregation in an old schoolhouse on State Route 28 with Williams as the first pastor. The first clerk was Virgil Lee Akins, one of the members who came from Cincinnati.[106] Akins was born in Wooldridge, Tennessee on September 9, 1902, and began working in the coal mines in Whitley County when he was a teenager.[107] The opportunity to work on the railroad brought him to Cincinnati from the coal mines in Harlan County in the late 1920s. Akins joined Bryant's church and was a delegate to the assembly from Cincinnati in 1933 and from Goshen from 1934 through 1936.[108] During that same time, he also served the Mountain Assembly as a Sunday School Evangel for the state of Ohio.

The Goshen church experienced early setbacks when the owner of the schoolhouse withdrew permission to use the building. For a time, the church rented the town hall for 75 cents each service. Though affordable, it proved an inconvenience as frequent use of the building by the community made hosting revivals impossible. The church grew slowly until Willis Yeary purchased another old schoolhouse and an acre of land for the church on Hill Station Road. The two-room schoolhouse served as both a sanctuary and a parsonage for the pastor's family. The church determined early on that it wanted a full-time pastor and endeavored to realize that vision despite the small membership.[109] From the outset, its pastors insisted the congregation support the tithe of tithes program. In 1937, Goshen trailed only Cincinnati and Monroe as the top tithing churches in the Mountain Assembly. The church's tithe of tithes in the amount of $60.12 represented 12.5 percent of the total received by treasurer that year despite its 18 members representing less than 1 percent of the Mountain Assembly's total from its 37 churches.[110]

After the churches in southwestern Ohio were established, the Mountain Assembly spread to the northeastern corner of the state. At the 26th Annual Mountain Assembly in 1932, the committee on divine services appointed Elder C.L. Price to preach the second morning service. His "real old time sermon" from Matthew 24 on the signs preceding Christ's return must have pressed upon the delegates an imperative for "this gospel of the kingdom" to "be preached in all the world." After the Assembly voted in the morning business session to appoint Price and Will Sharp as Field Evangels for the coming year, Sharp established a new church in Campbell County, Tennessee at Caryville near the church he had established at Lafollette the year before. Price, on the other hand, went further out into the field and established a church in Akron, Ohio.[111]

Charles "McKinley" Baird was born at Pine Knot, Kentucky on June 17, 1898, to Joshua and Nancy Perkins Baird.[112] As young child his parents moved the family to Elk Valley and attended the Mountain Assembly church there.[113] In 1918, McKinley married Maudie Ethel Stanfill at Elk Valley and shortly thereafter migrated to Arkon, Ohio, to obtain work in the burgeoning rubber industry.[114] In 1926, Ethel's brother, Kelly Oscar Stanfill, followed the Bairds to Akron where he and his wife found jobs in rubber manufacturing.[115] In 1925, Cale Yeary's daughter, Minnie, married James Wheeler Smith, a native of Whitley County, and moved to Cleveland, Ohio, where he worked in public transit as a street car conductor and city bus driver.[116] Already accustomed to commuting between Goshen and Cincinnati, driving from Cleveland to Akron to attend the church seemed no inconvenience for the Smiths.

Figure 6.14: *Virgil and Mattie Akins* Figure 6.15: *McKinley Baird*
c/o Jon Walden c/o Jon Walden

When Price established the church in Akron in 1933, Ethel Stanfill served as its first clerk, and Kelly Stanfill represented the church as a delegate at the assembly in Jellico.[117] The following year, Curd Walker, now living in Cleveland, Tennessee, split time between Akron and Adrian, Georgia, pastoring both churches. That year, McKinley Baird and Wheeler Smith joined Stanfill as delegates.[118] In 1935, Stanfill and Smith were joined by Perry Livingston as delegates from Akron. In 1927, Livingston had married Amy Shepherd, a charter member of the Whitley City church and daughter of Jesse Shepherd.[119] In 1935, Perry and Amy were living in Maple Heights and were driving down to Akron for services.[120] That same year, Earnie Yeary moved to Akron to pastor his first church, and Richard Litton moved from Sidney to pastor it in 1936.[121] In just three years, the church had grown to 35 members, and in 1936 it was the top giving church to the tithe of tithe fund.[122] The following year, the church selected McKinley Baird to be the pastor. By then, Baird had also already realized his vision to begin a work in Cleveland.

Akron's deacon, Wheeler Smith, lived in the Collinwood neighborhood on the east side of Cleveland and commuted to Akron for church services.[123] In late spring of 1936, a tent revival commenced at a vacant lot not far from Smith's home. Earnie Yeary and McKinley Baird came up from Akron and preached in some of the services that lasted for months. In October, Yeary and Baird organized a church with about ten members.[124] In addition to the Bairds, the Smiths, and Perry Livingston, Virgil and Mattie Akins joined the church after having just moved from Goshen. Another charter member was Frieda Steffani Yeary, the wife of Cale Yeary's son, Elmer. Elmer Benjamin

An Informal Triumvirate

Yeary had moved with his sister and brother-in-law in 1925 and found work as the manager of a Cleveland grocery store. He married Frieda in 1929, and she was the church's first convert in 1936.[125]

The church was able to rent a building on the corner of East 152nd Street and Aspinwall Avenue. The storefront was a duplex, with the church on one side and a bar on the other. Living quarters above the sanctuary provided space to accommodate the pastor's family.[126] Baird, however, chose not to move to Cleveland and, after commuting from Akron for almost a year, chose to return to that church to assume its pastorate.[127] The Cleveland church then elected Akins to be its second pastor after his ordination in Cincinnati earlier that year.[128] At the 31st Annual Mountain Assembly in September 1937, Smith and Livingston presented a letter from the church in Cleveland requesting membership in the Mountain Assembly. "After the letter was read and the usual investigation made, it was moved in order" to "accept into our fellowship the Church of God of Cleveland, O." before the "the usual hand of Christian love and fellowship was given the messengers of the new church."[129] The church was an immediate supporter of the financial program of the assembly and had sent in $20.91 for tithe of tithes that year.[130]

The Mountain Assembly's third decade saw it significantly expand outside the coal fields. In addition to the new churches at Hymera, Monroe, Sidney, Cincinnati, Goshen, Akron, and Cleveland, three more churches were started north of the Ohio River. In 1925, Thomas Sylvester Woods from the Siler's Chapel Church left Whitley County for Kokomo, Indiana, to become a vacuum cleaner salesman. With no Pentecostal churches in the area, he began attending Baptist churches and, in 1928, was asked to pastor Rock Prairie Separate Baptist Church. Forced to resign over his preaching of Pentecostal doctrine, he organized a Mountain Assembly church near Sharpsville with another twelve members who followed him in December 1929.[131] Joshua Baird also left Elk Valley for Indiana in 1925. Baird settled in Washington County in Oxonia just outside of the town of Salem. Nine years later, he established a church there with eleven members and brought its letter the annual Mountain

Figure 6.16: Thomas Woods
c/o CGMA

Figure 6.17: Joshua Baird
c/o CGMA

Assembly.[132] While pastoring in Monroe, Michigan in 1935, Morris Woolum established a church with eleven members on Roosevelt Avenue in Detroit. He installed W.W. Colvin as the pastor for the first year before Abraham Hubert Tribble began pastoring in 1936.[133]

Though the membership of these ten northern churches accounted for under 25 percent of the total membership of the 38 churches who sent letters to the 30th Mountain Assembly, their financial contribution represented more than 85 percent of the total tithe of tithes for the fiscal year that ended that September.[134] Thus, the expansion of the Mountain Assembly outside the mountains of southeastern Kentucky and northeastern Tennessee accelerated the growth of a central headquarters at Jellico. The ease of travel in the age of the automobile and United States Highway System connected the northern churches as well as the railroad had connected the first generation. The northern churches in the 1930s exchanged pastors and members as freely as the churches in the coalfields had done so in the 1910s and 1920s. For example, within the decade, Virgil Akins had been a member at Cincinnati, Goshen, and Cleveland, and later pastored Monroe. Earnie Yeary had been a member at Cincinnati and Goshen, and pastored Akron and Monroe. Roy Cornelius had been a member at Cincinnati and later pastored Goshen and Monroe. Clayton Lawson pastored Sidney and Cincinnati. Richard Litton pastored Sidney and Akron. Coy Laws pastored Sidney and Goshen. By 1937, it became apparent that the Mountain Assembly had outgrown the regional association of independent congregations of like faith patterned after the South Union Association of United Baptists. The Mountain Assembly of the Churches of God was becoming the Church of God of the Mountain Assembly.

Leadership Transition

In 1933, Curd Walker moved from Vidalia, Georgia to Cleveland, Tennessee, but continued to pastor Johnson's Chapel. The move facilitated travel between Adrian and the other churches he pastored and evangelized during the next five years and kept him close enough to Saxton to visit his eldest two daughters who had married and remained in Whitley County.[135] In January 1937, Walker's wife, Dosha, was diagnosed with a sarcoma of the hip.[136] By September her condition had worsened to the point she was unable to attend the 31st Annual Mountain Assembly in Jellico. Her husband "came only for a few minutes to request prayer for his wife."[137] She died the following month and was returned to Saxton for burial.[138] Perhaps Dosha Walker's repute as a prophetess influenced the way her words were interpreted in her final days. Recognizing that her death was imminent, she conveyed to Curd her desire for him to marry Lula Belle Johnson after her passing.[139] Johnson was the 19-year-old daughter of Johnson Chapel's founder and church clerk. The following November, the 61-year-old Walker married Johnson six weeks before her 21st birthday.[140]

Walker's courtship with Johnson occurred simultaneously with concerns about his government in the local church. While living in Saxton in 1917, Walker developed a "discipline" for church membership which included guidelines for conduct and dress. The rules included prohibitions against tobacco, jewelry, makeup, and immodest dress, just as the teachings of the Church of God Mountain Assembly. Walker also banned visiting "bathing pools, beaches, card parties, box suppers, ball games" and "picture shows." Family life was also strictly governed. Eloping was forbidden as "runaway weddings" did not allow the "sacred vow in the presence of some of the brothers or sisters in the Lord at the hands of some Godly minister." Birth control was also prohibited.[141] When he became pastor of Johnson's Chapel, the church had also been observing the "Discipline of the Holiness Baptist Church," its "articles of religion," and its doctrinal maintenances.[142] In relative isolation in southeastern Georgia from the rest of the Mountain Assembly, Walker's adoption of a different set of rules went unnoticed. In 1937, his home church at Saxton elected him again as its pastor for the first time in eight years. When Walker attempted to introduce his new regulations at Saxton, his proximity to Jellico invited the scrutiny of his fellow Elders. At the Assembly in 1938, the delegates voted that Walker "be called to order for deviating from our minutes discipline and teaching another contrary thereto." When he refused correction, the delegates removed him from the Board of Twelve Elders and chose Earnie Yeary to replace him. Later that week, the Mountain Assembly agreed to send the Elder Board to Adrian and Saxton to investigate those congregations regarding their "rules of discipline." Johnson Chapel chose to withdraw from the Mountain Assembly, and Saxton elected John Parks as its pastor for the coming year.[143]

The Mountain Assembly's unofficial triumvirate was reduced to a pair after the 1938 Assembly. Leadership by the duo of Stephen Bryant and John Parks came to an end on February 25, 1939, however, when Bryant passed away at the age of 70.[144] When the 33rd Annual Mountain Assembly opened in September, the delegates acknowledged that "all missed from our midst our beloved brother Moderator S.N. Bryant whom God in his infinite wisdom had called to his eternal home," but felt encouraged in the assurance that he was "with God and the Angels." The Assistant Moderator, Andrew Long, called the delegates to order for business and they elected him to succeed Bryant and elected Bryant's son, John Harrison Bryant, as the new Assistant Moderator. Bryant's vacancy on the Board of Twelve Elders was filled by Joshua Baird.[145]

Figure 6.18: Stephen Bryant
c/o CGMA

After Walker's defection and Bryant's death, the 78-year-old Parks recognized his ministry was nearing its completion. He chose not to run for re-election as pastor of the Jellico church that year, and the church selected Earnie Yeary to succeed him. At the Assembly, Parks dismissed the second morning's business session.[146] The following year the committee on divine services appointed him to preach the Sunday morning service, but he was too feeble to attend and was replaced by the moderator.[147] At the 35th Mountain Assembly on September 6, 1941, Parks fulfilled the appointment of the committee and preached from Colossians 4 and referred to his life's work "giving out good instructions to the saints and the ministry." He testified that in all his years of ministry, "that he had never seen the hour or day that he wanted to turn back." After fulfilling a request to sing "There's a Beautiful Home," the congregation "wishing to bless Brother Parks gave him a free-will offering of $52.46." It was the last sermon he preached at the general assembly. The following day, the last assembly sermons were preached in the tabernacle he had helped build twenty years earlier. "The tabernacle was filled to its capacity," and the Mountain Assembly recognized it had to act if it intended to accommodate the growth of the annual convention. In one of the final orders of business, the delegates directed the trustees to "enlarge the present tabernacle and make necessary improvements." The trustee chairman, Lewis Sharp, instead reported of the board's plans to build a new tabernacle.[148]

At a cost of just over $6000, the new tabernacle was completed when the 36th Mountain Assembly returned to Jellico, and Morris Woolum preached the introductory sermon on September 2, 1942. Two days later, "the people were glad on this day to see Elder J. H. Parks come into the new Tabernacle and stood up in token that they were pleased that God had blessed Brother Parks to live to see another Assembly."[149] On August 7, 1943, Parks "passed away at his home" in Jellico at the age of 82, and the Mountain Assembly remembered him for being "sound in his advice and exemplary in his deportment. He died in the Lord and his works will follow him, and his influence will reach out through the years. The world is made better by men like this man."[150] At the Assembly the following month, the delegates filled his vacancy on the Board of Twelve Elders with Luther Gibson.[151] Gibson had replaced Earnie Yeary as pastor at Jellico two years earlier and officiated the funeral of John Parks.[152]

Figure 6.19: John Parks & Ernie Yeary
c/o Allen Smith

Conclusion

The departure of four elected officials to the Church of God (Cleveland) from 1922 to 1925 left a leadership vacuum in the Mountain Assembly. For most of the next decade and a half, Bryant, Parks, and Walker, effectively influenced the direction of the association as its government became more centralized in significant ways. A new vacuity occurred between 1938 and 1943. This leadership void was filled by a group of seven in their various capacities. Andrew Long retained the office of Moderator until 1944 and during that time was assisted by John Bryant, Kim Moses, and Clayton Lawson. In 1940, J.E. Hatfield was elected Clerk and was assisted by Ira Moses, the grandson of John Parks. These six and Gibson provided leadership for the Mountain Assembly for the next three decades.

By the time Parks and Bryant died, they could see that what they organized had become something other than an association of independent congregationally governed churches. Elements of centralized government included associational officers with authority over local churches and a financial system that depended on the stewardship of the individual churches. The Mountain Assembly had also outgrown the coal regions of southeastern Kentucky and northeastern Tennessee, made possible by the mass production of the automobile and the development of a national highway system. While significantly more centralized, the Mountain Assembly still lacked the clear episcopal structure of the Church of God (Cleveland). Shortly after the death of John Parks, however, the new leadership of the Mountain Assembly would propose a bold new governmental transformation modeled after the group A.J. Tomlinson once led.

Figure 6.20: J.C. Taylor automobile, ca. 1917
From left to right: Emma Thomas, Sallie Taylor, S.N. Bryant, Newt Parks, John Parks, Savannah Taylor, J.C. Taylor, Daniel Thomas, Haywood Taylor, Hattie Privett. Children: James Thomas, Virgil Creekmore.

c/o Roxanna Chitwood

The Taylors presumably owned one of the first automobiles in the CGMA, but it would be another decade or two before highway travel spread the organization outside the mountains of Appalachia.

---

[1] Walker, "Just a Bit of History," 1.

[2] Janus Jones, *Happenings*, 52.

[3] Walker, "History," 2-7.

[4] Parks, 190.

[5] CGMA, *Minutes* (1907), 2.

[6] CGMA, *Minutes* (1912), 2-3.

[7] CGMA, *Minutes* (1913), 3.

[8] CGMA, *Minutes* (1915), 6.

[9] CGMA, *Minutes* (1916), 5.

[10] CGMA, *Minutes* (1930), 4.

[11] Holiness Baptist Association (HBA), *Minutes of the Thirty-Second Annual Session of the Holiness Baptist Association* (n.p.: by the association, 1925), statistical table.

[12] HBA, *Minutes of the Thirty-Fourth Annual Session of the Holiness Baptist Association* (n.p.: by the association, 1927), preface.

[13] CGMA, *Minutes* (1927), 11.

[14] HBA, *Minutes* (1927), 1-3.

[15] CGMA, *Minutes* (1928), 3, 8.

[16] CGMA, *Minutes* (1929), 5; CGMA, *Minutes of the Mountain Assembly of the Churches of God (Incorporated): The Thirty-First Annual Assembly of the Churches of God* (Jellico, TN: CGMA, 1937), cover.

[17] Clyde Edell Johnson, note found in her bible after her death, now in the possession of Stephen Curd Walker, Durango, CO.

[18] CGMA, *Minutes* (1930), 2.

[19] CGMA, *Minutes* (1922), preface.

[20] CGMA, *Minutes* (1928), 3; CGMA, *Minutes* (1926), 6.

[21] CGMA, *Minutes* (1931), 3; CGMA, *Minutes of the Mountain Assembly of the Churches of God (Incorporated): The Thirtieth Annual Assembly of the Churches of God* (Jellico, TN: CGMA, 1936), 9.

[22] CGMA, *Minutes* (1931), 3; CGMA, *Minutes* (1936), 6.

[23] CGMA, *Minutes* (1930), 3.

[24] Ibid., 4, 10.

[25] Ibid., 7-8, 10.

[26] Ibid., 10-11. This quorum of three was amended to nine in 9 in 1938 and to the full twelve or "as near that number as possible" in 1944. CGMA, *Minutes of the Mountain Assembly of the Churches of God (Incorporated): The Thirty-Second Annual Assembly of the Churches of God* (Jellico, TN: CGMA, 1938), 10; CGMA, *Minutes* (1944), 6.

[27] CGMA, *Minutes* (1930), 5-6.

[28] Ibid., 6, 17.

[29] CGMA, *Minutes* (1915), 6.

[30] CGMA, *Minutes* (1916), 5.

[31] CGMA, *Minutes* (1917), 4.

[32] CGMA, *Minutes* (1918), 4.

[33] Ibid., 5.

34 CGMA, *Minutes* (1917), 4.

35 CGMA, *Minutes* (1919), 4-5.

36 Ibid., 5.

37 CGMA, *Minutes* (1920), 5.

38 CGMA, *Minutes* (1922), 6, preface.

39 Jellico Church Minutes, 78.

40 CGMA, *Minutes* (1922), preface.

41 CGMA, *Minutes* (1924), 14.

42 CGMA, *Minutes* (1925), 13-14.

43 See CGMA *Minutes* (1927-1931).

44 CGMA, *Minutes* (1930), 10.

45 CGMA, *Minutes* (1931), 4.

46 Ibid., 7.

47 CGMA, *Minutes of the Mountain Assembly of the Churches of God (Incorporated): The Twenty-Sixth Annual Assembly of the Churches of God* (Jellico, TN: CGMA, 1932), 4-5.

48 CGMA, *Minutes of the Mountain Assembly of the Churches of God (Incorporated): The Twenty-Seventh Annual Assembly of the Churches of God* (Jellico, TN: CGMA, 1933), 5.

49 CGMA, *Minutes of the Mountain Assembly of the Churches of God (Incorporated): The Thirty-Third Annual Assembly of the Churches of God* (Jellico, TN: CGMA, 1939), 21; CGMA, *Minutes* (1940), 14.

50 CGMA, *Minutes of the Mountain Assembly of the Churches of God (Incorporated): Thirty-Sixth Annual Assembly* (1942), 11.

51 1930 United States Census, Harlan County, Kentucky, s.v. "Everett H. Ross," Ancestry.com; CGMA, *Minutes* (1930), 19.

52 CGMA, *Minutes* (1931), 9-10; CGMA, *Minutes* (1944), 14.

53 1930 United States Census, Campbell County, Tennessee, s.v. "Everett Creekmore," Ancestry.com.

54 CGMA, *Minutes* (1907), 2.

55 See CGMA *Minutes* (1932-1936).

56 CGMA, *Minutes* (1938), 16.

57 Sam W. Edmunds, *Hoosier Roots: A History of the Church of God in Indiana* ([Greenwood, In.]: [Indiana Church of God], n.d), 10.

58 1920 United States Census, Sullivan County, Indiana, s.v. "Morris Woolim," Ancestry.com.

59 Gibson, 17; CGMA, *Minutes* (1925), 6.

60 Edmunds, 10.

61 CGMA, *Minutes* (1920), 4, 7.

62 CGMA, *Minutes* (1925), statistical table.

63 CGMA, *Minutes* (1927), 12.

64 See CGMA *Minutes* (1922-1927).

65 J.L. Goins to H.L. Chesser, February 5, 1952, Goins file.

66 Drue Stanifer dropped the "d" from his family name in the 1920s.

67 CGMA, *Minutes* (1928), 10-11.

68 CGMA, *Minutes* (1923), 6, statistical table.

69 Ora Moore, *40th Year Anniversary Church of God Mountain Assembly of Monroe, Michigan* (Monroe, MI: Monroe Church of God Mountain Assembly, 1968), 1; Undated biographical sketch of Morris Woolum, Monroe County Historical Society.

70 CGMA, *Minutes* (1928), 12. James Milton Mayes and his second cousin, Hobart, were born in Claiborne County, Tennessee and had come to Monroe to find employment in the paper mills. See 1930 United States Census, Monroe County, Michigan, s.v. "Jim Mayer," and 1930 United States Census, Monroe County, Michigan, s.v. "Hobart Mayes," Ancestry.com. Jesse Allen was a native of Laurel County, Kentucky, but married Ollie Whitaker in Claiborne County in 1915 before relocating to Monroe to work in the paper mill. See 1930 United States Census, Monroe County, Michigan, s.v. "Jessie Allen" and Tennessee, Marriage Records, 1780-2002, s.v. "Jess Allen," Ancestry.com.

71 Moore, 1.

72 CGMA, *Minutes* (1936), 10.

73 CGMA, *Minutes* (1939), 16-17.

74 CGMA, *Minutes* (1929), 3.

75 Laurel Creek is listed in the 1910 Minute Book with 30 members, but there is no motion in the business to receive any new church into the association. As the church is not listed in the 1908 Minute Book and the 1909 Minute Book is nonextant, it appears safe to assume the church was organized before the 1909 Assembly rather than after.

76 CGMA, *Minutes* (1912), 2.

77 CGMA, *Minutes* (1915), 3; CGMA, *Minutes* (1916), statistical table.

78 CGMA, *Minutes* (1919), 3.

79 1930 United States Census, Shelby County, Ohio, s.v. "Myrtle Snowden," 1930 United States Census, Shelby County, Ohio, s.v. "Nannie L Baker," and 1930 United States Census, Shelby County, Ohio, s.v. "Eva Waters," Ancestry.com.

80 James E. Prewitt, unpublished book manuscript, ca 1986, now in the possession of Alfred Newton, Milford, OH.

81 John Longsworth, *History of the Sycamore Street Church of God* (Sidney, OH: Sycamore Street Church of God, 1949), 19.

82 CGMA, *Minutes* (1929), 8, 10.

83 Longsworth, 19.

84 Ibid.; CGMA, *Minutes* (1935), statistical table.

85 Charlie T. Yeary, "Testimonials," *GH* 1, no. 6 (December 1942): 3; "History of Our Church," *GH* 34, no. 10 (September 1973): 5.

⁸⁶ 1900 United States Census, Whitley County, Kentucky, s.v. "Adam Yeary," Ancestry.com.

⁸⁷ Kentucky, County Marriage Records, 1783-1965, s.v. "Nancy J Skuns," Ancestry.com. John Skeen and his son, Thomas Breckinridge Skeen, were ministers of the Buffalo Church of the Mount Zion Baptist Association, but several of Julia's relatives were delegates at the first Mountain Assembly in 1907. Mt. Zion Baptist Association, *Minutes of the Twenty-Third Annual Session of the Mt. Zion Baptist Association* (n.p.: by the association, 1907), 17. George Caddell, Lee Caddell, James Rountree, and Milton Ross were related by blood or marriage to Julia Caddell Skeen.

⁸⁸ Deed of Conveyance, *Whitley County Deed Book* 106, December 19, 1923, 84, Whitley County Court House, Williamsburg, KY; CGMA, *Minutes* (1917), 3.

⁸⁹ Kentucky, Death Records, 1852-1965, s.v. "Nancy Yeary" and 1920 United States Census, Whitley County, Kentucky, s.v. "James C. Yeary," Ancestry.com.

⁹⁰ CGMA, *Minutes* (1927), 5.

⁹¹ Personal Data sheet, Herman D. Williams file, Central Files and Records of the Church of God, Cleveland, Tennessee.; 1930 United States Census, Hamilton County, Ohio, s.v. "Herman Williams," Ancestry.com.

⁹² Lynch, *History of Elk Valley*, 61.

⁹³ 1910 United States Census, Campbell County, Tennessee, s.v. "Andrew J. Lawson" and 1920 United States Census, Hamilton County, Ohio, s.v. "Andrew Lawson," Ancestry.com.

⁹⁴ "History of [Cincinnati] Church," 5; Yeary, "Testimonials [Cincinnati]," 3; Ruby Shelton, "The Beginning of the Towne Street Church of God," undated letter in the possession of Debbie Shelton Cochran, Cincinnati, OH, 1.

⁹⁵ Shelton, 1.

⁹⁶ Kentucky, County Marriage Records, 1783-1965, s.v. "Rachel Creekmore," Ancestry.com.

⁹⁷ CGMA, *Minutes* (1929), 4-5, 12.

⁹⁸ CGMA, *Minutes* (1930), 15.

⁹⁹ Shelton, 1.

¹⁰⁰ CGMA, *Minutes* (1932), 15.

¹⁰¹ Kim Cornelius-Walden, Facebook message to author, December 18, 2019.

¹⁰² CGMA, *Minutes* (1934), 17.

¹⁰³ CGMA, *Minutes* (1933), 6.

¹⁰⁴ Shelton, 3.

¹⁰⁵ Ibid., 4-7.

¹⁰⁶ "Goshen Church of God," *GH* 34, no. 5 (May 1973): 7; CGMA, *Minutes* (1934), statistical table.

¹⁰⁷ Tennessee, Delayed Birth Records, 1869-1909, s.v. "Virgil Lee Akins" and 1920 United States Census, Whitley County, Kentucky, s.v. "Virgil Akins," Ancestry.com.

¹⁰⁸ Akins' wife, Mattie, was a first cousin to Bryant's wife, Fanny Moses Bryant.

¹⁰⁹ "Goshen," 7-8.

110 CGMA, *Minutes* (1937), 14-15, statistical table.

111 CGMA, *Minutes* (1932), 4-5; CGMA, *Minutes* (1933), 17.

112 U.S., World War I Draft Registration Cards, 1917-1918, s.v. "Charles Mc Kinley Baird," Ancestry.com.

113 Baird's maternal uncle, William Perkins, was a delegate from Elk Valley to the 1912 Assembly. His father represented the Elk Valley Church for most of the decade and was selected as one of the first twelve Elders of the Mountain Assembly in 1923.

114 Tennessee, Marriage Records, 1780-2002, s.v. "McKinely Baird" and 1920 United States Census, Summit County, Ohio, s.v. "Mckinley Baird," Ancestry.com.

115 Stanfill's wife, Ethel, was the daughter of Elk Valley's longtime clerk, Aaron Baird. Tennessee, Marriage Records, 1780-2002, s.v. "Kellie Stanfill" and 1930 United States Census, Summit County, Ohio, s.v. "Kelly Stanfill," Ancestry.com.

116 1930 United States Census, Cuyahoga County, Ohio, s.v. "James W. Smith," Ancestry.com.

117 CGMA, *Minutes* (1933), 17.

118 CGMA, *Minutes* (1934), 16-18, 20.

119 Amy had moved to the Cleveland area two years earlier with her first husband, John Mark White, the son of Whitley City pastor, Levi White. After their divorce, White returned to McCreary County.

120 "[Amy J. Livingston] Obituary," *GH* 2, no. 11 (May 1944): 3; CGMA, *Minutes of the Mountain Assembly of the Churches of God (Incorporated): The Twenty-Ninth Annual Assembly of the Churches of God* (Jellico, TN: CGMA, 1935), 19; 1920 United States Census, McCreary County, Kentucky, s.v. "Mark White" and 1940 United States Census, Cuyahoga County, Ohio, s.v. "Perry Livingston," Ancestry.com.

121 CGMA, *Minutes* (1935), 19; CGMA, *Minutes* (1936), 21. Litton's wife, Mary, was the maternal aunt of Ethel Baird Stanfill.

122 CGMA, *Minutes* (1935), 10, statistical table.

123 1930 United States Census, Cuyahoga County, Ohio, s.v. "James W. Smith," Ancestry.com.

124 "The Aspinwall Church of God," *GH* 35, no. 6 (June 1974): 7.

125 1930 United States Census, Cuyahoga County, Ohio, s.v. "Elmer B. Yeary," Ancestry.com; Glenn Yeary, Facebook message to author, December 18, 2019.

126 Aspinwall Church, "About us," church website, accessed December 19, 2019, http://www.aspinwallchurch.com/about-us.html

127 CGMA, *Minutes* (1937), 23.

128 Ibid., 16, 25.

129 Ibid., 5, 25.

130 Ibid., 15.

131 1930 United States Census, Tipton County, Indiana, s.v. "Thomas S. Woods," Ancestry.com; CGMA, *Minutes* (1930), 15; "Nevada, Indiana," *GH* 57, no. 12 (December 1996): 4.

132 1930 United States Census, Washington County, Indiana, s.v. "Joshua Baird," Ancestry.com; CGMA, *Minutes* (1934), 18, statistical table.

133 CGMA, *Minutes* (1935), 20-21; CGMA, *Minutes* (1936), 21.

134 CGMA, *Minutes* (1937), 14-15, statistical table.

135 1930 United States Census, Whitley County, Kentucky, s.v. "Elsie Davis" and 1930 United States Census, Whitley County, Kentucky, s.v. "Clara Shelton," Ancestry.com.

136 Tennessee, Death Records, 1908-1958, s.v. "Mrs. Dosha Walker," Ancestry.com.

137 CGMA, *Minutes* (1937), 10.

138 https://www.findagrave.com/memorial/122986680.

139 Polly Byers, Facebook message to author, December 22, 2019.

140 Clyde Edell Johnson, family bible record found, now in the possession of Stephen Curd Walker, Durango, CO.

141 Curd Walker, [Church Discipline], Johnson Chapel Holiness Church of God, Adrian, GA.

142 HBA, *Minutes* (1927), 13-17.

143 CGMA, *Minutes* (1938), 10, 14, statistical table.

144 Kentucky, Death Records, 1852-1965, s.v. "Stephen N. Bryant," Ancestry.com.

145 CGMA, *Minutes* (1939), 4-6, 12-13.

146 Ibid., 25, 9.

147 CGMA, *Minutes* (1940), 17.

148 CGMA, *Minutes* (1941), 7-8, 11-12.

149 CGMA, *Minutes* (1942), 17, 20, 23.

150 John Edward Hatfield, "John Parks, Beloved Minister, Called By Death," *GH* 2, no. 3 (September 1943): 1, 8.

151 CGMA, *Minutes of the Church of God of the Mountain Assembly Incorporated: Forty-Third Annual Assembly* (Jellico, TN: CGMA, 1943), 9.

152 CGMA, *Minutes* (1941), 14; Hatfield, "John Parks," 8.

7

Toward a Denominational Government

Introduction

Seven ministers rose to prominence in the wake of the first generation's passing to guide the Church of God Mountain Assembly in the 1940s. J.H. Bryant, A.J. Long, Kim Moses, J.E. Hatfield, Luther Gibson, Clayton Lawson, and Ira Moses inspired a new generation and faced new challenges. The formation of a new monthly periodical and the creation of ladies' and youth auxiliaries in the local churches promised to make the CGMA more like the Church of God (Cleveland) in practice. In addition, a new polity, patterned more closely after the Church of God, was implemented in 1944. The Mountain Assembly completed its shift from an association of independent congregations to a unified church denomination with a strong centralized government. While the Mountain Assembly had initiated an episcopal polity de jure, its de facto government was still very much independent and congregational.

The Second Generation of Leadership

When the 37th Annual Mountain Assembly opened on September 1, 1943, J.H. Bryant was the only remaining delegate from the first assembly in 1907. Bryant bridged the first generation of leadership with the second. He was an original delegate, as well as the son and grandson of original delegates. Kim Moses and Andrew Long were sons of original delegates, and Ira Moses was a grandson of John Parks. J.E. Hatfield, Luther Gibson, and Clayton Lawson were converted as adults. These seven played vital roles in the leadership and development of the Mountain Assembly.

John Harrison Bryant was born at Sheep Creek, Kentucky, on October 12, 1888 to Mary Rebecca (Davenport) and Stephen Nathan Bryant. Shortly after his birth, his father began preaching in the United Baptist Church at Wolf Creek. In January 1905, John was converted and was sanctified later that year when his father began preaching Wesleyan Holiness. In February 1909, he experienced the baptism of the Holy Ghost.[1] In 1914, John married Martha Jane Meadows of Ryan's Creek and moved to nearby Yamacraw, where he operated a general store and attended the Mountain Assembly church that his uncle had helped start there two years earlier. John stayed with the congregation when it relocated to Whitley City in 1919 and served as its clerk in 1923 when his father was elected pastor.[2] In February 1925, John was appointed postmaster of the new post office at Hill Top.[3]

Bryant continued to serve as clerk at Whitley City under Pastor Kim Moses and began preaching that same year.[4] He was ordained in 1926 and was called upon to pastor Whitley City the following year. After Bryant began to pastor, he decided to "put all [his] time into the work of the Lord" and gave up his jobs at the grocery store and post office.[5] His ordination and commitment to full-time ministry earned him an appointment to preach at the 21st Annual Mountain Assembly in 1927, and he became a frequent convention speaker for the next 35 years.[6] He was appointed to the Elder Board when it was reconstituted in 1930 and was elected Assistant Moderator after his father's death in 1939.[7]

Figure 7.1: J.H. Bryant *Figure 7.2: Kim Moses*
c/o Jeff Bryant   c/o the Moses Family

Kim Moses was born at Pleasant View, Kentucky on October 11, 1890 to Delphia (Strunk) and Thomas Deberry Moses.[8] His parents were converted shortly after Kim's birth at the United Baptist Church at Little Wolf Creek and were baptized by John Parks.[9] Tom Moses was among the seven ministers disfellowshipped from the South Union Association for preaching the holiness doctrine in 1905 and was a delegate at the first Assembly in 1907. On October 5, 1907, just days before the first Mountain Assembly met at Little Wolf Creek, Kim was united in marriage to Lucy Moses, a second-cousin, in Campbell County, Tennessee.[10] Kim was converted in August 1912, and was baptized with the Holy Ghost the following May.[11] Moses had begun preaching by the time he attended his first assembly as a delegate in 1917.[12] The following year, he began pastoral ministry assisting Stephen Bryant at Sheep Creek and in his home church at Little Wolf Creek.[13] In his first fifteen years of pastoral ministry, Moses pastored a dozen churches, sometimes as many as four congregations at a time.

The delegates at the 13th Mountain Assembly recognized Moses's spiritual maturity in 1919 and appointed him to the first Board of Twelve Elders and again when it was reconstituted in 1923. At the last reconstitution of the Board in 1930, however, Moses was not reappointed; but he was elected to fill the vacancy of Drue Stanifer when his eldership was revoked for tobacco use in 1938.[14] On September 2, 1925, delegates to the 19th Mountain Assembly elected Moses as the Assistant Moderator and the committee on divine services appointed him to preach that night for the first time at the assembly.[15] Moses preached at another eleven assemblies over the next twenty years. The Assembly elected him to assist Moderator Stephen Bryant another four years and twice elected him to assist Moderator Andrew Long.

Andrew Johnson Long was born in Whitley County, Kentucky, on August 21, 1892 to Sally (Lay) and John Long.[16] His parents were converted in the fall of 1903 and baptized by John Parks into the Baptist church at Zion Hill one year before the congregation was expelled from the South Union Association.[17] In October 1907, John Long represented Zion Hill as a delegate at the first assembly.[18] At the age of 17, Andrew was converted and joined the church at Zion Hill.[19] He represented the church as a delegate at the Sixth Annual Mountain Assembly in 1912.[20] The following year, the church ordained him as a deacon and elected him as church clerk.[21] At the age of 20, Long married Dessie Silcox, the daughter of Andrew J. Silcox, and was ordained into gospel ministry by John Parks and Kim Moses.[22] On February 26, 1916, Andrew and Dessie transferred their membership to Lower Elk Valley with Pastor Parks where it remained for seven years.[23] During this time, Long began his pastoral ministry. His first co-pastorate with Kim Moses in 1921 was at a newly constituted church at Upper Rock Creek, Kentucky, not far from his home church at Zion Hill.[24] Two years later, Long transferred his membership to Emlyn where it remained the rest of his life.[25] Long and Moses launched a new church at the coal camp in Packard, Kentucky in 1925 and assumed the pastorate of Siler's Chapel nearby the following year.[26]

In 1928, the delegates at the 22nd Mountain Assembly elected Long to the office of Assistant Clerk, and the committee on divine services selected him to preach. The "saints" were "refreshed with great joy," as Long "preached the word with power" using John 3:16 as his text.[27] Over the next 18 assemblies, Long returned to the pulpit 12 more times. In 1930, he was selected to the newly constituted Board of Twelve Elders, and he served as Assistant Moderator to John Parks and Stephen Bryant. After Bryant's death in 1939, Long was elected to his first term as Moderator.[28]

Figure 7.3: A.J. Long
c/o CGMA

Figure 7.4: Ira H. Moses
c/o North Monroe Street CGMA

Ira Hansford Moses was born just outside of Jellico in Whitley County, Kentucky on May 20, 1905 to Jalie (Parks) and William Elliott Moses. His mother was the second child of John and Rachel Parks, but he was their first grandchild. His father was an uncle of Lucy (Mrs. Kim) Moses and was a delegate from Little Wolf Creek beginning in 1913.[29] On July 31, 1927, Ira married Hester Marshall in Akron, Ohio, where he had relocated to find work.[30] After the birth of their first child, Vida on April 26, 1928, Moses returned to Whitley County to work in the coal mines.[31] Their first son, Hubert, was born in Jellico on July 19, 1930, but died from acute colitis that October.[32] On January 10, 1931, Moses was converted at a revival conducted by his grandfather and Kim Moses at the Tabernacle in Jellico. Two days later, Hester was converted.[33] On Easter Sunday, April 5, Ira and Hester were baptized and joined the Jellico church.[34] Two years later, he was elected clerk of the Jellico church and began assisting his grandfather at the general assembly by making announcements and directing visitors to lodging.[35]

In 1937, Moses began serving the church as a delegate, and two years later was elected by the Mountain Assembly as the Assistant Clerk.[36] The delegates elected him to this office three more times over the next four years. Moses began preaching about 1935, but was not ordained until July 25, 1943, by Luther Gibson, Andrew Long, and Kim Moses.[37] At the assembly, six weeks later, the divine services committee selected him to preach for the first time, and he preached from Proverbs 9:1 on the importance of wisdom and emphasized the importance of cooperation: "If we work together our work will connect in the building of God." Moses assumed his first pastorate that year in the coal camp at Kenvir, Kentucky.[38]

John Edward Hatfield was born in Wooldridge, Tennessee on April 30, 1904 to Hannah (Douglas) and Alexander Hatfield.[39] His mother's brother, Cleveland Douglas, was a delegate from Lower Elk Valley at the first assembly, and her brother-in-law, Emby King Creekmore, was a delegate and the first clerk at Hayes Creek.[40] Hatfield's first job at Falls Branch Coal Company in Oswego, near Wooldridge, was short-lived as he was unwilling to wait until the resolution of a labor strike. His older brother, Chet Francis Hatfield, had moved to Detroit six years earlier to work at Packard Motor Company and invited John to come to Michigan in the summer of 1924 and stay with him until he could gain employment. Hatfield worked in the "service division" for Packard for three years.[41] His marriage in 1926 produced two children but ended in divorce in 1929.[42] After his separation, Hatfield had returned to Jellico to work at Diamond Hosiery Mills. While working at the Appalachian Mills in Knoxville in 1930, he was converted and returned to Jellico to be baptized by John Parks and joined the church there on August 30, 1930.[43] Not long after, Hatfield began to preach and was ordained in November 1931 by Parks and Lewis Baird.[44]

Hatfield attended the Mountain Assembly for the first time as a delegate in 1931.[45] After his ordination, he was sent to Little Wolf Creek to pastor with Kim Moses.[46] The following year, the Mountain Assembly called upon him to read the letters from the churches on the first day's business. At the appointment of the committee on divine services, Hatfield preached the following morning. His "discourse being an admonition of unity among the saints of God," he delivered a "real edifying message" with "many hearty amens being heard during his sermon."[47] Delegates to the 28th Mountain Assembly elected Hatfield to the office of Assistant Clerk in 1934 and reelected him in 1937 and 1938.[48] The resignation of J.B. Spears from the Board of Twelve Elders in 1938 opened a vacancy that also was filled by Hatfield.[49] In 1940, the Mountain Assembly elected him to the office of Clerk.[50] Hatfield went on to serve in the offices of Elder and Clerk (later, General Secretary & Treasurer) for more than three decades.

A Bow Tied

Figure 7.5: J.E. Hatfield
c/o The Gospel Herald

Figure 7.6: Luther Gibson
c/o The Gospel Herald

Luther Gibson was born in Chenoa, Kentucky on January 18, 1914 to Rebecca (Overton) and Lee Roy Gibson, a coal miner in Fonde. Roy Gibson joined the church there by recommendation on August 7, 1930, along with his sons, Luther and Dewey, who were baptized by Pastor David McHenry Hammitte.[51] On May 6, 1932, Luther Gibson married Annette Engle at Fonde.[52] After having preached for several years, Hammitte and James Longsworth ordained him "as a minister of the gospel" on January 6, 1936.[53] The following September, the committee on divine services appointed Gibson to preach one night of the 31st Mountain Assembly. His message was "short but interesting and rich in the power of God."[54] Gibson's first assembly and first sermon there endeared his ministry to the members and ministers, and he went on to preach another two dozen times at the annual assembly including one stretch of eleven in a row.

Two years after his ordination, Gibson was called upon to pastor the church at Henderson Grove near the place where he was born, and shortly thereafter began pastoring a church at the coal camp in Stanfill, Kentucky, as well. For two years, Gibson pastored both churches until he took charge of the Mountain Assembly church in Kenvir and erected a new building there.[55] In 1941, the headquarters church at Jellico called on Gibson to be its pastor and he guided the church and the Mountain Assembly through the process of constructing a new tabernacle there in 1942.[56] Gibson preached the funeral message for John Parks at the tabernacle the following summer and took his place on the Board of Elders at the 37th Mountain Assembly.

A Denominational Government

Andrew Clayton Lawson was born on July 14, 1910 in Knoxville, Tennessee to Minnie (Baird) and Andrew Jackson Lawson. His mother had numerous relatives in the Mountain Assembly church at Elk Valley. His father had recently moved the family to Knoxville to work as a fireman with the railroad.[57] When the railroad moved the Lawson family to Cincinnati later that decade, Clayton's elder brother, Francis, was a charter member of the Mountain Assembly church established there in 1929. After a brief stint in the United States Navy, Clayton married Campbell County native Lassie Barley, and the two were converted at the Mountain Assembly church in Cincinnati under Pastor Herman Williams in 1934 before he left to organize the church at Goshen.[58] Lawson attended the assembly as a delegate from Cincinnati that year and began preaching around the same time.

Figure 7.7: Clayton Lawson
c/o The Gospel Herald

Lawson was ordained to gospel ministry in 1936 and called upon to pastor by the Mountain Assembly church in Sidney. The committee on divine services appointed him to preach at the assembly that year, and his message exhorted the congregation to cleanse themselves from sin and walk in the spirit of holiness.[59] Lawson went on to preach another 28 times at the general assembly.[60] His second year at Sidney saw him conducting extensive evangelistic work, and he reported to the 32nd annual assembly that he had witnessed 179 conversions. As a result, he was appointed an evangelist for the CGMA in 1938.[61] After another successful year in evangelism, Lawson was elected to pastor his home church in Cincinnati in 1939.[62] The following year, he was elected to serve one term as Assistant Clerk.[63] When the delegates at the 1943 assembly voted to remove Morris Woolum from the Board of Twelve Elders for "carrying a gun," they replaced him with Lawson.[64]

With the leadership of the Mountain Assembly in their hands, these seven proposed and implemented changes that further shifted the organization away from the congregationalism of its Baptist roots to an even more centralized denomination like the Church of God (Cleveland). At the conclusion of the 37th Annual Mountain Assembly in 1943, Bryant, Kim Moses, Long, Hatfield, Gibson, and Lawson comprised half of the Board of Twelve Elders. Long and

Moses served as moderator and assistant, and Hatfield and Ira Moses served as clerk and assistant. Over the course of the next twelve months, the group reinvented the Mountain Assembly.

A Denominational Periodical and Auxiliaries in the Local Church

In the early days of the Church of God (Cleveland), A.J. Tomlinson emphasized the need for a church paper and launched the first issue of *The Evening Light and Church of God Evangel* on March 1, 1910.[65] Jonah Shelton attempted to replicate a similar organ in the Mountain Assembly, first with *The Mountain Evangel* in 1912, and then with *The Old Paths* in 1916. Neither publication, however, lasted more than a year. Walker's promotion of the Holiness Baptist Association's *Gospel Standard* the following decade also failed to gain widespread circulation in the Mountain Assembly. The need for a magazine to keep ministers and members informed and connected with the churches was exacerbated as the organization became more widespread geographically in the 1930s. The key to the paper's success would be selecting a member suitably prepared to edit and publish it.

When the CGMA was organized, completion of elementary education at the "grammar school" concluded with the eighth-grade graduation. Secondary schools "trained youths to gain entry to particular colleges and universities in their vicinity." In 1910, nearly half of all high school graduates pursued higher education. During the "high school movement" from 1910 to 1940, local communities transformed secondary education from training "for college" to preparation "for life." As a result, the percentage of high school graduates in the United States increased from 9 percent to 40 percent over those three decades.[66]

Ministers in the Mountain Assembly fell below the national averages but were improving. In 1940, 73 ministers held ordination credentials in the Mountain Assembly.[67] One third of them had finished the eighth grade. Three, including Hatfield and Long, graduated from high school.[68] After graduating as valedictorian at Jellico High School in 1923, Hatfield entered Douglas Business School in Knoxville where he enrolled in bookkeeping and typing courses.[69] His election as clerk of the Mountain Assembly in 1940 gave him experience recording the minutes and preparing them for publication. On May 22-23, 1942, the Board of Twelve Elders met at the Tabernacle in Jellico and commissioned the Moderator and Assistant Moderator, Long and Bryant, to assist the assembly trustees with improvements to and enlargement of the tabernacle before the General Assembly in September. While in session, the Elders also discussed the value of a "church paper" and authorized Elder J.E. Hatfield to proceed with its publication as editor.[70]

Hatfield wasted no time soliciting member "testimonials," local church news, and sermons for print in *The Gospel Herald of the Church of God of the Mountain Assembly, Inc.* In July, the first issue was printed by *The Whitley Republican* of Williamsburg. Subscribers paid $1.00 for an annual subscription, and Hatfield sold advertisements to businesses in Jellico and Williamsburg to absorb the printing costs.[71] "The Editor soon saw that there was not enough space in the eight pages for these ads and the sermons and church news coming in for publication," and halted advertising to allow "only copy of a religious nature."[72] A cigar-smoking caricature in a local jeweler's advertisement also offended some readers.[73]

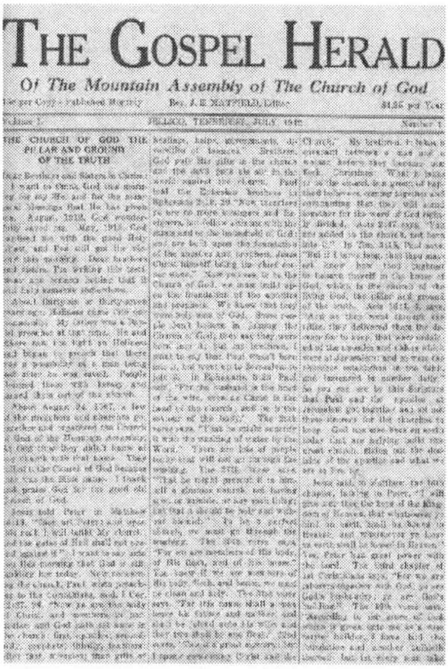
THE GOSPEL HERALD
Of The Mountain Assembly of The Church of God
THE CHURCH OF GOD THE PILLAR AND GROUND OF THE TRUTH

Figure 7.8: The Gospel Herald, Issue 1
c/o Alice Chitwood

The magazine operated as a network for congregations and individuals spread out geographically to connect them to the more centralized denomination. Staying connected to the Mountain Assembly through the periodical was especially important to the elder members who were no longer able to attend the annual convention in Jellico. Emma Woods had been "in the Mountain Assembly since it was organized." Her father, Baptist Minister Elijah Sylvester Carr, was recognized as a visiting minister and invited to a seat with the delegates at the first assembly in 1907.[74] When her son and pastor, Elder Thomas Sylvester Woods, returned from the elders meeting with news of the authorization of the church paper, Emma was delighted to write about her fond remembrance of *The Mountain Evangel.* She anticipated again "getting to hear from my brothers and sisters in Christ through the medium of our church paper, to hear them testify to His love and His power to save, sanctify and fill with the Holy Ghost."[75] Jane Silcox, the widow of Andrew Silcox, wanted readers to know that she was "still holy sanctified" despite having "been sick for a long time and not able to go to the house of the Lord." She testified that she was "ready to go and cross over to the Canaan land."[76] She died six months later.[77]

Hatfield did remarkably well with his solicitation of material for the first issue. The editor received another eight testimonials for the first issue along with those from Woods and Silcox. Hatfield, Luther Gibson, and Kim Moses wrote sermons for the inaugural publication, and 14 churches mailed news reports.[78] Early on, Hatfield emphasized that the paper's success depended on each church and expressed his ambitious desire "to hear from every church each month with news of their progress."[79] While failing to receive contributions from every church every month, *The Gospel Herald* featured news from 35 of the 39 churches during the first year.[80] The CGMA saw the paper as critical for building a national denomination. When the delegates to the 1942 Assembly voted to pay Hatfield $40 each month, he became the first official to draw a salary from the church's centralized government.[81]

To boost circulation, the editor appealed to youth groups to order rolls of 14 copies for $1.00 and sell them for ten cents per issue. In this manner, groups could raise funds while enlarging the paper's readership. In September 1942, *The Gospel Herald* sponsored a contest promising a prize to the individual who sold the most copies.[82] Twenty-eight-year-old Nora Caddell of Emlyn won the contest when she sold 46 copies and was awarded "a Precious Promise New Testament, with a complete index, and with a superb leather binding."[83] She realized that in "selling the paper that other people begin to see the light of the Church of God," which made her "eager to distribute the paper each month."[84] The magazine continued the sales contest for three more months, and Caddell sold the most each month with a total of 176 copies.[85] A month before the contest, Nora buried her ten-weeks old daughter, Jannas Fay, when the infant died from pneumonia.[86] Still raising seven more children under the age of nine, by March, Caddell had "not been blessed to go to church for some time," but found her new Bible a "prize to be highly appreciated by anyone."[87]

The solicitation of youth to circulate the magazine was part of Hatfield's strategy to appeal to the next generation. In his second issue, the editor announced his plan "to devote one page of the paper to young peoples' and Sunday School work," and beginning with the September issue, he did just that with Sunday school news, a Bible quiz, poetry, and a report from Emlyn's local youth program.[88] For more than a year, the "Young People's Page" continued to be a regular feature of each issue. The creation of a youth page in the first volume of the denominational periodical coincided with an effort to replicate the success the Church of God (Cleveland) had enjoyed in its churches for more than a decade, the Young People's Endeavor.

A Denominational Government

On April 3, 1923, Milo Parks Cross organized a youth auxiliary at the Church of God (Cleveland) congregation he pastored in Detroit, Michigan. Youth groups "from various Pentecostal missions cooperated by presenting programs from place to place in the city." The following year, Cross became the Church of God State Overseer and encouraged each congregation in Michigan to organize a youth society. Houston Ryland Morehead campaigned to that end and over the next year helped organize the Young Harvesters Club consisting of a dozen Church of God youth auxiliaries. In September 1926, Cross and Morehead directed the first state youth convention in the Church of God (Cleveland).[89]

About the same time that Cross was organizing a local youth auxiliary in Detroit, Alda Bert "Bertie" Harrison formed the Young People's Mission Band in the Church of God in Cleveland, Tennessee. The activities of Harrison's auxiliary were limited to the local congregation, but she soon saw the value of such a ministry for all the churches. In 1928, she proposed the idea of a national organization to the General Overseer, Flavius Josephus Lee. Lee pledged to work to that end, but his terminal diagnosis of liver cancer and untimely death at the conclusion of the 23rd General Assembly of the Church of God (Cleveland) impeded that goal. Harrison wrote to the *Church of God Evangel* in December to solicit interest in the program. The lone respondent was Florida State Overseer R.P. Johnson.[90]

Pastor E.L. Simmons and the Church of God in Miami had formed a Young People's Missionary Association in 1926. The auxiliary provided "young people a place to work in the Church, a place to promote fellowship," and Christian growth.[91] Church of God congregations in Florida saw the potential of the Miami youth society and replicated similar ministries of their own. After reading Harrison's plea in the *Evangel*, Johnson organized a statewide movement called the Young People's Endeavor.[92] When the Church of God (Cleveland) met for its 24th General Assembly in October 1929, Cross and Morehead submitted a resolution to create a national youth auxiliary. "In essence, the organization used in Michigan and the name used in Florida were adopted." The Church of God Young People's Endeavor (YPE) authorized the General Overseer with each State Overseer to choose state and district officers to "organize the above named organization in each local church, and to have general oversight of same throughout their state or district respectively." Local YPE officers were "under the jurisdiction of the pastor."[93]

As local congregations in the Church of God (Cleveland) began organizing YPE chapters, Mountain Assembly congregations became aware of such programs and instituted youth auxiliaries of their own, beginning in Michigan. Abraham Hubert Tribble was orphaned at age eight when his mother died of pneumonia and his aged father was unable to care for him.[94] A month after his 19th birthday, he enlisted in the United States Army and served two years.[95] While working in the rubber industry in Akron, he married Olive Stephenson in 1925.[96] After their son was born three years later, the couple moved to Detroit where Tribble found work in the automobile industry.[97] On February 17, 1935 Tribble was converted and joined the newly organized Mountain Assembly church on Roosevelt Street, where he soon experienced sanctification, baptism of the Holy Ghost, and a call to the ministry.[98] The following year, the Roosevelt Street Church selected Tribble to be its pastor.[99] Over the next five years, Tribble probably became acquainted with the Young People's Endeavor through the continuing work among Pentecostal missions that was launched by Cross and Morehead in Detroit for the Church of God (Cleveland). The Monroe church just to the south also developed "a good interest among the young people" during this time.[100]

In the summer of 1940, Tribble left his job as a gear grinder at Timken Detroit Axle and moved briefly to Ravenna, Ohio where Olive's father was living.[101] He began attending the Church of God (Cleveland) in nearby Warren, joined the church, was recommended for credentials as a Church of God bishop on July 31, and received them on August 24, 1940.[102] His pastor, James A. Lewis, had witnessed considerable church growth through Sunday school and youth ministry.[103] The Church of God at Warren had a prospering YPE. From Warren, Tribble began conducting evangelistic crusades. A four-week revival that concluded on Easter Sunday at the Church of God (Cleveland) in Jellico was "the greatest revival" the church had seen "for years."[104] By then, the Jellico YPE was a thriving ministry, having recently raised a $25.51 "mission offering" in a "Saturday night Y.P.E. service."[105]

In the fall of 1941, Tribble assumed the pastorate of the Mountain Assembly in Sidney, Ohio. By the 1940s, leadership changes in the Church of God (Cleveland) and the CGMA had helped reduce tensions between the two denominations. Doctrinal similarities often allowed ministers, like Tribble, to seamlessly transition between the organizations. In addition to serving as pastor, Tribble spent considerable time conducting revivals during the ten months he was there. He drove 25,000 miles, preached ten revivals between the 35th and 36th Annual Assemblies, and witnessed more than 250 conversions.[106] During one revival at Whitley City, Kentucky that winter, so stirred were the "great number of young people in the church" that they soon organized a young people's meeting on Tuesday nights where they experienced "large crowds" in attendance.[107] In the summer of 1942, Tribble moved to Oneida, Tennessee to assume the pastorate of the Mountain Assembly church there. He quickly organized a YPE and appointed Olive as its leader.[108]

Figure 7.9: Olive & Abraham Tribble
c/o The Gospel Herald

The YPE services were a source of inspiration to young people across the Mountain Assembly. In the fall of 1942, Dewey Lee Sexton attended a YPE meeting in Cincinnati with his 18-year-old brother, William "Bill" Philmore Sexton, and stirred the youths with his testimony. Dewey and William, along with three more brothers, had been orphaned when their father was shot and killed by prohibition officers when he resisted arrest for operating a still near his home in in Scott County, Tennessee.[109] As a result they grew up in the General Protestant Orphan Home in Cincinnati.[110] As a teenager, Bill was converted under Clayton Lawson and joined the church at Cincinnati.

Dewey was serving in the United States Navy during World War II and had been stationed on the aircraft carrier *USS Wasp*. On Tuesday, September 15, *Wasp* was among the aircraft carriers and a flotilla of warships escorting transports of reinforcements to Guadalcanal. At 2:45 that afternoon, the ship was attacked by a Japanese submarine and two torpedoes struck near the fuel tanks and ammunition magazines. The ensuing "fires continued to set off ammunition, bombs, and gasoline." By 3:20, the fires blazed uncontrollably, and Captain Forest P. Sherman unfortunately saw no recourse but to abandon ship. Rafts carried those severely injured, but many seamen were forced into the water because the fires limited access to rubber boats.[111]

At the YPE meeting in Cincinnati, Dewey Sexton shared how "some of the boys aboard the carrier had been having prayer meetings and how they were ridiculed by some." He testified that "he was in the water four hours before he was picked up by a rescue ship" and spent that time in prayer until he had "finally prayed through to God." His testimony encouraged the

Cincinnati youth group that "prayer changes things."[112] The same month his story appeared in *The Gospel Herald*, Hatfield published a list of 29 "boys in uniform" that readers might pray for those who "have left their homes to go into the service of our country."[113]

Like the Church of God (Cleveland), the Mountain Assembly established local youth auxiliaries to encourage young Christians to work in the church. The Emlyn church organized its Young People's Endeavor on March 22, 1942 with Clara Sproule as its leader, Kenneth Blythe as President, and Jeannette Sproule as Treasurer. They began meeting every Sunday night at 6:00.[114] That fall, the YPE held a "bake sale" to raise money for the church building fund.[115] By soliciting the service of its youth group, Emlyn was able to build a new church building three years later.[116]

The youth auxiliary was not the only Christian service organization the Mountain Assembly reproduced from the Church of God (Cleveland) during this same period. Local women's auxiliaries also became prevalent in Mountain Assembly congregations in the early 1940s. Women occupied a place in ministry and service in the Church of God (Cleveland) from its inception. Although women ministers were prohibited from administering the sacrament, baptizing believers, performing marriages, conducting business meetings, or pastoring churches, women evangelists enjoyed the liberty of freely preaching, and the number of credentialed women ministers in the Church of God greatly increased over its first few decades. While several states sponsored women's auxiliaries like the Ladies Prayer Band and the Dorcas Circle, there was no official national organization for laywomen.[117]

On November 16, 1929 Johnnie Belle Wood, wife of the Oklahoma State Overseer, organized a women's auxiliary in the local church whose primary function was to raise money for the church. Her idea spread and "within five or six years, congregations organized local chapters" of the "Ladies Willing Worker Band."[118] At the 31st General Assembly in October 1936, the Church of God (Cleveland) adopted a plan to officially recognize the women's auxiliary:

> That each local church organize and maintain an auxiliary which shall be generally known as "Ladies' Willing Workers Band." Officers of each organization shall consist of a president, vice-president, secretary & treasurer, which organization shall be under the jurisdiction of the pastor of each local church. The purpose of the said organization is to meet each week, or as often as convenient, to engage in such legitimate pursuits as may seem profitable to raise funds to be disbursed in behalf of the local church needs. It is further understood

that each local organization after consulting with their pastor, shall disburse their funds according to their best judgment. Where an organization of this type is functioning under a different name, it may continue if they so desire.[119]

Like the Young People's Endeavor, Mountain Assembly congregations copied the Ladies Willing Worker Band from Church of God (Cleveland) congregations nearby. Each church held "sisters' meetings" whenever most convenient for the women in the congregation. Little Wolf Creek began meeting on Saturday mornings at 10:00 before moving them to Monday afternoons, which was also the preference of women at Middlesboro, Emlyn, Jellico, Elk Valley, and Goshen.[120] The women at Marion, Tennessee preferred Monday morning, while the ladies at Sidney, Ohio met on Thursday afternoons, and those at Revelo, Kentucky met on Friday.[121]

Like the Church of God (Cleveland), the local women's auxiliaries in the Mountain Assembly churches functioned as a means for fund-raising. While the YPE at Emlyn were holding bake sales for the building fund, "the Willing Workers of the Emlyn Church" held "their regular Sisters meeting and quilting for the benefit of the building fund."[122] While "making quilts to help raise money to build the new church house," these gatherings also featured "singing and prayer" and divine healing. "The Lord touched one of the Sister's hands which [were] stiff from rheumatism so she could also help in the quilting work." "Special prayers for their children that are in the armed forces and in sin" highlighted the meetings, and as a result "the Baptist and Methodist sisters" met with them and enjoyed "the blessings of God."[123]

In this way, the ladies' ministry was also evangelistic, if not proselytizing. The "Willing Workers" in Cincinnati collected "old" copies of *The Gospel Herald* "to be given to shut-ins or those not able to buy one."[124] At a "Sisters Service" at Middlesboro, "Pastor Ottis Ellis made an altar call, and one came to the altar seeking to be saved" and "three were united to the Church." At the same meeting, "several were in the altar seeking the Holy Ghost."[125] The pursuit of a greater spiritual experience was a common purpose of LWWB meetings throughout the Mountain Assembly, and as a result, attendance increased. Starting with nine at their first meeting at Little Wolf Creek, the ladies' group grew to 25 in just a few months and they saw "several sanctified and filled with the Holy Ghost in these meetings."[126] The "sisters of the Jellico Church," likewise found themselves "trusting the Lord that He will Sanctify and fill with the Holy Ghost, those who have not yet received that blessing, and get us all ready for the testing time, which we believe is in the near future" and "expecting more of the Sisters to attend the meetings."[127]

Generally, the women's auxiliaries met at the church, but on occasion they met at a member's home. On August 17, 1942, "the Sisters of the Jellico Church met in the home of Elder J. H. Parks" for "their regular weekly prayer service." After a devotional lesson and singing, "there was a united prayer for Brother Parks as he was feeling very weak and wished prayer for his body." After the prayer, "Brother Parks testified that he was feeling much better" and additional "songs and testimonies" were presented, before a "closing song and the closing prayer was offered by Brother Parks."[128] A week later, "the Sisters of the Sidney Church met in the home of Sister Nancy Jones for prayer meeting." The ladies "read the Bible and testified of the goodness of the Lord."[129]

The youth and ladies' auxiliaries continued in the local churches throughout the 1940s without any official recognition at the annual Mountain Assembly or in its standard resolutions. In August 1948, however, the 42nd Mountain Assembly officially authorized both. A resolution creating the Ladies Willing Worker Band was adopted with the exact wording employed by the Church of God (Cleveland).[130] The women's auxiliaries functioned to assist the local churches for three decades before any national organization occurred.[131] The youth auxiliary, however, was organized nationally in 1948. It required some customization from the program adopted by the Church of God (Cleveland), and a committee was appointed to "to work out a program for the Young People" on Thursday, September 2. Luther Gibson, Morris Woolum, and Robert Newton "R.N." Ballinger proposed that the "Young People's Endeavor" would "consist of a national director and his assistant" who would "draft a program" to "stimulate interest among our young people, to assist in making our Sunday Schools better, and to promote the circulation of *The Gospel Herald*." The "local YPE president or youth leader" would "arrange for the weekly programs, to work in harmony with the pastor for the interest of the church, and to carry out the program submitted them by the National Directors."[132]

In September, the General Overseer announced the planning of "a Young People's Rally on Friday night of the Assembly" and urged the youth to attend.[133] Woolum served that same year on the committee on divine services and persuaded fellow-committeemen John H. Bryant and Clarence Ed Bray to place the Friday night service under the direction of his grandnephew, Edward Woolum. Robert Boyd Thomas, "a young evangelist

A Denominational Government

Figure 7.10: Edward Woolum
c/o Linda Woolum Coffman

Figure 7.11: Robert Thomas
c/o The Gospel Herald

preached the evening sermon," and "truly preached like a veteran."[134] The 16-year-old Thomas had conducted numerous successful revivals since he joined the Mountain Assembly in February. Nine were saved at Corbin in February, 18 were converted at Sidney and 25 at Cincinnati in April, and 76 made professions of faith at Kenvir in July.[135] Woolum had been "working for a large firm and making good wages" when God called him into the ministry earlier that April. At first, the 18-year-old struggled with obedience, but after nearly losing his fingers and arm on three consecutive days at work he left his job and surrendered to the call. Woolum began preaching that night at the CGMA church in Detroit. After a four-night revival where four were saved, Woolum conducted another revival in Middlesboro, Kentucky, and saw eight more converted.[136]

After the successful first youth service, the Assembly chose Woolum to be the first National Youth Director and Floyd Jordan to be his assistant.[137] Jordan had been elected the previous year as the YPE President at Middlesboro where Friday night youth services routinely boasted over 100 in attendance.[138] His "young people's class" also averaged over 60 in Sunday school attendance the following year.[139] On Sunday, October 17, 1948, Edward Woolum, Thomas, and

Figure 7.12: Floyd Jordan and YPE
c/o Middlesboro CGMA

Jordan were present in Middlesboro for the first State Youth Rally and rallies such as these soon became an important part of the national YPE program.[140]

The creation of a lasting monthly periodical along with local ladies' and youth auxiliaries adapted from the same programs in the Church of God (Cleveland) helped to unify the Mountain Assembly churches. Following the 1948 Assembly, the churches were "encouraged to maintain Young People's Meetings and Ladies Willing Workers Bands which can prove to be a great blessing to the Church of God," noting that they had "already proven their worth to the upbuilding of the church."[141] The church paper was promoted by the youth and ladies' ministries and in turn featured much content related to those programs in each issue. The Ladies Willing Workers Band often provided teachers and leaders for the Young People's Endeavor, and the two auxiliaries often raised funds toward the same projects. The three worked together to make the Mountain Assembly congregations more cohesive.

By adopting the same type of youth and ladies' auxiliaries, the Mountain Assembly congregations were often indistinguishable from each other. When a family left the South to find better work in the North, it could expect the local Mountain Assembly it joined to have a weekly LWWB meeting for mother to attend and a weekly YPE meeting for the children to enjoy. Comfort was found in the familiarity of the church experience in a sometimes otherwise alien culture. *The Gospel Herald* accounts of other youth and women's ministries also became a reservoir of ideas and inspiration. By reading the testimonies and church news from distant locations in other states, members recognized that they were part of something larger than simply a group of believers who met in their local community. The denominational periodical, then, served as a medium to connect otherwise independent congregations into a unified national church body. The published sermon content also helped unify the various members theologically. This became critically important as the Mountain Assembly moved toward formally changing its denominational polity. In its first year, *The Gospel Herald* published two sermons calling for stronger "church governments," one by C.L. Price and another by J.H. Parks.[142] As members studied the implications of these homilies, the next generation of leaders formulated a plan.

A New System of Government
As the congregations were becoming more interconnected through organization-wide ministries, the government of the Mountain Assembly continued its trend toward more centralization. One noteworthy

A Denominational Government

development was the creation of a new fund at headquarters from ministers' tithes. The Church of God (Cleveland) had experimented from 1920 to 1922 with a communal financial system where each church would send its tithes to headquarters and a committee would redistribute the funds for pastoral support.[143] This proved disastrous. By 1940, the Mountain Assembly had a growing number of ministers who had left secular employment and earned their living primarily through the ministry. This represented a substantial departure from their experience in the United Baptist Church where pastors seldom received significant financial compensation for their ministry service. As a result of this shift, the Mountain Assembly introduced a measure to assist ministers "who pastor churches that are not able to fully support them." The plan called for each minister to continue tithing on his income to the church where he was a member. The church treasurers were to remit ten percent of all ministers' tithes to "the general tithe treasureman [sic]." From this fund, pastors might receive financial assistance.[144]

Over the next year, 23 ministers sent $1,093.41 to Treasurer Lewis Sharp, and eight pastors received a total of $693.50 in assistance. Because some of the pastors chose to send the full amount of their tithes to headquarters, receipts for the new ministers' tithe fund came close to matching the $1,395 received by the tithe of tithes fund.[145] The creation of a second source of income for the Mountain Assembly headquarters coincided with a surging American economy at the outbreak of World War II. At the 38th Annual Mountain Assembly in 1944, Everett Creekmore reported he had received $4,931.96 in tithe of tithes that year, and Lewis Sharp reported $2,942.20 received in ministers' tithes. In addition, the balances of the two funds left the general treasury with a combined balance of $3,855.[146]

With revenue for operating expenses, the Mountain Assembly continued to support some of its pastors and to pay the traveling expenses of its Board of Elders and General Officials. In 1942, the Mountain Assembly also created an aged ministers' fund from monthly $1 donations by the local churches.[147] The same year the delegates voted to annul the standard resolutions pertaining to the assembly evangelists. Instead, they adopted a system whereby ministers who "see an opportunity to establish a new work" could "write to headquarters and apply for help." The "moderator and other proper assembly officials" would grant "assistance" from the tithe of tithes treasury for works deemed necessary.[148] The following year, the Mountain Assembly created the position of state evangelists, elected by the "churches of each state," to "expand and promote the work in their states and to assist the pastors in any

183

work needed to be done." Free-will offerings were intended to finance the office of state evangelist.[149]

As the headquarters treasury grew and the churches became more united, the Mountain Assembly's leadership began to envision a more centralized polity like that of the Church of God (Cleveland). One proponent of a new system of government was Clayton Lawson. Lawson had been converted under Herman Williams in Cincinnati. After pastoring in Cincinnati and then organizing and pastoring the church in Goshen, Williams left the Mountain Assembly and moved to the Los Angeles area and joined the Church of God (Cleveland) at Baldwin Park, California in November 1936.[150] From 1941 to 1943, Williams served as the Overseer for the State of Oklahoma.[151] As the Mountain Assembly began to prosper financially, Lawson became convinced his own organization could experience growth like his mentor's new organization by making changes to its government structure.

Lawson was not the only Mountain Assembly minister with eyes on the group in Cleveland. J.E. Hatfield subscribed to Church of God (Cleveland) publications. The stratagem he employed to boost circulation of *The Gospel Herald* in the fall of 1942 by sending rolls of extra copies that could be sold as a profit was hardly his own. The same roll-pricing plan for additional copies was employed by the Church of God (Cleveland) to boost circulation of its youth magazine, *The Lighted Pathway*, four years earlier. That fourteen copies of each magazine could be purchased for $1 and the suggested resale price of ten cents was hardly a coincidence, especially considering the *Pathway* was more than three times longer than the *Herald*.[152]

In August 1944, Andrew Long and Kim Moses visited John Bryant's home in Stearns, Kentucky, to discuss proposed changes to the system of government. Among the proposals, the Moderator and his Assistant desired to change the title of the offices to those used by the Church of God (Cleveland). Moses insisted, like Tomlinson had three decades earlier, "that the word overseer was a Bible term." It was also time to discontinue the use of "moderator," a holdover from "the old Baptist church." Moses also championed the idea of a "bishop's council," citing Acts 16:4-5 as evidence that the church's decrees should be "made by the apostles and elders."[153]

In 1921, the Church of God (Cleveland) attempted to solve some of its leadership woes in the middle of its greatest crisis. The Council of Seventy worked with the Council of Twelve and functioned as the "official Assembly." Other ministers and members were permitted to participate in discussions, but decision-making ultimately rested with the Councils. Each year, 14 members of the Council of Seventy were elected to a five-year term.[154] This form of government lasted only eight years before the Church of God abandoned it in favor of a "Bishops Council." From 1906 to 1921, business matters at the General Assembly were discussed freely by all the appointed delegates. From 1921 to 1929, business proposals originated in the Council of Twelve before they were discussed by the Council of Seventy. After both Councils had freely discussed the measures, the whole assembly heard them and voted for or against their adoption. In 1929, the Church of God (Cleveland) decided that all ordained ministers should form a council to replace the Council of Seventy. The following year, the Bishops Council began electing ministers to sit on the Council of Twelve.[155]

The question of who should participate in the business sessions of the association had been debated, settled, revisited, and revised multiple times in the South Union Association of United Baptists. In 1891, the Association asked its churches to restrict the number of delegates it sent one per 25 members. Seven years later, churches dropped the use of the word "delegate" in preference of "messenger."[156] In 1901, the Baptist association restricted its delegation to "ministers and elected messengers" and revisited it the following year by polling the churches to see whether they wanted a "restricted" or an "open" meeting. In 1904, it was agreed that no more than three lay members from each church should be permitted to sit with the members in the association's business.[157] When the Mountain Assembly organized in 1907, the first assembly offered no restrictions on the number of messengers each church sent, and the churches sent between four and ten.[158] With the Jellico church hosting each annual assembly, the number of its messengers reached ten in 1928 and the Mountain Assembly voted the following year to limit "each church to only three lay-member messengers with their ordained ministers."[159] The creation of a Bishops Council intended to remove all lay members from the major decision-making process.

On Tuesday, September 5, 1944, the Board of Twelve Elders convened the day before the 38th Mountain Assembly was scheduled to commence. At this meeting, the Elders discussed the need for a revised polity and appointed "committee of five brethren … to make plans for a new system of government for the assembly."[160] Kim Moses appointed to the committee Andrew Long, John Hatfield, Clayton Lawson, and Luther Gibson, and "expected to get the [final] appointment himself."[161] Instead, John Bryant rounded out the committee. Their plan proposed that a Bishops Council would meet "on Tuesday before the first Wednesday in each September" and "elect the officials of the Assembly." The "Elders and ordained ministers" would also become the "law-making body of the Assembly." Churches that wished to have business considered in the assembly could "petition the Bishop's Council" through their three delegates who would meet with the ministers after the Council finished its session.[162]

The committee further proposed that the moderator be replaced by the office of "General Overseer" whose duties included looking "after the general interest of all the churches, keeping a record of all the ministers, and to moderate the general assembly." The Assistant General Overseer replaced the assistant moderator who would "look after the general interest of all the churches as directed by the General Overseer." Both men were restricted to pastoring only one church each and were permitted to draw "traveling expenses from the tithe of tithes treasury." Following the model of the Church of God (Cleveland), the committee also proposed the creation of State Overseers "to look after the interest of the churches in their states, keeping a record of all the work in their state and reporting monthly to the General Overseer." Each minister was expected to report to his State Overseer each month. The office of Clerk and the two assembly treasurers were combined into one office, "General Secretary & Treasurer," and the Assistant Clerk became the Assistant General Secretary & Treasurer.[163]

The Board of Twelve Elders became "the judicial body of the Assembly" and had the final decision on any matter it was "called upon to decide." When a vacancy occurred, the Bishops Council elected a replacement. The General Officials, however, and the "Five General Trustees" would be elected annually, along with a new Committee on Finance. The latter would "audit the books of the treasurer every three months," authorize all expenses, and plan ways to increase the Assembly's income. To increase revenue immediately, the committee proposed that the "full amount" of all ministers' tithes paid into the local church should be sent directly to headquarters. In addition to these suggestions, the committee also examined the Standard Resolutions of the Mountain Assembly and recommended that 25 be deleted, seven be revised, and two be moved to the Teachings of the Church.[164]

When the General Assembly convened the following day, the delegates reelected Long as Moderator and Hatfield as Clerk. Lawson was elected Assistant Moderator, and Ira Moses was elected Assistant Clerk. When the committee to devise a new system of government presented its full plan to on Thursday, all the "revisions and recommendations" were adopted "by a large majority." The officers already elected assumed the new titles and new

A Denominational Government

job duties. Long, Bryant, Gibson, Ira Moses, and Kim Moses were appointed General Trustees, and Bryant, Gibson, and Lawson were selected as the Committee on Finance. The new State Overseers were Kim Moses for Kentucky, Gibson for Tennessee, Thomas Woods for Indiana, Roy Cornelius for Ohio, and Morris Woolum for Michigan. Woolum would also be re-elected to the Board of Twelve Elders.

Initially, the Mountain Assembly seemed to respond well to the new system of government. In the first six months, Long had "visited several of the churches" and found "a good spirit among our people." He discovered "a zeal and a mind to build in our churches."[165] Build, they did. The church at Oliver Springs, Tennessee, and four churches in Kentucky—Whitley City, Pine Hill, Williamsburg, and Emlyn—constructed new buildings in the spring of 1945.[166] Long had indicated his satisfaction that Lawson was elected his assistant because "he has a car and he can travel and visit the churches while I am going to other churches."[167] While Long pastored the Fonde church and visited southern churches, Lawson pastored the Linn Street church in Cincinnati and visited northern ones.[168]

One church Lawson visited was the new church in Dayton, Ohio. David Green Phelps moved from Corbin, Kentucky to Dayton the previous year. In early 1945, R.N. Ballinger from the Goshen area joined him there, and together they "worked hard to get this new church started." After a two-weeks revival conducted by Edd Prewitt of Emlyn, Lawson and State Overseer Roy Cornelius organized a church with nine members on February 11 with Ballinger and Phelps as pastors.[169] In addition to Dayton, five new churches sent letters requesting fellowship with the Mountain Assembly in 1945: churches in Kokomo, Indiana and Calloway, Kentucky; and second churches in Oliver Springs, Tennessee, and Cincinnati and Toledo, Ohio.

The first Mountain Assembly church in Toledo was launched in late 1943 while Roy Cornelius was pastoring in nearby Monroe, Michigan. Cornelius paid the first month's rent on a building on Summit Street, "built a rostrum, purchased seats, and took the piano out of his own house" to furnish the opening of the church. When the church was set in order, the charter members elected Silas Harold Mosingo of the Monroe church for pastor. The church soon moved to a building on George Street, and enjoyed immediate success.[170] Harvey Rose conducted a two-weeks revival there in May 1944 and saw ten saved, nine baptized, and eight join the church.[171] By the time the church was formally accepted into the Mountain Assembly in September, membership reached 30, and Sunday school attendance had reached 80.[172]

Figure 7.13: R.N. Ballinger
c/o Bev Halcomb

Figure 7.14: Roy and Mary Cornelius
c/o North Monroe Street CGMA

The second Toledo church was located on Blade Street and was pastored by Thomas Jackson. Jackson was an African American preacher who had become acquainted with Mosingo and Rose. Rose, now pastoring in Monroe after Cornelius returned to pastor the Goshen church, invited Jackson to preach for him on February 22, 1945. Visitors from the churches at Toledo and Monroe were present three days later when the "colored church" held its "first service in their new building."[173] Jackson appeared "before the Elders for questioning" at the Assembly in September and was approved for ordination. The following night, Jackson "took the stand to preach as Brother Lawson wanted him to preach in his place." The minister "brought a wonderful message which edified and was a blessing to the large congregation." Speaking from 1 Corinthians 13, he referred to love as evidence of the Holy Ghost. The Bishops Council also selected Jackson to serve as "State Overseer for the colored work in the State of Ohio."[174]

In addition to an increase in the number of churches, the Mountain Assembly's first year with the new system of government experienced significant financial growth, largely due to the changes in the minister's tithe fund. Now sending the full amount of their tithes to headquarters, ministers tithes increased 271 percent the first year.[175] Spiritually, the Mountain Assembly seemed in good shape as well. Before preaching the Saturday night service of the 39th Annual Mountain Assembly, Eldon Bowman "E.B." Rose remarked "that this was one of the best assemblies" he had attended. Edd Prewitt followed his sermon that night with one of his own and "expressed his view on what a great assembly we were having." Hatfield further concluded the minutes with his own commentary, "God was in the work from beginning to end, blessing His people in a wonderful way."[176]

Conclusion

Despite the seeming success of the new system of government, discontent remained. Many of the lay members disenfranchised by the new Bishops Council felt their voice was no longer heard. Their only recourse was through the "petition committee" appointed by the Bishops Council. Luther Gibson, Randall Watkins, and David Hammitte formed the committee in 1945 and received two matters to bring before the Council. A "question of modest apparel was taken up" and "the question of messengers and deacons voting with the ministers in the election of officers and on all questions" were brought before the bishops. After discussion, they voted to leave the issues as recorded in the "teachings as in the present minutes" and "to keep the rulings of last assembly."[177] The new polity patterned after the Church of God (Cleveland) remained in place, but so also did the independent congregationalist spirit of the Baptist roots of many members and churches. The tension between these two polities reached its zenith the following September and caused a divisive split as a result.

---

[1] Bryant, "Life Story," 3.

[2] CGMA, *Minutes* (1924), 3.

[3] U.S., Appointments of U. S. Postmasters, 1832-1971, s.v. "John H Bryant," Ancestry.com; Robert M. Rennick, *Kentucky Place Names* (Lexington: University Press of Kentucky, 1987), 141.

[4] CGMA, *Minutes* (1925), 8; Bryant, "My Story," 3.

[5] Bryant, "My Story," 3.

[6] CGMA, *Minutes* (1927), 10. Bryant preached at the General Assembly 25 times from 1927 to 1962, including the Introductory Sermon seven times.

[7] CGMA, *Minutes* (1930), 7; CGMA, *Minutes* (1939), 5-6.

[8] https://www.findagrave.com/memorial/12247310; U.S., World War I Draft Registration Cards, 1917-1918, s.v. "Kim Moses," Ancestry.com.

[9] CGMA, *Minutes* (1928), 15-16; Parks, 185.

[10] Tennessee, Marriage Records, 1780-2002, s.v. "Kim Mosis," Ancestry.com.

[11] Kim Moses, "The Church of God: The Pillar and Ground of Truth," *GH* 1, no. 1 (July 1942): 1.

[12] CGMA, *Minutes* (1917), 2.

[13] CGMA, *Minutes* (1918), statistical table.

14 CGMA, *Minutes* (1938), 10.

15 CGMA, *Minutes* (1925), 8-9.

16 Kentucky, Death Records, 1852-1965, s.v. "Andrew Johnson Long," Ancestry.com.

17 Parks, 190.

18 CGMA, *Minutes* (1907), 2.

19 James E. Prewitt, "In Appreciation of Their Many Years of Service: Reverend Andrew J. Long," *GH* 33, no. 12 (December 1972): 1.

20 CGMA, *Minutes* (1912), 2.

21 CGMA, *Minutes* (1913), statistical table.

22 Prewitt, "Appreciation: Long," 3.

23 Jellico Minutes, membership roster.

24 CGMA, *Minutes* (1921), 3.

25 CGMA, *Minutes* (1923), 10.

26 CGMA, *Minutes* (1925), 7; CGMA, *Minutes* (1926), 7.

27 CGMA, *Minutes* (1928), 6-7.

28 CGMA, *Minutes* (1939), 5.

29 CGMA, *Minutes* (1913), 2.

30 James E. Prewitt, "In Appreciation of Their Many Years of Service: Rev. and Mrs. Ira H. Moses," *GH* 33, no. 9 (September 1972): 3.

31 1930 United States Census, Whitley County, Kentucky, s.v. "Ira Moses," Ancestry.com.

32 Kentucky, Death Records, 1852-1965, s.v. "Hubert Mases," Ancestry.com.

33 Padgett, *Heritage*, 90-91.

34 Minutes of Jellico, membership roster; Prewitt, "Appreciation: Moses," 3.

35 CGMA, *Minutes* (1933), 3, 4, 11, 17.

36 CGMA, *Minutes* (1939), 6.

37 Prewitt, "Appreciation: Moses," 3; Ira H. Moses Ordination Certificate, in the possession of Roger Lands, Cookeville, TN.

38 CGMA, *Minutes* (1943), 20-21, statistical table.

39 Tennessee, Delayed Birth Records, 1869-1909, s.v. "John Edward Hatfield," Ancestry.com.

40 CGMA, *Minutes* (1907), 2.

41 John E. Hatfield, "Autobiography of John E. Hatfield, Youngest Son of A.L. and Hannah Hatfield," in J.E. Hatfield Minister File, Archives Room, Church of God Mountain Assembly Headquarters, Jellico, Tennessee.

42 Michigan, Marriage Records, 1867-1952, s.v. "Mr John Hatfield," Ancestry.com; Hatfield, "Autobiography."

43 Parks, 199; Jellico Minutes, membership roster; Hatfield, "Autobiography." Hatfield joined the Jellico Church on Saturday, August 30, 1930, and was baptized the following day.

A Denominational Government

44 Prewitt, "In Appreciation of Their Many Years of Service: Rev. & Mrs. J.E. Hatfield," *GH* 34, no. 6 (June 1973): 3.

45 CGMA, *Minutes* (1931), 15.

46 CGMA, *Minutes* (1932), 15.

47 CGMA, *Minutes* (1933), 3-4.

48 CGMA, *Minutes* (1934), 2; CGMA, *Minutes* (1937), 5; CGMA, *Minutes* (1938), 5.

49 CGMA, *Minutes* (1938), 13

50 CGMA, *Minutes* (1940), 6.

51 James E. Prewitt, "In Appreciation of Their Many Years of Service: Rev. and Mrs. Luther Gibson," *GH* 33, no. 11 (November 1972): 3; Minutes of Fonde, 173.

52 "A Tribute to Luther Gibson," 1, in Luther Gibson Minister File, Church of God Mountain Assembly Headquarters, Jellico, TN.

53 Fonde Minutes, 216.

54 CGMA, *Minutes* (1937), 13.

55 "Tribute to Gibson," 1.

56 CGMA, *Minutes* (1942), 20.

57 1910 United States Census, Knox County, Tennessee, s.v. "Andrew J Lawson," Ancestry.com.

58 1930 United States Census, Hamilton County, Ohio, s.v. "Robert C Lawson," Ancestry.com; CGMA, *Minutes* (1934), 17.

59 CGMA, *Minutes* (1936), 12-13.

60 No minister before or since has preached more times at the general assembly.

61 CGMA, *Minutes* (1938), 14.

62 CGMA, *Minutes* (1939), 24.

63 CGMA, *Minutes* (1940), 6.

64 CGMA, *Minutes* (1943), 9. That Woolum carried a gun, presumably for self-defense in Detroit, apparently offended several ministers who saw it as a lack of faith in God to protect him.

65 *CGE* 1, no. 1 (March 1, 1910).

66 Claudia Goldin and Lawrence F. Katz, "Human Capital and Social Capital: The Rise of Secondary Schooling in America, 1910-1940," *Journal of Interdisciplinary History* 29, no. 4 (March 1999), 685, 689.

67 CGMA, *Minutes* (1940), 25-26.

68 1940 United States Census, Ancestry.com. See table 7.1 at the end of the section.

69 Prewitt, "Appreciation: Hatfield," 3; Hatfield, "Autobiography."

70 Hatfield, "Elders' Meeting," *GH* 1, no. 1 (July 1942): 2.

71 *GH* 1, no. 1 (July 1942); *GH* 1, no. 2 (August 1942): 8.

72 Hatfield, "Reminiscing and Au Revoir," *GH* 28, no. 9 (September 1967): 12.

73 [advertisement], "Protect Your Watch," *GH* 1, no. 1 (July 1942): 2.

74 CGMA, *Minutes* (1907), 2.

75 Emma Woods, "Testimonials," *GH* 1, no. 1 (July 1942): 9.

76 Jane Silcox, "Testimonials," *GH* 1, no. 1 (July 1942): 9.

77 Kentucky, Death Records, 1852-1965, s.v. "Jane Silcox," Ancestry.com.

78 *GH* 1, no. 1 (July 1942).

79 Hatfield, "Editor's Note," *GH* 1, no. 3 (September 1942): 4; Hatfield, "The Editor's Message," *GH* 1, no. 4 (October 1942): 4.

80 *GH* 1 (July 1942 to June 1943). Gold Bug, Science Hill, Saxton, and Stanfill (all in Kentucky) were the four churches that failed to contribute.

81 CGMA, *Minutes* (1942), 11.

82 Hatfield, "The Editor's Message," *GH* 1, no. 3 (September 1942): 4.

83 Hatfield, "The Editor's Message," *GH* 1, no. 4 (October 1942): 4.

84 Nora Caddell, "A Note of Thanks," *GH* 1, no. 6 (December 1942): 1.

85 Hatfield, "October Sales," *GH* 1, no. 5 (November 1942): 8; Hatfield, "November Sales," *GH* 1, no. 6 (December 1942): 8; Hatfield, "December Sales," *GH* 1, no. 5 (January 1943): 8.

86 Kentucky, Death Records, 1852-1965, s.v. "Jannas Fay Caddell," Ancestry.com.

87 Caddell, *GH* 1, no. 6 (December 1942): 1; Caddell, *GH* 1, no. 9 (March 1943): 3.

88 Hatfield, "Editor's Note," *GH* 1, no. 2 (August 1942): 4; "Young People's Page," *GH* 1, no. 3 (September 1942): 5.

89 Conn, 252.

90 Ibid., 242-244, 251-252.

91 Simmons, 69-70.

92 Conn, 252.

93 Church of God, *Minutes of the Twenty-fourth Annual Assembly of the Churches of God* (Cleveland, TN: Church of God Publishing House, 1929), 24.

94 Tennessee, Death Records, 1908-1958, s.v. "Mattie Trible," Ancestry.com.

95 U.S., Department of Veterans Affairs BIRLS Death File, 1850-2010, s.v. "Abraham Tribble," Ancestry.com.

96 Summit County, Ohio, Marriage Records, 1840-1980, s.v. "Hubert Tribble," Ancestry.com.

97 1930 United States Census, Wayne County, Michigan, s.v. "Abraham H Trible," Ancestry.com.

98 Abraham H. Tribble, "Evangelistic Report," *GH* 1, no. 4 (September 1942): 1.

99 CGMA, *Minutes* (1936), 21.

100 [Agnes] Massingill, "Monroe Church," *GH* 1, no. 1 (July 1942): 5.

101 1940 United States Census, Wayne County, Michigan, s.v. "Abraham Trible" and 1940 United States Census, Portage County, Ohio, s.v. "Asa Stephenson," Ancestry.com.

A Denominational Government

[102] Church and Pastor's Endorsement and Report of Ordination, Abraham H. Tribble file, Central Files and Records of the Church of God, Cleveland, Tennessee.

[103] Treasel Mackey, "Brief Reports" and "Revivals," *CGE* 30, no. 6 (April 8, 1939): 4, 12; Mackey, "Conventions," *CGE* 30, no. 20 (July 15, 1939): 12.

[104] J.S. Walker, "Notices from the Field," *CGE* 32, no. 10 (May 3, 1941): 2.

[105] Herman Adkins, "Jellico, Tenn., District Convention," *CGE* 31, no. 24 (August 10, 1940): 11.

[106] Longsworth, Sidney *History*, 20; Tribble, "Evangelistic Report," *GH* 1, no. 4 (September 1942): 1.

[107] "Whitley City Church," *GH* 1, no. 2 (August 1942): 1.

[108] "Oneida Church," *GH* 1, no. 2 (August 1942): 5.

[109] Tennessee, Death Records, 1908-1958, s.v. "Fillmore Sexton," Ancestry.com.

[110] 1930 United States Census, Hamilton County, Ohio, s.v. "Dewey Sexton," Ancestry.com; https://www.findagrave.com/memorial/199902247; "Admissions Registers (1930-1947)," General Protestant Orphan Home Records (1849-1973) at the Cincinnati History Library & Archives, Cincinnati Museum Center, Cincinnati, Ohio.

[111] Robert J. Cressman, March 5, 2019, "Wasp VIII (CV-7), 1940-1942," Naval History and Heritage Command, Accessed January 15, 2020. https://www.history.navy.mil/research/histories/ship-histories/danfs/w/wasp-viii.html.

[112] Clayton Lawson, "Cincinnati, Ohio," *GH* 1, no. 6 (December 1942): 2.

[113] Hatfield, "Our Boys in Uniform," *GH* 1, no. 6 (December 1942): 8.

[114] Clara Sproule, "Emlyn Church, Young People's Endeavor," *GH* 1, no. 1 (July 1942): 4.

[115] "Emlyn, Ky," *GH* 1, no. 4 (October 1942): 2.

[116] Phronia Dinkins, "Dedication," *GH* 4, no. 12 (June 1946): 1.

[117] Conn, 296-297.

[118] Crews, 101-103.

[119] Church of God, *Minutes of the Thirty-First Annual Assembly of the Church of God* (Cleveland, TN: Church of God Publishing House, 1936), 35

[120] Middlesboro CGMA, Record Book For Sisters Service, Middlesboro, Ky. (1943), 19; Dora Moses, "Testimonials," *GH* 1, no. 1 (July 1942): 9; Luther Gibson, "Jellico, Tenn.," *GH* 1, no. 3 (September 1942): 2; "Emlyn, Kentucky," *GH* 1, no. 6 (December 1942): 6; Ione Rountree, "Little Wolf Creek, Ky," *GH* 1, no. 12 (June 1943): 2; Della Douglas, "Elk Valley, Tenn.," *GH* 2, no. 11 (May 1944): 6; Mary Golden, "Goshen, Ohio," *GH* 5, no. 1 (July 1946): 5.

[121] Edgar Strete, "Sidney, Ohio," *GH* 3, no. 1 (July 1944): 6; Ollie Thomas, "Revelo, Ky.," *GH* 5, no. 1 (July 1946): 5; Ruth Morgan, "Marion, Tenn.," *GH* 5, no. 1 (July 1946): 5.

[122] "Emlyn, Kentucky," *GH* 1, no. 8 (February 1943): 8.

[123] "Emlyn, Kentucky," *GH* 1, no. 6 (December 1942): 6.

[124] Randall Watkins, "Our Paper", *GH* 1, no. 2, (August 1942): 4.

[125] Middlesboro CGMA, "Record Sisters Service," 19.

126 Dora Moses, "Testimonials," *GH* 1, no. 1 (July 1942): 9.

127 Sisters of the Jellico Church, "Jellico, Tenn," *GH* 1, no. 4 (October 1942): 2.

128 "Jellico, Tenn.," *GH* 1, no. 3 (September 1942): 3.

129 "Sidney, Ohio," *GH* 1, no. 4 (October 1942): 2.

130 CGMA, *Minutes of the Church of God of the Mountain Assembly Incorporated: Forty-Second Annual Assembly* (Jellico, TN: CGMA, 1948), 8.

131 In 1976, General Overseer Jerome Walden appointed the first National Ladies Willing Worker Band officers. Two years later, the Mountain Assembly adopted a measure to add the department officially to its standard resolutions.

132 CGMA, *Minutes* (1948), 8, 10.

133 Luther Gibson, "Special from the General Overseer," *GH* 7, no. 3 (September 1948): 1.

134 CGMA, *Minutes* (1948), 9, 12, 15; "42nd Annual Assembly," *GH* 7, no. 4 (October 1948): 1.

135 Randall Watkins, "Corbin, Ky.," and "Kentucky Ministers' Meeting," *GH* 6, no. 10 (April 1948): 6, 8; Dover Kasee, "Cincinnati, Ohio," *GH* 6, no. 11 (May 1948): 5; Mildred Deal, "Sidney, Ohio," *GH* 7, no. 1 (July 1948): 3; Frank O'Rourke, "Kenvir, Ky.," *GH* 7, no. 2 (August 1948): 2. Church reports in *GH* during this same time period also mention revivals Thomas conducted at Coldiron, Middlesboro, Ages, Jellico, and East Bernstadt. Thomas's monthly minister reports printed in the church paper record him preaching 143 sermons from March through August 1948.

136 Edward Woolum, "Special to the Herald," *GH* 7, no. 2 (August 1948): 8.

137 CGMA, *Minutes* (1948), 13.

138 Middlesboro CGMA, YPE Ledger: 1946 to 1947, Middlesboro, Ky, 45.

139 Middlesboro CGMA, Junior Class Sunday School Record: 1949-1951., Middlesboro, Ky.

140 "Kentucky State Meeting," *GH* 7, no. 5 (November 1948): 1.

141 "42nd Annual Assembly," *GH* 7, no. 4 (October 1948): 1.

142 John H. Parks, "The Difference Between False Teachers and Gospel Teachers," *GH* 1, no. 2 (August 1942): 1; C.L. Price, "A Church Message," *GH* 1, no. 5 (November 1942): 3.

143 Conn, 198-202, 210.

144 CGMA, *Minutes* (1940), 11.

145 CGMA, *Minutes* (1941), 17-19.

146 CGMA, *Minutes* (1944), 13-16.

147 CGMA, *Minutes* (1942), 12.

148 Ibid., 11.

149 CGMA, *Minutes* (1943), 10.

150 Licensed Ministers Examination Blank, Williams file.

151 Personal Data, Williams file.

152 See Alda B. Harrison, "Everybody Read This," *The Lighted Pathway* 9, no. 12 (December 1938): 25.

153 John H. Bryant, "To Whom it May Concern," *GH* 5, no. 5 (November 1946): 8.

154 Conn, 208.

155 Ibid., 254-255.

156 The Mountain Assembly retained this preference until 1944 when "delegate" returned to common usage.

157 Jones, 14-15.

158 CGMA, *Minutes* (1907), 2.

159 CGMA, *Minutes* (1928), 11; CGMA, *Minutes* (1929), 3.

160 CGMA, *Minutes* (1944), 8.

161 Bryant, "Concern," 8.

162 CGMA, *Minutes* (1944), 8-9.

163 Ibid., 8-10.

164 Ibid.

165 Andrew Long, "General Overseer Speaks," *GH* 3, no. 9 (March 1945): 1.

166 Long, "General Overseers Report," *GH* 4, no. 12 (June 1945): 1.

167 Bryant, "Concern," 8.

168 Reports in the March 1945 issue of *GH* show Long visiting Kenvir, Marion, and Ages and Lawson visiting Monroe, Kokomo, and Dayton.

169 R.N. Ballinger, "Dayton, Ohio," and Roy Cornelius, "Greetings from the Ohio State Overseer," *GH* 3, no. 9 (March 1945): 5, 6.

170 "The Toledo Shelton Park Church," *GH* 33, no. 12 (December 1972): 7.

171 Mae Fitzpatrick, "Toledo, Ohio," *GH* 2, no. 12 (June 1944): 3.

172 CGMA, *Minutes* (1944), 26; Mae Fitzpatrick, "Toledo, Ohio," *GH* 3, no. 1 (July 1944): 3.

173 Agnes Massingill, "Monroe, Mich.," and Mae Fitzpatrick, "Toledo, Ohio," *GH* 3, no. 9 (March 1945): 3.

174 CGMA, *Minutes of the Churches of God Mountain Assembly Incorporated: Thirty-Ninth Annual Assembly* (Jellico, TN: CGMA, 1945), 7, 9-10.

175 Ibid., 17.

176 Ibid., 13-14.

177 Ibid., 9.

A Bow Tied

Minister	A	G	Profession	County, ED, Pg, Ln
Akin, V.L.	37	6	minister	Monroe, MI, 58-41, 2a, 39
Alder, A.C.	79	1	unable to work	Whitley, KY, 118-17, 8a, 34
Allison, William			*unable to locate*	
Baird, Joshua	67	8	minister	Washington, IN, 88-23, 3a, 23
Baird, Lewis	48	5	coal operator	Campbell, TN, 7-20, 8b, 52
Baird, Mckinley	41	8	Goodrich rubber	Portage, OH, 67-38, 8a, 16
Ball, TR	34	5	timber	Whitley, KY, 118-4, 6a, 29
Bolton, Neal	53	8	foreman	Whitley, KY, 118-13, 9b, 59
Broyles, L.M.	74	3	unable to work	Whitley, KY, 118-2, 8b, 47
Bryant, Bob	40	5	farmer	Laurel, KY, 39-3, 3a, 11
Bryant, J.H.	51	8	travel salesman	McCreary, KY, 74-3, 2b, 67
Byrd, Jim	66	5	unable to work	Scott, TN, 76-7, 1b, 67
Byrge, Mark	37	5	labor	Scott, TN, 76-5, 18a, 28
Chambers, Blag	40	5	section hand	Scott, TN, 76-8, 24b, 71
Cornelius, Roy	27	8	minister	Hamilton, OH, 91-305, 9a, 24
Creekmore, John	53	3	miner	Whitley, KY, 118-18, 10a, 26
Cupp, W.L.	39	8	farmer	Whitley, KY, 118-6, 17b, 72
Davis, H.C.	37	7	machinist	Clermont, OH, 13-4, 13b, 41
Douglas, R.L.	38	3	miner	Campbell, TN, 7-20, 15b, 60
Ellis, C.B.	51	8	miner	Bell, KY, 7-19, 11a, 31
Ellis, Ottis	30	5	miner	Bell, KY, 7-19, 11a, 5
Fore, Leslie	33	7	labor	McCreary, KY, 74-4, 10b, 42
Gibson, Luther	26	8	minister	Harlan, KY, 48-11, 11b, 41
Goins, Charlie	40	6	unable to work	Whitley, KY, 118-23, 10a, 20
Goins, William Lee	22	7	unable to work	Whitley, KY, 118-3, 3b, 74
Guy, Alex	52	0	miner	Campbell, TN, 7-1, 7a, 25
Guy, Carl	36	4	fireman	Howard, IN, 34-29, 7b, 51
Guy, E.L.	63	4	unable to work	Claiborne, TN, 13-22, 15b, 46
Hammitte, David	52	0	minister	Bell, KY, 7-26, 6b, 72
Harris, W.A.	63	4	unable to work	Pulaski, KY, 100-22, 8b, 43
Hatfield, John E.	35	12	bookkeeper	Campbell, TN, 7-20, 8b, 47
Huff, Briscoe	39	8	labor	Harlan, KY, 48-22, 6b, 57
Inman, Everett H.	38	8	auto mechanic	McCreary, KY, 74-3, 2a, 25
Isaac, Carl	28	8	rougher	Howard, IN, 34-16, 11a, 36
King, L.C.	67	8	tenant farmer	Whitley, KY, 118-17, 16a, 1
Laws, Coy	40	5	polisher	Shelby, OH, 75-9, 8a, 8
Lawson, Charles E.	18	12	housework	Whitley, KY, 118-7, 12a, 20
Lawson, Clayton	29	8	pastor	Hamilton, OH, 91-305, 8b, 58
Lawson, Wesley	53	0	coal loader	Bell, KY, 7-9, 11b, 50
Litton, R.D.	62	4	evangelist	Shelby, OH, 75-2, 61a, 18
Long, A.Z.	50	8	proprietor	Scott, TN, 76-7, 4a, 2
Long, Andrew	46	12	farmer	Campbell, TN, 7-12, 2b, 74

A Denominational Government

Minister	A	G	Profession	County, ED, Pg, Ln
Longsworth, James			unable to locate	
Lynch, Joe	52	5	unable to work	Campbell, TN, 7-20, 21a, 9
Mayes, James	55	3	janitor	Monroe, MI, 58-32, 24a, 18
Meadows, Mark	59	6	farmer	Whitley, KY, 118-20, 8b, 74
Miller, Walter	42	7	labor	Tipton, IN, 80-11, 3a, 14
Miracle, Bill	40	5	mining	Knox, KY, 61-5, 24a, 5
Moses, Emby	33	3	miner	Whitley, KY, 118-18, 20a, 25
Moses, Kim	49	7	farmer	Whitley, KY, 118-18, 19a, 22
Moses, Lewis M.	49	8	labor	Whitley, KY, 118-2, 12a, 1
Mowery, James	58	6		Pinellas, FL, 52-54, 1a, 9
Oliver, J.A.	42	5	farmer	Blount, TN, 5-29b, 6a, 16
Orrick, Scott	35	8	coal loader	Bell, KY, 7-32, 6b, 51
Parks, John H.	78	0	unable to work	Campbell, TN, 7-19, 3a, 29
Phelps, David G.	37	6	truck driver	Whitley, KY, 118-8, 2b, 63
Phelps, Harve	39	5	minister	Whitley, KY, 118-10, 2a, 14
Price, C.L.	65	4	unable to work	Whitley, KY, 118-10, 9a, 7
Pruitt, Ed	53	4	labor	Whitley, KY, 118-13, 5a, 10
Scalf, K.T.	67	8	unable to work	Knox, KY, 97-72, 2b, 76
Sharp, L.M.	53	9	telegraph op.	Campbell, TN, 7-20, 1B, 62
Sizemore, W.S.	51	5	evangelist	Laurel, KY, 63-6, 4a, 26
Smith, Bill	33	4	farmer	Whitley, KY, 118-4, 20b, 64
Smith, Davis	68	3	unable to work	Washington, OH, 84-6, 20b, 67
Smith, J.C.	53	3	unable to work	Rockcastle, KY, 102-5, 1b, 56
Spencer, J.D.	45	8	farmer	Putnam, FL, 54-29, 4b, 80
Stephens, Albert	45	6	taxi driver	Harlan, KY, 48-48, 2b, 63
Tribble, Abraham H.	39	3	gear grinder	Wayne, MI, 84-767, 1b, 78
Williams, John R.	47	1	coal loader	McCreary, KY, 74-4, 9a, 28
Woods, Thomas	52	8	pastor	Tipton, IN, 80-11, 1a, 26
Woolum, Clarence	33	4	carpenter	Wayne, MI, 84-504, 1b, 53
Woolum, M.E.	61	8	minister	Summit, OH, 89-225, 61a, 16
Yeary, Ernie	38	6	minister	Campbell, TN, 7-19, 2a, 35

Table 7.1: 1940 U.S. Census Data for CGMA Ordained Ministers. Key: Age, Highest Grade Completed, Enumeration District, Page number, Line Number.

8

Surviving a Schism

The creation of a strong centralized polity increased the prestige and power of the office of the General Overseer. His new duty "to look after the general interest of all the churches" required frequent travel. "When traveling on official business for the assembly," the Overseer was entitled to "draw his expenses from the tithes of tithes treasury."[1] The opportunity to preach in churches for a love offering and be reimbursed for traveling expenses appealed to ministers who desired full-time ministry and had a heart for evangelism. Annual elections provided ample opportunities for ambitious ministers to seek office and opened the door for divisive politics within the church.

The Ladies Willing Worker Bands became an integral part of the fund-raising efforts of the local churches. Weekly meetings of the sisters offered inspiration and fellowship to those who attended. In the mid-1940s however, several local churches experienced confusion due to excessive and abusive spiritual practices initiated in the sisters' meetings. The new episcopal polity presented a mechanism for its national leadership to assist in the resolution of church controversies. When mishandled, however, discord in the local churches led to conflict in the organization.

Ministry ambition, spiritual abuses, and general discontent over the change in government led to a change in leadership in 1946. The polarization of the issues created two distinct factions in the Mountain Assembly. Disgruntled ministers and those loyal to Andrew J. Long left the 40th Annual Assembly, created a new organization, and returned to the original polity. The Church of God of the Original Mountain Assembly met for its first assembly in Williamsburg, Kentucky, the following month. In the wake of the schism, the new leadership of John Bryant and Luther Gibson held the organization together and strengthened its still developing episcopal polity.

Desiring the Office of a Bishop

By the mid-1940s, two factions developed, one seeking to retain power and the other seeking to usurp it. Some saw it developing. Elder Ira Moses affirmed to Elder Lewis Baird in early 1946 that "you know there is a carnel [sic] sprit trying to rule the Assembley [sic]."[2] Gibson later admitted that, after the deaths of Parks and Bryant, "the spirit of politics got among us to a great extent, and politics and leadership caused our church to have another great struggle." He condemned such carnality.

> When we get to the place where we want to be leaders so bad that just before the assembly, we get our crowd and start drumming up votes, we are then out of the will of God. The Church of God is not run with a carnal mind. God will not allow it to go on that way. I think the Church of God today is in better condition than she has ever been. When we let political schemery [sic] get into the church, we are getting ready for a fall.³

Hindsight provided clearer perception than foresight. The Church of God (Cleveland) survived a devastating split over leadership twenty years earlier. Now after the Mountain Assembly modified its polity to match, it was headed for such conflict as well.

The change in government positioned the Mountain Assembly for another attempt to merge with the Church of God (Cleveland). In the winter of 1946, A.J. Long, Kim Moses, J.E. Hatfield, Clayton Lawson, Luther Gibson, and Ira Moses traveled to Cleveland after "The Cleveland Assembly wrote us about coming together and being one people." J.H. Bryant intended to go as well, but sickness prohibited him from making the trip. After a "favorable" meeting, word circulated among some of the uninvited Elders and ministers that the men "had gone to the Cleveland Assembly," and this rumor contributed to the growing tension in the organization.⁴

In its first forty years, the Mountain Assembly had grown from ten churches with 405 members to 47 churches with 2,133 members.⁵ By contrast, the Church of God (Cleveland) had grown from four churches at its first assembly to 1,970 churches with over 77,000 members in the United States with another 805 churches and 38,000 members in foreign countries.⁶ Some men believed the Mountain Assembly, now structured with the same government as the Church of God, was capable of experiencing similar growth. Clayton Lawson adhered to such and felt confident that his leadership could help realize that envisioned growth. Lawson had experienced success as an evangelist and as a pastor. As an evangelist, Lawson saw 179 converts in a single year before assuming the pastorate of his home church in Cincinnati.⁷ In his first ten years as its pastor, the Cincinnati church received 147 members by baptism and another 61 by letter and by recommendation, and tithe receipts increased by 400 percent.⁸ Under Lawson's leadership, the church purchased a larger building on Linn Street and then later another even larger building on the corner of 15th and Race Streets.⁹

While Lawson's vision for organizational growth formed the primary motivation for his leadership ambitions, he undoubtedly found the prospect of financial compensation for his ministerial services appealing as well. Lawson unsuccessfully sought the election of one of the Mountain Assembly's field evangels in 1937.[10] He was already engaged in full-time evangelism, and the ability to draw funds from the Assembly treasury for traveling expenses would have greatly assisted him. Lawson's success in evangelism earned him an election at the following assembly, and he drew $200 from the tithe of tithe fund that year.[11] As the Assistant General Overseer from 1944 to 1946, Lawson traveled extensively for the Mountain Assembly while pastoring the church in Cincinnati and drew nearly $1,000 from the tithe of tithes fund.[12]

Figure 8.1: Clayton and Lassie Lawson
c/o Debbie Cochran

Lawson and Luther Gibson had served on the committee to draft a new system of government for the Mountain Assembly, and they envisioned a time when the offices of General Overseer and Assistant would be compensated with full-time salaries.[13] Lawson's aspirations for the Mountain Assembly's highest office were no secret. He had run multiple times for Moderator and General Overseer, but Long's popularity and three decades of fidelity kept him in power. The new system of government presented the potential to change that. The election of officers by the Bishops Council under the new polity reduced the number of eligible voters to half the previous number.[14] At the first Bishops Council meeting during the 39th General Assembly in 1945, Long nevertheless won reelection for the office.[15] Defeating Long would require some injury to his reputation.

Long's dependence on his close circle of friends, with Kim Moses at the center, seemed to isolate other ministers and drove a "wedge" between the factions that were forming in the Mountain Assembly. Ira Moses had been elected to the Elder Board in 1945 with Long's endorsement, yet the Kenvir pastor felt like his opinion on any matter was discarded in favor of that of his distant cousin. Ira was convinced that if he told the General Overseer "that someone was killed here in Harlan and some one in Whitley Co[unty] would say I don't think that they are," Long would choose to believe "some fellows before he will listen to any body else." Moses's feelings were hurt when he learned that the General Overseer had driven by his house without stopping, but after a prophecy was given at Ages and not endorsed by Long, Moses's confidence in the General Overseer was "gone... all gone."[16]

Pentecostalism in Excess

From the earliest days of the modern Pentecostal movement, fanaticism, excess, and abuse were present. "From the start the Azusa Street Mission occupied experimental territory." A handful of New Testament passages guided the early church on the proper place of the gifts of the Holy Spirit, but their practice had been marginalized, if not eliminated, for centuries. No church leader in Los Angeles in 1906 could offer guidance to William J. Seymour on Pentecostal practice, nor correct Azusa Street worshippers "when they had gone too far."[17] One local pastor who visited the mission as an observer praised the revival for its evangelistic fervor but expressed concern that "certain of the enthusiasts might lose their reason through over zeal and become dangerous."[18] At the mission, "people spoke in tongues, prophesied, preached divine healing, went into trances, saw visions and engaged in other phenomena such as jumping, rolling, laughing, shouting, barking, and falling under the power of the Holy Spirit."[19] One such phenomenon was the perceived ability to write, as well as speak, in other "tongues."

In early 1901, Agnes Ozman had "written in tongues" while a student at Charles Fox Parham's Bethel Bible School in Topeka, Kansas. At the Azusa Street Mission revival in 1906, the practice was introduced there. Not finding any scriptural support for it, Seymour officially denounced it; but when missionaries left Azusa Street to evangelize Salem and Portland, Oregon, they carried the exercise with them.[20] Another practitioner of writing in tongues was sixteen-year-old Lillian Keyes. Lillian was the daughter of Dr. Henry Sheridan Keyes, a leading surgeon and hospital president who attended First New Testament Church in Los Angeles. Pastor Joseph Smale founded the congregation in September 1905 when the church board at his former pastorate, First Baptist Church, withdrew its support for his protracted prayer meetings for revival. The Keyes family were among the members of First New Testament Church who attended the revival at the Azusa Street Mission and experienced spiritual baptism. In July 1906, Lillian began to speak and write in tongues, prophesy, and lay in the floor, "slain in the Spirit."[21]

The practices caused conflict in First New Testament Church when Lillian delivered Smale a handwritten prophecy asserting that the pastor had "grieved the Holy Spirit" by being too stringent towards those who desired more spiritual liberty in the church. Smale responded by suggesting to Keyes that his daughter had "become a victim of fanaticism" and might possibly be under the influence of an evil spirit. Lillian delivered a second declaration to Smale in which she counseled him "to give up ambition in connection with his church work." Not long after the second judgment was delivered, Lillian stood up in a worship service and attempted to admonish the pastor publicly through prophecy. The pastor interrupted her and called the church "to ignore her as he led them in a song." After the congregation split over the events, Smale defended the authentic working of the Holy Spirit and gift of tongues while he recognized the existence of abuses. "Some of my people have it without a doubt and they are good, conscientious Christians, but the devil, as well as God is having a hand in this."[22]

As the Pentecostal Movement migrated east, the Church of God (Cleveland) and the Mountain Assembly were not exempt from fanaticism and excess. The Appalachian serpent-handling tradition, for example, began with the conversion of George Went Hensley at the Owl Hollow Church of God in 1908. Shortly after Hensley prayed through and renounced tobacco, moonshine, and worldliness, he carried a rattlesnake down from White Oak Mountain after a time of devout prayer. Hensley began to preach that "believers should practice *all* Jesus had commanded—including taking up serpents." By 1914, the Church of God (Cleveland) fully endorsed the practice. The *Church of God Evangel* published more than 80 reports of serpent-handling in Church of God services from 1914 to 1935. The practice was marginalized after deaths and maiming from serpent bites became more frequent in the 1920s.[23] While the Mountain Assembly and its leadership never endorsed the practices of serpent and fire handling, the church at Jellico Creek reported to the *Evangel* in 1915 that a sixteen-year-old boy "while under the power went to a grate of fire made of coal" and "took up a double handful of coals and carried them over the house without the least sign of fire on his hands." The same report included the account of a fifteen-year-old girl who also "dipped her hands in the fire then put them on her face and neck as if washing" with "no sign of fire on her, not even a hair singed."[24]

After the Mountain Assembly entered the Pentecostal Movement in 1909, tongues and interpretation of tongues became commonplace in the assembly meetings. At the 4th Annual General Assembly, for example, "the Lord wonderfuly [sic] blessed the people at Jellico Creek. Some were convert[ed], some were sanctified, [and] some filled with the Holy Ghost and spoke with new tongues the Lord working with them with Signs following."[25] The 8th Annual Session of the Mountain Assembly in Elk Valley in 1914 featured "many messages by speaking with other tongues as the Spirit gave utterance and the interpretation threw [sic] the spirit giving instructions for the assembly to be led by."[26] As tongue speech, interpretation, and prophecy grew more prevalent among the churches, signs of fanaticism began to appear. One member of the church at Jellico, though blind, testified that "after the Lord saved him and sanctified him, He baptized him with the Holy Ghost. Then sometime later He gave to him the gift of writing under the power of the Holy Ghost, in which he took great delight."[27]

By the 1940s this practice had spread to several churches. During a revival at Kenvir the first week of 1945, "the Holy Ghost worked in an amazing manner; moving on five sisters in order, all writing in plain English." Once completed the message was read by Pastor Ira Moses, "Therefore I have heard your prayers, and I am in your midst to bless this people; try me, and I'll prove my church."[28] As such practices spread, ecstatic spirituality ultimately created conflict when extremism dominated the weekly sisters' meetings in a handful of the local churches. Interpretation of tongues was often written down in the sisters' meetings and later brought to an individual at home or at church, where the prophetic word was delivered. As the messages of Lillian Keyes to Joseph Smale, the tone of these insights was often negative and condemning. Their predictions also rarely came to pass.[29]

No misuse of spiritual gifts in the 1940s was more grievous than the case of the family of Cordell Partin. Partin was born in Pound, Virginia on January 24, 1926 to Amanda Jane (Mullins) and James Henry Partin.[30] In the early 1930s, Jim Partin left his farm in Wise County, Virginia and moved to the coal camp at Pruden, Kentucky and began loading coal.[31] As a teenager, Cordell began attending the Mountain Assembly church at Fonde and became a devout and sincere Christian. On January 23, 1944, he attended a "wonderful meeting" at the Henderson Grove Church in nearby Frakes with several members of the Fonde church.[32] The following day, he registered for the selective service on his 18th birthday.[33] Four months later, he was drafted and reported to Fort Thomas in Newport, Kentucky on May 25.[34] At his last Sunday night service, the Fonde church surrounded him with prayer, and Glenn Rowe sang, "God Be With You Until We Meet Again." Some criticized him for his song selection, suggesting that it seemed ominous.[35]

Partin was assigned to the United States Army and sent to Camp Atterbury near Edinburgh, Indiana for combat training. Despite his circumstances, his faith and religious convictions remained strong. He wrote his mother four weeks later, "I got a pass today. I can go to Indianapolis if I want to. But I ain't [sic]." While many of his fellow enlistees took advantage of the weekend to visit any number of amusements the state capital had to offer, Cordell was interested in going only one place. He encouraged his family back home to "go to church, all of you. You couldn't go to a better place."[36]

Figure 8.2: PFC Cordell Partin
c/o Mike Partin

On August 2, Private First Class Partin was shipped to Camp Barkeley near Abilene, Texas.[37] Because his church taught "against going to war and killing," Partin held conscientious objections to combat. Twenty-five years earlier, the church at Fonde had excluded members who joined the army during World War I, but by the Second World War members had come to interpret the church teaching with the specification "but not against being subject in other dutys [sic] on a con objector."[38] Partin decided not "to carry any weapon for his self-defense. He believed that if it was the Lord's will that his life would be spared, he did not need any weapon. If it was God's plan that he die, a weapon would not protect him."[39] During World War II, the United States Army housed one of its three Medical Replacement Training Centers at Camp Barkeley.[40] Cordell's training in Texas prepared him to administer first aid to soldiers wounded in combat.[41] Partin continued to correspond with his mother back home, sending greetings to his church friends in the community and encouraging a sister "to go to church when she can" and his little brother to "be good and go to Sunday school ever time that they are any." His letters also pleaded with Mandy and Jim to "go to church not for my good only."[42]

From Camp Barkeley, Partin was shipped to Camp Beale near Marysville City, California. During World War II, the camp "served as a personnel replacement depot, which meant that soldiers were sent to Beale temporarily while waiting for their assignments."[43] As his departure for the Pacific theater grew more imminent, Mandy Partin grew more anxious, while her son's faith grew stronger. It was not uncommon for the local women's auxiliaries to devote time in their afternoon meetings for "special prayers for their children that are in the armed forces," and the church continued to pray for their young brother's safe return.[44] At one sisters' meeting that spring, a prophecy was written down for Mandy Partin that her prompt obedience was the key to her son's swift and safe return when he would answer the call to ministry and become a great preacher. Cordell urged his "dearest mother" to "do whatever that writing told you to do." The "wonderful sweet promise" of God given to Mandy was that her son would "be home quicker to do the things that God wants me to do." If Mandy would only "call upon Him," then God would save her and "deliver" her son, and "the quicker" she called, the "sooner" he "would be delivered home." Faced with the prospect of going to Japan soon, Partin acknowledged to Mandy that there were "things facing me that never faced me before, but Mother, by the help of my King, I'm trusting him until I die." Cordell conceded, "I don't know how long I will be here, but I will trust God until I die. I know he will deliver me."[45]

In May 1945, "Cordell joined the 32nd Infantry Regiment" on Okinawa and was "assigned to a rifle company as company aid man" where his excellence earned him "the confidence and admiration and gratitude of the men of the company." On June 8, his company attacked the "last escarpment on the southern end of Okinawa Island." As he rushed "to the aid of a wounded man, he was shot and instantly killed by a sniper" hidden in the steep slope "covered with large rocks, caves, and brush." A short time later, a "War Department announcement" arrived at the coal mines where Jim Partin worked and informed him that his son had been killed in action.[46] Glenn Rowe went down into the mines to deliver the devastating news to his co-worker.[47] The emotional pain of losing a child could not compare to what the Partin family was about to endure. One of the sisters prophesied that week that the news report was inaccurate, that Cordell was still alive, and would be home soon.[48]

When Mandy Partin received a letter from the Medical Corps Commanding Officer in July providing the details of her son's death in Japan, church members again prophesied that the report was false. While the family awaited the return of the fallen soldier's body, zealous church members encouraged them not to give up hope, but to trust in the Lord. As the emotional frenzy continued, the Fonde church broke out into spontaneous revival. Scott Orick did most of the preaching, and every morning and evening the evangelist waited at the train station expecting Cordell Partin to arrive. Additional prophecies promised Partin's return; one assured the church he was "so close to home, I can see the buttons on his uniform."[49]

Pastor Andrew Long generally commuted to Fonde from Elk Valley two weekends a month but was also consumed with visiting as many Mountain Assembly churches as he could in his new capacity as General Overseer. As a result, the church lacked strong leadership to intervene in the confusion. As the revival waned over the course of nine months, hope was lost, and the matter quickly became something no one discussed. Partin's remains finally returned to Pruden in February 1949, almost four years after he was killed in action in Okinawa.[50] The perplexed and despondent Jim and Mandy Partin buried their son at the Fonde-Pruden Cemetery.[51] Their only comfort could be found in the faith of their son evidenced by the words he scrawled on the back of his last letter, "Blessed are they that believe and yet have not seen."[52]

Amid the confusion at Fonde in 1946, the spiritual controversy spread to Middlesboro. One of the women at the center of this spiritual work relocated with her family amid the confusion and joined the church there. When she began attending sisters' meetings, the same manifestations of interpretation of tongues and prophecy continued now at Middlesboro. In the earliest days of the sisters' meetings at Middlesboro, Pastor Ottis Ellis often attended and led in prayer, sang, or offered commentary on one of the bible lessons taught.[53] After one female member falsely prophesied that a visiting minister had been smoking a pipe, Ellis knew action must be taken to remedy the problem.[54]

Figure 8.3: Dave Hammitte & Ottis Ellis c/oMiddlesboro CGMA

Local Church Schisms and Centralized Polity

The General Overseer, Andrew Long, visited the Middlesboro church in late winter 1946 but was not able to remedy the problem.[55] When Ellis brought charges against the offending member that spring, the church voted to exclude her. Several members in the church remained sympathetic to her, and they were also excluded as a result.[56] That spring, Long held "a meeting at Middlesboro" and took "sides with excluded members."[57] State Overseer and Elder C.L. Price visited the Middlesboro church at least three times during the controversy.[58] In May, Elders Morris Woolum and David Hammitte also visited the church.[59] The situation at Middlesboro was discussed when the Board of Twelve Elders met in Monroe, Michigan in July. The Elders determined that Long had "become out of order by violating the rules of our assembly by taking sides with excluded members against their pastors." Elder John H. Bryant warned Long at that time that "he would be counted out of order to run for Overseer" if he did not resolve the issue "before the assembly."[60]

When the 40th Annual Mountain Assembly opened and the Bishops' Council met on Tuesday, September 3, 1946, the Board of Twelve Elders ruled that "that the Bishops only be present for the business" and the assembly entered a closed session. Andrew Long and Clayton Lawson were nominated for General Overseer. Just as Bryant had warned, Long's nomination for General Overseer was challenged "as it is reported of him being out of order." Lawson "took charge of the meeting" and "the charges were presented against Brother Long for not upholding the government of the assembly, and the council found him guilty." After that, chaos ensued. Some wanted to "hear the different questions that concern the breaking of the government of the assembly." Others responded with comments and criticisms that were ruled out of order. After the council asked "Kim Moses to stay in order and obey the rules of decorum" and asked the General Overseer's older brother Azree Long "to apologize," the council also found Moses "guilty of being out of order with the assembly for not upholding the government of the assembly" and referred A.Z. Long "to the first Elders' meeting after the assembly as he failed to be reconciled to the council."[61] Moses, the Longs, and "some of the brethren left that day and never did return."[62]

In the aftermath of the disruption, the council rescinded "the first motion on the election of officers" and elected John H. Bryant as General Overseer. Bryant's father had served the Mountain Assembly as moderator longer than any other man, and the ministers perhaps felt like he was best suited to guide the organization "during those trying times."[63] To assist him, the council elected Esom Bert Bryant II, who had returned from the Church of God (Cleveland) two years earlier when the Mountain Assembly adopted its new system of government.

Figure 8.4: John H. Bryant

c/o CGMA

J.E. Hatfield was reelected Secretary & Treasurer with Ira Moses as his assistant. The following morning, the newly elected General Overseer preached the introductory sermon to those who remained and exhorted them to "walk in the spirit" and "not be desirous of vain glory, provoking one another, envying one another."[64]

The schism continued to affect the business. One minister advised his delegates not to submit their letter and was counted out of order. When it became apparent that Long and Moses were not coming back, the Bishop's Council voted to terminate their trusteeship and eldership. The following day, Elder Joshua Baird was removed for poor health, and Elder Lewis Baird was removed for not being "qualified for the place."[65] With little resistance to change remaining, the Mountain Assembly continued copying from the Church of God (Cleveland) what it saw as necessary for growth. These measures included the creation of an office building for the assembly, a second level of ministerial credentials, an appointing board, and an emergency fund for aged ministers.[66]

The office space in the tabernacle became a repository of assembly records, and place for the General Secretary & Treasurer to transact the assembly's business. When the Mountain Assembly appointed a committee the following year to "work out a resolution in regard to the General Overseer, and how to finance him for full time work," the General Overseer would also use the office on a regular basis. The committee—Luther Gibson, Ira Moses, and J.E. Hatfield—proposed that the General Overseer "not be allowed to pastor a church, but shall spend his full time in the work" and would be paid $65 per week, plus traveling expenses and "living quarters."[67]

The Baptist church had two offices, the ordained bishop and deacon. For its first forty years, the Mountain Assembly continued this tradition, and the only ministerial credentials it offered were to the ordained minister. The Church of God (Cleveland), however, "agreed to license some who were good evangelists but could not quite measure up to the requirements for ordination" at its second assembly in 1907.[68] In 1925, a third "order of ministry" was added to ministerial credentials. "Exhorters" who had the endorsement of their pastor and State Overseer might act in that capacity "for a year or two before he is set forth as an evangelist."[69] The Board of Twelve Elders of the Mountain Assembly had discussed in its 1945-46 meetings the possibility of issuing "Bishop's, Evangelist's, and Exhorter's papers." When presented to the delegates at the 1946 Mountain Assembly, "it was moved in order to have Bishop's and Evangelist's papers only." An application form was authorized, and the annually licensed evangelist was given "the right to preach the gospel, baptize believers, to administer the Lord's Supper, and washing of the saints' feet." A licensed evangelist might pastor a church "under the supervision of his State Overseer" in an "emergency," and all licensed and ordained ministers were required to pay tithes.[70]

As the Church of God (Cleveland) grew and the oversight of its congregations and appointments of its pastors became too great a burden for one man, the Assembly approved the office of State Overseers and appointed the first seven in 1911.[71] Two years later, the Assembly agreed that there existed "no better plan" than that "the State Overseers be appointed by the General Overseer."[72] When the Mountain Assembly created the office of State Overseers, like in the Church of God, they were selected by the Bishops' Council. Two years later, the Mountain Assembly created an "appointing board" to select the State Overseers. This board consisted of the General Overseer, Assistant Overseer, and General Secretary & Treasurer.[73]

The Great Depression forced into poverty many who had worked their whole lives. Most Americans continued to work for as long as they were physically able. While the Roosevelt administration investigated the feasibility of what became the Social Security Act of 1935, the Church of God (Cleveland) adopted a plan to assist its ministers who were "expected to work with scant recompense during their active years and then spend their later years with little or no provision."[74] The program called for each minister whose total income was greater than $50 per month to pay one percent of his income to "create a fund for the support of aged ministers" and that each church take a special offering each year in order to supplement the fund.[75]

The plan adopted by the Mountain Assembly in 1946 initially called for an "emergency fund, from which we may assist our aged ministers and the widows of aged ministers" to be funded from free-will offerings. Each church was encouraged to send a monthly offering for its support.[76] The assembly experimented with this endeavor over the next few years. One plan required ministers to send twelve percent of their income to headquarters, with the addition to their tithes designated to the "Aged Minister Fund."[77] Another designated three percent of his tithes to the fund.[78] The fund was abandoned in 1949 until a new one emerged in 1955.[79] The 1955-56 plan proposed by the Board of Elders gave that body discretion and oversight of the fund. Ministers reaching the age of 60 who had actively engaged for the past 15 years with ministry as his primary occupation would be entitled to a monthly allotment of one dollar for each year of service, plus a "rightful" amount determined by the Board "according to his record." No benefit was to exceed $65 per month. A minister's widow might also receive one-half the amount for which her husband would have been eligible.[80]

The departure of Long, Moses, and a significant number of ministers brought division and strain to the Mountain Assembly. It also simultaneously facilitated the further development of episcopal polity. The measures introduced and adopted at the 40th Annual Mountain Assembly contributed to a stronger centralized government and emphasized the organization at the heart of the church rather than the local congregations. Those sympathetic to Long and Moses used the occasion of his trial and ouster to form a new association modeled after their Baptist roots. For them, the spiritual revolution that began in 1907 had reached its pinnacle, and as a Thermidorian Reaction, they led the church back towards its congregationalist roots.

The Church of God of the Original Mountain Assembly

After Long, Moses, and the others left the Bishops' Council on Tuesday, September 3, they met in Williamsburg three days later. "Fifteen preachers and eight deacons and approximately two hundred members" gathered "for the purpose of re-establishing the old platform of the said Church of God, set in order at Ryons [sic] Creek, Ky., in the year of 1907."[81] John H. Bryant attended the meeting as an observer along with newly elected Elder R.N. Ballinger, and Ira Moses, Assistant General Secretary & Treasurer, who "took a record of the transactions of this meeting."[82] After preaching from Hebrews 2, Long called the delegation to order for business. The delegates voted to

> reaffirm and establish the principle and doctrine of the said Church of God. Herein from the date of its organization, the 24th day of August, 1907, which date appears in the Minutes 1917 of which organization was governered [sic] until 1944, which changed the government of the Assembly from the original principal to General Overseers and State Overseers and a Bishop's Council and Complser [sic] of certain rulings. Also evangelist and exhorters' papers and other rulings. We don't approve of such government and declare ourselves to be apart from this new set-up and to be on the old original platform and principles and foundation of the Church of God.[83]

They voted to restore the offices of Moderator and Clerk with assistants for each and to return the election and voting power to "a delegation sent by different churches to represent their churches, the preachers and deacons, and the delegation shall make up the delegation." They reinstated the 1917 Articles of Faith and Church Covenant as originally approved, adding back

Surviving a Major Schism

the final paragraph that had been deleted.[84] The group agreed to meet in October for its general assembly at the recently organized church in Williamsburg. Back in Jellico on the following morning, Bryant, Ballinger, and Moses reported on the group's activities, and the Mountain Assembly voted to "disqualify these ministers and deacons who took part and joined with these people who are leaving the assembly, calling in their credentials."[85]

At 10:00 a.m. on October 4, the Church of God of the Original Mountain Assembly convened in Williamsburg, and Scott Orick preached the introductory sermon. Long called the 84 delegates from 22 churches to order and appointed Paul Grubbs and Willis Yeary to read the letters from the churches. Andrew Long and Kim Moses were elected Moderator and Assistant Moderator, respectively. The delegation elected Paul Grubbs as Clerk with Byrd Bray as his assistant and Everett Creekmore as treasurer. Virgil Akins and Joe Moses were appointed evangelists, and the Original Mountain Assembly reverted to the previous financial system where the pastor's tithes remained in the local church to support evangelists. Three minister's meetings were scheduled. On November 15 at the McMicken Avenue Church in Cincinnati, twelve elders were appointed. Like the Mountain Assembly had done in 1930, the first three selected were authorized to appoint the remaining nine. Long, Moses, and Lewis Baird appointed Virgil Akins, McKinley Baird, William Baird, Roy Cornelius, Charlie Goins, Paul Grubbs, Joe Moses, Lewis Moses, and Willis Yeary to join them on the Board. At this meeting, the ministers also established qualifications for the Board of Elders and for the office of Moderator. A minister had to be ordained five years to be eligible for the office of Elder and ten years to be Moderator.[86]

Figure 8.5: Andrew J. Long
c/o CGMA

Figure 8.6: Kim Moses
c/o CGMA

Figure 8.7: Paul Grubbs
c/o Kim Walden

Nine churches withdrew from Mountain Assembly in 1946: Akron, Cincinnati (McMicken Ave.), and Cleveland in Ohio; Emlyn, Goldbug, Little Wolf Creek, and Saxton, in Kentucky; and Marion and Oneida in Tennessee. Another eleven congregations split to form churches in the new association: Ages, Corbin, Cawood, Fonde, Mountain Ash, and Henderson Grove in Kentucky; Hymera-Shelburn and Kokomo-Belmont in Indiana; Valley Creek and Newcomb in Tennessee; and Goshen, Ohio. Thirty-four ordained ministers surrendered their credentials in the Mountain Assembly and received new ones in the Original Mountain Assembly. In one year, the Mountain Assembly had dropped down to 38 churches and 1,574 members.[87]

As Long worked to restore what he believed was the original plan of John Parks and Stephen Bryant, he also replicated one of the most centralizing aspects of the Mountain Assembly. In 1947, the Original Mountain Assembly appointed Kim Moses, Azree Long, and Howard Lawrence Douglas as trustees to build a new tabernacle in Williamsburg. The delegates adopted a plan whereby each church would contribute between $50 and $500 to the building fund based on its membership.[88] The churches and members responded and raised $4,738.75 for the building fund and met in the new tabernacle on Second Street for the 1948 assembly.[89] Additional funds were raised the following year, and it was reported that a total of $ 8,615.48 had been spent on the completion of the tabernacle.[90] Completing construction of this project in such a short time with virtually no initial treasury was a testament to the charismatic leadership of Long and Moses and the generous response of the churches and members.

Success, however, was short-lived. Although one of the Mountain Assembly's oldest congregations, Siler's Chapel, left to join the Original Mountain Assembly when Kim Moses's son, Kelsie, became its pastor in 1947, the following year, however, saw the first returns of Original Mountain Assembly ministers and churches back to the Mountain Assembly.[91] Finley Gray was the first.[92] Over the next two years, dissident members began returning to the Mountain Assembly congregations at Newcomb, Mountain

Ash, Cawood, and Valley Creek, and the Original Mountain Assembly congregations in those locations dissipated as a result.[93] Long assumed the pastorate of the church at Emlyn in 1949 and eventually gave up the Fonde church. The Original Mountain Assembly church at Fonde soon closed, and many members returned to the Mountain Assembly church there as well.[94]

In 1950, the Original Mountain Assembly church at Marion was dismissed from the association, and Henderson Grove and the recently organized church at Crouches Creek, Tennessee left in support. Tension had built between Byrd Bray and Elery Barnes at Marion and leadership in the Original Mountain Assembly over the reception of prophecy and spiritual gifts within the organization. Barnes asserted that "the Spirit of God began to uncover sin, and they didn't like it." When some "began to try to do away with the Spirit," the church at Marion "took their stand for the Spirit of God." Barnes further maintained that "our leaders took sides with the ones that caused the trouble and took them in sister churches."[95] Once again conflict involving the use of spiritual gifts and the support of excluded members by Long and Moses led to a schism, and Bray and Barnes organized the Way of Holiness Church of God in Marion, Tennessee in 1950.

The Original Mountain Assembly dropped from 25 churches in 1948 to 15 in 1950 and had lost over 200 members. The delegation also voted that year to revoke the ordination credentials of Virgil Akins and McKinley Baird for "departing from the faith," creating two vacancies on the Board of Twelve Elders and further depleting the number of its ministers. The fifteen churches remaining in the Original Mountain Assembly in 1950 were pastored by 13 ministers.[96] One of those ministers, Joe Moses, had founded the Original Mountain Assembly church in Williamsburg and was also pastoring at Barton's Chapel in Corbin. His resignation from those pastorates and the Board of Twelve Elders in 1951 to return to the CGMA was a devastating loss for Long. With 100 members, Williamsburg was the largest church in the organization, but within three years, its membership plummeted to 23.[97]

Roy Cornelius also returned to the Mountain Assembly in 1950 and soon accepted the pastorate of its church at Trenton, Michigan.[98] In 1951, James Walden relocated from Jellico to Cleveland, Ohio and accepted the pastorate of the Original Mountain Assembly church there. Two years earlier, Walden had been a member and delegate from the church at Crouches Creek when it organized and joined the Original Mountain Assembly.[99] In 1953, he led the Cleveland church back into the Mountain Assembly.[100] The following year, the church on McMicken Avenue in Cincinnati also returned to the

A Bow Tied

Figure 8.8: *James Walden*
c/o Jon Walden

Figure 8.9: *Willis Yeary*
c/o CGMA

Mountain Assembly and dealt a serious financial blow to Long and Moses. In 1954, the Cincinnati church had contributed more than one-third of the tithe of tithes received by the Original Mountain Assembly.[101] In 1957, the church relocated to State Avenue, and its former pastor, Willis Yeary, returned to the Mountain Assembly.[102] Yeary had been an integral part of the Original Mountain Assembly since its inception, preaching often and serving on multiple committees. He rejoined the Mountain Assembly one year after Paul Grubbs returned and brought a church for membership that he had organized on Junction Street in Detroit on May 29, 1954.[103] Grubbs had been the first clerk of the Original Mountain Assembly and had served as its treasurer.

The departure of key churches and significant pastors left the Original Mountain Assembly struggling the way the schism had left the Mountain Assembly in 1946. Long continued to serve as moderator of the Original Mountain Assembly until 1956. By the time Kelsie Moses replaced him, morale was down, and the movement was already well into decline, with less than 600 members.[104] Of the 34 ministers who left the Mountain Assembly in 1946, at least fourteen eventually returned.[105] The rationales for ministers returning were as varied as the reasons they left in the first place. Long was popular and personable, and his leadership inspired the confidence and devotion of many ministers and laymen. Kim Moses was fiercely loyal to his friend, Andrew Long. His impassioned reaction to his and Long's removal from office at the 40th Mountain Assembly moved others to follow. In contrast to Long's warmth, Lawson was often aloof, if not abrasive. His deportment gave many the impression that he was arrogant and sometimes condescending. Many ministers made a spontaneous emotional decision over personalities that they regretted once passions cooled and reason returned.

Some left the Mountain Assembly over legitimate concerns over the change in polity, as Long and Moses claimed they did. While their Baptist roots recognized the offices of bishops and deacons and made democratic decisions through a majority vote of all the members, the new government modeled after the Church of God (Cleveland) denied deacons and members a voice in the new Bishops' Council. In the Baptist church, participation in the association was always voluntary. Each church sent its letter to the yearly meeting to join the association on an annual basis, and the association and its leadership never had any jurisdiction or authority over the congregation. Long's followers viewed the new polity with a General and State Overseers as an intrusion of their congregationalism, and their churches voluntarily withdrew. After the Mountain Assembly's experiment with modified episcopalism seemed to work to the satisfaction of the local churches, some of the ministers changed their mind and returned.[106] Those most loyal to Long and those committed to autonomous local churches remained in the Original Mountain Assembly.

Luther Gibson and Episcopal Polity

Despite the schism, General Overseer J.H. Bryant reported in February 1947 "the best spirit of unity and cooperation in the ministry we have had in many years." He encouraged the ministers to "work to each other's advantage" to "promote the church." Bryant urged his five State Overseers—Charles Lawson, Morris Woolum, Arvil Rountree, E.B. Rose, and Frank Croley—to visit all the churches in their states and for each minister to report regularly to his overseer.[107] Bryant's urging for everyone to do their part produced increases to the tithe of tithes and the ministers' tithes in the second half of the fiscal year.[108] The financial rebound and spirit of harmony notwithstanding, Bryant decided not to seek reelection for General Overseer when the 41st Mountain Assembly convened in September 1947. His assistant, E.B. Bryant, had had enough as well and chose to send his resignation letter to the General Overseer and not attend the Assembly.[109]

After the Bishops' Council gave J.H. Bryant a "vote of confidence" for "his faithful service" during the tumultuous year, it appointed a "committee to work out a resolution in regard to the General Overseer, and how to finance him for full time work." Luther Gibson, Ira Moses, and J.E. Hatfield met as the committee during a recess to deliberate on the advantages and disadvantages of the proposal. The schism the previous year led to a 14 percent decline in membership and a 17 percent decrease in the combined tithes' funds, but the committee believed that a General Overseer dedicated to the work of the organization could improve morale, increase financial support, and perhaps gain back some of the ministers and churches that left.[110] When reconvened that afternoon, the committee presented its resolution to revise the office of General Overseer by not allowing him to pastor a church, but to "spend his full time in the work." They recommended a salary of $65 per week and five cents per mile for "traveling expenses" to be paid from the ministers' tithes fund, and also provide him with "living quarters."[111]

Figure 8.10: Luther Gibson
c/o CGMA

Figure 8.12: Harvey Rose
c/o North Monroe Street CGMA

Once the committee's work was accepted, the Bishops' Council elected Gibson to serve as General Overseer and Harvey Luther Rose as his assistant. Rose was pastoring the church in Monroe, Michigan and had been elected the previous year to replace Andrew Long on the Board of Twelve Elders.[112] As a result of the election and the new resolution, Gibson resigned as pastor of the Jellico Church the following Saturday, and E.B. Rose, the brother of the Assistant General Overseer, moved from Toledo to assume the pastorate. Gibson wasted no time fulfilling his new duties, visited eleven churches within thirty days of the close of the General Assembly, and drove more than 1,500 miles.[113] Harvey Rose accompanied the General Overseer on four of those church visits and resigned from his pastorate at Monroe, Michigan on September 22 to "to work as Assistant General Overseer of the Assembly."[114]

Gibson and Rose strove to unite the local congregations into a single denomination with a stronger centralized government. They appointed

Newcomb Pastor Oscar Lee Bunch as Overseer for the eight churches in Tennessee. Sidney Pastor Anderson Miller McKenzie was appointed to oversee the five churches in Ohio, two in Indiana, and two in Michigan. William Randall Watkins, former Ohio Overseer, had relocated to London, Kentucky and was appointed to oversee the 16 churches in Kentucky.[115]

Bunch plunged into the task of growing the number of churches in Tennessee. In late September 1947, he conducted a tent revival in Campbell County at Royal Blue. "Many souls were saved, and God blessed in a great way." On October 5, Gibson organized a new church there with 14 members. His brother, Charles Cecil Gibson, was elected pastor.[116] Later that week, Bunch accompanied the General Overseer to visit the church at Shelburn, Indiana to "to help them in getting a pastor," as it had been vacant since E.B. Rose left to assume the pastorate in Toledo in 1946.[117] Bunch attempted to preach at Shelburn one week each month, depending on evangelists to fill the pulpit in the meantime.[118] His absence left the church vulnerable to schism, and Scott Kaiser led a group to nearby Hymeria to organize a congregation for the Original Mountain Assembly.[119] After his visit to Shelburn with the General Overseer, Bunch returned later that month for an extended revival. In December, he relocated from Newcomb and accepted the pastorate at Shelburn. His uncle, John Bunch, replaced him as Tennessee State Overseer, and Harvey Rose briefly assumed the pastorate at Newcomb.[120]

Figure 8.11: Oscar Bunch
c/o CGMA

John Bunch attended the Mountain Assembly as a delegate from Harlan and as pastor from Twila from 1917 to 1921.[121] He left the CGMA and the coal mines of Harlan County in the 1920s and began working as a carpenter and itinerant preacher. Before moving to Jellico in 1947, he had lived in Virginia, North Carolina, and New York.[122] Gibson met him on his first visit to the Jellico church after his election as Overseer and heard him preach "a wonderful sermon." When Bunch joined the Jellico church on October 19, the General Overseer was pleased and felt confident that Bunch would "make us a useful man in the ministry."[123] Gibson was right. Within weeks of his appointment as Overseer of Tennessee, Bunch scheduled a "campaign of

Tennessee" from January 20 to February 9 with two nights each at Royal Blue, Flat Hollow, Yoakum's Chapel, Valley Creek, Oneida, Oliver Springs, Elk Valley, Jellico, and culminated with a ministers' meeting at Newcomb.[124]

The ministers' meeting was moved to the Tabernacle at Jellico and convened for three days. More than eighteen ministers attended, including the General Overseer and Assistant. After Clayton Lawson delivered the "welcome sermon" on the importance of "the guidance of the Holy Ghost," Bunch presented a discourse on evangelistic work, and the ministers adopted a plan for the state of Tennessee. Churches were instructed to have "an evangelistic message and altar call each Sunday night." Each church was also expected to "organize and maintain a Women's Missionary Band." The ministers elected Isham McKinley Sharp to serve as a state treasurer, and each church was instructed to send a monthly offering to support the State Overseer. In the Friday morning service, Gibson preached on "Church Government" and "spoke of the necessity of both local and central government to successfully govern the church." He contended that the early church had such leadership, and the modern church needed the same. The Tennessee ministers also discussed a "building fund" and "decided that the State Overseer with the pastor[s] impress it upon each church the need of a parsonage."[125] Gibson took up the cause nationally and argued that "every church needs a parsonage" and suggested that the CGMA was "about 25 years behind with this work."[126] Several responded to his challenge, and over the next three months, three churches had bought parsonages, and at least one more was raising money to build one.[127]

In Ohio and Michigan, McKenzie began holding monthly fellowship meetings but was hampered personally with a bout of arthritis over the winter. His meetings in Toledo were well attended by the churches in Michigan but had weak support from Southern Ohio. Likewise, Goshen and Cincinnati were well represented at Dayton, but few from Detroit attended.[128] When Oscar Bunch took the church at Shelburn, the appointing board determined "that whoever pastored" the oldest church in Indiana would serve as the state overseer and named him to the office.[129] McKenzie remained overseer of Ohio and Michigan until the next Assembly but offered little to the development of the state office the way the Bunches did.

Gibson's priority in Kentucky was the church at Corbin. E.B. Bryant's departure to the Church of God (Cleveland) the previous year had left the new Fifth Street Church in Corbin "neglected," and Gibson sought to remedy that. After visiting to preach several times in his first two months as

Overseer, Gibson and Harvey Rose held an eight-night revival there in November with "a large crowd each night."[130] The General Overseer returned to preach a few more nights in January 1948 and helped negotiate the purchase of the property there.[131] On February 7, Gibson conducted a business meeting and received seven new members. The church elected State Overseer Randall Watkins to serve as its pastor that night.[132]

Watkins had been conducting revivals and writing extensively for *The Gospel Herald* as an associate editor but had done little in his capacity as State Overseer. The night before his election as pastor, however, Watkins attended the Tennessee State ministers' meeting at the headquarters tabernacle and heard John Bunch present his plans for his state.[133] Watkins responded by calling for a meeting of the Kentucky ministers and their wives on March 20-21 at Corbin to "understand one another better" and to "discuss the subject of evangelizing Kentucky and the advancement of the churches."[134]

When the meeting convened the following month, Watkins conducted it after the same manner as Bunch had conducted Tennessee's. J.H. Bryant preached a welcome message on "fellowship," followed by exhortations by the ministers present. After lunch, the ministers adopted a plan like that of Tennessee, including Sunday night evangelistic services. Each church agreed to receive a Sunday night offering for evangelistic work in the state and to receive an offering for the State Overseer when he visited. Ione Rountree, the wife of Stanfill Pastor William Arvil Rountree, was elected to serve as state treasurer.[135] Sixteen-year-old Robert Thomas of London was elected as the state evangelist, and churches were encouraged to "give this young successful minister" their support.[136]

After he was reappointed at the 1948 Assembly, Watkins continued to develop a state polity in the Mountain Assembly's largest state, including the YPE. Edward Woolum had been appointed National Youth Director, and Kentucky State Evangelist Robert Thomas had preached the first youth night at the General Assembly. Watkins invited both to participate in his state meeting in October at Middlesboro. After his appointment, Woolum announced his intention "to have a Christian Youth Organization in every church in the Assembly by the end of this fiscal year" and offered his assistance to local churches who desired to start a youth auxiliary or "helpful suggestions" for any existing works.[137] On October 17, the first state youth rally in the CGMA was held at Middlesboro, and "the young and old danced together under the power of the Holy Ghost."[138] Joe Asbury of Kenvir was elected state youth director, and Ione Rountree was elected state youth treasurer.[139] Asbury assisted Kentucky churches with organizing or reorganizing their youth auxiliaries and began holding monthly youth rallies.

As a result of the success of the Kentucky model implemented by Watkins and Asbury, the national youth department incorporated the ideas into its national program. At a ministers' meeting in Jellico on February 12, 1949, Edward Woolum and Floyd Jordan were replaced as National Youth Directors by Robert Thomas and John Thomas Longsworth, Jr.[140] Longsworth was a 22-year-old evangelist from Dayton, Ohio who had just joined the CGMA after having preached and pastored in the Church of God (Cleveland) for seven years.[141] To rectify the quandary experienced by churches in Ohio and Michigan where attendance at meetings required traveling a great distance, Thomas and Longsworth divided the states into "districts." They reasoned that such a move would increase participation among the churches. The Dayton district consisted of Sidney, Dayton, Cincinnati, and Goshen, and the Monroe district included Toledo, Monroe, Detroit, and the newly organized church at Trenton, Michigan. Kentucky had three districts centered around Harlan, Middlesboro, and Whitley City. Jellico and Powell Valley made up the two remaining districts in Tennessee. Lawrence Redmond of Jellico was appointed Tennessee state youth director, and later Gene Thompson and Ernest Rogers were appointed youth directors of Ohio and Michigan, respectively.[142]

In May, Thomas and Longsworth appointed Doris Athleen Garner as the first national youth secretary & treasurer. Garner's first order of business was to clarify the financial responsibilities of the local and state YPE leaders under the new centralized polity. Each church was expected to send its last YPE and "last Sunday School offering in each month to their state secretary-treasurer." The state treasurer would then forward half the amount to her. The offering of each rally under the direction of the state youth director would be divided with one-fourth staying in the local church, one-fourth to the state treasury, and one-half to the national youth department.[143]

During Gibson's first year as General Overseer, he attended 280 church services and visited nearly every CGMA congregation, and "every church seemed to need encouragement."[144] Wherever he went, Gibson encouraged members to subscribe to *The Gospel Herald* as he saw its circulation as a key to denominational growth.[145] To the General Overseer, every pastor was responsible for promoting the church paper and securing subscriptions. He suggested that each pastor "set a quota" in his church and do "something for the Church of God."[146] His earnest appeal, notwithstanding, *The Gospel*

Herald receipts dropped 35 percent Gibson's first year in office.[147] The General Overseer also appealed to the ministers to report to their state overseer every month.[148] The monthly report consisted of the number of sermons preached, homes visited, souls converted, sanctifications, and Spirit baptisms. Despite his pleadings for 100 percent participation from the ministers, the average month saw less than one-third reporting.[149]

Gibson's first year in office did enjoy financial increase. In addition to constant entreaties to sell subscriptions to the denominational periodical and to report to the State Overseers, the General Overseer also frequently reminded pastors to collect the $3.00 assessment for each member. This was used for general operating expenses at headquarters. Pastors were reminded that a labor union collected dues from its members without complaint and that members should not "growl" that the church was "all the time wanting money."[150] This "small sum" for the individual had the potential to generate more than $ 4,500 in revenue for the CGMA. Though his efforts produced only 40 percent of that goal, assessment receipts doubled from the previous year.[151] In addition to the increase in assessments, the Mountain Assembly also saw a 28 percent increase in tithe of tithes and a 40 percent increase in ministers' tithes during its first year with a full-time overseer. Gibson collected $ 4,765.90 from the tithes' treasuries for his services as General Overseer, and Hatfield collected $1,514.00 for his work as treasurer and editor.[152]

The experiment seemed to be working, and Gibson and Hatfield were reelected unanimously by the Bishops' Council in 1948.[153] Like E.B. Bryant the previous year, Harvey Rose left the CGMA for the Church of God (Cleveland).[154] To replace him as Assistant General Overseer, the Bishops' Council elected Ira H. Moses, who had also replaced Rose as pastor in Monroe the previous year. R.N. Ballinger was elected as the Assistant Secretary & Treasurer but resigned in November and was replaced by Randall Watkins.[155]

Gibson's second year in office did not see the same financial success as his first, and by Christmas, his frustration with the lack of support was evident. He wrote to "every member of the Church of God" Mountain Assembly, "you owe $3.00 assessment, and this should be sent to headquarters as soon as possible." To "every pastor and church," he added:

> the tithes of tithes and ministers' tithes should be sent in at least every two months. It should never go longer than that. There has been a lot of our ministers just playing church; but we need to get down to Church of God business. Now, you might say, Gibson! that is a little

too straight. To every reader and minister of this assembly: Our people get by, by doing less than any other organization I have ever heard of. Some of our people that are so bad to growl, if you were with some groups of people, I know of you would be taxed until you would have nothing left. Remember headquarters will be expecting every church to respond to all their obligations. Some preachers might say, I will pull out and be independent. Brother, when you pull out independent, God will not go with you.[156]

Despite Gibson's rebuke, finance did not come in during his second term the way it had during his first. Assessments dropped 37 percent, tithe of tithes fell 11 percent, and ministers' tithes plummeted 44 percent. With tithes receipts from the two funds down nearly $3,000 and Gibson's combined salary and travel expenses up to $5,127.61 for the year, some ministers expressed concern about the ability to maintain a full-time overseer.[157]

When the Bishops' Council met on Tuesday, September 6, 1949, Gibson was reelected General Overseer. Later that week, in the business session with the full delegation, there was some discussion about whether to require all ministers to send their tithes to headquarters. After the treasurer presented his fiscal report, the delegates decided to leave the current program in place and only require the pastors to send their tithes to headquarters. Despite the fiscal setback, they also decided to maintain the full-time office of General Overseer. After further consideration, however, this move was rescinded on the last day of business. The General Overseer would be permitted to pastor a church with official travel reimbursement from the ministers' tithes as his only compensation from headquarters.[158] Since the Jellico church had purchased a parsonage the previous spring, the General Overseer's parsonage became vacant when Gibson retuned to the pastorate there.[159] With an empty parsonage and the elimination of a salary, the Mountain Assembly decided to allow the General Secretary & Treasurer to live in the parsonage and agreed to compensate him for his work. J.E. Hatfield then received $25 per week.[160]

The changes seemed to be in the best interests of Gibson, the CGMA, and the Jellico Church. During his first year in office, Gibson had traveled extensively to visit nearly every church. While he traveled much his second year, at least five churches did not have a visit, and he attended Jellico more frequently. One reason was his concern for the church. Gibson pastored the church for six years prior to his election as General Overseer. Jellico enjoyed stability in its pastorates throughout its history as John Parks served as its primary pastor for its first three decades. During Gibson's first term as General Overseer, however, the Jellico church changed pastors three times.

Surviving a Major Schism

Eldon Bowman Rose encountered conflict with a few members during his first months at Jellico and called for a meeting with the Board of Twelve Elders on January 16, 1948 to help resolve it. Instead, the Elders "saw fit to change" pastors and appointed Brother Clayton Lawson as pastor for the rest of the term.[161] Many members, however, considered this action an affront to the church's congregationalism and criticized the Assembly's leadership and the new form of government as "lords over God's heritage" whereby "a few of them can rule the churches." They charged that "the twelve elders gave [Rose] a trial, said he was guilty," but neglected to tell "the church what the accusation was." As a result, 45 members left the church to organize another congregation, elected Rose as their pastor, and built a new church building on South Main Street. After an extended revival, another 37 joined the church.[162] Undaunted, Lawson launched the first of four revivals in five months the night after his appointment. Preaching many of the nights himself, he saw numerous converts.[163] Despite the success of the revivals, rumors persisted that the Jellico church was struggling. Gibson admitted that he had "heard that the Jellico Sunday School didn't have many in it," but welcomed those who "doubt about Jellico, just come and see."[164]

Figure 8.13: E.B. Rose
c/o Nicki Rose Smith

Figure 8.14: Jellico Main Street Church

c/o Bobby Wilson

Attendance at Jellico eventually picked back up, but tithes were down about 30 percent. Meanwhile, Lawson's previous church at Cincinnati had increased financially and purchased a parsonage for its pastor, Harvey Rose.[165] The Assistant Overseer, Rose, had resigned as pastor of Newcomb after two months to take the church in Cincinnati when Lawson moved to Jellico. Neither church seemed to be the right fit for either pastor; so, when Rose resigned on August 8, Lawson returned to Cincinnati to resume pastoral duties there.[166] Harvey Rose joined the Church of God (Cleveland) the following week, and his brother, E.B. followed him two years later.[167]

Figure 8.15: Ottis Ellis
c/o CGMA

After Lawson's resignation at Jellico, the church elected Ottis Ellis as its pastor. Ellis was appointed State Overseer of Tennessee in November and was also pastoring nearby Newcomb. In April 1949, Gibson and Ellis organized a new church at Tackett Creek in Claiborne County, and Ellis began taking care of it as well.[168] When E.B. Rose resigned at Jellico Main Street Church, Ellis began also preaching there. By doing so, he helped heal the rift and eventually reconciled the two congregations on Main Street.[169] Taking care of three congregations and overseeing the rest of Tennessee proved too much, and Ellis resigned all three pastorates and as State Overseer after the close of the 43rd Annual Assembly. Fonde Pastor Earl Heath was elected at the new church at Tackett Creek, and Ellis replaced him at Fonde. Gibson had often filled in for Ellis when the pastor preached away from Jellico, and after the assembly, the church chose him to pastor the coming year.[170]

Concern over the welfare of the headquarters church was a major reason that Gibson traveled less his second year in office, attended church at Jellico more frequently, and ultimately returned to its pastorate during his third year in office. He also had eight even more compelling reasons. The extensive travel of his first term saw Gibson spend at least 50 nights away from home, away from his wife, Annette, and their seven children.[171] The General Overseer was present in Jellico when his oldest son, Harold, was baptized by Lawson on May 29, 1948, and "sure was glad."[172] Over the next year, Gibson attended the Young People's Endeavor services at Jellico with his children more than a half dozen times.[173] Jellico rebounded during Gibson's final year as its pastor and his final year as General Overseer, receiving 17 new members. Nevertheless, Gibson chose not to seek reelection to either office. Again, he considered his children. Preferring pastoral ministry to keep him closer to home and knowing that the North promised better jobs after his children completed high school, Gibson took the pastorate of the church in Dayton, Ohio in 1950 and served as State Overseer of Ohio.[174]

Charting a Course for Growth

In addition to the changes in the General Overseer's duties and compensation, the 43rd Annual Mountain Assembly in September 1949 made four substantial changes, and two more significant things occurred at the 1950 Assembly. The first two initiatives dealt with ministerial credentials. One provided for membership at headquarters to allow the issuance of credentials for ministers joining the Assembly from another organization. A second granted credentials to women ministers. In 1949, delegates also voted to have the annual assembly at different sites. The return of Clayton Lawson to the office of Assistant General Overseer that same year positioned him to lead the organization for the next decade. In 1950, the term of the general officials was changed to two years, setting up biennial elections through the present time. At the same time, the office of General Overseer returned to a full-time position. Also at that assembly, five ministers from the Pentecostal Church of Christ (PCC) met with ministers from the Church of God Mountain Assembly to discuss a working relationship between the two organizations. The PCC would come to impact the program of the CGMA much like the Church of God (Cleveland) had influenced its polity.

The Mountain Assembly first began licensing evangelists in 1946, but the decision made no immediate impact. Three years later, the Assembly had just fourteen licensed evangelists to go with its 40 ordained ministers. The measured passed in 1949 facilitated the acceptance of new ministers into the organization, by allowing the General Overseer to issue credentials directly from headquarters. To replenish the number of ministers depleted by the split with the Long and Moses faction, Gibson and Lawson actively solicited ministers to join the fellowship and often appointed them to state and national offices. His appointment of John Bunch to the office of Tennessee State Overseer aided further recruitment. Bunch quickly secured preaching appointments for two well-known acquaintances whom he described as "mighty men in the gospel and great in revivals."[175]

Figure 8.16: Fate Creasman
c/o K.E. Massingill

Lawrence Taylor had lived on the same street with Bunch in Oakley, North Carolina, in 1940.[176] In 1946, he assumed the pastorate of the Moffitt Hill Church of God in nearby Old Fort. The church had been organized in 1918 by William Marquis Lafayette "Fate" Creasman "holding cottage prayer meetings" in the area. After Creasman died of typhoid in November 1919, his son, Ernest Preston Creasman, cared for the church. After a revival with Church of God (Cleveland) Minister Norman Jones in 1921, the church voted to join the "Tomlinson organization." After the schism of 1923, the church united with the (Original) Church of God until Taylor's pastorate.[177] Bunch arranged for Taylor to preach a revival in Jellico in February 1948 and another in Cincinnati that May.[178] After the Assembly, Gibson visited Taylor's pastor, E.P. Creasman, and visited the church at Old Fort eight more times over the next seven months, including to preach an eight-night revival. In the spring, he officially received the church and its 22 members into the fellowship.[179]

Bunch also procured preaching appointments for his friend, George W. Helmick, of Buckhannon, West Virginia. Helmick saw 35 souls saved in a revival at Elk Valley in February 1948 and preached another successful revival at Newcomb in May.[180] That fall, Helmick opened a new church in Washington, Pennsylvania with 26 members and brought it into the Mountain Assembly.[181] To accommodate the reception of new ministers who might be persuaded to join the CGMA, delegates to the 43rd Assembly voted to allow the General Officials "to receive ministers into the Assembly at Headquarters until their membership can be placed in some local church." In this manner, the General Secretary & Treasurer could issue the new "fellowship cards" quickly and allow the minister to pastor, evangelize, and start new churches.[182] An influx of ministers into the CGMA followed.

On the same day that the Mountain Assembly approved the motion to accept ministers' membership at headquarters, it also passed a motion to "license women evangelists, but not allow them to baptize, pastor churches, or minister the Lord's supper." The move had been made during Friday's session, but was postponed until Saturday. Before the meeting was adjourned on Friday, the committee on divine services, J.H. Douglas, David Hammitte, and Edd Prewitt, reported that the Friday evening preacher would be "the ten year old evangelist," Floy Marie Bell.[183] Bell, who also preached in the Tuesday afternoon service, attended a United Pentecostal Church in Memphis with her mother and sisters. At a young age, she received the Baptism of the Holy Ghost and felt the call to ministry. A ministry couple who rented a room at her mother's boarding house took the young girl under their wings and nurtured her for evangelism. The minister began scheduling her to preach with him at revivals and tent meetings across the Midwest.[184]

Friday night's service was "Young People's Night," and "a large crowd filled the tabernacle to overflowing." With "about as many people on the outside of the building as were inside," National Youth Director John Longsworth conducted the worship before Bell "preached a wonderful sermon" on "the four great sins connected with the slaying of John" from Mark 6. "People were made to wonder at the knowledge and wisdom of this child of God, being convinced that God was in her of a truth." Her message made such an impression that, the next morning, the tabled motion was renewed and adopted.[185] Longsworth was so impressed that he brought the young evangelist to Sidney for a revival the following spring.[186]

Figure 8.17: Floy Marie Bell
c/o Ramona Barger

Figure 8.18: Jessie Fearrl
c/o *The Youth Gateway*

Just 30 days after the close of the Assembly, Pastor Helmick and the church at Washington, Pennsylvania recommended Jessie Fearrl and Edith Frederick for evangelist's licenses, and CGMA headquarters issued the certificates.[187] Over the next decade, the Mountain Assembly issued

Figure 8.19: Jackie Ethridge
c/o Brenda Ethridge Demps

evangelist's licenses to an additional 21 female ministers, most from recently organized congregations. In fact, many of the churches organized in the Mountain Assembly in the 1950s utilized the ministries of women.[188] Although the Standard Resolutions did not permit women to pastor in the CGMA, such restrictions were sometimes overlooked. The first exception occurred when Joseph Cameron "Big Boy" Freeman left Oliver Springs in 1956 to pastor the church at Newcomb. On the Sunday following the Assembly, State Overseer George Douglas conducted business at Oliver Springs to receive Jackie Ethridge as a member of the church. That same night, she was selected as its pastor.[189] Ethridge began preaching in the 1940s and had been a member of the Assemblies of God in Dolomite, Alabama before moving to Oak Ridge in 1951.[190] She began fellowshipping with the Oliver Springs church not long after that.[191] Ethridge went on to pastor the church until 1961.[192]

As more women received credentials and more ministers joined the CGMA at headquarters, the number of licensed evangelists from the existing churches also continued to rise. A measure adopted in 1948 required an evangelist to be licensed for two years before he was eligible to be ordained.[193] Slowly, but steadily the number of ordained ministers increased along with the number of licensed ministers. Gibson and Lawson viewed the increase in ministers as important to rebounding from the schism and essential to the growth of the Mountain Assembly. More preachers meant more potential pastors. The number of credentialed ministers grew from 50 ordained and 22 licensed ministers in 1950 to 74 ordained and 91 licensed in 1960.[194]

The third significant change adopted by the 43rd Mountain Assembly was a decision to change the meeting place of the annual assembly, patterned after the Church of God (Cleveland). The Church of God outgrew its 4,000-seat headquarters tabernacle in less than fifteen years and, in 1934, moved the annual convention to Memorial Auditorium in Chattanooga for the next four years.[195] In 1938, approximately 6,000 people crowded into the auditorium "with hundreds standing," and at another service between 3,000 and 5,000 gathered outside the building. The Municipal Auditorium in Atlanta hosted

Surviving a Major Schism

the convention the following year. During the 1940s, the Church of God (Cleveland) held its annual assemblies in Chattanooga, Birmingham, Columbus, and Sevierville and found that large crowds attended regardless of its location and members were pleased by the variety of locations. The convention never returned to Cleveland.[196]

When the CGMA outgrew its first tabernacle, it was replaced with a new one in 1942. Attendance exceeded the new one's reasonable seating capacity immediately. Not even the split impeded attendance at the annual event in Jellico. By the second night of the 1949 assembly, Gibson asked "everyone to make as much room as possible because of the large crowd," as "the tabernacle was packed and people standing and many out around the building."[197] The Board of Twelve Elders discussed the possibility of "having the Annual Assembly at different places," and when its report was presented, the delegates voted to have the next one in Cincinnati, Ohio.[198]

The church in Cincinnati was prepared for just such an event. Just six months after Lawson returned to pastor, the church moved from its location on Linn Street to a building on the corner of 15th Street and Race Street. The building had been used by St. Paul's Evangelical Protestant Church before it merged with St. Peter's United Protestant Evangelical Church in 1948 to form the new St. Peter & St. Paul United Church of Christ.[199] Lawson was able to buy the church and its "eight-room parsonage" for $45,000. The main auditorium seated nearly five hundred and had "five rooms located in the rear of the auditorium with sliding windows where more seats may be set up." A balcony ran "the full length of the building on each side with a seating capacity of four hundred."[200]

Figure 8.20: 15th & Race Street Church

c/o North Monroe Street CGMA

The fourth significant change at the Assembly in 1949 was the election of Lawson to the office of Assistant General Overseer. He had served in that capacity from 1944 to 1946, determined to replace Andrew Long in the top office. The upheaval of the 1946 schism forced Lawson to reconsider his ambition and wait for a more auspicious time. His appointment to assist Gibson during a year when the General Overseer contemplated his own future ministry coincided with his preparations to host the annual assembly at his home church, where he could demonstrate his organizational and leadership abilities. Lawson rose to the occasion.

The pastor appointed Willie Goins to head the "music department," and the church spent $1,500 on musical instruments. Goins spent the year building a choir and band.[201] The 44th Annual Mountain Assembly featured the singing of Goins's choir and band every night, and Hatfield noted in the annual minute book how fortunate was the church "having a man like Brother Goins who has the ability to train a full band in a short time." Resolved to be good hosts, Lawson also "announced that the Cincinnati church would serve lunch each day for the people."[202] When the Bishop's Council met on Tuesday, August 22, it elected him to the office of General Overseer and Ira Moses as his assistant. Lawson served in that capacity for the next ten years, in part, because the election rules changed in 1950 as well.

Figure 8.21: 15th & Race Street Music Department
c/o North Monroe Street CGMA

After Lawson was elected, a motion was introduced Wednesday that the "Assembly Officials serve two years instead of one."[203] The Church of God (Cleveland) had made the move to biennial elections in 1944, the same year the Mountain Assembly adopted its new system of government patterned after that body. Church of God (Cleveland) ministers viewed the two-year term with a limit of one reelection as the key to avoiding autocratic leadership.[204] When the matter was introduced in the business session of the Mountain Assembly, delegates postponed it for further deliberation. The following day, they revived and amended it to also include the election of pastors by the local churches.[205] While the directive added stability to the general offices, it did not produce such in the local churches. So, in 1959, Lawson introduced a supplement for the annual minute book called "Powers of the Local Church," and concurrently called for annual pastors' elections.[206] The move was adopted and CGMA churches began electing their pastors annually again until 18 years later when a new resolution returned the elections to two-year terms.[207]

Two days after the Mountain Assembly extended Lawson's term to two years, it also restored the office of General Overseer to a full-time job and gave him a salary of $75 per week in addition to travel expenses. As required by the resolution Lawson resigned as pastor of the Race Street Church, and Dover Kasee succeeded him. Though Kasee had been a member of the church and began preaching under Lawson, the church experienced some decline which concerned Lawson who never relinquished his pastoral burden. The General Overseer resumed his pastorate of the Cincinnati church in 1952 when the Mountain Assembly revised its Standard Resolutions to allow him to pastor one church in addition to his duties to the organization. His salary was reduced to $40 per week as a result.[208] Income from ministers' tithes more than doubled in Lawson's first year as Overseer and remained steady the next three years.[209] By 1954, receipts totaled an all-time high, $7,621.19, more than adequate to cover a full-time weekly salary of $90. As a result, Resolution Committee Chairman Ira Moses presented a move to return the General Overseer to a full-time position. Race Street then chose J.H. Douglas, Earl Heath, and Willis Yeary in its next three elections before Lawson resumed the pastorate after leaving office in 1960.[210]

The General Secretary & Treasurer's salary was increased to $35 per week in 1951, and some felt he deserved another raise five years later. The delegates rejected the proposed increase of $15 to the weekly salary. Two days later, however, a resolution was adopted to raise the salary to $75 and require him to "spend full time in the work." A committee of Gibson, M.E. Woolum, and J.H. Douglas worked out the details for a full-time Secretary and Editor of *The Gospel Herald.*" In addition to keeping "an accurate account of all funds coming into the office," these included editing, distributing, and promoting the church paper, visiting as many churches as possible, and maintaining daily office hours five days per week.[211]

By 1957, ministers' tithes to headquarters had exceeded over $10,000 each year and discussion began about adding another salaried position. For looking "after the general interest of all the churches as directed by the General Overseer," his Assistant would receive $50 per month.[212] Luther Gibson had been serving in that capacity since 1952, and just as he had been the first General Overseer to receive a salary from headquarters, he became the first paid Assistant General Overseer as well.

While delegates at the 1950 Assembly in Cincinnati debated the merits of a full-time overseer and a two-year term. Five guest ministers were conspicuously present. Eldon L. Cyrus, Chester I. Miller, Joe Stanley, George K. Nickell, and Thomas L. Dooley represented the Pentecostal Church of Christ (PCC), and their presence would impact the Mountain Assembly for decades to come. The PCC was one of several Pentecostal organizations with which the leaders of the CGMA were familiar after having joined the Pentecostal Fellowship of North America the previous year. By 1950, CGMA members recognized that, as Pentecostals, they were part of a movement whose reach extended far beyond what their founders could have imagined.

Conclusion

Four decades of tension between congregationalism and episcopalism reached its breaking point in 1946 with the aid of some church politics. Those favoring a stronger centralized government faced the challenge of unseating an immensely popular General Overseer in Andrew Long. When Long failed to fulfill the duties of the new office, his adversaries used it as an occasion to undermine him and remove him from office. In retaliation, Long and Kim Moses split the Mountain Assembly into another congregational association. The CGMA meanwhile expanded its hierarchical government and continued to incorporate centralist measures into its polity by further development of the office of State Overseer and the creation of districts and district offices within the states. Centralized government required financial support from the churches and leaders continued to call on congregations to give. The increase in tithes made possible, for the first time, salaried officials. After waiting four years, Clayton Lawson pursued again the office of General Overseer and guided the Mountain Assembly through its greatest period of growth in the 1950s.

[1] CGMA, *Minutes* (1944), 8.

[2] Ira Moses to Lewis Baird, February 8, 1946, photocopy in the possession of the author.

[3] Luther Gibson, "The Church of God Moves On," *GH* 7, no. 11 (May 1949): 8.

[4] Moses to Baird, February 8, 1946; Ira Moses to Lewis Baird, February 15, 1946, photocopy in the possession of the author.

[5] CGMA, *Minutes* (1907), 2; CGMA, *Minutes of the Churches of God Mountain Assembly Incorporated: Fortieth Annual Assembly* (Jellico, TN: CGMA, 1946), 25; Church of God of the Original Mountain Assembly (CGOMA), *Minutes of the Churches of God of the Original Mountain Assembly 40th Annual Session* (Williamsburg, Ky.: CGOMA, 1946), statistical table.

[6] Church of God, *Minutes of the Forty-First Annual Assembly of the Church of God* (Cleveland, Tenn: Church of God Publishing House, 1946), 19.

[7] CGMA, *Minutes* (1938), 14.

[8] See CGMA *Minutes* 1939-1949.

[9] Leon Petree, "History of Our Church," *GH* 34, no. 10 (October 1973): 5.

[10] CGMA, *Minutes* (1937), 11.

[11] CGMA, *Minutes* (1938), 14; CGMA, *Minutes* (1939), 17.

[12] CGMA, *Minutes* (1945), 16; CGMA, *Minutes* (1946), 16.

[13] Luther Gibson, undated note in sermon manuscript collection, in possession of Mike Gibson, Knoxville, TN.

[14] By the early-1940s, the delegation at the General Assembly was restricted to three delegates from each church along with the ordained ministers. The 1943 minute book was the last to list the names of the church delegates. With 40 churches and 73 ordained ministers, the potential for a delegation of 193 delegates existed (the actual number of delegates was 84, plus the unknown number of ministers present). In 1945, the first election under the new system, only the 97 ordained ministers were eligible to vote for General Overseer.

[15] CGMA, *Minutes* (1945), 7.

[16] Moses to Baird, February 8, 1946.

[17] Cecil M. Robeck, Jr., *The Azusa Street Mission and Revival: The Birth of the Global Pentecostal Movement* (Nashville: Thomas Nelson, Inc., 2006), 110-111.

[18] Ibid., 83-84.

[19] Ibid., 12.

[20] Ibid., 112. Many historians see Parham's ministry in Topeka as the beginning of the Modern Pentecostal Movement. Parham was one of the first to articulate the doctrine of speaking in tongues as the initial evidence of the Baptism of the Holy Spirit. Ozman reportedly spoke in other tongues on January 1, 1901, and many others soon followed.

[21] Robeck, 58, 84, 198-204.

[22] Ibid., 200-204.

23 Ralph W. Hood, Jr. and W. Paul Williamson, *Them That Believe: The Power and Meaning of the Christian Serpent-Handling Tradition* (Berkley: University of California Press, 2008), 42-43, 62-65, 71-73.

24 J.P.M. Shepherd, "Parkers, Ky.," *CGE* 6, no. 13 (March 27, 1915): 4.

25 CGMA, *Minutes* (1910), back cover.

26 CGMA, *Minutes* (1914), 3.

27 CGMA, *Minutes* (1921), 5.

28 Frank O'Rourke, "Kenvir, Ky.," *GH* 3, no. 8 (February 1945), 3.

29 Padgett, *Heritage*, 54. For this work, the author interviewed multiple church members who shared anecdotes they had personally witnessed in the 1940s in the churches in Jellico, Middlesboro, and Fonde. Because of the sensitive nature of the subject and the living relatives of those involved, they wished to remain anonymous.

30 U.S. WWII Draft Cards Young Men, 1940-1947, s.v. "Cordell Partin," Ancestry.com.

31 1930 United States Census, Wise County, Virginia, s.v. "James Parton" and 1940 United States Census, Bell County, Kentucky, s.v. "Jim Partin," Ancestry.com.

32 Mildred Hamlin, "Henderson Grove, Ky.," *GH* 2, no. 3 (February 1944): 1.

33 U.S. WWII Draft Cards Young Men, 1940-1947, s.v. "Cordell Partin," Ancestry.com.

34 U.S., World War II Army Enlistment Records, 1938-1946, s.v. "Cordell Partin," Ancestry.com.

35 Michael Padgett, "A Tribute to a Hero," *GH* 61, no. 11 (November 2000): 12.

36 Cordell Partin to Mandy Partin, June 17, 1944, in the possession of Michael Partin, Harrogate, TN.

37 Cordell Partin to Mandy Partin, July 27, 1944, in the possession of Michael Partin, Harrogate, TN.

38 CGMA, *Minutes* (1944), 3. The quotation cited in this note is found written in the side margin of the 1944 minute book owned by Paul Grubbs, a friend of Partin and fellow member of the church at Fonde. Grubbs's minute book is in the personal collection of the author.

39 Major George Buehler to Mandy Partin, June 29, 1945, in the possession of Michael Partin, Harrogate, TN.

40 Robert J. Parks, Ed., *Medical Training in World War II* (Washington, D.C.: Department of the Army, 1974), 174, 199. https://history.amedd.army.mil/booksdocs/wwii/medtrain/default.htm

41 Buehler to Partin.

42 Cordell Partin to Mandy Partin, four undated letters from Camp Barkeley, in the possession of Michael Partin, Harrogate, TN.

43 Danny Johnson, "Camp Beale History," California Military History and Museums Program, Accessed February 7, 2020. http://www.militarymuseum.org/Beale.html

44 "Emlyn, Kentucky," *GH* 1, no. 6 (December 1942): 6; Rosa Jones, "Fonde, Ky.," *GH* 3, no. 8 (February 1945), 2.

45 Padgett, *Heritage*, 54; Cordell Partin to Mandy Partin, undated letter from Camp Beale, in the possession of Michael Partin, Harrogate, TN.

46 Buehler to Partin.

47 Padgett, "Tribute," 12.

48 Padgett, *Heritage,* 54.

49 Ibid.; Rosa Jones, "Fonde, Ky.," *GH* 4, no. 12 (June 1946): 5.

50 Cawood Funeral Home Ledger Book: January 1948 to December 1951, 28, Creech Funeral Home, Middlesboro, KY.

51 *U.S., Headstone Applications for Military Veterans, 1925-1963*, s.v. Cordell Partin, Ancestry.com; https://www.findagrave.com/memorial/19421978

52 Partin letter from Beale.

53 Middlesboro CGMA, "Record Sisters Service," 52-57.

54 Over the past 25 years, the author has had numerous conversations with members present at meetings related to this spiritual controversy in Middlesboro and Fonde. Because of the sensitive nature of the subject and the families involved, they wish to remain anonymous.

55 Admiral Ayers, "Middlesboro, Ky.," *GH* 4, no. 10 (April 1946): 5.

56 CGMA, *Minutes* (1946), 24. The statistical table shows that 16 members were excluded from the Middlesboro Church that year. The exact number of exclusions related to the controversy is unknown. The church clerk, one of the excluded members, refused to surrender the church minute book.

57 Bryant, "to Whom," *GH* 5, no. 5 (November 1946): 8.

58 Admiral Ayers, "Middlesboro, Ky.," *GH* 4, no. 6 (December 1945): 2; Admiral Ayers, "Middlesboro, Ky.," *GH* 4, no. 10 (April 1946): 5; Admiral Ayers, "Middlesboro, Ky.," *GH* 5, no. 1 (July 1946): 6.

59 Admiral Ayers, "Middlesboro, Ky.," *GH* 4, no. 12 (June 1946): 4.

60 Bryant, "Concern," 8.

61 CGMA, *Minutes* (1946), 3-4.

62 Gibson, *History,* 37.

63 Ibid.; CGMA, *Minutes* (1946), 4.

64 CGMA, *Minutes* (1946), 4.

65 Ibid., 5-7.

66 Ibid., 6-8.

67 CGMA, *Minutes of the Church of God of the Mountain Assembly Incorporated: Forty-First Annual Assembly* (Jellico, TN: CGMA, 1947), 8-9.

68 Church of God, General Assembly Minutes (1907), 22.

69 Church of God, *Minutes of the Twentieth Annual Assembly* (Cleveland, TN: Church of God Publishing House, 1925), 37; Flavius J. Lee, "Exhorter: Who, How, What," *CGE* 16, no. 48 (November 28, 1925): 2.

70 CGMA, *Minutes* (1946), 6, 8.

71 Church of God, *Minutes* (1911), 12.

72 Church of God, *Echoes* (1913), 34.

73 CGMA, *Minutes* (1946), 7.

74 Conn, 272.

75 Church of God, *Minutes of the Twenty-Ninth Annual Assembly* (Cleveland, TN: Church of God Publishing House, 1935), 51.

76 CGMA, *Minutes* (1946), 8.

77 CGMA, *Minutes* (1947), 11.

78 CGMA, *Minutes* (1948), 6.

79 CGMA, *Minutes of the Church of God of the Mountain Assembly Incorporated: Forty-Third Annual Assembly* (Jellico, TN: CGMA, 1949), 11.

80 CGMA, *Minutes of the Church of God of the Mountain Assembly Incorporated: Fiftieth Annual Assembly* (Jellico, TN: CGMA, 1956), 16-18.

81 CGOMA, *Minutes of the Churches of God of the Original Mountain Assembly, Inc. 43rd Annual Session* (Williamsburg, Ky.: CGOMA, 1949), 2.

82 Bryant, "Concern," 8.

83 CGOMA, *Minutes* (1949), 2.

84 Ibid.

85 CGMA, *Minutes* (1946), 8. That Bryant was permitted to observe the proceedings of the Long faction spoke of the esteem he held by both sides of the schism. The son of the former longtime moderator, Bryant was also the last remaining delegate of the first assembly. Likewise, Ira Moses was the grandson of John Parks, and was a relative of the eleven Moseses who were delegates at the first Original Mountain Assembly in Williamsburg that October.

86 CGMA, *Minutes* (1946), 2-3, 6, 12-13.

87 Ibid., statistical table; CGMA, *Minutes* (1946), 24-25; CGMA, *Minutes* (1947), 21-22.

88 CGOMA, *Minutes of the Churches of God of the Original Mountain Assembly 41st Annual Session* (Williamsburg, KY: CGOMA, 1947), 1, 4.

89 CGOMA, *Minutes of the Churches of God of the Original Mountain Assembly 42nd Annual Session* (Williamsburg, KY: CGOMA, 1948), 2, 17-18.

90 CGOMA, *Minutes* (1949), 10, 16.

91 CGOMA, *Minutes* (1947), 8.

92 CGMA, *Minutes* (1948), 21.

93 CGOMA, *Minutes* (1949), 17; CGOMA, *Minutes* (1950), statistical table; CGMA, *Minutes* (1950), 22-23.

94 CGOMA, *Minutes* (1949), 17; CGMA, *Minutes* (1950), 22-23.

95 The Way of Holiness Church of God, *Minutes of the Way of Holiness Church of God: 4th Annual Assembly* (Marion, TN: WYCG, 1953), 20-22.

96 CGOMA, *Minutes* (1948), 19; CGOMA, *Minutes* (1950), statistical table.

[97] CGOMA, *Minutes* (1950), statistical table; CGOMA, *Minutes of the Churches of God of the Original Mountain Assembly 47th Annual Session* (Williamsburg, KY: CGOMA, 1953), 15.

[98] CGMA, *Minutes of the Church of God of the Mountain Assembly Incorporated: Forty-Fifth Annual Assembly* (Jellico, TN: CGMA, 1951), 23.

[99] CGOMA, *Minutes* (1948), 13.

[100] CGMA, *Minutes* (1953), 10.

[101] CGOMA, *Minutes* (1948), 9.

[102] CGMA, *Minutes of the Church of God of the Mountain Assembly Incorporated: Fifty-First Annual Assembly* (Jellico, TN: CGMA, 1957), 46.

[103] CGMA, *Minutes* (1956), 26.

[104] CGOMA, *Minutes of the Churches of God of the Original Mountain Assembly 50th Annual Assembly* (Williamsburg, Ky.: CGOMA, 1956), 3, statistical table.

[105] These include Finley Gray (1948), Clarence Evans (1949), Stephen Rowland Fowler (1949), Roy Cornelius (1950), Joe Moses (1951), Elmer Steely (1954), Scott Orick (1955), Paul Grubbs (1956), William Lee Goins (1957), Willis Yeary (1957), Charles Wesley Goins (1958), Carl Guy (1962), J.M. Davis (1963), and Kelsie Moses (1976).

[106] Paul Grubbs and Roy Cornelius, for example, later became District Overseers in the Mountain Assembly.

[107] John H. Bryant, "The General Overseer Speaks," *GH* 5, no. 8 (February 1947): 1; CGMA, *Minutes* (1946), 8.

[108] After the first six months of the fiscal year, tithe of tithes receipts were $ 932.49, and ministers' tithes receipts were $ 2,082.89. During the second six months, tithe of tithes increased to $ 1,486.88 (59%), and ministers' tithes increased to $ 2,174.91 (4%). J.E. Hatfield, "Treasurer's Semi-annual Report," *GH* 5, no. 10 (April 1947): 6; CGMA, *Minutes* (1947), 14-15.

[109] CGMA, *Minutes* (1947), 7-8. E.B. Bryant left the Mountain Assembly in 1947 and returned to the Church of God (Cleveland) in which organization he remained until his death in 1954.

[110] CGMA, *Minutes* (1946), 16, 24-25; CGMA, *Minutes* (1947), 14-15, 21-22.

[111] CGMA, *Minutes* (1947), 9.

[112] CGMA, *Minutes* (1946), 6.

[113] Luther Gibson, "Report of the General Overseer," *GH* 6, no. 4 (October 1947): 1.

[114] Ibid.; Jean Bailey, "Monroe, Mich.," *GH* 6, no. 5 (November 1947): 4.

[115] CGMA, *Minutes* (1947), 18.

[116] "Royal Blue, Tenn.," *GH* 6, no. 4 (October 1947): 1.

[117] Gibson, "Report of the General Overseer," *GH* 6, no. 5 (November 1947): 1.

[118] "Shelburn, Ind.," *GH* 6, no. 1 (July 1947): 5.

[119] CGOMA, *Minutes* (1946), 2, statistical table.

[120] Gibson, "Report of the General Overseer," *GH* 6, no. 5 (November 1947): 5; Gibson, "Report of the General Overseer," *GH* 6, no. 7 (January 1948): 7; and Gibson, Harvey Rose, and J.E. Hatfield, "Notice," *GH* 6, no. 7 (January 1948): 1.

121 CGMA, *Minutes* (1917), 3; CGMA, *Minutes* (1921), 7.

122 1940 United States Census, Buncombe County, North Carolina, digital image s.v. "John Bunch," Ancestry.com; Maude and Nola Creekmore, "Jellico, Tenn.," *GH* 6, no. 6 (December 1947): 4.

123 Gibson, "Report of the General Overseer," *GH* 6, no. 5 (November 1947): 1.

124 John Bunch, "Tennessee State Meetings," *GH* 6, no. 7 (January 1948): 1.

125 "Tennessee Ministers' Meeting," *GH* 6, no. 9 (March 1948): 1, 8.

126 Gibson, "Stop – Look – Listen," *GH* 6, no. 9 (March 1948): 7.

127 Jellico, Monroe, Cincinnati purchased parsonages in the spring of 1948. Goshen completed the building of its parsonage at the beginning of 1950.

128 Jerry Garner, "Dayton, Ohio Fellowship Meeting," *GH* 6, no. 4 (October 1947): 3; J. H. Douglas, "Toledo, Ohio Fellowship Meeting," *GH* 6, no. 5 (November 1947): 4; Mildred Deal, "Sidney, Ohio," *GH* 6, no. 7 (January 1948): 4.

129 "Notice," *GH* 6, no. 9 (March 1948): 8.

130 Gibson, "Report of the General Overseer," *GH* 6, no. 6 (December 1947): 1.

131 Gibson, "Report of the General Overseer," *GH* 6, no. 8 (February 1948): 1, 7.

132 Gibson, "Report of the General Overseer," *GH* 6, no. 9 (March 1948): 1.

133 "Tennessee Ministers' Meeting," *GH* 6, no. 9 (March 1948): 1.

134 Randall Watkins, "Kentucky Ministers' Meeting," *GH* 6, no. 9 (March 1948): 1.

135 Arvil Rountree was the son of William Henry Rountree, a delegate from Little Wolf Creek at the first assembly. His name was almost always misspelled "Orville" in the CGMA minute book and in *The Gospel Herald*.

136 Randall Watkins, "Kentucky Ministers' Meeting," *GH* 6, no. 10 (April 1948): 8.

137 Edward Woolum, "Following the Gleam," *GH* 7, no. 4 (October 1948): 8.

138 Deward Hoskins, "Middlesboro, Ky.," *GH* 7, no. 5 (November 1948): 2.

139 Joe Asbury, "Attention, Kentucky Y.P.E.," *GH* 7, no. 6 (December 1948): 1.

140 "Young People's Endeavor of the Church of God (Mt. Assembly)," *GH* 7, no. 9 (March 1949): 2.

141 Longsworth, *History of Sidney*, 2; Church of God, *Minutes of the 39th Annual Assembly* (Cleveland, Tenn.: Church of God Publishing house, 1944), 82.

142 "Young People's Endeavor of the Church of God (Mt. Assembly)," *GH* 7, no. 9 (March 1949): 2; "Young People's Endeavor of the Church of God (Mt. Assembly)," *GH* 7, no. 11 (May 1949): 2.

143 Mrs. Raymond [Doris] Garner, "Thanks," *GH* 7, no. 12 (June 1949): 2.

144 Gibson, *History*, 40. In his history of the Mountain Assembly, Gibson states that he "visited every church but one."

145 Gibson, "A Reminder from the General Overseer," *GH* 6, no. 5 (November 1947): 1.

146 Gibson, "Remarks," *GH* 6, no. 11 (May 1948): 3.

147 CGMA, *Minutes* (1947), 15; CGMA, *Minutes* (1948), 19.

[148] Gibson, "A Reminder from the General Overseer," *GH* 6, no. 5 (November 1947): 1.

[149] From January 1948 through May 1949, the ministers' reports were published in *GH*. On average, 17.5 ministers reported during this period. There were 59 ministers listed in the 1948 minute book.

[150] Gibson, "Remarks," *GH* 6, no. 11 (May 1948): 3.

[151] CGMA, *Minutes* (1947), 15; CGMA, *Minutes* (1948), 19, 24.

[152] CGMA, *Minutes* (1947), 14-15; CGMA, *Minutes* (1948), 17-18.

[153] CGMA, *Minutes* (1948), 8.

[154] Report of Ordination, Harvey Luther Rose file, Central Files and Records of the Church of God, Cleveland, Tennessee; Church of God, *Minutes of the 42nd General Assembly* (Cleveland, Tenn.: Church of God Publishing House, 1948), 74.

[155] Gibson, "Remarks from the General Overseer." *GH* 7, no. 6 (December 1948): 8.

[156] Gibson, "Remarks by the General Overseer," *GH* 7, no. 7 (January 1949): 1.

[157] CGMA, *Minutes* (1948), 17-20; CGMA, *Minutes* (1949), 16-19.

[158] CGMA, *Minutes* (1949), 9, 11-13.

[159] Gibson, "General Overseer's Report for March," *GH* 6, no. 10 (April 1948): 7.

[160] CGMA, *Minutes* (1949), 8.

[161] Gibson, "General Overseer's Report," *GH* 6, no. 8 (February 1948): 7.

[162] Wheeler D. Perkins, *Teachings of the Jellico Church of God*, (Jellico, TN: by the church, ca 1948), 5-7.

[163] *GH* 6, nos. 8-12.

[164] Gibson, "General Overseer's Report," *GH* 7, no. 2 (August 1948): 7.

[165] CGMA, *Minutes* (1947), 14; CGMA, *Minutes* (1948), 17; Dover Kasee, "Cincinnati, Ohio," *GH* 6, no. 12 (June 1948): 2.

[166] Dover Kasee, "Cincinnati, Ohio," *GH* 7, no. 3 (September 1948): 3.

[167] Report of Ordination, Harvey Luther Rose file, Central Files and Records of the Church of God, Cleveland, Tennessee; Report of Ordination, Eldon Bowman Rose file, Central Files and Records of the Church of God, Cleveland, Tennessee; Church of God, *Minutes of the 44th Annual Assembly* (Cleveland, Tenn.: Church of God Publishing House, 1950), 63; CGMA, *Minutes* (1949), 23.

[168] "Notice to Tennessee Ministers," *GH* 7, no. 6 (December 1948): 6; [Rufus L.] Douglas, "Newcomb, Tenn.," *GH* 7, no. 7 (January 1949): 7; Gibson, "General Overseer's Report," *GH* 7, no. 11 (May 1949): 6; Gibson, "Report of the General Overseer," *GH* 7, no. 12 (June 1949): 5.

[169] Bobby Wilson, interview by author, Lakeland, FL, November 19, 2020.

[170] Betty Beach, "Tackett Creek, Tenn.," *GH* 8, no. 4 (October 1949): 3; Vivian Murray and Carrie Creekmore, "Jellico, Tenn.," *GH* 8, no. 5 (November 1949): 5.

[171] See reports of the General Overseer in *GH* (October 1947 – September 1948).

[172] Gibson, "Report," (July 1948): 1.

173 Gibson, "Report," (December 1948): 4; Gibson, "Report," (January 1949): 1; Gibson, "Report," (February 1949), 3; Gibson, "Report," (May 1949): 6.

174 CGMA, *Minutes* (1950), 19, 22-23.

175 John Bunch, "Your Overseer for the State of Tennessee," *GH* 6, no. 8 (February 1948): 1.

176 1940 United States Census, Buncombe County, North Carolina, digital image s.v. "John Bunch" and 1940 United States Census, Buncombe County, North Carolina, digital image s.v. "Lawrence Taylor," Ancestry.com.

177 "History of Old Fort, North Carolina Church," *GH* 39, no. 3 (March 1979): 4; North Carolina, U.S., Death Certificates, 1909-1976 s.v. "William F Creaseman," Ancestry.com.

178 Bunch, "Tennessee Report," *GH* 6, no. 9 (March 1948): 6; Gibson, "Report," *GH* (June 1948): 6.

179 Gibson, "From General Overseer's Desk," *GH* 8, no. 10 (April 1950): 1.

180 Bunch, "Tennessee Report," *GH* 6, no. 9 (March 1948): 6; [Rufus] L. Douglas, "Newcomb, Tenn.," *GH* 6, no. 2 (June 1948): 2.

181 Gibson, "From the Overseer's Desk," *GH* 8, no. 5 (November 1949): 7.

182 CGMA, *Minutes* (1949), 8.

183 Ibid., 11, 14-15.

184 Romona Ashworth Barger, Facebook message to the author, October 26, 2020.

185 CGMA, *Minutes* (1949), 11, 14-15.

186 Longsworth, *History*, 17.

187 Jessie Fearrl Evangelist's Examination and Recommendation Form, Jessie Fearrl File, CGMA Ministers Files, Jellico, TN; CGMA, *Minutes* (1950), 20.

188 For the number of female licensed evangelists, see the minister's addresses in the CGMA minute books from 1950 to 1960. For the churches and the use of women, see the dozens of church reports in *GH* over the same time period referencing women who preached in their services.

189 Bertha McCartt, "Oliver Springs, Tenn.," *GH* 15, no. 1 (September 1956): 7.

190 Brenda Ethridge Demps, text messages to author, March 6, 2021.

191 Lucy Clark and Pauline Rogers, "Oliver Springs, Tenn.," *GH* 11, no. 4 (December 1952): 5.

192 CGMA, *Minutes* (1960), 46. As General Overseer, Clayton Lawson's attitude toward women preachers stood in sharp contrast to that of Ira Moses's when he assumed the office in 1960. When the minute book was printed that year, no pastor was listed for Oliver Springs. Instead, it was noted, "Mrs. Charles Ethridge in charge."

193 CGMA, *Minutes* (1949), 7, 12.

194 CGMA, *Minutes* (1950), 19-20; CGMA, *Minutes* (1960), 34-38.

195 Conn, 270.

196 Church of God, *Minutes of the 33rd Annual Assembly of the Church of God* (Cleveland, Tenn.: Church of God Publishing House, 1938), 4.

[197] CGMA, *Minutes* (1949), 13.

[198] Ibid., 11.

[199] "Our History," St. Peter & St. Paul UCC, accessed February 27, 2020. https://www.spspucc.org/history

[200] Gibson, "General Overseer's Report," *GH* 7, no. 9 (March 1949): 6; Wanda Bell, "Cincinnati, Ohio," *GH* 8, no. 7 (January 1950): 6.

[201] Wanda Bell, "Cincinnati, Ohio," *GH* 8, no. 9 (March 1950): 3.

[202] CGMA, *Minutes* (1950), 9, 13-15.

[203] Ibid., 10.

[204] Conn, 315-316.

[205] CGMA, *Minutes* (1950), 11.

[206] CGMA, *Minutes* (1959), 5-10, 23.

[207] CGMA, *Minutes: Church of God of the Mountain Assembly, Inc.* (Jellico, TN: CGMA, 1967), 22. In 2002, the General Council adopted a resolution changing the pastor's term to four years. CGMA, *Church of God Mountain Assembly, Inc. 96th Annual Assembly* (Jellico, TN: CGMA, 2002), 11.

[208] CMGA, *Minutes* (1952), 13.

[209] CGMA, *Minutes* (1950), 17; CGMA, *Minutes* (1951), 17; CGMA, *Minutes* (1952), 18; CGMA, *Minutes* (1953), 17; CGMA, *Minutes* (1954), 20.

[210] Petree, "History," *GH* 34, no. 10 (October 1973): 5.

[211] CGMA, *Minutes* (1951), 13; CGMA, *Minutes* (1956), 27, 33.

[212] CGMA, *Minutes* (1955), 34; CGMA, *Minutes* (1956), 40; CGMA, *Minutes* (1957), 31; CGMA, *Minutes* (1958), 23.

9

Toward a Worldwide Movement

Under the leadership of Luther Gibson and Clayton Lawson, the Church of God Mountain Assembly claimed recognition as a Pentecostal denomination in the United States. Between 1947 and 1960, the CGMA extended its borders to the West Coast with the vision to become a nationwide and (ultimately) international denomination. Membership in the Pentecostal Fellowship of North America contributed to this end directly and indirectly. For the first four decades of its history, the impact of the Church of God (Cleveland) contributed directly to the development of CGMA. In the 1950s, the Pentecostal Church of Christ (PCC) replaced the Church of God as the most significant influence on the Mountain Assembly. The inception of a mission board and mission fund resulted in the organization doubling in size within a decade. The increase in ministers and churches brought the CGMA to its strongest point when the leadership mantle fell to Ira Moses in 1960.

Developing a Global Vision

When John Parks, Stephen Bryant, and Andrew Silcox formed what became the CGMA, the scope of their vision and the geographic borders of their organization mirrored that of the Baptist association that expelled them. As the coalfields of Appalachia became connected to others by rail, migrant miner-preachers sometimes launched new congregations far outside the bounds of Whitley County, Kentucky and Campbell County, Tennessee. The construction of highways and the ease of travel by automobile produced CGMA congregations in places with no mountains. By contrast, the Church of God (Cleveland) employed a national and international vision almost from its inception. In early 1910, Lillian Thrasher opened an orphanage in Egypt and devoted the rest of her life to that work with but little available financial support from the church. Almost simultaneously, Edmund S. Barr and R.M. Evans began evangelizing the Bahamas, winning converts, and planting churches. Tomlinson appointed Evans as Overseer of the Bahamas in 1911.[1]

The CGMA might have become part of a more nationwide or worldwide movement much sooner had any of the numerous discussions about merging with another group materialized. In addition to several conversations about unification with the Church of God (Cleveland), the Mountain Assembly briefly entertained discussions about a unity with the Holiness Baptist Association of South Georgia in 1927. That same year the CGMA received a letter from James Elijah Spence asking "to consider a unity between the Church of God and the Assemblies of God."[2] Spence had been ordained by the Fire Baptized Holiness Church and was a member when it merged with the Pentecostal Holiness Church to become the International Pentecostal Holiness Church in 1911. Spence attended the first General Council of the Assemblies of God three years later and, by 1917, had spent most of his ministry among Pentecostals outside the Wesleyan tradition, wrestling with whether sanctification was an instantaneous work of grace. After considering which organization to join, he settled on the Assemblies of God and was issued credentials in June 1917. After pastorates in Alabama, Mississippi, Missouri, and Tennessee, Spence was appointed South Florida District Superintendent in July 1927.[3] In response to Spence's letter, the Assembly appointed Parks to "write and ask the officials of the Assemblies of God to meet with us at our first quarterly meeting" on November 25, 1927. The following day, delegates approved a motion to "invite all holiness assemblies to come to our assemblies and consider a unity."[4] Nevertheless, no merger was ever consummated.

From the beginning of the modern Pentecostal movement, cooperation and/or consolidation were championed by many adherents, as evidenced by the success of the Azusa Street Revival. After the first generation of Pentecostals formed associations, denominations, and independent works, a new ecumenical call came from men like South African David Johannes du Plessis and London-born Donald Gee. In 1937, the General Council of the Assemblies of God invited Pentecostal leaders from around the world to attend its annual conference in Memphis. Gee, du Plessis, and others began discussing the possibility of conducting international conventions for Pentecostals. Within a few years, conferences had been held with some success in London and Stockholm before the Second World War made such mass gatherings in Europe impractical. The first Pentecostal World Conference (PWC) convened in Zurich in May 1947, organized by du Plessis and Swiss Pastor Leonard Steiner. A second conference in Paris in 1949 began a triennial gathering that continues to the present day.[5]

Du Plessis immigrated to the United States in August 1948 and hoped to assist in the organization of a similar conference to take place annually in North America. That month, 27 Pentecostal leaders met in Chicago for a second preliminary meeting "to further explore the possibility of promoting greater fellowship among the various Pentecostal groups in North America and to consider the advisability of calling a constitutional convention." Church of God (Cleveland) General Overseer John C. Jernigan chaired the meeting and "after a full and free discussion it was agreed by all that a constitutional convention be held in Des Moines, Iowa October 26-28, 1948." His hospitalization after a serious automobile-train collision hindered du Plessis from attending the constitutional convention, but the Pentecostal Fellowship of North America (PFNA) was organized at the Church of the Open Bible Standard with nearly 200 ministers representing various Pentecostal organizations in the United States and Canada.[6] The objectives of the Fellowship as adopted were:

> 1. To provide a vehicle of expression and co-ordination of effort in matters common to all; 2. To demonstrate to the world the essential unity of Spirit-baptized believers; 3. To provide services to its constituents which will enable them to accomplish more quickly and efficiently their responsibility for the speedy evangelization of the world; 4. To encourage the principles of comity for the nurture of the body of Christ. endeavoring to keep the unity of the Spirit until we all come to the unity of the faith.[7]

Though no representative from the CGMA attended this organizational meeting, once the letter of invitation to participate in the Fellowship reached Jellico, the Mountain Assembly joined, and General Overseer Luther Gibson represented it as a voting delegate at the Second PFNA conference in Oklahoma City in October 1949. Jellico Clerk Lewis M. Sharp accompanied Gibson on the trip as did Assistant General Overseer Clayton Lawson. Everything about the experience impressed Lawson. From the oil wells surrounding the Capitol to the "beautiful" civic auditorium, the locale set the tone for the meeting which was marked by "sincere and hearty" fellowship, the likes of which he had never witnessed. Awe-struck by the 300-member choir of Pentecostals from multiple congregations and the "remarkable job" of their director, Lonnie Rex, Lawson's heart was prepared to receive the message delivered by Tom Johnstone of the Pentecostal Assemblies of Canada. "The message that God had given Brother Johnstone did not fall on dull, unreceptive ears. The very air was seemingly charged with the attentiveness of the congregation." The following night, General Supervisor of the International Church of the Foursquare Gospel delivered a sermon titled, "What the Cross of Christ Means to Me." After which, Lawson conceded "I have never heard a greater sermon preached by any preacher."

Toward a Worldwide Movement

The final day featured a sermon on foreign missions in China by Sidney Correll and a report by du Plessis whose "report of the work in many foreign lands made us realize that God is everywhere" giving the Holy Ghost "to all men alike, be he black or white, and regardless of his nationality." The meeting also affected Gibson in a personal way. Having "never seen the Holy Ghost work any greater," the General Overseer felt like his organization fell short of all that "God wants us to have." He returned "with a determination to do more than I ever have to help build up the great Church of God."[8]

His first trip to a PFNA conference undoubtedly inspired Lawson with ways to conduct a conference and the 1950 General Assembly hosted by him in Cincinnati demonstrated just that. The experience also motivated him to become more involved in the global Pentecostal Movement. After representing the CGMA at the 3rd and 4th PFNA meetings in Memphis and Detroit, respectively, the General Overseer traveled to London in June 1952 for the 3rd PWC and made his first visit to the Holy Land. After sharing the details of his trip at the 46th Annual Mountain Assembly in August, the delegates voted to give him $250 to reimburse some of his travel costs.[9] That October, the CGMA received a high honor when Luther Gibson was chosen to preach an afternoon service at the 5th PFNA conference in Los Angeles.[10]

Gibson, now pastoring in Sidney, traveled across the country with his successor at Dayton, Efford Enix, and Silas Jones. They met Lawson at the convention at Angelus Temple, built in 1923 by Aimee Semple-McPherson, founder of the International Church of the Foursquare Gospel, with a seating capacity over 5,000. Three years earlier, Gibson had admitted to the PFNA Board of Administration that he was "embarrassed because" the CGMA was "so few in number," but was proud to represent such "conscientious" Christians as his fellow church members. After hearing Southwestern Bible College Founder Raymond Othel Corvin preach Tuesday night and the mention of his numerous degrees during his introduction, Gibson admitted that he still "felt sort of out of place."[11] Corvin's sermon was followed in the convention with messages from Pentecostal Holiness Church Bishop Joseph Alexander Synan, Church of God (Cleveland) General Overseer Hallie Louticious Chesser, and others. Gibson knew that his "Assembly would be judged" by his presentation of the Word and "sought the face of God," accordingly. He testified that he had never felt such freedom to preach and "saw people get blessed" in a way he had never witnessed. "Preachers, crying, shook my hand saying I had fed their souls. It looked as if everyone in the house was praising God." "Hundreds" asked him for prayer. One overseer invited him to be the camp meeting speaker for his organization. People followed him "out on the street" and begged for prayer.[12]

Gibson's success in California earned Lawson an opportunity to preach the Wednesday night service the following year when the PFNA convened in Charlotte.[13] Lawson continued to attend PFNA conventions throughout his tenure as General Overseer and returned to the PWC in Stockholm in 1955.[14] Once again the CGMA assisted him financially and reimbursed him $500 for his travel to Sweden.[15] Gibson returned to preach a service at the PFNA meeting when it returned to Des Moines in 1959, and "stirred the congregation as no other minister did throughout the entire convention."[16] The CGMA promoted the PFNA and PWC to its members and ministers through announcements and reports of the conventions and articles featuring the histories of member denominations in *The Gospel Herald*. Fellowship with sister organizations presented new opportunities for cooperation and new possibilities for consolidation.

One such group was the Pentecostal Church of Christ. John Stroup was a 54-year-old Wesleyan Methodist evangelist in South Solon, Ohio, when he was baptized with the Holy Ghost in 1907. An invitation to conduct a tent revival in Ironton, Ohio in 1913 introduced Pentecostalism to the Ohio/Kentucky/West Virginia tristate region and Stroup called together ministers and churches where his message had been received to meet in (what is now) Flatwoods, Kentucky on May 10, 1917 to "form an organization for their mutual comfort, fellowship, and encouragement." The PCC was organized in this meeting and it elected Stroup as its Bishop.[17] The previous year, Eldon Lindsey Cyrus experienced Spirit baptism shortly after being licensed as a Regular Baptist minister. In 1919, Cyrus was ordained by the PCC and was soon elected to serve as its General Secretary. In 1935, the PCC elevated him to the office of General Overseer. Under Cyrus's leadership, the PCC organized missionary efforts in Brazil in 1938, founded Faith Bible Institute in Ashland, Kentucky in 1941, and moved its headquarters to that city two years later.[18]

At the 34th Annual Conference of the Pentecostal Church of Christ in early August 1950, the PCC appointed a committee comprised of its Bishops, E.L. Cyrus and George Nickell, Secretary Chester Miller, Treasurer Joe Stanley, and Bible Institute President Thomas Dooley. It tasked the committee to "meet with a delegation from the Church of God, Mountain Assembly, for the purpose of studying with them the possibility of uniting these two denominations."[19] Two weeks later, during the 54th Mountain

Toward a Worldwide Movement

Figure 9.1: E.L. Cyrus
c/o IPCC

Figure 9.2: Chester I. Miller
c/o IPCC

Assembly at Cincinnati, "Bishop Cyrus of the Pentecostal Church of Christ, being present with us, was called upon to speak." Miller also addressed the delegates and spoke of his decade of missionary work in Brazil. Stanley, Nickell, and Dooley were also recognized by the General Overseer. The committee on divine services then announced that Cyrus and Gibson "would be the speakers for the night service." The Council also appointed Clayton Lawson, Luther Gibson, Ira Moses, J.H. Bryant, and J.E. Hatfield as a "committee to confer with the brethren of the Pentecostal Church of Christ."[20] The committee met that afternoon "for the purpose of bringing about a closer fellowship between the two organizations." The plan they proposed included "an interchange of ministers between the two organizations for pastoral and evangelistic work" and an "exchange of church papers, *The Pentecostal Witness* and *The Gospel Herald*. The PCC also extended an invitation to CGMA members to attend its Bible school.[21] Though no Mountain Assembly minister took advantage of the educational offer, some did utilize the additional magazine. Both an advertisement for his booklet, *Two Highways to Travel*, and a sermonette by CGMA Minister Roger Powell appeared in issues of *The Pentecostal Witness* within months of the arrangement made by the two organizations.[22]

This working agreement served as a basis of fellowship between the two organizations which lasted for decades. In January, the PCC committee attended a CGMA ministers meeting in Jellico where Miller again related "his experience as a missionary in foreign fields" and shared "a few of his many hardships" while in Brazil.[23] Cyrus and Miller went from Jellico to

Middlesboro and conducted a two-weeks revival with "four saved and five sanctified, and four filled with the Holy Ghost."[24] The Bishop was surprised at the good crowds which came "through rain, snow and cold" to "seek the face of the Lord," and 275 were present for Sunday school. Pastor Ulyess Graham and the congregation were "wonderfully blessed" by "some of the most soul-stirring messages from the word of God that this church has ever witnessed," and they willingly gave to advance the PCC work in Brazil.[25]

Figure 9.3: Middlesboro CGMA with Pastor Ulyess Graham
c/o Middlesbooro CGMA

The Missions Impetus

Miller's work in Brazil inspired the CGMA churches and ministers to work toward a foreign missions program. So, at the 45th Mountain Assembly on September 4, 1951, Lawson appointed the first Mission Board of Auza Vinson, Charles Lowery, Arvil Rountree, and J.H. Bryant, with Luther Gibson serving as Chairman. Four days later, the Assembly approved the final draft of the committee's plan. The Mission Board became a standing committee and would "meet as often as deemed necessary" to promote "our mission work at home and abroad." To finance the program, the CGMA designated the fourth Sunday of each month to receive a mission offering in each church and asked every minister to send one dollar each month. The board also solicited donations and pledges at the Friday and Saturday business sessions and received nearly $800 in cash and more than $2,000 in pledges.[26] By the next assembly, only 40 percent of the money pledged arrived and many churches and ministers failed to meet their obligations. Nevertheless, 16 churches sent offerings and mission receipts totaled $2,358.81 that first year. At the Assembly that August, Ottis Ellis replaced Lowery on the Mission Board and, with the remaining four, the committee stayed intact for another six years as they further developed the program by adding new directives.[27]

First, the committee recommended to "set aside one night of the General Assembly each year for the promotion of the Mission Work" and raise an offering in that service for missions. On Friday, August 15, 1952, Gibson and Vinson preached the first CMGA missions rally. The Assembly also adopted the board's proposal that its chairman be given discretion over mission fund disbursements along with the General Overseer. This oversight proved necessary as twelve ministers and 18 churches received financial support from the mission fund in the first three years.[28] After establishing the mission program, the board next sought to expand it hierarchically by adding State Mission Directors in 1954. At the same time, another ordinance was added that authorized the General Overseer to call a "Mission Meeting at least once each year."[29] Both directives were short-lived, however, and were revised the following year. Now, the Assembly would choose a "General Mission Director" to "promote the progress of the Mission, and the Mission Fund" by "visiting the churches" and with the pastors "draft a program for their states." The annual mission meeting became a board meeting with the General Mission Director in charge instead of the General Overseer. Gibson was then appointed to serve in this capacity.[30]

While Gibson served as General Mission Director, the CGMA mission fund averaged just over $2,000 a year. This income proved critical to the support of the new churches which sprang up throughout the organization in the 1950s. During the decade, no less than 45 congregations presented letters soliciting membership into the Mountain Assembly. The number of CGMA churches doubled during the decade and added churches in the states of Pennsylvania, West Virginia, Virginia, Utah, California, Georgia, and Illinois. Within fifteen years of the schism of 1946, the Mountain Assembly had more churches in more states than it ever had.

Perhaps no state was more decimated by the split than Indiana. The churches in Nevada and Salem had left the CGMA and the church in Shelburn split. By 1950, the lone Mountain Assembly congregation in Indiana was down to 28 members and had no pastor. It appeared that rebuilding the state would require recruitment and good leadership. Charles Harmon Lowery had been acquainted with John Longsworth before the latter joined the Mountain Assembly in early 1949 and assumed the pastorate of Sidney, Ohio.[31] In the spring of 1950, Lowery planted a church in Metamora,

Indiana with eight in attendance the first Sunday.[32] Gibson and Lawson visited there during a revival on April 17 and felt confident that "a great work" would be "accomplished there."[33] Lowery and the church presented themselves for membership at the General Assembly in Cincinnati that year and were accepted into the fellowship.[34] The young pastor's untimely death in an automobile accident three years later left the church without a pastor until his uncle, Thomas Lowery, briefly assumed the pastorate in 1957.[35]

A group of believers transplanted from McCreary County, Kentucky to Muncie, Indiana began meeting and worshipping together in that city in 1952. Everett Inman relocated that year from Cincinnati to oversee the fledgling mission. By the time the church organized and presented its letter for membership at the Mountain Assembly, however, Inman had resigned, and Robert Pike, relocated to Muncie from the Sidney church to pastor it. At the same time, R.N. Ballinger moved to Lawrenceburg, Indiana, started a church, and served as the overseer for the struggling state. The newly created mission fund supported Ballinger, Inman, Pike, and the Muncie mission that year.[36] By the next assembly, Ballinger also remodeled the building at Salem, reorganized the church, and installed George Cook as its pastor.[37]

Charles Leroy Weaver, and his wife, Jessie, lived 20 miles South of Muncie in New Castle, but commuted for church services after dissatisfaction with the Church of God (Cleveland). In June 1953, Pike recommended that Weaver start a church in the city where he had lived most of the last 30 years. On the first Monday of July, a service was held outdoors, but the Weavers soon found a two-room home, removed the wall partition, and began meeting there until a new brick building could be erected. Twenty-three attended the first Sunday school, and 32 came the first Sunday night. On June 7, 1954, Ballinger organized the mission with Weaver as pastor at an all-day meeting that featured preaching from the General Overseer and from Jess Neal who had already preached multiple revivals for Weaver.[38]

The Weavers proved to be just what the Mountain Assembly needed in Indiana. When Ballinger moved back to the Goshen, Ohio, area in 1955, Lawson

Figure 9.4: Charles L. Weaver
c/o *The Gospel Herald*

appointed C.L. Weaver State Overseer of Indiana. In this capacity, he built solidarity among the ministers and churches as they attended fellowship meetings and youth rallies and supported each other's revivals. Weaver also determined to grow the district by starting churches; the first was in Winchester. Lawson lauded the State Overseer in a report that winter. "Brother Weaver has a band of people in this Hoosier town who are rejoicing in the Lord in a great way." In 1959, Weaver organized three more churches at Shoals, Richmond, and Mitchell.[39] With eight churches now in the State, Lawson divided it into two districts on August 28 and appointed Salem Pastor James W. Leslie overseer of the southern district. The following month, Leslie opened a mission in Louisville, Kentucky.[40]

A crowning moment in organizational growth in Indiana occurred at the Elders' Meeting in New Castle in October 1956. To this meeting, "The Church of God of Nevada, Ind., sent a letter of solicitation for membership in the Assembly and was accepted with Bro. C.D. Blackburn, ordained minister, as pastor." Gibson held a revival with Charles Devenor Blackburn at Nevada for two weeks leading up to the meeting with the Board of Elders. Lawson also attended the revival and "extended our fellowship to them." Gibson credited Willis Yeary, who returned from the Original Mountain Assembly to pastor the Race Street Church in Cincinnati, and his brother and sister-in-law, Charlie and Dessie Yeary, for the "wonderful help in bringing about the reunion of the church with the Assembly."[41]

Gibson made saw reconciliation with the Original Mountain Assembly a key to growth and made it a priority. Gibson later recollected that one of his "greatest achievements" was going to Cleveland, Ohio and receiving that church and Pastor James Walden back into the fellowship. One reason Gibson so highly regarded this accomplishment was that three of Walden's sons, Jerome, James, and Jasper, ultimately became ordained ministers as well.[42] The senior Walden demonstrated his worth to organizational growth in his own right. When the states were divided into districts in 1954, Lawson appointed Walden District Overseer for Northern Ohio. The district began with two churches, but the new overseer determined to enlarge it.[43]

With Cleveland, the CGMA had a church in Akron to comprise the new Northern Ohio District. The first Mountain Assembly congregation there followed Long in 1946, but Lawson organized a new church on Ira Avenue on Thursday, May 24, 1951. His maternal first cousin, Jennings Baird, "through his untiring efforts to find a building and to gather the people together," facilitated the start of the church. Baird's older brother, Claude,

Figure 9.5: Jennings Baird
c/o CGMA

Figure 9.6: Claude Baird
c/o CGMA

pastor at Elk Valley, held the first revival to launch the initiative. Fellow Elk Valley Native Johnie H. Douglas was installed as the first pastor. Douglas began preaching at 16, was ordained at the General Assembly in 1944 at 21, and had pastored five different churches before taking this assignment at 28.[44]

Within two months of his appointment, James Walden organized another church in Cleveland on Detroit Avenue and installed Randolph Whitt as the pastor.[45] On February 8, 1955, he set another "church in order" with eleven members at the home of Elmer Lester in Wadsworth, with Whitt as its pastor. Elder Rufus Leonard Douglas, the son of Elk Valley Founder William B. Douglas, pastored the church when it lettered in to the 49th Annual Assembly that year. By then, the congregation found an old church building in Easton.

It used this building until the construction of a new highway claimed the property and it relocated to Rittman with Jennings Baird now its pastor.[46]

In early 1956, another church was set in order at South Amherst with William Matheny as pastor. Matheny did not stay long, and Walden found himself making multiple trips to keep open the doors of the struggling church. In 1960, he sent his son, Jerome, there to pastor.[47] Jerome had briefly pastored the church on Detroit Avenue in Cleveland a few years earlier.

Figure 9.7: Jerome Walden
c/o Al Newton, Jr.

James Walden organized a third church in the city of Cleveland on St. Clair Avenue on April 1, 1957, with eleven members and installed James C. Wimmer as the pastor.[48] Finally, just before the 1960 General Assembly, Walden set another church in order at Canal Fulton with Charles Wesley Goins as pastor.[49]

As Chairman of the Mission Board and General Mission Director, Luther Gibson was a church planter, himself. The church at Sidney had been instrumental in providing home missionaries for several years before Gibson and John Longsworth exchanged pastorates in late 1951. Longsworth did not stay at Dayton long. Bishop E.L. Cyrus had preached a revival for him while at Sidney in February 1951 where eight souls were saved.[50] That October, Longsworth preached a youth rally at the PCC in Jamestown, Ohio.[51] Months later, Longsworth took advantage of the accord between the PCC and CGMA to exchange pastors and minsters and resigned at Dayton to accept an appointment to pastor the PCC in Virginia Beach, Virginia.[52] Efford Enix, a grandson of John H. Parks, returned to Dayton to assume the pastorate there after pastoring two and a half years at Oliver Springs, Tennessee. Enix preached a revival at Oliver Springs with his father-in-law, Dayton Pastor Floyd Robinson, in later summer 1949 and stayed to pastor the struggling church. During his tenure there, Enix baptized 60 converts and left the church in solid condition.[53]

While at Sidney, Gibson helped start new churches in what would become the Central Ohio District. One of those was at Greenville. In the summer of 1953, Roger Powell began a tent revival at the fairgrounds. Powell was a native of Claiborne County, Tennessee, and was converted at the Mountain Assembly mission at Arthur a few years earlier. He soon dedicated his life to ministry and relocated to Randolph County, Indiana, in 1952, before moving to Greenville "not knowing one single person in that city." After Powell preached four weeks at the fairground, Gibson arranged for the purchase of a lot on the corner of 12th Street and Tilman Avenue, where a "basement church" was constructed. After nearly thirty had been saved, Gibson set a church in order with twelve members and Powell as the pastor on August 31, 1953. Powell left Greenville at the end of 1954 and was replaced by William Loudermilk, who had been converted and began preaching under Gibson at Dayton. The church enjoyed much success under Loudermilk, and in five years, set a new attendance record of 102.[54]

Figure 9.8: Roger Powell
c/o the Powell Family

After a brief stay in Barbourville, Kentucky, Powell initiated another tent revival in June 1955, this time in the Ohio state capital. By Sunday, September 4, he had secured a building on Parsons Avenue in Columbus and began having nightly meetings. The following Sunday, the Southern Ohio District Overseer organized the church with six members, four of whom were ministers. Two more ministers joined shortly thereafter, and the abundant preaching supply enabled the church to continue the revival for more than 400 consecutive nights.[55]

After launching the work in Greenville, Gibson began looking for a place to start a church in Piqua. Ancil Mat Laws had approached Pastor Gibson and expressed a burden for that city. Laws's father, John Melton Laws, and maternal grandfather, Thomas D. Moses, had been been delegates at the first Mountain Assembly in 1907. Gibson paid the first month's rent on a building from the mission fund, acquired seats and a pulpit, and launched the church with a revival before installing Laws as the pastor, where he remained for the next thirty years.[56]

In the fall of 1956, Ray Clark, another minister from Dayton, planted a church at "Wright View Heights" in nearby, Fairborn. Within a couple months, Sunday school attendance had reached near 50.[57] Almost simultaneously, Gibson organized a church at Troy on Sunday, November 23, 1956. All 56 seats in the building were filled at the first service, including "22 people from Troy." With $90 from the mission fund, Gibson purchased seats, a piano, and a pulpit. Everett Rogers of Sidney was installed as the first pastor.[58] Finally, just after the General Assembly in 1962, Gibson organized a church in Celina, in the home of his first cousin, John Gibson, and installed Elmer Rowe as pastor. After about six months, Rowe resigned, and Gibson's son, Harvey Merle Gibson, accepted the pastorate.[59]

To the north, a new mission was planted in the fall of 1953 in Holland, Ohio. Charles Arlando Freeman "took sick at work" in Toledo on the previous December 5 with "something wrong" with his heart. By the end of January, he lost 31 pounds. His brother took him to their father's home in Jellico where Lawrence Redmond, Claude Baird, and Joe Moses came to pray for him and "God was there in a mighty way." At church that Wednesday night, his "faith took hold of Jesus for the healing" of his body, and he began getting better and gaining weight back. The "kindness of the good people of Jellico" endeared Freeman to the Mountain Assembly and he attended a minister's meeting at the Toledo church in June. On October 9, Freeman had the first meeting with a congregation in a small building in Holland. The following morning, he started a Sunday school with 13 in attendance. State Overseer J.H. Douglas came to organize the church on November 7 with seven members. As the church began to grow, the building quickly became inadequate. "So small that some people had to stand outside to be in service," the members pressed to start a building fund. After the church bought a three-acre lot, it borrowed $200 from the CGMA to lay the foundation and paid back the loan within a year. Within three years, the church had a building with "ample room" thanks to generous contributions inside and outside the church. Even First Lady Mamie Eisenhower sent a donation.[60]

Figure 9.9: C.A. Freeman
c/o Janet Freeman

While the church at Holland worked to build a church, in late 1955, James Walden "preached a wonderful sermon" on Superior Street in Rossford before he "organized the body" there with four members and William Fitzpatrick as the pastor.[61] When its membership failed to double within a year, Fitzpatrick founded another congregation on Main Street in Toledo. This venture proved to be short-lived as well and both churches closed the following year.[62]

In 1950, the CGMA had three churches in Michigan: Monroe, Detroit, and Trenton. The latter was less than two years old. David Hammitte had been a member at Detroit since he moved to Michigan after organizing the Middlesboro church. He and Finley Gray began preaching in Trenton in the fall of 1948 and by January had small congregation. State Overseer M.E. Woolum organized the church that month with seven members.[63] After Roy Cornelius returned from the Original Mountain Assembly, he briefly pastored Trenton in 1951, before establishing a church on Biddle Avenue in nearby Wyandotte.[64] In September 1952, the Bagley Avenue Church in Detroit called upon Ottis Ellis to be its pastor.⁶⁵ Woolum began working with his grandnephew, Edward, the former National Youth Director, to start a church in Pontiac. The State Overseer set the church in order on March 29, 1953 with 17 members. When Edward resigned at the end of the year "to evangelize in South Carolina," Jesse D. Brown was appointed to take his place.⁶⁶ The elder Woolum, meanwhile, established another church in Detroit on Fort Street and resumed pastoring.⁶⁷ Paul Grubbs' return from the Original Mountain Assembly gave the CGMA a third church in Detroit on Junction Street in 1954.⁶⁸ The same year, Everett Brown, a minister from the Bagley Street Church, began taking care of the remnant of a church that disbanded in Ypsilanti. By the time a church was organized in 1964, C.A. Freeman's son, Ray Arnold Freeman, was the pastor.⁶⁹

Arvil Rountree assumed the pastorate at Goshen after the General Assembly in 1949. Two years later, Lawson appointed him to the Mission Board and as State Overseer of Ohio. As a result, mission work in the greater Cincinnati area increased. Two new churches in Northern Kentucky were received into the fellowship at the 46th General Assembly in 1952. Elmer Steeley had left the Cincinnati church on McMicken Street to pioneer a work in Newport, and yet another minister out of the Dayton church, Haskel Swain, started a church on Pike Street in Covington.⁷⁰ Almost immediately, Swain began conducting prayer meetings with another minister from Covington, William Warren on the other side of the Ohio River at the home of Charles Boggs in North Bend. Once organized, the church presented its letter for membership at the 1953 General Assembly and then found a building for rent in nearby Cleves. In February 1955, Goshen Minister James Gray went there to pastor and found another building for rent in Addyston.⁷¹

Near the end of 1952, another minister from the Goshen church, John Collins, started a church in "a little old barn by the side of the road" in Bantam.⁷² Within a year of its organization, some members of the church at Bantam attended every night of a revival Rountree held at Levanna. After the 1953 General Assembly, Rountree moved to North Carolina to pastor the church at Old Fort. His replacement at Goshen and the new Southern Ohio District Overseer, Claiborn Boyd "C.B." Ellis, Jr., organized a church at Levanna on August 6, 1954, with Vogel Boling as pastor.⁷³ Further down the Ohio River, a PCC mission at New Boston was established the same year when Everett Brown moved from Cleveland to Portsmouth. J.H. Douglas briefly pastored there before accepting the pastorate at Race Street Church in Cincinnati that August.⁷⁴

Toward a Worldwide Movement

In early 1955, Ellis helped another Goshen minister, Wade Moss Hughes, start a church between Goshen and Levanna, near Georgetown. Hughes had been raised in the Church of Christ but could not attend often for lack of transportation. Goshen Sunday School Superintendent Wymer Sumner, whose stepfather, Daniel Moses, was a delegate at the first Mountain Assembly, picked up young people for Sunday school in the back of his Chevy truck. Sumner's daughter, Delores, attracted the attention of teenaged Hughes the first time he rode to Goshen church, and the two married in 1949. Hughes accepted the call to ministry in his mid-20s and looked for opportunities to preach. He discovered a dilapidated building at Farmer's Chapel, remodeled it, and opened the church.[75] Hughes would go on to pastor the churches at Addyston and Covington before relocating to Nevada, Indina to pastor in 1960.[76]

Figure 9.10: Wade M. Hughes
c/o Al Newton

Figure 9.11: Arvil Rountree
c/o CGMA

Still on the Mission Board and now State Overseer of North Carolina, Arvil Rountree determined to see his district grow beyond the one CGMA church in his state at Old Fort. Not long after his arrival, he met a man in Marion who said that "God had laid on his heart to give a lot to build a church." Rountree began a prayer meeting in his home and accepted the lot with the promise to erect a church building. While building the church at Marion, he made the acquaintance of a group of "people there who love the Lord in the old fashioned way" in nearby Glenwood and began preaching in a "house using planks and blocks for seats." When a widow there made a similar offer to donate a lot to build a church, Rountree reasoned God opened another door in that community as well. Pastoring one church while attempting to build two others, Arvil and Ione Rountree were "in service almost every night." On August 10, 1955, the 49th General Assembly accepted both churches into the fellowship with Rountree listed as pastor of all three congregations in North Carolina. After the church at Marion was able to meet in its new building, Rountree sent a young minister from Old Fort, Lloyd Logan Camp, there to pastor and made plans to build at Glenwood. George William Douglas assumed the pastorate at the completed Glenwood church in 1957. Having tripled the size of his district in four years, Rountree moved to Michigan and assumed the pastorate of the church in Trenton. Camp returned to pastor his home church at Old Fort, and Evangelist Robert Morgan took care of Marion until June when another young minister from Dayton, Orville Clarence Bartee, Jr., came to pastor.[77]

Extending the boundaries of the Mountain Assembly into states with no churches seemed a priority for Gibson and Lawson. In 1950, the appointing board selected overseers for five states, Michigan, Indiana, Ohio, Kentucky, and Tennessee, and added North Carolina in 1952.[78] In 1954, the board divided Michigan and Kentucky into two districts each, and Ohio into three. It also selected overseers for Pennsylvania and Utah. Two years later, State Overseers were added for Virginia / West Virginia, and California.[79]

G.W. Helmick's 1949 appointment as the first State Overseer of Pennsylvania was short-lived. Helmick left the Mountain Assembly almost as quickly as he arrived. The two women evangelists that he licensed, however, continued to renew their credentials through headquarters. The church they attended in Monessen had divided from a congregation at Monongahela, just a few miles away on the opposite side of the Monongahela River. In 1953, Pastor Carl Lashinsky, of Monessen, received credentials with the CGMA but, in October, resigned from the church to pastor in Pine Hill, Kentucky. John Elrod briefly assumed the pastorate at Monessen. William Warren had been driving to Pine Hill from Covington for months to take care of the church before Lashinsky's arrival. Covington Pastor Haskel Swain took an interest in the Pennsylvania churches and sent Warren to Monessen to fill-in temporarily. In early spring 1954, John Parks, no relation to CGMA founder, took the church in Monongahela. Parks had been a member of the church in Covington and conducted revivals with Swain. Eventually, the care of both churches fell upon him. The following year, Dayton's Sunday School Superintendent Walter Vaughn took pastorship of both churches, reunited them into one congregation again, and moved them to Donora into a building that seated more than 200.[80]

After helping to establish the Pennsylvania District, Swain and his Covington ministers, set their sights on West Virginia. Swain and Warren conducted a revival in Ceredo and organized a church there with 21 members on September 5, 1954, and immediately made plans "for another new church" in the state, envisioning "West Virginia will be a great state in the Mountain Assembly." Swain and Lawson visited Ceredo on October 9 to record a deed for the property and to conduct a pastor's election for Carl H. Mayberry.[81]

Figure 9.12: Haskel Swain
c/o The Youth Gateway

On May 8, 1955, Swain helped bring into the Mountain Assembly an independent Church of God in Bluefield, and Parks left Pennsylvania to pastor this church with 60 members.[82] In early 1956, William Sparks opened a new mission in Kenova just west of Ceredo, and Jasper Combs began a mission to the east in Huntington.[83] Neither of these missions produced a church, and after Swain left the Mountain Assembly, the churches in West Virginia soon followed.

In the same month that Swain brought in the church in Bluefield, his former pastor at Dayton, Efford Enix, held a revival sixty miles away in Pulaski, Virginia, at a Church of God pastored by William Bentley Davis. About 35 indicated they had been saved or restored in the revival. At the conclusion of the week, Lawson was present and formally received the congregation into the Mountain Assembly.[84] Unfortunately, like West Virginia, the Mountain Assembly's presence in the state was fleeting. Within a few years, the church was gone, and it would be another seven years before another CGMA congregation was established in Virginia.

In 1952, Mark Byrge and William Riley Byrge moved from Huntsville, Tennessee, to Helper, Utah, and opened just the second Mountain Assembly church west of the Mississippi River the following year.[85] The Byrges were the sons of Clara Ward and George Washington Byrge. Their wives, Dirley and Florida, were the daughters of Sarah Abston and George Washington McCloud.[86] Members of the CGMA in Oneida, Mark was ordained in 1933, and his younger brother was ordained the following year.[87] They had left the coal mines of East Tennessee to work in the mines in Carbon County, Utah.

Figure 9.13: Helper, Utah CGMA

c/o David R. Duncan

They began having services "in a small building, isolated by itself, just west of the street" on which they lived. The church later moved to a stone building on the north side of town with living quarters "upstairs and the chapel was a downstairs large room."[88] The church was organized on January 30, 1954, with eight members. Lawson visited the congregation that spring on his way by bus to California.[89]

The purpose of Lawson's visit to Los Angeles may have been to arrange for a CGMA work there. That fall, Lawson ordained John E. Kennedy and Charles Grayson at the Race Street Church in Cincinnati as they prepared to move to Southern California for missionary work. Both ministers had been active in the church under Lawson's pastorate, and Kennedy had served as church treasurer for the past nine years. The Kennedys and Graysons visited area churches, held home prayer services, and conducted revivals for more than a year before Kennedy opened a mission in Ontario. Lawson held a revival there in the summer of 1957, and returned on November 3, to organize the church with seven members.[90]

That same year, John E. Elrod organized a church in Marietta, Georgia, with the hope that "many churches [would] spring up" in the state. After the churches in Pennsylvania withdrew from the assembly, Elrod had continued to renew his credentials with the CGMA despite not having a home church. He moved briefly to Cleveland, Ohio before relocating to the greater Atlanta area in 1957. Eighteen months after organizing the congregation in Marietta, as the new Georgia State Overseer, he set in order another church in Atlanta with 13 members.[91]

Elrod was not the only minister to leave Cleveland to establish a CGMA work in a new state in the late 1950s. In the spring of 1959, James Walden, Jr. moved to Waukegan, Illinois, and began a revival. In July, he organized a church with six members and was averaging forty in attendance within a year. In the spring of 1960, Walden organized another mission on Broadway in Chicago. Attendance climbed from four the first service to the building "filled to capacity" by August. On August 20, the new Illinois State Overseer set the church in order with Everett Brown as pastor.[92]

Figure 9.14: James Walden, Jr.
c/o Jon Walden

As the Mountain Assembly stretched its borders and extended itself into new states in the 1950s, it also started new works in the states where it began, Kentucky and Tennessee. George Jennings established a new church in Somerset, Kentucky in July 1953.[93] Five years later, a church was established about 25 miles south of Somerset at Day Ridge, Kentucky, with Robert Phillips as pastor, and began "progressing in a wonderful way."[94] When Everett Inman left the young church in Muncie, he evangelized out of Cincinnati, briefly pastored Monessen, and then took the small church at Trosper, Kentucky, after a revival he held there in the late fall of 1954. Inman remodeled the church and refurnished it with pews and a piano.[95] The following year, the mission fund sponsored him as he opened a new work in nearby Pineville where he also preached on the radio.[96]

In early 1954, Henry Vencil Lawson joined the Church of God Mountain and assumed the pastorate of the church at Ages, Kentucky. Lawson had been ordained in the Pentecostal Church of God and had recently been pastoring the First Pentecostal Church at nearby Loyall. Two years later, the appointing board selected him to be the overseer of the Harlan District. In the two years he served in that capacity, four new churches were organized in the district.[97] Within six months of assuming the office, Lawson "bought a 40 ft by 60 ft block building with three lots in a good location at Wallens [sic] Creek" for $1,500, and "organized a new church with fifteen members." Theodore Whitehead served as the first pastor.[98] In the spring, Eugene Lamb opened a new mission in the coal town of Kildav.[99] In 1958,

Lawson organized a church in an old school building, leased for ten years, at Ferndale with Archie Gaylor as pastor.[100] Lawson then established a church at Bledsoe, which he pastored until he left the Mountain Assembly in 1960.[101]

Figure 9.15: Lake City Homecoming, 1958

c/o Nellie Partin Yeary

Just south of CGMA Headquarters, Joe Moses held a two-weeks revival in Lafollette and opened a new church there in 1953. The church was organized and received into the Mountain Assembly in 1955.[102] The following year and just further south, Isham Sharp started a new church at Lake City (now Rocky Top).[103] After Sharp returned to pastor Mountain Ash in 1957, John Spurlock assumed the pastorate there until 1961. Still further south, a new Mountain Assembly church was planted in Knoxville in late 1955. Elk Valley Native Daniel Clifford Lynch had moved to the city a few years earlier. The General Overseer, Clayton Lawson, was among the first to donate toward the building fund. The home of his birth, Knoxville also held a special place in Lawson's heart because the Mountain Assembly had one of "the first full gospel church[es] to be in Knoxville." John Thomas's mission on Hill Street began in 1912 and grew to over 200 members before Thomas died in 1922. Although the church dissipated soon after its founder's death, Lawson contended that "many of the great Pentecostal Churches" in the city came from this mission. A church was organized and lettered into the General Assembly in 1956. After struggling for a couple of years, it merged with Faith Temple Church of God on the corner of 7th and Cecil Avenues and was reorganized.[104]

Toward a Worldwide Movement

Figure 9.16: Clayton Lawson
c/o Al Newton, Jr.

Figure 9.17: Auza Vinson
c/o Merele Vinson

Finally, in the summer of 1957, Mission Board Member Auza Vinson "purchased a 150' by 150' lot with a house on it for a new church" in Lawrenceburg, Tennessee. After removing the partitions and making repairs, it became "a very nice place to have meetings." Vinson had first attended the Mountain Assembly from Cleveland, Ohio in 1946. In the middle of the split, he aligned himself with the Original Mountain Assembly and was ordained by McKinley Baird, C.H. Randall, and Willis Yeary on November 12, 1947. The following year, he was elected pastor at Cleveland. Two years later, the church changed pastors and Vinson attempted to evangelize. When no one at the 1949 Original Mountain Assembly in Williamsburg scheduled him for revival, John Collins asked Vinson to replace him as pastor at Butlerville, Ohio. There, Vinson began to fellowship with the Goshen CGMA and befriended Arvil Rountree, who convinced him to return to the Mountain Assembly a year later. When the Butlerville church would not follow Vinson, Clayton Lawson took him to Old Fort and installed him as pastor. After erecting a new sanctuary there in 1952, he took the pastorate at Metamora for one year before returning to evangelism. Vinson then pastored Bantam from 1954 until his move to Lawrenceburg.[105] In his first seven years on the Mission Board, Vinson had pastored three young churches, built a new building at another, and done extensive evangelism among small struggling churches. When the Fiftieth Annual Assembly elected a new Mission Board for the first time in 1958, Vinson was selected as the chairman his by fellow committee members, Charles Creekmore, General Douglas, C.B. Ellis, Jr., and James Walden, Jr.[106]

A Bow Tied

Figure 9.18: Executive Board, 1958

c/o Alice Chitwood

During Clayton Lawson's ten years as General Overseer, the CGMA had doubled the number of its churches, thanks in large part to the new Mission Board and mission fund. He traveled extensively across the United States and made two trips to Europe. His trip to South America in January 1960, however, planted the seeds that grew into the first foreign mission work for the CGMA. Chester Miller picked up Lawson at the airport when he arrived in Recife, Brazil, on Saturday, January 16. After eating dinner, they went straight to a tent revival where Lawson preached through an interpreter. At 6:00 the next morning, they caught a bus bound for Caruaru on unpaved roads. The itinerary there included three church services and a funeral for a church member.[107] The General Overseer found the Brazilians to be gracious hosts who went to great lengths to make him comfortable despite the vast difference in living standards to which he was accustomed. He followed "the teachings of the Bible" and ate "what was set before" him.[108] Lawson impressed Miller with willingness to sacrifice for the ministry, especially at a time when his father was seriously ill.[109] He also made an impact on the people of Brazil. "His messages will not soon be forgotten, and the people continue to ask about 'Brother Clayton,'" Miller wrote. The missionary hoped that Lawson's pictures "turned out good" that "perhaps his visit will be a greater blessing than any of us at the present realize."[110] Indeed, as the General Overseer took the film of his first mission trip to church services and youth meetings, inspired congregations began to dream about the possibility that they might also send "missionaries to preach the word all over the world."[111]

Conclusion

The revolution of the 1940s that saw the Mountain Assembly modify its system of government and change its leadership had come and gone and left something different in its place. The most significant change in the 1944 Assembly had been the creation of a Bishop's Council modeled after that of the Church of God (Cleveland). The group in Cleveland, however, had created such a council to replace its Council of 70. It intended to make the law-making body of the organization more inclusive. The move had the opposite effect in the CGMA by limiting the number of eligible participants in the most important aspects of the church business. The exclusivity caused by this decision led to the split with the Original Mountain Assembly, but among those who remained, discontentment with the system still lingered. With a growing number of licensed evangelists who must hold credentials for two years before they were eligible to participate in the election of officers, there came a call for reform. In 1952, the Bishop's Council was discontinued after just eight years and replaced with a "General Council" comprised of "Ministers, Elders, and appointed Delegates," limited to two per church.[112]

Ironically, the Church of God of the Original Mountain Assembly voted to change the name of its Clerk to Secretary & Treasurer at its second assembly and revisited the nomenclature of its officials again in 1962. That year, delegates changed the name of the "Moderator" to "General Overseer."[113] Thus, within sixteen years of the split, the two groups had found common ground with the two major governmental differences that had separated them in the first place. In addition, Kelsie Moses, the son of Kim Moses, had replaced A.J. Long as Moderator of the Original Mountain Assembly in 1956 and continued to serve as General Overseer.[114] In the CGMA, Ira Moses replaced Clayton Lawson as General Overseer in 1960. Hence, both personalities at the center of the schism were no longer in leadership. Upon moving to Jellico, Ira Moses sought to improve fellowship between the groups and regularly attended the annual assembly in Williamsburg.[115] Although the relationship between them became cordial, no reconciliation was ever reached.

Lawson's strong personality had repelled many ministers in the 1940s. Over the course of ten years, it exhausted even some of his supporters. The same fears of an autocrat that plagued the Church of God (Cleveland) under A.J. Tomlinson gripped Mountain Assembly ministers with concerns about Lawson. By the end of his tenure, even his relationship with Gibson had become strained.[116] Lawson ran for reelection four times. Though twice, others were nominated, no one was willing to run against him.[117] He was reelected unanimously each time.[118] This was, in part, because the rules allowed for a voice vote in such cases. The 54th Annual Assembly in 1960 promised to be different. A new resolution adopted after the 1958 elections required the election of general officials by secret ballot, stipulating a yes/no vote when there was but one nomination.[119] Lawson may not have worried about losing a yes/no vote, but many negative votes would have seriously injured his ego. After a tense Elders' Meeting at Race Street in January 1960, Lawson decided not to seek reelection for General Overseer at the Assembly that year.[120] The General Council elected Ira H. Moses, the grandson of J.H. Parks, to succeed him.

Figures 9.19-9.20: General Council, 1958

c/o Alice Chitwood

Toward a Worldwide Movement

1 Conn, 146-147, 181-182; Phillips, 251.

2 CGMA, *Minutes* (1927), 10.

3 J.E. Spence Ordination Application; Spence to J.W. Welch, June 27, 1917; Spence Minister Card; all records in the J.E. Spence File, Flower Pentecostal Heritage Center, Springfield, Mo.; J. Samuel Rasnake, *Stones By The River: A History of the Tennessee District of the Assemblies of God* (Bristol, Tenn.: Westhighlands Church, 1975), 57.

4 CGMA, *Minutes* (1927), 10-11.

5 "Pentecostal World Conference," Stanley M. Burgess and Gary B. McGee, eds., *Dictionary of Pentecostal and Charismatic Movements* (Grand Rapids: Zondervan Publishing House, 1988), 707-709.

6 "David Johannes du Plessis," Burgess and McGee, 250-253; "Second Exploratory Conference of Pentecostal Leaders Held at Chicago, Illinois, August 3 and 4," *CGE* 39, no. 29 (September 25, 1948), 4.

7 J. Roswell Flower to Fellow Minister[s] of the Assemblies of God, November 20, 1948, Assemblies of God Ministers Letters, Consortium of Pentecostal Archives, available online at pentecostalarchives.org

8 Clayton Lawson, "What the Pentecostal Fellowship of North America Meant to Me," and Luther Gibson, "From the General Overseer's Desk," *GH* 8, no. 5 (November 1949): 1, 7-8.

9 Clayton Lawson, "Report of Convention," *GH* 11, no. 1 (July 1952): 1; CGMA, *Minutes of the Church of God of the Mountain Assembly Incorporated* (Jellico, Tenn: CGMA, 1952), 9, 16.

10 "Who's Who on the PFNA Convention Agenda," *The Foursquare Magazine* 25, no. 11 (November 1952): 19, 31.

11 Gibson, "Desk," *GH* 8, no. 5 (November 1949): 8.

12 Luther Gibson, "The Pentecostal Fellowship in Los Angeles, California," *GH* 11, no. 3 (November 1952): 4.

13 "Rev. Clayton Lawson," *GH* 12, no. 1 (September 1953): 7.

14 Clayton Lawson, "Report of the World Pentecostal Conference," *GH* 13, no. 11 (July 1955): 1-2.

15 CGMA, *Minutes of the Church of God of the Mountain Assembly Incorporated* (Jellico, Tenn.: CGMA, 1955), 24.

16 Clayton Lawson, "Report of Pentecostal Fellowship of North America," *GH* 17, no. 12 (December 1959): 2.

17 Thomas Dooley, "Historical Sketch of the Pentecostal Church of Christ," *GH* 15, no. 9 (June 1957): 1-2.

18 "International Pentecostal Church of Christ," Burgess and McGee, 465-466; "Wednesday Afternoon Speaker at PFNA Convention in Atlanta, Ga.," *GH* 15, no. 1 (September 1956): 8; Clyde M. Hughes, "International Pentecostal Church of Christ," in George Thomas Kurian and Sarah Claudine Day, eds., *The Essential Handbook of Denominations & Ministries* (Grand Rapids: Baker Books, 2017), 187-188; "History of the International Pentecostal Church of Christ," church website, accessed October 10, 2020 https://ipcoc.org/about/history/

19 Pentecostal Church of Christ, *Minutes of the 34th Annual Conference of the Pentecostal Church of Christ* (Ashland, KY: Pentecostal Church of Christ, 1950), 34.

20 CGMA, *Minutes* (1950), 10-11.

21 "Committee on Fellowship," *GH* 9, no. 4 (October 1950): 1.

22 [advertisement], *The Pentecostal Witness* 4, no. 3 (March 1951): 2; Roger Powell, "The Word of Truth," *The Pentecostal Witness* 4, no. 4 (April 1951): 10.

23 J.C. Murray, "Jellico, Tenn.," *GH* 9, no. 9 (March 1951): 1.

24 [Ulyess] Graham, "Revival," *The Pentecostal Witness* 4, no. 2 (February 1951): 7. Note: Graham's first name was commonly misspelled Ulysses. The preferred spelling, used in the body of this narrative, is consistent with U.S. Social Security records. Social Security Death Index, 1935-2014, s.v. "Ulyess L. Graham," Ancestry.com.

25 William Watson, "Middlesboro, Ky.," *the Gospel Herald* 9, no. 7 (January 1951): 7; Middlesboro CGMA, Church Treasury Ledger: 1946 to 1966, 103.

26 CGMA, *Minutes* (1951), 9, 10-13.

27 CGMA, *Minutes* (1952), 20-22.

28 Ibid., 9, 15; CGMA, *Minutes* (1953), 19; CGMA, *Minutes* (1954), 22.

29 CGMA, *Minutes* (1954), 12.

30 CGMA, *Minutes* (1955), 24. The reference to State (and later District) Mission Directors remained in the standard resolutions until a new mission program was drafted in 1967, but it does not appear that any were ever appointed. In practice, the work of home missions fell to the State (and District) Overseers, and, when the new program was adopted, the Mission Board became the District Overseers.

31 George Snowden, "Sidney, Ohio," *GH* 8, no. 5 (November 1949): 6; Snowden, "Sidney, Ohio," *GH* 8, no. 6 (December 1949): 6.

32 Charles Lowery, "Metamora, Ind.," *GH* 8, no. 10 (April 1950): 1.

33 Luther Gibson, "Report of General Overseer," *GH* 8, no. 11 (May 1950): 7.

34 CGMA, *Minutes* (1950), 11.

35 Indiana, Death Certificates, 1899-1911, s.v. "Charles Harmon Lowery," Ancestry.com; CGMA, *Minutes* (1957), 47.

36 CGMA, *Minutes* (1952), 21-22; Mae Spurlock, "Muncie, Ind.," *GH* 11, no. 4 (Dec 1952): 5; Mrs. Henry Davenport, "A Testimony," *GH* 11, no. 2 (August 1952): 1.

37 Carlos Ballinger, "National Spot News," *GH* 12, no. 1 (September 1953): 3.

38 Charles Leroy Weaver, "New Castle, Ind.," *GH* 17, no. 8 (August 1959): 1; "Victory at New Castle, Ind.," *GH* 12, no. 7 (March 1954): 1; Jessie Weaver, "New Castle, Indiana," *GH* 12, no. 11 (July 1954): 3; Henry Weaver, telephone interview with the author, March 20, 2021.

39 CGMA, *Minutes* (1955), 26-27; Clayton Lawson, "New Churches," *GH* 14, no. 7 (March 1956): 1; Charles Weaver, "New Church Shoales Indiana," and "Richmond, Indiana," *GH* 17, no. 5 (May 1959): 1; James W. Leslie, "Mitchell, Ind.," *GH* 17, no. 7 (July 1959): 4; CGMA, *Minutes of the Fifty Third Annual Assembly* (Jellico, Tenn.: CGMA), 41.

40 James W. Leslie, "Southern Indiana," and "Louisville Mission," *GH* 17, no. 10 (October 1959): 2, 11.

⁴¹ "First Elders' Meeting," *GH* 15, no. 3 (November 1956): 2; Luther Gibson, "Report of Assistant General Overseer," *GH* 15, no. 2 (October 1956): 5.

⁴² Gibson, *History*, 69.

⁴³ CGMA, *Minutes* (1954), 13, 65-66.

⁴⁴ Clayton Lawson, "Akron, Ohio," *GH* 9, no. 12 (June 1951): 2; CGMA, *Minutes* (1951), 22; Johnie H. Douglas, minister information card, J.H. Douglas File, CGMA Ministers Files, Jellico, Tenn.

⁴⁵ Darlyne Whitt, "Among the Churches: Cleveland, Ohio," *GH* 13, no. 5 (January 1955): 2.

⁴⁶ Stella Mae Dean, "News of the Churches: Wadsworth, Ohio," *GH* 13, no. 7 (March 1955): 5; CGMA, *Minutes* (1955), 17, 39; CGMA, *Minutes* (1957), 46; CGMA, *Minutes of the Fifty Second Annual Assembly* (Jellico, Tenn.: CGMA, 1958), 40; Sharon Triplett Vance, telephone interview by author, October 22, 2020.

⁴⁷ James Walden, "Northern Ohio," *GH* 15, no. 6 (February 1957): 3.; CGMA, *Minutes of the Fifty-Fourth Annual Assembly* (Jellico, Tenn.: CGMA, 1960), 43.

⁴⁸ "New Church," *GH* 15, no. 9 (June 1957): 4.

⁴⁹ "Spot News," *GH* 18, no. 8 (August 1960): 7.

⁵⁰ [revival notice], *The Pentecostal Witness* 4, no. 3 (March 1951): 6; E.L. Cyrus, "From Our Bishop," *The Pentecostal Witness* 4, no. 4 (April 1951): 2.

⁵¹ Carl O. Bachelor, Jr., "Good News from the "Hallalujah [sic] District," *The Pentecostal Witness* 5, no. 11 (November 1951): 7.

⁵² John Thomas Longsworth Card for Ministerial File, John T. Longsworth Ministerial File, International Pentecostal Church of Christ Archives, London, OH; Pentecostal Church of Christ, *Minutes of the 36ᵗʰ Annual Conference of the Pentecostal Church of Christ* (Ashland, KY: Pentecostal Church of Christ, 1952), 5, 34.

⁵³ CGMA, *Minutes* (1950), 23; CGMA, *Minutes* (1951), 22; Luther Gibson, "From General Overseer's Desk," *GH* 8, no. 10 (April 1950): 1.

⁵⁴ Gibson, *History*, 67; Roger Powell, "Greenville, Ohio," *GH* 12, no. 1 (September 1953): 6; Gibson, "Report of Assistant General Overseer," *GH* 12, no. 3 (November 1953): 8; Powell, *The Answer to Your Problems* (Columbus: Self-published, 1959), 4, 8; Alma Loudermilk, "Greenville, Ohio," *GH* 17, no. 5 (May 1959): 3.

⁵⁵ Powell, *Answer*, 8; Ralph A. Pope, "Columbus, Ohio," *GH* 14, no. 3 (November 1956): 1; Powell, "Columbus, Ohio," *GH* 15, no. 3 (November 1957): 3.

⁵⁶ Gibson, "Report of Assistant General Overseer," *GH* 12, no. 3 (November 1953): 8; Lawson, "New Churches," *GH* 12, no. 8 (April 1954): 1; Gibson, *History*, 68.

⁵⁷ Betty Pryor, "Dayton Youth Meeting" *GH* 15, no. 3 (November 1956): 11; Gibson, "Report of Assistant General Overseer," *GH* 15, no. 4 (December 1956): 5.

⁵⁸ "New Churches," *GH* 15, no. 5 (January 1957): 5; Gibson, *History*, 68.

⁵⁹ "New Church in Celina, Ohio," *GH* 22, no. 10 (October 1962): 7; Gibson, *History*, 6; CGMA, 68; "Spotlight on the Churches: Celina, Ohio," *GH* 23, no. 5 (May 1963): 2.

⁶⁰ C.A. Freeman, "A Testimony," *GH* 11, no. 8 (April 1953): 6; Artie Heaps, "Toledo, Ohio," *GH* 11, no. 11 (July 1953): 5; Freeman, "Two Years From Memory," *GH* 14, no. 8 (April 1956): 6; Freeman, "Holland, Ohio," *GH* 12, no. 4 (December 1953): 6; Lawson,

"Building Program," *GH* 14, no. 7 (March 1956): 1; Mae Fitzpatrick, "Holland, Ohio," *GH* 14, no. 9 (May 1956): 4.

[61] Mary L. Stacey, "New Church at Rossford, Ohio," *GH* 14, no. 1 (January 1956): 1.

[62] Clayton Lawson, "New Churches," *GH* 14, no. 7 (March 1956): 1; CGMA, *Minutes* (1957), 48.

[63] M.E. Woolum, "Detroit, Mich.," *GH* 7, no. 5 (November 1948): 2; David Hammitte, "Trenton, Mich.," *GH* 7, no. 8 (February 1949): 2.

[64] CGMA, *Minutes* (1952), 11, 27.

[65] Gibson, *History*, 97.

[66] Mrs. Elvan Smith, "New Church Set in Order," *GH* 11, no. 10 (June 1953): 1; "Notice," *GH* 12, no. 5 (January 1954): 1.

[67] CGMA, *Minutes* (1954), 32, 65.

[68] CGMA, *Minutes* (1956), 26.

[69] Lawson, "New Churches," *GH* 14, no. 7 (March 1956): 1; CGMA, *Minutes* (1964), 21; C.B. Ellis, "From the Assistant General Overseer's Desk," *GH* 24, no. 5 (May 1964): 2.

[70] CGMA, *Minutes* (1952), 11, 26-27.

[71] CGMA, *Minutes* (1953), 10, 25; CGMA, *Minutes* (1954), 65; CGMA, *Minutes* (1955), 39; Alverdia Eldridge, "Cleves, Ohio," 12, no. 6 (February 1954): 7; [photo caption], *The Youth Gateway (YG)* 2, no. 3 (April 1955): 3.

[72] Grace Dickson, "Bantam, Ohio," *GH* 11, no. 7 (March 1953): 1; CGMA, *Minutes* (1953), 10, 24.

[73] Ibid.; Shelby Maynard, "Georgetown, Ohio," *GH* 13, no. 2 (October 1954): 8.

[74] Lawson, "New Churches," *GH* 12, no. 8 (April 1954): 1; Louise Gardner, "Dayton, Ohio," *GH* 12, no. 12 (August 1954): 6; CGMA, *Minutes* (1954), 65-66.

[75] Carlos Ballinger, "National Spot News," *YG* 2, no. 3 (April 1955): 8; CGMA, *Minutes* (1955), 17, 39; Wade Martin Hughes, Facebook messages with the author, August 26, 2020.

[76] CGMA, *Minutes* (1956), 52; CGMA, *Minutes* (1958), 42; CGMA, *Minutes* (1960), 39.

[77] Lawson, "Building Program," *GH* 14, no. 7 (March 1956): 2; Jeanette Freeman, "Old Fort, N.C.," *GH* 13, no. 8 (April 1955): 5; CGMA, *Minutes* (1955), 17, 40; Freeman, "Old Fort, N.C.," *GH* 14, no. 3 (November 1955): 6-7; CGMA, *Minutes* (1957), 47; James McIntosh, "Marion Fellowship Meeting," *GH* 16, no. 5 (February 1958): 7; George Douglas, "Old Fort, N.C.," *GH* 16, no. 10 (July 1958): 7.

[78] CGMA, *Minutes* (1950), 19; CGMA, *Minutes* (1952), 22.

[79] CGMA, *Minutes* (1954), 13; CGMA, *Minutes* (1956), 29.

[80] [Mrs. Walter] Vaughn, "Monongahela, Pa.," *GH* 13, no. 9 (May 1955): 5; CGMA, *Minutes* (1953), 22; Carlos Ballinger, "Spot News," *GH* 12, no. 3 (November 1953): 3; CGMA, *Minutes* (1954), 66; Lawson, "New Churches," *GH* 12, no. 8 (April 1954): 1; W.M. Watson, "Middlesboro, Ky.," *GH* 11, no. 10 (June 1953): 6; Fonzie Mahan, "Kenvir, Ky.," *GH* 12, no. 4 (December 1953): 6; Ballinger, "National Spot News," *YG* 1, no. 11 (July 30, 1954): 4; Betty Pryor, "Revival Highlights," *YG* 2, no. 5 (June 1955): 7; Ballinger, "National Spot News," *YG* 2, no. 3 (April 1955): 8.

81 Janice Howe, "New Church Ceredo, West Va.," *GH* 13, no. 2 (October 1954): 1; Carlos Ballinger, "National Spot News," and Janice Howe, "One Member Added to Ceredo, W. Va. Church," *YG* 1, no. 14, (October 30, 1954): 4, 13.

82 Carlos Ballinger, "National Spot News," *YG* 2, no. 5 (June 1955): 5; CGMA, *Minutes* (1955), 39.

83 Clayton Lawson, "New Missions," *GH* 14, no. 7 (March 1956): 1.

84 Efford Enix, "As I Saw It," *YG* 2, no. 5 (June 1955): 12; Enix, "New State, Pulaski, Va.," *GH* 13, no. 9 (May 1955): 1.

85 In 1941, John R. Williams moved from Pine Hill, Kentucky, to Helm, Missouri, and sent a letter to the 35th Annual Assembly from a church there. The letter and church were received into the Assembly, but it was the only year it appeared in the minute book.

86 1910 United States Census, Cambell County, Tennessee, s.v. "George Byrge" and 1910 United States Census, Putnam County, Tennessee, s.v. "George McCloud," Ancestry.com.

87 CGMA, *Minutes* (1933), 20; CGMA, *Minutes* (1934), 19.

88 David R. Duncan to Bob Copeland, e-mail, January 12, 2020.

89 W.R. Byrge, "Helper, Utah," *GH* 12, no. 7 (March 1954): 5; Flora Bennett, "Helper, Utah," *GH* 12, no. 9 (May 1954): 1.

90 "Highlights from the Church of God 15th and Race St.," *GH* 13, no. 3 (November 1954): 4; "Highlights from the Church of God 15th and Race Streets," *GH* 13, no. 5 (January 1955): 4; Beatrice Kennedy, "West Coast Report," *YG* 2, no. 5 (June 1955): 8, 10; "New Mission," *GH* 14, no. 4 (December 1956): 9; Philip Yeary, "Cincinnati, Ohio," *GH* 15, no. 10 (July 1957): 12; "Ontario, Calif.," *GH* 16, no. 4 (January 1958): 9.

91 CGMA, *Minutes* (1954), 15; CGMA, *Minutes* (1957), 41; "New Church," *GH* 16, no. 4 (January 1958): 9; Hatfield, "New Church," *GH* 17, no. 7 (July 1959): 1.

92 "Spot News," *GH* 18, no. 8 (August 1960): 7; Roy C. Porter, "Grays Lake, Illinois," *GH* 18, no. 5 (May 1960): 2.

93 "Somerset, Ky.," *GH* 12, no. 3 (November 1953): 5.

94 CGMA, *Minutes* (1958), 20; [Martha] Bryant, "Day Ridge Fellowship," *GH* 17, no. 7 (July 1959): 1.

95 CGMA, *Minutes* (1953), 25; Beulah Turner, "Akron, Ohio," and Alice Bays, "Trosper, Ky.," *GH* 12, no. 3 (November 1953): 6; Alice Bays, "Trosper, Ky.," *GH* 12, no. 5 (January 1954): 1.

96 CGMA, *Minutes* (1955), 36. "News of the Churches: Visits Mt. Assembly Mission," *GH* 13, no. 8 (April 1955): 5.

97 Clayton Lawson, "New Churches," *GH* 12, no. 8 (April 1954): 1; CGMA, *Minutes* (1954), 65; CGMA, *Minutes* (1956), 43; H.V. Lawson, "Harlan District," *GH* 17, no. 3 (March 1959): 2.

98 H.V. Lawson, "The Overseer Speaks," *GH* 15, no. 6 (February 1957): 2.

99 H.V. Lawson, "Quarterly Meeting at Wallins Creek," *GH* 15, no. 11 (August 1957): 6.

100 CGMA, *Minutes* (1958), 20, 44; Geraldine Gaylor, facebook message to the author, August 29, 2020; H.V. Lawson to J.E. Hatfield, October 14, 1958, H.V. Lawson File, CGMA Ministers Files, Jellico, TN.

[101] CGMA, *Minutes* (1959), 23, 42; H.V. Lawson to J.E. Hatfield, August 9, 1960, H.V. Lawson file. By 1958, tension built between the district overseer and district youth director to the point neither was willing to work with the other. Factions formed in support and in opposition of Lawson as overseer. After two years, Lawson resigned in frustration and turned in his credentials.

[102] Joe Moses, "Lafollette, Tenn.," *GH* 12, no. 5 (January 1954): 2; CGMA, *Minutes* (1955): 17.

[103] CGMA, *Minutes* (1956), 23.

[104] Wilma Lynch, "Church of God Mission: Knoxville, Tennessee," *GH* 14, no. 8 (April 1956): 5; Clayton Lawson, "New Churches," *GH* 14, no. 7 (March 1954): 1; CGMA, *Minutes* (1912), 2; CGMA, *Minutes* (1917), statistical table; CGMA, *Minutes* (1956), 23; Volena Lynch, "Fellowship Meeting," *GH* 16, no. 5 (February 1958): 7; CGMA, *Minutes* (1958), 20.

[105] Auza Vinson, "Lawrenceburg, Tenn.," 15, no. 10 (July 1957): 2; Auza Vinson, autobiographical sketch, in the possession of Merele Vinson, Tecumseh, MI; CGOMA, *Minutes* (1949), statistical table; Jessie Ferman, "Metamora, Ind.," *GH* 12, no. 3 (November 1953): 6; CGMA, *Minutes* (1955), 39.

[106] CGMA, *Minutes* (1958), 19, 21.

[107] Clayton Lawson, "Report from Brazil," *GH* 18, no. 2 (February 1960): 4.

[108] Clayton Lawson (and Chester Miller), "From Brazil," *GH* 18, no. 3 (March 1960): 1-2.

[109] Andy Lawson died eight months later.

[110] Chester Miller to J.E. Hatfield, printed in *GH* 18, no. 3 (March 1960): 2.

[111] Ida Delaney, "Metamora, Ind.," *GH* 18, no. 4 (April 1960): 2; Jeanie Brock, "Jellico Y.W.C.," and Sylvia Bryant, "Race Street Y.W.C.," *GH* 18, no. 4 (April 1960): 5; June Moss, "Trenton, Michigan," *GH* 18, no. 5 (May 1960): 3.

[112] CGMA, *Minutes* (1952), 13.

[113] CGOMA, *Minutes* (1947), 1; CGOMA, *Minutes of the Churches of God of the Original Mountain Assembly, Incorporated: Fifty-Sixth Annual Assembly* (Williamsburg, KY: CGOMA, 1962), 6.

[114] CGOMA, *Minutes of the Churches of God of the Original Mountain Assembly, Incorporated: Fiftieth Annual Assembly* (Williamsburg, KY: CGOMA, 1956), 1.

[115] See Diaries of Ira Moses, 1960-1972.

[116] Luther Gibson, to J.E. Hatfield, December 24, 1960, Luther Gibson File, CGMA Ministers Files, Jellico, TN. In the letter, Gibson shares his frustration over Lawson (now a member of the Finance Committee) questioning his travel expense reimbursement as Assistant General Overseer. Lawson had run for the position at the Assembly that year, but Gibson was elected.

[117] CGMA, *Minutes* (1952), 10; CGMA, *Minutes* (1956), 19.

[118] Ibid.; CGMA, *Minutes* (1954), 24; CGMA, *Minutes* (1958), 19.

[119] CGMA, *Minutes* (1958), 21.

[120] Because of the sensitive nature of some of the details of that Elders Meeting, the minister who was present wished to remain anonymous.

10

Rise Up and Build

When Ira Moses declined to run for reelection as pastor of the Monroe Church on June 26, 1960, it ended his thirteen-year tenure as the longest serving pastor in the congregation's history. That distinction would be claimed by his successor. The church elected 25-year-old Fred Cornelius to replace him, and Cornelius pastored the church for the next four decades.[1] Moses, on the other hand, set his sights on Jellico. The headquarters church continued its search for a long-term pastor like John Parks. Instead, seven different pastors served the congregation in the 1950s. When William Fitzpatrick resigned as pastor to return to Toledo, an opportunity opened for Moses who came to the General Assembly in Jellico a week early to view his old homeplace, see his parents, and visit Fitzpatrick, J.E. Hatfield, and Clayton Lawson in the tabernacle office. He visited Sunday School at Jellico and preached the homecoming service at Newcomb before the 54th General Assembly convened on Tuesday, July 25. That day, the General Council elected Moses to the office of General Overseer, and he assumed the duties of moderating the business which he found to be "a very difficult task."[2]

Figure 10.1: Ira Moses
c/o North Monroe Street CGMA

Figure 10.2: Fred Cornelius
c/o North Monroe Street CGMA

Navigating the organization through its general business sessions and Elders' meetings over the next decade proved to be a challenge, indeed. The

Mountain Assembly was coming out of its greatest decade of growth, and yet it remained divided between those fiercely loyal to Lawson and those ready to move the Assembly beyond his influence. Although at times Moses had difficulty hiding his emotions, he never let resistance to change intimidate him. This proved to be an important quality as the Mountain Assembly underwent profound transformation during his leadership. First, a restructuring of the National Youth Department that began in the 1950s was completed in the 1960s and included a full-time National Youth Director, the commencement of a national youth camp program, and the construction of the Mountain Assembly's own campground. Second, the mission program that was responsible for numeric growth of congregations in the United States in the 1950s realized its vision of founding churches in foreign fields. The last half of Moses's tenure saw radical changes in the standard resolutions, many of which were designed to reverse the trend toward episcopalism of the first four decades and make the CGMA more democratic by the mid-1970s. By the time a third tabernacle was erected in Jellico, the second generation of leadership was nearing its end and a third was rising to take its place.

Youth Warriors for Christ

When the Mountain Assembly first adopted its Young People's Endeavor in 1948, the National Youth Directors were appointed by the Appointing Board of the General Overseer, Assistant General Overseer, and General Secretary & Treasurer. Gibson's desire to utilize young charismatic ministers and newcomers to the Mountain Assembly proved to be a double-edged sword. Generally, inexperience was a greater liability than zeal was an asset. As a result, a National Youth Director's appointment did not last long. The Board appointed Edward Woolum and Floyd Jordan as National Youth Directors at the 1948 General Assembly, but it replaced them the following February with Robert Thomas and John Longsworth.[3] By October, Longsworth was the National Youth Director with Thomas serving as his assistant.[4] After Longsworth left the Mountain Assembly for the Pentecostal Church of Christ in 1952, the Appointing

Figure 10.3: John Longsworth
c/o The Youth Gateway

Board chose Lawrence Redmond to replace him. Redmond had been at Jellico under Pastor Luther Gibson and was ordained by him.[5] As Sunday School Superintendent, Redmond was credited with helping rebuild the program in 1948 after the disastrous split left it destitute a year earlier.[6] After briefly pastoring at Mountain Ash and then at Newcomb, he returned to his home church to assume its pastorate in 1952.[7] Redmond's election as Jellico Pastor preceded his election as Assistant General Secretary & Treasurer and to the Finance Committee by a month.[8] Redmond remained on the Executive Board the rest of the decade, but the Appointing Board replaced him as National Youth Director with Haskel Swain at the General Assembly.

Swain had been converted at the church in Dayton and had just started the new church in Covington. Swain's appointment came just one year after the first major changes were made to the structure of the national youth department. Thomas and Longsworth had created the first state youth directors and divided the states into districts to accommodate travel by the churches to youth rallies. The need for more development in the Young People's Endeavor had been discussed by the Board of Elders and after its report, a committee was established to "work out plans for the Y.P.E." The committee consisted of Redmond, Earl Heath, Ulyess Graham, and C.B. Ellis, Jr. Their proposal was adopted the following morning and codified the monthly district youth rallies where half the offering would be sent to the National Youth Treasury. Each local YPE was also required to send an offering each month for this fund and the first national youth rallies would also serve as a fundraising opportunity for the treasury. Each year, the National Youth Director would host rallies in the North and in the South.[9]

Swain had written to *The Gospel Herald* just prior to the 1952 General Assembly that he believed the "future" of the Mountain Assembly "depends a lot upon the youth." He further "determined to see that in the coming year our youth will do greater things than they have ever done before." He made clear to his readers that he possessed "a great interest in the youth of the Church of God Mountain Assembly, to see them grow great and mighty" and meant "this just like it sounds."[10] Within a couple of weeks, he preached the youth service at the Assembly and was then appointed National Youth Director with Efford Enix as his assistant. Swain utilized *The Gospel Herald* to promote the youth program and its national rallies, and he was rewarded for his efforts. After his first year in office, the Mountain Assembly voted to supplement his income with ten dollars per week from the national youth treasury.[11]

That spring, Swain had introduced to the paper's readers, the "Youth Bible Question Board," and solicited queries from inquiring young people to assist them in their interpretation of scripture. The board was officially codified at the following assembly when a new set of directives governing the national youth department was adopted. In addition to the Bible Question Board, the General Council authorized the offices of "ambassadors, boosters, leaders, and reporters" and the creation of a general youth board. This board was required to submit any governmental directives to the General Assembly for approval, and "all youth work" was placed "under the jurisdictions of the General Assembly."[12] These measures were intended to temper Swain's zeal after the national youth director had already appointed many ambassadors, boosters, and reporters and announced them in the new youth magazine that he created in January without any authorization from the Assembly.

The first issue of *The Youth Gateway* was published January 25, 1954 to keep its readers "informed of the progress of our youth."[13] "After much discussion" the *Gateway* was officially endorsed by the Mountain Assembly in August, but "without assuming any financial responsibility."[14] At 20 pages, the magazine was more than twice as long as *The Gospel Herald* and soon found itself in competition for subscriptions. The youth paper, however, was short-lived. The following spring, Swain launched a subscription campaign offering more than 100 prizes for selling subscriptions. The grand prize was a 1950 Plymouth that had been donated for such a purpose.[15] When the contest ended in a tie that July, a bewildered National Youth Director awarded the prize to neither contestant. Amid the controversy, the General Council disbanded *The Youth Gateway* two weeks later, combined it with *The Gospel Herald*, and increased the official church paper from eight to twelve pages. Beginning in October, it included a "Youth Gateway" section.[16]

The subscription disgrace effectively ended Swain's tenure as National Youth Director and his ministry in the Mountain Assembly. Enix was appointed to succeed him, and Swain left the organization and later formed a fellowship of his own. His most significant accomplishment as National Youth Director was the creation of a new name for the youth auxiliary. The Mountain Assembly had used "Young People's Endeavor" since it copied the program from the Church of God (Cleveland) in the mid-1940s. In 1954, Swain began referring to the young people as "Youth Warriors for Christ," and the name was officially changed by the General Council at the 48th General Assembly that year.[17] Enix provided the Youth Warriors for Christ with the leadership stability it had lacked and went on to serve by the appointment of the board for seven years.

Enix and his assistant, Cecil Moses, continued to promote the national rallies which lasted two or three nights at some of the Assembly's largest churches and attracted visitors from multiple states. Enix and Moses also continued the tradition of having a parade through Jellico to launch the youth service during the General Assembly which was introduced by Swain in 1954. The parade began at the Tennessee state line at 4:00 p.m. and proceeded through town to the tabernacle. Swain and Enix served as grand marshals and carried the American and Christian flags. "Hundreds of cars, both decorated and undecorated were lined in between the groups of marching people representing" their local youth groups. "Hundreds of people lined the sidewalks to watch the parade as it passed by." Upon arrival at the tabernacle, the youth service began with reports by the state youth leaders and much singing before Swain brought the evening message.[18] The participants so loved the experience that Enix replicated it his first year as national youth director and scheduled one almost annually after that.[19]

Figure 10.4: Efford Enix
c/o The Youth Gateway

Enix's greatest contribution to the national youth department came in June 1962, just two months before his tenure came to an end, when he organized the first national youth camp. His first cousin, James Earl Prewitt, understood the importance of a camp program after seeing success with such in the Church of God (Cleveland) while attending Lee College. Prewitt chose not to return to Lee for the fall semester of 1961 when the church at Goshen elected him pastor. He preached the youth night service at the

Figure 10.5: Camp Matrina Flier
c/o Francis Yeary

277

general assembly that year and was scheduled to host the National Youth Rally at Goshen June 8-9, 1962.[20] After locating a campground at nearby Lake Matrina, Prewitt persuaded Enix to transform the rally into a youth camp meeting. The Goshen pastor organized the program while the National Youth Director conducted the services. To assist him, Prewitt drafted his close friend, Fred Cornelius. Though the two had been raised by Mountain Assembly pastors, they did not become Christians until their early 20s when they attended a revival in Detroit, Michigan in 1957. Both began preaching and pastoring soon afterward. Cornelius brought the teachers and kitchen workers from his congregation in Monroe to Camp Matrina.[21]

Services were conducted outside, some on an island in the middle of the lake. "Between services the lake was perhaps one of the main attractions, as both old and young took advantage of the boating and fishing facilities made available at this camp site." Young people sang hymns around the campfire. The Friday night service was held at Goshen church and featured the "great message offered by" General Overseer Ira Moses. On Saturday, four "outstanding young ministers" delivered messages "climaxing this rally." The unforgettable "message of Gene Douglas given on one of the islands as a large crowd resound[ed] the praises of our Lord and Savior at the Saturday morning" service was perhaps still on many minds when the CGMA made two significant changes to the Youth Warriors for Christ that August.[22]

On Thursday, August 9, 1962 the Resolution Committee of Clayton Lawson, J.H. Bryant, and Wade M. Hughes presented two significant resolutions concerning the general officials. The first created a full-time salary of $90 per week for the Assistant General Overseer and prohibited him from pastoring a church. Upon its adoption, C.B. Ellis, Jr., who had been elected two days earlier, became the first full-time Assistant General Overseer. The second resolution made the National Youth Director a full-time position and stipulated that he would no longer be appointed but elected by the General Council. Upon discussion, the question was divided, and the Assembly quickly decided that the national youth officials would be elected. The matter of his salary was postponed until the following day. After further consideration, the General Council voted to pay the National Youth Director a supplemental salary of $70 per week "as available from the Youth Treasury."[23] In practice, the newly elected Samuel "Gene" Douglas would earn the $3,640 salary provided he raised enough money to pay it after the additional youth expenses had been paid. That proved to be a difficult task, and the following year, the General Council authorized the payment of the

$640 deficit on his salary and gave him a $300 "gift of appreciation." Though certainly appreciated, the gesture was insufficient to convince Douglas to continue serving in that capacity, and he resigned to pastor the church in Knoxville. His assistant, Leon Petree, replaced him.[24]

Petree was born in Fonde, Kentucky on June 15, 1939 to Anna (Rose) and Simon Petree, who were converted and baptized by John Parks shortly after moving to Fonde in 1924.[25] His father was an itinerant coal miner and parttime lay minister, and his mother was a dedicated Christian whose brothers, Harvey and E.B. Rose, had pastored Mountain Assembly churches in the 1940s. Leon was converted in 1959 and soon began conducting revivals in Tennessee, Kentucky, Ohio, and Michigan. Many continued more than three weeks, and one, in Cincinnati, saw 80 people saved in 13 weeks.[26] By the spring of 1962, he had preached 24 revivals and witnessed 311 conversions.[27] Some of his early revivals were conducted jointly with his brother, Arlie Petree, whose testimony and songs inspired many.[28] Arlie had also been converted in 1959 under Efford Enix in Dayton. In February 1959, the 22-year old fell victim to an unexplainable and incurable sickness. "For seven months, the mysterious disease raged" in his body as he "shrunk steadily from a bustling 185 pounds to a feeble 95 pounds." On September 5, his mother fasted in Jellico and solicited church members there to join her in prayer for a miracle for her son. At 9:30 p.m., his wife, Jeannie, felt impressed to "let the [Dayton] church lay hands on her to pray" for her husband "by proxy." Across town, at that moment, "there was a change" and Arlie was "wondrously healed."[29]

Figure 10.6: Leon Petree
c/o Tonya Petree Mason

Figure 10.7: Arlie Petree
c/o Teresa Petree Holmes

While Arlie Petree showed himself "a living witness of the great healing power of God" in a revival at the Bagley Street Church in Detroit in January 1961, the pastor and district overseer, Ottis Ellis, met General Overseer Ira Moses in nearby Trenton to guide that church through the resignation of Arvil Rountree, who had left the Mountain Assembly to join the Church of God of Prophecy.[30] After Ellis assumed the care of the church for a short time, Arlie was selected for its pastor before Luther Gibson relocated to Trenton to pastor there in 1962. His brother, Leon, however, evangelized out of Jellico and served as National Youth Director from 1963 to 1968.

Under Petree's leadership, the Youth Warriors for Christ continued to draw large crowds for its national rallies and further developed the youth camp program. Douglas had returned to Camp Matrina for a four-day youth camp in June 1963, and Petree registered 115 young people for the camp in 1964.[31] Having outgrown the campground near Goshen, Petree took the YWC to an Assemblies of God campground at Lake Placid near Hartford City, Indiana, for a five-night camp in June 1965. At the Thursday evening service, an eight-year old boy from Chicago was healed after wearing a leg brace for 18 months. When "he lay down his crutches" and "ran and jumped around as though he had never been crippled," 26 young people "came running to the altar" to be saved.[32] Another 15 were saved throughout the week, and the camp proved so successful that Petree returned the following year and saw the number of registrants triple and another 40 converted.[33] An altar call by Efford Enix one night of the June 1967 camp at Lake Placid saw 75 come forward for salvation, and caused one of the Twelve Elders to remark that he had "never witnessed a move of God's power to save as great as I have seen here at Youth Camp."[34]

So successful were the early YWC camps that CGMA leadership began looking for a place to buy or build a campground almost immediately. General Overseers Ira Moses and C.B. Ellis looked at a potential site near Loveland, Ohio with Goshen Pastor J.E. Prewitt in June 1964. The following spring, however, Ellis and Goshen Deacon Charlie Yeary found nearly forty acres for sale in Highland County near Hillsboro, Ohio. On March 18, 1965, Moses, Ellis, Prewitt, and Yeary, met CGMA Trustees Glenn Rowe, Isham Sharp, Charles Weaver, and General Secretary & Treasurer J.E. Hatfield at the property and purchased the undeveloped land for just over $4,000 ten days later.[35] Yeary spearheaded a campaign to build a campground there beginning with a road in the spring of 1966. When limited contributions arrived, he introduced a motion at the General Assembly to build it.[36]

While Petree continued raising funds for the new campground, another opportunity presented itself in the fall of 1967. In Buford, also in Highland County, a 205-acre farm became available. Much of the land was undeveloped farmland leased by local farmers. The developed land included a large farmhouse, "spacious tabernacle," two dormitories to accommodate around 100 each, "fully equipped" kitchen and dining room, "an executive camp apartment building with bath in each room," concession stand, and large swimming pool. The property also included a stable with 35 "horses and ponies."[37] Seventeen ministers met at Lake Placid the first week of October 1967 for a ministers' retreat. As they discussed the Mountain Assembly and its future, those present thought the Buford property "would fit so well our own needs," and resolved to go view it two weeks later.[38] On October 23, two dozen CGMA ministers met to view the property, and in November, the General Trustees signed a lease with an option to buy the property for $100,000.[39] Petree conducted a successful youth camp at "Camp Canaan" the second week of July, but concern over the costs and controversy surrounding the pool caused the General Council to vote not to purchase the property.[40] Instead, Petree's successor would continue raising money to develop the property near Hillsboro.

Figure 10.8: Some of the ministers at the Lake Placid retreat

c/o Al Newton, Jr.

Clayton Lawson's resignation as pastor of the Race Street Church in Cincinnati in July 1967 brought three members of the church to Jellico to solicit the General Overseer's help in securing a pastor for the important church. Moses was with Petree the same evening and, not long after, sent the National Youth Director to Race Street with the exhortation to "go and preach like you did tonight."⁴¹ After Petree assumed the pastorate, his brother-in-law, Jasper Walden, was elected to replace him as National Youth Director in 1968. To assist him, the General Council elected a 19-year-old minister from his church in Kokomo, Donnie Hill. Over the next six years, Walden and Hill continued fundraising to build a YWC campground near Hillsboro. In the meantime, they rented one at Ludlow Falls near Troy, Ohio, with a large tabernacle, dining hall, dormitories, and cabins.⁴²

In his second year in office, Walden hired a professional architect to draw plans for the development of the camp property. To provide the YWC with capital to build, the plans called for 100 cabin lots to be leased by CGMA members for $300 and upon which they might build private cabins for use during the camps.⁴³ Some churches saw the value of the national camp program and responded to the call to build by raising funds to that end. The Rittman church, for example, raised $1,000 for the construction of the new youth camp amid a $12,000 campaign to remodel its own sanctuary.⁴⁴ In 1972, the General Council commissioned "the General Trustees, Finance Committee, and the National Youth Officials" to "go ahead with whatever is necessary to the get the youth camp program in motion."⁴⁵ Although several thousand dollars had been donated toward that goal, only about one third of the potential leased lots had been pledged by the time Walden's tenure came to an end in 1974.⁴⁶

His successor, Donnie Hill, reinvigorated the crusade soon after his election. Hill used his first national youth rally in November as a springboard for fundraising and encouraged attendees to bring their "check books and

Figure 10.9: Jasper Walden
c/o Jasper Walden

Figure 10.10: Donnie Hill
c/o Al Newton, Jr.

Rise Up and Build

Figure 10.11: YWC Groundbreaking

c/o *The Gospel Herald*

faith." Hill set aside Friday afternoon of the rally to take a busload from Cincinnati to view the campground and made plans to install sewage and water treatment as early as that winter.[47] In January, the General Trustees voted to install the system and expressed their willingness to borrow up to $50,000 to begin construction on additional facilities there.[48] At the General Assembly in August, the General Council voted "to mortgage Headquarters" for that amount for the development of the campground near Hillsboro.[49] The National Youth Director again used the November national youth rally to promote the cause and offered interested CGMA members the opportunity to sign a lifetime lease on a lot upon which they might construct a cabin at the new youth camp, and at least thirteen signed on Friday, November 7, 1975.[50] By the time a ground breaking ceremony was held on February 14, 1976, gravel roads had been constructed and the foundations for a shower house and cafeteria were laid.[51] On June 28, the first YWC camp on property owned by the Mountain Assembly commenced. With just two buildings on the property, guests stayed in tents, campers, and travel trailers. Services were conducted in a large tent, and Ray Landes preached the first night's message, "This is God's Place."[52] Despite the "heavy rains and storms that came" which caused many to take their belongings into the cafeteria to stay dry through the night, the people remained encouraged, and attendance the following year greatly increased.[53]

Settling in Jellico

That it took more than a decade to utilize the Hillsboro property had as much to do with timing as it did finances. The purchase of the camp property occurred in the middle of a drive to build a new tabernacle in Jellico. The Mountain Assembly outgrew its second tabernacle as soon as it was built in 1942. By the third night's service at the Assembly that year "the new Tabernacle was filled to its capacity."[54] When attendance remained high despite the split with the Original Mountain Assembly, the General Council attempted to remedy its crowd accommodation problem by voting to have "the annual assembly at different places."[55] After holding the 44th Annual Assembly in Cincinnati, however, delegates voted to return to Jellico for the following convention.[56] A motion to remain at the headquarters tabernacle was adopted each year for the next five general assemblies.[57] When the 50th General Assembly convened at the tabernacle in August 1956, the "imperative to arrange for a larger place to seat the people for the night meetings" was clear.[58] The tabernacle also had trouble seating "the largest voting delegation ever."[59] The city of Jellico had been a gracious host to the Mountain Assembly for three decades, and General Overseer Clayton Lawson "expressed his appreciation to the town's people who had so gladly received us for another Assembly." He also invited Mayor Robert L. Hicks to address the congregation who "enjoyed the message" from Deuteronomy 10:12-13 very much. That same night, Lawson received numerous $100 and $50 pledges toward a "project of the Assembly ground." The General Council appointed Isham Sharp, General Douglas, John H. Dobson, James Arthur Enix, and George Douglas as "a committee to look out a place for our new Assembly grounds."[60]

While a larger tabernacle was the top priority, the CGMA Executive Board hoped to utilize the headquarters grounds in a manner like the other Pentecostal groups with which they had fellowshipped for the past several years. The leaders especially desired to start a children's home. Even before the Church of God (Cleveland) was organized, A.J. Tomlinson and J.B. Mitchell established an orphanage in the North Carolina mountains. In 1911, the denomination itself opened the "Faith Orphanage and Children's Home Association" in Cleveland.[61] In the 1930s, Goshen Deacon Charlie Yeary had expressed his "desire for the Church of God of the Mountain Assembly to have a large farm that could be developed into an orphan's home, as well as adequate facilities for a home for the aged." He championed the purchase of Camp Canaan for that end in 1967.[62]

When H.V. Lawson joined the CGMA in 1954, he and the church he was pastoring had been associated with an orphanage in Barbourville, Kentucky, for at least two years.[63] The "Free Pentecostal Holiness Orphanage and Old Age Home" was organized on January 31, 1949, by William Gillis Martin and nine congregations in southeastern Kentucky.[64] Though the churches were independent and congregationally governed, many met for monthly fellowship meetings, and by the end of the year Martin proposed that they should "build a tabernacle where we could all come together and have a camp meeting."[65] By the time the association began construction on the "240 feet long and 80 feet wide" tabernacle building in April 1954, the orphanage had been opened with several children under the care of its superintendent.[66] On Thursday, August 12, 1954, the CGMA General Council heard "a brief outline on the orphanage in Barbourville," from "Brother Whitsitt and Sister Martin of the Pentecostal Organization."[67] The presentation by Whitsitt and Martin so impacted General Secretary & Treasurer J.E. Hatfield that he felt like an orphanage was "one of the great needs of this Assembly" in addition to "larger grounds and an open-air tabernacle."[68] General Overseer Clayton Lawson "stressed the need of an orphanage," and "was very much interested in having our own school."[69]

The Church of God (Cleveland) had opened its Bible Training School (now Lee University) on the first day of 1918 with a dozen students.[70] Though the Pentecostal Church of Christ made available enrollment to its Faith Bible Institute to Mountain Assembly members in 1951, none had taken advantage of the invitation. Lawson openly endorsed the idea of an educational institute on the "new assembly grounds" in churches where he preached and at a national youth convention in Cincinnati in December 1956.[71] Assistant General Overseer Luther Gibson also lamented that after fifty years of existence, the Mountain Assembly had "no school, no orphanage, no home for the aged," and that the organization lacked a "sound minister's pension plan" and bought "Sunday school literature from other sources." He envisioned assembly grounds sufficient to launch ministries such as these like he saw in other Pentecostal groups.[72]

In 1958, the General Council increased the amount of membership assessments from $3 to $5 and agreed to use the additional money "for the purpose of building a camp grounds and an administration building."[73] As a result, the Mountain Assembly saw a 20% increase in assessments the following year and also had several thousand dollars received or pledged toward the project.[74] The vision of the Executive Board, notwithstanding, the appointed committee was unable to produce a proposal for new grounds and another committee of Dan C. Lynch, William Fitzpatrick, and J.E. Hatfield was appointed in 1959.[75] When its report generated no serviceable plan, the General Council recommitted the assignment to C.B. Ellis, Arvil Rountree, and James Walden in 1960.[76] By 1962, $4,246.95 was reserved for the new tabernacle fund, but no committee had found suitable property for its construction. So, the General Council decided to "leave the buying of additional property at Headquarters in the hands of the Executive Committee and the General Trustees."[77]

The following spring, Campbell County Public Schools decided to close its junior high school in Jellico and put the property on Florence Avenue up for sale. This property adjoined the current tabernacle site and seemed the perfect solution to the Mountain Assembly's quest for a larger headquarters. On April 20, 1963, General Overseer Ira Moses and Assistant Overseer C.B. Ellis looked at the property with Jellico Pastor Glenn Rowe. Three days later, Trustee Chairman Clayton Lawson and Trustees Isham Sharp and Wade Hughes viewed the property with Moses.[78] At the General Assembly that August, the General Council authorized "the General Overseer and the General Trustees to purchase the Junior High School property" when it went up for auction that fall.[79] On October 5, Moses was pleased to discover he was the lone interested party, but "the school board rejected" his $8,000 bid. After having the property appraised for $14,000, Moses and Hatfield attended the school board meeting five days later and "split the difference" when the board approved their offer of $11,000.[80] The school itself was unusable and

Figure 10.12: Breaking Ground for the New Tabernacle, 1966

c/o CGMA

the Mountain Assembly demolished it in December 1965. The building that housed the home economics classrooms, however, was renovated to provide a new headquarters office for the organization. For nearly two years, Moses spent many days working to remodel the office building and delighted in entertaining out of town guests by offering tours of the newly acquired property.[81]

After the old school was demolished, Moses had plans drawn for the construction of a new tabernacle and marked off the lot on March 1, 1966. On Monday, March 21, a groundbreaking ceremony was held with special guests that included Jellico Mayor A.B. Forman and two aldermen. The Jellico High School Band performed and many CGMA ministers were present. The work commenced the following day and was completed on August 1, one week before the 60th General Assembly.[82] On August 8, 1966, Dayton Pastor Orville Bartee, Jr. opened the first service in the new tabernacle as the devotional leader, and J.B. Hammitte preached the first sermon, "Come, For All Things Are Now Ready." The following morning, Moses was re-elected to his fourth term as General Overseer. By the end of the week, the General Council adopted a resolution "to execute the renewal of all notes made" for security "by deeds of trust" for "money borrowed to construct the new open-air tabernacle." The organization took out $28,000 in loans for construction.[83] The resolution passed unanimously and "everyone seemed to be greatly pleased with the new tabernacle." During the business session, "a spirit of giving came upon the delegation and $3,100 was pledged immediately with $700 being paid instantly."[84] The National Youth Department itself had raised more than $3,000 "toward buying land and building a new tabernacle in Jellico."[85] As a result, the Youth Warriors for Christ would have to wait nearly a decade before the Mountain Assembly was fiscally sound enough to assume the debt of building a youth camp.

Into All the World

As the Mountain Assembly directed its attention toward building its youth camp program and new assembly ground in Jellico, the passion for missions during the tenure of Ira Moses waned somewhat. This was due, in part, to the absence of Luther Gibson from the Mission Board. Gibson had advocated for the need of a "director of evangelism or publicity manager for general evangelism and home missions."[86] As Chairman of the Mission Board, he attempted to incorporate some of the ideas he had proposed but lacked the resolute authority to accomplish it all. When he was not nominated for the board in 1958, Auza Vinson replaced him as chairman and General Missions Director.[87] Vinson left the mission he planted in Lawrenceburg, Tennessee to start another work in Scottville, Ohio in 1963, but by that time, the Mission Board and its Chairman had changed twice.[88]

In 1960, the General Council elected J.H. Douglas, Charles Creekmore, David Hammitte, and James Walden, Jr. to the Mission Board with Isham Sharp selected as Chairman.[89] Over the next two years, the board approved financial aid for two new missions in Chicago that Walden helped launch on Clark Street and on Damen Avenue.[90] The Board also assisted a new church in Sandusky, Ohio launched in the fall of 1961 with Pastor Bobby Wilson.[91] Several members of the Monroe church relocated to the area when a new Ford plant opened there in the late 1950s and formed the foundation of the new church. Wilson's parents were long-time members at Jellico, and he had been converted there in a revival under Lawrence Redmond in 1957. After pastoring the new work in Glenwood, North Carolina, Wilson relocated to Sandusky for one year to launch the church. In 1962, he assumed the pastorate at Nevada, Indiana.[92] The Mission Board also granted mission funds to plant a new work in Norwood, Ohio. James V. Freeman organized the church on Montgomery Avenue with thirteen members in 1962.[93]

In 1962, the General Council selected a new Mission Board of Willie Lee Partin, Dan C. Lynch, Azzie Brown, Carl Prewitt, and James Ledford Cox as the new Chairman and General Missions Director.[94] This board was also retained the next two elections.[95] Over the next five years, it designated almost one fifth of its allocated funds to support the mission works in the Chicago area.[96] In addition, an offering was given for the support of a new church organized in Kokomo, Indiana in the fall of 1962. Assistant General Overseer C.B. Ellis and National Youth Director Gene Douglas conducted a tent revival in the city, and Ellis organized a church with ten members and installed Kenneth Tinch as its pastor.[97] Jasper Walden relocated to Kokomo the following year and assumed the pastorate. About the same time that the mission in Kokomo was launched, a new mission by George Wood began on Main Street in nearby Muncie with help from CGMA Missions.[98] The following fall, Ellis brought his tent to Muncie and conducted a revival and witnessed 19 people testify of salvation.[99] A year later, Arlie Petree relocated to Muncie from Dayton and assumed the pastorate of the church.[100]

In the Spring of 1963, Ellis organized another church in Milford, Ohio and installed John Collins as pastor with financial support from the Mission Fund.[101] Collins did not stay long and the church declined over the next several years, but he founded another church, High Point CGMA, at nearby Blue Ash in 1967, and Ellis reorganized Milford and assumed its pastorate in 1969.[102] In July 1963, Ellis erected his tent in the city of Williamsburg, Kentucky and re-erected a smaller one when a windstorm tore it down and damaged it. Undeterred, he launched the revival and saw more than 40 conversions in the first eight nights. National Youth Director Leon Petree and his brother, Arlie, continued the revival after the General Assembly in the Whitley County Courthouse, and a total of 77 were saved. General Overseer Ira Moses organized a church with 24 members on September 1.[103] Joseph Martin "Mart" Prewitt was installed as its pastor. Moses attended there frequently and assisted in the building of a new church.[104] The General Mission Board also contributed to the church building financially.[105]

Figure 10.13: C.B. Ellis, Jr.
c/o Middlesboro CGMA

Meanwhile, Ellis held another revival in Ypsilanti, Michigan in April 1964, organized a church there with thirteen members, and installed Ray Freeman, the son of Holland, Ohio Pastor Charles A. Freeman, as the new pastor.[106] The young Freeman had assisted Ellis with music in the revival that launched the church at Kokomo.[107] In the fall of 1966, he moved into that area, accepted the pastorate at West Middleton, and later moved it to the east side of Kokomo.[108] Ellis's reputation as an evangelist and his success in church planting won him many admirers and he sought the office of General Overseer in 1966 after four years as the Assistant. Moses, however, had just built a new tabernacle, remained highly popular in the Mountain Assembly, and won the election with more than two-thirds of the votes.[109] Ellis was not nominated for Assistant General Overseer, and he was replaced by James Earl Prewitt, who resigned as Pastor at Goshen to accept the full-time position.[110]

Days after their elections, Moses and Prewitt traveled together to Middlesboro to conduct a pastor's election for David Carroll.[111] On September 8-9, Prewitt accompanied Moses to Cleveland, Tennessee to attend services at the General Assembly of the Church of God of Prophecy. From there, the trip took them to Wytheville, Virginia for an interdenominational fellowship meeting organized by Pastor Charles H. Davis.[112]

Figure 10.14: Ira Moses & J.E. Prewitt
c/o Al Newton, Jr.

Davis had contacted Moses two years earlier and invited him to preach. He presented his church for membership in the Mountain Assembly at the next General Assembly, and Moses returned to Wytheville for a homecoming and dedication service that October.[113] The visit by Moses and Prewitt was well received by Davis who was pleased that, after the "great oration" by Prewitt, "a precious soul found the joy and comfort of accepting Christ." The overseers were excited about visitors from a "mission church from Piney" and hoped to see the lone church at Wytheville develop into a district.[114]

In January 1967, Prewitt held a revival in Belle Vernon, Pennsylvania for Pastor James M. Bright. Bright had been a licensed evangelist for two years, but felt impressed to leave Cleveland, Ohio and return to the area where he was raised to start a new church. In a "community church where they were no longer having regular services," Bright donated "much time and money" to prepare the building. Supplied with names and addresses of past attendees, the minister began visitation, recruitment, and advertisement for the revival. After a church was organized that spring, it presented itself for membership in August and reopened the state of Pennsylvania for the CGMA.[115]

On March 2, Prewitt preached in "a great service" to open the mid-year Elders' Meeting at the Fullerton Avenue Church in Chicago, where James Walden, Jr. was pastor. Luther Gibson preached the following morning and J.H. Douglas preached that night. Moses referred to the event as "the best board meeting I ever attended."[116] The organization was doing well. Prewitt had ample opportunities to travel and preach. Despite the success, he began to grow frustrated that the office of Assistant General Overseer had no clear direction. The Standard Resolutions listed his vague duties as "to look after the general interest of all the churches as directed by the General Overseer" and "to promote the work of the Assembly, its Teachings, Doctrine, Financial Program."[117] Had he not already been doing that while pastoring the sound church at Goshen? Prewitt began to feel like he was doing nothing significant to earn his $100 weekly salary. Eventually, he discussed his frustration with Moses and confessed his contemplation of resignation. The General Overseer encouraged him to keep his office, lest he be labeled a "quitter." Prewitt patiently waited until a convenient alternative presented itself.[118]

Just a few months after the Elders' Meeting in Chicago, one of the members of the Fullerton Avenue Church felt called of God to be a missionary to Brazil. After praying about it for a couple of months, "the Lord confirmed this to her husband's heart."[119] Ronald and Mavis Amos immigrated to Chicago from Great Britain on January 4, 1960 and began attending the Mountain Assembly church there about five years later. Ron was born in Manchester, England on March 21, 1933, and was converted at the age of 19 when someone gave him George F. Dempster's book, *Finding Men for Christ*. Upon the realization that Christ died for the world and for him, personally, Amos gave his "heart and life to Him." Mavis Evans was born in Manchester on August 8, 1936, was orphaned four years later, and was raised in the "godless home of an aunt." At the age of twelve, she was converted while "reading from the Bible as a part of" her "homework assignment." As a teenager, she was introduced to Pentecostalism when another Christian woman told her she could be baptized with the Holy Ghost if she would ask. At home alone that night, she prayed for this experience and spoke in tongues. She shared her testimony with Ron after a Wednesday prayer service in the Nazarene church where they both attended, and he also experienced this baptism.[120]

After their spiritual empowerment, Ronald and Mavis believed they should train for the call of God on their lives and enrolled in the newly founded Nazarene Bible College in Thornleigh, Australia, a suburb of Sydney.[121] After graduation, they returned to Great Britain and were married. In 1960, Olivet Nazarene College in Kankakee sponsored their trip to the United States for further education. The Amoses immigrated with their oldest son, and three more children were born in Chicago. After the call to Brazil was established in their hearts, the Amos family attended the 61st General Assembly where they were introduced to the General Council by Pastor Walden on Thursday, August 10, 1967. Ron greeted the delegates and shared how that, one week earlier, God had instructed him to "go to the largest city" in Brazil in six months and "build indigenous churches."[122]

On the following morning, the Resolutions Committee introduced a measure to restructure the mission department, the Mission Board, and the office of Assistant General Overseer. The new plan put the Assistant General Overseer "in charge of evangelism," and required him to "hold mission rallies in each district," to "aid the District Overseers in building new churches," and to record and report mission offerings to *The Gospel Herald*. The General Council would no longer elect the Mission Board. Instead, the District Overseers served in this capacity with the Assistant General Overseer as the chairman. Each minister would send one dollar each month and each church would raise an offering for missions on the fourth Sunday of the month. In addition, Thursday night's service at the General Assembly was set aside for the promotion of missions. After the General Council adopted the revisions, it later voted to take $500 from the Youth Warriors for Christ treasury to assist the Amos family with its move to Brazil. [123]

The missionary call of the Amoses and the reorganization of the mission program gave Prewitt a new purpose and he approached the new duties of his office with great zeal. A mission rally he conducted later that month in Wytheville, Virginia, raised $50.[124] Prewitt proposed that "each district start and maintain a new church each year for five years," so that "at the close of five years, we will have more than doubled in size." He intended for his "keep the church alive and double in five" to be a statement of purpose rather than just a "catchy phrase."[125] By April, Prewitt reported "one double already realized" when mission receipts had surpassed the previous year's giving.[126] By the Assembly, his efforts contributed to a 366% increase in missions receipts from 1967 to 1968.[127]

While Prewitt conducted mission rallies and raised awareness to the new foreign mission program, Pastor Walden and the Amoses also solicited financial support from the churches in preparation for the work in South America.[128] In March, Ronald and Mavis Amos, and their four children,

Figure 10.15: the Amos Family

c/o The Gospel Herald

moved to Sao Paulo, Brazil, with no contacts and unable to speak Portuguese.[129] The Amoses naively pictured "thousands of souls yielding easily to God," but instead encountered hardship and "great spiritual warfare."[130] In the summer of 1968-69, the "fear of death" gripped their hearts when their two year-old son, Mark, fell sick and "three doctors had examined him and could not help him." God intervened and healed him, but the lack of adequate family medical care in the foreign country was always on their minds.[131] The Mission Fund had given them $2,345.25 in the first year and increased their salary to $4,460 in the second year, but the cost of living in the largest city in the country proved a great challenge.[132] When they relocated to Brasilia in 1969, little changed. Depending on less than reliable public transportation emphasized the importance of purchasing a used car.[133]

By June, Amos had relocated again to Itumbiara in southern Goiás, and launched a local radio broadcast with assistance from the Pentecostal Church of Christ.[134] Though he had picked up some Portuguese, he made the acquaintance of a Brazilian minister, José Amador da Silva, who assisted Amos by preaching on the radio and distributing tracts. The popularity of the radio broadcast led to numerous requests to hold house meetings with "50 to 70 people" in attendance. When God moved on the heart of a local businessman to help Amos, he located "an old furniture depository in the middle of town and after a lot cleaning and painting" a church was opened that September with 170 adults at the first service.[135] The Amos family returned to the United States in the late spring of 1970 and visited churches over the next few months reporting on the progress of the Brazilian mission and soliciting financial support.[136] On Thursday night of the 64th General Assembly, the Amoses testified of their work in Brazil and received a standing ovation for their dedicated service.[137] Despite the eventual success of the work in Itumbiara, financial support and interest in it waned. The Amoses intended to further their education before they returned to South America, but by that time, CGMA Missions shifted its focus to the West Indies and the work in Brazil was incorporated into the Pentecostal Church of Christ.[138]

Ultimately, lack of finances led to the demise of the CGMA presence in Brazil. CGMA Missions supported the Amos family with over $8,000 during their two years in Brazil but failed to raise more than $1,300 the following two years to send them back.[139] Several factors contributed to the loss of financial support. First, the ill-preparedness of the Amos family for foreign missions stymied the development of the first CGMA congregation on foreign soil. Impatience from donors who expected a faster return on their investment then frustrated giving. Second, Ronald Amos was an unknown when he came to the General Assembly in 1967 with a burden for foreign missions. He was unfamiliar with the personalities of the assembly's leadership, the development of the organization's government, and the cultural application of its holiness teachings. The prevailing attitude of many ministers was summarized by Luther Gibson in 1970: "If we are going to support someone in mission, why not get someone among us who has been brought up with this Assembly and knows what we stand for and knows how to represent our church organization?" Gibson also hinted that CGMA Missions should prioritize American evangelization until it was large enough to make a significant difference in foreign lands.[140] Third, when the Amos family returned from Brazil, CGMA Missions was looking elsewhere for foreign missions and a change in leadership helped complete this redirection.

Before the Amoses ever moved to Brazil, Walter Vaughn, who had been converted in Dayton under Efford Enix and had pastored in the 1950s in Monongahela, Pennsylvania, began evangelizing in Mountain Assembly churches again in the fall of 1967.[141] Vaughn, now based out of Rockledge, Florida, had returned recently from an evangelistic crusade in the Bahamas, and Prewitt hoped to "explore the possibilities" of mission work in the Caribbean before the next Assembly.[142] That Spring, Prewitt solicited financial support for the evangelist and accompanied Vaughn to the Bahamas.[143] Vaughn intended to launch a six-month campaign in Jamaica that fall.[144] Though no CGMA churches were established in the West Indies under Prewitt's leadership, contacts made facilitated the establishment of churches in Jamaica by his successor.

In the late spring of 1969, the Church of God of the Original Mountain Assembly congregation on Floral Avenue in Norwood, Ohio, had a pastoral vacancy. Prewitt and others conducted an extended successful revival there and the church petitioned the CGMA for membership at the General Assembly that August desiring Prewitt to be its pastor.[145] The General Council that year permitted Prewitt to pastor the church with the congregation assuming his full salary. Prewitt continued to serve as Assistant General Overseer & Missions Director for the next year and reasoned that the additional revenue received from the church without the outlay of expense for his salary might enable the organization to eliminate its debt by the time his term expired.[146] Although Prewitt continued to solicit funds for the mission in Brazil, his attention to missions was somewhat distracted by his pastoral duties and the work in the West Indies was placed temporarily on hold. On Tuesday, August 11, 1970, the General Council elected C.B. Ellis Jr. to succeed Prewitt as Assistant General Overseer, and Ellis resumed the pursuit of a mission in Jamaica.

Tweaking a Polity of Episcopalism and Congregationalism

The restructuring of the office of Assistant General Overseer and the Missions Department was part of a series of considerable changes that occurred from 1964 to 1976. Collectively, they were as significant as the change in government in 1944, but because they occurred over a decade, they failed to generate the same kind of negative consequences. Sensing the need for substantial change, the General Council elected a ten-member Committee on Resolutions to a two-year term in 1964. Five Elders—George Douglas, Ottis Ellis, Clayton Lawson, Glenn Rowe, and Luther Gibson—and five additional ministers—Fred Cornelius, Auza Vinson, Jerome Walden, Jennings Baird, and Bobby Wilson were elected.[147] Prior to this, the committee was selected at the beginning of business and met during the assembly to propose new adoptions and amendments. The much lengthier term allowed the committee to meet over the course of the term and prepare for changes far in advance of the convention. Over the next two years, the General Council adopted four amendments proposed by the committee related to the qualifications and procedures of the credentialling process.[148]

The committee also proposed changes to the Assembly government. In 1965, Lawson introduced a measure to add a "statute of limitation" to the number of terms that the Executive Board officers could serve. The following year, the committee proposed to remove the current members of the Executive Board from the Board of Twelve Elders while retaining them as part of "the judicial body of the Assembly."[149] Both measures failed, but the seed sown would ultimately produce fruit. One successful measure proposed by the Resolution Committee and adopted by the General Council in 1966 created a succession of office. Should the offices of General Overseer or General Secretary & Treasurer be vacated for any reason, their respective Assistants would assume the duties of the office until the next Assembly. Pleased with the committee's work, overall, the General Council voted to retain it for two more years.[150]

After the General Council adopted the committee's resolution to restructure the office of Assistant General Overseer and the Mission Board, it also approved one to change the duties of the Assistant General Secretary & Treasurer. Like the Assistant General Overseer, this office had no official

Figure 10.16: James L. Cox, Sr.
c/o James L. Cox, Jr.

duties except to "assist" the General Secretary & Treasurer. By 1967, J.E. Hatfield had served as the General Secretary & Treasurer since the office was created by combining the duties of the Clerk, General Treasurer, and Assembly Treasurer in 1944. He had also edited every issue of *The Gospel Herald* for 25 years. As the Mountain Assembly grew and the responsibilities of the full-time treasurer increased, "the duties of both offices became too much for one man," and the General Council approved a measure that made the Assistant General Secretary & Treasurer the Editor of *The Gospel Herald* and paid him $50 per month for his services.[151] By virtue of his office, Jellico Pastor Wade Hughes became the editor until his resignation in January when he left the CGMA and joined the Church of God (Cleveland). Hatfield resumed the editorial work until James Ledford Cox, Sr. was elected in 1968.[152]

The open position on the Executive Board and editorship of the paper attracted the attention of Wytheville Pastor Charles Davis, who presumptuously purchased a printing press prior to the General Assembly and sought the election that August. Davis had worked with Prewitt that spring to prepare a handbook on "Public Relations and Your Church."[153] With his publication experience underappreciated in 1968, Davis returned the following year with a resolution to create a "Public Relations Director" to "promote the Assembly and its local churches through all means possible" and to "maintain a file of photographs of the churches and ministers." Upon adoption of the resolution, Davis was elected to the position.[154] Davis's tenure as Public Relations Director was less than celebratory. After relocating to Sandusky to pastor the church there, he attempted to sell the church property in Wytheville in January. Unable to resolve the conflict amicably, General Overseer Ira Moses officiated a business meeting in Wytheville on April 5, and the church excluded Davis.[155] At the General Assembly in August, the General Council replaced him as Public Relations Director with Cleveland Pastor Jerome Walden.[156] Once again, Luther Gibson revealed his bias when he wrote "men that need jobs like this are men who know the assembly and about its activities" and endorsed the "good man in this position now."[157]

In 1968, the General Council set the size of the Resolution Committee to five men and elected Jerome Walden, Glenn Rowe, Bobby Wilson, Fred Cornelius, and Auza Vinson. Delegates in 1969 approved resolutions by the committee to eliminate the "appointing board" and to allow the ministers in each district to elect their District Overseers. The committee's attempt to make changes to the composition and tenure of the Board of Twelve Elders failed again in 1969, but its resolution to create tenure of office limitations on the Executive Board and National Youth Officers was approved.[158] Moses's tenure as General Overseer was approaching ten years and many eagerly awaited a change in leadership as they had under his predecessor. The Church of God (Cleveland) saw in its two-term limitation of offices a way to avoid autocratic leadership.[159] Many in the Mountain Assembly now believed term limits would reduce disunity and the political machinations of those who aspired for office. From 1950 to 1960, Lawson ran unopposed for General Overseer five times. Moses, on the other hand, ran without opposition in only one of six elections, and received less than 80% affirmatives in his unopposed secret ballot vote.[160] The General Council adopted a resolution that set the tenure of office limitations to two two-year terms and a maximum of eight consecutive years on the Executive Board.[161]

In 1970, the General Council adopted a resolution presented by the committee that required a nominee to receive a majority of votes to be elected. Prior to this, the elections were decided by plurality. This sometimes led to small margins of victory when multiple nominations were made. In the 1966 election for Assistant General Secretary & Treasurer, for example, two votes separated the three nominees and Wade Hughes was elected with 34% of the votes.[162] The new rule stipulated that a run-off between the two nominees with the highest number of votes would be held should no candidate receive a majority on the first ballot.[163]

Two significant resolutions were adopted by the General Council in 1973. One altered the process by which the Standard Resolutions could be amended. Previously, resolutions were presented by the committee as new business and required a simple majority vote. The new procedure specified that "proposed amendments or adoptions" must be submitted to each delegate in mimeograph form prior to the General Council and would require a 2/3 majority vote.[164] The second resolution removed a member of the Board of Twelve Elders upon his election to the Executive Board.[165]

Despite the challenge of obtaining a super majority to amend the current Standard Resolutions, the Mountain Assembly was ready for change and the

General Council approved two substantial amendments to the resolutions governing the Board of Twelve Elders over the next two years. First, qualifications for election to the Board were approved in 1974. One must have obtained the age of 40, been a member of the Mountain Assembly for 20 consecutive years and been ordained ten years to be eligible for election.[166] Second, in 1975, the General Council instituted an eight-year term on the election of the Board of Elders with three new Elders elected every two years. To facilitate the change, the three with the longest tenure would be replaced in 1976 and continue accordingly until 1982.[167] Younger ministers saw the initiative as an opportunity to serve and influence the organization more quickly. Older ministers saw it as an attempt to undermine their influence or push them to the side. Moses described the business meeting that day as the "worst business conference I have ever attended in 44 years."[168] Moses held out the hope that the amendment would be reconsidered the following year. The Board of Elders discussed a resolution to rescind the move. However, when its recommendation was tabled after a "hot debate" until it could be submitted in mimeograph form as specified by the new Standard Resolutions, it brough an end to the tenures of Ira Moses, Luther Gibson, and J.E. Hatfield, who had a combined 102 years on the Board. Rather than wait for the inevitable, Efford Enix, feeling cast to the side, resigned. Emotionally and physically exhausted, Moses did not return for business the following day.[169]

The amendments of 1973 and 1975 drastically changed the makeup of the Board of Twelve Elders. Although the new tenure of office limitations which went into effect with the elections of 1970 permitted Ira Moses to seek reelection again in 1972, he declined to run. He knew the Mountain Assembly was ready for change and chose to exit gracefully. He called August 8, 1972, a "day of decision," but the choice was probably made much earlier. The Board of Elders meeting in the old tabernacle in April was challenging for Moses as the moderator and as a member of the board. The first "day of much dispute and disagreement" was followed by "one of the darkest days in church business."[170] The 67-year-old minister was ready to lay that burden down. The General Council elected C.B. Ellis, Jr. to succeed Moses after having twice served as his Assistant.[171] When tenure of office brought an end to Hatfield's 34-year tenure as Secretary & Treasurer in 1974, the General Council elected Clayton Lawson to succeed him.[172] The election of Lawson and reelection of Ellis after the amendment of 1973 brought an end to their tenures on the Board of Twelve Elders and they were replaced by J.B. Hammitte and James L. Cox, Sr.[173]

Rise Up and Build

In 1976, Hatfield, Gibson, Moses, and Enix were replaced by Willie Lee Partin, Clayton Lawson, J.E. Prewitt, and Fred Cornelius.[174] When Partin died the following April, the General Council elected Bobby Wilson to complete his unexpired term.[175] The death of James Walden, Sr. in November 1977, and J.E. Prewitt's election to the Executive Board in 1978 created two vacancies in addition to the three regular elections. To fill these openings, the General Council selected Roy Cornelius, Claude Baird, Jennings Baird, Lloyd Camp, and Paul Grubbs.[176] After James Cox died on the day after the 1978 General Assembly and Bobby Wilson resigned later that year, the General Council replaced them with J.H. Douglas and J.C. Murray.[177] In 1980, Lawson's term was ended with his election to the Executive Board, and Fred Cornelius, Jerome Walden, Kenneth Massingill, and C.B. Ellis were elected to the Board of Twelve Elders.[178] Just 48 different men had served on the Board of Twelve Elders since its inception in 1919 until 1974. Over the following six years, however, another 14 joined their ranks. Only Douglas, whose previous term expired in 1978 before being reelected in 1979, remained from the pre-1974 Board. By the mid1970s it became obvious that the CGMA was entering its third generation of leadership.

Figure 10.17: J.E. Hatfield
c/o Evon Hatfield Tipton

Conclusion

Just as J.H. Bryant, Andrew Long, Kim Moses, J.E. Hatfield, Luther Gibson, Clayton Lawson, and Ira Moses guided the second generation of the Mountain Assembly for nearly thirty years, another seven men provided direction for the organization for most of the following three decades. Claiborn Boyd Ellis, Jr. was born on December 31, 1925 in Chenoa, Kentucky to Louise (Saylor) and Claiborn Boyd Ellis, Sr. His father began attending the Mountain Assembly as a delegate from Henderson Grove in 1918. By the time "Junior" was born, his father had served the church as a deacon and clerk. He was ordained into the ministry the following year and began pastoring in 1932. Junior was saved at Henderson Grove in 1939. When his father began pastoring at Flat Hollow, Tennessee the following

Figure 10.18: C.B. Ellis, Jr.
c/o K.E. Massingill

year, he met Dorothy Mae McCarty and married her two years later. Ellis moved to Monroe, Michigan and worked briefly for K & K Coal Company before serving in the United States Army from April 1944 through December 1946. Shortly after his discharge, Ellis relocated to Middlesboro where he began preaching. The church there recommended him for evangelist's license on October 23, 1950.[179]

After receiving credentials, Ellis began an itinerant ministry that saw him pastor briefly at Tackett Creek, Arthur, and Flat Hollow in Tennessee, and Middlesboro in Kentucky before relocating to Goshen, Ohio in 1953. In five years, Ellis built a new church building and moved the congregation out of the old schoolhouse that had long served as its place of worship. From 1958 to 1962, Ellis was appointed Assistant National Youth Director and spent most of that time evangelizing. His election to the office of Assistant General Overseer in 1962 coincided with the General Council's vote to pay a full-time salary for the position, and Ellis continued to evangelize and assisted with the establishment of numerous churches. Weary of the travel and time away from his family, Ellis settled in Milford, Ohio and began pastoring the Mulberry CGMA nearby. When he returned to the office of Assistant General Overseer in 1970, the duties included oversight of the foreign mission program, and he helped establish lasting Mountain Assembly works in Jamaica. He was elected General Overseer in 1972.[180]

James Earl Prewitt was born on December 15, 1933 in Wolf Creek, Kentucky to Bessie Jane (Enix) and Joseph Martin "Mart" Prewitt. His father began attending the Mountain Assembly as a delegate from Emlyn in 1919, served as a Sunday school evangelist for Kentucky for five years in the mid1930s, and pastored several churches. The Prewitt family moved to the Detroit area to find work in 1952. "Earl" served in the U.S. Army from 1953 to 1954. That year he met Alma Dean Stephens at the church on Junction Street, and they were wed in December. Alma had been raised at Jellico Creek CGMA where her maternal grandparents were charter members.[181]

Rise Up and Build

Prewitt was converted in January 1957 at the beginning of a three-week revival at Junction Street conducted by Robert Manis. His brother, Carl, was saved the last night, February 10. The following year, Earl began singing and leading the young people. After he began preaching that spring, he left his job at "Dodge Main," to pursue higher education and enrolled in Lee College in Cleveland, Tennessee that fall. His education would be cut short when the Goshen church called on him to pastor three years later. There, he helped coordinate the first national youth camps. From 1966 to 1970, he served as the Assistant General Overseer and helped develop the CGMA's first foreign mission program in Brazil. He returned to pastoral work in 1969 when he assumed the leadership of the Floral Avenue Church in Norwood, Ohio.[182]

Figure 10.19: Fred Cornelius, J.E. Prewitt, Homer Prewitt, Carl Prewitt
c/o Vonda Prewitt Morris

Virgil Glenn Rowe was born on March 8, 1921 in Sharp's Chapel, Tennessee to Mossie Artilia (Harmon) and Charlie Ondoff Rowe. His father was a coal loader, and Glenn followed in his footsteps near Fonde at the age of 14. He married Leatha Mae McKinney in 1941. Rowe was converted under Andrew Long and briefly followed his pastor during the schism, serving as clerk of the Fonde Original Mountain Assembly Church and assisting with reading the church letters at the General Assembly in Williamsburg. Rowe began preaching in 1947 and was licensed as an evangelist by the Mountain Assembly when he returned to the Fonde Church in 1951. The same year, Rowe assumed his first pastorate at nearby Henderson Grove and over the next nine years pastored at Fonde, Coldiron, and Middlesboro. In August 1960, General Overseer Ira Moses "appointed a committee to look for a pastor" at Jellico and conducted the business conference on September 3 when the church elected Rowe. He pastored the headquarters church until August 1966 when he relocated to Sidney, Ohio to assume the pastoral duties there. After five years, Rowe returned to Middlesboro where he was elected pastor on June 24, 1972. His third tenure at Middlesboro turned out to be his shortest, as six weeks later he was elected Assistant General Overseer & Missions Director.[183]

Figure 10.20: Glenn Rowe
c/o K.E. Massingill

Figure 10.21: Jerome Walden
c/o K.E. Massingill

Ancil "Jerome" Walden was born on August 15, 1933 in Jellico to Edna Lawrence (Douglas) and James Alton Walden, Sr. After his father relocated the family to assume the pastorate of the Church of God of the Original Mountain Assembly on Kipling Avenue in Cleveland, Ohio in August 1951, Jerome returned south in October to marry Charlene Eleanor Dykes in Saxton, Kentucky and brought her to Cleveland. In 1954, one year after the church returned to the CGMA, Jerome was converted and began preaching shortly thereafter. At the beginning of 1956, he received his minister's license and took the pastorate of the Detroit Avenue church on the west side of Cleveland. On February 6, 1958, he was ordained at Kipling Avenue by his father, Ira Moses, and Charles Creekmore. After pastoring for a couple of years at the new work at South Amherst, Walden returned to Kipling Avenue to succeed his father as pastor and immediately launched a building campaign. On January 1, 1965, Walden relocated the congregation to a new sanctuary on Aspinwall Avenue with a seating capacity of 280 and that Easter set a new attendance record with 236. After serving as Public Relations Director from 1970 to 1974, Walden left Cleveland and returned to Jellico upon his election as Assistant General Overseer & Missions Director.[184]

Kenneth Eugene "K.E." Massingill was born April 9, 1940 in Kenvir, Kentucky to Dorothy "Helen" (Fultz) and Claude Eugene Massingill. His father was a coal loader for the Black Mountain Coal Corporation. Kenneth enlisted in the U.S. Army in May 1957 and married Mildred Fuson on Christmas Eve before being sent to Germany the following month. Although his family attended the Mountain Assembly church at Kenvir since before his birth, Massingill did not become a Christian until he was in the mid-Atlantic on board the *USS Grant* en route to Europe. He began preaching a year later and received evangelist's license in June 1960 after his enlistment ended. He moved his family to pastor in Greenville, Ohio in 1961, and his father began pastoring at nearby Troy, Ohio the following hear. Kenneth returned to Kenvir to pastor his home church from 1963 to 1974, where he was ordained on November 29, 1965. After Mildred Massingill's untimely death on January 4, 1968, Kenneth married Linda Buress on November 17. The Kenvir church sponsored their first mission trip to Jamaica in January 1972, and the call to be a missionary that Massingill had felt since he was a teenager was confirmed on that trip.[185]

Figure 10.22: Kenneth Massingill
c/o K.E. Massingill

Another mission trip to Jamaica in early 1972 included C.B. Ellis and the Walden brothers, Jerome, James, and Jasper. Wiley Jasper Walden was born September 12, 1941, in Louisville, Kentucky to Edna Lawrence (Douglas) and James Alton Walden, Sr. He was converted in a service on New Year's Eve 1962 in Cleveland and began preaching in February 1963. On April 13, he married Mary Frances Petree and moved her to Kokomo, Indiana in September to pastor the young church. The church purchased a parsonage and new sanctuary on South Calumet two years later, and he was ordained there by C.B. Ellis and Bobby Wilson. After his brother-in-law brought the national youth camps to nearby Hartford City, Walden helped direct the camp and oversee counselors. In 1968, the General Council elected him to serve as National Youth Director, and he served in that capacity for six years, with the tenure of office limitations going into effect after his first term. Seeing nearly 1,000 people saved during the trip to Jamaica he took during his last term initiated a zeal for evangelism and foreign missions that characterized much of his ministry for the next two decades.[186]

Figure 10.23: Jasper Walden
c/o CGMA

Figure 10.24: James L. Cox, Jr.
c/o James L. Cox, Jr.

James Ledford Cox, Jr. was born on November 14, 1949 in Keavy, Kentucky to Ethel Mae (Parman) and James Ledford Cox, Sr. His father had served as Overseer of the General Assembly Church of God in the 1950s but joined the Mountain Assembly in 1961 to pastor the church at Mountain Ash. On May 21, 1964, "Jimmy" was converted and began serving in various capacities in the church. In January 1967, he began preaching for his father at the church and on his radio broadcast in Williamsburg. After high school graduation, he began evangelizing. Even before his 18th birthday, one member of the Executive Board recognized that he possessed the "the ability and Biblical knowledge to be a leader tomorrow." Auza Vinson's resignation as National Youth Secretary & Treasurer in the spring of 1969 created a potential nightmare for the National Youth Directors Jasper Walden and Donnie Hill as they prepared for their first youth camp. In April, Walden recommended to the Board of Twelve Elders that Cox be appointed to fill the position and he went on to serve the remainder of the term and was twice reelected in that capacity. In the meantime, he enrolled at Cumberland College and earned his bachelor's degree in 1975.[187]

Gibson, Lawson, and Moses led the Mountain Assembly for 25 years after its division with the Original Mountain Assembly. They succeeded in rebuilding the organization stronger than it ever had been, extending its geographic expanse across the country and into foreign lands, establishing a national youth program to ensure continued growth, and overseeing the further development of the headquarters property in Jellico as well as a new campground in Ohio. New resolutions established in 1973 and 1975 forced the three off the Board of Twelve Elders. Although Lawson would later return to the Elder and Executive Boards, Gibson and Moses would not.

Moses returned to pastoral ministry in Williamsburg after he left the General Overseer's office. He suffered a light heart attack the following summer which limited his preaching and travel. He began having chest pains again the first week of March 1979 but attended the Elders' Meeting in Jellico in the middle of the month, where he was troubled by several matters that were discussed. On Tuesday, March 27, he attended a revival service at the Baptist church in nearby Fairview and had another more serious heart attack the following day. He died in Lexington on Thursday.[188] By the time Moses passed away, Gibson's health had seriously declined. He had navigated through church conflict in Trenton for five years. On November 27, 1978, however, he suffered a stroke. The following week a massive stroke left him debilitated. Gibson spent most of the last ten years of his life in a nursing and rehabilitation center and died in Toledo on November 15, 1988.[189]

---

[1] Ira Moses, Personal Diary, June 25, 1960, in the personal collection of Jason Lands, Cookeville, TN; Fred Cornelius, "A Note from Pastor Cornelius to N. Monroe Church of God," *GH* 61, no. 7 (July 2000): 10.

[2] Ira Moses, Personal Diary, July 18 to 29, 1960.

[3] CGMA, *Minutes* (1948), 13; "The Young People's Endeavor of the Church of God (Mt. Assembly)," *GH* 7, no. 9 (March 1949): 2.

[4] "The Young People's Endeavor of the Church of God (Mt. Assembly)," *GH* 8, no. 4 (October 1949): 2.

[5] Luther Gibson, "How to Keep the Family Together," *GH* 17, no. 1 (January 1959): 9.

[6] Gibson, "Report of General Overseer," *GH* 7, no. 7 (January 1949): 1.

[7] Viola Moses, "Mountain Ash, Ky.," *GH* 9, no. 2 (August 1950): 6; Mildred Rigney and Geneva Lamb, "Newcomb, Tenn.," *GH* 9, no. 5 (November 1950): 6.

[8] CGMA, *Minutes* (1952), 10.

[9] CGMA, *Minutes* (1951), 8, 11-12.

[10] Haskel Swain, "World Upset," *GH* 11, no. 2 (August 1952): 1.

[11] CGMA, *Minutes* (1953), 12.

[12] CGMA, *Minutes* (1954), 56.

[13] Haskel Swain, "The Youth's Gateway," *YG* 1, no. 1 (January 25, 1954): 3.

[14] CGMA, *Minutes* (1954), 48.

[15] "Youth Gateway Magazine Subscription Selling Contest," *YG* 2, no. 5 (June 1955): 5.

[16] CGMA, *Minutes* (1955), 23; J.E. Hatfield and Efford Enix, "Let us Remember," *GH* 14, no. 1 (September 1955): 6; "Youth Gateway Section," *GH* 14, no. 2 (October 1955): 10.

[17] *YG* 1, no. 1 (January 25, 1954): 18; CGMA, *Minutes* (1954), 56.

[18] Haskel Swain, "2,000 Expected to Take Part in Assembly at Jellico, Tenn.," *YG* 1, no. 11 (July 30, 1954): 1; CGMA, *Minutes* (1954), 32-33.

[19] CGMA, *Minutes* (1956), 23. Although the parade was scheduled annually for most of Enix's tenure, the General Council voted on a few occasions to cancel it.

[20] Wade M. Hughes, "National Youth Rally," *GH* 16, no. 15 (December 1958): 6; J[ames]H. Johnson, "Goshen, Ohio," *GH* 18, no. 10 (October 1960): 6; "Large Crowds Overflow," *GH* 21, no. 9 (September 1961): 7; "National Youth Rally," *GH* 22, no. 5 (May 1962): 8.

[21] Fred Cornelius and James Earl Prewitt, in personal conversations with the author.

[22] Wade M. Hughes, "National Youth Rally Huge Success," *GH* 22, no. 8 (July 1962): 6.

[23] CGMA, *Minutes of the Fifty-Sixth Annual Assembly* (Jellico, TN: Church of God Mountain Assembly, 1962), 24-25.

[24] CGMA, *Minutes of the Fifty-Seventh Annual Assembly* (Jellico, TN: Church of God Mountain Assembly, 1963), 22, 40.

[25] Parks, Journal, 197-198; Fonde Minutes, 112.

[26] "The Evangelistic work of Rev. Leon Petree," revival record in the possession of Leon Petree, Cincinnati, OH.

[27] "Rev. Leon Petree," *GH* 22, no. 5 (May 1962): 1.

[28] "Spot News," *GH* 21, no. 5 (May 1961): 6; Lexie Busie, "Detroit, Mich. Bagley St.," *GH* 21, no. 7 (July 1961): 2.

[29] Arlie Petree, *He'll Be There* (Muncie, IN: by the author, ca. 1962), 11, 26, 28-29.

[30] Lexie Busie, "Detroit Michigan Bagley Street," *GH* 21, no. 2, (February 1961): 8; Ira Moses, "General Overseer's Report for December 1960, January and February 1961," *GH* 21, no. 3 (March 1961): 7; Moses, Diary, January 15, 1961; Roger Glenn Rountree, Facebook message to the author, October 7, 2019.

[31] "The 1963 Youth Camp," *GH* 23, no. 5 (Mary 1963): 6; Carol Bunch, "Youth Camp Huge Success," *GH* 24, no. 7 (July 1964): 8.

[32] Joseph Carder, "The Mountain Assembly Church of God Youth Camp," *GH* 25, no. 7 (July 1965): 10-12.

[33] Leon Petree, "God in the Midst of Youth Camp," *GH* 26, no. 7 (July 1966): 10; Petree, "National Youth Events: 65-66," *GH* 27, no. 9 (September 1966): 8.

[34] Petree, "1967 National Youth Camp," *GH* 28, no. 7 (July 1967): 3-4; Ira Moses, Diary, June 21, 1967.

[35] Ira Moses, Diary, March 18, 1965; Deed of Conveyance, *Highland County Deed Book*, March 28, 1965, Whitley County Court House, Hillsboro, Ohio; CGMA, *Minutes [of the] Church of God Mountain Assembly, Inc.: Fifty-Ninth Annual Assembly* (Jellico,

TN: Church of God Mountain Assembly, 1965), 34; T[homas] E. Bartee, "Central Ohio District Youth Rally Reports," *GH* 25, no. 5 (May 1965): 10.

[36] Charlie T. Yeary, "Youth Camp Ground," *GH* 26, no. 1 (January 1966): 2; CGMA, *Minutes [of the] Church of God Mountain Assembly, Inc.: Sixtieth Annual Assembly* (Jellico, TN: Church of God Mountain Assembly, 1966), 21.

[37] Yeary, "Possibilities for Progress," *GH* 28, no. 10 (October 1967): 5; Yeary, "Possibilities for Progress," *GH* 29, no. 1 (January 1968): 2; Petree, "Special Announcing Notice," *GH* 29, no. 4 (April 1968): 10.

[38] Ira Moses, "From the Overseer's Desk," *GH* 28, no. 11 (November 1967): 9; Moses, Diary, October 3-5, 1967.

[39] Moses, Diary, October 23, 1967 and November 10, 1967.

[40] CGMA, *Minutes* (1968), 23. The author has had multiple conversations about the potential purchase of Camp Cannon with several ministers over the past few decades. Their consensus has been the cost of the property while the Assembly was already in debt was of great concern to many of the elder ministers. Concerns over modesty created additional conflict from the most conservative faction.

[41] Moses, Diary, July 23, 1967; Leon Petree, Facebook message to the author, July 4, 2020.

[42] "Big National Youth Camp & Campmeeting," *GH* 30, no. 4 (April 1969): 6; *50th Anniversary Youth Warriors for Christ* (Jellico, TN: Church of God Mountain Assembly, 1998), 12.

[43] Jasper Walden, "Youth Warriors for Christ," *GH* 30, no. 12 (December 1969): 5; Walden, "Youth Warriors for Christ," *GH* 33, no. 9 (September 1972): 6.

[44] "Rittman Church Raises One Thousand Dollars...," *GH* 32, no. 9 (September 1971): 9.

[45] CGMA, *Annual Minutes [of the] Church of God Mountain Assembly, Inc.* (Jellico, TN: Church of God Mountain Assembly, 1972), 23-24.

[46] "Rittman Church," 9; CGMA, *Annual Minutes [of the] Church of God Mountain Assembly, Inc.* (Jellico, TN: Church of God Mountain Assembly, 1974), 47.

[47] Donnie Hill, "Attention," *GH* 35, no. 11 (November 1974): 12.

[48] Hill, "Youth Department News," *GH* 36, no. 2 (February 1975): 3.

[49] CGMA, *Minutes [of the] Church of God Mountain Assembly, Inc.* (Jellico, TN: Church of God Mountain Assembly, 1975), 28.

[50] Hill, "National Youth Rally" *GH* 36, no. 10 (October 1975): 10; Hill, "National Youth Rally" *GH* 36, no. 12 (December 1975): 4.

[51] Hill, "Progress on the Youth Camp at Hillsboro, Ohio," *GH* 37, no. 2 (February 1976): 3; Hill, "Are You Searching?," *GH* 37, no. 3 (March 1976): 3.

[52] Hill, "Y.W.C. Camp Report," and Jewel Griffith, "First Youth Camp at Hillsboro, Ohio," *GH* 37, no. 7 (July 1976): 2-4.

[53] Alma Prewitt, "Youth Camp of the Past and Youth Camp of Today," *GH* 45, no. 1 (January 1984): 2.

[54] CGMA, *Minutes* (1942), 23.

[55] CGMA, *Minutes* (1949), 11.

56 CGMA, *Minutes* (1950), 12.

57 CGMA, *Minutes* (1951), 13; CGMA, *Minutes* (1952), 16; CGMA, *Minutes* (1953), 13; CGMA, *Minutes* (1954), 55; CGMA, *Minutes* (1955), 24.

58 "50th General Assembly," *GH* 15, no. 1 (September 1956): 1-2.

59 Gibson, "The 50th General Assembly As I Saw It," *GH* 15, no. 1 (September 1956): 3.

60 CGMA, *Minutes* (1956), 31, 33. George Douglas was living in Speedwell in Claiborne County, Tennessee. The other four lived in Campbell County in or around Jellico.

61 Phillips, 259-260.

62 Yeary, "Possibilities," 5.

63 First Book of Minutes of Pentecostal Children's Home: 1949-1956, Barbourville Pentecostal Children's Home, Barbourville, Kentucky, 118, 132.

64 Ibid., 1-4.

65 Ibid., 30.

66 Ibid., 137, 150-151.

67 CGMA, *Minutes* (1954), 38. "Brother Whitsitt" mentioned in the minutes of the business session may have been John or Billy Whitsitt, Pentecostal preachers from Carmi, Illinois, long associated with the children's home. Neither is mentioned in the first minute book of the orphanage, however. "Sister Martin," was probably Lena Martin, who was appointed treasurer from Barbourville Free Pentecostal Church at the organizational meeting for the orphanage, and the mother of the founding president, William G. Martin. Her husband, John D. Martin, was believed to be the first Pentecostal adherent in Knox County, Kentucky. https://www.findagrave.com/memorial/73036406/john-d-martin

68 J.E. Hatfield, "A Great Need," *GH* 15, no. 3 (November 1956): 4.

69 William Watson, "Middlesboro, Ky. Quarterly Meeting," *GH* 15, no. 4 (December 1956): 7.

70 Conn, 186.

71 Jean Webb, "National Youth Convention," *GH* 15, no. 6 (February 1957): 10-11. Webb, the National Youth Secretary, was then a student at the University of Kentucky.

72 Gibson, "Assistant General Overseer & Mission Director Speaks," *GH* 15, no. 7 (March 1957): 2.

73 CGMA, *Minutes* (1958), 22.

74 CGMA, *Minutes* (1958), 30-31; CGMA, *Minutes* (1959), 33-34; CGMA, *Minutes* (1957), 36. In total, $1,823.25 had been received from Lawson's pledge drive at the 1956 Assembly with another $4,325.00 in extant pledges. By 1959, however, the fund still contained just $3,599.25.

75 CGMA, *Minutes* (1959), 26.

76 CGMA, *Minutes* (1960), 25-26.

77 CGMA, *Minutes* (1962), 26.

78 Ira Moses, Diary, April 20 and April 23, 1963.

79 CGMA, *Minutes* (1963), 22.

80 Moses, Diary, October 5 and October 10, 1963.

81 Moses, Diaries, 1963-1965; Moses, Diary, December 7, 1965.

82 Moses, Diary, March 1, 21-22, and August 1, 1966.

83 CGMA, *Minutes* (1966), 23, 18, 22, 30.

84 "Sixtieth Annual Assembly," *GH* 26, no. 9 (September 1966): 3.

85 Petree, "National Youth Events: 65-66," *GH* 27, no. 9 (September 1966): 8.

86 Gibson, "Department of Evangelism and Home Missions," *GH* 13, no. 6 (February 1955): 1.

87 CGMA, *Minutes* (1958), 19.

88 CGMA, *Minutes* (1963), 40.

89 CGMA, *Minutes* (1960), 24.

90 CGMA, *Minutes* (1961), 31; CGMA, *Minutes* (1962), 23, 31.

91 CGMA, *Minutes* (1961), 22, 31; CGMA, *Minutes* (1962), 31; Emma V. Brewer, "Sandusky, Ohio," *GH* 21, no. 9 (September 1961): 4.

92 Bobby H. Wilson, by author, Lakeland, FL, November 19, 2020.

93 CGMA, *Minutes* (1961), 31; "The Seven Hills Church of God," *GH* 34, no. 11 (November 1973): 7-8. The Norwood church organized on Montgomery Street later moved to Hopkins Avenue.

94 CGMA, *Minutes* (1962), 22.

95 CGMA, *Minutes* (1964), 23; CGMA, *Minutes* (1966), 23.

96 CGMA, *Minutes* (1963), 27; CGMA, *Minutes* (1964), 28-29; CGMA, *Minutes* (1965), 33; CGMA, *Minutes* (1966), 30.

97 CGMA, *Minutes* (1963), 20, 27; C.L. Weaver, "Indiana Youth Meeting," and [C.B. Ellis], "New Church in Kokomo, Indiana," *GH* 22, no. 10 (October 1962): 4, 7.

98 CGMA, *Minutes* (1963), 20, 27.

99 George Wood, "Tent Revival," *GH* 23, no. 11 (November 1963): 3.

100 Arlie Petree, "Just Two Years Old," 24, no. 10 (October 1964): 10.

101 Lida Creekmore, "New Church in Milford," *GH* 23, no. 5 (May 1963): 4; CGMA, *Minutes* (1963), 20, 27.

102 CGMA, *Minutes* (1967), 21, 50; CGMA, *[Minutes of the] Church of God Mountain Assembly Incorporated: Sixty-Third Annual Assembly* (Jellico, TN: Church of God Mountain Assembly, 1969), 20, 54.

103 Clarence Gibson, "Williamsburg Tent Revival," *GH* 23, no. 8 (August 1963): 6; Leon Petree, "The National Youth Director Reports," *GH* 24, no. 3 (March 1964): 5; "New Church Organized," *GH* 23, no. 9 (September 1963): 3; Ira Moses, Diary, September 1, 1963.

104 Moses, Diaries, 1964-1965.

105 CGMA, *Minutes* (1966), 30.

106 C.B. Ellis, "From the Assistant General Overseer's Desk," *GH* 25, no. 5 (May 1964): 2; CGMA, *Minutes* (1964), 29.

107 [photo captions], *GH* 22, no. 11 (November 1962): 3,4.

108 Twana Farmer, "West Middleton, Indiana," *GH* 27, no. 11 (November 1966): 5.

109 Moses, Diary, August 9, 1960.

110 CGMA, *Minutes* (1966), 19.

111 Moses, Diary, August 17, 1966; Minutes of the Middlesboro Church of God Mountain Assembly: Book Two, 1946-1969, Middlesboro, Kentucky, 231.

112 Moses, Diary, September 8-10, 1966.

113 Moses, Diary, September 12 and October 4, 1964; CGMA, *Minutes* (1965), 20; Moses, Diary, October 9, 1965.

114 Charles H. Davis, "Wytheville, Virginia," *GH* 26, no. 10 (October 1966): 7.

115 James E. Prewitt, "Spotlight on Belle Vernon, Pennsylvania," *GH* 28, no. 2 (February 1967): 10; CGMA, *Minutes* (1965), 39; CGMA, *Minutes* (1967), 21.

116 Moses, Diary, March 2-3, 1967.

117 CGMA, *Minutes* (1966), 9.

118 CGMA Missions, *I Have Set Before Thee An Open Door… Into All the World: A Brief History of CGMA Missions* (Jellico, TN: CGMA, 2017), 3; James E. Prewitt, personal conversations with the author, ca. 1995.

119 "Missionary Outreach – Chicago, Ill. Church," *GH* 28, no. 10 (October 1967): 7.

120 Illinois, U.S., Federal Naturalization Records, 1856-1991, s.v. "Ronald Amos" and "Mavis Amos," Ancestry.com; Ron Amos, "Ronald's Testimony," and Mavis Amos, "Sister Amos' Testimony," *GH* 28, no. 11 (November 1967): 11.

121 Now, Nazarene Theological College in Thornlands, Queensland.

122 Amos, 11; CGMA, *Minutes* (1967), 22.

123 CGMA, *Minutes* (1967), 23-24.

124 "Mission Rally," *GH* 28, no. 9 (September 1967): 5.

125 James E. Prewitt, "Keep the Church Alive and Double in Five," *GH* 28, no. 10 (October 1967): 4.

126 Prewitt, "One Double Already Realized," *GH* 29, no. 4 (April 1968): 4.

127 CGMA, *Minutes* (1967), 35; Church of God Mountain Assembly, *Annual Minutes of the Church of God Mountain Assembly, Inc.* (Jellico, TN: Church of God Mountain Assembly, 1968), 34.

128 James Walden, Jr., "From the Desk of the Chairman of the Y.W.C. Board," *GH* 29, no. 1 (January 1968): 5.

129 Prewitt, "One Double," 4; "Our Missionaries in Brazil," *GH* 29, no. 5 (May 1968): 2; Ronald Amos, "Sao Paulo, Brazil," *GH* 29, no. 7 (July 1968): 8.

130 Ronald Amos, "1st Anniversary: Let's Go up and Possess the Land… Brazil," *GH* 30, no. 4 (April 1969): 3.

131 Ronald Amos, "By My Spirit," *GH* 30, no. 2 (February 1969): 3.

132 CGMA, *Minutes* (1968), 34; CGMA, *Minutes* (1969), 39.

133 Amos, "1st Anniversary," 3.

134 Ronald Amos, "The World For Christ Missionary," *GH* 30, no. 6 (June 1969): 8.

135 Prewitt, "Mission Report," and Ronald Amos, "Itumbiara, Brasil," *GH* 30, no. 10 (October 1969): 4, 6-7.

136 Gene Ed Douglas, "A Burden for the Lost and Hungry," *GH* 37, no. 7 (July 1970): 9; Juanita Lambert, "Goshen Report" and Jessie Lyke, "The East Side Church of God, Inc.," *GH* 37, no. 8 (August 1970): 5, 8; Samantha Gibson, "Homecoming," *GH* 37, no. 10 (October 1970): 5.

137 CGMA, *Minutes* (1970), 27.

138 C.B. Ellis, Jr., *GH* 32, no. 1 (January 1971): 3; CGMA Missions, *Open Door*, 5.

139 CGMA, *Minutes* (1969), 38; CGMA, *Minutes* (1970), 36; CGMA, *Minutes* (1971), 39; CGMA, *Minutes* (1972), 40).

140 Gibson, *History* (1970), 89.

141 Betty Needham, "Dayton, Ohio," *GH* 29, no. 2 (February 1968): 7.

142 Prewitt, "Keep the Church Alive and Double in Five," *GH* 28, no. 11 (November 1967): 4.

143 Marie Wilson, "Dayton, Ohio," *GH* 29, no. 2 (February 1968): 5; Prewitt, "Thank You," *GH* 29, no. 4 (April 1968): 4.

144 Prewitt, "Evangelism Department," *GH* 29, no. 6 (June 1968): 2.

145 "Revival Booms at Floral Ave., Norwood, Ohio," *GH* 30, no. 7 (July 1969): 5; CGMA, *Minutes* (1969), 21.

146 CGMA, *Minutes* (1969), 23; Prewitt, "Mission Report," 4.

147 CGMA, *Minutes* (1964), 22-23; CGMA, *Minutes* (1965), 37. The 1964 minutes record that Willie Lee Partin, Bobby Wilson, Willis Yeary, J.B. Hammitte, and James Walden, Sr. were the five non-Elders elected to the committee. The next three minute books list the five who are named in the text. The author knows no way to reconcile this discrepancy.

148 CGMA, *Minutes* (1965), 21; CGMA, *Minutes* (1966), 21.

149 Ibid.

150 CGMA, *Minutes* (1966), 23.

151 J.E. Hatfield, "Reminiscing and Au Revoir," *GH* 28, no. 9 (September 1967): 12; CGMA, *Minutes* (1967), 24.

152 *GH* 29, no. 2 (February 1968): 2; CGMA, *Minutes* (1968), 20.

153 "Ministers Urged to Report," *GH* 29, no. 4 (April 1968): 2.

154 CGMA, *Minutes* (1969), 22-23; James L. Cox, Jr., personal conversations with the author.

155 Ira Moses, Diary, January 6 through 8, and April 5, 1970. Davis was asked to appear before the Board of Twelve Elders at its regular meeting on April 2, 1970. Instead, he sent a letter resigning from the Board of Trustees, as Public Relations Director, and as an ordained minister.

156 CGMA, *Minutes* (1970), 20.

157 Gibson, *History* (1970), 99.

158 CGMA, *Minutes* (1969), 21-24.

159 Conn, 315-316.

160 Ira Moses, Diary, August 13, 1968.

161 CGMA, *Minutes* (1969), 23-24.

162 CGMA, *Minutes* (1966), notes in the personal copy of Wade M. Hughes, in possession of the author.

163 CGMA, *Minutes* (1970), 22.

164 CGMA, *Minutes* (1974), 17. The Assembly voted in 1973 to dispense with the annual printing of a minute book and as a result, none was produced that year. In 1974, it rescinded this move and returned to its annual printing. As the 1974 minutes do not include reference to the adoption of this resolution, it is inferred that it was adopted in 1973.

165 Ibid., 9. See comment in previous note.

166 Ibid., 17, 26.

167 Church of God Mountain Assembly, *Minutes [of the] Church of God Mountain Assembly, Inc.* (Jellico, TN: CGMA, 1975), 10, 27.

168 Ira Moses, Diary, August 15, 1975.

169 Church of God Mountain Assembly, *Minutes [of the] Church of God Mountain Assembly, Inc.* (Jellico, TN: CGMA, 1976), 29; Ira Moses, Personal Diary, August 12-13, 1976.

170 Ira Moses, Diary, April 6-7 and August 8, 1972.

171 CGMA, *Minutes* (1972), 20.

172 CGMA, *Minutes* (1974), 21.

173 CGMA, *Minutes* (1976), 23.

174 Ibid., 30.

175 Church of God Mountain Assembly, *Minutes [of the] Church of God Mountain Assembly, Inc.* (Jellico, TN: CGMA, 1977), 21.

176 Church of God Mountain Assembly, *Minutes of the Church of God Mountain Assembly, Inc.* (Jellico, TN: CGMA, 1978), 21-22.

177 Church of God Mountain Assembly, *Minutes of the Church of God Mountain Assembly, Inc.* (Jellico, TN: CGMA, 1979), 20.

178 Church of God Mountain Assembly, *Minutes of the Church of God Mountain Assembly, Inc.* (Jellico, TN: CGMA, 1980), 21.

179 J.E. Prewitt, "In Appreciation of Their Many Years of Service: Rev. C.B. Ellis and Family," *GH* 34, no. 9 (September 1973): 3; CGMA, *Minutes* (1918), 3; CGMA, *Minutes* (1925), 6; CGMA, *Minutes* (1928), 11; CGMA, *Minutes* (1932); U.S., World War II Draft Cards Young Men, 1940-1947 s.v. "Claiborn Ellis," and U.S., Department of Veterans Affairs BIRLS Death File, 1850-2010 s.v. "Claiborn Ellis," Ancestry.com; Middlesboro Minutes, 46.

180 Prewitt, "Appreciation: Ellis," 3.

181 U.S., Social Security Applications and Claims Index, 1936-2007 s.v. "James Earl Prewitt," Ancestry.com; CGMA, *Minutes* (1919), 3; CGMA, *Minutes* (1933), 5; CGMA, *Minutes* (1934), 7; CGMA, *Minutes* (1935), 14; CGMA, *Minutes* (1936), 15; CGMA,

Minutes (1937), 17; Vonda Prewitt Morris, Facebook messages to the author, December 30, 2020.

[182] U.S., Department of Veterans Affairs BIRLS Death File, 1850-2010 s.v. "James Prewitt," Ancestry.com; Vonda Prewitt Morris, Facebook message with the author, December 30, 2020; Homer Prewitt, "Junction St. Church," *GH* 16, no. 5 (February 1958): 10; Homer Prewitt, "Detroit (Junction St.)," *GH* 16, no. 8 (May 1958): 10; Shirley Ann Woods, "Nevada, Indiana," *GH* 16, no. 11 (August 1958): 9; Wade M. Hughes, "National Youth Rally," *GH* 16, no. 15 (December 1958): 6.

[183] Funeral Obituary of Rev. Glenn Rowe in the possession of the author; CGOMA, *Minutes* (1948), 2; CGMA, *Minutes* (1951), 20; Ira Moses, Diary, August 20 and September 3, 1960; Joyce Carter, "Sidney, Ohio," *GH* 26, no. 8 (August 1966): 7; Minutes of the Middlesboro Church of God Mountain Assembly: Book Three, 1970-1987, Middlesboro, Kentucky, [June 3, 1972]; CGMA, *Minutes* (1972), 20.

[184] Padgett, *Heritage*, 89; Kevin Walden, Facebook message to the author, January 6, 2021; A.W. Reeves, "Church of God W. Cleveland Has Successful Revival," *GH* 14, no. 7 (March 1956): 3; "Cleveland, Ohio Aspinwall Church of God," *GH* 25, no. 7 (July 1965): 4; Jeannette Cacic, "News Flash," *GH* 25, no. 5 (May 1965): 10; CGMA, *Minutes* (1974), 21.

[185] Kenneth E. Massingill, Facebook message to the author, December 30, 2020;. Massingill, interview by author, Jellico, Tennessee, April 23, 2008; CGMA, *Minutes* (1960), 37.

[186] Gibson, *History*, 85; "Wedding," *GH* 23, no. 6 (June 1963): 3; Jasper Walden, "Kokomo Church in New Location," *GH* 25, no. 3 (March 1965): 6; "National Youth Camp," *GH* 26, no. 4 (April 1966): 8; Leon Petree, "National Youth Events," *GH* 26, no. 9 (September 1966): 8; Leon Petree, "1967 National Youth Camp," *GH* 28, no. 7 (July 1967): 4; CGMA, *Minutes* (1968), 21; Jasper Walden, "Report from National Youth and Sunday School Director," *GH* 33, no. 3 (March 1972): 10.

[187] [James L. Cox, Sr.], "Meet Our National Youth Secretary and Treasurer," *GH* 35, no. 5 (Mary 1969): 4; Michael Padgett, "In Loving Memory of Rev. James L. Cox, Jr.," *GH* 79, no. 8 (August 2020): 3; Wade M. Hughes, "Let's Get Acquainted," *GH* 28, no. 10 (October 1967): 11.

[188] Ira Moses, Diary, July 14 and 17, 1973; March 6, 15-16, 27-29, 1979.

[189] Ira Moses, Diary, November 26 and December 6, 1978.

11

Fruit That Remains

In the decade and a half that followed Ira Moses's tenure as General Overseer, the Mountain Assembly recovered from its aborted mission in Brazil to establish a permanent presence in the Caribbean. After the first national youth camp on property owned by the organization, the National Youth Directors further developed the property and expanded the program of the Youth Warriors for Christ. The creation of Public Relations Director in 1969 gave the Mountain Assembly seven elected general officials in addition to the various committees and boards. Within the next ten years, the General Council authorized the creatio.n of seven more offices to expand its centralized polity to highest number. As the new office of National Sunday School Superintendent metamorphosed into the National Christian Education Director, K-12 Christian Schools were founded across the organization, and the General Council imposed new educational standards upon candidates for ordination. All these measures made lasting impacts on the organization and formed the core of the modern CGMA.

In the Isles of the Seas

Although several Mountain Assembly congregations sponsored the missionary activity of Walter Vaughn to the Bahamas in 1968, nothing lasting materialized from it for CGMA Missions.[1] Six months after C.B. Ellis replaced J.E. Prewitt as Assistant Overseer, he traveled to Jamaica with a ministry acquaintance. Euliss Jasper "Jack" Cates, Jr. was born on September 10, 1922 in Haw River, North Carolina. In the late 1950s, Cates began preaching missionary crusades in Jamaica, and he invited Ellis to accompany him on one such trip in February 1971.[2] The Assistant General Overseer conducted "a few services there" and saw more than 70 "accept Christ." On this trip, Cates introduced Ellis to Elder M. Blair who pastored a New Testament Church of God (NTCG) in the village of Kinloss in Trelawny Parish.[3] The Church of God (Cleveland) organized the indigenous NTCG after J.S. Llewellyn traveled to the island in April 1918 in response to a petition from a Pentecostal preacher in Kingston, J. Wilson Bell. From the church Llewellyn organized in Kingston and five "preaching stations" he planted sprang a network of 53 churches by 1935.⁴ Ellis reported that God was "opening doors," and appointed Cates to serve as Island Overseer. CGMA Missions began supporting Cates, Blair, and his sons financially.⁵

Figure 11.1: Jack Cates
c/o *The Gospel Herald*

Figure 11.2: Elder M. Blair
c/o *The Gospel Herald*

Ellis returned to Jamaica three months later accompanied by Sidney Pastor Glenn Rowe. On this trip, Blair introduced the ministers to Ellis Vernon, who was affiliated with the Church of the Living God, the Pillar and Ground of Truth (CLGPGT). This church was organized by Mary Magdalena Lewis Tate in Greenville, Alabama in 1903.⁶ Ellis and Rowe distributed clothing, held outdoor services, and began construction on a "bamboo pole church" at Salt Spring in Hanover Parish, and persuaded Vernon to assume the pastorate there.⁷ Blair also introduced Ellis and Rowe to Pastor Sidney Innis and Deacon Stedman Barton who had a wood-framed church building at nearby Cousins Cove. Ellis negotiated the purchase of an adjacent lot with a house on it from Delbert Blair for $1,200.⁸ Barton, who later began to preach and to pastor, made such an impression on Rowe that he financially supported the Jamaican monthly for more than 25 years.⁹

Ellis returned to the United States and immediately began holding mission rallies to raise financial support for the new works. General Overseer Ira Moses, National Youth Director Jasper Walden, District Overseer James Cox, Sr., and Local Pastor Bobby Wilson planned and promoted the first one in Jellico. With preaching from Moses, Rowe, Goshen Pastor James Earl McKinney, Monroe Pastor Fred Cornelius, and Detroit Pastor Ottis Ellis, the rally attracted visitors from five states. The highlight of the week was the film footage Rowe shot on the trip which "gave everyone a visual challenge for promoting Missions."[10] In July, Ellis sent National Youth Secretary James Cox, Jr. to preach three nights at Ages and promote a district mission rally there the following two nights. The rally featured preaching from Ellis and Middlesboro District Overseer Willie Lee Partin and a slide show from Ellis's most recent trip to Jamaica and generated much "enthusiasm" for worldwide evangelism, especially in the heart of Harlan District Overseer Kenneth Massingill. The Kenvir pastor felt God's call to be a missionary when he was a teenager and began preaching while stationed in Germany in the late 1950s. After the rally, Massingill began preparing for a trip to Jamaica.[11]

At the General Assembly the following month, the church in Kinloss was officially recognized by the CGMA, and Cates reported on the progress of the work in Jamaica. Ellis recognized Cates, Massingill, and James Walden, Jr. as "men who have been or soon will be in the mission field."[12] Walden was accompanied to the convention that year by Thakkal V. Zachariah of India. Zachariah's uncle, Madappallil S. Skariah, had immigrated from Raipur in Madhya Pradesh, India, began attending the Antioch CGMA in Chicago where Walden pastored, and became a licensed minister in 1970.[13] With his uncle's encouragement, Zachariah had written to Walden about the possibility of attending Chicago Bible College. When Walden agreed to be his sponsor in the United States, he picked Zachariah up at the airport on January 10, 1971, and forged a lifetime friendship. When the pastor planned a trip to India that November, Zachariah arranged for him to preach in several churches including one pastored by his brother, K.V. Varughese, and another uncle, P.S. Samuel. Walden's trip to India ignited a passion for the nation that

Figure 11.3: James Walden, Jr.
c/o Jon Walden

Figure 11.4: James Walden, Jr.
c/o Jon Walden

never exhausted, and he spent the rest of his pastoral ministry investing in evangelism, benevolence, and ministerial training on the subcontinent. When Zachariah graduated from bible college in 1973, Walden offered to support his ministry financially upon his return to India. Instead, Zachariah chose to remain in the United States where his income from employment could sponsor "ten pastors" back home.[14]

Figure 11.5: Jerome, James, & Jasper Walden

c/o Jasper Walden

Walden had hardly returned from his first mission trip before his second was being promoted. He and his brothers planned a convention in Jamaica after the beginning of the year and Ellis recruited volunteers to join them on "The 5 Js Crusade: Jerome, James, and Jasper in Jamaica for Jesus." Joining them on the trip were R.N. Ballinger of Goshen, Cecil Johnson of Fonde, and George Wood of Muncie. From Jamaica, Ellis and Wood traveled on to Haiti to visit an orphanage there.[15] While visiting the work at Salt Spring, James Walden was grieved when no one in the community seemed to have any clothes. He felt like God told him to do something about that. In October, his church in Chicago filled five barrels with clothing to ship to the island. The *Christmas in October* tradition continued when Walden later moved to Cleveland

Figure 11.6: Myrlene & James Walden
c/o Jon Walden

and eventually grew into a joint venture of CGMA churches to send a shipping container to a different nation each year with scores of barrels filled with clothing, food, and other essentials.[16]

As the Walden expedition was arriving in Jamaica, Kenneth and Linda Massingill were returning home from the island. Their church in Kenvir sponsored the visit that had been burning in the pastor's heart since the spring. In the fall of 1971, Elder Blair and two of his sons visited the United States and preached in some of the Mountain Assembly churches to raise awareness and funds for the work in Jamaica. Their visit to the Bethel Tabernacle Church in Kokomo stirred the people to sponsor the purchase of a small van for ministry use on the island.[17] Perhaps, it was their visit to Southeastern Kentucky, though, that had the most significant impact on the future of CGMA Missions. The Massingills stayed with the Blairs on their visit to Jamaica in January 1972 and visited the fledgling churches. One day, while passing "a little house beside the sea" at Lucea, Kenneth asked his wife how she would like to live there. Linda assured him there was nothing wrong with the parsonage in Kenvir. Nevertheless, her initial reluctance would ultimately be replaced by the surety of God's call.[18]

Ellis brought the Blairs to the United States in August 1972 to preach in some of the churches and to attend the General Assembly. Assistant General Secretary & Treasurer James Cox kept them in his home during much of their stay, which included a revival at his church in Mountain Ash, Kentucky. During the annual convention in Jellico, they experienced great exultation. The brothers testified at the sisters' service on Tuesday afternoon. Harold and Nev Blair sang on Tuesday night. Their talent and reggae style music entranced the congregation so much so that they were asked to sing again in the services on Wednesday afternoon and Wednesday night. At the Thursday night mission service, the boys sang again, Harold gave his testimony, and "Daddy" Blair brought the evening message, "The Call That Made Me a Heavenly Citizen." They sang again at the final service on Saturday night.[19] That enthusiasm soon faded after a cultural misunderstanding.

On Tuesday, August 8, 1972, C.B. Ellis was elected to succeed Ira Moses as General Overseer. The General Council chose Middlesboro Pastor Glenn Rowe to assist Ellis and to direct the mission program. The following day, the Assembly officially recognized two more churches in Jamaica. Cates had started these churches in the late fall at Dias and Blenheim in Hanover Parish and installed Alphae Hibbert as their pastor.[20] Without Jack Cates and Elder Blair, CGMA Missions in Jamaica would not have materialized. Blair had been accustomed to receiving free will offerings in the churches where he ministered. Since his sons sang, testified, and conducted the altar service and he preached, he felt like he was entitled to the $1,400 offering that was received on Mission night. To no avail, Rowe tried to explain that the department's policy had been to divide that offering between home and foreign missions to accommodate the budget of multiple works. When he and Ellis visited Jamaica in October, he discovered that Blair had "dropped out of the mission work for the Church of God, Mt. Assembly in Jamaica." Despite the setback, Rowe was "not disturbed about our foreign work." When he saw the "beautiful spot of land" that a member from Blenheim had donated for the construction of another church, he was as excited as was Pastor Hibbert.[21]

Figure 11.7: Glenn Rowe at Salt Springs

c/o Leatha Rowe

Despite the remaining Jamaican pastors' satisfaction with CGMA missions and "prospects of another church building in a very remote section of the Island" in the spring of 1973, the leadership vacuum in Jamaica caused by the desertion of Blair and Cates was plain for Rowe to see. "What we really need," he wrote in April, "is someone to go to Jamaica and take care of the work." Cognizant of how many felt about the Brazil experiment a few years earlier, Rowe emphasized the importance of finding a "member long enough in the organization to understand its doctrine and teachings that they may be able to teach others."[22] He returned to Jamaica in May with Massingill and another Kenvir member, Roscoe Bray. Rowe's former church at Sidney, now pastored by Merle Laws, had raised $500 to build a church at Moreland Hill in Westmoreland Parish. Those who attended the "open air meetings" were "thrilled" at having the first full-gospel church in the area. Massingill's excitement over the 32 who were saved in the services at Moreland Hill and the 2 ½ hour baptismal service at Salt Spring brought him home singing the Jamaican chorus, "Something Got Hold of Me."[23] Something had. The teenage call to be a missionary and the pressing need for leadership in Jamaica were stirring the pastor to prepare for a considerable change.

In January, Massingill drove his father, Claude, to meet Rowe, who was returning to Jamaica accompanied by Cecil Johnson and Jellico Pastor Bobby Wilson. On this trip, construction began on a new "headquarters" building at the Cousins Cove property. The ministers also preached five nights and saw 122 souls saved.[24] That spring, Claude Massingill resigned his pastorate at Troy, Ohio and relocated to Tazewell, Tennessee. On May 13, Claude and Ken Massingill, with Glenn and Leatha Rowe, returned to Jamaica. Two days later, Ken learned by telegram that his son, Terry, was born the day he left. While in Jamaica, Ken calculated the "approximate cost of living," compared the costs of "importing [an] automobile and furniture" with purchasing them locally, and inspected schools. He met with the Jamaican pastors and attended various services, including one in the building at Moreland Hills where he had preached in the open air just one year earlier.[25]

Despite his pastoral success at Kenvir, including a "record" attendance on Easter Sunday 1974, Massingill was committed to relocation to the Caribbean. He declined to run for pastor in June, and the church chose Homer Prewitt to succeed him there.[26] At the 68th General Assembly in August, Glenn Rowe declined the nomination for reelection for Assistant General Overseer, and the General Council chose Jerome Walden to replace him. Walden, the fourth Missions Director in seven years, conducted a Mission Board meeting the following day. The board "voted unanimously" to allow Massingill to represent CGMA Missions in Jamaica and discussed the need for an overseer there to act as a liaison between headquarters and the indigenous pastors and churches. On Thursday, August 15, 1974, the board recommended to the General Council the creation of the office of "Island Overseer of the West Indies." After the measure was adopted, Massingill volunteered, and the delegates voted to send him to Jamaica in that capacity "for the next two years."[27] Later that month, he met with the new Missions Director and "discussed [the] progress of plans for Jamaica."[28]

Before Massingill could complete the necessary preparations for his move to Jamaica, he and Rowe met with Walden at headquarters on September 10 and received a call from the island informing them that Pastor Sidney Innis, who had been acting as overseer, passed away the previous day. Walden requested that Massingill and Rowe represent CGMA Missions at the funeral, and the two left the following morning for Jamaica. In addition to calling on Innis's family at home and expressing condolences at the funeral service, Massingill drove across the island "through rugged mountains" to the nation's capital. In Kingston, he visited the Minister of Labor and Minister of Trade about work permits and the importation of an automobile. He also visited the Jamaican pastors, Ellis Vernon, Stedman Barton, Rupert Ricketts, and Alphae Hibbert, and gave them financial support from headquarters. The overseer met with Hibbert about his resignation at Dias and investigated "a promising work" he had begun at Savana-La-Mar in Westmoreland Parish.[29]

On Tuesday, October 15, 1974, Massingill spent the night with his parents in Tazewell. The following morning, he and Linda left their three oldest children, Angelia, Kenny, and Dale, and started to Florida with their three youngest, Richard, Tammy, and Terry. The internal conflict surrounding leaving behind some of his children was resolved by three considerations. First, an adequate high school education in a foreign country was "not favorable." Second, Helen Massingill insisted on keeping her grandchildren and lobbied for her son to leave all six with her, including the five-month-old baby. The unique circumstances surrounding Angelia's birth provided a final rationale. His first child was born nine months after Massingill left the United States for Germany, and he did not see her until he returned two years later. The proud veteran had no regrets for the service he had rendered to his nation and reasoned that, if he could make such a sacrifice for his country, he could do it for the Lord.[30]

On Tuesday, October 22, the Massingill family arrived in Montego Bay in the afternoon and checked into a local motel in the heavy rains. The following day, Ken went to Cousins Cove to "check on the house" that had been purchased by Ellis and CGMA Missions three years earlier and discovered that the house had been relocated to another lot. Upon learning that the sales contract only included the purchase of the land, Massingill agreed to rent the house for $50 per month and planned to build

Figure 11.8: The Massingill Family
c/o K.E. Massingill

living quarters on the rear of the new church that was being constructed. That Friday, he picked up his familial belongings that had been shipped to Montego Bay, checked out of the motel, and moved his family into their home at Cousins Cove. Over the next week, the Island Overseer "registered Ricky in school," met with all the Jamaican ministers, and attended services at "Cove," Moreland Hills, Salt Spring, and Savanna-La-Mar. By Christmas, he had visited all six churches on a Sunday, in addition to numerous services throughout the week. Many weekday hours were spent building the church and his living quarters at Cove. In addition to frequent trips to the Lucea, the parish capital, several to Montego Bay, and one trip to the nation's capital, Massingill experienced delays connecting the water service at Cove and was never able to obtain a work permit. As a result, the Jamaican government allowed him to stay only six months at a time. Transportation woes also caused setbacks. Despite a "blowout" returning from "MoBay," pushing a motorcycle three miles home when he ran out of gas, and using a flashlight to guide his motorcycle ride coming home from Dias one night, Massingill persevered.[31]

Massingill felt his mission was "to work with the Jamaicans to spread the Gospel, to build churches, and to establish" the Mountain Assembly's presence in the island. He wasted no time serving in the capacity of an administrative bishop in the West Indies. One week after his arrival, Hibbert introduced him to Cutbert Kinglock who pastored in a 20 x 30 feet concrete building with electric lights at Delveland in Westmoreland Parish. A casual conversation with Kinglock about "coming into our fellowship seemed very favorable." An even "more fruitful visit" six weeks later featured "more complete arrangements for him to come into our body with the church." After preaching at Delveland the first time on December 15, Massingill received the minister and congregation into CGMA Missions in February. The Overseer also helped Hibbert with the rental of a building in Savanna-La-Mar and assisted Vernon with the signing of a new lease on the building at Salt Spring. At Salt Spring, he "had a ministers conference" and "discussed building plans, financial plans for the church," and showed the ministers how to use the "report blanks." To aid the ministers in their understanding of the teachings of the church, he "published 65 pieces of literature" on the subject. In November, Massingill also conferred with two of the ministers about issues raised in their churches and appointed "Buck" Buchanan to take care of the church at Moreland Hills for three months.[32]

At Cove, Massingill helped organize a YWC service and conducted a membership meeting where he discussed the church covenant and faithful stewardship. After completing the building, and "putting temporary seats in the new church" on December 21, the congregation sang choruses, read scripture, and had prayer in the new structure. At 4:00 the following morning the "first service in the new church" featured several addresses from the ministers present. The old building was dismantled at the end of the month.[33] The Island Overseer began reporting to *The Gospel Herald* to inform members of the progress of the mission work.[34] He also regularly corresponded with churches, family, and friends in the United States, including the Assistant General Overseer & Missions Director who sent $360 ($400 less tithes) each month to Massingill.[35] As the year, and his first two months, in Jamaica came to a close, the missionary found consolation for the loneliness he felt over a "divided" family on Christmas with the "presence of God." After a "watch service" at Cove on New Years Eve, he was able to attest that 1974 had "been a wonderful year."

Massingill was refreshed in January like "a cold drink of water on a hot summer day" by a visit from Jerome Walden, Bobby Wilson, Lloyd Camp, and others.[36] When their visas expired in April, the Massingills were forced to return to the United States and used this time to visit churches, hold mission rallies, show slide presentations, and raise financial support for the work in Jamaica.[37] Massingill returned to Jamaica for a week in May with James Earl McKinney and two men from the Goshen church.[38] Short-term mission trips such as this one, along with mission rallies in the districts, generated much enthusiasm in the Mountain Assembly churches and inspired members to give liberally. Having already returned to the island before the General Assembly, the Island Overseer's report was given by the Assistant Overseer. Linda Massingill, however, attended the missions' night service and "gave a moving testimony of the work and the need in the Isle of Jamaica" before a $ 3,700 offering was received. One of the needs that had been proposed for months was the construction of an orphanage at Cousins Cove to house and educate Jamaican youths, and the following morning, the General Council authorized the building of a children's home in Jamaica."[39]

In September, Walden and 20 others returned to Jamaica to host the first Jamaican CGMA Convention at Cousins Cove and to inspect the completed construction of the children's home. The group included CGMA Ministers Jasper Walden, James Walden, Jr., Donnie Hill, James Justice, Clayton Lawson, J.E. Lay, Roger Walden, and Elston Vaught, who assisted by preaching and teaching during the conference. By this time, the work in Jamaica included nine churches. Rupert Ricketts introduced Massingill to Eric Palmer who pastored an independent church at Grange Hill in Westmoreland Parish. Through Palmer, Massingill got acquainted with Sterling Nesbeth and another independent congregation at Riverside in Hanover Parish. Massingill also met William Pusey who pastored at Stonehenge in St. James Parish. By September, all three ministers and their churches had joined the CGMA. Once the construction of the orphanage was completed and the home was furnished, Massingill appointed 21-year-old Cleveland Walcott to oversee the facility which housed ten 6-10-year-old boys at its peak. The first of these, 9-year-old Kanhai "Conroy" Adams, had been raised at Darliston by his grandmother who attended Pusey's church. His father was dead, and his mother's whereabouts were unknown. For about $15 per month, CGMA Missions was able to house, feed, educate, and disciple the children until they finished high school.[40]

Figure 11.9: Cleveland Walcott
c/o K.E. Massingill

Figure 11.10: Conroy Adams
c/o K.E. Massingill

Massingill returned to the United States to attend the 70th General Assembly. Term limitations brought C.B. Ellis's tenure as General Overseer to an end on August 10, 1976, and the General Council elected Jerome Walden to replace him.[41] Those who had developed a deep passion for foreign missions faced the vacancy in the office of Assistant General Overseer & Missions Director with much apprehension. Some saw the "mission field" as "everywhere we look" and emphasized their own "back yard" over Christ's commission to go into all the world.[42] There was also concern that the foreign mission program might suffer from a job seeker elected by the

General Council because of his popularity. Indeed, Clayton Lawson made no secret his aspirations to return to office. In 1972, the former Overseer ran unsuccessfully for General Overseer and Assistant Overseer.[43] Two years later, Lawson was elected as General Secretary & Treasurer, when term limitations forced the retirement of J.E. Hatfield after 34 years in that position.[44] Despite his many gifts, accounting was not one of them, and Lawson's tenure as Treasurer was a disaster. To complete reports, he relied on James L. Cox, Jr., who worked part-time in the office while finishing his bachelor's degree at Cumberland College. Lawson ran unsuccessfully again for General Overseer in 1976 and was nominated for Assistant General Overseer.[45]

When Kenneth Massingill moved his family to Jamaica in 1974, he anticipated living there the rest of his life. Concern over the potential direction of the missions program under new leadership prompted him to leave his name in consideration for the office when he was nominated for Assistant General Overseer. After his election, the General Council discussed the office of West Indies Island Overseer and decided to allow the Executive Board to appoint Massingill's replacement. A new resolution approved at the end of the week, however, officially created the position to be appointed by the Mission Board. Despite its inclusion in the Standard Resolutions, no appointment was ever made, and the office was deleted the following year. Instead, Ellis Vernon was appointed as Overseer of Jamaica.[46]

Just before the General Assembly, Massingill made a visit to Haiti, and to the General Council, he "proposed to raise $ 25,000.00 during the coming year to start a medical clinic and feeding station" there.[47] Walden sent Massingill to Haiti to follow up on leads to two possible mission works in one of the poorest nations on earth. In the late 1940s, Doris Burke, a Jamaican emigrant opened an orphanage in Peguy-ville, Haiti. On one of several mission trips to Haiti in the 1960s, John Leslie Helman of Sidney, Ohio met Burke and began supporting the home financially and promoting it locally. Ozell Bunch, son of CGMA Elder Oscar Bunch, preached often at Sidney Full Gospel Church which were among the supporters of the home and informed his childhood friend, C.B. Ellis about the ministry there and the poor health of its founder. Ellis visited the home in 1971, but it was not until Burke died three years later that CGMA Missions got involved. After Burke's death, Sultane "Mammy Ge" Ganthier, who had been working with Burke, assumed the care of more than 20 children with her husband, Gerald "Pappy Ge," in their home. By that time, Helman's son, Richard, was serving on the board of a newly organized Christian school in Sidney and met Northtowne

CGMA Pastor Merle Laws when the latter offered the school the use of the church facilities. Laws relayed the needs of the Ganthiers to the CGMA Missions Director.[48]

In early 1974, Wayne and Sherry Jones invited a Haitian co-worker, Mona Cornet, to watch the film, "Thief in the Night," at the church they attended. Cornet was converted that night at Antioch CGMA in Chicago. She told Pastor James Walden, Jr. that she "wanted to go back home to tell my people about Jesus." Upon his advice, the young woman enrolled in Chicago Bible College that fall and began "studying God's word" for "training in order to minister effectively to the people in Haiti." Expecting her graduation the following year, the Missions Director commissioned Massingill to examine the feasibility of establishing a "Nutritional Center" in Port-au-Prince, where her parents owned a profitable hardware store.[49]

Figure 11.11: Mona Cornet
c/o The Gospel Herald

Figure 11.12: Nozor Augustin
c/o CGMA

In the nation's capital, Massingill met Isaiah and Nathan Dieudonne who pastored churches and operated a feeding ministry in the region. They helped guide Massingill on his visits to the nation and introduced him to Nozor Augustin, who desired to start a work in Croix-des-Bouquets but lacked the resources. Massingill also met Cornet and her parents. Ernie Ray, who assumed the pastorate at Antioch when James Walden returned Cleveland to succeed his older brother as pastor of Aspinwall CGMA, came to Haiti at the same time and preached in churches arranged by the Cornets. Massingill also met with James Walden and National Youth Director Donnie Hill, who had come to preach through contacts Cornet's family arranged.[50] By 1977, more than $ 16,000 had been raised by CGMA Missions and designated for work in Haiti.[51] Ultimately, the proposed commissioning of Cornet as a CGMA missionary never materialized, but early in Massingill's second term as Missions Director, the ministries of Augustin and Ganthier were recognized by CGMA Missions. Through the church and children's home in Peguyville, and the church, children's home, and food distribution ministry at Croix-des-Bouquets, the Mountain Assembly also added another four indigenous churches before the 1979 General Assembly. Augustin dedicated a new church and school on January 6, 1980, and by the General Assembly that year, Haiti had seven CGMA pastors and nine churches.[52]

While pastoring in the Chicago area for sixteen years, James Walden, Jr. encountered a wide variety of cultures and met numerous immigrants who presented possibilities for CGMA Missions. Walden sent the Amoses, immigrants from England, to Brazil. Cornet opened the door for Walden to preach in Haiti. Meeting Zachariah set in motion the pastor's first trip to India. His return to Cleveland neither smothered his evangelistic fire nor impeded his seeming knack for discovering opportunities. In 1976, a 76-year-old widow living in Vellore in the state of Tamil Nadu in India "received a call from God to serve Him." The husband of Mrs. Jessie Phillips "J.P." Strong had "passed away suddenly" and left her with "no one else to lean on." God revealed to her a purpose, and she "started an orphanage with a handful of children" in her own home and provided for them "with what little money" she "had managed to save." While she struggled to "carry on this work," her only daughter, Sheila Parker, was living in Cleveland, Ohio on Aspinwall Avenue. Pastor Walden visited his neighbors, witnessed to her family, and invited them to church. After learning about the struggling widow and the destitute orphans under her care, Walden began sending financial support to assist her. As funding increased, Strong received more children into the home and expanded its facilities.[53]

In January 1979, Walden and Massingill traveled to Vellore to inspect the home which now housed 32 children under the care of Strong and her helpers. CGMA Missions "officially endorsed Mrs. J.P. Strong as the representative of CGMA Missions for India and approved

Figure 11.13: Mrs. J.P. Strong
c/o Ion Walden

Figure 11.14: Sam Daniel
c/o CGMA

the operation of a children's home under her care." At the same time, a church and pastor, Arthur David, were received into the Assembly.[54] While sightseeing on a tour bus during a return visit to Vellore in October 1983, Walden got something in his eye and agonized in pain. The only person on the bus who spoke English was a Pentecostal preacher, Sam Daniel. Daniel took Walden to an ophthalmologist, and a lifetime friendship developed. Daniel began attending the General Assembly the following year and was recognized as a CGMA minister in 1985 with the two churches he pastored in the Vellore area.[55]

The expansion of CGMA Missions into Haiti and India was exciting, but Massingill's passion still lay in Jamaica. As Missions Director, he visited 50 churches per year, held mission rallies in the districts, showed slide presentations, and raised funds. Massingill also encouraged others to visit the mission field with him and continued the practice of the short-term mission trips. The Missions Director spent 67 days on the mission field during this third year in office, taking the trip to India, three trips to Haiti, and three more to Jamaica. One trip in December 1978 featured the distribution of 102 barrels of goods for the churches of Jamaica. Thirty-two others accompanied Massingill on mission trips, many making their first.[56] Two young women were especially impacted by the first trip they made to Jamaica in the 1970s.

While Massingill presented his slide show at a mission rally in Lake City, Tennessee in 1975, an overwhelming burden came upon 27-year-old Laura Taylor. After conferring with the Island Overseer, she learned her best opportunity for long-term mission work was to obtain a visa for education or medicine. Uninterested in becoming a teacher, Taylor pursued nursing. While she waited on acceptance into a crowded Licensed Practical Nursing (LPN) program at the local community college, she and her 8-year-old son traveled in a group with Massingill to Jamaica in February 1977. While visiting the churches, God confirmed her call to the island and its people. On June 12, she returned to conduct a week-long revival at Moreland Hill with her stepfather, Pastor Roger Powell, whose singing the Jamaicans especially enjoyed. That week, Vincent Cole, who pastored a small church at Petersfield in Westmoreland Parish, joined the Mountain Assembly. After Taylor started school, she and her son, John, made two more trips to the island during summer and Christmas breaks, preparing herself for a move to the island to provide support for the indigenous ministers of Jamaica and to assist in the boys' home at Cove.[57]

While Taylor made plans to relocate to Jamaica, Janey Hackler prepared herself for missionary work in Haiti. While "playing in the sand" as a small child in Jellico, Hackler first entertained the thought, "I would like to be a missionary" someday. She recalled that childhood desire when she took a short-term mission trip to Jamaica with others from her church led by Massingill, and the missionary impulse grew over the next few years. On Mission Night of the 1979 General Assembly, James Walden, Jr. preached from Mark 16:15 and emphasized that "the commission of GO is much greater than STAY." Massingill concluded the service by inviting those who "felt called to be missionaries" to come forward. Hackler did not go but admitted that she "should have." The next night, Floral Avenue Pastor James Bartee preached about being "totally committed," and she knew God was speaking to her. Not long after, her pastor, Ray Landes, spoke a word to her while she prayed in the altar that prompted her to announce that God had called her to Haiti. Hackler graduated with a B.S. in psychology from Cumberland College in 1974 and had a good job with the State of Tennessee, but she began preparing to leave it to relocate to the poorest nation on earth to teach English and the Bible to school children in Peguy-ville and Duval-Roche, where Augustin had just started another orphanage.[58]

Figure 11.15: Laura Taylor
c/o CGMA

Figure 11.16: Janey Hackler
c/o CGMA

Figure 11.17: Clayton Lawson
c/o CGMA

When the Mission Board met at the 74th General Assembly in August 1980, Taylor and Hackler appeared for approval and commissioning as missionaries in Jamaica and Haiti, respectively. Just days before, CGMA leadership underwent a radical transformation. Jerome Walden had been elected to pastor the church at Jellico as term limitations brought an end to his tenure as General Overseer. Many expected his assistant to succeed him as had been the case in three of the previous four such transitions. Instead, the General Council chose Clayton Lawson to begin a second tenure as General Overseer, 30 years after his first began.[59] At age 70, Lawson was the oldest man ever elected to the office of General Overseer.[60] Having reached his term limitation as Assistant General Overseer, Massingill turned his attention to home missions and planted a church in Corbin, Kentucky. To succeed him, the General Council elected James L. Cox, Jr. whose own term limitations brought an end to his tenure as General Secretary & Treasurer. Delegates then elected 76-year-old J.E. Hatfield to the office he previously held for more than three decades.[61]

As the new Missions Director, Cox oversaw the sending of Taylor and Hackler as the Mountain Assembly's third and fourth missionaries, respectively. Taylor moved to Jamaica with her husband, John Barton Taylor, and her son, John II, in January 1981, and stayed 18 months. While on the island, Taylor "helped a little" with the boys' home at Cove, attended services, and preached when she had the opportunity. She occasionally visited the church at Grange Hill and the Mint Road Basic School that Violet Palmer had started there in 1974. Long after her stay in Jamaica ended, Taylor continued to take short-term mission trips to the island, preaching and giving away clothes and food.[62]

On April 21, 1981, Cox, along with Glenn and Leatha Rowe, escorted Hackler to Haiti. Her first few days there were met with much loneliness, but God heard her prayer for companionship, and she met several Spirit-filled missionaries affiliated with Mission Possible. Although she minored in French at Jellico High School, Hackler found a challenge in mastering its Creole dialect in Haiti. On February 14, 1982, after ten months, Hackler "testified for the first time in Creole" in a church service near St. Marc. Pastor Augustin felt that teaching the Haitian children English would improve their chances for success and made it a top priority. Hackler experienced early frustrations with vocabulary and, later, still more with grammar.[63] Fanfan Janvier had been orphaned at the age of 6, and the teenager was determined to learn English. After Janvier was the only student who showed up for class during her first week commuting to Peguyville, Hackler decided instead to pay for his transportation and tuition and enrolled him in Christian school at Port-au-Prince. The investment paid in dividends. In 2006, Janvier opened Faith Academy in Lafferonney, and within 15 years, the school's enrollment grew to over 500 students.[64] After four years in the West Indies, Janey married another American missionary, Richard Donley. Donley had come to Haiti through Mission Possible and taught at the Christian school in Port-au-Prince. Not long after their first child was born in 1986, the Donleys briefly returned to the U.S. when local strife interrupted the operation of the school. When they returned to Haiti a few years later, they supported themselves through employment. By that time, many American and European churches and mission agencies had shifted their strategy from sending missionaries to utilizing and equipping indigenous ministers. The Mountain Assembly followed suit. The Donleys returned home for a final time in 1998 and settled in Jellico two years later.[65]

Cox promoted CGMA Missions outside the organization in a variety of ways. The service on Mission Night of the 75th General Assembly was video recorded and broadcast on local and Knoxville television stations. The following morning, the General Council voted to "look into participating in the World's Fair," scheduled to be held from May through October 1982. On March 10, the "Church of God Mountain Assembly officially became a part of the Association of Christian Denominations." The exhibit was an elaborate audio-visual presentation designed to demonstrate "The Church's Presence at the 1982 World's Fair."[66]

The publicity it generated along with the distribution of *The Gospel Herald* and the inclusion of CGMA Missions in various Pentecostal directories attracted the attention of numerous missionary works around the world. Many letters requesting support for indigenous ministries reached the Jellico headquarters. Overwhelmed with the oversight of the growing number of churches overseas, the support of two missionaries, and the constant pleas for help, the Missions Director lost sleep numerous nights worried about whether Hackler and Taylor had eaten that day when the program lacked sufficient funds. As a result, he chose not to follow up with many of the letters of solicitation. His successor would have to do it.[67]

By the time his tenure came to an end, Cox oversaw eleven churches in Jamaica, ten in Haiti, and one in India. Delegates to the 78th General Assembly elected Kenneth Massingill as General Overseer and Jasper Walden to replace Cox as Assistant General Overseer & Missions Director.[68] In his first year in office, Walden strengthened the existing works, but also began "forwarding the support of some of our folks that have a real burden for Africa to some real good relief organizations." These agencies included "Jimmy Swaggart Missions, World Vision, World Mission Press, Jerry Falwell Missions, New Tribes Missions," and Mission Aviation Fellowship. "Becoming well known to the great mission agencies all over the Christian world," led to further connections on the Dark Continent. By the following assembly, CGMA Missions had incorporated churches in Zambia under Peter Kiboko, in Malawi under Peter Sakwiya, in Nigeria under Job Ikemson, and in Liberia under Phillip Teah. With additional contacts in Zaire, Kenya, Tanzania, Ghana, and Cameroon, Walden predicted that CGMA Missions "could have an operation in half of the countries in Africa in the next five years."[69]

Although that goal was never realized, during Walden's four-year tenure as Missions Director, CGMA foreign missions grew to 27 churches in the West Indies islands, 14 on the Indian subcontinent, and 54 in African countries.[70] The incorporation of existing churches into the organization contributed to the growth of home missions as well, and from 1984 to 1988, 28 churches had been "started and brought into the Assembly." His final year in office, Walden saw a new record for missions contributions of $169,302.20 and over his tenure helped raise "almost a half a million dollars" for missions.[71] Although many CGMA churches in America continued to sponsor short-term mission trips, the program's focus had clearly shifted from attempting to send American missionaries to foreign countries to incorporating already existing indigenous ministries into the Mountain Assembly program through financial support.

The Expansion of the Youth Warriors for Christ Program

From 1968 to 1988, the foreign missions program established itself as a permanent and fruitful ministry of the Church of God Mountain Assembly. Simultaneously, the national youth department experienced a similar transformation. Jasper Walden played a role in both, concluding this era of the mission program after initiating this era of the youth program. Walden brought the Youth Warriors for Christ to the brink of hosting a camp on property owned by the Mountain Assembly, and his successor led them into the promised land. Not even the dreadful weather could dampen the fervor that accompanied that first camp on the property near Hillsboro, Ohio in 1976, and enthusiasm was what Donnie Hill intended to build upon. To assist with the building of new structures and new programs, the General Council created "a three member National Camp Board" in 1977. They would meet twice each year at the campground and discuss the needs of the camp and "oversee all camp building and activities." Upon its adoption, James Earl Prewitt, David Cornelius, and Ray Freeman were elected to serve.[72]

The General Council created the new Camp Board for general oversight, but also recognized that the mission program had enjoyed its greatest success when a member of the Executive Board took an active role in program development. The creation of a Second Assistant General Overseer to chair the new camp board resulted from a compromise to a proposal by General Overseer Jerome Walden to expand the centralized polity of the Mountain Assembly by adding two new general officials. The Mountain Assembly had just added two new offices the previous year, and Walden recognized the impracticality of adding two more salaries with travel expenses. Instead, he proposed deleting those two offices to implement his plan. The CGMA added the office of West Indies Island Overseer to the Standard Resolutions in 1976 but never filled the position. It also created a "National Evangelist." In the middle of Clayton Lawson's term as General Secretary & Treasurer, the Assembly conceived of an office better suited to his skills and suggested the creation of a full-time evangelist elected by the General Council. The Church of God (Cleveland) had often created positions for its retiring officials and, once again, the CGMA followed its lead. After Lawson served one year in this capacity, the General Overseer recommended the deletion of that office and that of the West Indies Island Overseer to be replaced by two new full-time positions.[73]

Walden submitted a resolution to divide the CGMA into a "Northern Conference" above Lexington, Kentucky and a "Southern Conference" below it. Each conference would have an overseer appointed by the Executive Board at the end of the General Assembly. The overseers would evangelize their conferences, raise money for missions, and "endeavor to establish new churches." James Earl Prewitt offered an amendment to the motion that would create the office of Second Assistant General Overseer. The "First" Assistant General Overseer would be the Southern Conference

Overseer as described by Walden's resolution, and continue to serve as Missions Director. The new officer would be the Northern Conference Overseer as the resolution called for and also chair the "Committee on the Camp Grounds." Such major overhaul of the polity concerned the delegates when it was proposed, and the motion was referred to a committee of Prewitt, James Walden, Jr., and the Executive Board—Jerome Walden, Kenneth Massingill, James L. Cox, Jr., and Ray Freeman—to consider any potential conflicts with the current Standard Resolutions. The measure then would be implemented in 1978.[74] The Church of God (Cleveland) had added "another assistant" to the General Overseer in 1941, and some reasoned that the Mountain Assembly had reached the point where the expansion of its episcopal polity was appropriate.[75]

Figure 11.18: J.E. Prewitt
c/o J.E. Prewitt

Figure 11.19: Donnie Hill
c/o K.E. Massingill

In the meantime, Donnie Hill continued to develop the youth camp with the general oversight of the Camp Board. The sale of cabin lots had generated revenue for the youth department and enabled it to build a cafeteria and bath house prior to the first camp. Before the second camp, the first cabin was erected on a lot leased by Clarence and Eva Jones of Goshen CGMA. The proximity of her cabin to the cafeteria was convenient to Eva who served as the camp cook for the week.[76] Two dormitories had also been erected in time for camp 1977, and a third was under construction. The Joneses' son, Danny, was pastoring the East Side CGMA in Kokomo and serving as the Northern Indiana District Youth Director. Roy Padgett of the Muncie church was serving as the Southern Indiana District Youth Director. Together, Jones and Padgett raised funds to build the Indiana Dorm in a race with Pastor James

Walden, Jr. and Aspinwall Church to build the first one. Pastor Ray Freeman and Rittman CGMA finished completion of their dormitory before the 1978 camp, and James Earl Prewitt and the Floral Avenue Church began building their dorm that summer.[77]

In preparation for the end of his tenure due to term limits, Hill pioneered a church in Harriman, Tennessee during his last year. He had been assisted by Michael Bartee in his first term and J.E. Lay in his second. At the 72nd General Assembly, the General Council elected Danny Jones to succeed Donnie Hill, and Nevada Pastor David Cornelius to assist him. Delegates also elected James Earl Prewitt to the office of Second Assistant General Overseer, and Prewitt resigned his pastorate at Floral Avenue CGMA to pioneer a new office for the Mountain Assembly like he had when he left Goshen eight years earlier.[78] Prewitt had pastored Jones at Goshen and mentored him as a young minister. As Chairman of the Camp Board, he would again mentor Jones and assist him in the development of the property.[79] A dormitory constructed by Leon Petree and the Cincinnati (Towne Street) Church and another by James Earl McKinney and Goshen CGMA provided six dormitories to accommodate nearly 300 people for the youth camps.[80] The construction of individual cabins occurred much more slowly. The standardized cabin plans called for a strict A-frame design leaving little room inside. When the General Council voted to "to adopt a revised A Frame Plan for the Cabins" to allow for a four-feet wall height in 1979, CGMA members built six more with that design over the next four years.[81]

Figure 11.20: Danny Jones
c/o K.E. Massingill

Figure 11.21: David Cornelius
c/o K.E. Massingill

Though advertised as youth camps, the summer program conducted by the National Youth Directors the previous sixteen years included guests of all ages. In 1979, Jones decided to introduce a true "youth camp" to precede the traditional week of "family camp." He separated the registered campers by age groups in the dormitories and assigned "counselors" to each group to oversee them. He closed the camp to "drive-ins," recreational vehicles, and unessential adults. He reasoned that adolescents would derive more benefit from the church services isolated from their parents and grandparents. To minister to the young people, Jones scheduled to preach all five nights, a 25-year-old African American from Cincinnati, Otis Lockett. Lockett had been saved four years earlier through Teen Challenge, a faith-based drug rehabilitation program. He was mentored there by James Gray of the Goshen church who highly recommended him to Jones.[82]

The experiment was not without its challenges, and it took a few more years to iron out the daily operations for the youth camp. Some opposed the change and pressured Jones to revert to a single week of family camp. Of the youth who attended, however, "everyone that went had a good time." The daily activities featured "a lot of games to play," a "trip to Seven Caves," and "karate demonstrations," by the General Overseer's son-in-law, Jack Anderson. The "classes on the influences of rock music" were "interesting" as well. Ultimately, the success of the camp was measured by the more than 80 who were saved and more than 40 "filled with the Holy Ghost."[83] Though the program was designed for the benefit of adolescents, the adult workers in attendance also found value in it. Anderson, for example, testified on Youth Night of the General Assembly in August to "how much he had been enlightened at camp this year."[84]

Though Jones planned another youth camp the following year, his first one was the only one he conducted. When his father died unexpectedly on the second day of Youth Camp 1980, Cornelius stepped up and directed the camp.[85] Despite the success of the program, Jones and Cornelius chose not to seek reelection at the 74th General Assembly in August 1980. The General Council elected Michael Bartee and Dennis McClanahan to succeed them. Bartee had pastored the former Akron church, now in Brimfield, for the previous four years. The 24-year-old McClanahan had just completed one term as Assistant General Secretary & Treasurer, the youngest man to ever serve on the CGMA Executive Board.[86] Soon after the Assembly, the new youth directors launched a campaign to build a tabernacle at the campground with the encouragement of the Mountain Assembly leadership. At a "special called meeting on September 9th," the Executive Board proposed, "Let's build a tabernacle where our people can worship the Lord," and unanimously approved the "construction of the first phase of a 72' x 106' tabernacle."[87] The dormitories provided ample accommodations for housing the campers, but outdoor services were inconvenient, and worshipping inside the cafeteria was uncomfortable. For just over $20,000, a large metal building was constructed in time for a dedication during family camp the third week of June 1981.[88] The tabernacle was mostly open-air with a gravel floor but provided a place for church services until a second phase could be completed.

Having expanded the facilities, Bartee enlarged the program. In June 1982, Bartee ambitiously conducted three weeks of camps. After "Family Camp," which featured family-themed teaching from IPCC General Overseer Tom Grinder, Bartee planned a "Teen Camp" for 7th graders through 21-year-olds. The final week of "Junior Camp" was designed for grades one through six and featured the "M & M Puppet Band." While pastoring at Kingston, Tennessee, Dennis and Paulette McClanahan developed a children's puppet ministry.[89] Richard Massingill, the 19-year-old son of the former Missions Director, attended Kingston while enrolled at the University of Tennessee, and assisted Dennis behind the curtains while "Sister McCranahan" attempted to keep order and teach Bible lessons to "Reggie" and his friends.[90] Camper registrations totaled 400 for the three weeks with 54 conversions.[91] Two years later, attendance grew to 532, and 109 were saved.[92] By YWC Camp 1983, Bartee completed a second phase of the tabernacle construction and added a wing on the side with six private furnished rooms including a large nurse's station.[93]

Figure 11.22: Paulette & Reggie
c/o Dennis McClanahan

In the middle of Bartee's tenure, term limits forced an end to Prewitt's stint as Second Assistant Overseer. In 1982, he moved to Whitley City to assume the pastorate of the church, and the General Council elected him to serve as Public Relations Director. Prewitt succeeded Leon Petree who had served the previous four years.[94] As Second Assistant Overseer, Prewitt was followed by Ray Landes, Jr., who had returned to Cleveland to pastor the

West Side Church two years earlier.⁹⁵ After his election, Landes moved his family to the youth campground when the Assembly purchased a double-wide mobile home to serve as a parsonage for the Northern Conference Overseer.⁹⁶

Figure 11.23: Ray Landes, Jr.
c/o Muncie CGMA

Figure 11.24: Michael Bartee
c/o CGMA

Term limitations brought an end to Bartee's tenure as National Youth Director in 1984, and he was elected to the office of Second Assistant General Overseer. Landes had declined to seek reelection after accepting the pastorate at Muncie, Indiana after the death of Pastor A.G. Padgett earlier that year. The following day, the General Council elected Dennis McClanahan as National Youth Director and Piqua Pastor Randy VanHoose as his assistant.⁹⁷ McClanahan completed the construction of the tabernacle, pouring a concrete floor and plumbing and wiring the V.I.P. rooms. He also "expanded the concession stand."⁹⁸ After VanHoose resigned in the spring of 1986, the General Council elected Richard Massingill to replace him in August.⁹⁹

As McClanahan and Massingill continued to conduct multiple weeks of camp divided by age groups, the resistance to the new format dissipated. One pastor's wife confessed "I never could understand why we had to have three camps until I came to Teen Camp this year." Her nostalgic view of camp "like it used to be" was allayed by the realization that "the change was for the best."¹⁰⁰ As attendance at "Family Camp" plummeted, and the "Youth Department was losing money on this endeavor," McClanahan discontinued it in 1988.¹⁰¹ To his critics, he reasoned that the January camp meeting in Florida had replaced it long ago.¹⁰² Indeed, attendance at the winter meeting increased simultaneously as the turnout in June fell. General Overseer C.B.

Ellis envisioned the camp meeting to offer fellowship to the fledgling Florida district geographically distanced from the rest of the CGMA churches.

The Florida district was created in 1969 when a church was organized in Eau Gallie, Florida. Goshen Deacon Charlie T. Yeary, and his wife, Dessie, were "snowbirds" who wintered in the Melbourne area. They approached Ellis for his assistance planting a church there. Ellis contacted Robert H. Adams, Jr., the brother-in-law of Public Relations Director Charles H. Davis, and persuaded him to join the effort.[103] Adams started the church in Eau Gallie that October, and Ira Moses visited and preached in the church the following month and appointed him to be State Overseer of Florida. From there, Moses visited Frank J. Williams in Tampa and "looked at the work he had started." Williams had contacted Moses in June 1966 "wanting to come into the assembly," and was recognized as an ordained minister the following year. After leaving Tampa, Moses preached to a dozen people gathered in the home of John and Mable Scott in Archer, Florida. The Scotts hoped to see a church established there in the Gainesville area.[104]

When Ellis, as Missions Director, visited Florida in early 1971, Adams indicated that he would like to appoint a pastor at Palm Bay so he could start another church. Together, they visited Gainesville and received "a big welcome to come and open up a church." They also visited Thomas and Ola Richardson in Intercession City. Ola became a licensed minister with the CGMA at West Milton, Ohio in 1969 and moved to Florida the following year. She and Tom were overseeing the Full Gospel Camp Ground and wanted to help Adams start a church in nearby St. Cloud.[105] Ellis returned to Archer the following year and organized a church with Ralph D. Moore as pastor.[106] Late in 1973, Williams sent notice to headquarters that he had organized a new church in Tampa.[107] The distance between the Florida churches made regular fellowship impractical, and the distance to the rest of the organization's churches left them detached. When the Richardsons invited readers of *The Gospel Herald* to attend the Full Gospel Camp Meeting in late February 1975, Ellis perceived a convention there would benefit the Mountain Assembly.[108]

Salvation Army Major W.W. Hinshaw and a group of friends purchased rural acreage in Osceola County in the 1960s to "establish a camp where those who shared his faith could worship the Lord freely."[109] The dormitories, dining hall, and tabernacle were made available in addition to numerous camper lots, and fourteen Mountain Assembly preachers attended the meeting from January 11 to 16, 1976. The camp served three meals per day and conducted three services per day. The evening speakers included James V. Freeman, C.B. Ellis, James Earl Prewitt, Bobby Wilson, Ray Freeman, and Jerome Walden.[110] Walden saw potential for growth from the meeting and hosted a second camp meeting there as General Overseer the following January.[111] CGMA leadership encouraged members to "plan your vacation for this week," pointing out the proximity to "Disney World," which had opened in Central Florida in 1971.[112] Attendance steadily grew for the annual meeting over its first ten years as a joint venture between the state overseer and the missions department. A significant change for the 1986 camp meeting magnified its importance on the Mountain Assembly calendar. In Monroe, Michigan on February 22, 1985, the Board of Twelve Elders voted to have its next mid-year meeting in conjunction with the Florida Camp Meeting.[113] The 1985 camp meeting was a "record breaker, but it was mild compared to" 1986.[114] By 1988, the success of the meeting in Florida rendered the additional family camp in Ohio unnecessary and it was discontinued by the National Youth Department.

The first Board of Twelve Elders' meeting held in the state of Florida significantly changed the National Youth Department in a more profound way than the eventual decision to cancel the family camp. After the General Secretary & Treasurer reported on the financial status of the organization, the Elders discussed "ways and means of increasing finance and cutting overhead expense" and appointed a committee to "study efficiency and conciseness with recommendations" to be offered to the General Council in August.[115] The committee consisted of James Earl Prewitt, Leon Petree, Lonnie Lyke, Jerome Walden, and Fred Cornelius, and it offered seven separate proposals to amend the Standard Resolutions. Two suggested relegating the General Secretary & Treasurer to part-time status and hiring a full-time administrative assistant, but neither was presented to the General Council in the business session. Two others authorized the bimonthly publication of *The Gospel Herald* and a provision for a housing allowance for the two Overseers living in the Jellico parsonages and requiring them to pay for their utilities, insurance, and home maintenance. These amendments passed along with another to delete the office of National Youth Secretary & Treasurer.[116] Robert Thomas had appointed Doris Garner to serve as the first National Youth Secretary & Treasurer in 1949.[117] Since 1962, all three national youth officers had been elected by the General Council. The committee determined it was fiscally responsible to add the accounting of the youth treasury to the duties of the General Secretary & Treasurer.[118]

However, the most significant change proposed by the committee and adopted by the Council was the elimination of "Conference Overseers." Under the new plan, the primary duty of the First Assistant General Overseer became the oversight of "world missions." The Second Assistant General Overseer would oversee evangelism and the "development" and rental of the youth campground. For the past eight years, he had served as chairman of the Camp Board, but the development of the camp was the responsibility of the National Youth Director. Bartee was reelected to the same job title, but the job description had significantly changed.[119] The resolution created a "camp development fund" but offered no guidance to differentiate between "youth" and "camp" expenses. Over the next two years, that ambiguity led to frequent difficulties. In the extreme, the standard resolutions suggested that the youth department was responsible for renting the campground from the camp development department. This absurdity necessitated a change.

At the beginning of the 82nd General Assembly, the Elder's Committee on Better Government presented a resolution to combine the duties of the "National Youth Director" with those of the "Second Assistant General Overseer" and create a new office, "National Youth Ministries & Camp Development Director." With the adoption of the resolution, the CGMA Executive Board was reduced again to four members. Since the "new" office was still a national youth office, the Board of Elders determined that the term limitations applied. Having served eight consecutive years as a national youth official, McClanahan's tenure came to an end. The General Council elected Rick Massingill to succeed him and chose Michael Manning as his assistant.[120]

Figure 11.25: Dennis McClanahan
c/o Dennis McClanahan

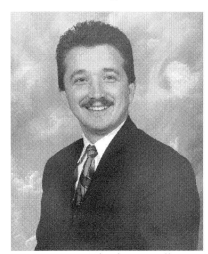

Figure 11.26: Richard Massingill
c/o CGMA

Mike Bartee had touted camp as a place where youth could "meet new friends," "have clean wholesome fun," "develop new skills," get away from harmful distractions, "learn from preachers that are uniquely interested in teens and their problems," find spiritual strength to overcome temptation, find godly counsel from "specialists," and to allow the Holy Spirit to guide them into their God-given calling.[121] Over the eight years that he and McClanahan conducted the Youth Warriors for Christ camps, that portrayal was demonstrated annually. Preaching on Youth Night of the 79th General Assembly, Jay Walden called attention to this phenomenon when he recognized five young men who had answered the call to preach the preceding month.[122] Dozens of young people announced a call to ministry, met their future spouse, or preached one of their early sermons at the campground in the 1980s.

To Religiously Educate Our Children

From 1977 to 1988, the General Council experimented with the National Youth Director's role in the development of the youth campground. Recognizing that building a campground distracted him from adequately emphasizing Sunday school, another resolution in 1977 separated it from the duties of the national youth department. The CGMA accentuated the development of Sunday schools in the 1920s and appointed Sunday school evangelists in each state to accomplish that end. By 1940, the Standard resolutions required each church to "maintain a Sunday School," and the Assembly voted to discontinue the evangelists.[123] When the YPE was instituted eight years later, the Assembly tasked the National Youth Director with "making our Sunday schools better."[124] The expansion of directives for the youth director in the 1950s and the increase of national, state, and district youth rallies led to the consideration of a separate department for Sunday school. In 1956, the General Council voted to create a "National Sunday School Superintendent" to collect attendance data from the churches and "seek ways and means to promote Sunday School work among adults and children." The Appointing Board selected Jellico Pastor Lawrence Redmond and Goshen Deacon Charlie T. Yeary as the first Superintendent and Assistant.[125] The new Sunday school department was dissolved the following year when the General Council voted to return "all Sunday School and youth work" to "the supervision of the National Youth Director."[126]

"Mart" Prewitt served as a Sunday school evangelist in the mid1930s, and his son, Carl, was the Sunday school superintendent at his home church in

Detroit in the 1970s.[127] As the primary focus of the National Youth Department shifted to the youth camp program and the construction of its own campground, Prewitt grew concerned that Sunday School was being neglected. On Friday, August 12, 1977, Prewitt submitted a resolution to create a "National Superintendent of Sunday Schools" who would "develop and promote Sunday School programs and literature," conduct a "Sunday School Convention each year with classes on the various methods and ways of teaching and building Sunday Schools," and "teach churches how to have an effective bus ministry." No one in the Mountain Assembly was more qualified to do the latter than Henry C. Taylor, and the General Council unanimously elected him to the position.[128]

Henry Taylor was saved at 15th & Race Street Church in Cincinnati under Pastor Leon Petree in February 1970 and was elected Sunday school superintendent a year later.[129] The church replaced its old 60-passenger bus with two brand new ones in 1972 and saw increases in Sunday school, including 490 that Easter with Cincinnati Mayor Tom Luken one of those in attendance.[130] In January 1973, Taylor and "a few members of the church" attended a seminar on bus ministry taught by Gardiner Gentry, "Bus Director and Assistant Pastor of the Beth Haven Baptist Church in Louisville." At Beth Haven, Gentry had grown a program that brought in 75 children on four buses to "2,250 riders on 20 buses" in 2½ years. His testimony "stirred and awoke" Taylor and the others, and his teaching offered practical instruction for the task.[131] By the time the church broke ground at its new location just off the Interstate 75 - Towne Street exit in the fall of 1973, "a fleet of six buses" contributed to a weekly Sunday school attendance near 400.[132] On Easter Sunday 1975, the Sunday school broke a new record with 1,025.[133]

During his first year in office, Taylor visited 14 Mountain Assembly churches and taught bus ministry techniques, conducted four district Sunday school conventions, and organized a large conference in Columbus, Ohio.[134] Dr. Paul E. Paino was the keynote speaker at the Downtown Holiday Inn on March 3-4, 1978. Paino pastored Calvary Temple Worship Center in Fort Wayne, Indiana where he averaged 2,000 in Sunday school "with a fleet of 40 buses."[135] The success of the first conference led Taylor to have two conventions after his reelection in 1978. The Southern Conference Sunday School Convention in Pigeon Forge that fall featured Gentry as the "guest speaker" and several workshops from CGMA ministers.[136] Taylor brought Gentry to Columbus in March for the Northern Conference Sunday School Convention, and another ten workshops were offered.[137]

Taylor invited Bruce Kirby of Nashville as the "special speaker" when he hosted another convention in Pigeon Forge in November 1979. In addition to various classes taught by CGMA members, one workshop was taught by Clyde Hughes, National Sunday School Superintendent of the International Pentecostal Church of Christ (IPCC).[138] In March, Taylor and Hughes coordinated a joint Sunday School Convention in Columbus.[139] Taylor declined to seek reelection at the 74th General Assembly, and the General Council chose James Bartee to succeed him. Bartee, the brother of National Youth Director Mike Bartee, had recently been elected pastor of the Bethel Tabernacle Church in Kokomo, Indiana and continued hosting two Sunday school conventions each year. Bartee moved the Southern Convention out of a hotel and into local churches but continued to conduct the joint IPCC meeting at the hotel in Columbus.[140]

Bartee did not seek reelection after his term, choosing instead to attend Beulah Heights Bible College (BHBC).[141] This school was founded in Atlanta in 1918 by Paul and Hattie Barth, who pastored a church founded eleven years earlier by Gaston Barnabas Cashwell after he was Spirit-filled at the Azusa Street Mission revival. The Atlanta church and a few others founded the Association of Pentecostal Assemblies in 1921 which united with International Pentecostal Church in 1936 to form the International Pentecostal Assemblies (IPA). On August 10, 1976, the IPA under General Overseer Tom Grinder merged with Chester I. Miller's Pentecostal Church of Christ (PCC) to form the International Pentecostal Church of Christ.[142] The PCC had entered formal discussions with the CGMA on three separate

Figure 11.27: Henry C. Taylor
c/o K.E. Massingill

Figure 11.28: James Bartee
c/o K.E. Massingill

occasions in the past to formulate a plan that might ultimately lead to a merger.[143] In 1980, the General Council appointed Jerome Walden, Paul Yeary, Michael Cornelius, Bob Vance, and James Walden, Jr., along with the Board of Trustees, to a committee "to look in closer with the Beulah Heights College."[144] Preliminary deliberations led to an opportunity for the CGMA to invest $100,000 in the school over a five-year period for joint ownership. The undertaking failed when a couple of the Trustees voiced strong reservations about the Assembly's ability to "raise the money."[145] Grinder and Massingill renewed discussions and formulated a plan for "closer fellowship" in the mid1980s. The resulting "agreement" included working together in Sunday school conventions, youth camps, ministerial training and exchange, and the acceptance of CGMA Students at BHBC with "financial assistance."[146] Bartee was joined at BHBC in the fall of 1982 by his first cousin, Tim Bartee, Robin Allen, Richard Massingill, and Steve Price.[147]

The General Council elected Ray A. Freeman as National Sunday School Superintendent in 1982. Freeman had pastored at Kokomo East Side (previously, West Middleton) since 1966, except for a two-year term in Rittman, from 1976 to 1978, while he also served as Assistant General Secretary & Treasurer and Editor of *The Gospel Herald*.[148] During Freeman's first year in office, the department's focus shifted from exclusive Sunday school work to broader areas of discipleship and training, and he submitted a resolution to change the name of the office to "National Christian Education Director." Freeman also submitted a resolution stipulating that "any minister applying for Ordination shall have completed a study of the Old and New Testament Survey, through a study course approved by the Elder Board."[149] This educational requirement for ordination was the result of an initiative launched by James Cox and Ronald Shelton.

Shelton was the nephew of General Overseer Clayton Lawson and had been elected General Secretary & Treasurer in 1982. J.E. Hatfield's untimely death during the 75th General Assembly left the position vacant for a year. In the meantime, the duties of the office were performed by the Assistant Overseer's wife, Jackie Cox, and by his brother, Charles. In the headquarters' office, James Cox and Ron Shelton discussed adding an educational requirement to the ordination process and inquired into the Assemblies of God's (AG) ministerial training correspondence courses through Berean School of the Bible. They proposed a course of study for ordination to the Board of Twelve Elders at its meeting in Kokomo on February 25, 1983.

Figure 11.29: Ray A. Freeman
c/o the Freeman Family

Some of the Elders balked over the use of AG curriculum; others were hesitant to require any scholastic requisite at all.[150]

Freeman had recently returned from Dallas, Texas where he completed "training with the A.C.E. staff, getting ready to open East Side Christian Academy" in Kokomo.[151] Accelerated Christian Education (ACE) was founded in 1970 by Donald and Esther Howard at a Fundamentalist Baptist Church in Garland, Texas. The curriculum was designed in self-instructional workbooks, or Packets of Accelerated Christian Education (PACEs).[152] Within ten years, over 3,000 Christian schools had been started using the ACE curriculum.[153] Freeman suggested the ACE New Testament and Old Testament Surveys as a compromise between completion of a formal certificate program and no educational component. The Board of Twelve Elders approved the study courses, and the General Council approved Freeman's resolution that August.[154]

Once the bible survey courses had been mandated, the Board of Twelve Elders sought to add a supplement on the "history and doctrine" of the organization and commissioned the Christian Education Director with developing it. Freeman submitted his proposed study in one PACE to the Board at its meeting in Monroe on February 22, 1985. After making some corrections, the Elders approved the course and recommended it be added to the requirements for ordination. At the same time, Freeman was tasked with writing a "mastery test" to be administered to ordination applicants who had taken Old and New Testament surveys through a course other than the one the Board of Elders had approved.[155] Both measures were adopted by the 79th General Assembly that August.[156]

During Freeman's last year as National Christian Education Director, the Southern Sunday School Convention was discontinued and replaced by a joint "leadership conference" at Ridgecrest, North Carolina in conjunction with the IPCC, Pentecostal Freewill Baptist Church, and the Congregational Holiness Church.[157] Five weeks after the joint Sunday school convention held with the IPCC in Dayton the next March, Freeman resigned as Christian Education Director when he and his church withdrew from the CGMA.[158]

In August, the General Council elected Henry Taylor to the position he had held the first three years of its existence, and Taylor continued to co-conduct the joint leadership conference and the joint Sunday school convention and to administer the appropriate survey courses for ordination candidates.[159]

When Freeman opened the doors of the East Side Christian Academy in the fall of 1983, it was the fourth such school in the CGMA. At the 75th General Assembly, Pastor Dale Whatley presented his church in Brooksville, Florida for membership in the CGMA. Whatley, a former missionary to Central America, had opened the "Saylor Christian Academy" the previous fall with seven students. When the schoolyear began in August 1981, 61 students enrolled under its new name, "Mountain Assembly Christian Academy."[160] At the same time, Luther and Janice Whitehead opened Lighthouse Christian Academy at the Palm Bay church.[161] The church later added an ACE college as well.

Figure 11.30: A.G. Padgett
c/o Alisha Padgett Landes

Another ACE school in Muncie, Indiana opened its doors in the fall of 1981. Pastor A.G. Padgett and his brother, Roy, took a short-term mission trip to Jamaica and Haiti with James Cox in January 1981. Flying out of Florida, the Padgetts visited Whatley's church and school in Brooksville. Already concerned about what his nine-year-old daughter, Alisha, was learning in public school, A.G. Padgett determined to provide a Christian education alternative for his congregation and community. After four years on Indianapolis television, the church canceled its weekly "Sound the Alarm" broadcast to redirect funds for the Sound the Alarm Christian Academy that fall.[162]

While Freeman was planning the start of his school in Kokomo, some of the ministers in the Jellico vicinity considered the possibility of opening a Christian school there. After discussion during the business session of the 77th General Assembly appeared unfavorable, J.H. Douglas withdrew his motion that the Assembly "allow the use of the Old Tabernacle for a Christian School."[163] Instead, the school began at nearby Fairview where James Ulrich pastored, and Bruce Dixon served as the first supervisor in the fall of 1984.[164] During the planning stages at Fairview, Ulrich and others presented the ACE curriculum to several churches in the area. One of them was the church at Fonde.¹⁶⁵ Pastor Cecil Johnson felt impressed to open an academy in his community and with help from James Cox, whose term limitations on the Executive Board were expiring, opened the school with 35 students. After two years in the Sunday school rooms, the church spent $150,000 to build a school and gymnasium to accommodate the needs of the academy.¹⁶⁶

After two years at Beulah Heights, James Bartee accepted the pastorate of the CGMA in Celina, Ohio, in 1984. Two years later, he founded the Myrtle Orick Christian Academy. At the same time, another Christian school opened in Cleveland. The Aspinwall Church had operated a daycare in the inner-city since 1967. Pastor James Walden, Jr. proposed the opening of a Christian school while in the middle of an ambitious building program. Richard and Janey Donley, returning from Haiti over conflict in the Port-au-Prince school, moved to Cleveland to assist with the opening of Aspinwall Christian Academy in the fall of 1986.¹⁶⁷

Nine Mountain Assembly churches opened ACE schools in the 1980s, and two more opened in the decade that followed. Pastor Tim Bartee and the Victory Center CGMA in Wapakoneta, Ohio opened a school in the fall of 1999, and Pastor Leslie Gilreath opened one the following year at Revelo, Kentucky. Many of the schools remained opened long enough for their initial student bodies to complete high school before closing due to lack of interest and funding. By the 2021-22 school year, only the schools at Fonde and Revelo remained. The impact of ACE on the organization lingered, however. At least six pastors had earned their high school diplomas with the curriculum, and nearly 2/3 of the ordained ministers had taken Old and New Testament surveys through the National Christian Education Department.¹⁶⁸

National Ladies Willing Workers Band

While CGMA Foreign Missions was establishing itself in the West Indies, the YWC were building a permanent place to have national youth camps, and the Christian Education Department was developing future leaders, another organizational department was growing into a vital ministry for the Mountain Assembly. The Ladies Willing Workers Band (LWWB) was authorized for local ladies' auxiliaries in 1948 but had no national charter. Beginning with the 59th General Assembly the women began hosting a devotional service during the annual convention. The first one, on Friday August 13, 1965, was under the direction of Jessie Weaver of New Castle and featured singing by "the sisters of the Race Street church" and the "Rowe family." After "several testimonies were given," Weaver preached "a timely sermon greatly needed."[169] Lassie Lawson conducted a similar service on Tuesday afternoon of the 1966 Assembly, but none was held the following year.[170] In 1968, Weaver resumed leading and preaching in the Tuesday afternoon service and continued to do so for the next four years.[171] In 1973, the Program Committee decided to fill the afternoons with a YWC talent contest and workshops on "stewardship," "missions," and "modest apparel." The latter was conducted by Dessie Yeary.[172] The following year, the afternoon program was repeated except for the "modest apparel" seminar. Instead, the Jellico Willing Workers officers led a LWWB workshop.[173]

Figure 11.31: Charlene Walden
c/o The Gospel Herald

Figure 11.32: Linda Massingill
c/o The Gospel Herald

The Assistant General Overseer's wife, Charlene Walden, directed a LWWB Workshop on Wednesday afternoon of the 1975 General Assembly, and the following year, she convened the first "National LWWB Meeting."[174] One day after his election as General Overseer, Jerome Walden, called the women to order for business on August 11, 1976. They voted to elect national officers, to "continue the Christmas in October project for Jamaica," to collect dues from the members, and to hold a retreat for ministers' wives at the youth campground in October. The ladies present elected Charlene Walden the first National LWWB President, Linda Massingill the vice-president, and Linda Bartee the secretary & treasurer.[175] With two big projects slated for October, the trio hit the ground running. After helping coordinate the effort to collect clothing in the local churches for missions, the officers conducted the first women's retreat at the YWC campground with 14 ministers' wives in attendance. With limited facilities, the women held three classes and a prayer meeting, ate, and slept in the cafeteria. After a successful retreat, the ladies turned their attention to collecting testimonies, recipes, and fundraising ideas to share.[176]

At the second national ladies' business session, another retreat was scheduled for Old Fort, North Carolina, and a decision was reached to publish a cookbook to raise funds for "a large lighted sign for the Headquarters grounds" in Jellico.[177] The sign the National LWWB erected in front of the tabernacle featured the new CGMA logo. While Missions Director, James Earl Prewitt had discussed the need for a distinct and recognizable insignia. In 1970, the General Council adopted the "church emblem" he presented consisting of a cross and flame inscribed in a triangle.[178] Over the next few years discontent grew over the symbol because its cross and flame too closely resembled that of the United Methodist Church. In early spring 1978, Missions Director Kenneth Massingill asked his son, Richard, to draw something with a more intense fire. His drawing became the basis for the new logo, and the Mission Department sponsored the construction and sale of signs to the local churches.[179] The ladies purchased the large sign and installed it in front of the tabernacle prior to the 72nd General Assembly.[180]

Figure 11.33: CGMA Logo
c/o The Gospel Herald

At the assembly that week, Jerome Walden and Kenneth Massingill presented a resolution to officially "authorize" the National LWWB Department. After it was adopted, Charlene Walden, Linda Massingill, and Linda Bartee were reelected to their offices.[181] The following August, the ladies transformed their business session to a luncheon with guest speaker, Annie Hill of Beulah Heights Bible College.[182] In 1980, the National LWWB elected Jacqueline "Jackie" Cox to serve as president, Beulah Fry as vice-president, and Jean Jones as secretary & treasurer. Within months of her election, Cox began submitting a monthly ladies' column to *The Gospel Herald*, often featuring a testimony from a saintly woman.[183] At the 75th General Assembly in 1981, she organized a "create a hat contest" and a diamond anniversary celebration parade through Jellico.[184] When attendance at the fall retreat remained small after five years, Cox proposed that the women, instead, meet twice a year at one of the local churches for a "Northern and Southern National Ladies' Day"[185] The first National Ladies' Day was held October 23, 1981 at Middlesboro with seven churches represented. With three classes, a craft, a skit, and lunch, everyone in attendance indicated on a survey "that they enjoyed" the program.[186] In May, the Northern National Ladies' Day in Goshen followed a similar format and had 80 in attendance from twelve churches.[187] By that time, the recently published *LWWB Handbook* was available with a ministry manual and numerous fund-raising ideas.[188]

Figure 11.34: Jackie Cox
c/o The Gospel Herald

Figure 11.35: Beulah Fry
c/o Susan Silcox

Cox and Fry were reelected at the 1982 General Assembly. Jones declined to run and was replaced by Debbie Shelton. In the summer of 1983, the National LWWB launched a "Pennies for Jamaica" campaign with a goal of collecting $500 in pennies from the Vacation Bible Schools in local churches, but in the end three times that amount was raised.[189] In 1984, Cox declined to seek a third term, and the LWWB elected Fry to succeed her, with Joan Marler as vice-president, and Vivian Murray as secretary & treasurer.[190] Fry had long served as the local ladies' president at Jellico where her artistic talents led to numerous craft projects. As President, Fry changed the format to the National Ladies' Days by replacing some of the teaching sessions with singing and testimonies.[191] Fry and Murray were reelected in 1984, but Marler chose to step down. She was replaced by Murray's daughter, Vijaya Long. Under Fry and Murray, income from dues increased from $ 246 in 1984 to more than $ 2,700 in 1988 and the Ladies were able to contribute

$1,500 to a project to add a drop ceiling in the Tabernacle.[192] Fry was elected to an unprecedented third term in 1988. Long replaced her mother as treasurer, and Paulette McClanahan was elected vice-president.[193] By then, the National Ladies' Days had become a permanent fixture on the Assembly Calendar and an event greatly anticipated by the local women's auxiliaries.

Conclusion

When he awoke on the morning of August 7, 1984, Kenneth Massingill intended to seek election as Missions Director, and had already informed his church in Corbin of that desire. However, on the way to Jellico for the business meeting that morning, he felt God speak to him, "You can promote missions from the top."[194] After he was elected General Overseer that morning, he did just that. Over the next four years, Massingill made three trips to Haiti, two to Jamaica, and one to Africa. In addition to promoting missions from the top, Massingill backed the entire CGMA program as overseer, including the national youth and Christian education departments. He attended five national youth rallies and four weeks of YWC camp and worked more than ten days wiring the new tabernacle at the youth campground. He attended the last southern Sunday school convention, the first three joint leadership conferences, and all four Northern joint Sunday school conventions while he was General Overseer. He also participated in the groundbreaking ceremony at Fonde Christian Academy and served on the Board of Trustees for Beulah Heights Bible College.[195]

Massingill's activity during his tenure typifies what the office became in the 1970s. The General Overseer still looked "after the general interests of all the churches." Massingill visited between 58 and 68 CGMA churches each year in office, preaching 16 homecomings and 15 pastor's appreciations, and participating in 19 building dedications or mortgage burnings.[196] But the Overseer's calendar was also filled with numerous national meetings as the organizational bureaucracy expanded significantly. At the beginning of Lawson's first tenure as General Overseer, the CGMA Calendar consisted of the General Assembly, a mid-year Elders' meeting, and a national youth rally. By the end of his second stint, another national youth rally, two conference rallies, three weeks of youth camp, a national camp meeting in Florida, two Sunday school conventions, and two national ladies' days had been added. From 1972 to 1988, the episcopal polity of the organization had been expanded into the various auxiliaries. Seven foreign national overseers served at the appointment of Assistant General Overseer & Missions Director.[197]

Now, with a National Camp Board to help guide the building and activity of the Youth Warriors for Christ, its officials conducted a year-long campaign that culminated with up to three weeks of youth camps. After just six years of existence, the National Christian Education Director promoted leadership development opportunities, while overseeing the ministerial educational requirements for ordination. The Ladies Willing Workers Band that had served local churches for more than three decades through fundraising, fellowship, worship, and discipleship, was now organized nationally to fulfill the same functions for the CGMA organizationally. "From the top," the General Overseer's office had come to oversee much more than local churches and ministers, and the leadership of C.B. Ellis, Jerome Walden, Clayton Lawson, and Kenneth Massingill provided the Mountain Assembly with long-lasting fruits.

---

[1] Marie Wilson, "Dayton, Ohio," *GH* 29, no. 2 (February 1968): 5; Prewitt, "Thank You," *GH* 29, no. 4 (April 1968): 4.

[2] https://www.findagrave.com/memorial/160842268/euliss-jasper-cates; Florida, U.S., Arriving and Departing Passenger and Crew Lists, 1898-1963 s.v. "Eulis J. Cates," Ancestry.com;

[3] C.B. Ellis, "From the Assistant General Overseer's Desk," *GH* 32, no. 3 (March 1971): 3; Jack Cates to C.B. Ellis, March 1971, letter printed in *GH* 32, no. 5 (May 1971): 3.

[4] https://ntcogjamaica.org/home/forward-in-faith-the-jamaica-story

[5] CGMA, *Minutes* (1970), 39-40.

[6] http://www.houseofgodclg.org/mother-mary-tate

[7] Ellis, "Report on the Mission Fields," *GH* 32, no. 7 (July 1971): 3; Kenneth E. Massingill, interview by author, Jellico, TN, April 23, 2008.

[8] Memorandum and Contract of Sale, May 26, 1971, copy in the possession of Kenneth E. Massingill, Old Fort, NC.

[9] Leatha Rowe, interview by author, Middlesboro, KY, May 6, 2008.

[10] Ellis, "Glimpse of the National Mission Rally," *GH* 32, no. 6 (June 1971): 4, 7.

[11] K.E. Massingill, "District Mission Rally," *GH* 32, no. 8 (August 1971): 5-6; James L. Cox, Jr., interview by author, Williamsburg, KY, February 26, 2008.

[12] CGMA, *Minutes* (1971), 22, 26-27.

[13] CGMA, *Minutes* (1970), 46.

[14] T.V. Zachariah, telephone interview by author, January 5, 2021.

[15] C.B. Ellis, "Special Announcement," *GH* 32, no. 12 (December 1971): 6; Jasper Walden, "Report from National Youth and Sunday School Director," *GH* 33, no. 3 (March

1972): 10; CGMA, "Mission Report," *GH* 33, no. 3 (March 1972): 4; Ellis, "Report to Gospel Herald," *GH* 33, no. 4 (April 1972): 4, 9.

[16] Jon Walden, Text messages to the author, January 10, 2021. The October 2020 container to Liberia contained 201 barrels in addition to many boxes.

[17] Colleen Farmer, "Bethel Tabernacle," *GH* 32, no. 11 (November 1971): 6.

[18] Massingill, interview; Massingill, *GH* 33, no. 6 (June 1972): 4.

[19] CGMA, *Minutes* (1972), 25-29; Cox interview.

[20] CGMA, *Minutes* (1972), 20-21, 63; C.B. Ellis, "Report on Missions," *GH* 32, no. 12 (December 1971): 3.

[21] Glenn Rowe, *GH* 33, no. 12 (December 1972): 3-4.

[22] Rowe, "Mission Report," *GH* 34, no. 4 (April 1973): 3.

[23] Rowe, "Mission Department" and Massingill, "Something God Hold of Me," *GH* 34, no. 6 (June 1973): 4-5, 12.

[24] Massingill, personal diary, January 7, 1974; Rowe, "Mission Report," *GH* 35, no. 3 (March 1974).

[25] Massingill, diary, May 13-20, 1974.

[26] Ibid., April 14 and June 8, 1974.

[27] Ibid., August 14-15, 1974; CGMA, *Minutes* (1974), 21, 23-24; Massingill, interview.

[28] Massingill, Diary, August 27, 1974.

[29] Ibid., September 10-17, 1974; Massingill, "Foreign Missions," *GH* 35, no. 10 (October 1974): 3.

[30] Massingill, Diary, May 14 and October 15, 1974; Massingill, interview by author, Old Fort, NC, January 4, 2021.

[31] Massingill, Diary, October 22 – December 31, 1974.

[32] Ibid.

[33] Ibid.

[34] Massingill, "Go Ye," *GH* 35, no. 12 (December 1974): 3, 5.

[35] As of January 1, 2021, the official currency exchange rate valued one Jamaican Dollar (JMD) at $ 0.007 U.S. Dollars (USD), or $1 (USD) = $141 (JMD), because of exponential devaluation over the past 35 years. In 1974, however, the official exchange rate was $1 (USD) = $0.91 (JMD). In remote areas, like where Massingill lived, his purchasing power was generally 80 cents on the dollar. Massingill, interview (2021); see also https://jablogz.com/2019/11/how-the-jamaican-dollar-has-devalued-over-time/

[36] Massingill, "From the Field," *GH* 36, no. 3 (March 1975): 3, 15.

[37] Lola Newton, "North Monroe Street Church of God" and Charlotte May, "Troy, Ohio Church of God," *GH* 36, no. 7 (July 1975): 6, 10; Jim Bell, "Goshen Church of God," *GH* 36, no. 8 (August 1975): 6.

[38] Jim Bell, "Goshen Church of God," *GH* 36, no. 6 (June 1975): 5.

[39] CGMA, *Minutes* (1975), 22, 27; Jerome Walden, "Good News From Jamaica," *GH* 36, no. 7 (July 1975): 4.

[40] Jerome Walden, "Mission: Life," *GH* 36, no. 11 (November 1975): 6-7; CGMA, *Minutes* (1976), 87-88; Jerome Walden, "Mission: Life," *GH* 37, no. 4 (April 1976): 4-5; Conroy Adams, interview with the author, May 3, 2021. As of May 2021, Conroy Adams, now in his 50s, still lives at Cousins Cove and oversees the property there on behalf of CGMA Missions.

[41] CGMA, *Minutes* (1976), 23.

[42] Gibson, 89.

[43] CGMA, *Minutes* (1972), 20.

[44] CGMA, *Minutes* (1974), 21.

[45] CGMA, *Minutes* (1976), 23; James L. Cox, Jr., personal conversations with author.

[46] Massingill, Interview (2021); CGMA, *Minutes* (1976), 23, 34, 87; CGMA, *Minutes* (1977), 24.

[47] Jerome Walden, "Greetings From the Missionary Department," *GH* 37, no. 7 (July 1976): 16.

[48] Ralph Stallard, telephone interview by author, May 7, 2008; Fan Fan Janvier, telephone interview by author, April 13, 2021; Joyce Snowden, e-mails to the author, April 23-24, 2021; Doris Jeune, telephone interview by author, May 11, 2021.

[49] Jerome Walden, "Greetings From the Missionary Department," *GH* 37, no. 7 (July 1976): 16; Mona Cornet, *GH* 38, no. 8 (August 1977): 5.

[50] Massingill, Interview (2008); Massingill, Telephone Interview by author, January 9, 2021; Donnie Hill, Telephone Interview by author, January 9, 2021.

[51] CGMA, *Minutes* (1977), 50.

[52] CGMA, *Minutes of the Church of God of the Mountain Assembly, Inc.: 1979* (Jellico, TN: CGMA, 1979), 72; Massingill, "Mission Reflections," *GH* 41, no. 5 (May 1980): 2-3; CGMA, *Minutes of the Church of God of the Mountain Assembly, Inc.: 1980* (Jellico, TN: CGMA, 1980), 73.

[53] J.P. Strong, "Report from India," *GH* 42, no. 7 (July 1981): 5; James Walden, Telephone Interview by author, February 26, 2008.

[54] Massingill, "Mission Report," *GH* 39, no. 4 (April 1979): 1; Massingill, "Reaching the Unreached," *GH* 39, no. 8 (August 1979): 2.

[55] CGMA Missions, *An Open Door*, 13; CGMA, *Minutes of the Church of God of the Mountain Assembly, Inc.: 1985* (Jellico, TN: CGMA, 1985), 26; Jasper Walden, Foreign Mission Report, 79th General Assembly Delegate Booklet (1985). Strong's children's home continued to operate with financial support from Aspinwall CGMA through CGMA Missions until 1996 when the final orphan graduated from high school and Strong retired at the age of 96.

[56] CGMA, *Minutes* (1979), 71; Massingill, "World News and Views," *GH* 39, no. 4 (April 1979): 1.

[57] Laura Taylor, interview by author, Jacksboro, TN, April 21, 2008; Colleen Allen, "Church of God Mountain Assembly Cousins Cove," *GH* 38, no. 11 (November 1977): 10.

[58] Janey Donley, interview by author, Jellico, TN, May 6, 2008; Janey Hackler, "Missionary Department," *GH* 42, no. 5 (May 1981): 12; CGMA, *Minutes* (1979), 28.

[59] CGMA, *Minutes* (1980), 19, 69.

60 S.N. Bryant was, however, eight days older when he was elected to his last term as "Moderator" in 1938. When Lawson was re-elected to his second term in 1982, he became (and remains) the oldest elected without any differentiation between the offices.

61 CGMA, *Minutes* (1980), 19.

62 Taylor, interview. As of 2020, Taylor has made dozens of trips over the past four decades.

63 Hackler, "Learning to Trust God on the Mission Field," *GH* 42, no. 9 (September 1981): 3; Hackler, interview.

64 Fanfan Janvier, telephone interview with the author, April 13, 2021; *Minutes of the] 113th Annual Assembly of the Church of God Mountain Assembly* (Jellico, TN: CGMA, 2019), 58; https://www.sifministries.org/index.php/projects-partnerships/faith-academy.

65 Janey Donley, Facebook message to the author, January 11, 2021.

66 CGMA, *Minutes of the Church of God of the Mountain Assembly, Inc.: 1981* (Jellico, TN: CGMA, 1981), 27; Home Missions Department, "1982 World's Fair Update," *GH* 43, no. 5 (May 1982): 7.

67 Cox, interview.

68 CGMA, *Minutes of the Church of God of the Mountain Assembly, Inc.: 1984* (Jellico, TN: CGMA, 1984), 16-17, 58-59.

69 Jasper Walden, "C.G.M.A. Missions," *GH* 46, no. 6 (June 1985): 14; Walden, Mission Report, Delegate Booklet (1985).

70 CGMA, *Minutes* (1988), 82-85.

71 Jasper Walden, First Assistant Overseer / Missions Director Report, 82nd Annual Assembly Delegate Booklet (1988), 7-9.

72 CGMA, *Minutes* (1977), 23.

73 CGMA, *Minutes* (1975), 27-28; CGMA, *Minutes* (1976), 26; CGMA, *Minutes* (1977), 26.

74 CGMA, *Minutes* (1977), 24-25.

75 Conn, 310.

76 James E. Prewitt, "A Look at the Assembly Camp Grounds," *GH* 39, no. 1 (January 1979): 14-15.

77 Ibid.; Alma Prewitt, "Youth Camp in the Past and Youth Camp Today," *GH* 41, no 1 (January 1984): 2, 9; "Youth Camp 77," and "Indiana District," *GH* 38, no. 8 (August 1977): 7-8, 14.

78 CGMA, *Minutes* (1978), 19-20.

79 Danny Jones, conversations with the author, ca. 1996.

80 Alma Prewitt, "Youth Camp," 9.

81 Ibid.; CGMA, *Minutes* (1979), 24.

82 1977 National Youth Camp Flyer and Application, insert in *GH* 39, no. 4 (April 1979); "Our Legacy," Church of God in Christ: North Carolina Second Jurisdiction, accessed January 12, 2021, https://www.nc2cogic.org/our-legacy/; David Cornelius, Facebook message to the author, January 12, 2021.

[83] "Norwood, Ohio (Hopkins Avenue)," and Cathy Grubb, "Norwood, Ohio (Floral Avenue)," *GH* 39, no. 9 (September 1979): 6; Jones, conversations.

[84] CGMA, *Minutes* (1979), 28.

[85] Jones, conversations.

[86] CGMA, *Minutes* (1980), 20.

[87] Mike Bartee, "Y.W.C. Camp," *GH* 41, no. 11 (November 1980): 9.

[88] "It's Camp Time 1981!" *GH* 42, 42, no. 6 (June 1981): 7.

[89] "C.G.M.A. Camp – 1982," *GH* 43, no. 5 (May 1982): 8.

[90] Dennis McClanahan, personal conversations, ca. 1994.

[91] Mike Bartee, National Y.W.C. Report, 77th General Assembly Delegate Booklet (1983); [Mike Bartee], "It's Almost Camp Time to Attend: C.G.M.A. Camp -1983," *GH* 44, no. 5 (May 1983): 4.

[92] Mike Bartee, National Y.W.C. Report, 78th General Assembly Delegate Booklet (1984).

[93] Bartee, Report, Delegate Booklet (1983).

[94] CGMA, *Minutes of the Church of God of the Mountain Assembly, Inc.: 1982* (Jellico, TN: CGMA, 1982), 23. A discussion on the "need for proper understanding on the tenure of office for Public Relations Director" took place prior to the election. The Standard Resolutions specified that there were term limitations on the Executive Board and National Youth Officers, but not the PR Director. In practice, however, no Public Relations Director had served more than two consecutive terms. Because Jerome Walden served from 1970-74 and Robert Wilson served from 1974-78, many assumed tenure of office limitations applied and that Petree was ineligible to be reelected after serving from 1978-82. As a result of that consensus view, he declined to run for office.

[95] Ibid., 22.

[96] J.H. Douglas, Board of Trustees Report, Delegate Booklet (1983).

[97] CGMA, *Minutes* (1984), 17-18.

[98] Dennis McClanahan, National Youth Department, Delegate Booklet (1985).

[99] CGMA, *Minutes* (1986), 21.

[100] Mary Cornelius, "Looking Back at Youth Camp 1986," *GH* 48, no. 1 (January/February 1987): 5.

[101] Elder's Meeting, Delegate Booklet (1988), 61.

[102] Dennis McClanahan, personal conversations with the author.

[103] Kenneth Ellis, "Living Waters Church of God Mountain Assembly Church History," 2018.

[104] Moses, diary, November 1-7, 1969; Moses, diary, June 3 and July 26, 1966; CGMA, *Minutes* (1967), 41; Alma Adams, "Eau Gallie, Fla. Church," *GH* 30, no. 12 (December 1969): 9; Mable Scott, "Gainesville, Fla.," *GH* 31, no. 3 (March 1970): 9.

[105] C.B. Ellis, "Assistant General Overseer Report," *GH* 32, no. 2 (February 1971): 3.

[106] Barbara Meredith, "The Church of God of the Mountain Assembly," *GH* 33, no. 2 (February 1972): 10.

107 "New Church Established in Florida," *GH* 35, no. 1 (January 1974): 4.

108 "Invitation," *GH* 36, no. 1 (January 1975): 3.

109 Full Gospel Bible Camp, "About the Full Gospel Bible Camp," accessed January 12, 2021, https://www.fullgospelbiblecamp.org/about_the_full_gospel_bible_camp.php

110 "Florida State Campmeeting of the Church of God Mountain Assembly," *GH* 36, no. 12 (December 1975): 5; "Florida State Camp Meeting," *GH* 37, no. 2 (February 1976): 4-5.

111 "Florida Campmeeting," *GH* 38, no. 2 (February 1977, misprinted as "March" on cover): 10.

112 "Campmeeting," (December 1975): 5

113 Minutes of the Elders Meeting, Delegate Booklet (1985).

114 Jasper Walden, "Florida Campmeeting," *GH* 47, no. 4 (April 1986): 3.

115 Elder's Meeting, 80th General Assembly Delegate Booklet (1986).

116 CGMA, *Minutes of the 80th Annual Assembly of the Church of God of the Mountain Assembly, Inc.* (Jellico, TN: CGMA, 1986), 19.

117 Mrs. Raymond [Doris] Garner, "Thanks," *GH* 7, no. 12 (June 1949): 2

118 CGMA, *Minutes* (1962), 25. James L. Cox, Jr. finished was serving as National Youth Secretary & Treasurer when the job was deleted. The following day, he was elected General Secretary & Treasurer. That continuity ensured a smooth transition.

119 CGMA, *Minutes* (1986), 19-20.

120 CGMA, *[Minutes of the] 82nd Annual Assembly of the Church of God Mountain Assembly, Inc.* (Jellico, TN: CGMA, 1988), 21, 23-24.

121 [Mike Bartee], "Who Needs Camp?" *GH* 43, no. 3 (March 1982): 3

122 Jay Walden, "Let Us Rise Up & Build," *GH* 47, no. 2 (February 1986): 8-9.

123 CGMA, *Minutes* (1940), 14, 21.

124 CGMA, *Minutes* (1948), 8.

125 CGMA, *Minutes* (1956), 29, 34.

126 CGMA, *Minutes* (1957), 20.

127 U.S., Social Security Applications and Claims Index, 1936-2007 s.v. "James Earl Prewitt," Ancestry.com; CGMA, *Minutes* (1919), 3; CGMA, *Minutes* (1933), 5; CGMA, *Minutes* (1934), 7; CGMA, *Minutes* (1935), 14; CGMA, *Minutes* (1936), 15; CGMA, *Minutes* (1937), 17.

128 CGMA, *Minutes* (1977), 23-24.

129 Henry C. Taylor, "What Sunday School Has Meant to Me," *GH* 38, no. 11 (November 1977): 3.

130 "Progress Report – Church of God 15th & Race Streets – Cinn., Ohio," *GH* 33, no. 5 (May 1972): 6-7.

131 Beverly Halcomb, "Blessings, Blessings and More Blessings," *GH* 35, no. 9 (September 1974): 5-6; "Here Are Some Facts About Gardiner Gentry: Bus Ministry," *GH* 34, no. 4 (April 1973): 10.

132 Leon Petree, "History of Our Church," *GH* 34, no. 10 (October 1973): 5-6.

133 Beverly Halcomb, "Towne Ave. Church of God," *GH* 36, no. 5 (May 1975): 6.

134 Henry C. Taylor, "National Sunday School Superintendent," Report to the 72nd General Assembly (1978).

135 "Up with Sunday School," *GH* 39, no. 2 (February 1978): 16; "Report from the Ohio State Sunday School Convention," *GH* 39, no. 5 (May 1978): 3-5.

136 Dennis A. McClanahan, "Southern Sunday School Convention Highlights," *GH* 39, no. 1 (January 1979): 8.

137 "Northern Conference Sunday School Convention," *GH* 39, no. 3 (March 1979): [back cover].

138 "Sunday School Convention," *GH* 40, no. 11 (November 1979): 11.

139 "Together We Work," *GH* 41, no. 2 (February 1980): 11.

140 CGMA, *Minutes* (1980), 20-21, 62; "200 Years and Still Counting!" *GH* 41, no. 10 (October 1980): 10; "Northern Sunday School Rally," *GH* 42, no. 3 (March 1981): 6; "Church of God Mountain Assembly, Inc. Calendar: 1981-1982," *GH* 42, no. 10 (October 1981): 10.

141 Timothy A. Bartee, Facebook messages to the author, January 14, 2021.

142 Burgess and McBee, eds., "International Pentecostal Church of Christ," *Dictionary*, 465.

143 Under Clayton Lawson and E.L. Cyrus, the CGMA and PCC, respectively, in the early 1950s discussed possible ways in which the two groups might work together. The groups renewed discussion in the late 1950s after Miller became General Overseer of the PCC. After Ellis's election in 1972, the two groups again considered ways they might unite in a cooperative effort. See discussion in chapter 9, various documents in Mountain Assembly File, IPCC Archives, London, OH; "Fellowship Between the Church of God Mountain Assembly and the Pentecostal Churches of Christ," *GH* 33, no. 9 (September 1972): 11; "Ministers Retreat," *GH* 34, no. 7 (July 1973): 3.

144 CGMA, *Minutes* (1980), 23.

145 Kenneth E. Massingill, Facebook messages with the author, October 14-15, 2017.

146 CGMA, *Minutes* (1986), 66.

147 Tim Bartee, Facebook messages.

148 CGMA, *Minutes* (1982), 23; CGMA, *Minutes* (1976), 23, 80.

149 CGMA, *Minutes of the Church of God Mountain Assembly, Inc.: 1983* (Jellico, TN: CGMA, 1983), 17.

150 James L. Cox, Jr., Personal conversations with the author, ca. 1994; Cox, Facebook messages with the author, October 13, 2017.

151 Ray A. Freeman, "Sunday School Report," 77th Delegate Book (1983). The school was later renamed "Christian Heritage Academy."

152 Bruce Gerencser, "My Life in an ACE School Part One," The Life and Times of Bruce Gerencser, October 22, 2015, accessed January 14, 2021 https://brucegerencser.net/2015/10/my-life-in-an-ace-school-part-one/

153 W.M. Fred Stoker and Robert Splawn, "A Study of Accelerated Christian Education Schools in Northwest Texas," abstract, unpublished study at West Texas State University (June 1980).

154 Cox, conversations; CGMA, *Minutes* (1983), 17.

155 Minutes of the Elders Meeting, 79th Delegate Booklet (1985).

156 CGMA, *Minutes* (1985), 21.

157 K.E. Massingill, General Overseer's Report, 80th Delegate Booklet (1986).

158 Ray A. Freeman to Kenneth Massingill, April 22, 1986, Ray Freeman File, CGMA Ministers' Files, Jellico, TN.

159 CGMA, *Minutes* (1986), 21.

160 CGMA, *Minutes* (1981), 22; "Saylor Academy Changes Name," *GH* 42, no. 12 (December 1981): 11.

161 Woodrow E. Martin, "Palm Bay," *GH* 42, no. 11 (November 1981): 7.

162 The author's personal and family recollections.

163 CGMA, *Minutes* (1983), 19.

164 Padgett, *Heritage*, 96.

165 Jerry Reynolds, Facebook messages with author, January 15, 2021.

166 Cecil Johnson, "Report on Fonde CGMA," (1992), 2.

167 Padgett, *Heritage,* 96; Richard Donley, Telephone interview with the author, January 11, 2021.

168 CGMA, *Minutes* (1983), 34-37; CGMA, *[Minutes of the[113th Annual Assembly of the Church of God Mountain Assembly* (Jellico, TN: CGMA, 2019), 16-17, 48-57.

169 CGMA, *Minutes* (1965), 27-28.

170 CGMA, *Minutes* (1966), 24.

171 CGMA, *Minutes* (1968), 24; CGMA, *Minutes* (1969), 25; CGMA, *Minutes* (1970), 24-25; CGMA, *Minutes* (1971), 23; CGMA, *Minutes* (1972), 25.

172 "Assembly Theme – "Occupy Till I Come," *GH* 34, no. 6 (June 1973): 8-9.

173 "Speakers and Program for the Sixty-Eighth General Assembly of the Church of God," *GH* 35, no. 7 (July 1974): 8-9.

174 "Speakers and Program for the Sixty-Ninth General Assembly of the Church of God," *GH* 36, no. 7 (July 1975): 8-9.

175 CGMA, *Minutes* (1976), 27.

176 "Attention! Ladies Who Missed the Retreat – You Really Missed it," *GH* 37, no. 12 (December 1976): 18.

177 CGMA, *Minutes* (1977), 28.

178 CGMA, *Minutes* (1970), 21.

179 [cover art], *GH* 39, no. 4 (April 1978); CGMA, *Minutes* (1978), 42; CGMA, *Minutes* (1979), 29.

180 "72nd General Assembly," *GH* 38, no. 10 (October 1978): 7; CGMA, *Minutes* (1979), 29.

181 CGMA, *Minutes* (1978), 22, 46.

182 "A Look at 73rd General Assembly," *GH* 40, no. 10 (October 1979): 6.

183 Jackie Cox, "Good News for Women," *GH* 42, no. 1 (January 1981): 7.

184 Jackie Cox, "Good News for Women," *GH* 42, 20. 7 (July 1981): 6.

185 Jackie Cox, "Good News for Women," *GH* 42, no. 9 (September 1981): 7.

186 Jackie Cox, "Good News for Women," *GH* 42, no. 12 (December 1981): 4.

187 Jackie Cox, "Good News for Women," *GH* 43, no. 7 (July 1982): 10.

188 National LWWB, *Church of God Mountain Assembly Ladies Handbook* (Jellico, TN: CGMA, ca. 1982).

189 Jackie Cox, "Good News for Women," *GH* 44, no. 7 (July 1983): 4; [Jackie Cox], "Celebrating 25 Years of Ladies Ministry," *GH* 61b, no. 8 (August 2001): 8.

190 CGMA, *Minutes* (1984), 50.

191 Beulah Fry, "For Ladies Only," *GH* 45, no. 12 (December 1984): 10.

192 Debbie Shelton, National L.W.W.B. Treasury Report, Delegate Booklet (1984); Vivian Murray, National L.W.W.B. Treasury Report, Delegate Booklet (1988).

193 CGMA, *Minutes* (1988), 67.

194 Massingill, interview (2021).

195 Massingill, General Overseer's Report, Delegate Booklet (1985); Massingill, General Overseer's Report, Delegate Booklet (1986); Massingill, General Overseer's Report, 81st General Assembly Delegate Booklet (1987); Massingill, General Overseer's Report, Delegate Booklet (1988).

196 Ibid.; CGMA, *Minutes* (1984), 6.

197 CGMA, *Minutes* (1988), 82-85.

12

Grounded and Settled

The seeds sown by the Church of God Mountain Assembly in the 1970s and 1980s produced lasting fruit. The final two decades of the 20th century were a period primarily of maintenance with steady financial growth. While CGMA Missions extended its reach abroad in Africa, the Caribbean, and into Central America, the number of churches at home modestly increased. After a decade that saw eight new offices created, the Mountain Assembly launched just one new national ministry over the next 25 years. The absence of significant structural change, and the tension that often accompanies it, created an environment of high morale and fiscal stability that positioned the CGMA at its strongest moment before the end of the millennium. As a result, the Assembly successfully navigated multiple potential setbacks in the 1990s.

Kenneth Massingill was elected General Overseer on August 7, 1984 and served two terms in that capacity. Over his tenure, tithe of tithes and ministers' tithes receipts saw an average annual increase about 33% though the total number of churches remained the same. His successor, Jasper Walden, saw a 13% increase in the number of churches while the tithe funds averaged annual gains of 30% over his six years in office. Cecil Johnson served as General Overseer from 1994 to 2000, and though the number of churches remained steady, the more than 50% increase in average tithe receipts helped the organization prepare financially for the setbacks it would experience under the next administration. The financial stability allowed the organization to pay off all its outstanding debt in 1993, and the General Council recognized with "heart-felt and sincere appreciation" the labor of the General Officials in making this a reality.[1]

An Era of Good Feelings

The resolution to create tenure of office limitations that went into effect with the elections of 1970 contributed to the stability the Mountain Assembly experienced the following decade. Two term limits on the Executive Board and National Youth Department often meant aspiring leaders needed only to wait four years for an opportunity to serve. As a result, it became increasingly rare for an incumbent to face opposition for reelection.[2] By 1988, the sentiment of unity had reached the point that, when all four members of the Executive Board were nominated unopposed, the General Council willingly ignored its own rules requiring election by ballot and elected the officers by acclamation.[3] Jasper Walden ascended to the office of General Overseer at the 82nd General Assembly after having served four years as the Assistant Overseer. After completing his two terms as General Overseer, Kenneth Massingill returned to Assistant Overseer & Missions Director. James L. Cox, Jr. was re-elected to a second term as General Secretary & Treasurer, and Bob J. Vance became his Assistant.[4]

The 1988 election of Richard Massingill to the newly-revised office of National Youth Ministries & Camp Development Director brought significant change to the national youth department and to the entire organization. Massingill's fundraising efforts on behalf of the youth department led to an 84% increase in annual average receipts over his tenure. The financial boost enabled him to make considerable improvements to the youth campground during his first year in office, including remodeling the bath house, installing a sound room in the tabernacle, and expanding the length of the cafeteria by attaching a new concession stand to its end.[5] In addition to numerous minor projects over the next few years, Massingill installed bathrooms and shower facilities to several dormitories that had been constructed without them.

In addition to working on the campground an average of 112 days each year of his tenure, Massingill preached an average of 139 sermons.[6] His effective sermons and affable personality endeared him to young people in local church youth revivals, district and national youth rallies, and at national youth camp. By the end of his third year in office, his popularity among the youth led to the circulation of a petition that garnered 150 signatures requesting the General Council to consider amending Standard Resolution 62 to allow the National Youth Ministries & Camp Development Director to serve more than two consecutive terms. At the conclusion of business at the 85th General Assembly, Lonnie Lyke read the petition on behalf of the young people. Once again, the spirit of harmony that so pervaded the organization led the General Council to ignore its own amendment procedure. During the discussion of the petition, a motion was made to amend the Standard Resolutions by extending the tenure of office limitations for all Executive Board and National Youth Officers. Its adoption permitted the officers to succeed themselves twice for a total of six years.[7]

A Bow Tied

Figure 12.1: Kenneth Massingill
c/o CGMA

Figure 12.2: Jasper Walden
c/o CGMA

The extension of tenure eligibility combined with a little chaos over the 1990 election of Assistant General Overseer contributed to a brief hiccup a few years later. Kenneth Massingill's tenure on the Executive Board was interrupted by the somewhat surprising election of Clayton Lawson as General Overseer in 1980. After succeeding Lawson in that capacity for four years, Massingill returned to the Missions Department as the Assistant General Overseer under Jasper Walden in 1988. Over the next two years, Massingill continued to cultivate the mission works in Africa, India, and the West Indies. One month after his election, Hurricane Gilbert became "the first Category 5 hurricane to make landfall in the western hemisphere" in nearly 20 years when it "traversed the entire length of Jamaica."[8] Five churches were destroyed, and another seven were damaged. Massingill took a work group in November and began reconstruction of the churches.[9] The expense of rebuilding the churches in Jamaica forced the mission program to operate "on a very tight budget" the following year, but the setback did not prevent the Mountain Assembly from entering new territory. Through the efforts of Nozor Augustine in Haiti, CGMA Missions was able to receive 30 existing churches in the Dominican Republic under Neal Maxi as the National Overseer. With the works in Haiti, the Mountain Assembly, now had 45 churches and two children's homes on the island of Hispaniola.[10]

In the summer of 1990, the church at Old Fort called upon Massingill to fill the pastoral void left by the death of Lloyd Camp in May.[11] Because the ministers had grown accustomed to patience and deference in pursing full-time national offices, the General Council was ill-prepared to replace

Massingill with two years remaining on his tenure of office limitations. When the 84th General Assembly convened in August, thirteen men were nominated for Assistant General Overseer. After eleven declined, Johnie H. Douglas was elected. At the beginning of the business session the following morning, Douglas admitted his haste in accepting the nomination and offered his resignation. In the prevailing spirit of solidarity of the times, a motion was offered to allow Massingill to continue to serve in the office while simultaneously pastoring the Old Fort church. After some discussion, the matter was referred to the Board of Twelve Elders and the election was postponed until the last business session. When the Elders considered the matter on Thursday, they voted unanimously to reject the proposal. The General Council, instead, elected Bob J. Vance, the following morning.[12]

By the time the Board of Elders met for its mid-year meeting in January 1991, Vance had not resigned his pastorate in Columbus, Indiana and relocated to the vicinity of Jellico as required by the Standard Resolutions of the Assembly.[13] When he was questioned about his compliance to the Assembly's bylaws, Vance "tendered his resignation as of March 1, 1991, citing his poor health, damaged home, and proximity to specialists." The Board reconvened at the end of March and determined to leave the duties of the Missions Director in the hands of the General Overseer until the 85th General Assembly. At this time, the General Council would elect a replacement to fulfill the unexpired term. The Elders also decided that the additional year would not count "toward tenure of office and tenure of the Executive Board."[14] In August, the General Council elected Cecil Johnson to complete the remainder of the term.[15] After a few years, this combination of incomplete terms, staggered tenure, lengthened term limits, and inconsistently enforced rules led to ambiguous understandings of *fulfilled* tenure and contributed to the decline in harmony among the brethren.

Figure 12.3: Bob J. Vance
c/o CGMA

Strengthening What Remains

In his three years as Missions Director, Johnson saw a 33% increase in the average annual missions receipts. Though his reports to the General Council included no works in new foreign countries, the existing CGMA mission fields enjoyed relative stability despite political unrest in Haiti and Liberia.[16] Midway through Johnson's tenure, CGMA Missions made the acquaintance of Kabango Kapizya Muzinga who oversaw a fellowship of more than 30 ministers and churches in Zaire (later, the Democratic Republic of the Congo). Within two years, the mission department began supplementing Muzinga with a meager salary, and he and his now over 100 churches identified with CGMA Missions.[17] About that same time, the mission program also attracted the attention of Edward Chitsiku of Zimbabwe. Chitsuku was affiliated with almost 60 ministers and congregations throughout southern Africa, including churches in his native country, Botswana, Namibia, South Africa, Mozambique, Tanzania, Angola, Senegal, and Zambia. The Assembly began sending support to Chitsiku in 1994 and those indigenous ministries joined CGMA Missions.[18] By 1995, CGMA Missions reported more than 350 churches in 14 foreign countries, more than three times the number in the United States.[19]

The exponential growth of the number of foreign churches was largely attributed to the need of financial support for already existing indigenous ministries. The home missions fund assisted domestic churches as well. These churches tended to be startups planted by CGMA Ministers. Existing churches often sought the Mountain Assembly for fellowship as opposed to finances. In 1994, at the conclusion of Jasper Walden's tenure on the Executive Board, he reported 55 churches had been added to the Mountain Assembly under his leadership as Missions Director and General Overseer. Unfortunately, 21 of those startups had closed during the period in addition to a number that had left the organization. Still, the 116 churches listed in the roll call of churches at the 88th General Assembly was the most ever.[20]

Having fulfilled his tenure as General Overseer, the General Council elected Cecil Johnson to succeed Walden in 1994. Cecil Ray Johnson was born in Valley Creek, Tennessee on October 4, 1939 to Anna (Turner) and Horace Johnson. He was converted in a revival at Fonde in the Spring of 1963 and ordained as a deacon in August 1967. He began preaching two years later and was ordained as a gospel minister on December 31, 1971.[21] From 1974 to 1991, Johnson pastored his home church at Fonde before being elected to serve as Assistant General Overseer. To succeed Johnson, the General Council elected Lonnie Lyke.

Lonnie Clark Lyke was born in Fonde, Kentucky on August 8, 1943 to Helen (Seal) and James Cornelius Lyke. He was converted in a revival at Fonde in 1960 and began preaching within a year. In 1966, his home church called upon him to pastor, and he was ordained there in August 1967. In 1974, Lyke relocated to nearby Middlesboro where he pastored for the next 18 years before returning to pastor Fonde for two years.[22] Upon his election as Assistant General Overseer, Lyke indicated his intention to continue to strengthen the existing foreign works while also emphasizing home missions to start churches in the United States. As a result, he reported 18 new churches in his first term.[23]

Among the churches established in the mid-90s, perhaps none were as significant as the Mountain Assembly's first Hispanic churches. In the early 1990s, Jessie Stevens got acquainted with Puerto Rican native Raphael Santiago while the two worked together in pest control. Stevens was pastoring Bibleway CGMA in Fort Myers, Florida, and offered the use of an outbuilding behind the church to Santiago to open a mission for a Spanish-speaking congregation in 1994. After a short time, the Hispanic congregation moved into the church alternating between English-speaking and Spanish-speaking services until a storefront could be located. At Stevens's invitation, Jay Walden held a revival for the Hispanic congregation that spring, and General Overseer Jasper Walden received Santiago and First Spanish CGMA into the Assembly at the revival's conclusion.[24]

Figure 12.4: Cecil Johnson
c/o CGMA

Figure 12.5: Lonnie Lyke
c/o CGMA

Around the same time, Kentuckiana District Overseer Woodrow Johnson was working to bring the Mountain Assembly to the Southwest. Johnson "met several ministers and Christian brethren" in Tucson, Arizona through his brother, Lesly, who was living there. On his second trip to hold revivals in the area in December 1995, Johnson also traveled to Agua Prieta near the U.S. border in the Mexican state of Sonora. Johnson returned to Tucson in February 1996 and secured a building with support from CGMA Missions and appointed Ruben Rangel to pastor the congregation. On another trip the following month, Johnson preached an extended revival in Tucson and met David Martinez, an associate of Rangel's. Martinez, an evangelist living in Mexico, agreed to work as a CGMA missionary in his country, and through his connections, Johnson reported to the General Council that August that he had "united six churches in Mexico and one in Tucson" with the Mountain Assembly and the possibility of adding more that fall.[25] While Johnson was working to add churches in Mexico, another door in Latin America was also opening.

In his first report to the General Council as Missions Director, Lyke conveyed the "possibility of opening new works in Puerto Rico."[26] In June 1995, he had traveled to the island with Santiago and preached one night in Moca, where he met several ministers, including David Badillo. By the end of the year, Badillo opened the first CGMA congregation in Puerto Rico with 23 in attendance at the first service.[27] Badillo was a gifted administrator with numerous ministry contacts in the Caribbean and Central America. In the Spring of 1997, Badillo traveled to Costa Rica to preach in churches associated with Javier Chavarria, who indicated his willingness to join CGMA Missions.[28] At the General Assembly, Lyke reported a church in Costa Rica with Chavarria as pastor and contact from a minister in the Philippines. Malachi Galing, who was also interested in joining the organization.[29] Through the network of ministers that began with Badillo, CGMA Missions added more than 75 churches in Puerto Rico, Costa Rica, Honduras, Dominican Republic, Guatemala, El Salvador, Nicaragua, and Venezuela within a decade.[30]

Although the churches he pastored placed among the top 20 in missions giving for 24 straight years, Lyke had never traveled outside the United States when he was elected Missions Director in 1994. Instead, he spent and was spent in the communities he pastored. Once he got his passport, however, Lyke made up for lost time, making 19 trips to the mission field during his six-year tenure.[31] As his predecessors had done, Lyke invited multiple CGMA ministers from various congregations to accompany him. Kenneth Massingill had used slide presentations to bring the mission field to the churches but recognized from the beginning that taking members to the foreign churches was the most effective way to impact Christians for missions. As more and more pastors saw the work firsthand, financial support increased as did the number of short-term trips sponsored by local churches. Between the 93rd and 94th General Assemblies, no less than 14 short-term mission trips were taken by CGMA ministers and churches.[32] With so many members and churches actively involved, giving skyrocketed to nearly three times the annual average under the previous Missions Director. In 2000, for the first time, Mission Receipts surpassed Tithes of Tithes Receipts.

Local churches and the missions department were not the only groups sponsoring short-term mission trips. In July 1995, the Youth Warriors for Christ sponsored its first mission to Jamaica. National Youth Director Kenneth Ellis had promoted the trip for months and enlisted six zealous teenagers—Jason Fahnestock, Aaron Fahnestock, Holly Henderson, Laurie Moses, Holly Reedy, and Chris Halcomb—and five chaperones—Ralph Watkins, John Keefer, Roger Prewitt, Glenda Newton, and Alfred "Al" Newton, Jr.—to accompany him on a soul-winning crusade on the island. With "great success" on this first trip, Ellis made it a regular part of the national youth program. By that time, he had begun already promoting and conducting "home missions trips" as well.[33]

At the Northern National Youth Rally in Monroe, Michigan, young people distributed 1,400 handbills to promote the event in the community. Ellis proposed to do the same for "one of our new churches" to promote a new mission work.[34] In June, the mission recently founded by Dennis Martin in Union City, Ohio was the first to benefit. With help from Newton, Michael Laforme, Tim Bartee, Jerald McGuire, Kevin Keller II, Charles Helton, Walter Davenport, and James Jonathan "Jon" Walden IV, Ellis distributed 1,000 fliers in the community and conducted special weekend services. Walden preached "God is a deliverer," and Davenport preached "If you build it, they will come."[35] In September, youth leaders and teenagers from several CGMA youth groups came together to assist mission works in Kingston, Tennessee and Dugger, Indiana with maintenance and upkeep on their buildings.[36] The foreign and domestic mission projects were just two of the innovations of the new youth director since his appointment to the office.

Near the end of his six-year tenure as National Youth Ministries & Camp Development Director in 1994, Richard Massingill accepted the pastorate of the High Point CGMA in Greater Cincinnati. To succeed him, the General Council elected Dennis "Wayne" Halcomb with Kenneth Ellis as his Assistant.[37] Shortly after the conclusion of the 88th General Assembly, Halcomb regretfully resigned. Because the CGMA Standard Resolutions did not provide explicit guidance for succession of office, newly elected General Overseer Cecil Johnson convened the Board of Twelve Elders for counsel on this matter. He reported to the Elders that Ellis "had committed" to accepting the office "if offered." On August 26, 1994, the Board "referred this decision to the Executive Board to appoint until the next General Council."[38] The Executive Board appointed Ellis National Youth Director with Jay Walden his Assistant.

Ellis resigned his pastorate in Nevada, Indiana and relocated to the youth campground to assume the duties of maintenance and development of the property and youth program. Massingill had added a third week of youth camp in 1992, and Ellis continued conducting junior, junior high, and teen camp, along with two national youth rallies, and fall and spring retreats for young adults and Christian workers. After implementing the home and foreign mission trips in his first year, Ellis added the "Ministers Life Institute" to the program of the National Youth Rallies. These morning workshops featured teaching on a wide variety of ministerial topics.[39] Next, through his leadership, the YWC sponsored a national Bible Quiz competition. Winners in the local church youth group would compete at the district level. District winners would then participate in the final round at the General Assembly.[40] In the national competition, Jessica Gaylor, Matthew Myers, Sarah Griffith, Sam Welch, and Jennifer Cox won in their respective categories.[41]

In addition to enhancements in the program, Ellis made considerable improvements to the campground. During his four-year tenure, he finished adding bathrooms and showers to the remaining dormitories, rendering the bathhouse virtually unnecessary. He purchased the first cabin constructed at the camp and converted it into an office building for the youth department. A new pole barn was erected to store equipment and tools, and the walls of the tabernacle were studded and drywalled to improve the sound.[42] In June 1998, Ellis was elected to pastor the Sidney, Ohio church upon the retirement of longtime Pastor Merle Laws. Under Ellis's leadership, the YWC enjoyed the steady financial growth experienced by the general fund and missions, with average annual receipts up by 55%. His final year in office, total youth receipts exceeded $100,000 for the first time.[43]

Figure 12.6: Kenneth Ellis c/o CGMA   *Figure 12.7: Jay Walden* c/o CGMA

While the other departments experienced steady increases and stability, the National Ladies Willing Worker's Band was no exception. Initially, fundraising served as the one of the primary purposes of the ladies' auxiliaries at the local and national levels. For this reason, income could fluctuate drastically from year to year depending on the nature of any projects the women might pursue. Nevertheless, the LWWB under Fry enjoyed a 36% increase in average annual receipts during her six-year tenure. In 1990, the ladies elected Judy "Paulette" McClanahan to succeed her. Jackie Cox returned to the national ladies' office as vice president, and Paula Keefer was elected secretary & treasurer. In addition to the fall and spring ladies' days, McClanahan initiated a luncheon during the Florida Camp Meeting and raised funds to install a baby changing station in the ladies' restroom at the tabernacle and special projects for missions.[44]

Midway through McClanahan's tenure as president, the national ladies' department experience structural changes due to the adoption of new resolutions from the General Council. In 1991, the Mountain Assembly adopted a resolution that required the General Secretary & Treasurer to read the qualifications for each office before nominations began.[45] After doing so before the elections the following year, the lack of substantial qualifications for the general officials became apparent, and a motion was passed to have "the Elder Board and the Executive Board establish qualifications for all the officers in our assembly during the Florida Elders' meeting and submit a resolution to that effect to the resolutions committee by July 1, 1993."[46] On January 30, the Board of Elders referred the initial drafting of the qualifications to the Resolution Committee and Executive Board to be approved by the full Board of Elders prior to the deadline.[47] When the committee failed to address the national ladies' officers in its recommendation, the officers themselves discussed the matter. McClanahan, Keefer, and Lorinda Grubbs, now serving as vice president recommended changing the name of the LWWB to "Ladies Ministries," encouraging each member to send $12 each year for national dues, instituting three-term / twelve-year tenure limitations like the Executive Board, authorizing district ladies' coordinators, and establishing qualifications for each office. Their proposal was submitted to the General Council by McClanahan's husband, Dennis.[48]

On Thursday, August 12, 1993, with nearly no discussion, the resolution was adopted. On the following day when the Resolution Committee presented the recommendations of the Elder Board, however, the General Council was overwhelmed with the scope of the changes. After a motion failed to divide the question into separate amendments to be considered for each individual office, the main motion was laid on the table and died at the conclusion of business.[49] As a result, the national ladies' offices were the only general officials to have significant qualifications for election. For McClanahan's third term as president, Robin (Allen) Bartee served as vice president, and Wanda Davis served as secretary & treasurer.[50]

With her tenure fulfilled, McClanahan was replaced by Nancy Vance in 1996. Bartee continued to serve as vice president, and Tammy Massingill was elected as secretary & treasurer.[51] In addition to the changes in the format of the ladies' days, Vance raised funds to purchase a new sign for the youth

Figure 12.8: Paulette McClanahan
c/o CGMA

Figure 12.9: Nancy Vance
c/o CGMA

campground and to remodel the stage at the Jellico tabernacle. To keep the women better informed, she returned to publishing a monthly column in *The Gospel Herald* and requested that the names and addresses of the local ladies' officials from each church be added to its annual church statistical letter.[52] Instead of mailing announcements and fliers to pastors, Vance and Massingill maintained direct contact with the local ladies' ministries auxiliaries which contributed to better attendance.

Attendance at some national ladies' days had already reached over 150 under McClanahan and continued to draw large numbers under Vance, especially the spring meeting in the South. Originally, these meetings featured several classes, a craft, and a skit. Beulah Fry added singing and testimonies, and McClanahan added to the worship a devotional sermon by one of the pastors. Vance envisioned a service with a devotional message brought by a female speaker. While planning her first ladies' day for October 19 at High Point CGMA in Cincinnati, she felt God impress upon her to ask 27-year-old Elena Petree Gibson to speak. Despite having grown up in a pastor's home, and her father, Leon Petree, having been one of the organization's most gifted speakers, Gibson had not done any public speaking. When Vance called Karen Petree for her daughter's number, she gave it to her with the assurance that Elena would not accept that invitation. Gibson responded that "she had something she had been wanting to speak about to ladies but didn't know where" it might happen.[53] Gibson made an immediate impact on the women who attended the meeting, and the success had two immediate and lasting effects. First, Vance continued to schedule female speakers to provide inspirational messages at the fall and spring events, and second, Gibson began receiving numerous invitations to speak at ladies' meetings and conferences, including one as the keynote speaker for the ladies' track at the 2000 joint leadership conference in Pigeon Forge, Tennessee.[54]

Henry Taylor returned to the office of Christian Education Director in 1986 and held the position until 2000. Maintaining the survey courses required for ordination and promoting the Joint Church Leadership Conference and Sunday School Convention (now Leadership 2000) continued to comprise his primary responsibilities. Since 1977, churches were asked to send one offering each month to the department, and the director's travel and actual expenses were taken from these funds. In 16 of the first 17 years, income exceeded expenses, but the balance reverted to the general fund treasury. In 1994, Taylor moved to retain "excess Christian Education Department funds received in order to start a CGMA children's home in the

United States."⁵⁵ The move was superseded the following year when an opportunity presented itself to participate with an already existing children's home. In the 1950s, Clayton Lawson, Luther Gibson, and others had expressed interest in founding an orphanage in the Church of God Mountain Assembly. In 1954, representatives from the Pentecostal Children's Home in Barbourville, Kentucky attended the Mountain Assembly and shared the mission and vision of the home and offer practical advice on the subject. The vision, however, never materialized.⁵⁶

In early 1995, the orphanage in Barbourville found itself in a desperate financial crisis. Glenn Rowe had been acquainted with numerous ministers associated with the children's home through the years, and the board of directors reached out to him, living in nearby Middlesboro, for assistance. Rowe pledged financial support from his church at White Rock, Virginia and was added to the home's board of trustees in accordance with its bylaws. When he indicated the possibility that CGMA Missions might also contribute regularly, the board of directors amended the home's articles of incorporation to allow an "association of churches" to "send up to ten trustees" as voting representatives at the annual meeting in July of each year.⁵⁷

At the 89th General Assembly, Rowe "discussed a proposal for the CGMA to be in association with and financially supportive of the Pentecostal Children's Home." Leon Petree, like Rowe, had long been acquainted with numerous ministers associated with the home and was a frequent guest minister at the Pentecostal Camp Meeting in Barbourville. After Rowe made his presentation, Petree moved to rescind the previous year's motion and use the excess funds to support the Barbourville home. Because $300 in annual support entitled an independent church to a voting trustee, the General Council voted to reserve up to $3,000 for the support of the home in Barbourville. The Executive Board, Finance Committee, and Trustee Board were appointed as CGMA voting representatives at the annual trustees meeting at the Pentecostal Children's Home for the following year.⁵⁸ Rowe called for and was granted a suspension of the order of business in order to consider the proposal at the beginning of the General Council Meeting because he felt it was of such importance that he did not want to wait until the number of delegates had dwindled at the end of the week. The move considerably shifted the scope of the Christian Education Department. However, with fifty fewer delegates on Friday, a far more significant measure with respect to Christian Education was adopted.⁵⁹

Grounded and Settled

The International Institute of Ministry

During miscellaneous business on August 11, 1995, Tim Walden discussed the need for an institute of higher education for the organization. Clayton Lawson and Luther Gibson had championed the idea in the 1950s, but nothing came of it. In the first year of his tenure as General Overseer, Walden's father, Jerome, had helped lay groundwork for what would have become The Gospel Herald Institute of the Bible. Having been remodeled to provide dormitory-style accommodations, the old tabernacle was envisioned as a residence hall, dining hall, and classroom space. James Cox, Jr. was to serve as the first academic dean and numerous potential teachers were lined up "to train people in all areas of church work ranging from layman to the position of elder."[60] Concerns over the ability to recruit students to Jellico along with a perceived "undercurrent of opposition to formal education" caused the venture to fail before it had a chance to begin.[61]

After this scholastic mission was aborted, James Earl Prewitt undertook a similar endeavor. For several years, Prewitt had sponsored educational ventures through "Central Christian Ministries" while pastoring the Floral Avenue CGMA in Norwood. The "New Media Bible" developed by "the Genesis Project" was a multimedia study of the Bible that incorporated filmstrips of the Holy Land with narration by leading experts in a variety of fields. Students received a certificate upon completion of the program. General Overseer Jerome Walden "encouraged the pastors to book this presentation of the Bible in their churches" and Prewitt presented the material at several CGMA and IPCC congregations.[62]

In collaboration with Pastor Leon Petree at the new building on Towne Street, the Cincinnati church opened its doors on January 16, 1978 to host Central Christian Ministries Institute. Prewitt taught a course on Genesis, Henry Taylor taught on Sunday School Evangelism, and Jerry Williams taught on Youth Ministry.[63] Although the school enjoyed modest success in its first semester, its life was cut short when Prewitt accepted the newly created office of Second Assistant General Overseer that August. After declining the opportunity to invest in Beulah Heights Bible College in the early 1980s, the Mountain Assembly's aspirations for higher education lay dormant for more than a decade. Tim Walden's motion at the 89th General Assembly to "form an exploratory committee" to determine the feasibility of "establishing a CGMA College" passed, and the General Council selected Henry Taylor, Michael Cornelius, Jasper Walden, Michael Padgett, and

James Walden, Jr. to form the committee with the Executive Board.[64] As Christian Education Director, Taylor was named chairman.

The committee met for the first time at the YWC campground on November 17, 1995 and invited Beulah Heights Bible College President Samuel R. Chand for consultation. Chand discussed a wide range of topics including the selection of trustees, mission statement, faculty and administration credentials, budget, long-range plans, curriculum, incorporation, name and site selection, operations manual, course catalog, and accreditation. He recommended the organization "begin with a one-year focused institute" and "use this year to establish feasibility." After putting "operations into place," procuring personnel, and building financial support, the Assembly could to determine whether to proceed.[65]

Figure 12.10: Henry Taylor
c/o CGMA

The committee met again in December, January, March, and June and determined that because of the "number of young ministers and Christian workers, the increased effectiveness that such training would provide, and the desire to see the Church of God Mountain Assembly continue to preserve its place in the mainstream of powerful Pentecostal movement into the 21st century," such an institution was not only feasible but "deemed of utmost importance." Its report to the General Council recommended the establishment of the "C.G.M.A. International Institute of Ministry" with the General Officials serving as its initial board of directors. It proposed the hiring of a full-time administrator funded from the tithe of tithe treasury, and the administrator and board would work toward "preparing staff and curriculum for the opening of school by the fall of 1997." The committee had surveyed CGMA members and determined the "most favorable location" for the school was the YWC campground.[66]

The General Council rejected the portions of the report that would have situated the institute at the campground. The Council approved the report with two additions. First, the exploratory committee was retained to serve on the board of directors along with the General Officials. Second, the directors and Board of Twelve Elders would hire the administrator within one month of the General Assembly from applicants whose resumes had been submitted before September 3.[67] The board met later that day to discuss its direction and determined the necessity of a new survey regarding the site and to set a date for the consideration of applications. Two applicants submitted resumes and were invited to attend a meeting with the Board of Elders and board of directors on September 5, 1996 at the Cincinnati Towne Street Church. After the meeting was called to order, "Leon Petree read a proposal from the Towne Street CGMA which granted" the "use of their grounds and facilities for the purpose of starting a college." This included the use of a newly constructed multi-purpose building. The consensus of the board was to accept this offer and locate the school in Cincinnati. When one of the applicants expressed his unwillingness to relocate to the area, his application was not considered. The board then considered the application of James Kilgore and interviewed him for the position. After hearing his vision and his responses to questions, the board voted to hire Kilgore as the administrator.[68]

From 1990 to 1996, James W. Kilgore served as General Secretary & Treasurer. As a member of the Executive Board, he participated in the college exploratory committee meetings. After the fulfillment of three terms in office, Kilgore was elected as the Assistant General Secretary & Treasurer at the Assembly the previous month and used *The Gospel Herald* to promote the International Institute of Ministry (IIM) over the next year. He began with soliciting funds to build a library before Nancy Vance undertook the library as a special project for the ladies' ministries.[69] Kilgore also solicited donations for the establishment of scholarships and at least seven families made memorial donations to assist students with tuition, which was set at $825 per semester or $70 per semester hour.[70]

During the preparation year, the IIM took a decidedly different path than the one that had been recommended. Chand proposed the organization determine its foremost need and design a one-year training program to meet it. Instead, Kilgore developed a one-year "Certificate of Christian Ministries program" along with a two-year "Associates Degree in Christian Ministries" with one of five areas of

Figure 12.11: James W. Kilgore
c/o CGMA

emphasis: pastoral ministry, youth ministries, missions, Christian education, and praise and worship. The school also offered more than ten general education courses.[71] In addition to the denominational periodical, Kilgore promoted the school at National Youth Rallies, Teen Camp, and the General Assembly.[72] Pre-registration at these events and the standard registration day on September 3 produced 13 students when the Institute opened in the fall of 1997, and the spring 1998 semester saw it increase to 15.[73] Most of the students the first year enrolled in just one course. The largest class in the spring semester was a Bible course taught by Tim Bartee, who commuted from his pastorate in Wapakoneta. As most of his students also commuted from the Central Ohio District where he was Overseer, Bartee petitioned the Board of Directors in June to allow him to teach courses in his district where the convenience of the location might boost attendance further. Concerned that opening regional sites would negatively impact enrollment at the main campus, the board decided not to pursue that course of action.[74]

During its second year of operation, the IIM reported 14 (3 full-time) students in the fall semester and 16 (4 full-time) enrolled for spring.[75] For the 1999-2000 academic year, 20 (4 full-time) students registered for fall courses, and 15 (1 full-time) signed up in the spring. When the Board of Directors met in June, it discussed the need for a formal job description and annual performance evaluations for the administrator. After establishing minimum expected duties, the board indicated it would like to see a 100% increase in enrollment over the next academic year. To promote the school and hopefully boost attendance, the board decided to offer one course each semester free of tuition and approved the offering of courses at regional campuses.[76] The following month, Kilgore was elected pastor of the CGMA in Butlerville, Ohio and resigned as the IIM Administrator effective at the conclusion of the 94th General Assembly. In his final act in that capacity, he presented Kevin Human with the first and only 2-year diploma granted by the institution during the youth night service on Wednesday, August 9.[77]

Figure 12.12: Kevin Human
c/o CGMA

Conclusion

During the 1980s and 1990s, the Church of God Mountain Assembly grew relatively larger with a net increase of 23 churches in the United States and exponentially wider with 13 times more foreign churches in 17 countries than it had in three countries two decades earlier. The organization grew fiscally as its general fund, missions, and youth receipts each increased by more than 400%, and total receipts at Headquarters in the 1999-2000 fiscal year exceeded $1,000,000 for the first time. The Assembly failed to grow significantly broader as it had in previous decades adding only one new ministry and national office. Through its commitment to leadership development in the Christian Education department, one might argue that the Assembly intended to grow deeper, but its most profound growth may have been in an area impossible to quantify. In the 1980s and 1990s, the Mountain Assembly grew warmer. In his first five "From the General Overseer" columns in *The Gospel Herald*, Cecil Johnson wrote to his fellow members about being merciful, forgiving, peaceful, and loving, and the importance of being "a kinder and gentler church."[78] In the stability of that era of good feelings, spiritual and emotional bonds were strengthened that kept the organization from splintering in the first decade of the new millennium.

---

[1] CGMA, *[Minutes of the] 87th Annual Assembly of the Church of God Mountain Assembly, Inc.* (Jellico, TN: CGMA, 1993), 23.

[2] After C.B. Ellis faced opposition in his 1974 reelection, it would be another 30 years before an incumbent General Overseer was challenged when he was eligible for another term.

[3] Standard Resolution 61 required "the General Officials of the Assembly, and all local pastors" to be elected "by secret ballot vote." Because the Standard Resolutions offered no provision for the suspension of the election rules, the move was technically out of order. The General Secretary & Treasurer objected to the procedure even concerning his own re-election, but the sentiment of the meeting prevailed because the move had been accepted in the recent past in the interest of saving time and the precedent continued over the next several decades.

[4] CGMA, *Minutes* (1988), 15, 22-23.

[5] Richard Massingill, Report of the National Youth Ministries and Camp Development Director, 83rd Annual Assembly Delegate Booklet (1989), 12.

[6] Ibid.; Massingill, Report of the National Youth Ministries and Camp Development Director, 84th Annual Assembly Delegate Booklet (1990), 14; Massingill, Report of the National Youth Ministries and Camp Development Director, 85th Annual Assembly

Delegate Booklet (1991), 10; Massingill, Report of the National Youth Ministries and Camp Development Director, 86th Annual Assembly Delegate Booklet (1992), 13; Massingill, Report of the National Youth Ministries and Camp Development Director, 87th Annual Assembly Delegate Booklet (1993), 13; Massingill, Report of the National Youth Ministries and Camp Development Director, 88th Annual Assembly Delegate Booklet (1994), 13.

[7] CGMA, *[Minutes of the] 85th Annual Assembly of the Church of God Mountain Assembly, Inc.* (Jellico, TN: CGMA, 1991), 25. Standard Resolution 75 required any proposed amendment to have been received by the Resolution Committee postmarked by July 1. The spontaneous amendment to the Standard Resolutions on the delegation floor, therefore, was out of order. That the overwhelming majority of those present seemed to be pleased with the organization's leadership suggested that following protocol by waiting until the following assembly was unnecessary.

[8] Hurricanes: Science and Society, "1988-Hurricane Gilbert," accessed March 6, 2021, http://hurricanescience.org/history/storms/1980s/gilbert/.

[9] Kenneth Massingill, Foreign Missions Report, Delegate Booklet (1989), 6; Massingill, "Mission News," *GH* 50, no. 2 (February 1989): 18-19.

[10] Kenneth Massingill, Foreign Mission Report, Delegate Booklet (1990), 6; CGMA, *[Minutes of the] 84th Annual Assembly of the Church of God Mountain Assembly, Inc.* (Jellico, TN: CGMA, 1990), 79.

[11] "In Memory of Bro. Lloyd Camp," *GH* 51, no. 7 (July 1990): 1; Massingill, "Report," Delegate Booklet (1990), 8.

[12] CGMA, *Minutes* (1990), 21-22, 25.

[13] When the Overseers' parsonages were demolished in 1986 to accommodate additional parking at the tabernacle, the General Council amended the Standard Resolutions to provide the General Overseer and his Assistant an allowance to provide their own housing. Standard Resolution 2 specified that the General Overseer's housing must be "in the vicinity of the headquarters property," defined as within a local telephone call. The general understanding was that both Overseers must live in the Jellico vicinity despite the oversight that Standard Resolution 4 did not include those words. As Vance was still pastoring, he was nevertheless in violation of the restriction that he "not be allowed to pastor a church."

[14] Minutes of the Elder's Meeting, and Special Elder's Meeting, Delegate Booklet (1991), 69, 71.

[15] CGMA, *Minutes* (1991), 22.

[16] Cecil Johnson, Foreign Missions Report, Delegate Booklet (1992), 9-10; Johnson Foreign Missions Report, Delegate Booklet (1993), 7-8; Johnson Foreign Missions Report, Delegate Booklet (1994), 7-8.

[17] CGMA, *[Minutes of the] 86th Annual Assembly of the Church of God Mountain Assembly, Inc.* (Jellico, TN: CGMA, 1992), 84; CGMA, *[Minutes of the] 88th Annual Assembly of the Church of God Mountain Assembly, Inc.* (Jellico, TN: CGMA, 1994), 54, 89-91.

[18] CGMA, *Minutes* (1994), 92-93; CGMA, *[Minutes of the] 89th Annual Assembly of the Church of God Mountain Assembly, Inc.* (Jellico, TN: CGMA, 1995), 53; Lonnie Lyke, Foreign Missions Report, 90th General Assembly Delegate Booklet (1996), 8.

[19] CGMA, *Minutes* (1994), 73-93.

[20] Jasper Walden, General Overseer's Report, and [James Kilgore], [Roll Call of Churches], Delegate Booklet (1994), 3, 17-26.

[21] "News Flashes," *GH* 24, no. 4 (April 1964): 3; Ira Moses, Diary, August 27, 1967; Linda Lyke, "Fonde Church," *GH* 30, no. 10 (October 1969): 8; Ordination Service Program of Jeffery Lance Brooks, Middlesboro, KY, April 21, 2018.

[22] Lonnie Lyke, Facebook message to author, March 9, 2021.

[23] Lonnie Lyke, Home Missions Report, 89th General Assembly Delegate Booklet (1995), 14; Lyke, Home Missons Report, Delegate Booklet (1996), 10.

[24] Jay Walden, text messages to the author, July 15, 2017; Cecil Johnson, Home Missions Report, Delegate Booklet (1994), 9.

[25] [Woodrow Johnson], "Tucson, Arizona CGMA Launched," *GH* 57, no. 4 (April 1996): 13; Woodrow Johnson, Kentuckiana/Mexico – Arizona District, Delegate Booklet (1996), 36.

[26] Lyke, Foreign Missions Report, Delegate Booklet (1995), 13.

[27] Lyke, "C.G.M.A. Missions," *GH* 56, no. 8 (August 1995): 3; Lyke, Foreign Missions Report, 92nd General Assembly Delegate Booklet (1998), 6.

[28] Lyke, "C.G.M.A. Missions," *GH* 58, no. 5 (Mary 1997): 19.

[29] Lyke, Foreign Missions Report, 91st General Assembly Delegate Booklet (1997), 6; Lyke, "CGMA Missions," *GH* 58, no. 9 (September 1997): 18.

[30] CGMA Missions, *Brief History*, 16-17.

[31] Lyke, Facebook message to author, March 9, 2021; Lyke, Foreign Mission Reports, Delgate Booklets (1995-2000).

[32] The author found references to fourteen different trips in *The Gospel Herald* from October 1999 through September 2000. It is highly likely that additional trips were taken but not reported in the magazine.

[33] Kenneth Ellis, "Youth Warriors for Christ," *GH* 56, no. 9 (September 1995): 15.

[34] Kenneth Ellis, "Youth Warriors for Christ," *GH* 56, no. 6 (June 1995): 13.

[35] "Union City, Ohio," *GH* 56, no. 8 (August 1995): 12; Jon Walden, text messages to the author, March 10, 2021.

[36] Kenneth Ellis, "Youth Warriors for Christ," *GH* 56, no. 11 (November 1995): 4.

[37] CGMA, *Minutes* (1994), 24.

[38] James Kilgore, Special Elders Meeting, Delegate Booklet (1995), 83.

[39] Kenneth Ellis, "Youth Warriors for Christ," *GH* 56, no. 10 (October 1995): 4.

[40] Kenneth Ellis, "Youth Warriors for Christ," *GH* 57, no. 2 (February 1996): 4.

[41] Kenneth Ellis, "Youth Warriors for Christ," *GH* 57, no. 10 (October 1996): 17.

[42] Kenneth Ellis, National Youth Ministries and Camp Development Report, Delegate Booklet (1995), 20-21; Kenneth Ellis, National Youth Ministries and Camp Development Director's Report, Delegate Booklet (1998), 38-39.

[43] CGMA, *[Minutes of the] 92nd Annual Assembly of the Church of God Mountain Assembly, Inc.* (Jellico, TN: CGMA, 1998), 50.

44 Paulette McClanahan, National Ladies President Report, Delegate Booklet (1992), 70; McClanahan, National Ladies President Report, Delegate Booklet (1994), 68.

45 CGMA, *Minutes* (1991), 24.

46 CGMA, *Minutes* (1992), 26.

47 James Kilgore, Minutes of the Elders' Meeting, Delegate Booklet (1993), 71.

48 Resolution to Amend and Replace Resolution 77, Delegate Booklet (1993), 73-74.

49 CGMA, *Minutes* (1993), 25-28.

50 CGMA, *Minutes* (1994), 72.

51 CGMA, *[Minutes of the] 90th Annual Assembly of the Church of God Mountain Assembly, Inc.* (Jellico, TN: CGMA, 1996), 72

52 [Jackie Cox], "Celebrating 25 Years of Ladies' Ministry," *GH* 61b, no. 8 (August 2001): 8-9.

53 Nancy Vance, Facebook messages to author, October 19, 2017.

54 "Joint Leadership Conference 2000," *GH* 61, no. 11 (November 2000): 9.

55 CGMA, *Minutes* (1994), 28.

56 See discussion in Chapter 10.

57 Amended Articles of Incorporation of Pentecostal Children's Home, Inc. (Barbourville, KY), July 18, 1995.

58 CGMA, *Minutes* (1995), 24

59 Ibid., 29.

60 "Church of God Announced Opening of Bible Institute in March," *The Jellico Advance-Sentinel*, August 9, 1977, 1.

61 Michael Cornelius, Facebook message to author, October 26, 2020.

62 *The Flame and the Sword* [ca. Spring 1977]. This publication was the official newsletter of Central Christian Ministries. Prewitt began publication of the periodical shortly after he assumed the pastorate of Floral Avenue Church. He suspended its production during his tenure as editor of *The Gospel Herald* from 1972 to 1976. Of the surviving issues that the author has located, none have a volume or issue number or date. The issue cited in this note states it is the first in four years, reports on an event in February and announces another upcoming event in October.

63 Buck Lewis, "Cincinnati, Ohio (Towne Street)," *GH* 39, no. 3 (March 1978: 6

64 CGMA, *Minutes* (1995), 29.

65 Samuel R. Chand, "Meeting of Church of God Mountain Assembly and Samuel R. Chand, President of Beulah Heights Bible College," November 17, 1995. In the possession of the author.

66 Henry Taylor, Report of the College Feasibility Exploratory Committee, Delegate Booklet (1996), 80-81.

67 CGMA, *Minutes* (1996), 28.

68 Alfred Newton, Jr., "Minutes of the Elders Meeting," September 5, 1996.

⁶⁹ James Kilgore, "CGMA International Institute of Ministry," *GH* 57, no. 11 (November 1996): 15; [Jackie Cox], "Celebrating 25 Years of Ladies Ministry," *GH* 61b, no. 8 (August 2001): 8.

⁷⁰ International Institute of Ministry Student Handbook / Course Catalog, 6-7.

⁷¹ Kilgore, "Students Invited," *GH* 58, no. 2 (February 1997): 19; IIM Handbook, 17; Kilgore, IIM Administrator's Report, Delegate Booklet (1997), 24.

⁷² Kilgore, "Graduates, March This Way," *GH* 58, no. 6 (June 1997): 19;

⁷³ Kilgore, "God Lifts IIM Into Orbit with 13 Aboard," *GH* 58, no. 10 (October 1997): 3; Kilgore, "Retrofitted and Relaunched with 15 Aboard," *GH* 58, no. 3 (March 1998): 19.

⁷⁴ Michael Cornelius, IIM Board Minutes, June 12, 1998.

⁷⁵ Michal Cornelius, IIM Board Minutes, September 25, 1998 and March 11, 1999.

⁷⁶ Michael Cornelius, IIM Board Minutes, September 21, 1999, March 10, 2000, and June 6, 2000.

⁷⁷ CGMA, *[Minutes of the] 94th Annual Assembly of the Church of God Mountain Assembly, Inc* (Jellico, TN: CGMA, 2000), 19.

⁷⁸ Cecil Johnson, "Blessed are the Merciful," *GH* 55, no. 10 (October 1994): 2; Johnson, "Be a Forgiving Servant," *GH* 55, no. 11 (November 1994): 2; Johnson, "Peace on Earth," *GH* 55, no. 12 (December 1994): 2; Johnson, "Love Your Enemies," *GH* 56, no. 1 (January 1995): 2; Johnson, "A Kinder and Gentler Church," *GH* 56, no. 2 (February 1995): 2.

13

Strong Local Churches

On his 57th birthday, Lonnie Lyke was elected General Overseer of the Church of God Mountain Assembly. The "delegate count" of 203 was the highest ever recorded, and the General Council returned James L. Cox, Jr. to the office of Missions Director 20 years after his first tenure in the office began. The same day, Alfred Newton, Jr. was elected to his third term as General Secretary & Treasurer, and Michael Padgett was elected Assistant General Secretary & Treasurer and editor of *The Gospel Herald*. Retiring General Overseer Cecil Johnson had indicated to the Program Committee that he would not preach the annual introductory sermon in deference to the newly elected Overseer. Lyke preached from Matthew 16:18 about Christ building His church and shared his vision for the CGMA: "to build strong local churches." He pledged "that this administration would be united in thought, labor, and service" and promised that when you saw one member of the Executive Board, you would "see all."[1]

Lyke made good on the promise. During the first year of his tenure, he conducted at least seven district ministers' banquets with all four members of the board in attendance. In addition to regular and special committee and board meetings, the four also attended both national youth rallies, both

Figure 13.1: Executive Board, 2000
Michael Padgett, Al Newton, Lonnie Lyke, James Cox   c/o CGMA

leadership conferences, and the Pentecostal World Conference in Los Angeles.[2] Lyke envisioned regular "staff meetings" with all the general officials, but coordinating schedules proved to be a difficult task. Leon Petree had been elected to an unprecedented ninth term as Public Relations Director.[3] Nancy Vance was serving her final term as Ladies President, and Jay Walden was elected to a second term as National Youth Director. In the Christian Education Department, Tim Bartee followed Henry Taylor's sixteen consecutive years as its director. The General Overseer believed the organization and its officials existed for the benefit of the local churches and thought of the national offices as agencies to undergird the ministry done in communities by pastors and congregations.

The Church of God Mountain Assembly, Inc. had been built into an international denomination through the financial and spiritual support of strong local churches, and Lyke believed that returning the emphasis to the churches was critical to organizational growth. He proposed several measures to realize this end, but three significant factors contributed to financial reverses which threatened the organization's fiscal stability and growth. The combination of a crisis with the benevolent funds, the significant purchase of adjoining property in Jellico, and the General Secretary & Treasurer's election of 2002 effectively brought an end to Lyke's tenure and threatened the organization's survival. The Church of God Mountain Assembly in the 21st century, cannot be understood outside the context of the events within the first four years of the millennium.

Strong Local Churches and a Strong Association

From 1928 to 1937, Mountain Assembly congregations were established in Monroe, Michigan, and Cleveland, Sidney, Cincinnati, and Goshen, Ohio. Those churches quickly became leading congregations in the organization and remained so throughout the century. During the final decade of the 20th century, all five were among the top ten in total finance sent to headquarters each year and sent more than a combined $ 1.3 million. In addition to their age, two denominators common to those five were pastoral longevity and building programs. Along with these five, the congregations in Old Fort, North Carolina, Piqua and Blue Ash, Ohio and Muncie and Kokomo, Indiana rounded out the top ten in total finance for the decade and consistently supported the missions and youth programs with finance and attendance.

Figure 13.2: Merle & Marlin Laws
c/o The Gospel Herald

Figure 13.3: Jerry Wilson
c/o CGMA

Merle Laws and his wife, Marlin, were saved in 1955 at the newly founded CGMA mission in Piqua, Ohio where his uncle, Ancil Laws, was pastoring, and the couple worked in the church in numerous capacities over the next fifteen years. In August 1971, the Sidney church elected Laws to succeed Glenn Rowe as its pastor. Three years later, the congregation constructed a new edifice to seat 270 people. The church actively supported the foreign missions and youth ministry throughout Laws' 27-year tenure as pastor.[4] In 1998, he retired from full-time ministry and the church chose National Youth Director Kenneth Ellis to succeed him.

Ancil Laws pastored the Piqua church for 30 years before his retirement in 1984. After a brief pastorate by Randall VanHooose, Jerry Wilson assumed the pastorate there in October 1985. Wilson was saved under Ancil Laws in 1962 and began working in various capacities in the church. Under Wilson's leadership, the Piqua church became one of the top ten giving churches in the Assembly in 1990s. In 1995, the Piqua church relocated from Linden Avenue to Looney Road and constructed a new sanctuary.[5]

In 1974, James Walden, Jr. left a thriving church in Chicago to pastor his home church in Cleveland. Already a solid church, the congregation continued to flourish under Walden's leadership. In addition to overseeing the October mission barrel project and assuming the primary sponsorship of the children's home in India, the Aspinwall CGMA supported the YWC with attendance and finance. In 1986, Walden finished construction of a new sanctuary, and, in its second Sunday, the church drew 820 people for Easter.[6] Walden retired in 2014 after leading the church nearly 40 years.

Ten years into Walden's tenure in Cleveland, his brother-in-law, Ray Landes, assumed the pastorate of the church in Muncie, Indiana. Landes had been serving as Northern Conference Overseer but had also enjoyed brief pastorates in Peru (Indiana), Jellico, and on the west side of Cleveland. Everywhere he went, Landes remodeled or built, and Muncie was no different. After completing construction on a new multipurpose building, the congregation became one of the top ten financing churches in the 1990s. Landes pastored the church until 2002 when he relocated to Jellico to assist Jerome Walden before his retirement.

Figure 13.4: James Walden, Jr.
c/o CGMA

Figure 13.5: Ray Landes, Jr.
c/o CGMA

When Leon Petree assumed the pastorate of the 15th & Race Church in Cincinnati in 1967, it had been one of the premier congregations in the organization for most of its history. In 1974, Petree relocated the church from downtown to just off Interstate 75 at the Towne Street exit and built a large edifice there to accommodate the Sunday school that was then averaging near 400 in attendance and ultimately saw a record attendance of 1,035.[7] Under Petree's 40 years of leadership, Towne Street was the top tithing church in the organization 23 times, and more than 40 ministers were called.[8]

Just east of Cincinnati, the church at Goshen enjoyed similar success under its forty year pastorate of James Earl McKinney. McKinney was raised in Fonde but was not converted until he was an adult in Goshen. In 1966, he was called upon to pastor the church and labored faithfully in the rural community for four decades. In 1993, the church built a new 840-seat sanctuary. During the 1990s, no church sent more finance to headquarters than the congregation at Goshen.

Figure 13.6: Leon Petree
c/o CGMA

Figure 13.7: James Earl McKinney
c/o CGMA

Number two in total finance for the decade was the church in Monroe. Fred Cornelius's retirement in July 2000 concluded a remarkable pastoral career in that community. Cornelius conducted nearly 600 funerals and officiated approximately 1,000 weddings over a span of 40 years in Monroe. In 1971, he relocated the congregation from Franklin Street to build a much larger edifice on North Monroe Street. In 1995, another building campaign saw the construction of a 700-seat sanctuary adjoining the former facility. At his retirement, the church averaged over 500 on Sunday mornings.[9]

In Kokomo, Indiana, his brother, David Cornelius, also guided the Bethel Tabernacle Church to one of the leading congregations in the

Figure 13.8: Fred Cornelius
c/o CGMA

Figure 13.9: David Cornelius
c/o CGMA

Strong Local Churches

organization. Cornelius pastored the Kokomo church from 1984 to 2015. In 1995, the church relocated from Monroe Street to a 20-acre property on Highway 26 and built a new sanctuary to seat 450.[10]

When Lloyd Camp passed away after pastoring for 34 years in Old Fort, Kenneth Massingill left the Missions Department to assume the pastorate in 1990. Already a solid church, under Massingill's leadership Living Waters Tabernacle grew to one of the organization's top contributing churches. After extensive remodeling projects in the 1990s, the church launched a building campaign and completed construction on a $1 million sanctuary in 2005.[11] Massingill went on to pastor the church until his retirement in 2016.

While Kenneth Massingill was turning the church at Old Fort into one of the Assembly's most supportive churches, his son, Richard, was doing the same thing at the Cincinnati High Point CGMA. John Collins founded the church in the Blue Ash area in 1967. After several pastoral changes in the 1970s, Tim McGlone led the church from 1980 to 1990 before returning to his home church at Goshen to work with his father-in-law, J.E. McKiney. William Lee Sweet pastored the church for the next four years, until "Rick" Massingill assumed the pastorate during his final year as National Youth Director. Over the next three years, the church jumped to fourth place in total finance sent to headquarters. In September 1997, Massingill resigned to become Assistant Pastor in Monroe where he was elected pastor upon Fred Cornelius's retirement three years later. Succeeding him at High Point was Philip Russel who had recently transferred credentials from the IPCC. Under Russell, the church continued to be a top-supporting church.[12]

Figure 13.10: Lloyd Camp
c/o CGMA

Figure 13.11: Tim McGlone
c/o CGMA

A Bow Tied

In addition to pastoring strong churches, James Walden, Ray Landes, Leon Petree, J.E. McKinney, Fred Cornelius, David Cornelius, and Kenneth Massingill served terms on the Board of Twelve Elders during the 1990s. Additional Elders during the decade included Michael Cornelius, Johnie H. Douglas, Wayne Ison, Donnie Hill, Jasper Walden, and Jerome Walden. Each enjoyed a long-term pastorate. During his 13-year tenure as pastor at Rittman, Ohio, James Michael Cornelius built a large sanctuary before relocating to Norwood, Ohio to assume the pastorate of the Floral Avenue Church after the retirement of longtime Elder J.H. Douglas.[13] Cornelius went on to pastor the church 27 years. Wayne Ison began pastoring the Mountain Assembly church in Metamora, Indiana in 1980. From 2003 to 2004, he led the church in the purchase of 24 acres and the construction of over 20,000 square feet of new facilities.[14] Ison went on to pastor the church for more than 40 years. During his last year as National Youth Director, Donnie Hill launched a new work, built a church in Harriman, Tennessee, and pastored it for 28 years. Similarly, Jasper Walden assumed the pastorate of the church in Lafollette, Tennessee during his final year as National Youth Director. The church there had dwindled to the point that it nearly closed. Walden pastored the church from 1974 until his election to the Executive Board ten years later. At the end of his tenure, he resumed the pastorate and remained there for more than 26 years. His brother, Jerome Walden, was elected pastor of the Jellico church after his tenure as General Overseer in 1980. He pastored the church until his retirement in 2008.

Figure 13.12: Michael Cornelius
c/o CGMA

Figure 13.13: J.H. Douglas
c/o CGMA

Strong Local Churches

Figure 13.14: Wayne Ison
c/o CGMA

Figure 13.15: Donnie Hill
c/o CGMA

Figure 13.16: Jasper Walden
c/o CGMA

Figure 13.17: Jerome Walden
c/o CGMA

At the 99th General Assembly, the General Council voted "to enter into a lease with [the] Jellico CGMA for their church to be located at the Headquarters Tabernacle." The matter was referred to the Board of Twelve Elders and the General Trustees to negotiate the terms of the lease.[15] The two parties agreed that after the organization replaced the existing roof on the tabernacle, the local church would assume all renovations, maintenance, utilities, and insurance on the building in exchange for a 99-year lease.[16] Over the next twelve months, Jerome Walden and Ray Landes with the Jellico church transformed the limited use open-air tabernacle into a weekly worship center. The CGMA borrowed $100,000 to replace the roof of the tabernacle, but the Jellico church borrowed four times that amount to complete major renovations on the building in time to host the 100th General Assembly.[17]

Figure 13.18: CGMA Tabernacle, 1999

c/o the author

Figure 13.19: Jellico CGMA Tabernacle, 2007

c/o Jellico CGMA

The remodeling of the tabernacle was the culmination of intended improvements on the headquarters property that began in 1995 with the erection of a memorial stone placed "at a prestigious place on our grounds" in honor of deceased ministers.[18] Just before the first service of the 90th General Assembly a $10,000 "granite stone" engraved with 268 names was set on a concrete pad in front of the old tabernacle. "Flanked by flagpoles holding the Christian and the CGMA flags and two benches, it serves as an inspirational and envisionary [sic] landmark."[19]

Figure 13.20: Ministers' Memorial
c/o the author

Figure 13.21: Elders & Officials at the old tabernacle, 1998

Two years later, the CGMA launched another major improvement project with the construction of a new office building. The first office spaces for full-time general officials were installed in the tabernacle in the 1950s. When the school property was purchased to build a new tabernacle in 1965, one of its buildings was converted into general offices. By 1998, both the office and the old tabernacle had dilapidated and became liabilities. In its annual report at the 92nd General Assembly in August 1998, the Board of Trustees recommended the demolition of both buildings and the construction of a new office building on the old tabernacle site.[20] The General Council approved the proposal and the work commenced that fall. The CGMA borrowed $265,000 to complete the demolition and new construction.[21]

By 2000, the CGMA owned significant acreage on Florence Avenue in Jellico due in part to its acquisition of several adjoining or nearby properties. In the late 1970s, three such lots became available and General Overseers C.B. Ellis and Jerome Walden encouraged the organization to purchase them even if it required borrowing.[22] The faithful stewardship of churches and ministers enabled the payoff of all outstanding debts during Jasper Walden's final term as General Overseer. The relative prosperity of the 1990s reassured the Board of Trustees and Finance Committee about borrowing so heavily again. A final purchase was made in 1998. An adjoining lot had been a source of conflict with the neighbor in the mid-1980s and ultimately required legal adjudication.[23] In 1998, the owner made the property available to the CGMA contingent on the additional purchase of his mother's property across the street. In November, after the demolition of the old tabernacle but before construction began on the new office building, the Trustees and Finance Committee approved the purchase of the property for $100,000, with 90% to be financed.[24] By the time Lonnie Lyke assumed office as General Overseer, the Mountain Assembly was over $300,000 in debt and would nearly double that amount within a year. That the organization was poised to borrow the money from itself was a double-edged sword.

Figure 13.22: Dedication of New Office

c/o Al Newton, Jr.

The Benevolent Fund Crisis

Though the CGMA had substantial debt when the 1999-2000 fiscal year ended on June 30, it also boasted more than $800,000 in its benevolent and burial funds.[25] The organization first recognized the need to assist its "aged ministers" in the 1940s and created a benefit funded by freewill offerings from the churches. Seven years after it was discontinued, a new "pension plan for aged ministers" went into effect from 1956 to 1966.[26] That year the General Council adopted a resolution whereby the Assembly would return up to one-half the amount that each full-time minister "contributed to Social Security from other than the wages from public employment" provided the minister had sent his tithes to headquarters.[27] In 1976, the General Council elected Clayton Lawson, James Cox, Jr. and James Walden, Jr. as a committee "to bring before this delegation next year a retirement plan for our Ministers."[28] After its report, the committee was retained for further study on the subject and a new plan was presented to the General Council in 1978.[29]

The new plan retained the ½ Social Security benefit for full-time ministers, offered ministers the opportunity to "Participate in the Nationwide Insurance Company's Group Retirement program," created a new "benevolent fund" for senior ministers, and constituted a three-member "Board of Review on Retirement" to "review the plan and make necessary recommendations" beneficial to the ministers. The benevolent fund would be subsidized by 2% of annual ministers' tithe receipts and 1% of the tithe of tithes each year. From this fund, ministers over the age of 65 with 25 consecutive years of full-time ministry with no other retirement besides Social Security would be eligible for a $100 monthly allotment. Lawson, Cox, and Walden were retained as the Board of Review and "to act as a liaison" between Nationwide and the CGMA.[30] When after five years, only a few ministers had participated in the retirement insurance program, the agency dropped the coverage.[31]

On January 31, 1986, the Board of Twelve Elders elected "a committee to study [the] efficiency" of the Assembly's government. Among their proposals to the 80th General Assembly in August, Jerome Walden, Fred Cornelius, Leon Petree, James Earl Prewitt, and Lonnie Lyke suggested an overhaul of the retirement program. The plan called for the creation of two "retirement" funds and a burial fund. The latter would be financed from ten percent of the tithe of tithes sent by the local churches. Most credentialed ministers would be eligible for a death benefit that began at $500 and increased to $850 and $1,200 with 10 and 20 years of service, respectively. The first retirement fund was financed from ministers' tithes. Ten percent of each ministers' tithes sent to headquarters were to be "set aside for the benefit of the particular minister providing he or she remains with the CGMA until age 65." At that time, the minister would be entitled to the accumulated interest and balance in a lump sum or monthly payments. The second retirement fund would have established "a voluntary contribution plan" that could not be forfeited and would be available for the minister after ten years in the plan. The minister would have the option of contributing his ½ Social Security payment into this plan.[32] On August 14, 1986, the General Council adopted all but the second retirement fund but retained the committee "to study the latter parts of the Retirement Plan."[33]

In December, the committee met with Dr. James B. Keiller who had helped the International Pentecostal Church of Christ develop the retirement program upon which this plan was based. The following month, the committee met again and proposed that instead of a "voluntary contribution" program, the Assembly would retain the ½ Social Security benefit of each minister in a second retirement account. Participants in the program would be "fully vested in five years" and at retirement age could request a lump sum or payments like the first account. The Executive Board recommended that the committee continue to oversee the development of the program and be constituted as a standing committee with its initial term set at five years.[34] In August, the General Council adopted both measures and, "to maintain a consistency in operations," created an election procedure whereby at least three members of the committee would be retained each election.[35]

The previous retirement plan was set to expire after ten years in 1988. The Retirement Committee recommended that the burial fund continue the support of the three ministers covered by the plan, Clayton Lawson, Luther Gibson, and Roy Cornelius, until their deaths.[36] Two years after the plan expired at Lawson's death, the Finance Committee revisited the policy and submitted a resolution to provide a monthly benefit for the ministers' widows, Lassie Lawson, Annette Gibson, and Mary Cornelius, for the remainder of their lives.[37]

Nine years after its creation, the burial fund's closing balance exceeded $90,000, and the Committee on Benevolent Funds recommended that it be capped at $100,000 and the excess "be redirected to benevolent fund #1 participants in equal amounts." At the same time, the death benefits from the burial fund were doubled.[38] In addition to benevolent payments and death benefits, the burial fund also provided small loans for local congregations. The low interest rates of such loans benefited the churches but yielded a higher return than was available in a standard checking account. The Committee on Benevolent Funds exercised discretion by limiting the amount available for loans at any given time.

From the onset, the committee recognized that wise investment would be critical to the success of the benevolent program. In the first year, a $10,000 certificate of deposit (CD) was purchased from the $19,064.16 received in the benevolent and burial funds.[39] Initially, benevolent fund 1, funded from each ministers' tithes sent to headquarters, earned passbook savings rates of 5.5% and benevolent fund 2, funded from ministers' tithes through the ½ Social Security calculation, earned 9%.[40] The General Secretary & Treasurer occasionally found banks offering such interest rates on CDs, but prudence required the availability of some funds in general checking. The difference between interest earned through investments and the interest paid to the minister's "account" in the benevolent fund was reconciled from the general fund. In the early years, when the account balances were relatively low and fewer ministers participated, the availability of high-yielding CDs required less money from the general fund to reconcile the difference.

By the time Lonnie Lyke was elected General Overseer, the combination of increased participation, climbing balances, and declining interest rates presented a quandary. In the first ten years, the number of ministers participating in benevolent fund 2 (½ Social Security) rose almost 33%, and the number who sent tithes to headquarters (and were thus eligible for benevolent fund 1) rose over 55%.[41] The closing balance in the combined benevolent and burial funds grew from just over $19,000 in 1987 to more than $814,000 in 2000. More than half of this amount was in benevolent fund 2 which still paid 9% interest to its participants.[42] Over the same period, average interest rates on a 5-year CD dropped from over 7% to under 5%.[43]

As the rates continued to drop, General Secretary & Treasurer Al Newton conveyed the grim reality to the Benevolent Committee whose responsibility it was to set the interest rates. In January 2002, he reported that, at the close of the fiscal year, the general fund would be expected to transfer more than $50,000 to reconcile the difference between the interest received from CD investments and the interest paid to the benevolent fund accounts. In addition, he estimated the need to transfer nearly $100,000 from the ministers' tithes and tithe of tithes for the regular amounts set aside for the burial fund and benevolent fund accounts. He asked the committee to lower the interest rate on benevolent fund 1 from 5.5% to 3.5% and the rate on benevolent fund 2 from 9% to 6% to save the Assembly more than $20,000. The committee reluctantly agreed, admitting "we knew at some point we'd have to do this." As CD renewal rates continued to plummet, in May, Newton asked the committee again to consider lowering the benevolent fund rates to match the interest rates earned from CDs. Concerned that some of the participants would withdraw their funds, the committee declined to lower the rates again so soon.[44] Few saw the problem and fewer were willing to address it until it was unavoidable. In a joint meeting with the Board of Elders and Finance Committee in September 2003, for example, James Walden, Jr. observed "we have created a situation with our benevolent & burial funds that, if we do not fix, will kill us." No one responded.[45] By the close of the 2001-2002 fiscal year, the balances of the benevolent and burial funds exceeded $1,000,000. To exacerbate the problem further, nearly 25% of that amount was unavailable to invest even if CD rates had not been so poor.[46] The general fund had borrowed $235,000 from benevolent fund 2 to purchase adjoining property.

A Bow Tied

Figure 13.23: Diamond Hosiery Mills

c/o Johnny Walker

The "Cantrell Property"

Diamond Hosiery Mills opened in Jellico in 1916 to manufacture socks for American soldiers in the First World War. In 1924, two years after the Mountain Assembly built the first tabernacle beside it, the business and property were sold to "Cumberland Knitting Mills."[47] The following year, James Henry Cantrell founded Imperial Bronze Manufacturing Company in a small metal building on London Avenue. Its eight employees "manufactured replacement parts for the mining industry." In 1936, Cantrell purchased the Hosiery Mill and expanded operations in the much larger facility to build air compressors. After the Second World War, the company began utilizing its foundry to manufacture bronze bearings for heavy equipment. After it incorporated in 1948 as Imperial Cantrell Manufacturing Company, it expanded its production to include an "increasing variety of bronze items."[48] After 75 years in business, Imperial Cantrell closed in 2000.

In the spring of 2001, corporate executives approached CGMA headquarters to inquire of its interest in purchasing the property before it was exposed to public sale. On May 8, Lyke convened a joint meeting with the General Trustee Board and Finance Committee. After meeting at the office for communion, the ministers toured the prospective real estate and authorized the Executive Board to negotiate its purchase, contingent on a clean report from the Environmental Protection Agency, and to sell the rental house on Florence Avenue if the Cantrell property could be obtained. The Finance Committee authorized the purchase for $175,000 and indicated its willingness to extend the offer to $225,000, if necessary.[49] When the Cantrell

Company held firm on its price of $235,000, a joint meeting was set for June 5 to discuss it further. In the meantime, the Executive Board attended the Pentecostal World Conference in Los Angeles on May 29-31. During the conference, Lyke met with the rest of the Executive Board to discuss the impending meeting, and the General Overseer informed James Cox, Al Newton, and Michael Padgett that he had decided not to recommend the purchase of the property. He reasoned that tying up such a significant amount of financial resources in real estate would severely hamper the organization's ability to grow ministries. The rest of the Board agreed.

Figure 13.24: 2001 PWC Chairman Thomas Trask with Lonnie Lyke
c/o the author

When the Trustee Board, Finance Committee, and Benevolent Committee met the following week, the General Overseer presented the offer of Imperial Cantrell and updated the ministers on the current financial obligations of the general fund, including $150,000 owed on the office building and another $80,000 on the houses. For more than an hour, Lyke shared his vision for future ministry in the CGMA and suggested better ways to spend that kind of money. After his impassioned speech, one of the committee members insisted it was possible for the organization to purchase the building and to develop and launch new ministries simultaneously. Accordingly, the Board of Trustees voted to purchase the Cantrell property for $235,000, and the Finance Committee voted to borrow the amount, amortized for 15 years with the intention of making $2,500 monthly payments for seven years with a balloon payment of $113,000. The Committee on Benevolent Funds and Insurance then voted to loan the full amount to the general fund from benevolent fund 2 at 7% interest.[50]

The general reaction to the purchase was mixed. Many ministers were frustrated at the decision made by a handful that had wider implications for the entire organization. At the beginning of Kenneth Massingill's tenure as General Overseer, the Executive and Trustee Boards and Finance Committee had discussed the prospect of relocating headquarters and voted to appraise the property for a potential sale. The "joint committee" determined it was "feasible to move General Headquarters in phases" whether the Jellico property was sold or retained.[51] After considerable discussion of its report at the 79th General Assembly on August 14, 1985, a motion was made "to move General Headquarters." The motion failed, but 40% voted in favor of it.[52] Two years later, a resolution was presented to "place all properties – three houses, two tabernacles, office building and parking grounds in Jellico, Tennessee for sale at fair market prices as soon as possible" and "rent an office in the greater Cincinnati area and move Headquarters to this city within eight months of the close of the Eighty First General Assembly." Proceeds from the sale of property were to be used to acquire property for a new headquarters and the Executive Board would be expected to "rent a suitable convention site" for the General Assembly. Though this second attempt also failed, more than a decade later many were still hopeful of relocating headquarters and saw the building of a new office and acquisition of additional property as impediments to that goal.[53] Furthermore, some of the ministers were angered that the purchase was made through the benevolent fund program. Not a true "retirement" program, the benevolent gift did not belong to a minister until he asked for it at retirement. Still, some viewed it as if the Assembly had borrowed their money without their consent. They also appreciated the security of knowing the money was invested in CDs. Now, more than half of the balance in benevolent fund 2 was allocated in the internal loan to headquarters.

Some ministers, however, were excited about the expansion of the headquarters property and envisioned the possibilities of ministry uses for the building. These included the relocation from Cincinnati of the International Institute of Ministry (IIM), local missions work, and a recreation center. Jellico residents were encouraged by the possibility that the CGMA might rent the facility to potential industry and boost the struggling local economy. Lyke trusted the judgment of the trustee board in its confidence that the Mountain Assembly could buy property and build programs simultaneously and presented his vision to the General Council two months after he shared it with the joint committees. In his booklet, *Following the Calling: Building Strong Local Churches*, the General Overseer shared his "heart for caring, supporting, and strengthening our members, ministers and local Churches." First, he called for "an international prayer network" and offered materials from headquarters for local churches to "establish a strong prayer program." He pledged his and Newton's willingness to present the material personally to the local congregations. The Assistant National Youth Director, Nick Hill, had also volunteered "to help begin a young people prayer group" wherever he was invited. Lyke also committed to "caring for our pastors" by facilitating "spiritual restoration and renewal in clergy families," hosting "complimentary gatherings for ministers and their spouses," providing "pastoral resources," offering crisis management, and instituting a pastoral mentoring program.[54]

The proposal included "a pastoral support team" comprised of "men of integrity" to strengthen and fulfill "the vision God has given the Pastor," and Lyke implemented the national men's ministry right away by appointing Henry Taylor as its first director. Taylor had just completed 14 consecutive years as National Christian Education Director, and Lyke was certain that Taylor could pioneer the new program as successfully as he done the first. Taylor wasted no time delving into his duties. Launching a column in *The Gospel Herald* in September 2001, Taylor promoted the first "Armor Bearers Meeting" in the form of a National Men's Ministry Retreat at the YWC Campground in October.[55] Eight pastors and about two dozen laymen convened on October 12-13 for fellowship and instruction. Taylor shared the "Principles and Pitfalls of Men's Ministry," David Holmes taught a workshop on men's small groups, and Wayne Ison instructed on becoming "Better Husbands, Fathers, Providers, and Spiritual Leaders as Priest in the Home."[56] Taylor reported at the 96th General Assembly the following year that, among his other activities, he had conducted three district men's meetings during the year, and the General Council elected him for a two-year term.[57]

Figure 13.25: 2001 Men of Integrity Retreat

c/o the author

To further strengthen pastors and local churches, Lyke advocated for evangelism through the creation of "outreach directors" and offered "partial financial assistance for his salary with those churches that cannot do so themselves." In the first year, three churches took advantage of the program and Steve Branstutter, Nick Hill, and Rich Holmes received supplemental salaries from headquarters[58]

Lyke conducted a "round table meeting" at King's Island, Ohio during the Leadership 21 Conference on March 8, 2001 and included some of the ideas proposed at this meeting in the *Following the Calling* guide. James Walden, Jr. contributed some suggestions for member care through a visitor retention program. Kenneth Ellis recommended "caring for our communities" through a local mission director in each church. The vision also contained ways to incorporate the national Youth Warriors for Christ, CGMA foreign missions, and the National Christian Education Department into the ministry of the local churches. In particular, the General Overseer emphasized the IIM as critical to the future of the organization and imagined "expanding the extension sites to give every district access," as well as "high quality professional video correspondence courses" and the ability to access coursework through the internet. [59]

Lyke's vision was ambitious especially when tenure of office limitations gave him a maximum of five more years to fulfill it. Just as ambitious was the Finance Committee's faith that the organization could pay its new mortgage as planned in addition to its other debts. In June 2002, the Assembly sold one of its rental properties and a vacant lot and paid off the balance previously owed on it.[60] But, the combination of high debt and the impending benevolent fund crisis was about to be complicated further by a transition in the office of General Secretary & Treasurer.

The Treasurer Election of 2002

Tenure of office limitations imposed by the new resolution in 1969 were aimed at creating smooth transitions in the office of General Overseer. The unforeseen consequence was the impact the measure had on the office of General Secretary & Treasurer. J.E. Hatfield served in that capacity for 30 consecutive years until the new guidelines brought an end to his tenure in 1974. That the General Council reelected Hatfield in 17 consecutive elections was a testimony to its confidence in his ability, but this should not suggest that no one else was capable or willing to serve, or that some did not desire change. In fact, from 1956 to 1964, Hatfield ran unchallenged only once in five elections, and he received nine "no" votes when he ran unopposed in 1966.[61] Wade Hughes was twice elected to serve as Hatfield's assistant and was approached numerous times by ministers asking him to run for General Secretary & Treasurer. Hughes' admiration for and loyalty to his mentor would not allow him to consider it.[62]

Clayton Lawson's election to succeed Hatfield in 1974 demonstrated that, while some men could fulfill the duties of the office, others could not. After James L. Cox, Jr. worked in the office to assist Lawson with accounting for the Assembly's funds, the General Council elected him to his own terms in 1976 and 1978. In 1980, Lawson returned to the position of General Overseer and Hatfield returned to the job of General Secretary & Treasurer. Their reunion in the offices they held 30 years prior was short-lived as Hatfield died during the 75th General Assembly the following year. From 1982 to 1986, the General Council elected Lawson's nephew, Ronald Shelton, to the position before James Cox returned for a second tenure from 1986 to 1990.

James Kilgore's election in the last order of business of the first session of the 1990 General Assembly was not without controversy. Although the Standard Resolutions did not require members of the Executive Board to be ordained, some ministers felt they should be, and that the requirement was implied. When another licensed minister was nominated for Assistant General Secretary & Treasurer later in the week, he was declared ineligible.[63] The change in term limitations the following year extended Kilgore's tenure and allowed him to serve six years. In 1996, a resolution was submitted to extend the term and tenure limitations of the office to five successive elections and twelve consecutive years on the Executive Board. When the General Council voted not to suspend the order of business to consider it prior to the election, its purpose became moot, and it was withdrawn.[64]

On August 13, 1996, the General Council of the 90th General Assembly elected Alfred Newton, Jr. as the General Secretary & Treasurer. Once again, a question was raised about the nominee's eligibility since he was not yet ordained. The General Council voted in a separate motion that Newton was eligible, and he was elected accordingly.[65] To clear up future confusion, the Assembly adopted a resolution the following year that required "nominees for the Executive Board" to "have been ordained for a period of two years."[66] Newton served four years with Cecil Johnson and two under Lonnie Lyke before term limitations concluded his tenure.

When the General Council met for the 96th General Assembly on August 13, 2002, it reelected Lyke for General Overseer and James Cox for his Assistant. Both men ran unopposed. The General Council nominated three men for General Secretary & Treasurer, but two declined. The remaining nominee was subjected to a secret ballot yes/no vote as called for by the bylaws. After nearly two-thirds voted in the negative, the floor was reopened for nominations. After ten nominees declined running, the Council voted to table the election until Wednesday morning and have "the Executive Board meet in Executive Session to discuss the office of General Secretary & Treasurer." After the election the following day filled the office, a new resolution was adopted to create "an Administrative Assistant," hired by the Executive Board to work in the headquarters office.[67] Amy Lyke Profitt had been working as the office secretary with Kilgore and Newton for the past ten years, and assumed the new position when it was constituted. After the conclusion of a two-week training period for the incoming Secretary & Treasurer, the Finance Committee met on September 10, 2002 to audit Newton's books a final time. The closing balances in the general fund, missions, and youth ministries ledgers were reconciled with the August bank statements at this time.[68]

On March 10, 2003, Profitt resigned, effective at the conclusion of her two-week notice. She indicated she would work three days that week before taking two days off and requested her vacation time and pay the following week, along with severance.[69] The General Overseer called a joint meeting with the Executive Board and Finance Committee the following day to accept her resignation, approve the compensation requested, and discuss the qualifications, duties, and wages of a new hiree.[70] Ultimately, the position was never filled, and Profitt's absence the final month of the fiscal year's third quarter was evident when the Finance Committee met on May 13 to audit the ledgers.[71] The procedure took considerably longer than usual due to numerous inconsistencies in data entry. At the final quarterly meeting on July 29, the treasurer's books had not been closed by the July 10 deadline, the ledgers were not ready for audit, and the Finance Committee faced the grim reality that that the General Secretary & Treasurer's report may not be ready when the 97th General Assembly opened the following week. Such a fear was realized when the report failed to include disbursements for the general fund, youth department, or foreign missions. Also noticeably absent was a report on the benevolent and burial funds.[72]

After a motion to "commit the report to the Finance Committee to await completion," the General Secretary & Treasurer pledged to conclude his report by the end of August. After a series of amendments to the main motion, the General Council voted "to authorize the Finance Committee and General Secretary & Treasurer to bring to completion the financial report and that the General Overseer call a special session of the Board of Elders and

Finance Committee and empower them to act on behalf of the delegation to receive this report." Each delegate was to receive "the printed report after its completion and prior to the meeting of the Board of Elders."[73]

The Finance Committee met accordingly on September 2 and discovered that the Treasurer's "report was still incomplete" and the "ledgers were not ready for audit and approval."[74] Lyke then informed the pastors that the meeting with the Board of Elders and Finance Committee "to act on behalf of the delegation" was scheduled for September 30.[75] Four weeks later, the meeting convened at Headquarters, and the Finance Committee Chairman updated the Board of Elders on the situation. He said the treasurer "had asked him this morning if he wanted to look at his final report before it would be distributed to the Elders," and he declined, "saying there was no way to certify the report in such a short time." The Board voted to adjourn for lunch while the Finance Committee audited the report. Three hours later, the committee recalled the Elder Board, recounted numerous discrepancies in the report, and "summarized the committee's findings by stating that there was no way to send this report to the delegates at this time." The Board of Elders then voted to hire James Kilgore to spend 15 days in the office as soon as convenient to assist in the closing of the books and completion of the report, though no timetable was "set for the completion of this report."[76]

Another version of the report was presented to the Finance Committee when it met on November 11, 2003 to audit the first quarter of the 2003-2004 fiscal year.[77] When the report was not complete and the ledgers for the new fiscal year were not prepared for the audit, the Chairman indicated the committee would return the following week and complete its assignment or ask for the Treasurer's resignation. On November 18, the Treasurer presented a fifth edition of the report and indicated some hindrances to the preparation of the ledgers. The following week, he mailed the latest version of the report to the pastors and asked for their "help." He wanted "each Pastor and Church Treasurer to closely review the financial information credited to [their] church" and "report any corrections."[78] After the next two quarterly finance meetings failed to produce a reliable report or ledgers that could be audited satisfactorily, the Finance Committee Chairman asked for an Elders Meeting.

On May 20, 2004, the Board of Twelve Elders convened and voted that "due to non-compliance to job responsibilities and to orders from the General Overseer, Finance Committee, and Board of Twelve Elders," the General Secretary & Treasurer "be suspended from his office duties with pay and benefits until the 2004 Assembly election." The Assistant General Secretary

& Treasurer, Michael Padgett, assumed "many of the office duties until the General Assembly," and Kilgore was asked to continue working with previous treasurer's reports and the benevolent and burial funds.[79] When the local bank President recommended the CGMA close checking accounts and open new ones, Padgett took the advice and began new ledgers as well. As a result, two finance reports were presented to the 98th General Assembly in August. The one from Padgett opened on May 25 with balances using the reconciled bank statements from the closed checking accounts and concluded on July 10. Kilgore's report opened on July 11, 2003 using ending balances from his most recent edition of the 2002-2003 fiscal year report and concluded on May 24, 2004. The differences between the May 24 closing balances and May 25 opening balances as reported to the General Council totaled more than $172,000.[80]

After the May 2003 Finance Committee meeting when inconsistencies in the ledgers were first noticed, the Board of Twelve Elders met in regular or called meetings in July, August, September, December, and January, before finally suspending the Treasurer in May 2004. That it took six meetings for the Board to take corrective action was a reflection on the attitude of some Elders that "he was elected by the delegation to do the job," and, therefore, they lacked the authority to remove him.[81] As the dilemma lingered and leadership failed to rectify it, morale plunged. Some blamed the Board of Elders, while some blamed the Executive Board. In August, a bitterly divided Assembly gathered for the 98th General Council Meeting with a record number of delegates. Only once in the past three decades had another minister ran against an incumbent General or Assistant Overseer.[82] Nine votes separated Fred Cornelius from Lonnie Lyke as General Overseer, and four made the difference between Jay Walden and James Cox for Assistant. James Kilgore returned to the office of General Secretary & Treasurer, and W. Scott Isham was elected unopposed as his Assistant.[83] In 2020, it remained the only General Assembly where every member of the Executive Board changed.[84]

A Perfect Storm

The combination of scruples in the Treasurer's report, the benevolent fund crisis, and unmanageable debt eventually brought the CGMA to near financial collapse. The new officers understood the challenge in front of them. During the first quarter of the fiscal year, more than half the churches failed to send any tithe of tithes to headquarters, and 41 of the 116 churches sent no finances at all. Cornelius felt a personal "sense of accountability to God the Father to always communicate clearly and openly" and asked for the "help and cooperation" of the pastors and churches to "work hard and work together."[85] Total general fund receipts received at headquarters in the 2001-2002 fiscal year were a record-high, $655,377.22.[86] Three years later, they dropped nearly 19%.[87] It would be 2008 before the general fund receipts reached that amount again but, adjusted for inflation, remained almost 20% off that mark.[88] The decrease in revenue was especially intensified by the financial strain of one of the local churches. In November 2001, the Finance Committee received two requests for CGMA Headquarters to cosign on loans for local church construction projects.[89] The committee often granted such requests when local churches were unable to secure financing without a guarantor. When one of the churches fell behind on its monthly payments five years into its 15-year $300,000 mortgage, the general fund began making payments and paid more than $75,000 before the church became stable enough to resume the responsibility.[90]

Fortunately, by that time, the Assembly was attempting to resolve the crisis with the benevolent funds. On May 13, 2003, the Committee on Benevolent Funds and Insurance had met with the Finance Committee and reviewed the interest rates on the benevolent fund accounts. It was reported that "CD interest rates have declined," were "now at 2.5%," and that no banks in the area could come close to matching the 3.5% and 6.0% rates the Assembly would pay on benevolent fund 1 and 2, respectively. Faced with no choice, the committee agreed to make the adjustment and ultimately set the rates to match what was earned through certificates of deposit.[91]

However, the organization did not recover quickly from the low morale, as quantified by ways other than a lack of financial support. Attendance at the spring leadership conference, national youth rallies, and the General Assembly declined significantly. While general attendance at the latter was not counted and recorded, the number of "delegates" in the General Council was. The number of participants registered in election years was always significantly higher than the odd-numbered years. In the 1980s, the delegate count at the beginning of business sessions in election years averaged 147. In the 1990s, it climbed to 170 before it peaked at 203 in 2000 and hit an all-time high of 216 in 2004. Two years later, it dropped to 176.[92]

In an effort designed to increase attendance, a resolution was presented to the 102nd General Assembly to relocate the 2009 convention to "the vicinity of Pigeon Forge / Gatlinburg," Tennessee. After some discussion, the General Council voted 66-50 to lay the motion on the table. When the business session concluded shortly thereafter without having brought the motion from the table, the measure died.[93] Two days later, the discussion was revived at the meeting of the Board of Twelve Elders. As "interpreters of the current bylaws of the CGMA, and since the current bylaws do not state where the annual Assembly is to be held," the Elders determined "that the Executive Board is empowered to choose that location."[94] The explanation ignored a century-old practice rooted in the tradition of the South Union Association of United Baptists that the delegates have the power to choose the association meeting place. The Executive Board moved the General Assembly to the Grand Resort Convention Center in Pigeon Forge the following year and the Smoky Mountain Convention Center in 2010.[95]

The relocation did little to increase attendance and further damaged morale. Many preferred meeting in the Jellico tabernacle that had become a monument to cherished memories of worship and fellowship. Some were so disheartened that they chose not to attend at all.[96] Even if they supported the move, many ministers expressed displeasure at what they perceived to be a circumvention of the will of most of the General Council.[97] The first four election years in Pigeon Forge averaged 136 "delegates" at the beginning of the General Council, including the lowest total in decades with 122 in 2014.[98]

Another measure of low morale may be found in the number of ministers and churches leaving the fellowship. Such numbers fluctuate any given year based on several factors. But in the five years prior to 2000, the CGMA averaged five "ministers who left the fellowship" each year. In the five years following 2003, that average climbed to nearly 15.[99] When the "roll call of churches" was presented at the 102nd General Assembly in 2008, the General Council voted that "next year non-supporting churches will not be listed in the Roll Call of Churches report and the Pastors of those churches would not have their credentials renewed."[100] As a result, nearly 40 ministers left the CGMA or failed to have their credentials renewed over the next two years.[101] Over the same time frame, 23 churches were removed from the roll call.[102]

The financial reverses and lack of participation led to the discontinuation of the evangelism outreach director program, the cancelation of the spring leadership conference, and the practical cessation of the IIM. From 2001 to 2008, eight total ministers received monthly allotments from headquarters at various times for their services to local churches. After seven years, the program was discontinued for budgetary concerns.[103] The northern Sunday School Convention was held in Columbus, Ohio its first five years before it relocated to Dayton in 1983.[104] After four years there, the conference moved to the Kings Island Inn just north of Cincinnati and became a two-day event filled with multiple workshops and seminars.[105] In 1994, the convention was rebranded as "Leadership 2000" and featured four separate tracks for pastors, teachers, youth, and music with nine sessions in each track.[106] By the time it was renamed for the new millennium, "Leadership 21" had added a fifth track for "laity" or "changemakers."[107] At its peak, the convention drew more than 400 registrants, but attendance sharply declined in the first decade of the 21st century. In 2011, it relocated to a more cost-efficient location in Dayton where it was discontinued after two more conventions.[108]

Until a replacement for James Kilgore could be hired, the oversight of the IIM fell to Tim Bartee after his election as Christian Education Director in 2000. Bartee envisioned "expanding the extension sites to give every district access" to the school.[109] In the fall 2000 semester, 29 students completed courses at four different sites. Enrollment increased to 50 students at six locations that spring.[110] IIM added two more campuses the following year, and enrollment increased to 52 and 73 students in the fall and spring semesters.[111] By that time, no application had been received for the vacancy in the school administrator's position, and at a meeting of the IIM Board of Directors on May 31, 2002, General Overseer Lonnie Lyke "opened the discussion concerning the long term plan for IIM." He appointed James Cox to chair a subcommittee of the Board "to establish and implement a five-year plan for the College."[112] The task force consisted of Bartee, Michael Cornelius, Ray Landes, Michael Padgett, Roger Webb, Jerry Bastien, Steve Ireland, and Al Newton. In March, Cox assigned six tasks to groups of two to three members with goal of reorganizing the institute, and the committee met again in April.[113] Meanwhile, another possibility presented itself.

Bartee had projected the potential for "making the IIM internet accessible" and "providing high quality professional video correspondence courses."[114] In December 2002, the latter looked like it was on the horizon after five members of the IIM Board attended a presentation by the Church of God School of Ministry in Cleveland, Tennessee. Four years earlier, "the executive leadership of the" Church of God (Cleveland) "decided that the best

Figure 13.26: Tim Bartee

c/o CGMA

way to address the educational needs of ministers who could not attend" traditional college "was to develop non-traditional educational offerings." As a result, the School of Ministry launched a Certificate in Ministerial Studies (CIMS) program that featured "476 video lessons with 70 different instructors" in 19 college level courses in Biblical, doctrinal, and practical studies. The first courses were offered in January 2000, and the School of Ministry offered the CGMA the opportunity to participate in the still brand-new program. The CGMA General Overseer was invited to record an introduction to the videos to replace the one by the Church of God (Cleveland) General Overseer for tapes distributed in the Mountain Assembly, and the CGMA would pay only the costs of video duplication.[115] Ultimately, the situation in the General Secretary & Treasurer's office derailed both projects, and the last IIM courses taught regularly were offered during the 2004-2005 academic year.[116]

Conclusion: The Road to Recovery

After one term as General Overseer, Fred Cornelius decided not to seek reelection at the 100th General Assembly, and the General Council elected Walter "Donnie" Hill to succeed him, and Jay Anthony Walden followed him six years later. Midway through Hill's tenure, the CGMA showed signs of economic recovery with tithe of tithes reaching an all-time high of $410,752.70.[117] As James Kilgore's tenure as General Secretary & Treasurer was nearing an end, concerns over a negative impact from a transition in the office led to a proposal to double the length of tenure limitations. A resolution adopted at the 103rd General Assembly in 2009 permitted the General Secretary & Treasurer to "succeed himself five times for a total of twelve years," and Kilgore continued to serve in that capacity.[118] The perception of economic stability, however, proved to be a mirage as regular general fund receipts plummeted to the lowest point in more than two decades in the 2017-18 fiscal year.[119] The fiscal year was salvaged, however, from the proceeds of an insurance claim.

On Saturday, June 3, 2017, the "Cantrell building" burned as the Jellico Fire Department fought the blaze "all night and contained the damage."[120] In September, the insurance company settled the claim for $580,900.[121] Paying off the Assembly's debts was the first priority. In 2001, the Finance Committee had envisioned paying off the Cantrell property halfway through its 15-year mortgage with a balloon payment. Instead, at the conclusion of the 2015-2016 fiscal year, the Assembly still owed benevolent fund 2 almost two-thirds the original loan.¹²² The Executive Board met with the Finance Committee and General Trustees on December 5, 2017, to make decisions about the allocation of the proceeds. By that time, the Assembly had paid off the balances of the Cantrell property loan, the tabernacle roof loan, and a loan for one of the local churches for which headquarters had assumed payments. The demolition of the factory building was underway, and funds were already set aside to cover those costs. From the remaining proceeds, the joint committees approved funding to recarpet and repaint the office, repave the headquarters parking lot, purchase new office equipment, repair the sewage treatment plant at the youth campground, repair one of the dormitories there, install a new roof on one of the youth parsonages, transfer $36,000 to the missions funds for foreign work and church planting, and to reserve $125,000 in certificate of deposit for future use.¹²³

Necessity forced the organization to become more fiscally responsible. James Coffey's resignation as National Youth Director in the fall of 2013 presented an opportunity for the organization to reduce the budget of the general fund. The Executive Board and Finance Committee proposed that his assistant, Douglas Walden, be permitted to assume the duties of the office with a part-time salary while continuing to pastor his congregation in Ferguson, Kentucky. At the 108th General Assembly the following year, the General Council adopted a resolution to keep the plan in place for a two-year trial period.¹²⁴ While the absence of a full-time youth director saved money for the general fund, it cost the YWC fund. Total YWC receipts fell 12% in the first five years with a part-time youth director from the last five years with a full-time director.¹²⁵ Despite the economic losses and the lack of a full-time promoter, the camp program remained stable.

After the virtual dissolution of the IIM, Tim Bartee began a rebrand of CGMA ministry training as AIM: Advancement In Ministry in 2008 and launched a website to serve as a digital repository of leadership materials.¹²⁶ He continued to offer Bible survey courses periodically to serve the needs of ministers interested in ordination. In 2015, AIM launched a "Minister's Training Program," of twelve "monthly projects" that combined formal lectures, selected readings, and practical assignments with pastoral mentoring.¹²⁷ The Christian Education Department continued offering live and cybernetic alternatives to the bible correspondence courses and redesigned a history and doctrine course.

In 2018, James Walden, Jr. II succeeded his first cousin as General Overseer. Walden committed to restoring the sense of brotherhood so prevalent 25 years earlier by maintaining regular contact with pastors and district overseers, by soliciting the assistance of ministers and empowering them for service, and by championing ministerial training. The rise of social media helped bring together members of the Assembly and keep them connected in ways that John Parks never envisioned. The challenges that reached a critical point in 2004 threatened to unravel the Church of God Mountain Assembly, but perhaps the "bow tied" at Elk Valley 90 years earlier meant something more than a connection of the organization with its sister church in Cleveland. Maybe the CGMA congregations were tied together in such a way that nine decades of tension between two ecclesiologies and numerous ecclesiastical conflicts could not undo what hath God wrought.

---

[1] CGMA, Minutes (2000), 5-6, 19.

[2] Lonnie Lyke, General Overseer's Report; James L. Cox, Jr. Assistant General Overseer's Report; Alfred Newton, Jr., General Secretary & Treasurer's Report; Michael Padgett, Assistant General Secretary & Treasurer's Report, 95th General Assembly Delegate Book (2001), 2-5, 10-11, 36.

[3] Petree went on to serve until 2006. In two tenures, he served a total of 24 years as Public Relations Director.

[4] Merle Laws, "The Sidney, Ohio Church of God," *GH* 36, no. 3 (March 1975): 5-7.

[5] "Piqua Celebrates Fifty Years," *GH* 63, no. 1 (January 2004): 4.

[6] Jerry Bunn, "Aspinwall Church of God," *GH* 47, no. 6 (June 1986): 10; http://www.aspinwallchurch.com/about-us.html

[7] "History of Our Church," *GH* 34, no. 10 (September 1973): 5; "Now Read This," *GH* 35, no. 7 (July 1974): 3.

[8] "History of Towne Street CGMA," *GH* 60, no. 1 (January 1999): 9; Leon Petree, Facebook messages to the author, October 13, 2017.

[9] "Church Hosts 70th Homecoming," *GH* 59, no. 11 (November 1998): 19; Fred Cornelius, "A Note From Pastor Cornelius," *GH* 61, no. 7 (July 2000): 10.

[10] "We've Come This Far By Faith," *GH* 56, no. 10 (October 1995): 8-9.

[11] Kenneth Massingill, North Carolina District Report, 99th General Assembly Delegate Booklet (2005), 56.

[12] Top Ten Total Finance, Delegate Booklet (1997), 51; "High Point CGMA #5 Total Finances Sent to Headquarters," *GH* 6, no. 2 (February 1999): 10; "Monroe, Michigan," *GH* 58, no. 9 (September 1997): 14.

[13] When Douglas's term ended in 1996, he had served 42 of the previous 43 years on the Board of Elders due to his being elected to fulfill several unfulfilled terms. Only Clayton Lawson served more years on the Board of Twelve Elders (43 years).

14 "Metamora, Indiana," *GH* 62, no. 9 (September 2003): 8; "Metamora Indiana CGMA Celebrates New Church Facility Grand Opening," *GH* 63, no 12 (December 2004): 20.

15 CGMA, *[Minutes of the] 99th Annual Assembly of the Church of God Mountain Assembly* (Jellico, TN: CGMA, 2005), 9.

16 Lease Agreement between Church of God Mountain Assembly Inc. Headquarters and Jellico Tennessee Church of God Mountain Assembly, February 1, 2006.

17 Tennessee Deed of Trust, *Campbell County Trust Book* T464, November 15, 2005, 70, Campbell County Court House, Jacksboro, TN; Tennessee Deed of Trust, *Campbell County Trust Book* T531, June 9, 2006, 860, Campbell County Court House, Jacksboro, TN.

18 CGMA, *Minutes* (1995), 28-29.

19 James Kilgore, "Church of God Mountain Assembly Deceased Ministers Memorial," *GH* 57, no. 10 (October 1996): 18; CGMA, *Minutes* (1996), 46.

20 Jasper Walden, Board of Trustees Annual Report, Delegate Booklet (1998), 42.

21 Alfred Newton, Jr., Facebook message to the author, October 20, 2017.

22 Tennessee Deed of Trust, *Campbell County Trust Book* T94, August 15, 1975, 473, Campbell County Court House, Jacksboro, TN; Warranty Deed, *Campbell County Warranty Deed Book* 224, March 7, 1978, 49, Campbell County Court House, Jacksboro, TN; Warranty Deed, *Campbell County Warranty Deed Book* 224, September 13, 1976, 49, Campbell County Court House, Jacksboro, TN.

23 J.H. Douglas, Board of Trustees Report, Delegate Booklet (1985).

24 "Progress on New Construction at Headquarters in Jellico, TN," *GH* 60, no. 2 (February 1999): 20; Warranty Deed, *Campbell County Warranty Deed Book* 359, November 12, 1998, 203, Campbell County Court House, Jacksboro, TN.

25 CGMA, *Minutes* (2000), 32.

26 CGMA, *Minutes* (1942), 12; CGMA, *Minutes* (1956), 32; See further discussion in Chapter 8.

27 CGMA, *Minutes* (1966), 22-23. The ½ Social Security benefit required each minister to provide proof that he had paid the Social Security tax and that his tithes reflected the full amount of the income he had received from full-time ministry.

28 CGMA, *Minutes* (1976), 34.

29 CGMA, *Minutes* (1977), 26.

30 CGMA, *Minutes* (1978), 17-18, 20-21.

31 James L. Cox, Jr., Facebook message to the author, October 19, 2017. Nationwide proposed the plan to the CGMA with the expectation that 100 ministers would participate. Instead, four did.

32 "Elders Meeting," and "Minister's Retirement Plan and Death Benefits," CGMA, Delegate Booklet (1986).

33 CGMA, *Minutes* (1986), 22.

34 "Report of the Committee on Retirement and Insurance," Delegate Booklet (1987).

35 CGMA, *Minutes* (1987), 22.

36 CGMA, *Minutes* (1988), 27.

37 CGMA, *Minutes* (1996), 29. The plan expired in 2012 with the death of Annette Gibson.

38 CGMA, *Minutes* (1995), 27). The Committee on Retirement and Insurance was renamed the Committee on Benevolent Funds and Insurance in 1991. This was due, in part, to the recognition that the program was not a true *retirement* plan that might be subject to regulation by the Internal Revenue Service, but a benevolent gift offered to the minister at his/her request.

39 CGMA, *Minutes* (1987), 38.

40 CGMA, *[Minutes of the] 83rd Annual Assembly of the Church of God Mountain Assembly, Inc.* (Jellico, TN: CGMA, 1989), 40.

41 CGMA, *Minutes* (1988), 36-37; CGMA, *[Minutes of the] 91st Annual Assembly of the Church of God Mountain Assembly, Inc.* (Jellico, TN: CGMA, 1997), 34-35, 41.

42 CGMA, *Minutes* (1987), 38; CGMA, *Minutes* (2000), 32.

43 https://www.bankrate.com/banking/cds/historical-cd-interest-rates

44 Committee on Benevolent Funds and Insurance, Agenda, January 30, 2002; Al Newton, "Benevolent Fund Action," January 30, 2002; Personal recollections of the author.

45 Minutes of the Joint Meeting of the Board of Elders and Finance Committee, September 30, 2003; audio recording of the meeting in the possession of the author.

46 CGMA, *Minutes* (2002), 27-28.

47 Gail Douglas Garrett, Facebook post in "Jellico, America's Home Town," January 11, 2021; Tennessee Warranty Deed, *Campbell County Warranty Deed Book* 73, 306, August 30, 1924, Campbell County Court House, Jacksboro, TN.

48 "Imperial Cantrell was founded in 1925," *The [Jellico] Advance Sentinel*, July 1, 1981.

49 Minutes of Joint Meeting Executive and Trustee Board along with Finance Committee, May 8, 2001.

50 Minutes of Joint Meeting of Executive & Trustee Board Benevolent & Finance Committee, June 5, 2001; Agenda (with author's original notes), Joint Meeting of Executive & Trustee Board Benevolent & Finance Committee, June 5, 2001.

51 Minutes of Joint Committee Meetings, Delegate Booklet (1985).

52 CGMA, *Minutes* (1985), 20.

53 CGMA, *Minutes* (1987), 23.

54 CGMA, *Following the Calling: Building Strong Local Churches* (Jellico, TN: CGMA, 2001), 1-3.

55 Ibid., 4; Henry Taylor, "Armor Bearer's Meeting," *GH* 61b, no. 9 (September 2001): 9.

56 Taylor, "Introducing Men of Integrity," *GH* 61b, no. 10 (October 2001): 7; Taylor, "Developing Armor Bearers," *GH* 61b, no. 11 (November 2001): 7.

57 Henry Taylor, Men of Integrity Report, 96th General Assembly Delegate Booklet (2002), 47; CGMA, *Minutes* (2002), 5.

58 *Following the Calling*, 5-8.

59 *Following the Calling*, 9-20.

60 Tennessee Warranty Deed, *Campbell County Warranty Deed Book* 390, 724, June 7, 2002, Campbell County Court House, Jacksboro, TN; CGMA, *Minutes* (2002), 23.

61 CGMA, *Minutes* (1956), 20; CGMA, *Minutes* (1958), 19; CGMA, *Minutes* (1960), 23; CGMA, *Minutes* (1962), 22; CGMA, *Minutes* (1964), 20; Wade M. Hughes, notes in his personal copy of CGMA, *Minutes* (1966), 48.

62 Wade M. Hughes, conversation with the author, ca. 2002.

63 CGMA, *Minutes* (1990), 21, 25.

64 Resolution A, CGMA Delegate Booklet (1996), 82; CGMA, *Minutes* (1996), 24, 28.

65 CGMA, *Minutes* (1996), 24.

66 CGMA, *[Minutes of the] 91st General Assembly* (Jellico, TN: CGMA, 1997), 25-26.

67 CGMA, *Minutes* (2002), 4-5, 12-13.

68 Agenda – Finance Committee Meeting, September 10, 2002; Finance Committee Report, September 10, 2002.

69 Amy Profitt, Memorandum to the Executive Board of the Church of God Mountain Assembly, March 9, 2003.

70 Agenda – Joint Executive Board and Finance Committee Meeting, March 11, 2003.

71 Agenda for Finance / Benevolent Committee, May 13, 2003.

72 Treasurer's Report, 97th General Assembly Delegate Booklet (2003).

73 Minutes of the 97th General Assembly.

74 Lonnie Lyke, to the distinguished Board of Elders and Finance Committee, September 2, 2003.

75 Lonnie Lyke, to the pastors of the CGMA, September 2, 2003.

76 Minutes of the joint meeting of the Board of Elders and Finance Committee, September 30, 2003.

77 Agenda for Finance Committee, November 11, 2003.

78 Roger L. Webb, to the Pastors of the CGMA, November 25, 2003.

79 Minutes of the Meeting of the Board of Twelve Elders, May 24, 2004; Lonnie Lyke, to the pastors of the CGMA, May 29, 2004.

80 Treasurer's Reports, 98th General Assembly Delegate Booklet (2004), 37-53, 55-64. The discrepancy in the General Fund was reportedly $70,268.74, in the Missions Treasury $4,431.55, in the youth treasury $47,438.46, in the Benevolent Funds $22,414.37, and in the Burial Fund $28,208.83. In every case, the bank reconciled balances showed *more* money in the bank than reported in the ledgers. This suggests that numerous *deposits* made from September 2002 through May 2004 were never properly recorded in the ledgers.

81 Minutes, September 30, 2003.

82 CGMA, *Minutes* (1998), 24.

83 CGMA, *[Minutes of the] 98th Annual Assembly of the Church of God Mountain Assembly* (Jellico, TN: CGMA, 2004), 7-8.

84 The "Executive Board" was created with the new system of Government in 1944. Some early minute books fail to record who was elected to each position, but it does not

appear that any prior assembly saw a change in all four offices (Moderator, Assistant Moderator, Clerk, and Assistant Clerk) as well.

[85] CGMA, Finances Received July 11th through October 10th, 2004; Fred R. Cornelius, [to the ministers and treasurers of the CGMA], October 18, 2004.

[86] CGMA, *Minutes* (2002), 26.

[87] CGMA, *Minutes* (2005), 33.

[88] CGMA, *[Minutes of the] 102nd Annual Assembly of the Church of God Mountain Assembly* (Jellico, TN: CGMA, 2008), 40.

[89] Agenda for Finance Committee [with the author's notes], November 13, 2001.

[90] CGMA, *[Minutes of the] Church of God Mountain Assembly 100th Annual Assembly* (Jellico, TN: CGMA, 2006), 32; CGMA, *[Minutes of the] Church of God Mountain Assembly 101st Annual Assembly* (Jellico, TN: CGMA, 2007), 31.

[91] Agenda for Executive Board, Benevolent and Insurance Committee, and Finance Committee with attached report, May 13, 2003.

[92] CGMA Minute Books, 1980 to 2006.

[93] CGMA, *Minutes* (2008), 13-14.

[94] Donnie Hill, [to the pastors of the CGMA], August 19, 2008.

[95] CGMA, *[Minutes of the] 103rd Annual Assembly of the Church of God Mountain Assembly* (Jellico, TN: CGMA, 2009); CGMA, *[Minutes of the] 104th Annual Assembly of the Church of God Mountain Assembly* (Jellico, TN: CGMA, 2010).

[96] The author knows numerous ministers and ministers who attended the General Assembly in Jellico for decades but have never or rarely attended a service since its move to Pigeon Forge.

[97] The author talked to numerous ministers who were displeased with *how* the change came about even if they were pleased to have the convention somewhere else.

[98] CGMA Minute Books (2010 to 2016).

[99] CGMA Minute Books (1995 to 2009).

[100] CGMA, *Minute Book* (2008), 12.

[101] CGMA, Minute Books (2009 to 2010).

[102] Church Statistical Information, 102nd General Assembly Delegate Booklet (2008), 21-23; 104th General Assembly CGMA Financial Statement, 1-3.

[103] CGMA, *Minutes* (2002), 26; CGMA, *Minutes* (2005), 34; CGMA, *Minutes* (2006), 33; CGMA, *Minutes* (2007), 33; CGMA, *Minutes* (2008), 38. The ministers were: Steve Branstutter (Kokomo), Rich Holmes (Knoxville), Nick Hill (Harriman), James Coffey (Williamsburg), Doug Walden (Middlesboro), Joe Riggs (Harriman), Jon Walden (Jellico), and Jeremy Walden (Brimfield).

[104] Church Calendar, *GH* 43, no. 10 (October 1982): 12.

[105] "Joint Sunday School Convention & Pastors' Conference," *GH* 48, no. 1 (January/February 1987): 19.

[106] "Leadership 2000 Schedule," *GH* 55, no. 3 (March 1994): 16.

[107] "Leadership 21—Equipping Leaders for Ministry in the 21st Century," *GH* 61b, no. 2 (February 2001): 16.

108 Tim Bartee, National Christian Education Department report, 105th General Assembly Delegate Booklet (2011).

109 Tim Bartee, The International Institute of Ministry Regional Coordinator Packet, 2000-2001.

110 Tim Bartee, National Christian Education Department report, 95th General Assembly Delegate Booklet (2001), 39-40.

111 Tim Bartee, National Christian Education Department report, Delegate Booklet (2002), 41.

112 Minutes of IIM Board of Directors Meeting, May 31, 2002.

113 Record of IIM Board of Directors Organizational Sub-Committee Meeting, March 15, 2003.

114 Bartee, IIM Coordinator Packet.

115 Church of God of the Mountain Assembly and Church of God School of Ministry Agenda, December 10, 2002; "CIMS Overview," included in handouts distributed at the meeting.

116 CGMA, *Minutes* (2005), 32. Under the auspices of the IIM, the author taught bible survey courses in 2007-2008 in his local church to meet requirements for ordination.

117 CGMA, *Minutes* (2009), 38.

118 CGMA, *Minutes* (2009), 10. At a meeting of the Board of Twelve Elders on August 6, 2015, the Board inexplicably interpreted the passage of the resolution to imply that Kilgore's tenure began anew with the election of 2010 and was entitled to continue serving in that capacity until 2022 and ignored the clause in the bylaws that states explicitly that "but in no case shall nay person serve more than twelve consecutive years on the Executive Board." As a result, Kilgore continues to serve in the office as of 2021.

119 CGMA, *[Minutes of the] 112th Annual Assembly of the Church of God Mountain Assembly* (Jellico, TN: CGMA, 2018), 36.

120 James Kilgore, e-mail to the CGMA pastors, June 6, 2017.

121 James Kilgore, text message to the author, September 6, 2017.

122 CGMA, *[Minutes of the] 110th Annual Assembly of the Church of God Mountain Assembly* (Jellico, TN: CGMA, 2016), 39.

123 Minutes of the Joint Meeting of the CGMA Board of Trustees, Finance Committee, and Executive Board, December 5, 2017.

124 CGMA, *[Minutes of the] 108th Annual Assembly of the Church of God Mountain Assembly* (Jellico, TN: CGMA, 2014), 8-9. In 2016, the trial was extended an additional two years, and in 2018, the trial was extended with slight modifications for another two years. The 2020 expiration of the trial was postponed by the canceled General Assembly due to COVID-19 and remains in place until at least August 2021.

125 See CGMA Minute Books, 2009-2013, 2015-2019.

126 Tim Bartee, "Christian Education Department – Teaching Tips," *GH* 67, no. 1 (February 2008): 5.

127 https://www.timbartee.com/cgma-ministers-training-program, accessed May 6, 2021.

14

Summary, Analysis, and Conclusion

Summary

The South Union Association of United Baptists summarily dismissed seven ministers for preaching the Wesleyan doctrine of entire sanctification and the danger of apostasy in 1905. These ministers and the churches under their influence met two years later to form a new association of churches modeled after the polity of their Baptist heritage. When the members of the Mountain Assembly became aware of the Church of God (Cleveland) in 1911, they discovered a like-minded group of Pentecostal believers with a Wesleyan Holiness background. Doctrinally, the groups were so similar that in the 1920s the Mountain Assembly took its standard teachings directly from the group in Cleveland. Where the groups differed, however, was in polity. Almost from its beginning, the Church of God (Cleveland) governed itself with an episcopal polity with its founder A.J. Tomlinson at the head as General Overseer. State, and later District, Overseers completed the hierarchical government of the church with a Board of Elders to assist the General Overseer with national administration. A failed merger between the Mountain Assembly and the Church of God (Cleveland) in 1912 was the result of these conflicting polities.

Dozens of Mountain Assembly ministers left the organization for the Church of God (Cleveland) in favor of its polity and sometimes took entire congregations with them. Many who stayed with the Mountain Assembly sought reform to structure the organization's government after the model of the Church of God (Cleveland) perceiving that as the key to replicate the numerical success of the larger group. In 1944, the Mountain Assembly adopted a new more episcopal system of government. The major changes accomplished through this broad action led directly to a schism, and the opposing group reorganized as the Church of God of the Original Mountain Assembly and reverted to the polity adopted in 1907.

Empowering leadership with "general oversight of all the churches" was ultimately ineffective without the consent of those churches. Episcopalism went only so far as each congregation was willing to submit its own authority to the hierarchy. Thus, during its first 40 years, the history of the Church of

Summary, Analysis, and Conclusion

God Mountain Assembly is best understood as a narrative between two tensions, the competing influences of congregationalism from its Baptist heritage and episcopalism from its exposure to the Church of God (Cleveland). After 1950, the Mountain Assembly gravitated back toward its congregationalist roots and abandoned the Bishop's Council for the more democratic General Council. The direct influence of the Church of God (Cleveland) diminished as the Mountain Assembly began to fellowship with the Pentecostal Church of Christ and experienced national and international growth through its emphasis on a general missions program. Maintaining the episcopal offices of the Church of God (Cleveland) without redefining the scope of their power sustained the tension within the organization as denominational leaders sometimes asserted authority over churches and congregations sometimes rebuffed. By the end of the century, an emphasis on the primacy of ministry at the local level over denominational ministries rekindled the conflict.

Analysis

The tension between two polities existed throughout the Mountain Assembly's history. Sometimes, its occurrence was subtle, and on other occasions it was obvious. Three clear demonstrations of this may be found by analyzing the process of church membership, the selection of pastors, and the permanency of organizational membership. In each example, the ecclesiastical polity is best understood as a mixture of the two polities held in tension.

In the Baptist church, membership typically took place at the monthly conference meeting. The prospective member testified of his or her conversion experience and answered questions. By majority vote, the church received the convert into the fellowship upon water baptism. Baptized members pledged themselves to abide by the covenant of the church.[1] Baptist churches also believed that the right to discipline members rested solely with the church body and developed a procedure for excluding members that included a trial and a vote from the membership.[2] Baptist ecclesiology emphasized that "no outside ecclesiastical authority possesses jurisdiction over the local church" and that "the final court of appeal is the congregation."[3] The sole authority for the reception and exclusion of church members rested in the church body with every member having the right to vote.

As ecclesiology developed in the Church of God (Cleveland), its membership process looked altogether different. First, it disassociated water baptism from membership. The 7th General Assembly raised the question of whether the Church of God can "fellowship one who has not taken on the Lord in baptism" and concluded that "water baptism is not a door into the church."[4] In November 1914, the 10th General Assembly recommended in cases where "a person wishes to unite with the church," but cannot presently be baptized, "they shall not be denied the privilege of membership." While the church expected that new members would seek baptism as soon as possible, their right to membership was unquestioned.[5] Second, a procedure for the reception of new members gradually developed and was formally adopted as practiced in 1954. This process required the pastor to read the teachings of the church publicly before calling "prospective members to stand before the altar and face the congregation" and then charging them to fulfill the expectations of the church. "By the authority vested in" him "as a minister of the Church of God," the pastor received new members into the church, prayed, and invited the congregation to offer "the right hand of fellowship."[6] Instead of a business conference, the rite occurred during a worship service and was performed by the pastor, without a vote by the congregation. The exclusion process developed in such a way that a member could be excluded from the Church of God (Cleveland) by a vote of the congregation, by the pastor and pastor's council, or by state or district overseer alone.[7]

The founders of the Mountain Assembly maintained the process of church membership they had practiced as Baptists. During its first year of organization in 1918, the Mountain Assembly church in Fonde received 36 new members by baptism during its regular monthly business conferences. During the same time, the church also excluded three of its members "for walking disorderly."[8] The sentiment of water baptism's relationship to membership was so strong that in 1921, the Mountain Assembly adopted two related measures. Members "must be baptized by a legal ordained minister of the Church of God [Mountain Assembly]," and ordained ministers shall "baptize no one who will not take up fellowship with the church." The same year, it resolved that "each local Church shall have the final decision as to excluding their members."[9] Over the next two decades, however, the membership process in the Mountain Assembly morphed into a hybrid of the Baptist church and the Church of God (Cleveland).

Elery Barnes moved to Fonde in the early 1930s and began attending the Mountain Assembly church after his daughter joined there. Barnes was a member of the Baptist church but was intrigued by the joyful expressiveness of Pentecostal worship and the "good clean life" that the Mountain Assembly members appeared to live. As he studied scripture and prayed for God's direction in his life, he had an epiphany after work one day that confirmed he needed to join the Mountain Assembly. That night, he "went and joined the Church of God [Mountain Assembly] and they gave [him] the right hand of fellowship."[10] The Fonde church allowed Barnes to come forward and present himself for membership during a revival service in the late winter of 1933 and gave him the right hand of fellowship. Having been baptized by a Baptist minister, however, Barnes was required to be re-baptized soon after.[11]

When the Mountain Assembly adopted its new system of government in 1944, it also removed the stipulation for baptism by a Mountain Assembly minister. The new rule allowed Christians satisfied with their baptism to join the church provided it was by immersion using the Trinitarian formula.[12] Three years later, the Mountain Assembly annulled its prohibition on ministers baptizing nonmembers.[13] By 1950, water baptism was still a requirement for membership in the Mountain Assembly, but the process now allowed for prospective members to join any time the pastor *opened the doors of the church*. It still included assent to the church covenant but was also generally accompanied by the *right hand of fellowship*. Most significantly, the church membership continued to vote by majority to receive members and to exclude them.

A second illustration of the tension between the two ecclesiological roots of the Mountain Assembly may be seen in the method of pastoral selection. In Baptist ecclesiology, the church's responsibility "of settling a minister" included the "call and invitation of some church, and his accepting the call on the terms proposed, or such as they may agree upon."[14] United Baptist churches in Whitley County, Kentucky, typically elected their pastors to a one-year term. This annual review facilitated a convenient transition if the pastor or the congregation grew dissatisfied. The church elected its pastor by a majority vote of its members and reserved the right to remove him by the same procedure. Such was the case of John Parks at Jellico Creek United Baptist Church from 1900-1902. One month after his second reelection, Parks was removed from the pastorate by motion and a vote of the church.[15]

When the Church of God (Cleveland) appointed its first State Overseers in 1911, it empowered them to "see that every church is supplied with a pastor as much as lies in his power."[16] Five years later, Tomlinson expressed his concern of "each church being an independent government of its own, and bordering on to independent democracy instead of real Bible theocracy" and urged the Assembly not to dismiss before a better process for pastoral selection could be adopted.[17] Ultimately, churches were urged to "refrain from taking action on the selection of pastors until authorized to do so by the state overseer" and the said overseer was given authority to "direct such a procedure as is suited in his judgment for the welfare of the church in the selection of said pastor."[18] In 1954, the Church of God (Cleveland) returned the privilege of voting to the members of the local church. This voting, however, was understood to be a "preference for pastors" and upheld the idea that "the authority of the appointment of pastors is vested in the state overseer."[19] Without a United Baptist tradition of annual elections, Church of God (Cleveland) pastors never faced the re-election process.

Again, the pastoral selection process of the Mountain Assembly and the role of the district overseer should be viewed as a hybrid of the two. Six resolutions were adopted at the first Mountain Assembly in 1907, one of which dealt implicitly with the right of churches to elect their pastors. Churches were called to "examine such preachers as they may have in mind to call for pastors to see if they are in the faith of holiness of heart and life."[20] Seven years later, churches were urged to "choose for their pastors, ministers that are able to care for the churches."[21] In 1941, the Mountain Assembly explicitly placed in its standard resolutions what had already been an accepted practice throughout its history. Churches would elect their pastors, and for the sake of uniformity, the pastoral election in each church would be conducted in August.[22]

The new system of government in 1944 created the first state overseers in the Mountain Assembly. Given general oversight of the churches in his state, the overseer's authority in the local churches remained limited. When trouble arose in a church that could not be resolved locally, the overseer, "with the pastor and church, shall endeavor to bring about a satisfactory settlement."[23] A new resolution in 1951 required pastors to consult with the district overseer before resigning. In such cases, the overseer was then empowered to appoint a pastoral replacement.[24] CGMA pastors continued to be elected for a one-year term until 1950 when the length was doubled, and elections became bi-annual.[25] The office of district overseer was modeled after the state overseers in the Church of God (Cleveland). However, it lacked the same kind of authority in the Mountain Assembly, and pastor elections continued to be a privilege of congregational government.

One final analysis worth consideration examines the relationship between the local churches and the organization. Central to Baptist ecclesiology was the autonomy of the church. While Baptists recognized that no higher

Summary, Analysis, and Conclusion

authority existed outside the members collectively, they also saw the importance of cooperation between local churches. Joining an association in proximity allowed the church to participate in collaborative ventures and mutually benefit from fellowship in Christian service. United Baptist churches typically included the formal drafting of a letter to the association in the business of the monthly conference before the associational meeting. The United Baptist Church of Christ at Little Rock Creek in southeastern Whitley County did just that at its meeting on August 15, 1896. The letter, prepared by Pastor John Parks and Clerk Isham Anderson read:

> We the United Baptist Church of Christ now in session at Little Rock Creek sendeth greetings to the West Union Association when convened with the messengers and delegates at Black Creek Church, Scott County, Tenn. We send this short spirited by the hands of our beloved bretheren [sic] who we have chosen from among us to sit with you in a Godly consultation and counsel whom we trust you will invite to seat with you.[26]

Letters such as these included membership statistics, named church messengers, and were read at the associational meeting. Participation in the association was voluntary, and the church could and did choose whether to send a letter annually.

As ecclesiology developed within the Church of God (Cleveland), the church came to be understood as one church in perpetual union, howbeit that met in multiple locations. The church made this clear in 1920 by declaring that

> the names of all the local churches recorded in various minutes including this one are the result of the faithful services of the ministers and representatives of the General Assembly and when thus received by the said representatives of the General Assembly they then became and composed a part of the General Assembly. We, therefore, do not recognize the right of any local church to withdraw from the General Assembly as a whole.[27]

When the Mountain Assembly organized in 1907, its commitment to congregationalism was evidenced by their retention of the custom of lettering to each annual association meeting. Local church members understood this as voluntarily joining the Mountain Assembly for another year or withdrawing from it by withholding the letter. Just six weeks before the 20th Annual Mountain Assembly, for example, the Mountain Assembly church at Jellico voted that "the clerk prepare a letter to the Assembly."[28] Likewise, the church at Fonde voted three weeks later in its monthly conference "that the church letter up to the Assembly."²⁹ Even after the Mountain Assembly stopped reading the letters in 1975, and instead instituted a statistical form to be completed by the local church clerks, many older churches continued the practice of formally voting to send a letter.

On the concept of voluntary participation in the association in Baptist ecclesiology as opposed to a perpetual union in the Church of God (Cleveland), the Mountain Assembly tended toward autonomy like the Baptist church. So, even while the CGMA was growing more episcopal in its polity and leadership, local churches found flexibility to exercise their own will. For this reason, during the first forty years of the Mountain Assembly's history, no less than 127 different congregations were members of the Mountain Assembly, although at no time was the total number higher than 47.³⁰ The departure of churches from the Mountain Assembly with Fore and Goins to the Church of God (Cleveland) in the 1920s and the churches that followed Long and Moses in 1946 must be understood in this context.

Conclusion

The first four decades of Mountain Assembly history demonstrate the strain between its Baptist roots and the influence of the Church of God (Cleveland). While ministers continued to transfer to and from the Church of God (Cleveland) over the next six decades, its direct influence over the Mountain Assembly effectively culminated by 1950. When J.H. Bryant chose not to seek reelection after one year in office, the CGMA decided its General Overseer should serve the organization with a full-time salary and housing provided from its tithes' funds. Luther Gibson was elected General Overseer from 1947 to 1950. In 1950, the Mountain Assembly amended its standard resolutions to elect officers biennially, and Clayton Lawson served as General Overseer from 1950 to 1960. Ira Moses followed Lawson and served until a new resolution creating term limitations forced him out of office in 1972. Both measures, the two-year term and the two-term limit, were duplicated from the Church of God (Cleveland). Two years later, term limitations brought J.E. Hatfield's 34-year tenure as General Secretary & Treasurer to an end as well. By the time the third generation of leadership took over the Mountain Assembly in the 1970s, its constitutional governmental structure was a near carbon copy of the Church of God (Cleveland).

Clayton Lawson's leadership as General Overseer in the 1950s sought to situate the Mountain Assembly among the broader Pentecostal movement by participation in the Pentecostal Fellowship of North America. Lawson also

Summary, Analysis, and Conclusion

sought to double its size and impact by merging with the Pentecostal Church of Christ. Although this pursuit failed, it did introduce the Mountain Assembly to foreign missions through the PCC's works in South America. While Lawson failed to launch a missions program during his tenure of office, his successor, Ira Moses, successfully planted the first Mountain Assembly congregation in Brazil in 1968.

Moses's twelve-year tenure as General Overseer followed Lawson's decade in office. Gibson served ten of those years as the Assistant General Overseer, and Hatfield served the entire 22 as General Secretary & Treasurer. By 1970, the Mountain Assembly recognized the potential for another schism over personalities existed within the denomination. So, it enacted measures designed to allow more men to lead. Thus, the second generation of leadership came to an end by resolution. The General Council imposed a two-term limit on each of the officials with a maximum of eight consecutive years on the Executive Board. It also created an eight-year term for members of the Board of Elders with three members leaving the Board every two years.

In the 1970s, the Mountain Assembly continued to develop its centralized government with the creation of a Second Assistant General Overseer, a Christian Education Director, and national ladies' officers. By 1980, the organization had five officials earning a full-time salary, despite having only 95 congregations in the United States. This number continued to fluctuate by as much as 20 over the next three decades as new churches joined, while others left at will. Thus, the impulse of independent congregationalism remains deeply ingrained in the culture of many Mountain Assembly congregations just as it was in the 1910s when Hayes Creek and Zion Hill rejected the directive of the association to discontinue the use of tobacco. This book has limited its scope to the tension in ecclesiastical polity in the first 100 years of the history of the Mountain Assembly. Further research will demonstrate the long-term impact of the 98th General Assembly and the various ways leadership responded to the challenges that resulted from it over the next two decades.

---

[1] Wills, in Devers, *Polity*, 22-23.

[2] Benjamin Griffith, *A Short Treatise Concerning a True and Orderly Gospel Church* (Philadelphia, 1743) in Dever, *Polity*, 106-110.

[3] Wellum and Wellum, in Dever and Leeman, *Foundations*, 64, 67.

[4] Church of God, *Echoes* (1912), 19.

[5] Church of God, *Echoes* (1914), 3.

[6] Church of God, *Minutes of Forty-Fifth General Assembly* (Cleveland, TN: Church of God Publishing House, 1954), 27.

[7] Church of God, *Minutes 2016: Church of God Book of Discipline, Church Order, and Governance* (Cleveland, TN: Church of God Publishing House, 2016), 143-144. The Church of God gave pastors the right to dismiss members at the 10th General Assembly in 1914. Church of God, *Echoes* (1914), 31.

[8] Fonde Minutes, 4-25.

[9] CGMA, *Minutes* (1921), 4.

[10] Elery Barnes, "God's Blessings to Me," *GH* 2, no. 8 (February 1944): 1, 6.

[11] Fonde Minutes, 190.

[12] CGMA, *Minutes* (1944), 10.

[13] CGMA, *Minutes* (1947), 10.

[14] Samuel Jones, *A Treatise of Church Discipline, and a Directory* (Lexington: T. Anderson, 1805) in Dever, *Polity*, 146-148.

[15] Minutes of Jellico Creek Baptist.

[16] Church of God, *Minutes* (1911), 12.

[17] Church of God, *Minutes of the Twelfth Annual Assembly* (Cleveland, TN: Church of God Publishing House, 1916), 13.

[18] Church of God, *Minutes of the Twenty-Sixth General Assembly* (Cleveland, TN: Church of God Publishing House, 1931), 38.

[19] Church of God, *Minutes* (1954), 34.

[20] CGMA, *Minutes* (1907), 3.

[21] CGMA, *Minutes* (1914), 3-4.

[22] CGMA, *Minutes* (1941), 10.

[23] CGMA, *Minutes* (1944), 9.

[24] CGMA, *Minutes* (1951), 10.

[25] CGMA, *Minutes* (1950), 11.

[26] First United Baptist Church of Christ, Clerk's Journal: 1887-1912, no pagination, transcription available at Historical and Genealogical Room, Whitley County Public Library, Williamsburg, Kentucky.

[27] Church of God, *Minutes of the Fifteenth Annual Assembly* (Cleveland, TN: Church of God Publishing House, 1920), 50.

[28] Jellico Minutes, 112.

[29] Fonde Minutes, 135.

[30] CGMA, *Minutes* (1945), 26-27.

Appendix One

General Officials

The Church of God Mountain Assembly selected by motion its first officers beginning with the First General Assembly in 1907. In 1934, the Assembly began using the nomination procedure to select its officials. Elections were held annually until 1950 when a two-year term was instituted. In *1968* the rules were changed to require a majority vote for election. Tenure of office limitations began with the elections of 1970.

Term	*Moderator*	*Assistant Moderator*
1907-08	Andrew J. Silcox	James J. Sammons
1908-09	Andrew J. Silcox	Stephen N. Bryant
1909-10	unknown	unknown
1910-11	Andrew J. Silcox	Edom J. Rountree
1911-12	Stephen N. Bryant	John H. Parks
1912-13	Stephen N. Bryant	John H. Parks
1913-14	Stephen N. Bryant	John H. Parks
1914-15	Stephen N. Bryant	Newton K. Parks
1915-16	Stephen N. Bryant	Newton K. Parks
1916-17	Stephen N. Bryant	Newton K. Parks
1917-18	Stephen N. Bryant	George A. Fore
1918-19	Stephen N. Bryant	George A. Fore
1919-20	Stephen N. Bryant	George A. Fore
1920-21	Stephen N. Bryant	George A. Fore
1921-22	Stephen N. Bryant	none
1922-23	George A. Fore	James L. Goins
1923-24	Stephen N. Bryant	Charles H. Standifer
1924-25	Stephen N. Bryant	John H. Parks
1925-26	Stephen N. Bryant	Kim Moses
1926-27	Stephen N. Bryant	Kim Moses
1927-28	Stephen N. Bryant	Curd Walker
1928-29	Stephen N. Bryant	Kim Moses

1929-30	Stephen N. Bryant	Kim Moses
1930-31	Stephen N. Bryant	Kim Moses
1931-32	Stephen N. Bryant	Kim Moses
1932-33	Stephen N. Bryant	Kim Moses
1933-34	Stephen N. Bryant	John H. Parks
1934-35	John H. Parks	Andrew J. Long
1935-36	Stephen N. Bryant	Andrew J. Long
1936-37	Stephen N. Bryant	Andrew J. Long
1937-38	Stephen N. Bryant	Andrew J. Long
1938-39	Stephen N. Bryant	Andrew J. Long
1939-40	Andrew J. Long	John H. Bryant
1940-41	Andrew J. Long	John H. Bryant
1941-42	Andrew J. Long	John H. Bryant
1942-43	Andrew J. Long	Kim Moses
1943-44	Andrew J. Long	Kim Moses
	General Overseer	***Assistant Overseer***
1944-45	Andrew J. Long	Clayton Lawson
1945-46	Andrew J. Long	Clayton Lawson
1946-47	John H. Bryant	Esom B. Bryant II
1947-48	Luther Gibson	Harvey Rose
1948-49	Luther Gibson	Ira H. Moses
1949-50	Luther Gibson	Clayton Lawson
1950-52	Clayton Lawson	Ira H. Moses
1952-54	Clayton Lawson	Luther Gibson
1954-56	Clayton Lawson	Luther Gibson
1956-58	Clayton Lawson	Luther Gibson
1958-60	Clayton Lawson	Luther Gibson
1960-62	Ira H. Moses	Luther Gibson
1962-64	Ira H. Moses	Clayborn B. Ellis Jr.
1964-66	Ira H. Moses	Clayborn B. Ellis Jr.
1966-68	Ira H. Moses	James E. Prewitt
1968-70	Ira H. Moses	James E. Prewitt
1970-72	Ira H. Moses	Clayborn B. Ellis Jr.
1972-74	Clayborn B. Ellis Jr.	Glenn Rowe

Appendix 1: General Officials and Committees

Term		
1974-76	Clayborn B. Ellis Jr.	Jerome Walden
1976-78	Jerome Walden	Kenneth E. Massingill
1978-80	Jerome Walden	Kenneth E. Massingill
1980-82	Clayton Lawson	James L. Cox Jr
1982-84	Clayton Lawson	James L. Cox Jr
1984-86	Kenneth E. Massingill	Jasper Walden
1986-88	Kenneth E. Massingill	Jasper Walden
1988-90	Jasper Walden	Kenneth E. Massingill
1990-92	Jasper Walden	Bob J. Vance[1]
		Cecil Johnson
1992-94	Jasper Walden	Cecil Johnon
1994-96	Cecil Johnson	Lonnie Lyke
1996-98	Cecil Johnson	Lonnie Lyke
1998-2000	Cecil Johnson	Lonnie Lyke
2000-02	Lonnie Lyke	James L. Cox Jr.
2002-04	Lonnie Lyke	James L. Cox Jr.
2004-06	Fred R. Cornelius	Jay A. Walden
2006-08	Donnie Hill	Jay A. Walden
2008-10	Donnie Hill	Jay A. Walden
2010-12	Donnie Hill	Lonnie Lyke
2012-14	Jay A. Walden	Lonnie Lyke
2014-16	Jay A. Walden	James Walden Jr. II
2016-18	Jay A. Walden	James Walden Jr. II
2018-21[2]	James Walden Jr. II	Jay A. Walden

Term	*Second Assistant Overseer*
1978-82	J.E. Prewitt
1982-84	Ray Landes, Jr.
1984-86	Michael Bartee
1986-88	Michael Bartee

---

[1] Bob Vance resigned in March 1991, and the General Council elected Cecil Johnson to replace him that August.
[2] The cancellation of the 113th General Assembly due to COVID-19 extended the terms of current officials by one year.

A Bow Tied

Term	Clerk	Assistant Clerk
1907-08	Joseph T. Richardson	Jacob C. Taylor
1908-09	Joseph T. Richardson	Jacob C. Taylor
1909-10	unknown	unknown
1910-11	unknown	unknown
1911-12	Jonah L. Shelton	Jacob C. Taylor
1912-13	Jacob C. Taylor	John Thomas
1913-14	Jacob C. Taylor	John Thomas
1914-15	Jacob C. Taylor	Joe L. Jones
1915-16	Jacob C. Taylor	Joe L. Jones
1916-17	Jacob C. Taylor	Joe L. Jones
1917-18	Jacob C. Taylor	Jonah L. Shelton
1918-19	Jacob C. Taylor	none
1919-20	Jacob C. Taylor	George A. Fore
1920-21	Jacob C. Taylor	George A. Fore
1921-22	Jacob C. Taylor	none
1922-23	Starling Smith	Francis M. Thomas
1923-24	Curd Walker	Samuel M. Sexton
1924-25	Everett H. Ross	Curd Walker
1925-26	Esom B. Bryant II	Gilbert Weaver
1926-27	Esom B. Bryant II	Gilbert Weaver
1927-28	Esom B. Bryant II	Jacob C. Taylor
1928-29	Esom B. Bryant II	Andrew J. Long
1929-30	Lewis M. Sharp	Curd Walker
1930-31	Lewis M. Sharp	Curd Walker
1931-32	Curd Walker	Lewis M. Sharp
1932-33	Curd Walker	Lewis M. Sharp
1933-34	Lewis M. Sharp	Curd Walker
1934-35	Lewis M. Sharp	John E. Hatfield
1935-36	Lewis M. Sharp	Curd Walker
1936-37	Lewis M. Sharp	Richard D. Litton
1937-38	Lewis M. Sharp	John E. Hatfield
1938-39	Lewis M. Sharp	John E. Hatfield
1939-40	Lewis M. Sharp	Ira H. Moses
1940-41	John E. Hatfield	Clayton Lawson

Appendix 1: General Officials and Committees

1941-42	John E. Hatfield	Ira H. Moses
1942-43	John E. Hatfield	Ira H. Moses
1943-44	John E. Hatfield	Ira H. Moses
	Secretary & Treasurer	***Assistant Sec. & Treas.***
1944-45	John E. Hatfield	Ira H. Moses
1945-46	John E. Hatfield	Everett Creekmore
1946-47	John E. Hatfield	Ira H. Moses
1947-48	John E. Hatfield	Ira H. Moses
1948-49	John E. Hatfield	Robert N. Ballinger / Randall Watkins
1949-50	John E. Hatfield	John T. Longsworth
1950-52	John E. Hatfield	John T. Longsworth
1952-54	John E. Hatfield	Lawrence Redmond
1954-56	John E. Hatfield	Lawrence Redmond
1956-58	John E. Hatfield	Lawrence Redmond
1958-60	John E. Hatfield	Lawrence Redmond
1960-62	John E. Hatfield	Wade M. Hughes
1962-64	John E. Hatfield	James E. Prewitt
1964-66	John E. Hatfield	James E. Prewitt
1966-68	John E. Hatfield	Wade M. Hughes
1968-70	John E. Hatfield	James L. Cox Sr.
1970-72	John E. Hatfield	James L. Cox Sr.
1972-74	John E. Hatfield	James E. Prewitt
1974-76	Clayton Lawson	James E. Prewitt
1976-78	James L. Cox Jr.	Ray A. Freeman
1978-80	James L. Cox Jr.	Dennis A. McClanahan
1980-82	John E. Hatfield	Arlie Petree
1982-84	Ronald Shelton	Arlie Petree
1984-86	Ronald Shelton	James E. Prewitt
1986-88	James L. Cox Jr.	James E. Prewitt
1988-90	James L. Cox Jr.	Bob J. Vance
1990-92	James W. Kilgore	Dennis A. McClanahan
1992-94	James W. Kilgore	Dennis A. McClanahan
1994-96	James W. Kilgore	Dennis A. McClanahan

1996-98	Alfred Newton Jr.	James W. Kilgore
1998-2000	Alfred Newton Jr.	Bob J. Vance
2000-02	Alfred Newton Jr.	Michael Padgett
2002-04	Roger Webb	Michael Padgett
2004-06	James W. Kilgore	W. Scott Isham
2006-08	James W. Kilgore	W. Scott Isham
2008-10	James W. Kilgore	W. Scott Isham
2010-12	James W. Kilgore	J. Jonathan Walden IV
2012-14	James W. Kilgore	J. Jonathan Walden IV
2014-16	James W. Kilgore	J. Jonathan Walden IV
2016-18	James W. Kilgore	J. Jonathan Walden IV
2018-21	James W. Kilgore	J. Jonathan Walden IV

The office of "General Treasurer" was created in 1917 and accounted for funds spent on "ministry," such as distributing tithes to evangelists. The "Assembly" or "Finance" Treasurer was created in 1923 and functioned as an administrative treasurer responsible for building expenses, printing, etc.

Term	*General Treasurer*	*Assembly Treasurer*
1917-18	Francis M. Thomas	
1918-19	Francis M. Thomas	
1919-20	Francis M. Thomas	
1922-23	Francis M. Thomas John H. Parks	
1923-24	Everett H. Ross	William C. Brock
1924-25	Everett H. Ross	William C. Brock
1925-26	Everett H. Ross	Lewis M. Sharp
1926-27	Everett H. Ross	Lewis M. Sharp
1927-28	Everett H. Ross	Lewis M. Sharp
1928-29	Everett H. Ross	Lewis M. Sharp
1929-30	Everett H. Ross	Lewis M. Sharp
1930-31	Everett H. Ross	Lewis M. Sharp
1931-32	Everett Creekmore	Lewis M. Sharp
1932-33	Everett Creekmore	Lewis M. Sharp
1933-34	Everett Creekmore	Lewis M. Sharp

Appendix 1: General Officials and Committees

1934-35	Everett Creekmore	Lewis M. Sharp
1935-36	Everett Creekmore	Lewis M. Sharp
1936-37	Everett Creekmore	Lewis M. Sharp
1937-38	Everett Creekmore	Lewis M. Sharp
1938-39	Everett Creekmore	Lewis M. Sharp
1939-40	Everett Creekmore	Lewis M. Sharp
1940-41	Everett Creekmore	Lewis M. Sharp
1941-42	Everett Creekmore	Lewis M. Sharp
1942-43	Everett Creekmore	Lewis M. Sharp
1943-44	Everett Creekmore	Lewis M. Sharp

Term	***To oversee printing and distribution of the Minutes***
1910-11	John Thomas & the Clerks
1911-12	Jonah L. Shelton
1912-13	John H. Parks
1913-14	Jonah L. Shelton
1914-15	John Thomas
1915-16	Jacob C. Taylor
1916-17	Jonah L. Shelton and Jacob C. Taylor
1917-18	Jonah L. Shelton
1918-19	Jacob C. Taylor
1919-20	Jacob C. Taylor. George A. Fore
1920-21	John H. Parks, George A. Fore, Stephen N. Bryant
1991-22	Jacob C. Taylor
1922-23	Starling Smith (appointed, but left the Assembly)
1923-24	John H. Parks, Curd Walker
1924-25	Everett H. Ross, Curd Walker
1925-26	Esom B. Bryant II
1926-44	responsibility of the Clerk and Assembly Treasurer

From 1948 to 1962, the national youth directors were chosen by the Appointing Board, and they in turn appointed the youth secretary & treasurer. In 1962, the General Council began electing the position to fulfill a two-year term. Since then, four National Youth Directors have resigned before their term was expired.

Term	National Youth Director	Asst. Youth Director
1948-49	Edward Woolum	Floyd Jordan
1949	Robert Thomas	John T. Longsworth
1949-50	John T. Longsworth	Robert Thomas
1950-52	John T. Longsworth	
1952	Lawrence Redmond	
1952-55	Haskel Swain	Efford Enix
1955-58	Efford Enix	Cecil Moses
1958-62	Efford Enix	Clayborn B. Ellis Jr.
1962-63	Samuel G. Douglas	Leon Petree
1963-64	Leon Petree	Samuel G. Douglas
1964-66	Leon Petree	Samuel G. Douglas
1966-68	Leon Petree	Orville C. Bartee Jr.
1968-70	Jasper Walden	Donnie Hill
1970-72	Jasper Walden	Donnie Hill
1972-74	Jasper Walden	Donnie Hill
1974-76	Donnie Hill	Michael Bartee
1976-78	Donnie Hill	Jesse E. Lay
1978-80	Danny Jones	David Cornelius
1980-82	Michael Bartee	Dennis A. McClanahan
1982-84	Michael Bartee	Dennis A. McClanahan
1984-86	Dennis A. McClanahan	Randall VanHoose
1986-88	Dennis A. McClanahan	Richard Massingill
1988-89	Richard Massingill	Michael Manning
1989-90	Richard Massingill	James Walden Jr. II
1990-92	Richard Massingill	James Walden Jr. II
1992-94	Richard Massingill	James Walden Jr. II
1994	Wayne Halcomb	Kenneth Ellis
1994-96	Kenneth Ellis	Jay A. Walden
1996-98	Kenneth Ellis	Jay A. Walden
1998-2000	Jay A. Walden	Michael Padgett
2000-02	Jay A. Walden	Nicholas Hill
2002-04	Jay A. Walden	Nicholas Hill
2004-06	Nicholas Hill	J. Jonathan Walden IV
2006-08	J. Jonathan Walden IV	Jeff Hill

Appendix 1: General Officials and Committees

2008-10	J. Jonathan Walden IV	Jeff Hill
2010-12	James Coffey	Douglas Walden
2012-13	James Coffey	Douglas Walden
2013-14	Douglas Walden	Scott Landes
2014-15	Douglas Walden	Scott Landes
2015-16	Scott Landes	Randall Halcomb
2016-18	Scott Landes	Randall Halcomb
2018-21	Scott Landes	Randall Halcomb

Term	Youth Secretary	Youth Treasurer
1949-50	Doris Garner	Doris Garner
1950-51	Anna Lucille Snowden	Anna Lucille Snowden
1952-53	Nellie Swain	Lawrence Redmond
1953-54	Phyllis Carlisle	Lawrence Redmond
1954-56	June Shiflet-Allen	Lawrence Redmond
1956-58	Jean Webb	Lawrence Redmond
1958-60	Wade M. Hughes	Lawrence Redmond
1960-62	Wade M. Hughes	
1962-64	Wade M. Hughes	
1964-66	Wade M. Hughes	
1966-68	Auza Vinson	
1968-70	Auza Vinson	
	James L. Cox Jr.	
1970-72	James L. Cox Jr.	
1972-74	James L. Cox Jr.	
1974-76	Jasper Walden	
1976-78	Jasper Walden	
1978-80	Ronald Shelton	
1980-82	Ronald Shelton	
1982-84	James Angel	
1984-86	James L. Cox Jr.	

The office of Public Relations Director was created in 1969 and the office of National Sunday School Superintendent / Christian Education Director was created in 1977. Neither are subject to term limitations.

Term	Public Relations Director	Christian Ed. Director
1969-70	Charles H. Davis	
1970-72	Jerome Walden	
1972-74	Jerome Walden	
1974-76	Bobby H. Wilson	
1976-78	Bobby H. Wilson	
1977-78		Henry C. Taylor
1978-80	Leon Petree	Henry C. Taylor
1980-82	Leon Petree	James Bartee
1982-84	James E. Prewitt	Ray A. Freeman
1984-86	James L. Cox Jr.	Ray A. Freeman
1986-88	Leon Petree	Henry C. Taylor
1988-90	Leon Petree	Henry C. Taylor
1990-92	Leon Petree	Henry C. Taylor
1992-94	Leon Petree	Henry C. Taylor
1994-96	Leon Petree	Henry C. Taylor
1996-98	Leon Petree	Henry C. Taylor
1998-2000	Leon Petree	Henry C. Taylor
2000-02	Leon Petree	Timothy A. Bartee
2002-04	Leon Petree	Timothy A. Bartee
2004-06	Leon Petree	Timothy A. Bartee
2006-08	David Cornelius	Timothy A. Bartee
2008-10	David Cornelius	Timothy A. Bartee
2010-12	David Cornelius	Timothy A. Bartee
2012-14	David Cornelius	Timothy A. Bartee
2014-16	W. Scott Isham	Timothy A. Bartee
2016-18	W. Scott Isham	Timothy A. Bartee
2018-21	W. Scott Isham	Timothy A. Bartee

The National Ladies Willing Workers Officers were first elected in 1976 and were officially constituted in the Standard Resolutions in 1978. The Ladies' officers are elected at the National Ladies Meeting at the General Assembly. The first National Men of Integrity Director was appointed in 2001. The General Council began electing the position the following year. It was officially constituted in 2010.

Appendix 1: General Officials and Committees

Term	Men's Ministry Director	Ladies' Ministry President
1976-78		Charlene Walden
1978-80		Charlene Walden
1980-82		Jackie Cox
1982-84		Jackie Cox
1984-86		Beulah Fry
1986-88		Beulah Fry
1988-90		Beulah Fry
1990-92		Paulette McClanahan
1992-94		Paulette McClanahan
1994-96		Paulette McClanahan
1996-98		Nancy Vance
1998-2000		Nancy Vance
2000-02	Henry C. Taylor (2001)	Nancy Vance
2002-04	Henry C. Taylor	Beverley Halcomb
2004-06	Henry C. Taylor	Beverley Halcomb
2006-08	Henry C. Taylor	Lois Centers
2008-10	Henry C. Taylor	Lois Centers
2010-12	Heath Hunter	Lois Centers
2012-14	Faron Cole	Misty Hill
2014-16	Faron Cole	Misty Hill
2016-18	James Couch	Misty Hill
2018-21	James Couch	Nicole Walden

Term	Ladies Vice-President	Ladies Sec. & Treas.
1976-78	Linda Massingill	Linda Bartee
1978-80	Linda Massingill	Linda Bartee
1980-82	Beulah Fry	Jean Jones
1982-84	Beulah Fry	Debbie Shelton
1984-86	Joan Marler	Vivan Murray
1986-88	Vijayah Long	Vivian Murray
1988-90	Paulette McClanahan	Vijayah Long
1990-92	Jackie Cox	Paula Keefer
1992-94	Lorinda Grubbs	Wanda Davis
1994-96	Robin Bartee	Wanda Davis
1996-98	Robin Bartee	Tammy Massingill

1998-2000	Robin Bartee	Tammy Massingill
2000-02	Beverley Halcomb	Glenda Kilgore
2002-04	Connie Taylor	Glenda Kilgore
2004-06	Lois Centers	Glenda Kilgore
2006-08	Linda Massingill	Kim Walden
2008-10	Linda Massingill	Kim Walden
2010-12	Linda Massingill	Vanessa Petty
2012-14	Dawn Paul	Ashlee Hill
2014-16	Nicole Walden	Ashlee Hill
2016-18	Nicole Walden	Ashlee Hill
2018-21	Angie Walden	Jessalynn Cornett

The primary purpose of the Field Evangel was to conduct revivals in new areas where prospective churches might be established. The Church Evangel coordinated with the Field Evangels and the Board of Twelve Elders to look after destitute churches and appoint pastors. A new position of National Evangelist was constituted briefly in 1976. He was to work under the direction of the Assistant General Overseer conducting revivals in the local churches.

Term	*Field Evangelist / Church Evangel / National Evangelist*
1915-16	Henry Mobley
1916-17	Henry Mobley
1917-18	C.L. Price, Lewis M. Broyles, George A. Fore
1918-19	George A. Fore, John H. Parks, Hubert O. Harris, John Thomas, Lewis M. Broyles, James L. Goins, C.L. Price
1919-20	George A. Fore, James L. Goins, William S. Sizemore, Starling Smith, John H. Parks, Walters, John Thomas, Horace M. Bates
1924-25	Stephen N. Bryant
1925-26	Stephen N. Bryant
1926-27	Henry Mobley
1927-28	unknown
1928-29	Kim Moses, Stephen N. Bryant
1929-30	C.L. Price, Curd Walker, M.E. Woolum, Drue Stanifer

Appendix 1: General Officials and Committees

1930-31	C.L. Price, Curd Walker, Kim Moses, M.E. Woolum, Drue Stanifer
1931-32	Kim Moses, Andrew J. Long, M.E. Woolum
1932-33	Kim Moses, Andrew J. Long, M.E. Woolum, C.L. Price, Will Sharp
1933-34	Will Sharp, Richard D. Litton, Esom B. Bryant II
1934-35	Will Sharp, Esom B. Bryant II
1935-36	Kim Moses, Andrew J. Long
1936-37	M.E. Woolum, Andrew J. Long
1937-38	M.E. Woolum, Kim Moses
1938-39	Clayton Lawson, M.E. Woolum, Will Sharp, Kim Moses
1939-40	Richard D. Litton, M.E. Woolum
1940-41	Kim Moses, Richard D. Litton, Carl Isaac
1941-42	David Hammitte, Richard D. Litton, Kim Moses
1976-78	Clayton Lawson

Boards and Committees

The Church of God Mountain Assembly has delegated authority to boards and committees since its inception. Most "Standing Committees" were chosen annually until 1950 when two-year terms were created. "Special" or "Select" Committees have been chosen periodically to fulfill a specific function.

Resolutions Committee

The committee on resolutions was generally appointed annually at the beginning of the General Assembly. The committee was elected for the first time in 1962 and 2-year terms began in 1964.

1907	Milton F. Ross, James Allen Moses, Curd Walker
1910	Newton K. Parks. James Allen Moses, William Hicks. Henry Watters. Reucanny P. Creekmore
1911	Pleasant I. Cox, Edom J. Rountree, James M. Rountree, William Hicks

1912	Newton K. Parks, John Smiddy, Terrell F. Hamblin, Levi White, Curd Walker,
1913	John H. Parks, Joseph T. Richardson, Curd Walker, George A. Fore, Milton F. Ross
1914	John Thomas, Curd Walker, William R Hamblin, William Hicks, George A. Fore, John H. Parks
1915	Committee of the whole
1926	Henry Mobley, William Wilder, Sherman Sizemore, John H. Parks, Anderson Alders
1928	John H. Parks, Lewis M. Sharp, James B. Spears, Thomas Woods, Henry Mobley
1929	John H. Parks, Stephen N. Bryant, Curd Walker
1930	John H. Parks, Stephen N. Bryant, Curd Walker
1932	John H. Bryant, Thomas Woods, Andrew J. Long
1933	Curd Walker, Will Sharp, Esom B. Bryant II
1934	Stephen N. Bryant, Curd Walker, Thomas Woods
1935	Will Sharp, Richard D. Litton, Kim Moses
1936	Thomas Woods, Ernie E. Yeary, Andrew J. Long
1937	John H. Parks, Kim Moses, Morris E. Woolum
1938	John H. Parks, Curd Walker, Will Sharp
1939	Clayton Lawson, Ernie E. Yeary, Virgil L. Akins
1940	Morris E. Woolum, David Hammitte, Kim Moses
1941	Lewis Baird, Will Sharp, Kim Moses
1942	Will Sharp, Luther Gibson, Joshua Baird
1943	Clayton Lawson, Will Sharp, John H. Bryant
1948	Morris E. Woolum, Rufus L. Douglas, David Hammitte
1949	Ira Moses, Morris E. Woolum, John H. Bryant
1950	John H. Bryant, Morris E. Woolum, Ira Moses
1952	Morris E. Wollum, Ira H. Moses, Rufus L. Douglas
1953	Ira Moses, Robert N. Ballinger, Luther Gibson
1954	Ira Moses, John H. Bryant, Morris E. Woolum
1955	Ira Moses, Arvil Rountree, Luther Gibson
1956	John H. Bryant, J.H. Douglas, C.B. Ellis Jr.
1957	John H. Bryant, Joe Howard, Arvil Rountree
1958	Ottis Ellis, Willis Yeary, Paul Grubbs

Appendix 1: General Officials and Committees

1959	Charles Creekmore, Isham Sharp, Hayes Harp
1960	Willis Yeary, Paul Grubbs, Dan Lynch
1961	Glenn Rowe, Clayton Lawson C.B. Ellis Jr.
1962	Clayton Lawson, Wade M. Hughes, John H. Bryant
1963	John H. Bryant, Ottis Ellis, C.A. Freeman
1964-66	Ottis Ellis, Glenn Rowe, Luther Gibson, Auza Vinson, George Douglas, Bobby Wilson, Willis Yeary, Jerome Walden, Fred Cornelius, Clayton Lawson
1966-68	Ottis Ellis, Glenn Rowe, Luther Gibson, Auza Vinson, George Douglas, Bobby Wilson, Willis Yeary, Jerome Walden, Fred Cornelius, Clayton Lawson
1968-69	*Glenn Rowe*, Fred Cornelius, Auza Vinson, Jerome Walden, Bobby Wilson
1969-70	*Glenn Rowe*, Leon Petree, Lloyd Camp, Fred Cornelius, Jerome Walden
1970-72	*Glenn Rowe*, Leon Petree, Fred Cornelius, Lloyd Camp, Jerome Walden
1972-74	J.H. Douglas, Bobby Wilson, Everett Rogers, Clayton Lawson, James Walden Jr.
1974-76	James Freeman, J.H. Douglas, Ray Freeman, Jennings Baird, James Walden Jr.
1976-78	*James Walden Jr.*, Bob Vance, Paul Grubbs, Lonnie Lyke, Ray Freeman
1978-80	*James Walden Jr.*, Paul Ellis, Ernest Ray, Ray Freeman, Fred Cornelius
1980-82	*James Walden Jr.*, Bob Vance, Paul Yeary, Dan Lynch, Fred Cornelius
1982-84	*James Walden Jr.*, Fred Cornelius, Paul Yeary, Ray Freeman, J.H. Douglas
1984-86	*Fred Cornelius*, Glenn Rowe, Roger Walden, Ray Freeman, J. H. Douglas
1986-88	*James Walden Jr.,* Claude Massingill, Fred Cornelius, Dan Lynch, Ray Landes
1988-90	*James Walden Jr.,* Claude Massingill, Fred Cornelius, Ray Landes, Dan Lynch

1990-92	*James Walden Jr.*, Kenneth E. Massingill, Cecil Johnson, Michael Cornelius, Leon Petree
1992-94	*James Walden Jr.*, Lee Sweet, Carl Prewitt, Lonnie Lyke, James Bartee
1994-96	*James Walden Jr.*, Michael Cornelius, Tim McGlone, Ray Landes, Dan Lynch
1996-98	*Michael Cornelius*, Uly Cox, Tim Walden, Alan Laws, Richard Massingill
1998-2000	*Michael Cornelius*, Uly Cox, Tim Walden, Alan Laws, Richard Massingill
2000-02	*Michael Cornelius*, Richard Massingill, David Cornelius, Tim Walden, James Walden Jr.
2002-03	*Michael Cornelius*, Richard Massingill, David Cornelius, Tim Walden, James Walden Jr.
2003-04	*James Walden Jr.*, Richard Massingill, David Cornelius, Tim Walden
2004-06	*James Walden Jr.*, Kevin Walden, Tim Slaughter, Wayne Ison, Earl Hisle
2006-08	*James Walden Jr.*, Jack Anderson, Earl Hisle, Lee Sweet, Tim Slaughter
2008-10	*James Walden Jr.*, Earl Hisle, Tim Slaughter, Kenny Ellis, Heath Hunter
2010-12	*James Walden Jr.*, Kenny Ellis, Earl Hisle, Heath Hunter, Tim Slaughter
2012-14	*James Walden Jr.*, Lee Sweet, Earl Hisle, Tim Slaughter, J.R. Simpson
2014-16	*James Walden Jr.*, Jerry Grubbs, Nick Hill, Earl Hisle, Michael Padgett
2016-18	*James Walden Jr.*, Michael Padgett, Jeremy Walden, Earl Hisle, Donnie Hill
2018-20	*James Walden Jr.*, Douglas Walden, Tim Walden, Michael Padgett, Nicholas Hill
2020-21	*Michael Padgett,* Douglas Walden, Tim Walden, Nicholas Hill

Appendix 1: General Officials and Committees

Committee to read the church letters

The process of enrolling delegates originally consisted of a committee reading letters from the local churches. By the mid1940s that task fell to the General Secretary & Treasurer. The formal reading of the letters was discontinued in the mid1970s when a "roll call of churches" was presented to the General Council.

1907	James J. Sammons, Alvin Ross
1908	Joseph T. Richardson, Henry N. Creekmore
1909	unknown
1910	Henry N. Creekmore, Josiah M. Thomas
1911	Josiah M. Thomas, Ambrose J. Tomlinson
1912	Josiah M. Thomas, Joe L. Jones
1913	Josiah M. Thomas, Joseph T. Richardson
1914	Josiah M. Thomas, Joe L. Jones
1915	T.J. Wood, Joe Silcox
1916	Virgil Snavely, Richard D. Litton
1917	Virgil Snavely, James D. Taylor
1918	Virgil Snavely, John Bunch
1919	Virgil Snavely, Joseph T. Richardson
1920	Virgil Snavely, Horace M. Bates
1921	Joshua Baird, Curd Walker
1922	Horace M. Bates, Benjamin H. Enix
1923	Horace M. Bates, Benjamin H. Enix
1924	Will Sharp, Samuel M. Sexton
1925	Gilbert Weaver, Jim Chadwell
1926	Curd Walker, Squire Broyles
1927	Curd Walker, Jim Chadwell
1928	Curd Walker, Andrew J. Long
1929	Richard D. Litton, Lewis M. Sharp
1930	Azree Long, Gilbert Weaver
1931	Richard D. Litton, Azree Long
1932	Lewis M. Sharp, Curd Walker
1933	Joe L. Jones, J.E. Hatfield
1934	Joe L. Jones, Curd Walker
1935	Richard D. Litton, Curd Walker

1936   Richard D. Litton, Will Sharp
1937   Richard D. Litton, Will Sharp, A.J. Long, J.E. Hatfield
1938   Andrew J. Long, J.E. Hatfield
1939   Clayton Lawson, Joe Silcox
1940   Clayton Lawson, Luther Gibson
1941   Will Sharp, Ira Moses
1942   Clayton Lawson, Ira Moses
1943   Clayton Lawson, Ira Moses
1944   Clayton Lawson, Ira Moses
1945   Clayton Lawson, Ira Moses

Finance Committee to Receive Assembly Offerings

A Committee to Receive Finance during the Assembly was first appointed in 1907. From 1933 to 1944, the responsibility fell to the Finance Treasurer, Lewis M. Sharp. In the late 1940s, the Assembly returned to annual elections / appointments.

1907   Henry N. Creekmore, John Selvia
1910   Henry N. Creekmore, Aaron Thomas
1911   James M. Rountree, Francis M. Thomas
1912   George F. Lucas, Martin S. Haynes
1919   Curd Walker, Squire Broyles
1920   Benjamin H. Enix, John Bunch
1922   Benjamin H. Enix, Will Brock
1925   Esom B. Bryant II
1926   Curd Walker, Squire Broyles
1927   Curd Walker, Jim Chadwell
1928   Curd Walker, Andrew J. Long
1929   Richard D. Litton, Lewis M. Sharp
1930   Azree Long, Gilbert Weaver
1931   Richard D. Litton, Azree Long
1932   Lewis M. Sharp, Curd Walker
1948   Randall Watkins, Arvil Rountree, John Bunch
1949   C.E. Garrett. Arvil Rountree, Clayton Lawson
1951   J.H. Douglas, Charles Lowery, Roy Cornelius
1952   J.H. Douglas. Lawrence Redmond, Arvil Rountree

Appendix 1: General Officials and Committees

1953	Robert Pike. C.B. Ellis, Lawrence Redmond
1954	James Walden Sr., Deward Hoskins, Joe Moses
1955	Lawrence Redmond, J. H. Douglas, James Walden Sr.
1956	James Walden Sr., General Douglas, Lawrence Redmond
1957	Joe Moses, C. B. Ellis., Lawrence Redmond
1958	Joe Howard, C.A. Freeman, Joe Moses
1959	Jerome Walden, C. B. Ellis, J.H. Douglas
1960	C.B. Ellis, Joe Moses, Willis Yeary, Lawrence Redmond, Charles Creekmore
1961	U.P. Gray, Jennings Baird, Dan Lynch
1963	Fred Cornelius C.L. Weaver, J.B. Hammitte
1964	George Douglas, Jennings Baird, Leon Petree, Dale Workman
1965	Jennings Baird, Leon Petree, J.H. Douglas
1966	Dan Lynch, Jerome Walden, Clayton Lawson
1967	Bobby Wilson, Wade M. Hughes, Fred Cornelius, Jennings Baird
1968	Glenn Rowe, Leon Petree, Bobby Wilson, Charles Davis, James Walden Jr.
1969	Glenn Rowe, Edward Angel, J.E. Lay, C.D. Blackburn, Donnie Hill
1970	Edward Angel, Chester Broughton, Elston R. Vaught, Dan Lynch, Claude Massingill
1972	Fred Cornelius, Glenn Rowe, C.B. Ellis
1975	Cecil Johnson, Lonnie Lyke, Roy Padgett, Ray Landes, Claude Massingill
1976	Charles Vance. Bob Vance. Roy Padgett, Paul Ellis. Clayton Sharp, Claude Massengill
1977	Roy Padgett, Scott Thornton, Randy Duncan, Randall VanHoose, Ralph Johnson

Committee on Queries

1908 Milton F. Ross, James Allen Moses, James M. Rountree, John Smiddy, John Thomas

Committee on Bible Questions

1924	Joshua Baird, J.L. Goins, Charles H. Standifer
1925	Kim Moses, C.L. Price, John Parks, N.K. Parks, William Douglas
1926	John H. Parks, Charles H. Standifer, Kim Moses

Committee on Grievances

1921	John H. Parks, Henry Mobley, G.A. Fore, J.L. Goins, John Thomas, Herbert O. Harris, Horace M. Bates
1924	Joshua Baird, J.L. Goins, Charles H. Standifer
1925	Kim Moses, C.L. Price, John Parks, N.K. Parks, William Douglas
1926	Lewis M. Broyles, Curd Walker, Joshua Baird
1927	Lewis M. Broyles, Crit Smith, John H. Parks
1928	John H. Parks, RD Litton, CL Price
1929	John H. Parks, Curd Walker, Thomas Woods
1930	John H. Parks, Curd Walker, ME Woolum
1931	John H. Parks, CL Price, JB Spears
1932	John H. Parks, Thomas Woods, AJ Long
1933	John H. Parks, AJ Long, Thomas Woods
1934	Stephen N. Bryant, Curd Walker, Thomas Woods
1935	John H. Parks, Morris E. Woolum, Thomas Woods
1936	Thomas Woods, Ernie E. Yeary, Andrew J. Long
1937	Thomas Woods, Will Sharp, Ernie E, Yeary

Committee on Miscellaneous Business

1923	John H. Parks, Lewis M. Broyles, Newt K. Parks, William S. Sizemore, Curd Walker
1933	Curd Walker, Thomas Woods, Andrew J. Long
1936	Will Sharp, Virgil L. Akins, Alvin Black
1938	John H, Bryant, Kim Moses, Harve Phelps
1939	Clayton Lawson, Ernie E. Yeary, Virgil L. Akins
1942	Kim Moses, Virgil L. Akins, Fred Cummins
1943	Clayton Lawson, Will Sharp, John H. Bryant

Appendix 1: General Officials and Committees

Committee on Sunday Schools

1912 Curd Walker, Peter Huddleston, F. M. Thomas, William Hicks, J.F. Norman

1913 Squire Broyles, M.F. Ross, Aaron Hackler, R.D. Litton, M.H. Layn, J.M. Rountree

1930 John M. Laws, Gilbert Weaver, George Kidd

1931 Curd Walker, Felder Miracle, Mae Johnson, Joe Jones, Kim Moses, Gilbert Weaver, Francis Lawson, Melt Laws, James Mays, Matthew Douglas, Lewis Baird, R.D. Litton, E.E. Yeary, Drue Stanifer, Thomas Woods, Paul Raubb, M.E. Woolum, Jess Allen

1932 Gilbert Weaver

1933 James M. Prewitt, Gilbert Weaver, Virgil Akins, Lewis Birdwell, Sam Cadle, A.A. Snipes, J.W.D. Johnson

1934 James M. Prewitt, John M. Laws, Gilbert Weaver, Virgil Akins, Lewis Birdwell, Sam Cadle, A.A. Snipes, Felder Mimbs, E.D. Henry

1935 James M. Prewitt, John M. Laws, Gilbert Weaver, Virgil Akins, Lewis Birdwell, Ebb Bailey, A.A. Snipes, Felder Mimbs, E.D. Henry

1936 James M. Prewitt, John M. Laws, Gilbert Weaver, Virgil Akins, Alvin Black

1937 James M. Prewitt, Ebb Bailey, Arthur Enix, Alvin Black, Glen Spurgeon

1938 Lee Caddell, Arthur Enix, Robert Ballinger, Clyde Pierce, Glen Spurgeon

1939 Lee Caddell, Arthur Enix, Willis Yeary, Clyde Pierce, Glen Spurgeon

General Trustees

Trustees were first appointed in 1920 to hold property to be purchased for the first tabernacle (then planned in Williamsburg). After the tabernacle was built in Jellico, a new set of trustees was appointed in 1923. The list was modified as necessary until 1944 when the new system of government called for the election of trustees annually, and then biennially in 1950.

1920	Francis M. Thomas, George A. Fore, Jacob C. Taylor
1923	Gilbert Weaver, John Shepherd, Joseph T. Richardson
1926	Lewis M. Sharp replaced Richardson
1930	S.N. Bryant Will Sharp replaced Shepherd and Weaver
1937	Alvin G. Ross and E.B. Rose were added to the three
1939	Herbert Higginbotham replaced Bryant
1944-45	*Andrew J. Long,* Kim Moses, Luther Gibson, Ira Moses, J.H. Bryant
1945-46	*Andrew J. Long,* Kim Moses, Luther Gibson, Ira Moses, J.H. Bryant
1946-47	*Luther Gibson,* Clayton Lawson, Robert N. Ballinger, J.H. Bryant, Ira Moses
1947-48	C.L. Price, Anderson McKenzie, Ottis Ellis, J.H. Bryant, Ira Moses
1948-49	C.L. Price, Anderson McKenzie, Ottis Ellis, J.H. Bryant, Ira Moses
1949-50	C.E. Bray, Edd Prewitt, John Longsworth, J.H. Bryant, Ira Moses
1950-52	*Ira Moses*, John Longsworth, Lawrence Redmond, Morris E. Woolum, J.H. Bryant,
1952-54	*Ira Moses*, Arvil Rountree, Luther Gibson, J.H. Douglas, J.H. Bryant
1954-56	*Ira Moses*, Arvil Rountree, Luther Gibson, J.H. Douglas, J.H. Bryant
1956-58	Ira Moses, Arvil Rountree, J.H. Bryant, J.H. Douglas, General Douglas,
1958-60	*Arvil Rountree*, J.H. Bryant, J.H. Douglas, Ottis Ellis, James Walden Sr.
1960-61	*Arvil Rountree*, Dan Lynch, C.B. Ellis, Willis Yeary, Lawrence Redmond
1961-62	*Clayton Lawson*, Dan Lynch, C.B. Ellis, Willis Yeary, C.A. Freeman
1962-64	*Clayton Lawson*, Isham Sharp, Wade Hughes, Ottis Ellis, J.H. Douglas

Appendix 1: General Officials and Committees

1964-66	*Glenn Rowe*, C.L. Weaver, Isham Sharp, Jennings Baird, James Walden Sr.
1966-68	*C.B. Ellis*, Bobby Wilson, Glenn Rowe Fred Cornelius, J.H. Douglas
1968-69	Bobby Wilson, J.B. Hammitte, George Douglas, Fred Cornelius, Charles H. Davis
1969-70	Clayton Lawson, J.B. Hammitte, George Douglas, Fred Cornelius, Charles H. Davis
1970-72	Fred Cornelius, J.H. Douglas, Glenn Rowe, J.B. Hammitte, Bobby Wilson
1972-74	Roy Cornelius, J.B. Hammitte, James Walden Jr., Clayton Lawson, James Cox
1974-76	J.H. Douglas, Ray Freeman, Wesley Dupuy, Glenn Rowe, James Walden Jr.
1976-78	*Bobby Wilson*, Glenn Rowe, Wesley Dupuy, Jasper Walden, J.H. Douglas
1978-79	*Bobby Wilson*, Ray Landes, Clayton Lawson, Glenn Rowe, Jasper Walden
1979-80	*Fred Cornelius*, Ray Landes, Clayton Lawson, Glenn Rowe, Jasper Walden
1980-82	*J.H. Douglas*, Michael Cornelius, Jerome Walden, Fred Cornelius, Glenn Rowe
1982-84	*J.H. Douglas*, Cecil Johnson, Glenn Rowe, Lloyd Camp, Michael Cornelius
1984-86	*J.H. Douglas*, Cecil Johnson, Glenn Rowe, Lloyd Camp, Michael Cornelius
1986-87	*J.H. Douglas*, Donnie Hill, Glenn Rowe, Danny Jones, Jerry Reynolds
1987-88	*J.H. Douglas*, Donnie Hill, Glenn Rowe, Danny Jones
1988-90	*Glenn Rowe*, James E. McKinney, Cecil Johnson, Fred Cornelius, J.H. Douglas
1990-92	*Glenn Rowe*, James E. McKinney, Cecil Johnson, Fred Cornelius, J.H. Douglas
1992-94	*Glenn Rowe*, J.H. Douglas, Donnie Hill, Steven Colyer, James E. McKinney

1994-95	*Kenneth E. Massingill*, J.H. Douglas, Glenn Rowe, Donnie Hill, Steven Colyer
1995-96	*Kenneth E. Massingill*, J.H. Douglas, Glenn Rowe, Donnie Hill, Henry C. Taylor
1996-98	*Jasper Walden*, Donnie Hill, Glenn Rowe, J.H. Douglas, Wayne Ison
1998-99	*Jasper Walden*, Donnie Hill, Glenn Rowe, J.H. Douglas, Wayne Ison
1999-2000	*Jasper Walden*, Donnie Hill, J.H. Douglas, Wayne Ison, Fred Cornelius
2000-02	*Jasper Walden*, Fred Cornelius, Rick Massingill, Donnie Hill, Scott Isham
2002-04	*Jasper Walden*, Donnie Hill, Ray Landes, Scott Isham, Fred Cornelius
2004-06	*Jasper Walden*, Wayne Flower, James Walden Jr. II, Donnie Hill, Wayne Ison
2006-08	*Jasper Walden*, Wayne Flower, Dennis McClanahan, Nick Hill, James E. McKinney
2008-10	*Jasper Walden*, Nick Hill, James Justice, John Keefer, Scott Landes
2010-12	*Jasper Walden*, Nick Hill, Heath Hunter, Scott Landes, David Cornelius
2012-14	*Jasper Walden*, Scott Landes, Kenny Ellis, Jerry Grubbs, Jerry Wilson
2014-16	*Jasper Walden*, Donnie Hill, Jerry Grubbs, Scott Landes, Jerry Wilson
2016-18	*Jasper Walden*, Donnie Hill, Jerry Grubbs, Scott Landes, Jerry Wilson
2018-21	*Scott Landes*, Donnie Hill, Jasper Walden, Tim Walden, Joe Hill

Committee on Retirement and Insurance (Benevolent Committee)

The committee constituted in 1987 and replaced special committees previously appointed by the General Council.

Appendix 1: General Officials and Committees

1987-92	J.E. Prewitt, Fred Cornelius, Leon Petree, Lonnie Lyke, Jerome Walden
1992-94	J.E. Prewitt, Fred Cornelius, Leon Petree, Lonnie Lyke, Jerome Walden
1994-96	Jasper Walden, Jerome Walden, Kenneth Massingill, Leon Petree, Fred Cornelius
1996-98	Jasper Walden, Jerome Walden, Kenneth Massingill, Leon Petree, Fred Cornelius
1998-2000	Jasper Walden, James Walden Jr., Kenneth Massingill, Leon Petree, Fred Cornelius
2000-02	Jasper Walden, James Walden Jr., Kenneth Massingill, Leon Petree, Fred Cornelius
2002-04	Jasper Walden, James Walden Jr., Kenneth Massingill, Michael Cornelius, Fred Cornelius
2004-06	Jasper Walden, James Walden Jr., Kenneth Massingill, Michael Cornelius, James E. McKinney
2006-08	Jasper Walden, James Walden Jr., Kenneth Massingill, Jerry Wilson, James E. McKinney
2008-10	Jasper Walden, James Walden Jr., Kenneth Massingill, Jerry Wilson, James E. McKinney
2010-12	Jasper Walden, James Walden Jr., Kenneth Massingill, Cecil Johnson, David Cornelius
2012-14	Jasper Walden, James Walden Jr., Kenneth Massingill, Cecil Johnson, David Cornelius
2014-16	Jasper Walden, James Walden Jr., Kenneth Massingill, Cecil Johnson, David Cornelius
2016-18	Donnie Hill, James Walden Jr., Kenneth Massingill, Cecil Johnson, Ray Landes
2018-20	Donnie Hill, James Walden Jr., Kenneth Massingill, Lonnie Lyke, Ray Landes
2020-21	K.E. Massingill, Donnie Hill, Lonnie Lyke, Ray Landes

Camp Committee

The Committee on the youth campground was constituted in 1977. The Second Assistant Overseer served as its chairman from 1978 to 1988. Since then, the National Youth Director has served as chairman.

1977-78	James E. Prewitt, Ray Freeman, David Cornelius
1978-80	Danny Jones, Ronald Shelton, Randy VanHoose
1980-82	James E. McKinney, Michael Bartee, Orville Bartee
1982-84	James E. McKinney, Marion Shelton, Michael Bartee
1984-86	Donnie Hill, James E. McKinney, Dennis McClanahan
1986-88	J.E. Prewitt, J.E. McKinney, Dennis McClanahan
1988-90	James Bartee, James E. Prewitt, Marion Shelton
1990-92	J.B. Brewer, Bill Gaylor, Ray Landes
1992-94	Kenneth Ellis, Tim Padgett, James Walden Jr.
1994-96	Richard Massingill, J.B. Brewer, James Walden Jr. II
1996-98	Richard Massingill, J.B. Brewer, James Walden Jr. II
1998-2000	J.B. Brewer, Roger Webb, Paul Wigginton
2000-02	Tim Adkins, John Hoover, Jerry Grubbs
2002-04	Tim Adkins, Jerry Grubbs, James Walden Jr II
2004-06	Tony Shaw, Jerry Grubbs, James Walden Jr. II
2006-08	Jerry Grubbs, Willard Cole, James Walden Jr. II
2008-10	Jerry Grubbs, Willard Cole, James Walden Jr. II
2010-12	Willard Cole, Jerry Wilson, Rick Massingill
2012-14	Jerry Wilson, Sean Landes, James Walden, Jr. II
2014-16	Joe Hill, Nick Hill, Jerry Wilson
2016-18	Joe Hill, Nick Hill, Jerry Wilson
2018-21	Joe Hill, Nick Hill, Richard Massingill

Mission Board

The first Mission Board was created in 1951 to develop a plan for planting and financing new churches. In 1967, the District Overseers became the Mission Board with the Assistant General Overseer serving as chairman and Missions Director.

1951-52	*Luther Gibson*, Arvil Rountree, Auza Vinson, Ottis Ellis, John H. Bryant
1952-54	*Luther Gibson*, Arvil Rountree, Auza Vinson, Ottis Ellis, John H. Bryant
1954-56	*Luther Gibson*, Arvil Rountree, Auza Vinson, Ottis Ellis, John H. Bryant

Appendix 1: General Officials and Committees

1956-58	*Luther Gibson*, Arvil Rountree, Auza Vinson, Ottis Ellis, John H. Bryant
1958-59	*Auza Vinson*, C.B. Ellis, James Walden Jr., Charles Creekmore, General Douglas
1959-60	*Auza Vinson*, C.B. Ellis, James Walden Jr., Charles Creekmore
1960-62	*Isham Sharp*, Charles Creekmore, James Walden Sr., J.H. Douglas, Dave Hammitte
1962-64	*James Cox Sr.,* Dan Lynch, Azzie Brown, Carl Prewitt, Willie Lee Partin
1966-66	*James Cox Sr.,* Dan Lynch, Azzie Brown, Carl Prewitt, Willie Lee Partin
1966-67	*James Cox Sr.,* Dan Lynch, Azzie Brown, Carl Prewitt, Willie Lee Partin

Finance Committee

The 1944 new system of government created a General Finance Committee to devise means of increasing the Assembly's income, to approve Assembly expenses, and to audit the books of the General Secretary & Treasurer.

1944-45	J.H. Bryant, Luther Gibson, Clayton Lawson
1945-46	J.H. Bryant, Luther Gibson, Clayton Lawson
1946-47	J.H. Bryant, Luther Gibson, Clayton Lawson
1947-48	J.H. Bryant, Luther Gibson, Edd Prewitt
1948-49	Ottis Ellis, Robert N. Ballinger, J.E. Hatifeld
1949-50	John H. Bryant, John Longsworth, J.E. Hatfield
1950-51	J.H. Bryant, Lawrence Redmond, Uyless Graham
1951-52	J.H. Douglas, Charles Lowery, Roy Cornelius
1952-54	J.H. Bryant, J.H. Douglas, R.N. Ballinger
1954-56	J.H. Bryant, Lawrence Redmond, R.N. Ballinger
1956-58	J.H. Bryant, Arvil Rountree, Lawrence Redmond
1958-60	*J.H. Bryant,* Arvil Rountree, Lawrence Redmond
1960-62	*J.H. Bryant,* Clayton Lawson, J.H. Douglas
1962-64	*Glenn Rowe,* Fred Cornelius, Willis Yeary
1964-66	*Luther Gibson,* Clayton Lawson, J.H. Douglas

1966-68	*Luther Gibson*, Clayton Lawson, James Walden, Sr.
1968-70	*Paul Grubbs*, Glenn Rowe, Jerome Walden
1970-72	*Glenn Rowe*, Ray Freeman, Jerome Walden
1972-74	*Jerome Walden*, Ray Freeman, Bobby Wilson
1974-76	Fred Cornelius, Ira Moses, Glenn Rowe
1976-78	*Glenn Rowe*, Bobby Wilson, Leon Petree
1978-79	*Glenn Rowe*, Lonnie Lyke, Bobby Wilson
1979-80	*Glenn Rowe*, Lonnie Lyke, J.E. McKinney
1980-82	*Glenn Rowe*, Lonnie Lyke, J.E. McKinney
1982-84	*Glenn Rowe*, K.E. Massingill, Michael Cornelius
1984-86	*Jerome Walden*, Glenn Rowe, Michael Cornelius
1986-88	*Jerome Walden*, Lonnie Lyke, Glenn Rowe
1988-90	*Jerome Walden*, Lonnie Lyke, Glenn Rowe
1990-92	*Jerome Walden*, Lonnie Lyke, Glenn Rowe
1992-94	*Lonnie Lyke*, Jerome Walden, Glenn Rowe
1994-96	*Glenn Rowe*, K.E. Massingill, Jerome Walden
1996-98	*Jerome Walden*, K.E. Massingill, Glenn Rowe
1998-2000	*Jerome Walden*, K.E. Massingill, Tim McGlone
2000-02	Jerome Walden, K.E. Massingill, Ray Landes
2002-04	*K.E. Massingill*, Michael Cornelius, Ray Landes
2004-06	Donnie Hill, K.E. Massingill, Tim Walden
2006-08	K.E. Massingill, David Davis, Tim Walden
2008-10	K.E. Massingill, David Davis, Tim Walden
2010-12	Scott Isham, Glen Hall, Tim McGlone
2012-14	Tim McGlone, Tim Bartee, Glen Hall
2014-16	*Tim Bartee*, Josh Stephens, Glen Hall
2016-18	*Tim Bartee*, Faron Cole, Scott Isham
2018-21	*Faron Cole*, Scott Isham, Lonnie Lyke

Committee on Publications *(to solicit subscriptions to The Gospel Herald)*

1948   Ottis Ellis, Edd Prewitt, Robert Thomas, Edward Woolum, Ione Rountree, George Douglas, Finley Gray

1949   Iona Rountree, Lassie Lawson, Betty Hammitte, Hester Moses, Dessie Yeary

1951   Lawrence Redmond, Dover Kasee, Ulysses Graham

Appendix 1: General Officials and Committees

1959 Lassie Lawson, Iona Rountree, Jackie Ethridge
1960 Lassie Lawson, Bessie Douglas, Jackie Ethridge
1961 Lassie Lawson, Bessie Douglas, Jessie Weaver
1962 Lassie Lawson, Bessie Douglas, Jessie Weaver
1964 Roy Estes, Leon Petree, Auza Vinson, Orville Bartee, Gene Douglas
1965 Bobby Wilson, Dessie Yeary, Jessie Weaver, Charles Weaver
1967 Roger Walden, Gladys Brown, Leon Petree, Clayton Sharp

Committee on Entertainment
1948 Luther Gibson, Ira H. Moses, John Bunch
1949 M. E. Woolum, Clayton Lawson, Luther Gibson, David Hammitte, Ira H. Moses
1952 Haskel Swain, Joe Moses, Efford Enix, Auza Vinson
1954 R.N. Ballinger. Lawrence Redniond, Efford Enix, Haskel Swain, General Douglas
1955 Lawrence Redmond, J. H. Douglas, James Walden, Archer Engle, R. N. Ballinger, Auza Vinson.
1956 George Douglas, Barton Bryant, Hayes Harp
1957 J.H. Douglas, Lawrence Redmond, George Douglas
1958 Willis Yeary, Efford Enix, J.H. Douglas, J.C. Freeman, Joe Moses, William Loudermilk, Glenn Rowe
1962 Efford Enix, James L. Burke
1963 T.J. Watters, J.B. Hammitte, Clarence Slaven
1964 Fred Cornelius, Efford Enix, Gene Douglas
1966 Gene Douglas, J.B. Hammitte, T.J. Watters
1967 Fred Cornelius, George Douglas, Willis Yeary
1968 Gene Douglas, Homer Prewitt, Stanley Taylor
1970 Dan Lynch, J.C. Murray, Roger Powell
1971 J.C. Murray, Ray Freeman, Orville Bartee
1972 J.C. Murray, Orville Bartee, TJ Watters
1973 Bobby Wilson, Stanley Taylor, Jerome Walden
1974 James Cox Jr., Durand Dixon, Bobby Wilson
1975 J.C. Murray, Durand Dixon, James Cox Jr.
1978 Ron Shelton, James Angel, Ray Freeman
1979 Michael Cornelius, Philip Yeary, Marvin Busie

Committee on Music
1958 James Burke and Efford Enix
1959 Efford Enix, Lawrence Redmond, Fred Cornelius
1961 Paul Grubbs, Samuel G. Douglas, Joe Asbury
1962 James Walden Jr., George Douglas, Fred Cornelius
1964 Fred Cornelius, Efford Enix, Gene Douglas
1974 James Cox Jr., Durand Dixon, Bobby Wilson

Committee on Publicity
1958 J.E. Hatfield, James Burke
1959 Wade Hughes, J.E. Hatfield
1963 Roy M. Estes, J.C. Freeman, Azzie Brown
1964 George Douglas, Glenn Rowe, J.E. Hatfield
1966 J.C. Murray, J.E. Hatfield
1967 Wade Hughes, Mit Walden
1968 JC Murray, James Cox Sr.
1970 J.E. Hatfield, James Cox Sr.
1971 J.E. Hatfield, James Cox Sr.
1972 Jerome Walden, J.E. Hatfield, James Cox Sr.
1973 Jerome Walden, Lonnie Lyke, J.E. Hatfield
1974 Jerome Walden, J.E. Hatfield, J.E. McKinney
1975 Bobby Wilson, Clayton Lawson, James Cox Sr.
1976 Bobby Wilson, Clayton Lawson, James Cox Sr.
1977 Bobby Wilson, Cecil Johnson, James Cox Jr.
1978 Bobby Wilson, Jasper Walden, James Cox Jr
1979 Leon Petree, Dennis McClanahan, Ray Landes
1980 Leon Petree, Ray Landes, Dennis McClanahan
1981 Leon Petree, J.E. Hatfield, Arlie Petree
1982 Leon Petree, Arlie Petree
1983 J.E. Prewitt, Ron Shelton, Arlie Petree
1984 Arlie Petree, J.E. Prewitt, Ronald Shelton

Board of Twelve Elders

The first Board of Twelve Elders was appointed in 1919 and was discontinued two years later. A board of six was appointed in 1922 and reconstituted as a board of twelve the following year. In 1930, a fourth

Appendix 1: General Officials and Committees

Board of Twelve was reconstituted. The current board is a continuation of the 1930 body. An eight-year term was instituted beginning in 1974.

John H. Parks, 1919-1921, 1923-1925, 1925-1930, 1930-43
Stephen Bryant, 1919-1921, 1922-23, 1923-1925, 1925-1930, 1930-39
Newton K. Parks, 1919-1921, 1923-1925, 1925-1930
Curd Walker, 1919-1921, 1930-38
Kim Moses, 1919-1921, 1923-1925, 1925-1930, 1930-46
Levi M. White, 1919-1921, 1923-1925
Joshua Baird, 1919-1921, 1922-23, 1923-1925, 1925-1930, 1939-46
George A. Fore, 1919-1921, 1922
James L. Goins, 1919-1921, 1922-23, 1923-1925
Henry Mobley, 1919-1921, 1922-23
Starling Smith, 1919-1921
John Thomas, 1919-1921
Lewis M. Broyles, 1922-23, 1923-1925, 1925-1930
Charles H. Standifer, 1923-1925, 1925-1930
C.L. Price, 1923-1925, 1925-1930, 1930-50
John Sharp, 1923-1925, 1925-1927
William B. Douglas, 1923-1925, 1925-1930
Benjamin H. Moses, 1925-1930
Esom B. Bryant II, 1925-1930, 1946-47
James B. Spears, 1930-38
Morris E. Woolum, 1930-43, 1944-60
Andrew J. Long, 1930-46
Thomas Woods, 1930-45
William Sharp, 1930-44
Drue Stanifer, 1930-38
John H. Bryant, 1930-65
Lewis Baird, 1930-46
Ernie E. Yeary, 1938-41
John E. Hatfield, 1938-76
David Hammitte, 1941-67
Luther Gibson, 1943-76
Clayton Lawson, 1943-74, 1976-80, 1986-1994

A Bow Tied

Ira H. Moses, 1945-76
Harvey Rose, 1946-48
Edd Prewitt, 1946-50
Robert N. Ballinger, 1946-49
Ottis Ellis, 1947-78
Rufus L. Douglas, 1948-60
George Douglas, 1949-78
Arvil Rountree, 1950-61
Oscar Bunch, 1950-53
J.H. Douglas, 1953-78, 1979-82, 1982-88, 88-96
Efford Enix, 1959-76
C.B. Ellis, Jr., 1960-74, 1980-82
Glenn Rowe, 1961-80, 1982-90, 1994-98
Willis Yeary, 1966-1980
James Walden Sr., 1967-78
J.B. Hammitte, 1974-82, 1984-90, 1990-98
James L. Cox Sr., 1974-78
Willie Lee Partin, 1976-77
James Earl Prewitt, 1976-78, 1982-84
Fred Cornelius, 1976-80, 1980-88, 1990-98, 1999-02, 2002-10
Bobby Wilson, 1977-78
Roy Cornelius, 1978-82, 1982-90
Claude Baird, 1978-84
Jennings B. Baird, 1978-86
Lloyd Camp, 1978-86
Paul Grubbs, 1978-86
J.C. Murray, 1979-84
Jerome Walden, 1980-88, 1990-98, 2000-08
Kenneth E. Massingill, 1980-84, 1992-2000, 2004-10, 2012-18, 2018-
Leon Petree, 1984-92, 1994-2002
James Earl McKinney, 1984-92, 1998-2006
Lonnie Lyke, 1984-92, 2018-
James Walden, Jr., 1986-94, 1998-2006
Charles Creekmore, 1986-94
Arlie Petree, 1988-1996, 2006-14

Appendix 1: General Officials and Committees

Ray Landes, Jr., 1988-96, 1998-06, 2010-18
David Cornelius, 1992-2000, 2002-10, 2012-14
Donnie Hill, 1992-2000, 2002-06, 2012-21
Jasper Walden, 1994-2002, 2004-12, 2014-
James L. Cox, Jr., 1996-2000
Michael Cornelius, 1996-2004
Wayne Ison, 1996-04, 2008-16, 2018-
Cecil Johnson, 2000-08, 2010-18
James W. Kilgore, 2000-04
Henry Taylor, 2000-04
Richard Massingill, 2004-12
Jerry Wilson, 2004-12, 2014-
Tim Bartee, 2006-2014, 2016-
James Walden, Jr. II, 2006-10
Ulys Cox, 2008-16
John Keefer, 2008-16
Jay Walden, 2010-12
Kenneth Ellis, 2012-21
Tim McGlone, 2014-
Scott Isham, 2014-21
Michael Padgett, 2016-
Jerry Grubbs, 2016-

Select / Special Committees
Committee on Articles of Faith (1907): Andrew J. Silcox, Steven Bryant, John H. Parks, John J. Sammons, Edom J. Rountree
Committee on constitutional name (1907): John Smiddy, John H. Parks, Isaac Jones, James Jones, J. Allen Moses
Committee to develop an order of proceedings (1907): Steven Bryant, John H. Parks, J. Allen Moses
Committee on ordinations and establishment of new churches (1915): John Thomas, John H. Parks, Steven Bryant
Committee to buy a tent (1916): John H. Parks, John Thomas, Curd Walker

Committee to find a location for our assembly (1920): F.M. Thomas, Henry Mobley, G.A. Fore, J.L. Goins, John Thomas, Squire Broyles, Steven Bryant, John H. Parks

Committee to raise finance for the new tabernacle (1920): J.C. Taylor, G.A. Fore, Harrison Enix

Building Committee (1920): S.N. Bryant, John Bunch, W.C. Brock, G.A. Fore, J.L. Goins, Mat Witt, F.M. Thomas, Squire Broyles

Building Plans Committee (1920: W.C. Brock, John Bunch

Committee to dispose of printing press (1921): G.A. Fore, F.M. Thomas, Squire Broyles

Committee to develop a system to receive church letters (1922): J.H. Parks, S.N. Bryant, J.L. Goins

Committee to develop the work of an Elder (1922): J.H. Parks, S.N. Bryant, Henry Mobley, G.A. Fore, Starling Smith

Committee to decide whether to have Elders (1922): F.M. Thomas, L.M. Broyles, Kim Moses, J.L. Goins, Joshua Baird

Committee to select the Board of Elders (1922): Henry Mobley, S.N. Bryant

Committee to handle the tabernacle finance (1922): Squire Broyles, W.C. Brock, L.M. Sharp

Committee to dispose of printing press (1922): G.A. Fore, F.M. Thomas, Squire Broyles (retained)

Committee to appoint three trustees (1923): Curd Walker, S.N. Bryant, J.H. Parks

Committee on Printing Press (1923): Squire Broyles, Will Sharp, Will Brock

Committee to handle the tabernacle finance (1923): Squire Broyles, W.C. Brock, L.M. Sharp (retained)

Committee to plan a mess hall (1924): J.H. Parks, Curd Walker, J.L. Goins, Squire Broyles

Building Committee for Mess Hall (1924): J.H. Parks, L.M. Sharp, W.C. Brock

Committee to handle the tabernacle finance (1924): Squire Broyles, W.C. Brock, L.M. Sharp (retained)

Committee to meet with building committee and trustees (1925): C.B. Ellis, R.D. Litton, W.S. Sizemore

Appendix 1: General Officials and Committees

Mess Hall Planning Committee (1926): J.H. Parks, C.H. Standifer, Gilbert Weaver, S.N. Bryant, Curd Walker

Committee on Assembly Finance (1926): Gilbert Weaver, J.H. Parks, Squire Broyles

Committee to schedule first quarterly meeting and write to Assemblies of God (1927): unnamed

Committee to lay out the Bible way of paying tithes (1930): J.H. Parks, S.N. Bryant, Curd Walker

Committee to appoint a Sunday school committee (1930): J.H. Parks, S.N. Bryant, Curd Walker

Committee to appoint trustees (1930): J.H. Parks, S.N. Bryant, Curd Walker

Committee on building fund for new churches (1933): assembly trustees

Committee on hospitality (1936): J.H. Parks, Ira Moses, Squire Broyles, R.D. Litton

Committee to look up the Assembly's charter (1938): McKinley Baird, L.M. Sharp, Kim Moses

Building Committee to enlarge tabernacle (1940): Assembly trustees

Committee to plan a new system of government (1944): Luther Gibson, A.J. Long, J.E. Hatfield, Clayton Lawson, J.H. Bryant

Petition Committee (1945): Luther Gibson, David Hammitte, Randall Watkins

Petition Committee (1946): C.E. Bray, David Hammitte, Harvey Rose

Committee to work out a plan to finance a full-time General Overseer (1947): Luther Gibson, Ira H. Moses, and J.E. Hatfield

Committee to work out a program for the young people (1948): M.E. Woolum, R.N. Ballinger, Luther Gibson

Committee to work out a program for an old age minister fund (1948): M.E. Woolum, R.N. Ballinger, Clayton Lawson

Committee to work out a plan for governing pastor's elections (1949): J.E. Hatfield, Ira Moses, Arvil Rountree

Committee to confer with the Pentecostal Church of Christ (1950): Clayton Lawson, Luther Gibson, J.H. Bryant, Ira Moses, and J.E. Hatfield

Committee on a property for an orphanage (1952): Clayton Lawson, Luther Gibson, J.E. Hatfield, Ira Moses, J.H. Bryant, Arvil Rountree, J.H. Douglas

Committee on the Minutes (1954): Ira Moses, R.N. Ballinger, Lawrence Redmond

Committee on Aged Ministers Plan (1954): J.H. Bryant, R.N. Ballinger, Ira Moses

Committee on Vacation Bible School (1954): Beatrice Kennedy, [Sister] Hobbs, Lassie Lawson, Nellie Swain, Haskel Swain, Efford Enix, C.B. Ellis, Jr.

Committee to propose wording for a resolution on pension plan (1956): Clayton Lawson, Luther Gibson, J.E. Hatfield

Committee to work out duties for a full-time treasurer (1956): M.E. Woolum, Luther Gibson, J.H. Douglas

Committee to look for a place for new assembly grounds (1956): Isham Sharp, General Douglas, J.H. Dobson, J.A. Enix, George Douglas

Committee to work with the Resolutions Committee to revise some of the standard resolutions (1957): Luther Gibson and two unnamed

Committee on publicity to prepare to take care of people at the next assembly (1958): General Douglas, James Burke, J.E. Hatfield

Committee to look for a location for a new tabernacle and campground (1959): Dan Lynch, William Fitzpatrick, J.E. Hatfield

Committee to look for a place to build a new tabernacle (1960): Arvil Rountree, C.B. Ellis, James Walden Sr.

Committee on minister's retirement (1966): added Paul Yeary to previous committee

Committee to work with the Pentecostal Church of Christ (1974): added Jerome Walden to previous committee

Committee to bring a minister's retirement plan before the General Council the following year (1976): *James Walden, Jr.*, James Cox, Jr., Clayton Lawson

Committee to investigate conflicts with the current resolutions over newly adopted creation of Second Assistant Overseer (1977): Executive Board, J.E. Prewitt, Rev. James Walden, Jr.

Board of Review on Retirement (1978): *James Walden, Jr.,* James L. Cox, Jr., Clayton Lawson (retained until 1986)

Appendix 1: General Officials and Committees

Committee to confer with Beulah Heights Bible College (1980): James Walden, Jr., Bob Vance, Paul Yeary, Mike Cornelius, Jerome Walden, J.H. Douglas, Glenn Rowe

Committee to study the potential for a credit union (1980): Executive Board, Finance Committee

Committee to confer with International Pentecostal Church of Christ (1985): Executive Board, Christian Education Director, National Youth Director

Committee on minister's retirement (1986): J.E. Prewitt, Leon Petree, Lonnie Lyke, Jerome Walden, Fred Cornelius

Committee to clarify the relationship between the funds and duties of the Second Assistant Overseer and National Youth Department (1986): Camp Board, Finance Committee Chairman, Trustee Chairman

Exploratory Committee to research establishing a CGMA college and report at next assembly (1995): Executive Board, Jasper Walden, Henry Taylor, Michael Padgett, Michael Cornelius, James Walden

Committee to research the CGMA formation date (1996): J.E. Prewitt, Leon Petree, Michael Padgett

Committee to find a more practical and time efficient way to distribute plaques at the general assembly (1997): Fred Cornelius, Bill Gaylor, Rick Massingill

Committee on Church Planting (2010): Donnie Hill, Jasper Walden, James Kilgore, Cecil Johnson

Committee to study the issue of teaching 25; to research the scriptural, historical, etymological, and legal aspects; to report to the executive board; and to submit resolutions for proposed wording changes for the next general assembly (2015): Michael Padgett, Jasper Walden, Donnie Hill, Scott Isham, Rick McKinney

Committee for further study and suggestions of teaching 25 (2016): previous committee retained

Committee to study and propose an amendment to Article XII, Section A requiring background check for applicants for ministerial credentials (2017): no committee appointed

Appendix Two

General Assembly Speakers

Following the tradition of the Baptist association from which they came, the founders of the Church of God Mountain Assembly chose the location of the next annual meeting at the conclusion of business each year. After the first tabernacle was built on Florence Avenue in Jellico in 1922, the delegates ceased the annual vote on the assembly location. After the second tabernacle (built in 1942) proved inadequate to accommodate the large crowds, the Board of Twelve Elders recommended "having the Annual Assembly at different places" in 1949, and the General Council voted to hold the 44th General Assembly at the 15th & Race Street Church in Cincinnati, Ohio. After one assembly outside the mountains, the Council voted each year to hold the next assembly at Jellico until 1956 when it appointed a committee to "look out a place for our new Assembly grounds." In 1966, the Assembly built a third tabernacle in Jellico more than sufficient to host each annual convention thereafter.

In 2008, the Board of Twelve Elders determined that, since the CGMA Constitutional Declaration & Bylaws did not specify that the General Council had the sole authority to choose the location of the annual convention, "the Executive Board is empowered to choose that location." As a result, the 103rd General Assembly convened at the Grand Resort Convention Center in Pigeon Forge, Tennessee in 2009. The following ten conventions were held at Smoky Mountain Convention Center nearby. The 113th General Assembly had been planned for The Ramsey in Pigeon Forge until the Board of Twelve Elders canceled it in July 2020 due to the COVID-19 pandemic. Due to rescheduling conflicts, the 2021 Assembly is slated for the Music Road Hotel in Pigeon Forge.

Along with choosing the location of the next annual assembly, each business session concluded with choosing a speaker (and an alternate) for the next Introductory Sermon. The Mountain Assembly founders continued this practice from the Baptist association until 1964 when the General Council voted to have the General Overseer preach the sermon each year. Originally, the Introductory Sermon preceded the opening of the business session. A new 'order of business" adopted in 1944 with the new system of government

Appendix 2: Assembly Speakers

placed the sermon at the beginning of the "General Assembly" on Wednesday after the "Bishops' Council" convened on Tuesday. Eight years later, the "General Council" replaced the Bishops' Council, but the Introductory Sermon remained on Wednesday morning. In 1998, the Mountain Assembly instituted a full-day's business session on Tuesday and created a scenario where, on several occasions, the business session concluded before the Introductory Sermon was delivered. In 2010, the General Council voted to place the Introductory Sermon on Monday night of the General Assembly.

From 1907 to 1953, delegates appointed a Committee on Divine Services after the election of officers. This committee announced the additional speakers for the evening and morning worship services during the business sessions. In the Baptist association, the delegates from the host church would customarily serve as the committee, and the Mountain Assembly followed this tradition until 1935. In 1953, the Board of Twelve Elders began choosing a "Program Committee" at its last meeting prior to the General Assembly. This committee selected speakers and devotional leaders, chose a theme, prepared a printed program prior to the General Assembly, and often appointed music and entertainment committees and a publicity committee. In 1971, the adoption of a new resolution created a Program Committee, consisting of three licensed/ordained ministers, elected annually by the General Council.

The table that follows provides the dates and locations for each General Assembly, the speaker for the Introductory Sermon, and, when known, additional speakers, theme, and the appropriate committee.

1st General Assembly

October 11-12, 1907   Little Wolf Creek, Kentucky

Introductory Sermon: John Parks
Committee on Divine Services: "the delegates of the association"

2nd General Assembly

September 12-13, 1908   Zion Hill, Kentucky

Introductory Sermon: Alvin J. Ross
Committee on Divine Services: Milton F. Ross, John D. Lay, James Lay, Lewis M. Angel, Solomon Barley, Newt Parks

3rd General Assembly
October 1-2, 1909   Hayes Creek, Kentucky
Introductory Sermon: John Parks

4th General Assembly
September 30-October 2, 1910   Jellico Creek, Kentucky
Introductory Sermon: Edom J. Rountree (Revelation 13:6)
Additional Speakers: William Douglas
Committee on Divine Services: J.C. Taylor, Alex Cornelius, Loney Lovitt, Thomas Higginbotham

5th General Assembly
October 6-8, 1911   Siler's Chapel, Kentucky
Introductory Sermon: John Parks (Ephesians 4:1-17)
Additional Speakers: S.N. Bryant, Peter Smith, John Parks, Joseph S. Llewellyn, A.J. Tomlinson, John Thomas, Joshua Sharp, Andrew J. Silcox, Edom J. Rountree
Committee on Divine Services: Terrel Siler, Ferd Siler, John Q. Siler, John H. Fulton, Aaron Faulkner

6th General Assembly
October 4-6, 1912   Lower Elk Valley, Tennessee
Introductory Sermon: S.N. Bryant (Acts 3:21)
Additional Speakers: Thomas L. McLain, George F. Lucas, A.J. Tomlinson, A.J. Tomlinson, Martin S. Haynes, Peter Smith, S.N. Bryant, A.J. Tomlinson, Thomas D. Moses, Aaron Thomas, Edom J. Rountree and others, John Parks, A.J. Tomlinson
Committee on Divine Services: John Smiddy, Squire Broyles, Aaron Hackler, Terrell F. Hamblin

7th General Assembly
October 3-4, 1913   Saxton, Kentucky
Introductory Sermon: S.N. Bryant (Ezekiel 2:19-20)
Additional Speakers: John Thomas, Crise Irvin, John Parks, Newt Parks, S.N. Bryant, John Parks
Committee on Divine Services: Joe L. Jones, Curd Walker, Walter Willie, Pete Huddleston, George Perkins, J.B. Spears, L.K. Kinley

Appendix 2: Assembly Speakers

8th *General Assembly*

October 2-4, 1914   Elk Valley, Tennessee

Introductory Sermon: John Thomas (Acts 20:28)
Additional Speakers: John Thomas, Billy Wilder, William R. Hamblin
Committee on Divine Services: William B. Douglas, Mathew Douglas, Joshua Baird, John Sharp, Lee Lynch

9th *General Assembly*

October 1-3, 1915   Jellico Creek, Kentucky

Introductory Sermon: Henry Mobley (1 Peter 2)
Additional Speakers: Curd Walker, D.B. Vess, Curd Walker, John Parks
Committee on Divine Services: Henry N. Creekmore, Joseph Walker, Lawrence Cornelius, William F. Cornelius, Tyra J. Wood, John Baird, Silvester Baird, Albert Shepherd, Arthur Patrick, Tandy Gallamore, Loney Lovitt, J.C. Taylor, James D. Taylor, Elihu H. Privett

10th *General Assembly*

October 6-8, 1916   Lower Elk Valley, Tennessee

Introductory Sermon: Levi M. White (1 Corinthians 12)
Additional Speakers: John Thomas, S.N. Bryant, John Parks
Committee on Divine Services: Albert Bell, Roy Todd, Joe Daniels, Henry Mobley, N.K. Parks, R.D. Litton, John Meeks, Aaron Gaylor, Charles Cox

11th *General Assembly*

October 5-7, 1917   Lower Elk Valley, Tennessee

Introductory Sermon: Hubert O. Harris (2 Timothy 2)
Additional Speakers: S.N. Bryant, S.N. Bryant, John Thomas
Committee on Divine Services: Newt Parks, R.D. Litton, John Bates, Aaron Gaylor, John Creekmore, A.Z. Long

12th *General Assembly*

October 4-6, 1918   Emlyn, Kentucky

Introductory Sermon: S.N. Bryant (1 Corinthians 3:9)
Additional Speakers: John Thomas, Levi M. White, James Daniels, Joseph Daniels, Edom J. Rountree, Craig Griffitts, Billy Wilder, John Parks, C.H. Standifer, C.L. Price, James Mowery
Committee on Divine Services: John Calchera, Billy Griffitts, Billy Wilder

13th *General Assembly*
October 3-5, 1919   Lower Elk Valley, Tennessee

Introductory Sermon: George A. Fore (Ephesians 1)
Additional Speakers: A.A. Carpenter, William S. Sizemore, George T. Brouayer, S.N. Bryant, Cal King, John Bunch
Committee on Divine Services: Charles Cox, Jerry Wilson, John Sively, Henry Mobley, Harve Mobley, Aaron Gaylor, R.D. Litton, Newt Parks, E.H. Ross, Albert Bell, John Smith

14th *General Assembly*
October 1-3, 1920   Lower Elk Valley, Tennessee

Introductory Sermon: John Parks (Hebrews 5:8)
Additional Speakers: John Thomas, J.L. Goins, S.N. Bryant, G.A. Fore, John Stooksbury
Committee on Divine Services: Newt Parks, R.D. Litton, Albert Bell, Henry Mobley, W.C. Brock, E.H. Ross, Aaron Gaylor, Arthur Enix

15th *Annual Assembly*
September 30-October 2, 1921   Lower Elk Valley, Tennessee

Introductory Sermon: G.A. Fore (Acts 3:22-23)
Additional Speakers: unknown
Committee on Divine Services: R.D. Litton, A.J. Long, Henry Mobley, Harve Mobley, Newt Parks, E.H. Ross, Charles Smith, Charles Cox, Aaron Davis, Albert Bell, Squire Broyles, Gilbert Weaver, William C. Brock, Jerry Wilson, Aaron Hackler

16th *Annual Assembly*
October 6-8, 1922   Jellico, Tennessee

Introductory Sermon: S.N. Bryant (1 Corinthians 3:9)
Additional Speakers: George A. Fore, J.L. Goins, C.H. Standifer
Committee on Divine Services: Newt Parks and others

Appendix 2: Assembly Speakers

17th Annual Assembly
October 1-5, 1923   Jellico, Tennessee

Introductory Sermon: none
Additional Speakers: Squire Broyles, C.H. Standifer, Curd Walker, Samuel Sexton, John Parks, Matt Morgan, Joshua Baird, Curd Walker, C.L. Price

18th General Assembly
October 1-5, 1924   Jellico, Tennessee

Introductory Sermon: C.H. Standifer (Mark 16:17-20)
Additional Speakers: S.N. Bryant, James A. Cole, John Parks, J.L. Goins
Committee on Divine Services: Gilbert Weaver, Will Sharp, Henry Mobley, Harve Mobley, William C. Brock, John Parks, Albert Bell

19th General Assembly
September 2-6, 1925   Jellico, Tennessee

Introductory Sermon: J.L. Goins (Romans 12)
Additional Speakers: Kim Moses, C.H. Standifer, C.L. Price, Matt Morgan, Ed Johnson, B.H. Moses, James M. Bilbrey, Horace M. Bates, Sim A. Wilson, S.N. Bryant
Committee on Divine Services: Gilbert Weaver, W.S. Heatherly, Will Sharp, Henry Mobley, John Parks, Harve Mobley

20th General Assembly
September 1-5, 1926   Jellico, Tennessee

Introductory Sermon: S.N. Bryant (1 Corinthians 3:9)
Additional Speakers: Curd Walker, C.H. Standifer, Moss Dalton, Kim Moses, C.L. Price, Drue Stanifer, E.B. Bryant, John Parks, Henry S. Scalf, Matt Morgan, S.N. Bryant, William S. Sizemore
Committee on Divine Services: Squire Broyles, Fred Puckett, Lee Lynch, Frank Standifer, Harve Mobley

A Bow Tied

21ˢᵗ *General Assembly*
September 7-11, 1927   Jellico, Tennessee

Introductory Sermon: E.B. Bryant (Revelation 3)
Additional Speakers: Curd Walker, Moss Dalton, C.H. Standifer, B.H. Moses, J.H. Bryant, Lewis M. Broyles, Matt Morgan, Kim Moses, Henry Mobley, John Parks, S.N. Bryant
Committee on Divine Services: R.D. Litton, Harve Mobley, Henry Mobley, John Parks, Newt Parks, Albert Bell, John R. Smith, Gilbert Weaver

22ⁿᵈ *General Assembly*
September 5-9, 1928   Jellico, Tennessee

Introductory Sermon: S.N. Bryant (Hebrews 13:13)
Additional Speakers: Curd Walker, Thomas Woods, Kim Moses, James A. Oliver, E.B. Bryant, A.J. Long, C.L. Price, John M. Yancy, Louis Woods, S.N. Bryant
Committee on Divine Services: John Parks, Newt Parks, Gilbert Weaver, Henry Mobley, Alvin G. Ross, Elliott Moses, Will Sharp, R.D. Litton, W.S. Heatherly, Albert Bell

23ʳᵈ *General Assembly*
September 4-8, 1929   Jellico, Tennessee

Introductory Sermon: Thomas Woods (1 Timothy 1:3)
Additional Speakers: Drue Stanifer, M.E. Woolum, Curd Walker, Lewis M. Broyles, E.B. Bryant, James C. Leatherwood, J.H. Bryant, Kim Moses, Drue Stanifer, S.N. Bryant, John Parks
Committee on Divine Services: Alonzo Douglas, E.B. Rose, Aaron Hackler

24ᵗʰ *General Assembly*
September 3-7, 1930   Jellico, Tennessee

Introductory Sermon: Curd Walker (2 Timothy 2:15)
Additional Speakers: M.E. Woolum, Matt Morgan, Drue Stanifer, C.L. Price, E.B. Bryant, A.J. Long, J.H. Bryant, Kim Moses, S.N. Bryant, John Parks, Curd Walker
Committee on Divine Services: William C. Brock, Gilbert Weaver, Harve Mobley, John Parks, Alvin G. Ross

Appendix 2: Assembly Speakers

25th *General Assembly*
September 2-6, 1931   Jellico, Tennessee

Introductory Sermon: Kim Moses (Acts 16)
Additional Speakers: Curd Walker, Thomas Woods, Willard Cress, B.H. Moses, J.H. Bryant, John Parks, R.D. Litton, M.E. Woolum, E.B. Bryant, A.J. Long, Curd Walker, B.H. Moses
Committee on Divine Services: J.E. Hatfield, Alvin G. Ross, Arthur Enix, John Parks

26th *General Assembly*
September 7-11, 1932   Jellico, Tennessee

Introductory Sermon: John Parks (2 Timothy 4:1-18)
Additional Speakers: Curd Walker, C.L. Price, J.H. Bryant, A.J. Long, Joshua Baird, Thomas Woods, George W. Hensley, Hurston Chambers, E.B. Bryant, John Parks
Committee on Divine Services: W.S. Heatherly, Arthur Enix, Aaron Hackler, John Parks, Gilbert Weaver, Harve Mobley, Alvin G. Ross

27th *General Assembly*
September 6-10, 1933   Jellico, Tennessee

Introductory Sermon: E.B. Bryant (1 Corinthians 10)
Additional Speakers: Curd Walker, Thomas Woods, J.E. Hatfield, A.J. Long, H.D. Williams, J.H. Bryant, James C. Leatherwood, Harve Phelps, M.E. Woolum, Drue Stanifer, Jonah L. Shelton, John Parks, E.B. Bryant
Committee on Divine Services: E.E. Yeary, E.B. Rose, George Perkins

28th *General Assembly*
September 5-9, 1934   Jellico, Tennessee

Introductory Sermon: S.N. Bryant (John 13:34-35)
Additional Speakers: K.T. Scalf, Joshua Baird, Curd Walker, Thomas Woods, Kim Moses, William L. Miracle, B.H. Moses, E.B. Bryant, S.N. Bryant, John Parks
Committee on Divine Services: J.A. Enix, Gilbert Weaver, George Perkins

A Bow Tied

29th General Assembly
September 4-8, 1935   Jellico, Tennessee

Introductory Sermon: J.H. Bryant (1 Peter 2:1-5)
Additional Speakers: Curd Walker, Thomas Woods, Kim Moses, A.J. Long, M.E. Woolum, Will Sharp, Drue Stanifer, E.E. Yeary, John Parks
Committee on Divine Services: Curd Walker, M.E. Woolum, Thomas Woods

30th General Assembly
September 2-6, 1936   Jellico, Tennessee

Introductory Sermon: John Parks (2 Peter 1)
Additional Speakers: A.J. Long, E.E. Yeary, Thomas Woods, J.H. Bryant, Curd Walker, M.E. Woolum, Clayton Lawson, Will Sharp, David Phelps, Edd Prewitt, B.H. Moses, Curd Walker
Committee on Divine Services: Thomas Woods, A.J. Long, E.E. Yeary

31st General Assembly
September 1-5, 1937   Jellico, Tennessee

Introductory Sermon: Thomas Woods (1 Corinthians 16:13)
Additional Speakers: Kim Moses, Virgil L. Akins, M.E. Woolum, McKinley Baird, David Hammitte, Joshua Baird, Abraham H. Tribble, Luther Gibson, Lewis Baird, B.H. Moses, John Parks, S.N. Bryant
Committee on Divine Services: Lewis Baird, Alvin G. Ross, Johnny Jones, Ira Moses

32nd General Assembly
September 7-11, 1938   Jellico, Tennessee

Introductory Sermon: John Parks (1 Corinthians 15:58)
Additional Speakers: Charles Goins, Clayton Lawson, J.B. Spears, Clarence Woolum, Virgil L. Akins, Will Sharp, Luther Gibson, William Baird, J.H. Bryant, Roy Cornelius, E.E. Yeary, M.E. Woolum
Committee on Divine Services: M.E. Woolum, E.B. Rose, Curd Walker

Appendix 2: Assembly Speakers

33rd *General Assembly*

September 6-10, 1939   Jellico, Tennessee

Introductory Sermon: E.E. Yeary (1 Corinthians 15:58)
Additional Speakers: Will Sharp, J.H. Bryant, Joshua Baird, Luther Gibson, A.J. Long, William Baird, Abraham H. Tribble, Thomas Woods, M.E. Woolum, Virgil L. Akins, Clayton Lawson, Edd Prewitt, John D. Spencer
Committee on Divine Services: J.H. Bryant, Will Sharp, Joshua Baird

34th *General Assembly*

September 4-8, 1940   Jellico, Tennessee

Introductory Sermon: Kim Moses (1 Corinthians 14:1)
Additional Speakers: Charles Goins, R.D. Litton, Carl Isaac, John R. Williams, J.H. Bryant, E.E. Yeary, Luther Gibson, Thomas Woods, Edd Prewitt, Will Sharp, A.J. Long, J.E. Hatfield
Committee on Divine Services: Charles Goins, R.D. Litton, Kim Moses

35th *General Assembly*

September 3-7, 1941   Jellico, Tennessee

Introductory Sermon: J.H. Bryant (Ephesians 2:19-22)
Additional Speakers: Edd Prewitt, Fred Cummins, Joshua Baird, David Hammitte, Clayton Lawson, M.E. Woolum, Will Sharp, John Parks, Andy Campbell, C.E. Bray, R.D. Litton, William S. Sizemore
Committee on Divine Services: Edd Prewitt, Fred Cummins, Joshua Baird

36th *General Assembly*

September 2-6, 1942   Jellico, Tennessee

Introductory Sermon: M.E. Woolum (Song of Solomon 6)
Additional Speakers: Fred Cummins, William L. Goins, J.H. Bryant, Ottis Ellis, Clayton Lawson, Thomas Woods, Roy Cornelius, Kim Moses, Joshua Baird, Abraham H. Tribble, Luther Gibson, Will Sharp, Virgil L. Akins
Committee on Divine Services: J.H. Bryant, M.E. Woolum, Clayton Lawson

A Bow Tied

37ᵗʰ *General Assembly*
September 1-5, 1943   Jellico, Tennessee

Introductory Sermon: A.J. Long (1 Corinthians 3)
Additional Speakers: Charles Gibson, Charles Goins, J.H. Bryant, Ira Moses, Charles E. Lawson, Will Sharp, Joe Moses, Silas Mosingo, Luther Gibson, Neal Bolton, Harvey Rose, William L. Miracle, Joe Moses
Committee on Divine Services: Kim Moses, Luther Gibson, Will Sharp

38ᵗʰ *General Assembly*
September 6-10, 1944   Jellico, Tennessee

Introductory Sermon: J.H. Bryant (Philippians 1:27)
Additional Speakers: E.B. Bryant, Thomas Woods, Ottis Ellis, Paul Grubbs, M.E. Woolum, Charles E. Lawson, Willis Yeary, Clayton Lawson, A.J. Long, Luther Gibson, McKinley Baird, Starling Smith, E.B. Bryant
Committee on Divine Services: Luther Gibson, Kim Moses, Lewis Baird

39ᵗʰ *General Assembly*
September 5-9, 1945   Jellico, Tennessee

Introductory Sermon: A.J. Long
Additional Speakers: Coy Laws, Thomas Jackson, C.B. Ellis Sr., Randall Watkins, Silas Mosingo, M.E. Woolum, E.B. Bryant, David Hammitte, E.B. Rose, Edd Prewitt, William S. Sizemore, Ira Moses, Charles Gibson, Harvey Rose
Committee on Divine Services: J.H. Bryant, Harvey Rose, C.L. Price

40ᵗʰ *General Assembly*
September 4-8, 1946   Jellico, Tennessee

Introductory Sermon: J.H. Bryant (Galatians 5:25-26)
Additional Speakers: Maynard L. Woods, Edd Prewitt, Ottis Ellis, Charles Gibson, Clayton Lawson, Anderson McKenzie, Harvey Rose, E.B. Rose, David Phelps, C. L. Price, Ira Moses, "Brother Henson"
Committee on Divine Services: E.B. Rose, Luther Gibson, M.E. Woolum

Appendix 2: Assembly Speakers

41ˢᵗ General Assembly
September 3-7, 1947   Jellico, Tennessee

Introductory Sermon: Clayton Lawson (2 Corinthians 4:1)
Additional Speakers: J.H. Bryant, Randall Watkins, Edd Prewitt, J.L. Goins, Harvey Rose, Leslie E. Strunk, E.B. Rose, Luther Gibson, Floyd Robinson
Committee on Divine Services: Ira Moses, J.E. Hatfield, Anderson McKenzie

42ⁿᵈ General Assembly
September 1-5, 1948   Jellico, Tennessee

Introductory Sermon: J.E. Hatfield (Matthew 28:19-20)
Youth Night: Robert Thomas
Additional Speakers: George Douglas, Charles Gibson, Lawrence Taylor, C.H. Randall, Ottis Ellis, Clayton Lawson, "J.W. Roberts," John Bunch, M.E. Woolum, Arvil Rountree, Rufus L. Douglas, Ira Moses, Ottis Ellis
Committee on Divine Services: C.E. Bray, M.E. Woolum, J.H. Bryant

43ʳᵈ General Assembly
September 6-11, 1949   Jellico, Tennessee

Introductory Sermon: Luther Gibson
Youth Night: Floy Marie Bell
Additional Speakers: Floy Marie Bell, "C.E. Garrett," Rufus L. Douglas, Ira Moses, J.H. Bryant, "Rev. Turner," M.E. Woolum, Ulyess Graham, "James Hutson," George W. Helmick, J.H. Douglas, J.H. Douglas
Committee on Divine Services: J.H. Douglas, David Hammitte, Edd Prewitt

44ᵗʰ General Assembly
August 22-27, 1950   Cincinnati, Ohio

Introductory Sermon: J.H. Bryant (Ephesians 6)
Youth Night: John T. Longsworth
Additional Speakers: Ira Moses, Efford Enix, Eldon L. Cyrus, Luther Gibson, M.E. Woolum, George K. Nickell, Lawrence Redmond, David Hammitte, J.H. Douglas, J.H. Douglas, Arvil Rountree
Committee on Divine Services: M.E. Woolum, J.H. Bryant, Floyd Robinson

A Bow Tied

45th *General Assembly*
September 4-9, 1951 Jellico, Tennessee

Introductory Sermon: Clayton Lawson (1 Corinthians 4:1)
Youth Night: Efford Enix, C.B. Ellis Jr.
Additional Speakers: Ira Moses, Anderson Owsley, Auza Vinson, J.H. Bryant, Luther Gibson, Roy Cornelius, Dover Kasee, Arvil Rountree, John Collins, Ottis Ellis, M.E. Woolum, Joe Moses, Joe Moses, Ira Moses
Committee on Divine Services: M.E. Woolum, Ira Moses, Arvil Rountree

46th *General Assembly*
August 12-17, 1952 Jellico, Tennessee

Introductory Sermon: Clayton Lawson (1 Timothy 1)
Youth Night: Haskel Swain, Efford Enix, Archer Engle,
Additional Speakers: J.H. Douglas, M.E. Woolum, J.E. Hatfield, Arvil Rountree, Maynard L. Woods, Lawrence Redmond, Ira Moses, Luther Gibson, Auza Vinson, Earl Heath, Deward Hoskins, Joe Moses.
Committee on Divine Services: Ottis Ellis, David Hammitte, Ira Moses

47th *General Assembly*
August 11-16, 1953 Jellico, Tennessee

Introductory Sermon: J.H. Bryant (1 Peter 2:1-5)
Youth Night: Efford Enix, Archer Engle
Additional Speakers: J.E. Hatfield, Clayton Lawson, Ira Moses, Luther Gibson, Auza Vinson, Arvil Rountree, J.H. Douglas, Earl Heath, Hestle Ball.

48th *General Assembly*
August 10-15, 1954 Jellico, Tennessee

Introductory Sermon: Clayton Lawson (2 Timothy 2:2)
Youth Night: Haskel Swain
Additional Speakers: Dan Lynch, Arville Shepherd, Hayes Harp, M.E. Woolum, Luther Gibson, J.H. Bryant, Ira Moses, David Hammitte, Arvil Rountre, Ira Moses

Appendix 2: Assembly Speakers

49th *General Assembly*
August 9-14, 1955   Jellico, Tennessee

Introductory Sermon: Ira Moses (1 Timothy 4)
Youth Night: Hayes Harp
Additional Speakers: J.H. Douglas, J.H. Bryant, Luther Gibson, Auza Vinson, Clayton Lawson, Lawrence Redmond, Arvil Rountree, "Brother Klutz," Isham Sharp

50th *General Assembly*
August 7-12, 1956   Jellico, Tennessee

Introductory Sermon: Luther Gibson (Psalm 78:41)
Youth Night: Efford Enix
Additional Speakers: Hestle Ball, Earl Heath, James Walden Sr., William Sheffield, Charles Gibson, General Douglas, J.H. Bryant, Robert Hicks, Clayton Lawson, Isham Sharp, Everett Rogers, Joe Howard, Silas Lay

51st *General Assembly*
August 13-17, 1957   Jellico, Tennessee

Introductory Sermon: Arvil Rountree (Acts 20:28)
Youth Night: Efford Enix
Mission Night: Luther Gibson, Clayton Lawson
Additional Speakers: J.H. Douglas, Ira Moses, Lawrence Redmond, David Hammitte, M.E. Woolum, Auza Vinson

52nd *General Assembly*
August 12-16, 1958   Jellico, Tennessee

Introductory Sermon: J.E. Hatfield (Acts 2:14-39)
Youth Night: C.B. Ellis Jr.
Additional Speakers: Ottis Ellis, J.H. Bryant, Hayes Harp, Clayton Lawson, Luther Gibson, Walter Vaughn, Willis Yeary

53rd *General Assembly*
August 11-15, 1959   Jellico, Tennessee

Theme: "Jesus Christ, the Hope of the World"
Introductory Sermon: Lawrence Redmond
Additional Speakers: Charles Creekmore, Arvil Rountree, Luther Gibson, James A. Cross, David Hammitte, Willis Yeary, Ira Moses
Program Committee: Luther Gibson, Lawrence Redmond, J.E. Hatfield

A Bow Tied

54th *General Assembly*

July 25-30, 1960   Jellico, Tennessee

Introductory Sermon: Ira Moses (Acts 15:28)
Youth Night: Fred Cornelius
Additional Speakers: Frank Croley, Jerome Walden, George Douglas, Chester I. Miller, George K. Nickell, Charles A. Freeman, Clayton Lawson, Willie Lee Partin, Dan Lynch

55th *General Assembly*

August 8-12, 1961   Jellico, Tennessee

Theme: "Reaching Forward"
Introductory Sermon: Willis Yeary (Philippians 2:5)
Youth Night: J.E. Prewitt
Additional Speakers: J.B. Hammitte, James Walden Sr., J.H. Douglas, J.E. Hatfield, Ira Moses, J.H. Bryant, Maynard L. Woods

56th *General Assembly*

August 7-11, 1962   Jellico, Tennessee

Theme: "He is Able"
Introductory Sermon: J.H. Bryant
Youth Night: Leon Petree
Additional Speakers: Jennings B. Baird, Luther Gibson, Ottis Ellis, Charles Creekmore, Ira Moses, J.H. Douglas, Gene Douglas

57th *General Assembly*

August 13-17, 1963   Jellico, Tennessee

Theme: "A Better Way"
Introductory Sermon: David Hammitte (Isaiah 62:10)
Youth Night: Jerome Walden
Additional Speakers: Dan Lynch, James Cox Sr., Efford Enix, C.B. Ellis Jr., Ira Moses, Azzie Brown, Arlie Petree
Program Committee: J.E. Prewitt, Clayton Lawson, Efford Enix

Appendix 2: Assembly Speakers

58th General Assembly
August 11-15, 1964   Jellico, Tennessee

Theme: "The Lord is My Helper" (Hebrews 13:6)
Introductory Sermon: C.B. Ellis Jr.
Youth Night: J.E. Prewitt
Additional Speakers: Charles Creekmore, Luther Gibson, Ira Moses, Ottis Ellis, Clayton Lawson, Gene Douglas, James Cox Sr.
Program Committee: Luther Gibson, Willis Yeary, Glenn Rowe, Ottis Ellis, George Douglas

59th General Assembly
August 10-14, 1965   Jellico, Tennessee

Introductory Sermon: Ira Moses (Matthew 16:18)
Youth Night: Leon Petree
Additional Speakers: Roy Cornelius, J.E. Hatfield, Donnie Hill, Everett Rogers, James Walden Jr., James V. Freeman, George Douglas, Bobby Wilson, Clayton Lawson, Jessie Weaver, Fred Cornelius, Willie Lee Partin

60th General Assembly
August 9-16, 1966   Jellico, Tennessee

Theme: "To Preach the Acceptable Year of the Lord" (Luke 4:19)
Introductory Sermon: Ira Moses (Luke 4:19)
Youth Night: Jasper Walden
Additional Speakers: J.B. Hammitte, James Walden Jr., Willis Yeary, James Laudermilk, C.B. Ellis Jr., Charles H. Davis, J.H. Douglas, David Carroll, Ken Massingill
Program Committee: J.E. Prewitt, Clayton Lawson, Willis Yeary, Bobby Wilson, Charles Creekmore

61st General Assembly
August 8-12, 1967   Jellico, Tennessee

Theme: "Evangelize" (Mark 16:15)
Introductory Sermon: Ira Moses (Mark 16:15)
Youth Night: Jerome Walden
Additional Speakers: Paul Grubbs, James Walden Sr., J.E. McKinney, Arlie Petree, Donnie Hill, Jerry Bunn, Larry Shanks, Paul Dobson, Ottis Ellis, Merle Laws, Luther Gibson, Orville C. Bartee, Roger Walden, J.E. Prewitt, Charles H. Davis, Roger Powell

Program Committee: Glenn Rowe, J.B. Hammitte, Ottis Ellis, James Walden Jr.

62nd General Assembly
August 13-17, 1968   Jellico, Tennessee

Theme: "Day of Deliverance" (Exodus 13:3)
Introductory Sermon: Ira Moses (Hebrews 7:11-16)
Youth Night: James Gray
Mission Night: Bobby Wilson
Additional Speakers: Wesley Dupuy, Jessie Weaver, Glenn Rowe, Larry Hopkins, Donnie Hill, Lonnie Lyke, George Douglas, James Cox Jr., Fred Cornelius, Lewis Young
Program Committee: George Douglas, Efford Enix, Fred Cornelius, Ottis Ellis, Leon Petree

63rd General Assembly
August 11-16, 1969   Jellico, Tennessee

Introductory Sermon: Ira Moses (Acts 1:8)
Youth Night: Leon Petree
Mission Night: Luther Gibson
Additional Speakers: James Cox Sr., J.H. Douglas, Jessie Weaver, Lloyd Camp, Clayton Lawson, Charles H. Davis, Jerome Walden, Merle Gibson, James Walden Jr., James Laudermilk

64th General Assembly
August 10-15, 1970   Jellico, Tennessee

Theme: "Christ for '70"
Introductory Sermon: Ira Moses (Matthew 20:1-15)
Youth Night: C.B. Ellis Jr.
Mission Night: J.E. McKinney
Additional Speakers: Willie Lee Partin, J.B. Hammitte, Jessie Weaver, Ottis Ellis, Philip Yeary, Ken Massingill, Claude Baird, Hiram Ellis, Gene Douglas, Bobby Wilson
Program Committee: Willis Yeary, Clayton Lawson, C.B. Ellis Jr.

Appendix 2: Assembly Speakers

65th *General Assembly*

August 9-14, 1971   Jellico, Tennessee

Theme: "Government in Action"
Introductory Sermon: Ira Moses (2 Timothy 1:1-9)
Youth Night: Donnie Hill
Mission Night: Clayton Lawson
Additional Speakers: George Douglas, Ken Massingill, Jessie Weaver, Thomas Bartee, James Walden Sr., Henry Weaver, Charles D. Blackburn, James Crisp, Efford Enix, Lonnie Duff
Program Committee: J.H. Douglas, Orville C. Bartee, Willie Lee Partin

66th *General Assembly*

August 7-12, 1972   Jellico, Tennessee

Theme: "Our Day of Visitation"
Introductory Sermon: Ira Moses (Psalms 11:1-3)
Youth Night: Ray Landes
Mission Night: Elder M. Blair
Additional Speakers: Ray Freeman, Everett Rogers, Jessie Weaver, Bobby Wilson, Roy Cornelius, James Justice, Jennings B. Baird, Ross Randolph, Arlie Petree, James Cox Jr.
Program Committee: Fred Cornelius, Bobby Wilson, James Walden Jr.

67th *General Assembly*

August 6-11, 1973   Jellico, Tennessee

Theme: "Occupy Till I Come" (Luke 19:13)
Introductory Sermon: C.B. Ellis Jr.
Youth Night: Michael Bartee
Mission Night: Fred Cornelius
Additional Speakers: Hiram Ellis, James Walden Jr., Paul Grubbs, Willis Yeary, Michael Cornelius, Luther Gibson, Dan Lynch
Program Committee: J.B. Hammitte, Dan Lynch, Ottis Ellis.

68th *General Assembly*

August 12-17, 1974   Jellico, Tennessee

Theme: "What Does Pentecost Mean to Us" (Ephesians 5:8; Acts 5:18)

Introductory Sermon: C.B. Ellis Jr.
Mission Night: Clayton Lawson
Youth Night: Jerome Walden
Additional Speakers: William Fitzpatrick, George Douglas, J.E. Prewitt, Leon Petree, Claude Baird, Charles D. Blackburn, James C. Murray
Program Committee: J.H. Douglas, Roy Cornelius, Donnie Hill

69th General Assembly
August 11-16, 1975   Jellico, Tennessee

Theme: "For the Coming of the Lord Draweth Nigh" (James 5:8)
Introductory Sermon: C.B. Ellis Jr (Matthew 24)
Mission Night: Glenn Rowe
Youth Night: Jasper Walden
Additional Speakers: Ernest Ray, Roger Powell, Efford Enix, James Walden Sr., J.B. Hammitte, J.E. McKinney, Lonnie Lyke
Program Committee: Ira Moses, Ottis Ellis, James Walden Jr.

70th General Assembly
August 9-14, 1976   Jellico, Tennessee

Theme: "The Anointing" (Luke 4:18)
Introductory Sermon: C.B. Ellis Jr. (Exodus 29:36)
Mission Night: Merle Laws
Youth Night: Michael Bartee
Additional Speakers: Fred Cornelius, Luther Gibson, Leon Petree, Ira Moses, James Walden Jr., Willie Lee Partin, Arnold Guy
Program Committee: J.B. Hammitte, Jasper Walden, Ray Freeman

71st General Assembly
August 8-13, 1977   Jellico, Tennessee

Theme: "Year of Evangelism"
Introductory Sermon: Jerome Walden (Luke 24:45-48)
Mission Night: C.B. Ellis Jr.
Youth Night: Donnie Hill
Additional Speakers: James Justice, Bobby Wilson, Michael Cornelius, Ray Landes, J.E. Hatfield, Conard Profitt, Leon Petree, Ray Freeman, James Walden Jr.
Program Committee: Leon Petree, Ray Freeman, James Walden Jr.

Appendix 2: Assembly Speakers

72nd General Assembly

August 7-12, 1978   Jellico, Tennessee

Theme: "Maranatha: Behold, He Cometh" (1 Corinthians 16:22)
Introductory Sermon: Jerome Walden
Mission Night: J.E. Prewitt
Youth Night: Darroll Alexander, Kenneth Ellis, James Walden Jr. II
Additional Speakers: W.P. Sawyer, David Cornelius, James Cox Jr., J.H. Douglas, Lloyd Camp,
Program Committee: Ray Landes, Fred Cornelius, J.E. Prewitt

73rd General Assembly

August 6-11, 1979   Jellico, Tennessee

Theme: "The Church Triumphant – Alive and Well" (Matthew 16:18)
Introductory Sermon: Jerome Walden (Matthew 16:18)
Mission Night: James Walden Jr.
Youth Night: James Bartee
Additional Speakers: David Ellis, James C. Murray, Jerry Reynolds, Arlie Petree, Cecil Johnson, Earl Heath, Ulys Cox
Program Committee: Bob Vance, David Ellis, Clayton Lawson

74th General Assembly

August 11-16, 1980   Jellico, Tennessee

Theme: "I am Not Ashamed of the Gospel of Christ" (Romans 1:16)
Introductory Sermon: Jerome Walden (1 Corinthians 2:2)
Mission Night: Ken Massingill
Youth Night: Marvin Busie
Additional Speakers: Randy Duncan, J.B. Hammitte, Fred Cornelius, Leon Petree, Clayton Lawson, Samuel Walden,
Program Committee: Michael Cornelius, J.H. Douglas, James Walden Jr.

75th General Assembly

August 10-15, 1981   Jellico, Tennessee

Theme: "We've Come This Far By Faith" (Hebrews 11:9)
Introductory Sermon: Clayton Lawson (2 Timothy 4)
Youth Night: Danny Jones
Mission Night: J.E. Prewitt
Additional Speakers: Thomas J. Watters, Ray Landes, Ray Freeman, C.B. Ellis Jr., Lonnie Lyke, J.E. McKinney, Durand Dixon

A Bow Tied

Program Committee: Michael Cornelius, Danny Jones, Jasper Walden

76th *General Assembly*

August 9-14, 1982   Jellico, Tennessee

Theme: "And God Giveth the Increase"
Introductory Sermon: Clayton Lawson (1 Thessalonians 2:9-14)
Youth Night: Dennis McClanahan
Mission Night: J.H. Douglas
Additional Speakers: Jasper Walden, Jennings B. Baird, Carl Prewitt, Robert Hughes, Bob Vance, J.B. Hammitte, Richard Massingill
Program Committee: Lonnie Lyke, Carl Prewitt, Leon Petree

77th *General Assembly*

August 8-13, 1983   Jellico, Tennessee

Theme: "Awake, Arise, and Call on God"
Introductory Sermon: Clayton Lawson
Youth Night: James Angel
Mission Night: J.E. McKinney
Additional Speakers: David Cornelius, Randy VanHoose, Glenn Rowe, Merle Laws, Claude Massingill, Wayne Ison, James Ulrich
Program Committee: J.H. Douglas, Fred Cornelius, Ken Massingill

78th *General Assembly*

August 6-11, 1984   Jellico, Tennessee

Theme: "Going Forward"
Introductory Sermon: Clayton Lawson (Revelation 1:10-20)
Youth Night: Michael Bartee
Mission Night: Michael Cornelius
Additional Speakers: Harley Hensley, James Walden Jr., Leon Petree, J.E. Prewitt, Charles Gibson, Rick Acomb, Billy Paul
Program Committee: Lonnie Lyke, Glenn Rowe, Leon Petree

79th *General Assembly*

August 12-17, 1985   Jellico, Tennessee

Theme: "Let Us Rise Up and Build"
Introductory Sermon: Ken Massingill (Nehemiah 2:17-18)
Youth Night: Jay Walden

Appendix 2: Assembly Speakers

Mission Night: James Bartee
Additional Speakers: Tom Grinder, Lonnie Lyke, Jerome Walden, Thomas Bartee, Danny Jones, James Justice, Durand Dixon
Program Committee: Michael Cornelius, Ray Freeman, James Bartee

80th General Assembly

August 11-15, 1986   Jellico, Tennessee

Theme: "Let Us Love One Another"
Introductory Sermon: Ken Massingill (1 John 4:7-11)
Youth Night: Richard Massingill
Mission Night: James Walden Jr.
Additional Speakers: Jerry Castle, Arlie Petree, Fred Cornelius, J.H. Douglas, Michael Manning, Donnie Hill
Program Committee: Leon Petree, Bob Vance, David Cornelius

81st General Assembly

August 10-14, 1987   Jellico, Tennessee

Theme: "A Worshipping Church" (John 4:21-24)
Introductory Sermon: Ken Massingill (John 4:21-24)
Youth Night: Michael Bartee Jr.
Mission Night: Leon Petree
Additional Speakers: Tim McGlone, Clyde Hughes, Ray Landes, Conard Profitt, Jennings B. Baird, Ralph Johnson
Program Committee: James Bartee, Leon Petree, James Walden Jr.

82nd General Assembly

August 8-12, 1988   Jellico, Tennessee

Theme: "If I (Jesus) Be Lifted Up" (John 12:32)
Introductory Sermon: Ken Massingill (John 12:32)
Youth Night: Johnny Paul
Mission Night: Jay Walden
Additional Speakers: Michael Cornelius, Jerome Walden, J.E. McKinney, Merle Laws, James Laudermilk, Ray H. Hughes
Program Committee: Cecil Johnson, J.E. McKinney, Lonnie Lyke

83rd *General Assembly*
August 7—11, 1989   Jellico, Tennessee

Theme: "A People For His Name" (Acts 15:14)
Introductory Sermon: Jasper Walden
Youth Night: James Walden Jr. II
Mission Night: Lonnie Lyke
Additional Speakers: Kenneth Ellis, Henry Taylor, Wayne Ison, Glenn Rowe, Woodrow Johnson, J.E. Prewitt
Program Committee: Michael Bartee, Charles Vance, James Walden Jr.

84th *General Assembly*
August 6-10, 1990   Jellico, Tennessee

Theme: "And When They Prayed" (Acts 4:31)
Introductory Sermon: Jasper Walden
Youth Night: Joe Prewitt
Mission Night: Fred Cornelius
Additional Speakers: Jerry Wilson, James Cox Jr., J.H. Douglas, Jessie J. Stevens, James Justice, Ray Landes
Program Committee: Merle Laws, Glenn Rowe, James Walden Jr.

85th *General Assembly*
August 12-16, 1991   Jellico, Tennessee

Theme: "Pentecostal Priorities" (Acts 2:1-4)
Introductory Sermon: Jasper Walden (1 Thessalonians 5:22-23)
Youth Night: Richard Massingill
Mission Night: Vincent Cole
Additional Speakers: Jerome Walden, Gerald Fritz, Leon Petree, Merle Laws, Wayne Ison, Conard Profitt
Program Committee: Cecil Johnson, Jay Walden, Wallace Justice

86th *General Assembly*
August 10-14, 1992   Jellico, Tennessee

Theme: "Doing Always to Please Him" (John 8:29)
Introductory Sermon: Jasper Walden (2 Timothy 3:1-5; 4:1-5)
Youth Night: Kenneth Ellis
Mission Night: Lee Sweet

Appendix 2: Assembly Speakers

Additional Speakers: Ulys Cox, James Laudermilk, Ken Massingill, Jerry Noe, Robert Hughes, Daryl Petree
Program Committee: Glenn Rowe, Leon Petree, Donnie Hill

87th General Assembly
August 9-13, 1993   Jellico, Tennessee

Theme: "Wilt Thou Not Revive Us Again?" (Psalms 85:6)
Introductory Sermon: John Nichols (2 Samuel 6)
Youth Night: Wayne Halcomb
Mission Night: James Walden Jr.
Additional Speakers: Tim Walden, Hiram Ellis, Bob Vance, Jack Anderson, Ralph Johnson, James Bartee
Program Committee: James Bartee, Tim Walden, Jay Walden

88th General Assembly
August 8-12, 1994   Jellico, Tennessee

Theme: "The Cost of True Salvation" (Luke 14:25-35)
Introductory Sermon: B.E. Underwood (Psalms 133)
Youth Night: Richard Massingill
Mission Night: Leon Petree
Additional Speakers: Jay Walden, James Kilgore, Scott Isham, Lonnie Lyke, Glenn Rowe, Fred Cornelius
Program Committee: Ralph Johnson, Jerome Cox, Jessie Stevens

89th General Assembly
August 7-11, 1995   Jellico, Tennessee

Theme: "Who Will Go For Us?" (Isaiah 6:8)
Introductory Sermon: Cecil Johnson (Ephesians 6:10-18)
Youth Night: Alfred Newton
Mission Night: Jerry Wilson
Additional Speakers: David Cornelius, J.E. McKinney, Jasper Walden, Woodrow Johnson, Wayne Flowers, Joe Prewitt
Program Committee: Scott Isham, Bryan Thompson, Jay Walden

90th General Assembly
August 12-16, 1996   Jellico, Tennessee

Theme: "Dare to Be a People of Faith" (Mark 10:27)
Introductory Sermon: Cecil Johnson (Psalms 27:13-14)
Youth Night: Alfred Newton
Mission Night: Ralph Johnson
Additional Speakers: Jerome Walden, Tim Bartee, Ray Landes, Henry Taylor, Mark Tolson, Robert Johnson
Program Committee: Wayne Ison, John Keefer, James Walden Jr. II

91st General Assembly
August 11-15, 1997   Jellico, Tennessee

Theme: "Our Heritage, His House; Our Hope, His Glory" (Haggai 2:3-9)
Introductory Sermon: Cecil Johnson (Ezra 3:12)
Youth Night: Alan Laws
Mission Night: Vincent Cole
Additional Speakers: James Walden Jr. II, Tim Adkins, Wayne Ison, Arlie Petree, Michael Padgett, Donnie Hill
Program Committee: Arlie Petree, Ray Landes, Tim Walden

92nd General Assembly
August 10-14, 1998   Jellico, Tennessee

Theme: "Our Eyes are Upon Thee" (2 Chronicles 20:12)
Introductory Sermon: Cecil Johnson (2 Chronicles 20:12)
Youth Night: John Keefer
Mission Night: Kenneth Massingill
Additional Speakers: Merle Laws, Michael Cornelius, J.H. Douglas, Bryan Thompson, Leon Petree
Program Committee: Alan Laws, Richard Massingill, Tim Walden

93rd General Assembly
August 9-13, 1999   Jellico, Tennessee

Theme: "Holiness is God's Standard" (Hebrews 12:14)
Introductory Sermon: Cecil Johnson (Ephesians 5:1-17)
Youth Night: Scott Isham
Mission Night: Ray Landes

Appendix 2: Assembly Speakers

Additional Speakers: Dennis McClanahan, Lee Sweet, Carl Prewitt, Steve Wilson, Fred Cornelius
Program Committee: Jasper Walden, John Keefer, Joe Prewitt

94th General Assembly
August 7-11, 2000   Jellico, Tennessee

Theme: "A Firm Foundation, A Fresh Anointing, A Promising Future" (Acts 2)
Introductory Sermon: Lonnie Lyke (Acts 2:41)
Youth Night: Joe Prewitt
Mission Night: Sam Daniel
Additional Speakers: James Walden Jr., Kenneth Ellis, Jack Anderson, Orville C. Bartee, Jerome Walden
Program Committee: Tim Bartee, Tim Walden, James Walden Jr. II

95th General Assembly
August 6-10, 2001   Jellico, Tennessee

Theme: "The Word of God: Our Weapon, Our Tool" (Psalms 149:6; 1 Corinthians 3)
Introductory Sermon: Lonnie Lyke (Philippians 2:1)
Youth Night: Eric Petree, Richie Holmes, Jon Walden
Mission Night: David Cornelius
Additional Speakers: Conard Profitt, Richard Massingill, Jerome Cox, Stewart J. Carmical, James Laudermilk
Program Committee: Donnie Hill, James Kilgore, Ken Massingill

96th General Assembly
August 12-16, 2002   Jellico, Tennessee

Theme: "God Empowering His Church ... For Such a Time as This" (Ephesians 4:1-16; Esther 4:14)
Introductory Sermon: Lonnie Lyke
Youth Night: Bruce Dixon
Mission Night: David Badillo
Additional Speakers: Scott Isham, Ray Landes, Wayne Ison, Tim Bartee, Leon Petree
Program Committee: David Cornelius, Alan Laws, Lee Sweet

97th General Assembly
August 2003   Jellico, Tennessee

Theme: "Preparing This Generation for the Glory of Christ"
Introductory Sermon: Lonnie Lyke
Youth Night: Jon Walden
Mission Night: Ken Massingill
Additional Speakers: Tim Adkins, J.E. McKinney, Ronnie Steele, Alan Laws, Donnie Hill
Program Committee: Kenneth Ellis, Scott Isham, Ken Massingill

98th General Assembly
August 2-6, 2004   Jellico, Tennessee

Theme:
Introductory Sermon: Lonnie Lyke
Youth Night: Richard McKinney
Mission Night: Kenneth Massingill
Additional Speakers: James Walden Jr. II, Jack Anderson, Michael Padgett, John Rice, Fred Cornelius
Program Committee:

99th General Assembly
August 1-5, 2005   Jellico, Tennessee

Theme: "Fanning the Flame of Evangelism" (Acts 1-2)
Introductory Sermon: Fred Cornelius (Psalms 51:1-12)
Youth Night: Kenneth Ellis
Mission Night: Wallace Justice
Additional Speakers: Arlie Petree, Tim Walden, Ulys Cox, Henry Taylor, Jody Moore
Program Committee: Michael Padgett, Leon Petree, James Walden Jr. II

100th General Assembly
August 7-11, 2006   Jellico, Tennessee

Theme: "There is Yet Much to Do!" (Joshua 13:1)
Introductory Sermon: Fred Cornelius (Joshua 13:1)
Youth Night: Scott Isham
Mission Night: James Walden Jr.
Additional Speakers: Donnie Hill, J.E. McKinney, Sam Daniel, Ray Landes, Leon Petree

Appendix 2: Assembly Speakers

Program Committee: the Executive Board

101ˢᵗ *General Assembly*

August 6-10, 2007   Jellico, Tennessee

Theme: "A Positive Past / A Promising Future" (2 Kings 19:30; 1 Timothy 1:18)
Introductory Sermon: Donnie Hill (Matthew 4:23-25)
Youth Night: Nicholas Hill
Mission Night: Tim McGlone
Additional Speakers: Jerry Grubbs, Douglas Walden, Vincent Cole, Gerald Warf, Tim Slaughter
Program Committee: Willard Cole, Nicholas Hill, James Walden Jr.

102ⁿᵈ *General Assembly*

August 4-8, 2008   Jellico, Tennessee

Theme: "Holding Fast While Reaching Forth" (Revelation 1-3; Phil. 3)
Introductory Sermon: Donnie Hill (Ezra 9:5-6)
Youth Night: Joshua Adkins
Mission Night: Joe Prewitt
Additional Speakers: Lee Sweet, Jimmy Ison, James Coffey, Lonnie Lyke, Richard Massingill
Program Committee: Tim Bartee, Wayne Ison, Jerry Wilson

103ʳᵈ *General Assembly*

August 3-7, 2009   Pigeon Forge, Tennessee

Theme: "Draw Night to God as He Draws Night" (James 4:8; 5:8)
Introductory Sermon: Donnie Hill (2 Corinthians 12:7-10)
Youth Night: Jeremy Walden
Mission Night: Kenneth Ellis
Additional Speakers: Tim Bartee, Scott Isham, Thedford Branson Jr., Michael Winner, Greg Wilson
Program Committee: Scott Landes, Richard Massingill, Lee Sweet

104th General Assembly
August 2-6, 2010   Pigeon Forge, Tennessee

Theme: "Restoration for the Greater Harvest" (Lamentations 5:21)
Introductory Sermon: Donnie Hill (1 Chronicles 12)
Youth Night: Scott Landes
Mission Night: Alva Robinson
Additional Speakers: James Walden Jr. II, Arlie Petree, Heath Hunter, Wayne Ison, Jerry Wilson
Program Committee: Faron Cole, Jerome Cox, Douglas Walden

105th General Assembly
August 1-5, 2011   Pigeon Forge, Tennessee

Theme: "Listen"
Introductory Sermon: Donnie Hill (Proverbs 8:33)
Youth Night: Joe Prewitt
Mission Night: Tim McGlone
Additional Speakers: Jay Walden, Faron Cole, John Keefer, Kenneth Massingill, Cecil Johnson
Program Committee: Kenneth Ellis, Nicholas Hill, Scott Isham

106th General Assembly
July 30 – August 3, 2012   Pigeon Forge, Tennessee

Theme: "Be Ready; Get Busy" (John 9:4; Luke 12:40)
Introductory Sermon: Donnie Hill (Colossians 4:17)
Youth Night: Steve Branstutter
Mission Night: Tim Bartee
Additional Speakers: David Cornelius, Lee Sweet, Randy Halcomb, Joe Hill, Ulys Cox
Program Committee: Sean Landes, Tim McGlone, Thedford Branson Jr.

107th General Assembly
August 5-9, 2013   Pigeon Forge, Tennessee

Theme: "We Have Past Promises and Present Power for Future Growth" (Acts 2)
Introductory Sermon: Jay Walden
Youth Night: Douglas Walden
Mission Night: Lonnie Lyke

Appendix 2: Assembly Speakers

Additional Speakers: Jon Walden, Wayne Ison, Tim McGlone, Darryl Gaunce, Thedford Branson Jr
Program Committee: Randall Halcomb, Lee Sweet, James Walden Jr. II

108th General Assembly
August 4-8, 2014   Pigeon Forge, Tennessee

Theme: "Rise and Shine" (Isaiah 60:1)
Introductory Sermon: Jay Walden
Youth Night: Scott Landes
Mission Night: Faron Cole
Additional Speakers: J.E. McKinney, Tanner Schulte, David Grise, Nicholas Hill, James Walden Jr.
Program Committee: Tim McGlone, Joshua Stephens, Joseph Hill

109th General Assembly
August 3-7, 2015   Pigeon Forge, Tennessee

Theme: "Repair, Rebuild, Reinforce" (Nehemiah)
Introductory Sermon: Jay Walden (2 Chronicles 7:14)
Youth Night: Jeremy Walden
Mission Night: Ken Massingill
Additional Speakers: Nicholas Hill, Michael Winner, Joshua Stephens, Wayne Ison, Kenneth Ellis
Program Committee: Randall Halcomb, Tony Shaw, Jon Walden

110th General Assembly
August 1-5, 2016   Pigeon Forge, Tennessee

Theme: "Making New Footsteps on the Old Paths of Acts with Apostolic Anointing" (Jeremiah 6:16; Ephesians 4:11-12; Acts 2:16)
Introductory Sermon: Jay Walden (Acts 3:1-8)
Youth Night: Chris Davidson
Mission Night: Ken Massingill
Additional Speakers: Jon Walden, John Keefer, Don White, Richard McKinney, Scott Isham
Program Committee: Darryl Gaunce, Nicholas Hill, Jacob Walden

111th General Assembly

July 31 – August 4, 2017　　　　　　Pigeon Forge, Tennessee
Theme: "Rooted" (Ephesians 3:17)
Introductory Sermon: Jay Walden
Youth Night: Nicholas Hill
Mission Night: Tim Bartee
Additional Speakers: Douglas Walden, Ulys Cox, Tony Shaw, Matthew Griggs, Donnie Hill
Program Committee: James Couch, Nicholas Hill, Jeremy Walden

112th General Assembly

July 30 – August 3, 2018　　　　　　Pigeon Forge, Tennessee
Theme: "Vision"
Introductory Sermon: Jay Walden
Youth Night: Brady Hill, Patrick Halcomb
Mission Night: James Walden Jr.
Additional Speakers: Lonnie Lyke, Michael Padgett, Michael Moore, Wayne Ison, James Couch
Program Committee: Tim Bartee, Carl McNeill, Tony Shaw

113th General Assembly

July 29 – August 2, 2019
Theme: "Forward Together" (Exodus 14:15)
Introductory Sermon: James Walden Jr. II (Exodus 14:13-15)
Youth Night: Jonathan Muncy, Jaylin Walden
Mission Night: Joseph Campbell
Additional Speakers: Tim Walden, Randall Halcomb, Thedford Branson Jr., Ralph Johnson, Bruce Dixon
Program Committee: Jon Walden, Sean Landes, Michael Padgett

Bibliography

Primary Literature

Church of God. *The Church of God Evangel*. Available in "Church of God Publications, 1901-1923" on DVD-ROM from the Dixon Pentecostal Research Center, Cleveland, TN and, in later years, online at pentecostalarchives.org

Church of God. *Minutes of the General Assembly of the Church of God*. Available in "Church of God Publications, 1901-1923" on DVD-ROM from the Dixon Pentecostal Research Center, Cleveland, TN and, in later years, online at pentecostalarchives.org

Church of God. Minister Files. Available in Central Files and Records of the Church of God, Cleveland, TN.

Church of God Mountain Assembly. General Assembly Delegate Booklets. Available in the personal collection of the author, Middlesboro, KY.

Church of God Mountain Assembly. *The Gospel Herald*. Available in photocopies, digital scans, and originals in the personal collection of the author, Middlesboro, KY.

Church of God Mountain Assembly. *Minutes of the Church of God Mountain Assembly*. Available in photocopies, digital scans, and originals in the personal collection of the author, Middlesboro, KY.

Church of God Mountain Assembly. Minister Files. Available in Archives Room at Church of God Mountain Assembly Headquarters, Jellico, TN.

God's Revivalist [also called *The Revivalist*]. Journals available on microfilm in the Campus Archives and Special Collections, R.G. Flexon Memorial Library, God's Bible School and College, Cincinnati, OH.

Holiness Baptist Association. *Minutes of the Holiness Baptist Association*. Available in the personal collection of Donnell Sellers, Lenox, GA.

Jellico Creek Baptist Church. *Records: Jellico Creek Baptist Church, Whitley County, Kentucky, 1846 to 1928*. Available at the History and Genealogy Room, Whitley County Public Library, Williamsburg, KY.

Jones, Janus, ed., *Happenings Around Pleasant Hill: Pleasant Hill Baptist Church (1868-2018): Celebrating 150 Years*. Williamsburg, KY.: Pleasant Hill Baptist Church, 2018.

Massingill, Kenneth E. Personal Diary: 1974. Available in the personal collection of Kenneth Massingill, Old Fort, NC.

Minutes of the Fonde Church of God Mountain Assembly, Book One: 1917 to ca. 1940. Available in the personal collection of Jerry P. Grubbs, Lincoln Park, MI.

Minutes of the Holiness Church of God at Hayes Creek, Book One: 1907 to 1945. Available in the care of Joy Ball, church clerk, Stearns, KY.

Minutes of the Jellico Church of God Mountain Assembly, Book One: 1916 to 1943. Available at the Tabernacle Church of God Mountain Assembly, Jellico, TN.

Moses, Ira H. Personal Diaries: 1958-1979. Available in the personal collection of Jason Lands, Cookeville, TN.

Mount Zion Baptist Association. *Minutes of the Mount Zion Association of United Baptists*. Available at the Mission Office of the South Union / Mount Zion Association, Williamsburg, KY.

Parks, John H. Unpublished Journal: 1917-1937. Available in the personal collection of Jason Lands, Cookeville, TN.

Pratt, Mrs. C.T. [Minnie]. *We Walked Alone: Part of the Story of My Life*. Dalton, GA: The Southerner Press, 1955.

South Union Association of United Baptists. *Minutes of the South Union Association of United Baptists*. Available at the Mission Office of the South Union / Mount Zion Association, Williamsburg, KY.

Spurling, Richard G. *The Lost Link*. Turtletown, TN: self-published, 1920.

Tomlinson, Ambrose J. *Diary of A.J. Tomlinson: 1901-1924*, eds. Hector Ortiz and Adrian Varlack. Cleveland, TN.: White Wing Publishing House, 2012.

_____. *The Last Great Conflict*. Cleveland, TN.: White Wing Publishing House, 1913.

West Union Association of United Baptists. *Minutes of the West Union Association of United Baptists*. Available at the Southern Baptist Theological Seminary Archives, Louisville, KY.

Bibliography

Secondary Literature

Brasher, J. Lawrence. *The Sanctified South: John Lakin Brasher and the Holiness Movement.* Chicago: University of Illinois Press, 1994.

Burgess, Stanley M. and Gary B. McGee, eds. *Dictionary of Pentecostal and Charismatic Movements.* Grand Rapids: Zondervan Publishing House, 1988.

Cady, David. *Religion of Fear: The True Story of the Church of God of the Union Assembly.* Knoxville: University of Tennessee Press, 2019.

Carroll, James Milton. *The Trail of Blood... Following the Christians Down Through the Centuries* or *The Present History of Baptist Churches: From the Time of Christ, Their Founder, to the Present Day.* Lexington, KY: Ashland, Baptist Church, 1931.

Catholic Church. *The Catechism of the Catholic Church*, 2nd ed. Vatican: Libreria Editrice Vaticana, 2012.

The Church of God of Kentucky: A History, 1911-1987. Charlotte: Delmar Company, 1987.

Coulter, Dale M. "The Development of Ecclesiology in the Church of God (Cleveland, TN): A Forgotten Contribution?" *Pneuma* 29 (2007): 59-85.

Conn, Charles W. *Like a Mighty Army: A History of the Church of God, 1886-1995.* Definitive ed. Cleveland, TN.: Pathway Press, 1994.

Crews, Mickey. *The Church of God: A Social History.* Knoxville: University of Tennessee Press, 1990.

Crosby, Thomas. *The History of the English Baptists*, 4 vols. London, 1738-1740.

Davidson, Charles T. *Upon This Rock.* 3 vols. Cleveland, TN.: White Wing Publishing House, 1973.

Davis, Marshall. *The Baptist Church Covenant: Its History and Meaning.* Sandwich, NH: self-published, 2013.

Dever, Mark E. ed. *Polity: Biblical Arguments on How to Conduct Church Life.* Washington: Nine Marks Ministries, 2001.

_____ and Jonathan Leeman. eds. *Baptist Foundations: Church Government for an Anti-Institutional Age.* Nashville: B&H Publishing Group, 2015.

East Tennessee Land Company. *Two Years of Harriman, Tennessee.* New York: South Publishing Company, 1892.

Estep, William R. *The Anabaptist Story.* Nashville: Broadman Press, 1963. Revised ed., Grand Rapids: William B. Eerdmans Publishing Company, 1975.

General Assembly Churches of God, Inc. *Centennial History Book: 1906-2006.* Pine Knot, KY: General Assembly Churches of God, Inc., 2007.

Gibson, Luther. *History of the Church of God Mountain Assembly: 1906-1970.* Jellico, TN: Church of God Mountain Assembly, Inc., 1970.

Grudem, Wayne. *Bible Doctrine: Essential Teachings of the Christian Faith.* Edited by Jeff Purswell. Grand Rapids: Zondervan, 1999.

_____. *Systematic Theology: An Introduction to Biblical Doctrine.* Leicester: Inter-Varsity Press, 1994.

Hills, Aaron Merritt. *A Hero of Faith and Prayer; or, Life of Rev. Martin Wells Knapp.* Cincinnati: Mrs. M.W. Knapp, 1902.

Horton, Wade. ed. *Glossolalia Phenomenon.* Cleveland, TN: Pathway Press, 1966.

Hollenweger, Walter J. *Pentecostalism: Origins and Developments Worldwide.* Peabody, MA.: Hendrickson Publishers, 1997.

Hood, Ralph W., Jr. and W. Paul Williamson. *Them That Believe: The Power and Meaning of the Christian Serpent-Handling Tradition.* Berkley: University of California Press, 2008.

Hudson, Winthrop S. "Baptists Were Not Anabaptists." *The Chronicle* 16 (October 1953): 171-179.

Hunter, Harold D. "A.J. Tomlinson's Emerging Ecclesiology." *Pneuma* 32, no. 3 (2010): 369-389.

Jones, Janus, ed. *1990 Annual of South Union Baptist Association: 175th Anniversary.* Williamsburg, KY: South Union Baptist Association, 1990.

_____. *200 Years of Associational Missions: A History of the South Union Association 1815-1997 And the South Union Mount Zion Association 1997-2015.* Williamsburg, KY: South Union Mount Zion Association, 2015.

Kärkkäinen, Veli-Matti. "Church as Charismatic Fellowship: Ecclesiological Reflections from the Pentecostal-Roman Catholic Dialogue." *Journal of Pentecostal Theology* 9, no. 1 (2001): 100-121.

Bibliography

Longsworth, John. *History of the Sycamore Street Church of God.* Sidney, OH: Sycamore Street Church of God, 1949.

Lynch, Elizabeth Brown. *A History of Elk Valley, Tennessee.* Knoxville: self-published, 1991.

McBeth, H. Leon. *The Baptist Heritage.* Nashville: Broadman Press, 1987.

Moore, Ora. *40th Year Anniversary Church of God Mountain Assembly of Monroe, Michigan.* Monroe, MI: Monroe Church of God Mountain Assembly, 1968.

Noll, Mark A. *A History of Christianity in the United States and Canada.* Grand Rapids: William B. Eerdmans Publishing Company, 1992.

Padgett, Michael. *A Goodly Heritage: A History of the Church of God Mountain Assembly, Inc.* Middlesboro, KY: self-published, 1995.

Phillips, Wade H. *Quest to Restore God's House: A Theological History of the Church of God (Cleveland),* Vol. 1, 1886-1923, *R.G. Spurling to A.J. Tomlinson: Formation-Transformation-Reformation.* Cleveland, TN.: CPT Press, 2014.

Presbyterian Church (USA). *The Book of Order 2017-2019.* Louisville: The Office of the General Assembly Presbyterian Church (USA), 2017.

Powell, Roger. *The Answer to Your Problems.* Columbus: Self-published, 1959.

Rasnake, J. Samuel. *Stones By The River: A History of the Tennessee District of the Assemblies of God.* Bristol, Tenn.: Westhighlands Church, 1975.

Richey, Russell E., Kenneth E. Rowe, and Jean Miller Schmidt. *American Methodism: A Compact History.* Nashville: Abingdon Press, 2010.

Robeck, Cecil M., Jr. *The Azusa Street Mission and Revival: The Birth of the Global Pentecostal Movement.* Nashville: Thomas Nelson, 2006.

Roebuck, David G. "Restorationism and a Vision for World Harvest: A Brief History of the Church of God (Cleveland)." *Cyberjournal for Pentecostal-Charismatic Research* 5 (February 1999): 1-34.

Siler, James Hayden. "A History of Jellico, Tennessee: Containing Historical Information on Campbell Co., Tenn., and Whitley Co., Ky," unpublished manuscript, 1938. Available at Jellico Public Library, Jellico, TN.

Simmons, Ernest L. *History of Church of God: With Headquarters at Cleveland, Tennessee.* Cleveland, TN: Church of God Publishing House, 1938.

Spencer, J.H. *A History of the Kentucky Baptists*. 2 Vols. Cincinnati, 1885. Reprint, Gallatin, TN: Church History Research & Archives, 1984.

Stephens, Randall J. *The Fire Spreads: Holiness and Pentecostalism in the American South*. Cambridge: Harvard University Press, 2008.

Synan, Vinson. *The Pentecostal-Holiness Tradition: Charismatic Movements of the Twentieth Century*, 2nd ed. Grand Rapids: Eerdman's Publishing Company, 1997.

Thornton, Wallace. "The Revivalist Movement and the Development of a Holiness / Pentecostal Philosophy of Missions." *Wesleyan Theological Journal* 38, no. 1 (Spring 2003): 160-186.

Tull, James E. *A History of Southern Baptist Landmarkism in the Light of Historical Baptist Ecclesiology*. New York: Arno Press, 1980.

Underwood, A.C. *A History of the English Baptists*. London: Kingsgate Press, 1946.

Vedder, Henry C. *A Short History of the Baptists*. Valley Forge: Judson Press, 1907.

Wacker, Grant. *Heaven Below: Early Pentecostals and American Culture*. Cambridge: Harvard University Press, 2001.

Whitsitt, William H. *A Question in Baptist History*. New York: Arno Press, 1980.

General Index

Accelerated Christian Education, 346-348, 359
Adrian, Georgia. *See* Johnson's Chapel, Georgia
Africa, 332, 352, 362, 364, 366
Ages, Kentucky, 261
Akins, Virgil Lee, 150-154, 162, 211-213
Akron, Ohio, 143, 151-154, 168, 176, 212, 251, 269, 271, 336
Alder, Anderson Cheek, 30, 33, 77
Amos, Ronald and Mavis, 73, 291-294, 310-311
Apostasy, 1, 8, 26, 32, 34, 38, 103, 418
Assemblies of God, 228, 243, 267, 280, 345
Azusa Street Revival, 6, 8, 62, 201, 233, 243, 344
Baird, Charles McKinley, 151-152, 211-213, 263
Baird, Claude, 254, 299
Baird, Jennings, 251-252, 295, 299
Baird, Joshua, 78-79, 153, 156, 164, 208
Baird, Lewis, 106, 138, 169, 198, 208, 211, 233
Baird, William, 37, 211
Ballinger, Robert Newton, 180, 187, 195, 210-211, 221, 250, 268, 270, 271, 317
Bantam, Ohio, 256, 263, 270
Barnes, Elery, 213
Bartee, James, 329, 344, 348
Bartee, Michael, 335-336, 341-344, 357-358
Bartee, Orville Clarence Jr., 258, 287
Bartee, Robin, 345, 372

Bartee, Timothy, 345, 348, 359, 369, 378, 385, 409, 411, 416-417
Bell, Floy Marie, 227
Blackburn, Charles Devenor, 251
Blair, Elder M., 314, 318
Blue Ash, Ohio, 289, 370, 373, 385, 389, 412
Board of Trustees, 124, 286, 345, 352, 357, 374, 393, 398, 399, 413, 414, 417
Board of Twelve Elders, 10, 49, 77, 87, 98, 104-106, 112, 118, 123, 126, 137-145, 155-157, 167-172, 183-187, 207-213, 216, 223, 229, 251, 275, 291, 295-299, 304-305, 340-341, 345-346, 365, 370-372, 376-377, 390-395, 397, 404-408, 412-418
Bray, Byrd, 211, 213
Brimfield, Ohio, 336, 416
Brouayer, George Tyre, 78, 129
Broyles, Lewis Marion, 73, 77-79, 85, 109, 125, 139
Broyles, Squire, 73, 97, 99, 150
Bryant, Esom Bert II, 172, 221, 235-237, 271-272
Bryant, John Harrison, 9, 24, 51, 53, 58, 62, 106, 138, 146, 156, 165, 171, 180, 184-187, 195-199, 207, 210, 215, 219, 237, 247, 248, 278
Bryant, Stephen Nathan, 1-3, 10, 16, 22, 25, 30-39, 46-48, 51, 56-58, 77-79, 105-109, 118, 134-141, 146, 156, 164-168, 212, 242, 356,
Bryant, William F., 2
Buffalo, Kentucky, 85, 101, 118, 147, 148, 162
Bunch, John, 98, 121, 125, 217, 219, 225, 238, 240

Bunch, Oscar Lee, 151, 217, 218, 325
Byrge, Mark, 259
Byrge, William Riley, 259
Calchera, John, 86-87, 94
Camp, Lloyd Logan, 258, 299, 323, 364, 380, 389
Cass Station, Georgia, 74-75
Cates, Jack, 314-319, 353
Cawood, Kentucky, 212-213, 235
Chicago, Illinois, 17, 243, 261, 267, 280, 288-291, 310, 316-317, 326-327, 386
Church Evangels, 141-142
Church of God (Cleveland), 4, 8, 15-18, 51, 60-69, 71-75, 79-84, 87-88, 92, 95-96, 100-112, 117, 120-131, 134, 137-139, 144, 148, 150, 157-158, 165, 171-180, 182-184, 186, 189, 199, 202, 207-209, 215, 218, 220-221, 224-226, 228, 230, 237, 242-245, 250, 265, 276-277, 284-285, 296-297, 314, 333-334, 409, 412, 418-419, 420-424
Church of God (Union Assembly), 71, 75, 91
Church of God Evangel, 74, 83-89, 120, 126, 172, 175, 202
Church of God of Prophecy, 8-9, 117, 130, 280, 289
Church of God of the Original Mountain Assembly, 198, 210-217, 233, 236-237, 251, 255-256, 263-265, 272, 284, 294, 301-304, 418
Cincinnati, Ohio, 19, 26, 50-51, 98, 141-143, 147-154, 162, 171, 177-179, 181, 184, 187, 193-194, 199-200, 211-214, 218, 220, 224, 226, 229-232, 238-241, 245-247, 250-251, 256, 260-261, 271, 279-285, 306, 335-336, 343, 370, 373-375, 377, 382, 385, 387, 389, 400, 408
Cleveland, Ohio, 153, 163, 302, 313, 326, 327, 335, 348, 355, 386
Coffey, James, 411

Collins, John, 256, 263, 288, 389
Columbus, Ohio, 254
Congregational Holiness Church, 346
Congregationalism, 12, 13, 21, 295
Cornelius, David B., 333, 335, 356, 388, 390
Cornelius, Freddy Ray, 273, 278, 295-299, 305-306, 315, 340, 388-390, 395, 406, 410-412
Cornelius, James Alexander, 36
Cornelius, James Michael, 345, 375, 382-383, 390, 409
Cornelius, Roy, 149, 154, 187, 195, 211, 213, 237, 255, 299, 396
Covington, Kentucky, 256-259, 275
Cox, Jackie, 345, 350, 361, 371, 382
Cox, James Ledford Jr., 304, 311-318, 325, 330-331, 334, 345-348, 353-355, 358-359, 363, 375, 384, 394, 399, 403, 406, 409, 412-413,
Cox, James Ledford Sr., 288, 296, 299, 304
Cox, Pleasant Isaiah, 69, 84
Creekmore, Charles, 263, 288, 302
Creekmore, Charles Everett, 142, 160, 183, 211
Cyrus, Eldon Lindsey, 232, 246-247, 253, 269, 359
Daniels, James Madison, 43, 110, 116
Davis, Charles H., 290, 296, 310, 339
Dayton, Ohio, 6, 187, 195, 218, 220, 225, 238, 245, 253-256, 258-259, 269-270, 275, 279, 287-288, 294, 311, 346, 353, 408-409
Detroit, Michigan, 143, 154, 169, 175-176, 181, 191, 214, 218, 220, 245, 252, 255-256, 270, 278, 280, 300, 302, 306, 313-315, 343
Dixon, Bruce, 347
Donley-Hackler, Janey, 329-330, 348, 355
Douglas, General, 263, 284
Douglas, George, 228, 270, 284, 295, 308

General Index

Douglas, Johnie H., 227, 231, 252, 255-256, 269, 288, 290, 299, 347, 357, 365, 390, 413
Douglas, Rufus Leonard, 252
Douglas, Samuel Gene, 278, 288
Douglas, William Baird, 10, 37, 79, 258
Dusina, James, 85-87, 94
Elk Valley, Tennessee, 38, 42, 54, 96, 141, 148, 151, 153, 162-163, 171, 179, 193, 203, 206, 218, 226, 252, 262, 412
Ellis, Claiborne Boyd Jr., 256, 263, 270, 275, 278, 280, 286, 288, 295, 298-299, 303, 309-314, 318, 324-325, 339-340, 353-354, 357, 379, 393
Ellis, Kenneth, 357, 369-370, 381, 386, 402
Ellis, Ottis, 179, 196, 206, 224, 249, 256, 280, 295, 315
Emlyn, Kentucky, 43, 65, 82, 84-87, 96, 98, 106, 118, 122, 126, 139, 167, 174, 178-179, 187, 193, 212, 213, 234, 300
Enix, Benjamin Harrison, 85, 98, 109, 121, 460
Enix, Efford Ferrous, 245, 253, 259, 271, 275, 279-280, 294, 298, 306
Enix, James Arthur, 125, 284
Episcopalism, 12, 295, 418
Ethridge, Jackie, 228, 240
Fearrl, Jessie, 227, 240
Field Evangels, 141, 151
Finance Committee, 272, 275, 282, 374, 393, 396-399, 402-407, 410-411, 414-417
Fire Baptized Holiness Church, 243
Fitzpatrick, William, 255, 273, 286
Flat Hollow, Tennessee, 218, 300
Fonde, Kentucky, 42-43, 55-56, 72, 91, 109-111, 115-116, 170, 187, 191, 203-206, 212-213, 224, 234-235, 279, 301, 306, 317, 348, 352, 360, 366-367, 381, 387
Fore, George Arlow, 3, 43, 68-69, 78-79, 82, 85, 97-99, 109, 112-114, 118-125, 131-132, 136-137, 139-140, 147, 196
Freeman, Charles Arlando, 254, 289,
Freeman, James V., 288, 340
Freeman, Joseph Cameron, 228
Freeman, Ray Arnold, 256, 289, 333-335, 340, 345, 359-360
Fry, Beulah, 350-351, 373
Gaylor, Archie, 262
General Assembly Church of God, 69-71, 90, 304
Gibson, Luther, 9, 20, 157, 165, 169-170, 174, 180, 185, 189-194, 198-200, 208, 215, 232-233, 237, 242-248, 253, 267-269, 272, 275, 280, 285, 287, 290, 294-299, 305, 374-375, 396, 424
Gilreath, Leslie, 348
Glenwood, North Carolina, 257-258, 288
Goins, James Lee, 3, 77-79, 97-99, 109, 118, 123, 132-133, 139-140, 144, 161
Gold Bug, Kentucky, 70, 73-74, 118-119, 147, 192
Goshen, Ohio, 147, 150-154, 162, 171, 179, 184, 187-188, 193, 212, 218, 220, 238, 250, 256-257, 263, 277, 278, 280, 284, 289-290, 300-301, 306, 311, 315, 317, 323, 334-336, 339, 342, 351, 354, 385, 387, 389
Graham, Ulyess, 248, 275
Gray, Finley, 212, 237, 255
Gray, James, 256, 336
Greenville, Ohio, 253-254, 269, 303, 315
Grubbs. Paul, 211, 214, 234, 237, 256, 299
Haiti, 317, 325-330, 332, 347-348, 352, 364, 366
Halcomb, Dennis Wayne, 370
Hamlin, William Riley, 43, 68, 70, 73, 109, 234
Hammitte, David McHenry, 189, 206, 227, 255, 270, 288
Hammitte, J.B., 287, 299, 311

Harlan, Kentucky, 65, 80, 85, 93, 118, 121, 124-126, 133, 142, 150, 160, 196-197, 200, 217, 220, 261, 271, 316
Harriman, Tennessee, 80, 82-83, 97, 109, 113, 335, 390, 416
Harris, Hubert O., 109, 139
Hatfield, John Edward, 51, 91, 157, 164-165, 169-174, 178, 184-186, 189-193, 196, 199, 208, 215, 221-222, 230, 237, 247, 271-273, 280, 285-286, 296-299, 306, 308, 311, 325, 330, 345, 402-403, 424-425
Hayes Creek, Kentucky, 34, 39, 44, 48, 54, 56, 58, 70, 90, 95, 135, 146, 169
Heath, Earl, 224, 231, 275
Helmick, George W., 226, 227, 258
Helper, Utah, v, 259, 271
Henderson Grove, Kentucky, 170, 203, 212-213, 234, 299-301
Hensley, George Went, 202
Hicks, William, 3, 58, 65-69, 84, 89
Hill, Nicholas, 402
Hill, Walter Donnie, 282, 304, 307, 323, 326, 333-335, 355, 390, 410, 416
Holland, Ohio, 254-255, 269-270, 289
Hughes, Wade Moss, 257, 278, 286, 296-297, 306, 312-313, 402
Human, Kevin, 378
Hymera. *See* Shelburn, Indiana
India, 316, 327-328, 332, 355, 364, 386
Inman, Everett, 250, 261
International Institute of Ministry, 375-378, 382-383, 400-402, 408-411, 417
International Pentecostal Assemblies, 344
International Pentecostal Church of Christ, 267, 269, 337, 344, 346, 359, 375, 389, 395
International Pentecostal Holiness Church, 243
Irwin, Benjamin Hardin, 15, 62

Ison, Wayne, 390, 401
Jackson, Thomas, 188
Jamaica, 294-295, 300, 303, 314-320, 323-325, 328-330, 332, 347-354, 364, 369
Jellico Creek, Kentucky, 25, 30-31, 36-37, 44, 46-48, 53-56, 69, 81, 88, 95-96, 119, 134, 146, 149, 202, 300, 421
Jellico, Tennessee, 3, 18, 20, 25, 30-31, 36-37, 44-48, 50, 53-57, 66, 69, 73, 81-100, 109-116, 119, 122-126, 130, 134-137, 140, 142, 144, 146-150, 152, 154-160, 163-164, 168-173, 176, 179-180, 185, 190-195, 202-203, 211, 213, 216-218, 220-226, 229, 233-241, 244, 247, 254-255, 265-269, 271-277, 279-281, 284, 286, 287-288, 296, 300-315, 318, 320, 329-331, 340, 342, 347-361, 365, 373, 375, 379-387, 390-393, 398-400, 408, 410, 413-417, 421-423
Johnson, Cecil Ray, 317, 320, 348, 360, 362, 365-366, 370, 379-381, 383-384, 403
Johnson, Woodrow, 368, 381
Johnson's Chapel, Georgia, 135-136, 154-155
Jones, Danny, 334-335, 356
Jordan, Floyd, 181, 220, 274
Justice, James, 323
Kasee, Dover, 194, 231, 239
Keefer, John, 369
Kenvir, Kentucky, 41, 169, 170, 181, 194-195, 200, 203, 219, 234, 270, 303, 316-320
Kilgore, James W., 377-383, 403-406, 409-413, 417
Knapp, Martin Wells, 26, 51
Kokomo, Indiana, 153, 187, 195, 212, 282, 288-289, 303, 309, 313, 318, 334, 344-347, 385, 388-389
Ladies Willing Workers Band, 178-182, 194, 198, 348-353, 361, 371-372
Lafollette, Tennessee, 151, 262, 272, 390

General Index

Landes, Ray, 283, 329, 337, 387, 390-391, 409
Lashinsky, Carl, 258
Laws, Ancil Mat, 254, 386
Laws, John Melton, 138, 254
Laws, Merle, 319, 326, 370, 386, 412
Lawson, Andrew Clayton, 149, 154, 157, 165, 171, 177, 184-186, 193, 199, 207, 214, 218, 223-225, 230-232, 240-244, 247, 262-273, 278, 281, 284-286, 295, 298-299, 323, 325, 330, 333, 345, 353, 359, 364, 374-375, 394-396, 403, 412, 424
Lawson, Henry Vencil, 261, 271-272, 285
Lay, J.E., 323, 335
Lee, Flavius Josephus, 78, 128
Little Wolf Creek, Kentucky, 2, 23-25, 28, 31-34, 37, 39, 47, 55, 58, 62, 76, 95, 101, 135, 166-169, 179, 193, 212, 238
Litton, Richard Dewey, 109, 147, 152, 154, 163, 196
Llewellyn, Jospeh Steel, 60, 66, 78, 88-89, 108, 127-129, 314
Long, Andrew Johnson, 106, 138, 141, 150, 156-157, 165-169, 184-186, 190, 195, 198-199, 206-207, 211, 214-216, 230-232, 265, 299-301
Long, Azree, 207, 212
Longsworth, John T., 161, 227, 249, 253, 274
Loudermilk, William, 253
Lovitt, Caswell, 23, 24, 25, 34, 76
Lovitt, Edom Lonzo, 70
Lower Elk Valley, Tennessee, 3, 36, 39-43, 50, 58, 65, 67, 70, 74, 78, 85, 96-100, 104, 109-111, 122, 167, 169
Lowery, Charles, 248, 249
Lyke, Lonnie Clark, 244, 340, 363, 367, 380-381, 384, 394-396, 403-406, 409, 412, 415
Lynch, Daniel Clifford, 262, 286-288

Maples, John Henderson, 85, 109, 124
Massingill, Claude Eugene, 303, 320
Massingill, Kenneth Eugene, 299, 303, 316-320, 323-329, 332, 334, 350-353, 360-364, 369, 380, 389-390, 399
Massingill, Linda, 349
Massingill, Richard, 321, 337-338, 341, 345, 350, 363, 369, 379, 389
McClanahan, Dennis, 336-338, 342, 357
McClanahan, Paulette, 337, 352, 371-372, 381
McGlone, Tim, 389
McKenzie, Anderson Miller, 217-218
McKinney, James Earl, 301, 315, 323, 335, 387, 390
Middlesboro, Kentucky, 75, 118, 123, 143, 179-182, 193-194, 206, 219-220, 234-238, 248, 255, 268, 270, 289, 300-302, 308, 310-313, 316, 318, 351-353, 367, 374, 381
Miller, Chester I., 232, 246-247, 264, 272, 344
Mobley, Henry, 43, 78, 97, 104, 110, 138
Monroe, Michigan, 143-145, 151-154, 161, 176, 187-188, 193-197, 207, 216, 220-221, 237-238, 255, 273, 278, 288, 300, 305, 315, 340, 346, 354, 369, 385, 388-389, 412
Morgan, Matthew Hayden, 68, 109, 149
Moses, Cecil, 277
Moses, Ira Hansford, 149, 157, 165, 168, 172, 186-187, 190, 198-200, 203, 208-210, 215, 221, 230-233, 236, 240-242, 247, 251, 265-266, 272-273, 278-280, 286-289, 296, 298-302, 305-315, 318, 339, 381
Moses, James Allen, 34, 39, 58, 101
Moses, Joe, 211-213, 237, 254, 262, 272
Moses, Kelsie, 212, 214, 237, 265

Moses, Kim, 78, 141, 157, 165-171, 174, 184-189, 199-200, 207, 211-214, 232, 265, 299
Moses, Lewis, 211
Moses, Thomas Deberry, 34, 54, 76, 91, 141, 166, 254
Mountain Ash, Kentucky, 212, 213, 262, 275, 304, 305, 318
Nevada, Indiana, 163, 249, 251, 257, 288, 313, 335, 370
New River Baptist Association, 25, 36, 101
Newcomb, Tennessee, 98, 212, 217-218, 224-228, 239-240, 273-275, 305
Newton, Alfred Jr., 369, 382-384, 397-399, 403, 409, 412-413
Old Fort, North Carolina, 226, 240, 256-258, 263, 270, 350, 353-354, 364-365, 385, 389
Oliver Springs, Tennessee, 187, 218, 228, 240, 253
Oneida, Tennessee, 141, 146, 177, 193, 212, 218, 259
Orick, Scott, 205, 211, 237, 348
Padgett, A.G., 338, 347
Padgett, Michael, 375, 384, 399, 406, 409, 412
Parham, Charles Fox, 201, 233
Parks, John Hansford, 1-3, 10, 22, 28, 30-34, 39, 45-48, 51, 55, 58, 65, 68-79, 90, 93, 96-101, 108-110, 117-119, 122, 125, 134-139, 149, 155-158, 164-170, 180, 194, 212, 222, 236, 242, 253, 273, 279, 412, 421-423
Parks, Newton K., 1, 34, 58, 68, 70, 77-79, 109
Partin, Cordell, 203-205, 234-235
Partin, Willie Lee, 288, 299, 311, 316
Patterson Creek, Kentucky, 33-36 39, 47, 58
Pentecostal / Charismatic Churches of North America, 244-246, 267
Pentecostal Children's Home, 308, 374, 382

Pentecostal Church of Christ, 225, 232, 242, 246-248, 253, 256, 344, 359
Pentecostal Church of God, 261
Pentecostal Freewill Baptist Church, 346
Pentecostal World Conference, 243-246
Petree, Arlie, 279-280, 288-289, 306, 309
Petree, Leon, 279, 289, 306-309, 313, 335-337, 340, 343, 358, 373-377, 385-387, 390, 395, 412
Phillips, Wade H., 9, 18
Piqua, Ohio, 254, 338, 385-386, 412
Pleasant View, Kentucky, 27-28, 36, 39, 44, 52, 58, 71, 80-84, 92, 114, 118-121, 166
Powell, Roger, 247, 253, 268-269, 328
Pratt, Charles Thomas, 73-75, 91
Prewitt, Carl, 237, 258-259, 269, 288, 301
Prewitt, Edd, 187-189, 227
Prewitt, James Earl, 161, 190-191, 277, 289, 294, 300, 306, 310-312, 333-335, 340, 350, 356, 358, 375, 395
Prewitt, Joseph Martin, 289, 300, 342
Price, C.L., 79, 106, 109, 138-1141, 146, 151, 182, 194, 206
Puerto Rico, 368
Rains Grove, Tennessee, 65, 119
Redmond, Lawrence, 220, 254, 275, 288, 342
Revelo, Kentucky, 179, 193, 348
Richardson, Joseph Thomas, 39, 58, 69, 99, 122, 129
Rittman, Ohio, 252, 282, 307, 335, 345, 390
Robinson, Floyd, 253
Rock Creek, Kentucky, 70, 167
Rock Prairie, Indiana. *See* Nevada, Indiana
Rocky Top, Tennessee, v, 262, 328
Rogers, Everett, 254

General Index

Rose, Eldon Bowman, 188, 215-217, 223, 239, 279
Rose, Harvey Luther, 187, 216-219, 221, 224, 237, 239, 279
Ross, Alvin Jones, 23, 36, 58, 70, 140
Ross, Everett Harmon, 99, 140, 160
Ross, Melton Franklin, 39, 69, 70
Rountree, Edom John, 36, 39, 45, 69
Rountree, James Madison, 69, 142
Rountree, William Arvil, 215, 219, 238, 248, 256-258, 263, 280, 286, 306
Rowe, Virgil Glenn, 203-205, 280, 286, 295-297, 301-302, 313-315, 318-321, 330, 348, 353-354, 374, 386
Ryan's Creek, Kentucky, 1, 24, 30, 31, 36, 37, 39, 58, 136, 165
Sammons, James Jackson, 30, 39, 45, 58
Sanctification, 1, 2, 7, 8, 19, 26, 27, 28, 30, 32, 33, 34, 36, 38, 39, 62, 65, 118, 176, 243, 418
Sandford, Frank, 2, 15, 63, 97
Santiago, Raphael, 367
Saxton, Kentucky, 29-30, 39, 58, 69, 71, 74, 77, 96, 134-135, 154-155, 192, 212, 302
Seymour, William, 8, 201
Sharp, Isham McKinley, 218, 262, 280, 284, 286, 288
Sharp, John, 79, 119, 123, 131
Sharp, Lewis, 140, 157, 183
Sharp, William M., 99, 106, 138, 141, 150, 151
Sheep Creek, Kentucky, 24, 32, 34, 36, 39, 58-59, 165-167
Shelburn, Indiana, 123, 141-144, 212, 217-218, 237, 249
Shelton, Jonah Love, 65, 80, 83, 89, 93, 109, 172
Shelton, Ronald, 345, 403
Sidney, Ohio, 143-147, 152-154, 161, 171, 176, 179-181, 193-194, 217, 220, 227, 238, 245, 249-250, 253-254, 268, 302, 313-315, 319-320, 325, 370, 385-386
Silcox, Andrew Jackson, 22-26, 32-39, 45-48, 50-51, 66, 76, 101-103, 114, 141, 167, 173-174, 192, 242
Siler's Chapel, Kentucky, 36, 43, 48, 60, 66-67, 70, 95, 103, 108, 126, 153, 167, 212
Sizemore, William Sherman, 85, 125, 197
Smiddy, John P., 36, 39, 58
Smith, Starling, 78, 85, 109, 118-119, 132
South Union Association, 1, 10, 17-18, 22, 24-25, 31-38, 41, 44-48, 50-54, 57, 60, 66, 69, 95, 101-103, 106, 154, 166-167, 185, 408
Spears, John B., 106, 138, 169
Spurling, Richard G., 2, 8, 14-15, 18-19, 60-63, 71, 76
Standifer, Charles Hampton, 79, 123-124, 143-144
Stanifer, Joseph Drue, 106, 138, 141, 144, 161, 167
Stevens, Jessie James, 367
Storey, Mary, 26-29, 36, 51-52
Swain, Haskel, 256-259, 275-277, 305-306
Sweet, William Lee, 389
Taylor, Henry C., 343, 347, 358-359, 373-375, 382, 385, 401, 414
Taylor, Jacob C., 36, 39, 98
Taylor, Laura, 328-330, 355
The Gospel Herald, 51, 173-174, 178-184, 219-220, 231, 238, 246-247, 275-276, 292, 296, 323, 331, 339-340, 345, 350, 373-384, 401
The Gospel Standard, 136, 172
The Lighted Pathway, 184, 195
The Mountain Evangel, 84, 172-173
The Old Paths, 84-85, 93, 109, 172
The Pentecostal Witness, 247, 268, 269
The Youth Gateway, 270, 276
Thomas, Aaron, 1, 28, 34, 58, 119
Thomas, Francis Marion, 58, 78, 82, 97, 118-119

Thomas, John, 30, 77-78, 84, 97, 109, 118, 135, 139, 220, 262, 269
Thomas, Josiah Martin, 3, 58, 66, 68, 109
Thomas, Robert Boyd, 180, 219-220, 274, 340
Tobacco, 42, 66-71, 75, 85, 87, 107-108, 117, 135, 155, 167, 202
Tomlinson, Ambrose Jessup, 2-3, 8-9, 14-15, 18-21, 60-91, 97, 102-103, 105-109, 112, 117, 120-122, 126-132, 158, 172, 184, 226, 242, 265, 284, 418, 421
Tribble, Abraham Hubert, 154, 176-177, 192-193, 197
Troy, Ohio, 254, 282, 303, 320, 354
Valley Creek, Tennessee, 212-213, 218, 366
Vance, Bob J., 269, 345, 363-365, 380-382
Vance, Nancy, 372, 377, 385
VanHoose, Randall, 338, 386
Vaughn, Walter, 258, 294, 314
Vaught, Elston, 323
Vinson, Auza, 248-249, 263, 272, 288, 295-297, 304
Walden, Ancil Jerome, 194, 251-252, 295-299, 302-303, 317, 320, 323-324, 330, 333-334, 340, 345, 349-350, 353-357, 375, 387, 390-395
Walden, Charlene, 302, 349-350
Walden, Douglas, 411
Walden, James Alton, 213, 251-255, 263, 269, 286, 290, 299, 302-303, 310-311, 355, 376, 402
Walden, James Jonathan IV, 369
Walden, James Jr., 251, 261-263, 288-290, 303, 310, 316-317, 323, 326-329, 334-335, 345, 348, 376, 386, 394, 397, 402
Walden, James Jr. II, 411
Walden, Jay Anthony, 342, 358, 367, 370, 381, 385, 406, 410
Walden, Roger, 323
Walden, Wiley Jasper, 251, 282, 288, 303-304, 307, 313-317, 323, 332, 353-358, 362-367, 375, 380, 390, 393, 413
Walker, Alec Curd, 29-30, 39, 52-53, 58, 69, 77-78, 99, 106, 109, 134-138, 141-145, 152-159, 164, 172, 193
Watkins, Randall, 189, 194, 217, 219, 221, 238
Way of Holiness Church of God, 213, 236
Weaver, Charles Leroy, 250-251, 268, 280
Weaver, Gilbert, 99, 122, 138
Weaver, Jessie, 250, 268, 348
Wesley, John, 1, 6, 26
West Union Baptist Association, 24, 25, 37, 38, 46, 54, 101, 423, 496
White, Levi Milton, 78, 79, 146
Whitehead, Luther, 347
Whitley City, Kentucky, 29, 119, 146, 152, 163, 166, 177, 187, 193, 220, 337
Wilder, William Jesse, 27, 29
Williams, Herman David, 148, 150, 162, 171, 184
Williamsburg, Kentucky, 27, 33, 48, 51-57, 78, 98-99, 113-114, 121-122, 162, 173, 187, 198, 210-213, 233, 236-237, 263-265, 272, 289, 301-305, 309, 353, 416
Wilson, Bobby, 239, 288, 295-299, 303, 311, 315, 320, 323, 340
Wilson, Jerry, 386
Wolf Creek, Kentucky, 24-25, 32-33, 47, 54, 103, 119, 165, 300
Woodhaven, Michigan, 213, 220, 255, 258, 270, 272, 280, 305
Wood, George, 288, 309, 317
Woods, Thomas Sylvester, 106, 138, 141, 153, 187
Wooldridge, Tennessee, 36, 39, 41, 58, 59, 65, 84, 150, 169
Woolum, Edward, 180-182, 194, 219-220, 238, 256, 274
Woolum, Morris Edgar, 106, 138, 141, 154, 157, 161, 171, 180, 187, 206, 215, 231, 255, 270

General Index

Wytheville, Virginia, 290-292, 296, 310

Yamacraw. *See* Whitley City, Kentucky

Yeary, Charlie T., 147-150, 161, 251, 280, 284, 307, 339, 342

Yeary, Earnest Esco, 149, 152-157

Yeary, James Caleb, 109, 147

Yeary, Paul, 345

Yeary, Willis, 149-151, 211, 214, 231, 237, 251, 263, 311

Young People's Endeavor, 174-182, 193-194, 219-224, 238, 274-276, 305, 342

Youth Warriors for Christ, 274-278, 280, 287, 292, 307, 314, 332-333, 342, 353, 369, 381, 402

Ypsilanti, Michigan, 256, 289

Zion Hill, Kentucky, 31, 33, 36, 39, 47, 48, 55, 58, 70, 95, 101, 167

Made in the USA
Middletown, DE
15 August 2021